Crimewarps

Crimewarps

GEORGETTE BENNETT

Crimewarps

The Future of Crime in America

ANCHOR PRESS/DOUBLEDAY
GARDEN CITY, NEW YORK
1987

The author and the publisher thank the following for permission to use the respective material:

Excerpts from "Silicon Valley Drugs" and "Farm Crisis," MacNeil/Lehrer NewsHour © 1986, Educational Broadcasting Co. and GWETA. All rights reserved.

Excerpts from ABC News "20/20," "Seeds of Hate," © 1985 American Broadcasting Companies, Inc.

Excerpts from "Our Romance with Violence," © CBS Inc., 1981. All rights reserved. Originally broadcast on October 19, 1981, over the CBS Television Network as part of the "Up to the Minute" program series

Library of Congress Cataloging-in-Publication Data

Bennett, Georgette.
  Crimewarps: the future of crime in America

  Bibliography: p.
  Includes index.
    1. Crime forecasting—United States.   2. Crime and criminals—United States.   3. Criminal behavior, Prediction of.   4. Twenty-first century—Forecasts.
I. Title.
HV6791.B45   1987   364'.973   86-10885
ISBN: 0-385-23090-7
Copyright © 1987 by Georgette Bennett
All Rights Reserved
Printed in the United States of America

To my darling husband, Marc, and dear mother, Sidonie—
Twin beacons who light up my life.
I hope I have contributed in some small way to your safe future.

Acknowledgments

This book had its beginnings in happenstance. I was making a routine visit to the Insurance Information Institute (III), which had retained me as a crime prevention consultant and media spokesperson. When I arrived, I was asked to drop by the Planning and Issues Analysis Department before going to my regularly scheduled meeting. The III was in the process of organizing its industry report on the year 2000 and wanted to consult with me about the state of crime in the future.

The request took me by surprise. I'd never given any thought to the subject and made it clear that I would be speaking strictly off the cuff. By the time an hour had passed, an unexpected stream of ideas and predictions had come pouring out of me. I turned to Ruth Gastel, a III staffer, and asked whether she would send me a copy of the notes she had taken of my remarks. This book was born from those notes.

At about the same time, Dr. Gerald Lynch, president of John Jay College of Criminal Justice of the City University of New York, had invited me to be a panelist at a press conference. We were to discuss the merits of the crime proposals put forward by two New York State gubernatorial candidates. I found myself evaluating the proposals on the basis of future changes in crime patterns.

The III and John Jay sessions convinced me that crime in the year 2000 was a natural for a magazine article. I wrote one with the guidance of my friend and mentor Earl Ubell. Earl, health editor for *Parade* magazine and health and science editor at WCBS-TV in New York, taught me television, popular writing, computers, and serious tennis. I owe him more than I can ever repay. Over the years, his leads have always proven to be on target. So when he suggested that I expand my article into a book, I listened.

I put together the proposal for this book with the help of the Charlotte Sheedy Literary Agency. Although writing has long been part of how I make my living, I used to dislike it. But agents Charlotte Sheedy and Linda Nelson were so enthusiastic and supportive, they inspired me. I wanted to write for *them*.

Charlotte and Linda took my concept to Doubleday, where they found me a smart, witty, and wonderful editor, Philip Pochoda. Unfortunately, I lost Phil to Simon and Schuster. But his early suggestions helped to carry me.

The blow of Phil's departure turned out to be an opportunity. *Crimewarps* was turned over to Paul Bresnick, an editor every bit as delightful, insightful, easy to work with, and encouraging as Phil. I am most grateful to Paul for so avidly jumping into this project.

Paul's assistant, Karen Suben, was a patient and solid bulwark. She contributed refinements of style and substance with suggestions that were always germane

Of course, this book could never have been written in the short time it was if not for my husband, Marc. Marc, whom I cherish as one of the world's special people, has long prodded me to do a book about my life of crime. He enabled me to put my quotidian concerns on the shelf for a year, chain myself to a computer, and get lost in a blitz of prose.

Gary Phillips, dear friend and assistant, helped out with the research and follow-up tasks on parts of *Crimewarps*. His eagle eye and keen mind were great assets in checking the accuracy of the text.

Finally, I owe thanks to the countless people who gave so generously of their time and knowledge in providing the accumulated information that has found its way into these pages.

In ten years, I'd want to feel like I wouldn't have someone watching my back to be safe.

A safe world? It would be like heaven. . . . We could go out and leave our doors unlocked. We wouldn't have to use keys. We wouldn't have to kill or have guns. . . . It would be perfect.

Statements of Crime Victims in Flora Colao and Tamar Hosansky, Your Children Should Know *(Bobbs-Merrill, 1983)*

Contents

Preface

The Fear Wave

Crime. We fear it. We're fascinated by it. Our notions about crime—molded mostly by what we read and hear—are often distorted. Yet those perceptions determine our sense of safety at home and on the streets, in a store or in an office, in the investments we make and the air we breathe. Because we feel vulnerable on every front, we need to understand the state of crime today and what it tells us about the time to come. That's why I've written this book on the future of crime in America.

Crime is not static. Existing patterns get displaced by new ones. *Crimewarp* is the term I've coined to describe the bends in today's trends that will affect the way we live tomorrow. This book is organized around six crimewarps, each of which represents a set of major social transformations:

CRIMEWARP I: THE NEW CRIMINALS. Traditional criminals—young, male, poor, uneducated—will increasingly be displaced by older, more upscale offenders. The number of crimes committed by women will accelerate, not only in stereotyped areas like prostitution, but in white-collar crime and domestic violence. Teenagers will commit fewer, but more terrible crimes. Senior citizens will enter the crime scene as geriatric delinquents.

CRIMEWARP II: THE MARCH OF CRIME. Crime will become freer of geography. Less of it will take place at the neighborhood level. Where crime is spatially bound, it will shift from the Northeast to the Sunbelt and into rural areas.

CRIMEWARP III: RING AROUND THE WHITE COLLAR. The street crimes that scare us will decrease in relation to more impersonal, far-reaching white-collar crimes. Computers, cashless money, technological secrets will become the new booty. Patterns of consumer fraud will mold themselves around changed demographics, and we will find new ways of cheating old institutions.

CRIMEWARP IV: THE POLITICS OF PLEASURE. Despite a deeply rooted Puritan ethic and its contemporary expression in the New Right, some consensual crimes—drug abuse, homosexuality, prostitution, gambling—will be legalized. Others, like pornography, will be subject to stricter regulation.

CRIMEWARP V: THE UPS AND DOWNS OF BIG BROTHER. Long entrenched crime-fighting strategies will be displaced by leaner, more focused, less personal tactics. Efficiency and coverage will be enhanced by the proliferation of computers and high-tech listening/detection devices. Self-help, security hardware, and private police will reduce the reliance on traditional law enforcement. New architectural designs will build crime-proofing into the environment.

CRIMEWARP VI: PAYING THE TAB FOR THE BILL OF RIGHTS. Some of our civil liberties will be displaced in an effort to stem crime and the moral anarchy that underlies it. The erosion will occur in the process of ceding our privacy to computer files and our moral judgment to ultraconservatives.

The six crimewarps—displacements in crime patterns—we face are the sum of complex social forces: demographics, economics, religion, politics, technology, education, biology, law, values. These trends are varied and sometimes inconsistent, tied in as they are to the patchwork of our pluralistic society. In our panic, we tend to think of crime as something alien. It isn't. Crime is simply a form of behavior that reflects myriad intersecting forces. Crime occurs when there is a conflict in social norms and/or a breakdown in social controls. It provides a mirror in which we can view how our society functions.

The law and the public are often at odds over which acts to label as criminal. Crimes are defined in and out of existence relative to the social, economic, and political climate of the times. Prohibition and abortion are two cases in point. As with other social changes, shifts in crime occur gradually. In making predictions about crime, one has to take into account the currents that are likely to buffet definitions one way or the other. That is precisely the task of this book. But before tackling it, it's important to understand how fear molds our attitudes toward crime.

Sunday, December 2, 1984. A quiet New York Street. A lone woman returning from the theater entered the elevator of her West End Avenue building. At 1:40 A.M., the stillness was shattered by her screams. Caroline Isenberg, a twenty-three-year-old Harvard graduate, had been forced to the roof at knife point. There, twenty-one-year-old Emmanuel Torres robbed her of twelve dollars, tried to rape her, and repeatedly stabbed her.

For days, the details of the crime exploded in the headlines: Caroline's dying words about the bitter price she paid for not giving in to the rape; the forty detectives who were assigned to the case; the grief of her mother and psychiatrist father; her prep school; her promising life; her nascent acting career. Then there was the killer: whom a prosecutor described as the irresponsible drifter son of the building's superintendent; his estranged parents; his inability to complete high school; Emmanuel's doctor-brother who made good; the remorseless confession in which Torres described the murder in all its horror.

And, a week after Caroline's death, the vigil. The neighbors and strangers—Hispanic, black, white—who lit candles and stood watch outside 929 West End Avenue, while one mourner intoned: *"Yis gadal v'yiskadash sh'mei rabba,"* the life-affirming Jewish prayer for the dead.

That's how the life of an upscale, bright young white woman was extinguished by a reportedly unemployed, dope-smoking, black Hispanic on a crisp winter night in the season of goodwill. It was the stereotypical crime with the stereotypical cast of characters—the apotheosis of all our most primitive fears and prejudices about crime.

Crimes like this are the ones that fire the imaginations of press and public alike. Their luridness precludes a reasoned separation of fact and frenzy.

I'm a sociologist and criminologist. I'm also a journalist. So I work both sides of the street—fact and frenzy. I've spent most of my career dealing with criminals, victims, law enforcers, attorneys, prison officials, court personnel. I've taught thousands of college, graduate, and professional students; advised police commissioners; designed programs for federal, state, and city governments; counseled corporations. I've developed stories for "60 Minutes," "20/20," "MacNeil/Lehrer NewsHour"; worked crime beats for local news programs and covered the nation for NBC News.

I've reported on the body found in the trunk of a car at Newark Airport; the rapist who, after he got his power fix, coolly reached over and strangled his victim; the distraught parents whose seven-year-old daughter was forced to watch in a mirror as her killer butchered her with a knife. Having done all that, you'd think I'd be inured to crimes like the Isenberg murder. But this story made me sick—not only because of the heinousness of the act itself, but because it's so misleading. As a journalist, I know that stories like hers sell papers and boost ratings. As a social scientist, I know that this crime and others like it are anomalies today; *they'll be even more rare tomorrow.*

Today's normative victim and criminal share this profile: young, male, black or Hispanic, undereducated, unmarried, unemployed. Emmanuel Torres fits. Except for her age, Caroline Isenberg doesn't. She was a fluke. And so was the crime.

The prototypical street crime is not interracial. Blacks prey on blacks, whites on whites. Street punks usually victimize their own neighbors. Torres traveled a relatively long way to menace Caroline but, because of his father's job, he was no stranger to her apartment building. The majority of murders are committed by people who have some knowledge of their victims, even if only in passing. Among violent crimes, robberies and assaults are committed mostly against strangers. (The data on rape are inconclusive.)

Caroline was an unlikely street crime victim. As a woman, her odds of being targeted were half that of a man's. As a white, they were a little more than half that of a black's. As an affluent person, they were half that of a poor person's. Finally, her kind of tragedy is only an infinitesimal part of the total crime picture. Yet, it's the kind of crime that conditions our sense of safety.

If you're like most people, you think of crime in terms of violence—rape, murder, assault. Your fear attaches not to just any crime, but specifically to a random attack by a stranger lurking in the street. Most people believe we're in the midst of an unprecedented crime wave. Maybe you're one and I don't blame you. You turn on your local "Action News" and 20 percent of the airtime is devoted to a body count.

My friend Joan watches too. She says her daily exposure to TV news makes her afraid to walk around her West Hollywood neighborhood at night. This thirty-nine-year-old lawyer loves her home, her city, and her work, but her fear of crime makes her constantly uneasy. "With what I hear, I'm afraid to go out. I always lock my door when I'm driving. I always keep my eyes to the ground. I never make eye contact. I've always been careful—but now I'm careful and scared."

Like most people, Joan has never been a street crime victim. The odds are she never will be, because she's white, female, and no longer in the crime-prone fourteen- to twenty-four-year-old age group. But media-manufactured myths about crime have robbed her of her sense of safety.

It's not surprising. According to a recent *Newsweek* poll, 62 percent of Americans get most of their news from television. A National Opinion Research Center (NORC) study shows that 56 percent read a newspaper every day. But, says an American Society of Newspaper Editors survey, more people trust what they learn from TV. Heavy TV viewers, maintains the influential *Figgie Report on Fear of Crime* (conducted by Research & Forecasts, Inc., for Ruder & Finn), are the ones most rattled by the myth of a crime explosion. Sporadic TV viewers tend to be less fearful. (This is consistent with the findings of Dr. George Gerbner, an authority on media violence research, at the University of Pennsylvania's Annenberg School of Communications.)

At various times, Joan has turned on her TV and seen an account of a driver plowing his car into a crowd of people on Westwood Boulevard; or a mass murderer gunning down unsuspecting patrons of a McDonald's; or a mad rapist stalking women in the hills.

A disproportionate number of TV crime stories are violent. A recent study conducted by Michael Robinson, visiting scholar at the American Enterprise Institute, and Maura Clancy at the University of Maryland avers: "Violent crimes are more memorable as news events than all but the most dramatic political occurrences." But government statistics show that only a tenth of all crimes are violent. The majority of offenses are petty thefts, the kind in which a wallet is taken off a counter or a coat is stolen off a hanger. You'd never know that from most press reports. The crimes considered most newsworthy have little in common with the routine purse snatchings, family squabbles, and drunken cavorting that dominate the police blotter.

Joan's morning and evening news binges have convinced her she's in terrible danger. Twenty years ago, she might have been. There was a crime boom in the 1960s. The fear it generated has not abated, despite the fact that crime rates leveled off in the 1970s and (according to the National Crime Survey) have taken a nosedive in the 1980s. What we've got now is not a crime wave, but a *fear* wave.

Fear waves affect the way people live. The National Crime Survey shows that nearly half the residents of large cities have altered their lifestyles because of crime. They've moved their homes, changed their transportation routes, curtailed their activities, switched jobs. The same government research reveals that crime is one of the two most frequent complaints residents cite about their own neighborhood.

The 1980 *Figgie Report on Fear of Crime* disclosed a resounding 70 percent of respondents who took precautions against crime as they went about their daily lives. More than half owned guns to protect their homes. But a NORC study shows that only a fifth of the population has ever actually been threatened with or shot at with a gun.

Even hard-nosed business people have capitulated to fear. A recent study of the Joint Economic Committee of Congress reported that perceived quality of life is the single greatest factor in making business location and expansion decisions. The critical factor in assessing quality of life is crime.

The closer to home a crime takes place, the more vulnerable we feel, according to a twenty-six-city study. Hearing a neighbor or our friendly local newscaster tell how the Jones house down the street was broken into last week worries people more than a network story on a hijacked plane in Iran.

Regardless of their experiences, people are more afraid of crime than they are of dangers they face more often. In a given year, the odds are twice as great that we'll commit suicide than be the victim of a homicide; twice as great that we'll die of heart disease than be raped; thirty-two times as great that we'll be hurt in a car accident than on the receiving end of a serious assault.

None of this is to deny that we have a massive crime problem in America. Even with the latest decreases, more than a quarter of all households are touched by crime each year. And the Bureau of Justice Statistics estimates that the lifetime odds of being a crime victim are far greater than the annual ones. Over the long haul, the probability of being murdered is 1 in 133. If you're a black male, your odds rise to a staggering 1 in 21. For a white female, they sink to a reassuring 1 in 369.

We can't blame the press for the frightening toll crime takes on our lives.

Nevertheless, the "body count" school of covering crime makes it harder for us to deal with the problem. News reports rarely help us assess our own risks or learn how to protect ourselves. For example, a reported "rape wave" in San Jose left a lot of women terrified. As it happens, more than half the victims were prostitutes. Although that fact doesn't make rape acceptable, we should be aware that most women are simply not exposed to random violence in the same way as a streetwalker.

In the midst of all this fear, people like Joan feel very vulnerable. Consecutive Harris surveys, starting in 1967, reveal that a growing part of the population—four fifths as of this writing—doesn't believe law enforcement deters crime. A *Newsweek* poll reveals that half of the respondents have very little confidence in the ability of police to protect them against violent crime. So here we are walking around with all this free-floating fear and very little faith in government's power to shield us.

My work with government, business, foundations, and a wide variety of street, white collar, and vice offenders has taught me that crime and our responses to it can't be isolated from the social context in which they occur. Crime control is just a form of social control, a term we behavioral scientists use to describe the arsenal of weapons society levels at its members to keep them in line. They are effective only to the extent that they are meaningful to those on the receiving end.

The hold of social controls is weak when people relate to each other distantly —say as colleagues rather than family, football fans instead of close friends. If the fragmentation is extensive, the result is a state of rootlessness and normlessness called "anomie." The anomic individual floats free of bonds, accountabilities, and restrictions. Suicide, crime, and innovation all arise from that state.

Norman Washburne, in his classic book, *Interpreting Social Change in America,* identifies two macrotrends in our society, urbanization and bureaucratization, which imply a movement toward greater anomie and fragmentation. More recently, John Naisbitt in *Megatrends* and Alvin Toffler in *Future Shock* have identified derivative trends—heightened religiosity, ethnic identification, and decentralization—that are leading toward greater connectedness and more powerful social controls.

Without social controls, we would exist in anarchy, subject to leviathanlike aggression, hedonism, and brutality. Sounds like life in any big city? Well, that's why the temperance movement pushed us into Prohibition and the New Right is lobbying for a moral revival backed by strong restraints.

It's hard to argue with the need for restraints. The problem is, *whose* morality will define *what* controls? When you talk about crime, you are perforce talking about politics. In a society as complex as ours, competing value systems operate simultaneously. That the Moral Majority and the American Civil Liberties Union (ACLU) can function within the same national boundaries is a tribute to American pluralism.

The group whose values come to be defined as mainstream—the values to which the rest of us are expected to conform—has a lot to do with power. The group with power will find its values echoed in legislatures, schoolrooms, police procedures, and cocktail parties. A mortal battle for the national conscience is being waged as I write and you read. The jousting is both a product and producer of forces that will determine what we, in the future, will label as "crime" and how we react to it. This book explores those forces, places them in the context of our fears, and separates the crimes that are a growing threat from those that are declining.

Introduction

The New Demographics
of Crime

In 1983, Robert Nascimben, a twenty-seven-year-old technician for Texas Instruments, found himself at the center of several crimewarps. He made a nice salary and was living the good life in Houston with his wife. Finding a house was his major preoccupation, and crime was very far from his mind. Then it happened. Not at the hands of a mugger or a burglar as you might expect, but through the manipulations of a swindler.

Timothy Leighton, thirty-nine, a mobile-home salesman, had used a stolen computer terminal provided by a confederate to access Nascimben's credit information. Investigators say he used the data to open accounts with Visa, MasterCard, and First City National Bank of Dallas. Bank losses of $10,000 were incurred in Nascimben's name. His credit rating could have been destroyed, and his sense of privacy was profoundly violated.

Nascimben's experience is typical of the kind of crime that will bedevil us in the future: a white-collar offense taking place in the Sunbelt, involving an older victim and criminal, abetted by a computer, detected by new investigation techniques, and deeply impacting our right to privacy.

Nascimben's victimization stands in stark contrast to the street crimes that are normative today. The case of Michael "Meathead" McReynolds, a nineteen-year-old black Atlantan, illustrates a kind of crime that is on the wane. Early in 1983, McReynolds was shooting baskets with his friends when he was shot by his neighbor, eighteen-year-old Bobby Lester, also black. Two months before, Lester's brother had burglarized McReynolds' home and stolen his father's .38. Thinking that his former victim was out to get even, Lester launched a preemptive strike: five bullets in the back on a Love Street basketball court. Lester pleaded guilty to aggravated assault.

Had McReynolds died of his wounds, the crime with which Lester could have been charged is murder, a felony whose rate plummeted 22 percent between 1980 and 1985. But he survived. In the future, his odds of being a street crime victim will be greatly reduced. Crimes like the ones his family suffered—burglary and aggravated assault—have declined, as have all crimes (except for minor ones like stealing a bicycle or throwing your best friend a light punch). The decrease in crime is no longer a blip on a graph.

The start of a new millennium is almost upon us. As we approach it, we are seeing dramatic changes in the way we live. This Introduction provides an overview of how key parts of those changes—crime, criminals, and crime-fighting—are being transformed into the six crimewarps that make up the balance of this book. But before dissecting the crimewarps, it is helpful to sample the major themes we'll be dealing with—demographic shifts in age, ethnicity, labor markets, education, technology, religion, and politics—and their specific impact on the crime scene.

The good news: *The chances of being a street crime victim are getting smaller and will continue to shrink for the next several decades.* Today, each household has 2.6 chances in 10 of being touched by crime. That's an average drop of 19 percent in victimization by personal and household crimes since 1975. If the odds keep decreasing at that rate, the year 2000 will see the risk drop to about 2 in 10.

One reason crime will continue to ebb is the aging of our population. Most street criminals are young, with ages fourteen to twenty-four being the most dangerous years. By the time they reach their twenty-fifth birthday, most of the hell-raising is over. Come the year 2000, more than three quarters of the population will have cleared the crime-prone age barrier. Today only 60 percent have crossed that threshold. The median age, which is now thirty, will creep steadily to nearly forty-two by the year 2050. *The rate of conventional crime will drop as the median age rises.*

Now the bad news.

In the future, when crime strikes, it could well be less violent, less personal, more tricky, and more profitable. *The criminal will be older, more sophisticated. And so will the victim.* As the population ages, we can expect more crimes like the credit fraud that ensnared Robert Nascimben and several Houston banks. White-collar crimes are usually committed by older, "respectable" criminals against older, more affluent victims. Reliable baselines don't exist, but since this part of the population is growing, we can expect the rate of white-collar crime to grow too.

The signs are everywhere:

- Detroit: A trust officer for the National Bank of Detroit embezzled over $1 million from wealthy clients of the bank.
- New York: Two Dean Witter account executives used a phony account to make at least $80 million in unauthorized trades and hundreds of thousands of dollars in profit for themselves.
- Houston: A psychologist, football coach, and accountant each got taken for $5,000 in a con game.
- San Jose: A technician at a major laser manufacturing plant offered to sell a rival company the plans for his employer's latest product.
- Jackson: A lawyer converted to his own use a $223,000 trust fund belonging to a local Co-op.

White-collar crime isn't the sole province of individuals. Business entities are voluminous offenders. The eighties have spun off two simultaneous and opposite trends: corporate mergers and growth of cottage industries. Members of the corporate food chain—airlines, communications, oil, and insurance companies —swallow each other whole, adding no new equity to the economy. But Joe Duncan, chief economist for Dun & Bradstreet, is quick to point out that mergers are "not where the action is in the economy." The action is in the fragile rustle of sole proprietorships that add virgin blood to the economic stream.

"*This* business cycle is unique in that the big companies are keeping their overhead low, refusing to add white collar employees," argues Duncan. Instead of doing everything in house, big business is buying services—public relations, advertising, back-office operations—from small companies that add new productive capacity to the Gross National Product. This gives us a "diversified employment base," concludes Duncan, "which cushions workers against downturns in the economy."

Unfortunately, small struggling businesses are among the most prolific tax cheats and often engage in a variety of stealthy practices to survive.

On the other hand, the sheer size of the merger-bloated supercompanies creates its own pressures for fraud. In 1985 a number of America's elite corporations were caught with their gray flannel pants down. Most of the Defense Department's contractors, including General Electric and General Dynamics, were nailed for out-and-out theft from the taxpayers. E. F. Hutton, a bastion of Wall Street solidity, was convicted for kiting millions of dollars worth of checks.

The New York *Times* attributed this phenomenon to profit pressures in a tight economy, a relaxed regulatory environment, and diminished corporate ethics. All of those explanations for a breakdown in controls are valid, but there's one the *Times* missed: An excess of mergers concentrates power in the hands of a few corporations. Consumers are the natural prey. Add to this the explosion in credit fraud and computer crime, and you have a crimewarp.

The ubiquitous computer has created a crimewarp that's free of geographical constraints. Experts agree that computer crime in all its colorful variations—"data diddling," "superzapping," "logic bombs," "salami slicing," "Trojan horse"—*will be the single greatest crime generator we face in the future.* The new criminals will include computer operators, programmers, tape librarians, and electronic engineers. They will be wealthier, older, and better educated, like the convicted computer expert who used a Federal Reserve access code to electronically transfer $10 million in embezzled money from a Los Angeles bank to his own Swiss bank account.

The national Chamber of Commerce estimates computer crime losses to range from $100 million to $300 million per year. More and more, our paychecks, bank accounts, and pensions are being converted from hard cash to electronic data bytes. We will become increasingly vulnerable to computer bandits. Unlike the street punk who mugs just one victim at a time, the high-tech highwayman can divert an entire payroll or bleed a complete stock offering. Each crime can create thousands of casualties.

While violent crime will decrease, it won't disappear. The murders, rapes, robberies, and thefts that make us shudder are generally the province of young criminals and young victims, who are disproportionately black and Hispanic. Here the new demographics contain a time bomb: Census Bureau projections indicate that by the year 2050, there will be a 7 percent smaller proportion of whites in this country. Blacks and Hispanics will make up about one quarter of the population, compared to less than one fifth today.

According to Lawrence Sherman, former research director for the Police Foundation, high-crime-risk minorities have suffered "destruction of the family and increasing illegitimacy. That has to have an effect." The effects will be felt, asserts Sherman, in more domestic violence. It will also be felt in more thefts. Because future job creation will take place in the crime-prone service industries that hire minorities, "theft will go off the wall!" according to Sherman.

This may be so. But Marvin Wolfgang, one of the nation's leading criminologists, feels it won't be due to greater numbers of criminals. He asserts that *the volume of juvenile offenders is shrinking, but the crimes committed by the remaining ones are growing in number and violence.* To this I would add that the "remaining ones" won't be sufficient to bring us back to the sky-high crime levels of the 1960s and 1970s. The reason will be shifts in the job market, education, and law enforcement strategies.

Internal migration patterns follow employment. The concentration of crime will shift from old cities of the Northeast to job meccas of the Sunbelt and West coast. When those economic wells dry up, the least skilled will be trapped while the more mobile go off to new hunting grounds. *A geographic crimewarp will sour the prosperity of the energy and electronics boomtowns.*

On the other hand, the large urban households most vulnerable to crime are a shrinking part of our national profile. *Suburban and rural migration and a trend toward smaller families are hastening the plunge in the crime rate.*

The small family and the graying of America will produce labor shortages by the year 2000. Minorities and women will be the chief beneficiaries. In 1983, for the first time, white men were outnumbered in the labor force. "By the turn of the century," predicts *U.S. News & World Report,* "two-thirds of American wives and most female single parents will hold full time jobs." The Rand Corporation concludes: "Higher wages should help persuade young women and older workers who face retirement to hold on to their jobs. These job opportunities will discourage women in the labor force from having many children, and may persuade some to have none at all."

Low birthrates and high work rates will leave a plethora of unattended homes as prime burglar bait during the day. However, "defensible space" architecture and greater watchfulness among neighbors will reduce the attractiveness of these crime targets. In addition, staggered work hours, communal living, and a growing trend toward home-based work sites will reduce the number of empty structures. Self-employed workers, who are likely to toil in a home-office, have among the lowest street crime victimization rates of private sector, nonagricultural workers.

But most cottage and small businesses don't have big budgets or big profits, leaving them prone to a host of white-collar schemes. According to Wayne Gray, a caring and diligent postal inspector based in California, "boiler room" sales scams are victimizing small businesses to the tune of $100 million a year. Misleading advertising specialties offers—a low-cost way to publicize businesses —are one of the most troublesome frauds. Then there are the office supply salesmen who take advantage of the perpetual need to save money by promising brand-name products at cut-rate prices. The goods often turn out to be phony and inferior, doing fatal damage to office machines. So while the self-employed may be somewhat reprieved from muggers and burglars, they are beloved by con artists.

Some students of crime and the business cycle have observed enigmatic spasms of crime during times of high employment. During such times, people can afford to travel, eat out, go to theaters—leaving their homes unattended. They have money to burn on the lightweight TVs, stereos, VCRs, and "ghetto blasters" that tempt thieves. They indulge in drugs, liquor, and handgun purchases that encourage violence.

During recessions, on the other hand, unemployment and lower incomes mean people can't afford to go out and party. By virtue of their presence, their homes are less likely to be broken into. But they still drink or take drugs and remain subject to violent fights and wanton destruction—the crimes bred by cabin fever, frustration, and poverty.

The future will feature a bipolar economy of simultaneous boom and bust. In the suburbs of Atlanta, New York, Boston, Phoenix, and Dallas, thousands of high-tech and service jobs go begging. The rich will live in glossy splendor, enjoying the fruits of a sensurround wonderland. The poor, however, will be trapped in the inner cities, unable to reach the abundant temporary and permanent jobs in the suburbs.

At the same time, tens of thousands of blue-collar laborers will be dumped out of their highly paid, highly skilled jobs in car plants and machine tooling factories. These will be displaced workers caught in the transition from smokestack to white-collar economy. Left behind by the coming boom in fields calling for technological wizardry—systems analysis, electrical engineering, solar energy, communications, asteroid mining, robotics, hazardous waste management—they have nowhere to go except entry-level service jobs at Burger King that pay less than half of their former wages. The alternative is unemployment. Both options are demoralizing and leave these marginal workers ripe for frustration-induced crime. Even if they are not the perpetrators, the outlook is dim: Laborers and service workers have the highest victimization rate of any occupational group.

Such retrenchments will erode our middle class—the crucial stabilizing and moderating force in society—and leave America ripe for upheaval. Domestic antiterrorist activity will become a police priority in the future.

Whether our lot as individuals is diamonds or dust depends to a great extent on how many people were born at the same time that we were. By the turn of the twenty-first century, slowing population growth will reduce the demand for goods and services. Prices will drop, the good things in life will become more accessible—too late for some.

Those born at the tail end of the postwar baby boom will, by 1995, be the ones struggling hardest to make ends meet. Crowded out of employment markets by earlier boomers and confronted with housing costs driven up by those same boomers, they will watch in frustration as the smaller generation behind them walks off with all the goodies. Their best hope for solvency will be a two-income marriage, just at a time when single-headed families are becoming a growth industry. The new bifurcated job market will, however, create opportunities in the service sector for the high-risk young. Those trapped in cycles of poverty will have a chance to rise up out of the ghetto.

The *good* career opportunities will require computer literacy and superior education. As the school-age population dwindles, more students will have access to computers and individual attention. (School enrollments have dropped 12 percent since 1974, according to the National Education Association, while staffing levels have dropped just 1 percent. There will, however, be a temporary rise in enrollments through the 1990s as the children of the baby-boom generation reach school age.) Computer teaching will pervade every phase of a lifelong learning process.

The presence of three- to five-year-olds in the classroom has been mounting steadily since 1970. As droves of mothers continue to enter the job market, they will send more children to school at the earliest possible age. Preschool software packages will employ a kaleidoscope of computer-generated graphics to teach toddlers basic learning concepts—position, color, letters. Early education benefits parents, children, and society. Studies reveal that children in preschool programs go on to jobs or post–high school education at a rate nearly twice that of others. They exhibit fewer arrests, detentions, and teenage pregnancies. Such programs cost several thousand dollars a year per child, but they ultimately save taxpayers money because of the reduced need for remedial education down the road. In short, the high-tech kindergarten will make a big contribution toward keeping the streets safe in the future.

As children progress through school, use of computer simulation gaming will enhance the teaching of current events, history, geology, writing. A 1984 report of the U.S. Department of Education found that half the students seeking a college diploma never get it; Graduate Record Examination scores—especially those dealing with verbal skills—have dipped since 1964; college curricula have become excessively vocational and narrow; one out of eight highly able high school seniors chooses not to go to college at all. Electronic educators hope they can overcome the deficiencies that plague today's halls of ivy. Futurists predict that within fifty years, 60 percent of Americans will have attended college—that's twice today's percentage. Almost all will have grown up with computers.

Many corporations have chipped in with advanced or remedial training run by their own state-of-the-art hardware and instructional programs. The Rand Corporation offers a Ph.D. curriculum. Wang Laboratories and Northrop Corporation offer master's degrees. Xerox, RCA, and Holiday Inns have built sophisticated educational facilities, and a number of corporations run joint programs with universities. In 1984, IBM gave over $6 million worth of equipment to Yale University.

Today's education prepares pupils for a post–Industrial Revolution economy that is rapidly becoming extinct. Tomorrow's *computer classroom* will promote the flexible thinking needed to support the new Information Age. *The marketable skills it produces will be our best anticrime insurance.*

There are, however, downsides to growing up with galvanic data processors. We are creating whole generations of computer "hackers" skilled in making criminal and innocent mischief by breaking into hospital, military, and financial data banks. In 1984, for instance, students infiltrated the University of Southern California's computer system, falsified grades, and went into business selling phony degrees for as much as $25,000 each.

We are also widening "the gap between the educated haves and have-nots," warns the Carnegie Foundation's Ernest Boyer. Affluent neighborhoods will be able to provide their schools with superior computer facilities, and children whose families can afford a home computer will have an edge over those whose families can't.

The gap will be further widened by the surging enrollments in private schools, even at a time when overall enrollments are shrinking. Department of Education statistics show the increase is not in traditional Roman Catholic parochial schools (down 5 percent) but in other religious (up 22 percent) and nonsectarian schools (up 36 percent). Hidden in these figures is a massive expansion in ultra-right Fundamentalist academies that eschew "secular humanism" and focus on a literal interpretation of the Bible—and whose standardized test scores show they are ill prepared for the Post-Industrial society.

Meanwhile, back in the ghetto, those trapped in the squalor of urban public schools find the battle for truth and marketable skills more ambiguous. College Board figures tell us that Scholastic Aptitude Test scores have risen for all minority groups, but most still trail the national average. While test results for blacks have improved, their share of the college-going population has slipped. Cities such as Chicago and New York are reporting astoundingly high dropout rates for black pupils. According to a federal study of high school sophomores, Hispanic students have the highest rate of all.

Language and basic skills are the reasons. Most dropouts come out of high-stress families in which school has little significance. Often students are driven out of class by early marriage, pregnancy, drugs, and, above all, financial need. In countless cases, the call of the streets is more powerful than the lure of a textbook. The intimate link between lack of schooling, idleness, and juvenile crime bodes poorly for the futures of minority youngsters.

A variety of innovations are moderating the bleak outlook. In New York, STEP (School to Employment Project) is offering employers large wage subsidies to hire high-risk teenagers. The program provides needy children with early work experience as well as income. In many cases a little cash is all it takes to attack the strongest incentive for dropping out of school. STEP's benign blackmail forces kids to choose between school and money or no school and no money. Other places—like the Neill Academy in the Midwest; the Alternative School in Richmond, Indiana; the Cooperative High School in New Haven, Connecticut; or the Cities-in-Schools program in Atlanta, Houston, and New York City—focus on intensive counseling, small classes, and constant monitoring of would-be dropouts. Still others, like the community colleges in North Carolina, work with those who have already dropped out and would otherwise be abandoned.

The most effective stay-in-school device will be the millions of part-time, entry level job opportunities made available by virtue of the burgeoning service economy and shrinking teenage population. There are proportionately more young people in the black and Hispanic communities than there are among whites. Therefore, minority youngsters will be the primary occupants of these jobs. Working at a local McDonald's, dry cleaner, or senior citizen center will provide teens with the money they need to stay in school. Those who drop out anyway will have a productive alternative to the street life.

In sum, *fewer students will drop out of school to drop into a life of crime.* Career criminals will increasingly be replaced with career technocrats. According to Wharton Econometric Forecasting, the unemployment rate will drop to 5.3 percent over the next decades. Individuals from all sectors of society will have access to the 14 million new jobs that Forecasting International predicts will be created by the year 2000. Both legitimate and criminal opportunities will shift accordingly.

Our means for fighting white collar and street crime will shift also. Police and corporations are developing an arsenal of new weapons. In Silicon Valley we have the first high-tech criminal task force—detectives trained to talk "lasers," "microchips," and "integrated circuits." Credit card companies, like Southwestern States Bankcard Association, maintain platoons of special investigators to nab interlopers like Timothy Leighton, who pleaded guilty to theft. Private corporations are learning to protect their computers and data tapes with audit trails, talking alarms, passwords, and log-in procedures. They are coming to rely on lie detectors to screen out dishonest employees. The FBI has set up a white-collar-crime hot line and the Houston Police Department has created a "con squad."

Information will be the key to crime control in the future. The computer, the greatest potential crime generator, is also becoming our greatest crime fighter. By giving public and private agencies the capability to keep track of us, it will become, according to Ira Lipman, president of a major private security firm, "a tool to protect and inhibit us."

Already, government and business have created electronic dossiers that track nearly every aspect of our lives: debts, insurance claims, crimes, welfare payments, taxes, medical status, work history, psychological profiles. Mark Monsky, a television news executive, predicts that computers will allow us to "frisk people for their minds."

A small percentage of offenders is responsible for the majority of street crimes. Computerized data banks can tell us who they are. Once identified, they will fall under the scrutiny of a "career criminal program." Anthony Bouza, police chief in Minneapolis, explains how to target the chronic offender: "One of the obvious solutions is to give them special attention in terms of surveillance, control, manipulating them through the system, warehousing them."

Minneapolis' version of the career criminal program is called "Target 8." Rory Rowles, twenty-three at the time I interviewed him, was a self-proclaimed habitual offender—one of eight targeted for special surveillance by police. He'd been in and out of prison for years. His problem? Cocaine. The habit turned him into a burglar and a dealer in stolen goods.

Although still in the younger drug-prone age group (fourteen to twenty-four), Rory told me he'd had enough. When on the loose, his mug shot, criminal record, address, type of car, and list of criminal associates were circulated to all Minneapolis police officers. Armed with information, they kept a casual watch on him with extra patrols and spot checks on the street. Rory got to feeling downright harassed.

There's no question career criminal programs work. They now operate in about one hundred cities, and there will be many more in the future. Programs such as this raise the hackles of civil libertarians. "It really amounts to an all-points bulletin on a certain group of people," says Gara LaMarche, formerly of the New York Civil Liberties Union. "You can trigger a police state atmosphere, not on the basis of ongoing or imminent criminal activity, but on the basis of unproven allegations or time already served." When Chief Bouza gazes into his crystal ball, he concurs with LaMarche: "We will become incrementally repressive."

The computers that store our secrets will increasingly be programmed to talk to each other. The IRS will flash information to the FBI. The Social Security Administration will transmit data to the Department of Social Services. We will stand exposed before a voltaic tyrant, with only a stripped down Freedom of Information Act to protect us.

While the computer gnaws away at our privacy—a constant worry to civil libertarians—people will hide behind multiple, fluid identities. "Anonymity will be our revenge," quips Mark Monsky. Identity will be tied to computers and will become the most critical issue of the future, he claims. "Cash is anonymous, but credit comes with a number." So does Social Security and almost every other aspect of modern life. Therefore, we will need various identities to do the things we want to do. "Anonymity will breed a broader spectrum of acceptable behaviors," postulates Monsky. Crime included.

Computers are only part of a general attack on civil liberties that is fueled by both fear of crime and fear of moral erosion. A 1981 Gallup Poll reports that 40 percent of its respondents believe that a breakdown in morality is responsible for what they perceive as an increase in lawlessness. In exchange for a moral renaissance, *large segments of the population are willing to compromise vital parts of the Bill of Rights.*

Freedom of expression is at risk from ultraconservative drives to control the airwaves, schools, books, and libraries. The New Right aims to neutralize ideas that contradict a literal reading of the Bible. Course work in Fundamentalist Bible schools emphasizes solid Christian values as an antidote to crime, hedonism, and political wrongheadedness. The concerns are valid, and supporters of such academies have every right to their own dogma. But by claiming to hold a monopoly on truth, they may inadvertently be setting the stage for a moral and political totalitarianism that reinforces many of the very problems it is intended to solve. Book burnings, a painful reminder of the Nazi horror, have occurred in places like Wichita, Kansas, and Gastonia, North Carolina. While right-wing Fundamentalism is not Naziism, the analogy is relevant. It illustrates that crime can emerge from intolerance.

The Fundamentalist revival—a sincere answer to the search for stability, certainty, and meaning at a time of chronic social change and mobility—contains the unintended seeds of political violence and terrorism. Encouraged by a climate that legitimates monism and ethnocentrism, neo-Nazis, Ku Klux Klanners, and abortion vigilantes will flourish.

Mainstream values mold our responses to crime. Because American values have always gravitated toward the moderate middle, the New Right will not prevail in the coming decades. But it will influence legislators and attitudes. In openly trying to Christianize America, New Right Fundamentalists seek to have particularist values reflected in the law of the land, and their generously funded, sophisticated public relations campaigns—such as those of the Moral Majority, Liberty Federation, and the Christian Roundtable—will help form our responses to crime. If they preside, due process may well be redefined, and crimes made and unmade according to the tenets of the new religio-political gospel. Lobbyists of the New Right are striving to eliminate the "exclusionary rule" that protects us from unreasonable search and seizure, alter bail practices, and introduce preventive detention. To some extent, they have already succeeded.

The gospel according to Jerry Falwell points to communism as the gravest crime of all. Conversely, anything that promotes a free-market economy is considered God's work. Falwell's New Right mentor, Richard Viguerie, views federal regulations as a form of socialism: "Businessmen are so over-regulated and harassed by bureaucrats that they are approaching the point of zero economic freedom." According to some critics, the renewed emphasis on laissez-faire business practice and the growing attack on regulatory agencies, allows minions of the right to "render laws protecting health and safety of workers and consumers meaningless" and "legitimate the violence caused by socially irresponsible practices of businesses." In a recent survey, Amitai Etzioni found that more than half of Fortune 500 corporations were involved in illegal practices—price-fixing, bribes, fraud, overcharging—between 1975 and 1984. The top one hundred boasted more shady incidents than all the others combined. The regulatory mechanisms set up to contain them, charges Etzioni, have become "increasingly supine." A free market left unchecked will leave companies, whose practices are now defined as fraudulent or criminally negligent, freer to victimize us in the future—another example of good intentions gone awry.

The New Right's family agenda is similarly fraught with unintended consequences. According to its precepts, the sanctity of the family is inviolate. Government is debarred from interfering in education, sex training, contraception, rights of parents over children, rights of husbands over wives. Rigid patriarchalism may unwittingly encourage domestic violence. Laws protecting battered children and abused spouses have already been weakened in some states. The repression of sex information feeds rising illegitimacy. Unwanted, antisocial, abused children will become our most fearsome criminals.

Social and public supports, which might offset these calamities, are thought to interfere with the God-given processes of natural selection and survival of the fittest—a paradoxical conclusion from those who disparage Darwin's theory of evolution. Ultraconservatives will spearhead tax revolts and cuts in municipal services. Recent attempts have failed. But where they succeed, streamlined budgets will force a reevaluation of priorities and lead to de facto decriminalization of the very acts the New Right considers immoral. Laws against prostitutes, drug abusers, and other consensual criminals will simply become too expensive to enforce, but those who kill, rape, and rob will be subject to the full wrath of an increasingly punitive criminal justice system. The religious, economic, family, and constitutional priorities of the Radical Right will be a strong contender in the marketplace of ideas that determine what is a crime and how we respond to it.

Displacements in crime will touch the most basic aspects of our existence: safety on the streets and in our homes, financial security, work life, government, morality, and freedom. This book is devoted to anticipating how. The search for answers will lead us through the violators, scenes, offenses, and responses to crime that will make up the six crimewarps of the future.

Crimewarp I

The New Criminals

- A woman executive embezzles $10 million in federal funds.
- A devil-worshiping teenager mutilates and kills a schoolmate in a drug feud.
- An eighty-two-year-old woman is caught trying to steal contraceptives.
- The sixty-three-year-old leader of an armed gang is foiled in an attempt to break out of jail, where he is serving time for robbery.

Traditionally, criminals have been thought of as young, unemployed, undereducated punks. But as we move into a new era of crime, they will gradually be displaced by older, smarter, more sophisticated operators.

The newest recruits for a life of crime will be drawn from pools of women and senior citizens. The number of young criminals will decline, but those who remain will be more dangerous.

1

Women Alone

I met Fran O'Leary after she'd gone straight for ten years, but her previous life was the stuff of which some criminologists say a new female crime wave is being made.

Her life started out conventionally enough: She was a middle-class kid who spent eleven years in Catholic school. Mama wanted her to be a nurse, because that's how you meet and marry rich doctors. But round about eighth grade, mama's plans went awry. O'Leary started breaking rules. She'd cut classes and smoke; she'd hang out with boys, but preferred football and basketball to dating.

"I couldn't fit into the role they had picked out for me," reflects O'Leary. "I was just a tomboy. I used to get from my friends that something was wrong with me because I didn't like boys. From the nuns and my family, I would get, 'You're a tramp because when we see you, we see you with ten boys.' The amazing thing is I was probably the only virgin left in my neighborhood at sixteen."

Virginity didn't last very long. That summer, her parents sent her to an aunt's house in upstate New York. There she met a nineteen-year-old youth with a car and a line: "If you love me, you'll do it." She had no sexual feelings yet, but it was clear to her that shedding her chastity was her visa to being accepted. It was also her entree to motherhood. At age sixteen, she was pregnant with her first daughter. Marriage and a second pregnancy followed in short order. Fran didn't know how not to get pregnant and was too embarrassed to ask. By age seventeen, she had two daughters. She went to visit her parents that Christmas and never returned to her husband. But she didn't know what to do with two children. A mere teenager herself, all she wanted to do was hang out on the corner.

And she did.

The corner was Broadway and Forty-second Street. She ran away from her parents and children and into the arms of passing strangers who would pay her for sexual favors. She'd never worked a day in her life, but prostitution was something she understood. "I'm sure my mother never meant it the way it came out, but [when she said] to save your virginity for that man who has the money, sex and money got put together at a very young age."

O'Leary plied the skin trade for eight years—and still felt nothing sexually. She was arrested for the first time after five years. Lots of arrests followed, but, Fran theorizes, because she was white she was always released.

Finally she did time at the Women's House of Detention. That was a turning point. Her fellow convicts taught her that "pross" was a penny-ante crime, not worthy of doing time. She learned to set her sights higher to robbery, burglary, and check forgery. Something told her to head West.

California became her laboratory, and her crimes expanded. "I wanted to be bigger and badder than any man. I couldn't compete in any other world, but I could compete in that world. All my crime partners were men, and I had to be better than them."

A slew of grocery clerks and barkeeps got to stare down the barrel of this petite armed robber's gun. A bunch of banks ended up on the receiving end of her forged checks. A number of acquaintances got a firsthand taste of this tough-talking redhead's rage.

"I was going through a real craziness in my life," she claims. "The violence was building and I wanted to hurt someone. The violent crimes were all very personal. It was people I knew that I felt had hurt me and that was my way of hurting back."

But O'Leary was the one who got hurt. She was arrested in Los Angeles, and this time she ended up doing *serious* time: six months to fourteen years in a maximum security prison. She was alone, scared, and three thousand miles away from home.

Parole was finally granted and O'Leary went to New Jersey. There, she learned the hard way what happens to ex-cons looking for a job. It was Question 6 on the job application—"Have you ever been arrested?"—that always queered her chances. The job search was a failure. She decided to go back to work she could count on—armed robbery. In planning her heist, she found an item in a newspaper about the Fortune Society, a support group dedicated to helping ex-convicts stay straight. She figured that would be a great place to recruit a partner for the Fort Lee robbery she was plotting.

The Fortune Society outsmarted Fran. Not only did it keep her straight, she eventually became its president. But not before she engaged in a lot more self-destructiveness. "When I first came to Fortune, I did stop committing crimes. What I did was internalize it. I wasn't hurting other people anymore; I was now going to hurt myself. I went from relationship to relationship, marriage to marriage. I wasn't dealing with my kids.

"Fortune could not have helped me. I was the only female there. They were all men, men who adored my kids. I didn't want two minutes with [my kids]. How do I go to a bunch of men who think my kids are great and I want to say I don't want them?"

What Fortune wasn't able to do for O'Leary, school was. "I started going to college and, by accident, got caught up in a course called Women in Society. It's like a Pandora's box came open." After a year of consciousness-raising, she concluded that the roots of her criminal behavior were to be found in the way she was raised as a woman. At a speaking engagement she blamed part of the distortion on religion.

"The first thing you ever taught me," she told a priest, "was the reason I was here, and the most beautiful and blessed thing I could ever do with my life was to bear children. The next thing you taught me was the dirtiest, filthiest thing I could do was to have sex. Well, Father, how do you do one without the other? How could you possibly give birth and not feel guilty over what you did to have that baby? You destroyed me. All of a sudden, you're a teenager and you're fighting with these feelings. And if you get told you're bad long enough, you'll be bad."

Fran O'Leary was "bad" from age sixteen to twenty-eight—a span that includes the normative crime-prone years. Her badness started with the status offenses, like running away and sexual misbehavior, that characterize most female juvenile crime; advanced through prostitution and check forgery, the stereotypical female crimes; and culminated in serious property and violent crimes that people don't usually associate with women. Some experts are saying that we can expect a tidal wave of Fran O'Learys in the future.

☐ ☐ ☐

An unmarried woman with three illegitimate children was in prison for brutalizing her two-and-a-half-year-old daughter. She had been punishing the child for refusing to eat and soiling her pants. For a whole day she intermittently whipped the tot with a hose and an electric cord and placed her in a tub of cold water. The last beating of the child's life ended when she was thrown into that tub and hit her head on a faucet. The mother left the room. When she returned twenty minutes later, she found her infant lying face down in the water, dead— one of the children who make up an estimated 20 percent of the victims of female killers. The mother, who went to prison for her crime, had been drinking for four days straight.

Women who commit such crimes tend to be woefully ignorant about child development. Many expect their children to understand the difference between right and wrong before the age of one. Others take a baby's yawn or burp as a personal affront. Most are premature in their demands for obedience and comprehension. Such unrealistic expectations set the stage for an extreme frustration that can erupt into punitive aggression. Add to this volatile mix a mother who is single, poor, young, undereducated, and without close community ties, and you have the classic abusive family. Tragically, this is precisely the kind of mother of whom we'll be seeing more.

□   □   □

A woman cited in a staff report to the National Commission on the Causes and Prevention of Violence had been convicted of murder in the second degree for killing her husband. She and her husband argued constantly in their brief six months of marriage, especially when they'd been drinking. In these bouts, the woman claimed, her husband would often slam her around. One night they had a trivial argument over a television show: The husband wanted to watch a political program about the Kennedys and the wife protested. He then called his mother to complain that his wife was a Republican and that all Republicans should be killed. The argument escalated, and it was "the Republican" who ended up doing the killing. She stabbed her husband with a paring knife while he sat on a kitchen stool.

In a high percentage of the cases in which women attack family members, the violence is provoked by the victim—especially in the case of mate killings. Frequently, the victim is a male who has been drinking. The victim may have been the first to show a gun, make a threat, call the assailant a "bitch," abuse her for having done a poor job of washing the dishes, or throw her across the room. The chronic surplus of women and growing conflicts over sex roles will spawn more such violence in years to come.

□   □   □

Several years ago, Sandra Brown, a successful New York businesswoman, was convicted of grand larceny and conspiracy for forging and falsifying business records. The former publisher of *Executive Woman* magazine and *The American Express Handbook for Women* had reportedly embezzled $10 million in federal funds earmarked to provide seed money for women's businesses. She and two male accomplices were said to have set up dummy corporations to divert the stolen money into a variety of fashionable amusements. Among these, a plane, a helicopter, several boats, a horse farm, and a Southampton condominium.

A growing number of women have broken the "pink-collar" job barrier. They've joined the 8 out of every 1,000 employed women who hold a high-level executive, managerial, or administrative job. That number may seem paltry, but it represents an 84 percent increase since 1972. The leap into the executive suite has opened up vast career vistas for women. Along with it has come access to a motley array of new criminal opportunities.

In 1970, which was about the time that Fran O'Leary committed her last crime, the imprisonment rate for women hit its lowest point since 1925. But Fran's experience was a harbinger of the future. By 1985, that rate had more than tripled to 17 per 100,000. At the same time, according to a Roper poll, the percentage of women who admitted to having been arrested for crimes other than traffic violations increased by half.

If you look at raw numbers, the population of the United States has grown by 18 percent since 1970. Because women now make up 51 percent of the population, more than half that growth—is attributable to them. Their arrest rate, however, is growing at a much faster pace than their rate of increase in the population. Women commit far fewer serious crimes than men—only 1 arrest to every 5 arrests of men. But there's no denying that this ratio masks a quantum leap in apprehensions of women. What's going on?

Some experts say nothing is going on. The jump in statistics merely reflects a greater willingness on the part of law enforcement agents to arrest, prosecute, and jail women—an end to chivalry, if you will. Others say the women's movement has encouraged equality in crime just as it has in the home, at school, and at work. To these I add another explanation.

The woman of the future will find herself living in a world of increasing *singleness;* escalating *feminization of poverty;* and burgeoning access to *new work opportunities.* These three central trends will have far-reaching repercussions on female crime patterns. The first two go hand in hand and will erupt in bolts of domestic violence and economic crimes of survival; the last will trigger crimes of both survival and greed.

CRIME AND THE IMBALANCE OF THE SEXES

The prospects of steady male companionship for women are not good. Since World War II, there has been a shortage of men and a resulting "marriage squeeze." With insufficient numbers of men to go around, more members of both sexes have been marrying later, divorcing and not remarrying, or remaining single.

A good number of my women friends have been caught in the squeeze—and they're not necessarily losers. Many attractive, accomplished people don't understand why they can't find a man who'll make a commitment or treat them kindly.

Custom dictates that a woman marry a man two or three years older than herself and of equal, if not better, educational and social standing. When you consider those factors, the prospects for eligible men become even more narrow. Some women deal with the shortage by violating the traditional norms.

Phoebe (not her real name), a forty-year-old professional with an Ivy League education, did just that in two marriages. In her second one, she blundered into a short, disastrous marriage with a psychopathic drifter who was several years younger than she.

In an earlier marriage, she was financially and emotionally dependent on a man much older and more sophisticated than she. He was also a traditional man, and Phoebe's independent career ideas were a threat to the total dependency he required. The more he realized he couldn't control her, says Phoebe, the more violent he became. The beatings started with hitting and progressed to near-murder. Her husband, a pillar of his community, forcibly held her under a cold shower, pitched her outdoors, naked, into freezing weather; threatened, with his brother, to kill her; strangled, humiliated, and defamed her. The final blow came when he pinioned Phoebe so his grown daughters could have a go at her.

By the time Phoebe left him, she had accumulated an injury scorecard that included bruises, loss of consciousness, and three occasions of hospital treatment. Today, after years of having no contact with her first husband, Phoebe still claims: "If I had stayed, I would have become very physically violent with him. My hatred would have grown so strong. Even now, there are times I wish I could kill that man."

Her other liaisons were not so catastrophic. The men were simply scared, ambivalent, or otherwise engaged. And why not? With only 81 unmarried men for every 100 unmarried women, males have a surplus of over 5 million females with whom to play musical relationships. Phoebe, on the other hand, is among the one fifth of women aged 14 and older who, as of 1970, have not had potential male partners.

Her story is not unusual. She used to search her soul to find the fatal flaw that kept her from finding a relationship that would work. The fact is there is no fatal flaw in her; the flaw is in the skewed demographics that will persist right through the year 2050. The men Phoebe and so many other women encounter are behaving as one might expect under circumstances in which males have the upper hand both in numbers and power. For men, it is a buyer's market.

The excess of women gives men little incentive to make commitments and put up with inconvenience, restrictions, or hard times. Given the number of romantic options they have available, it is easy for them to decide that the woman they're with is too much trouble and that the grass will be greener elsewhere. They are in the happy situation of being able to demand much and give little in return.

In this context, an extraordinary number of men, like Phoebe's first husband, feel free to be emotionally and physically abusive. The women who depend on them have few options, so many put up with it. But if mistreated long enough, many women retaliate with violence. Just as Fran O'Leary did. Just as Phoebe might have.

Police, who are often the only recourse available to a woman trapped in a violent situation, have not been much help. I've spent hundreds of hours on patrol with officers and found that they have little sympathy for women who are unchaste, unwed, or unsober.

I remember the woman who frantically begged a desk sergeant to arrest the estranged husband who had been beating her and stealing her possessions. The sergeant refused to act. The husband—who turned out to be a bigamist—was acting within his rights, the man behind the badge insisted.

Then there was the dispatch to a tenement in what used to be known as "Fort Apache." It was a missing child call. Our team was greeted by a forty-seven-year-old black woman and her lover. She was throwing him out because she didn't "want to be sexed." Both were drunk, and they had been steady customers of this precinct during previous drinking bouts. But this night the woman was frantic over her young child. Instead of empathy, she got disparagement for her "breeding habits." Said the indignant men in blue, "You can have children but you don't know where they are?" As an aside, the officers informed me that, now that the woman had had her fun, she wanted to get her child back.

Finally, there was the young couple whom we found lying naked and dead in a demolished bedroom—mattress and bed turned over, chairs askew, dressers broken. Both had .22-caliber slugs in their chests. The investigative premise was that the young woman was an adulteress whose husband had caught her with her lover. As it happened, the man splayed on the floor *was* her husband. It hadn't dawned on these officers that she might have been raped, or that the male might have been the adulterer, or that an armed burglar might have chanced upon a legitimate couple making love in the late afternoon.

Incidents such as these illustrate the sexism with which women are confronted when they turn to those who are expected to treat their plight objectively. Of course, the police can rebut with countless war stories about women who insisted on having an abusive boyfriend arrested only to renege when it came to pressing charges and testifying against him. The police can regale you with tales of the family fights in which they took the man away and were later invited to come back for a roll in the hay with the female disputant. They'll also show you the scars they acquired when they tried to forcibly remove some tough who was beating up his wife—and the outraged wife jumped on the astounded cop for picking on her husband! And all these stories would be true. They form the backdrop that makes police so cynical about domestic violence.

But the police have learned that making an arrest *does* make a difference. They can prevent further violence against men and women by taking the aggressor away. Until the word spreads around the country, however, many of our law enforcers are simply sealing the trap that leads women to attack and kill.

Phoebe wrenched herself out of the maelstrom before she reached her boiling point. With no children to support and no man to abuse her, she manages to eke out a modest living and steer clear of frustrations and economic pressures that turn some women into violent felons. The two-and-a-half-year-old girl who died in a cold bath was just one among thousands of male or female children and adults who, every year, find themselves in the vortex of feminine rage—rage induced by a low sex ratio that is trapping women in cycles of poverty, abuse, or despair.

In 1960, when Phoebe was first starting to think about boys, there were only about 4¹/₂ million women living alone; today, she is one among almost 13 million. About one sixth of all white family households have a female head with no husband present; among blacks, the sex ratio is much lower—only 73 men to each 100 women—and the problem proportionately more severe. "In 1970," asserts one study, "for the age cohorts most eligible for marriage, there were almost two black women for every man." Nearly half of all black households are now headed by a woman.

Tragically, the shortage problem is self-perpetuating, especially for blacks. There is a small difference in the rate at which blacks and whites conceive male children, with whites producing boys 3 percent more often than do blacks. Male babies of all races are less hardy than female babies and therefore suffer a higher death rate at infancy. But among disadvantaged minorities, a lack of money and education for child care leads to infant mortality more often. Finally, conceiving a male requires higher concentrations of sperm. When a potential father is highly active sexually, eight emissions or more a week, his ejaculate is often too weak to produce a male. In a culture characterized by surpluses of women as well as an absence of constraints on sexual behavior, we can expect a high male activity level—and fewer surviving boy babies.

The imbalance in the sex ratio has led to an astronomical increase in births out of wedlock. Since 1940, the illegitimacy rate has steadily climbed from 7.1 per thousand unmarried women to 29.6 per thousand. More than half of these births occur among blacks, even though they make up only 12 percent of the population. That's high, but it's a lot lower than it was in 1955, when 65 percent of all out-of-wedlock births were black. The shift in these racial proportions shows the extent to which whites are sharing the problem.

Today, more than one fifth of all births take place out of wedlock. A growing number of upscale mature women, like Phoebe, are considering becoming bachelor mothers. Many women thirty-five and older have gone ahead and done it. But the vast plurality of such births occur among the poor and the underaged: close to 40 percent of all illegitimate babies are born to women younger than nineteen. Speaking at the 1985 annual conference of the Children's Defense Fund, Dr. Aaron Shirley, director of a school-based teenage pregnancy program, reported: "I identified 90 mothers in a school of 960 and learned that half of them had given birth before starting high school."

The current conservative trend in government discourages sex education. In the future, as in the present, high school pregnancy classes will remain a needed antidote to ignorance. A recent Alan Guttmacher Institute study compared U.S. teenage pregnancy rates with those of other developed countries: Ours is by far the highest. The report attributed much of the difference to government perception of its role in family planning. In countries like France, Sweden, and the Netherlands, the government gives priority to preventing pregnancy through free or inexpensive contraception. Sex is treated as just another part of human relations. By contrast, our government, with strong prompting from religious conservatives, has decreed that teenage sex is sinful. Its oft declared priority is to promote premarital chastity. The result has been not less sex, but more pregnancy.

Under these circumstances, prenatal care, nutrition, and knowledge of child care are apt to be inadequate. Out-of-wedlock babies are often born with a low birthweight and a variety of diseases, defects, and addictions. This reduces the odds of survival for male babies even further. As it is, nonwhite male babies die before the age of one at a rate almost twice that of white male babies and 23 percent higher than black female babies.

All of this is partially offset by differences in black and white birthrates and overall improved infant mortality rates. Birthrates are declining across the board, but more slowly for blacks than for whites. Blacks produce 21 births per 1,000; whites, only about 15 per 1,000. Simultaneously, death rates for black infants have declined from 52 per thousand in 1960 to 19 per thousand today, a 65-percent decrease. The mortality rate among black female infants has decreased as well. Therefore, the larger pool of female babies means this decline does nothing to redress imbalance in the sex ratio. As a result, says one demographer, "American blacks present us with the most persistent and severest shortage of men in a coherent subcultural group that we have been able to discover during the era of modern censuses."

These dry demographic realities contain the seeds of the crime patterns of the future. There is good evidence that women who are single heads of families with young children suffer a higher rate of depression and criminal behavior than women with mates. If these women are poor and young, their children are more apt to be neglected or abused. If these same women have been consistently exploited or abused by men, they are more apt to be angry and violent. Many of the children they raise will in turn grow up to abuse others and engage in antisocial behaviors.

Such a situation is germinating in the Midwest. A few years ago, a court found a mother to be guilty of neglect. She had allowed her live-in boyfriend to share a twin bed with her eleven-year-old daughter and to abuse the child's younger sister. The rapist went to jail, but the eleven-year-old was already impregnated by him. The mother refused the child permission to abort the fetus. I can only speculate on the desperation that allowed this mother to tolerate the sexual abuse of her children. Perhaps the strains of caring, single-handedly, for two youngsters led to criminal neglect. Yet, underlying that was a rigid, Fundamentalist Right-inspired notion of morality that induced her and a juvenile court judge to force a raped preadolescent to carry a pregnancy to term. I wonder about the kind of future that awaits the eleven-year-old victim of this quagmire. Perhaps, like Fran O'Leary, she will find the responsibilities of premature motherhood too much to bear. Will she, too, run away from them and become a prostitute, armed robber, burglar, and check forger? Or will she become an abusive and neglectful mother or a battered wife? Perhaps she will become all those things.

This case raises red flags about the dangers inherent in the low sex ratios we face over the next sixty-five years. For women who have short- or long-term partners, we can anticipate weaker commitments, greater abuse, more exploitation. Both they and their children will suffer. For women who have children but no partner, despair, drift, and frustration will be enhanced. Above all, we will see more domestic violence committed by women who are either alone or in bad relationships.

When the availability of men is scarce, jealousy over infidelity or the end of a relationship looms large as a motive for domestic violence. I once came across a case in which a woman shot her husband seven times with a .22-caliber pistol after he announced that he was divorcing her and would take all the property they owned. When he refused to discuss the matter with her, she opened fire.

A more celebrated jealousy murder took place a few years ago in the prosperous village of Scarsdale. Jean Harris was the archetypal sex-ratio casualty. For years, this genteel Virginia school administrator had been the devoted mistress of Herman Tarnower, the celebrated physician who popularized the "Scarsdale Diet." But Tarnower—wealthy and eligible at age seventy—had his pick of Westchester divorcées to warm his bed between Jean's visits. Reportedly, he even proposed marriage to one of them, a much younger nurse who worked for him. Friends of Tarnower's told me that he had grown tired of Jean and wanted to dump her but knew that Jean, being a "tough" woman, would "never take no for an answer." Jean, who had, for the bulk of her middle years, assumed that she and Hy were a couple, was understandably devastated upon learning of her hero's alleged perfidy. She went back one last time to the Scarsdale estate she regarded as home. There, she confronted her longtime lover and shot him. Harris alleged that it was herself she had intended to kill, but a court found her guilty of premeditated murder.

When men are scarce and women plentiful, it is easy for older men like Tarnower to dump aging mates in favor of younger women—who, in turn, may be having trouble finding a mate among their contemporaries. The older man–younger woman partnership is one way to cope with the sex-ratio problem. But it leaves middle-aged females like Jean Harris with nowhere to go—sometimes with fatal consequences.

A prominent lawyer once said to me of Tarnower, "He needed killing." The same might be said of other targets of female ferocity. A woman's violent rage is often preceded by a history of emotional or physical abuse from her victim.

Women are victims of family violence three times more often than men. But when siblings attack each other, as they do an estimated 19 million times a year, the male and female rates equalize. When females attack other relatives, it is three times more likely to be another woman than it is a man. When women kill, in 86 percent of the cases their victim is male. (Men's victims, on the other hand, are almost always other men.)

A 1973 study of domestic murders highlights the chronic nature of family violence. In 85 percent of the cases, police had been summoned to at least one previous disturbance call at the victim's home. In half the cases, they had been there five or more times. A more comprehensive nine-year special report of the National Crime Survey found that victims of family violence had, in a quarter of the cases, been similarly assaulted at least three times in the previous six month period.

Living together is less dangerous than living apart. One study discovered that disturbances involving physical force are more prevalent among separated or divorced spouses. This finding foreshadows an increase in violence during periods of escalating divorce rates. Fortunately, after reaching a record high in 1981, the divorce rate has been inching downward.

The murder that follows a series of fights is frequently an expression of intolerable despair. Great blues songs capture the feeling when they describe a woman's agonizing love for a man who hurts or abuses her. That is precisely how Phoebe felt about her brutal husband—until she came to her senses. A letter introduced as evidence at her trial indicates that this must be the way Jean Harris felt about Tarnower. But like so many others trapped in emotionally or physically destructive relationships, Jean baled out with violence.

In 1984 millions of us were treated to the spectacle of Farah Fawcett setting her husband's bed on fire and immolating him in a movie called *The Burning Bed*. It told the true story of Francine Hughes, a frequently battered wife who burst out of her personal purgatory by incinerating her tormentor. Francine, acquitted on grounds of temporary insanity, had been unable to leave her husband for good in any other way.

Her solution was not as unusual as you might think. The surprise that consistently appears in the family violence literature is that wives kill husbands about as often as husbands kill wives. But there's a difference: When wives kill, the odds are 7 to 1 that they are acting in self-defense.

And they're apt to get away with it. In a Dade County study, only one quarter of female killers actually went to state prison. A host of new criminal defenses have evolved that allow their crimes to be viewed as justifiable. The "battered-wife syndrome" defense was successfully used in the trial of Cindy Hutto in South Carolina. In April 1979 a jury acquitted her of the murder of her husband Bubba. She shot him, while he was lying in bed, with the same gun he had earlier handed her after threatening to kill her. After the repeated batterings she had suffered at his hands, she wasn't taking any chances. The PMS (premenstrual syndrome) defense is being employed in similar ways. Shirley Santos, a twenty-four-year-old mother of six, pleaded guilty to harassment, but defended the beating of her four-year-old daughter by claiming premenstrual fatigue and depression.

Such defense strategies are creating a double standard of justice. Many women are exonerated for crimes for which men would be held accountable. While PMS and battered-wife defenses help some deserving women, they inadvertently reinforce damaging stereotypes of female instability. Their use, however, will increase, because there really *are* extenuating circumstances that elucidate much female violence.

□ □ □

It is astounding that nearly two thirds of family homicides relate to conflicts over sex roles, according to a Detroit study. In Francine Hughes' case, it was a husband who used violence to thwart her educational and career aspirations. But it can just as easily be a man like Phoebe's ex-husband, who humiliates his wife and feels she ought to take it passively. Then there is the woman who criticizes her husband in front of his friends and is subsequently "put in her place." In the majority of such killings, the parties define each other as objects, property to be possessed.

Such frenzies reach across the social spectrum to the rarified atmosphere of our country's Scarsdales. But violence is a more prevalent response among the poor, who have nothing, not even the words, with which to safely ventilate their frustrations.

Years ago, while doing some field research, I ran an after-school club for a group of black and Puerto Rican teenage girls in a low-income section of the Bronx. Among our activities was a series of improvisations based on real situations I had encountered in their school or which the girls had drawn from their private experiences. There was the pregnant girl bringing a drug-addict boyfriend home to her mother; the girl who came home from school to find her mother with a new man, a drug addict; the mother summoned to school to answer for her child's discipline problems; the teacher confronting her pupils with an alleged theft.

In enacting how they, as mothers, daughters, and teachers, would cope with such conflagrations, battering always emerged as a prime strategy. The violence trigger in each case was a verbal repertory too limited to adequately express powerful feelings. Words would tumble out until, like a broken record, the girls would get stuck on one phrase. Not being able to get past the frustration of endless repetition, they would inevitably lash out with their hands.

In this Bronx neighborhood, as in so many slums, resorting to violence was not restricted to family matters; nor was it confined to males. Boys and girls were expected to fight as a means of both defending their honor and showing disdain for another person. The fights took place not only between persons of the same sex, but between males and females as well.

A host of slights could trigger a sentiment like the one I found scrawled in a school's third floor Girls' Room: "I am going to beat Carolyn's ass." One teen, for example, was assaulted for asking another whether she "became a lady at school." The assailant would allow only her own mother the liberty of asking such a personal question about the onset of menstruation.

One student, the oldest of three sisters, was often charged with cooking for, and safeguarding, the other two. She described fighting on her siblings' behalf as an important part of her duties. "If they bother my little sister, then they're botherin' me." Fights were often started by "talkin' all that big talk." But this young warrior had a strict code: "If I beat somebody's behind, I tell them to their face. I don't start fights. I just finish them."

Finishing a fight sometimes required a return match. One day I came across two girls in the bathroom. They were trying to figure out a way to leave the school unseen so that one of them would not be found by a classmate who was looking to fight her. To my amazement, the girl they had been trying to avoid actually walked in. She was asked by the others, "Why do you want to have a second fight?"

"Because I haven't finished the first one."

"Hey, you! Why do you want to fight her?"

"Because I got my reason."

Students seldom tried to hide their fights. Fighting ability was a source of equal pride to girls and boys. This widely accepted mode of settling disputes kept many teenagers out of class and gave the school its foremost discipline problem. As a result, physical skills got honed while verbal skills remained undeveloped, thus reinforcing the need for violence.

It is such childhoods that set the stage for the convicts who inhabit our women's prisons. Many studies, in which teenagers report on their own behavior, maintain that patterns of delinquency are very similar for boys and girls, with the increase in violence being greater among juvenile females than it is among adult women.

In "The Masculinity of Crime—Some Second Thoughts," Nanci Koser Wilson, of Southern Illinois University, argues that female violence has been escalating at a much faster pace than most people think. She writes:

"Traditionally, the female had a ready alternative to the use of violence in the protection of a man. It was the female's father, brother, or husband who might use violence to protect her honor or person. Further, a woman who became personally aggressive would lose her status as a 'lady' . . . it is at least clear that women who are 'on their own,' whether as heads of families or as barroom customers, are not in a position to receive this protection." (The barroom hazard was vividly displayed in the 1983 gang rape of a lone female patron in a New Bedford, Massachusetts, saloon.)

The low sex ratio has changed that tradition of passivity, and escalating female violence will be part of the fallout: A long-term study on female homicide offenders since 1940 supports this prediction. Today's incarcerated female killers are younger and far less likely to be married or living with a man than were their predecessors. They are also much more likely to have children, but not the means to support them. Most were on welfare or working at menial jobs at the time of their arrest. Others were peddling their bodies.

One thing hasn't changed: Like earlier cohorts, they are in prison for having killed a mate, a child, a cousin, a crony, or a pimp. The motive? Revenge or a response to physical abuse prevailed among the 1940–66 group. But today's imprisoned woman, claims the study, is most likely to have killed during a robbery.

Today, a female is arrested for 1 out of every 10 violent crimes that come to the attention of police. That proportion has remained relatively unchanged for thirty years, despite the spiraling effects of the low sex ratio. But it's important to see what's buried in that number.

The FBI indexes four crimes in the category "violent crimes": murder and nonnegligent manslaughter, forcible rape, robbery, and aggravated assault. In her controversial study, Nanci Wilson recalculates arrest rates and concludes that the growth in adult female violence has outpaced that of males—an increase of 250 percent versus 225 percent—since 1960. For girls, the jump is 7½ times the 1960 rate, whereas for boys it is only 4½. Wilson's calculations have some weaknesses that are inherent in all arrest statistics. But keep reading: You'll see there's good reason to believe that at least some of that increase is real.

One of the violent crimes, forcible rape, is extremely difficult for a woman to commit. The low ratio of female arrests for that crime, 1 in 1,000, artificially pulls down the violent crime average for women.

Robbery statistics also skew the picture, although there are many more female robbers than rapists. Patricia Joyce Brown, arrested in 1985 after purportedly holding up the Union Street branch of Wells Fargo Bank in San Francisco, is one of the 7 percent of arrested robbers who are women (in 1960, women accounted for fewer than 5 percent). Brown, who was caught with a .22-caliber pistol and her "take" of $1,767, was suspected of robbing four other local banks as well. She was never prosecuted because the district attorney failed to file a complaint. Yet, Brown's alleged "M.O." is consistent with that of many female robbers. A gun, "the great equalizer," is almost always present; and the heists are ongoing, rather than isolated, events.

If we turn to Fran O'Leary, the profile gets rounded out. Most female robbers are, as she was, single heads of families who need money. Perhaps, like Fran, they simply cannot get a straight job. But they treat crime like a job. Fran carefully planned her Fort Lee, New Jersey, stickup. She always worked with male accomplices but took an active part in the theft. A prior history of delinquency, Fran's teenage prostitution, contained the germs of her future career as a robber.

Of course, not all female robbers make a *career* of crime. Some are drunk, or strung out, or in crisis; some get goaded by friends and others get duped by lovers. For them, robbery is a fluke with few criminal antecedents. But whether the career or situational variety, there was a nearly 43-percent increase in arrests of female robbers between 1971 and 1981, compared to less than 30 percent for men. If you go back to 1960, the scoreboard reads closer to 300 versus 200 percent. By 1985, robbery arrests eased across the board, but more for males than females.

□ □ □

A more common female crime is aggravated assault. Arrests for such crimes have increased by 45 percent in the 1971-to-1981 time period, 5 percent less than the growth rate for men. However, after 1981, when arrests declined, the drop-off was steeper for men than for women. Aggravated, as opposed to simple, assault describes crimes which result in serious bodily injury. When a weapon is involved, the seriousness of the injury is irrelevant; the mere presence of a deadly weapon is sufficient to "aggravate" the assault.

In 1985, Oranette Mays of Cleveland tried to hijack a Pan Am plane making a stopover in her city on its way to New York. When ground personnel tried to prevent her from boarding, she pulled a gun and shot her way in. There, she held four hostages for six hours before being wounded by police who stormed the plane. Mays herself hurt a ticket agent and shot an officer in the chest (that bullet was deflected by his bulletproof vest). The presence of a gun as well as her threatening behavior qualify this incident as an aggravated assault. One out of every eight aggravated assaults is committed by a woman. Storming a plane with a gun, however, is not characteristic of them.

Women's assaults have more in common with murders. Not surprisingly, the percentage of women arrested for murder is almost identical to that of aggravated assaults: 12.7, or 1 in every 8. The actual number of such arrests, however, declined by one eighth between 1971 and 1981, while men's increased by over 20 percent. But within four years, murder arrests for both sexes dipped by about two fifths.

When focusing only on assaults and murders—*crimes that often arise out of close relationships*—we find that women account for 1 out of every 8 arrests, a proportion 20 percent higher than that of their overall violent-crime ratio. The gap between male and female narrows even more when one factors in simple assaults. These crimes, which cause little or no injury, are not included in the FBI's index for serious violent crime. Yet, today, 1 out of every 6 people arrested for simple assault is a woman, an increase of nearly 22 percent since 1971.

In 1984, the violence statistics were boosted by seven when a mostly female gang was arrested for the kidnapping and murder of a Long Island insurance man. Police found the victim in a Harlem apartment where, stripped to his undershorts, he had been tortured and starved for two weeks. Among his convicted captors were a four-hundred-fifty-pound woman who rarely left her apartment, a "swinging" twenty-year-old housewife who had recently walked out on her husband, and a charismatic Filipino-born shopgirl.

A case like this makes great copy, but assaults and murder committed by women rarely involve such deliberate acts of gratuitous violence. As described by Fran O'Leary, they are more likely to be intensely personal, spontaneous eruptions committed against "people I knew that I felt had hurt me and that was my way of hurting back."

□ □ □

Sometimes, the hurt is displaced. A convicted child killer had beat her three-year-old son with a shoe until he was covered with bruises. It wasn't the first time she had punished him severely; in the past she had used belts, electric cords, and her fists. But on this occasion, she had spent the previous evening with the boy's father, a man she hated so much that she transferred the hostile emotions to her son.

Statistics indicate that child abuse is proliferating wildly—reports increased by more than 40 percent in the first half of the 1980s alone. But such numbers, based on statistics from only thirty states, may reflect nothing more than intense media exposure. In truth, we don't know whether child abuse has increased or not. Only in 1962 did we first become aware of the "battered child syndrome." It wasn't until twelve years later that laws were passed requiring the reporting of all suspected child-abuse cases.

Few statistics on child beatings and sexual molestation are compiled nationally. The American Humane Association attempts to make broad-based estimates, but for the most part we must rely on nonstandardized local records, which are more reflective of a jurisdiction's zeal than the actual incidence of child abuse. In sum, we have no reliable before-and-after records on which to base conclusions about the extent of child abuse.

The odds are that cruelty to children was far more prevalent in the harsh rigors of the colonial era and the industrial revolution. After all, it wasn't until 1870 that we saw a legal challenge to the absolute rights of parents over their children. That's when Mary Ellen, a severely beaten and neglected child, came to the attention of a group of church workers. They appealed to the only organization that might have any jurisdiction in such a case: the Society for the Prevention of Cruelty to Animals. The SPCA sued to remove the girl from her home on the grounds that Mary Ellen was a member of the animal kingdom and therefore entitled to the same protection as a dog or a cat. That famous case led to the creation of the Society for the Prevention of Cruelty to Children in 1871. Prior to that, the concept of child abuse simply did not exist.

Cases like Mary Ellen's make it clear that the range of permissible assaults on children was much broader in the past than it is today. Given modern conditions, however, it is safe to say that child abuse will grow in the future. On the one hand, we have an expansion of religious fundamentalism, which, in some extreme forms, preaches the biblical virtues of beating the inborn evil out of children. (A past president of the American Psychological Association was quoted as saying, "Soon we won't be able to tell the difference between child abuse and an excess of Christian zeal.") On the other, we have swelling ranks of young, single, poor, undereducated mothers who lash out against their children out of frustration and ignorance.

All this is not to say that violence occurs only among the poor. Affluence brings its own explosive stresses. But the evidence is clear: the lower parental income, employment, and education, the higher the rate of violence.

☐ ☐ ☐

The overall increase in arrests of women for violent crimes was almost 22 percent between 1971 and 1985, about 5.5 percent more than men. Ordinarily, we criminologists frown on using arrest statistics as the basis for conclusions about crime patterns. Most crimes never end in an arrest. For those that might, police policy has much to do with who gets arrested for what.

In the case of women, there has traditionally been a strong "chivalry factor." Police have been reluctant to arrest women for a crime for which they would not hesitate to arrest a man. The same applies to prosecutors and judges at later points in the criminal justice process.

Chivalry is evoked partially by the demeanor of the suspect. If she behaves in a ladylike way, she is likely to be treated with more indulgence than if she violates female stereotypes by using foul language or fighting. Some researchers argue that the kind of crime she commits makes a difference in the female offender's treatment as well. If it is a "feminine" crime, like shoplifting, she stands a greater chance of being diverted from the criminal justice system.

Fran O'Leary was treated leniently as long as she restricted her criminal activities to selling her body, but when she was caught for a "masculine" crime, like robbery, she did harder prison time. As Fran herself admits, the fact that she is white helped a lot. But if more of her victims had pressed charges, that would have overridden any chivalrous or racial considerations, and she would have been arrested more often.

There is strong evidence that the chivalry factor is going the way of the lace handkerchief. As more women, either by choice or circumstance, are forced to make it on their own, *feme sapiens* is being released from long-standing social controls imposed by the traditional paterfamilias. To the extent that informal social controls in the home are no longer operative, formal legal controls begin to fill the breach. Many women, who under previous conditions would not have committed a crime—or have been punished for it if they had—are now feeling the full weight of the law. The female "crime wave" may, in part, be an artifact of the greater willingness to treat women like criminals.

All female arrest statistics are thus flawed. But in the case of violent crime, they are nevertheless a revealing indicator of who is doing what to whom. Assault and murder are the crimes with the highest clearance rates. The fact that they tend to be unplanned and involve people who know each other makes most of them relatively easy to solve.

If anything, arrest rates underestimate the number of women actually involved in violence. Men, when victims of domestic assaults, are injured more often than their female counterparts. Yet, because of the implied slight to their masculinity, they are reluctant to report having been on the receiving end of a closet pole wielded by a woman. Children, the frequent victims of battering at the hands of women (though proportionately less than at the hands of a man), are in a poor position to tell anyone of their abuse. Above all, much personally motivated violent crime is never reported to police because it is considered to be a private matter. Since most assaultive behavior by women falls into this category, it is likely that only a small percentage of the actual incidents becomes known to the authorities who compile statistics.

When we bypass those authorities and talk directly to victims, we see that lower income people and those in the twenty to thirty-four age range are more likely than others to be involved in family violence. In the case of child abuse and neglect, for example, 64 percent of known female perpetrators are between the ages of twenty and thirty-four. Most of the time, however, the victims of family violence are older than their assailants. This is significant in light of the fact that women tend to marry men older than themselves. When men become embroiled in fatal family fights, half of the time they are the ones who end up dead.

The unexpectedly high male fatality rate is linked to the weapons that women use to assault men. Most often, it's a gun; the second weapon of choice is a knife. Because these two are more efficient killing implements than a fist or a candlestick, attacks that might have been nothing but assaults become homicides instead. To the extent that increasing numbers of people keep guns at home or in their cars, we can expect to see an accretion of these kinds of deaths.

The presence of a gun is one of the common threads in the examples of intimate violence I've cited (the woman who shot her husband when he asked for a divorce; Jean Harris who shot her lover when he wanted to leave her; Christine Hutto who shot her husband with the same gun he had used earlier to menace her). Another is a history of violent disputes (Phoebe's and Francine Hughes' chronically abusive mates). A third is alcohol (the "Republican" who knifed her husband as he sat on a kitchen stool; the mother who beat to death her two-and-a-half-year-old daughter).

In many of the cases, either the victim or the assailant, or both, were drinking. A Roper survey of drinking habits covering the years 1977 through 1980 detects a 22-percent increase in women who report overindulging. This compares to a slight downward turn for men. The increases are most dramatic at the lowest income level and for those aged eighteen to twenty-nine. It's no coincidence that these are also the groups most heavily represented among the perpetrators of family violence.

The same Roper poll reports the rise in problem drinking is greater among blacks than whites. While there is no difference between victimization rates for blacks and whites for violent crime by current or ex-spouses, there is one for assaults by other relatives: Blacks report a higher rate than whites.

If the poll has identified a long-term trend, the combination of guns, drinking, youth, race, and poverty will prove to be a lethal one. Young, low-income, poorly educated minority families are the ones most likely to be affected by a low sex ratio and its attendant explosive pressures. They are also, proportionately, the most violent.

THE FEMINIZATION OF POVERTY

The poor stratum of society is not the one that produces militant feminists. On the contrary, the women who get arrested tend to come from the most traditional and exploited segments of society. Like Fran O'Leary, they are the ones saddled with young children at an early age. While powerful as mothers, they are apt to be oppressed as mates. "Liberation" is thrust upon them by poverty and male abdication rather than choice.

I remember my days as a young activist in the women's movement. In the late sixties and early seventies, it was a crusade of white, middle-class women who had traditionally enjoyed the protections of a paternalistic society. Our less-privileged sisters regarded us with some mirth and thought, "Hell, we've always been on our own. We'd like to have a little of what you're trying to get away from!"

Nevertheless, there is a popular theory that the women's movement accounts for the explosion in female crime. According to the foremost proponent of that theory, Freda Adler, "Just as women are taking on such traditionally male roles as stevedores, airline pilots and telephone linesmen, they're becoming assassins,

too." Sara Jane Moore and "Squeaky" Fromme aside, assassination and impersonal murder are not the detonators that have set off the female crime bomb. A
close examination of the statistics shows that the hottest flash points are economic crimes that tie in to the increasing feminization of poverty.

□   □   □

Between 1971 and 1981, women experienced an increase of arrests for burglary, larceny, car theft, and arson that exceeded 50 percent; in the same decade, men's arrests for those crimes rose only 29 percent. The areas in which
women most sharply outstripped men, however, were forgery/counterfeiting
and fraud, followed by burglary and larceny. These surges in arrests ranged from
50 to 169 percent. In the prior decade, the jumps were even steeper, rising at a
rate nearly three times faster than men's. Even with decreasing arrests since
1981, women now account for almost one third of those collared for such
offenses. In 1960, they made up less than one sixth. Note that these trends were
evident *before* the women's movement had made any major inroads.

The numbers are deceptive. Some argue, for example, that most of the increase in fraud is accounted for by a crackdown on welfare cheating; that the
free-for-all in larcenies is mostly petty shoplifting made possible by the expansion of self-service stores; and that the forgeries and counterfeiting are simply
irregularities in cashing government support checks. In short, the motives are
wholly economic. The criminals, mainly destitute women trying to get by, are
engaging in traditional female crimes.

Feminization of poverty flows from the growing singleness of women. The
number of families maintained by women has almost doubled since 1960. About
a third of those families are black, a percentage far out of proportion to the
number of blacks in the population. While two thirds of female-headed families
are white, their share of the total has actually dropped by 10 percent since 1960;
the percentage for blacks has increased by 8 percent.

All together, 16 percent of American families are headed by a woman: 44
percent among blacks, 23 percent among Hispanics, and 13 percent among
whites. The median income for all female-headed families is between one third
and one half of the income for all other family arrangements. For black and
Hispanic female-headed families taken alone, the median income is $2,000 be-
low the poverty threshold.

Almost two thirds of such families contain minor children, a cumulative
increase of 14 percent since 1960. The children born to these families have
replaced the elderly as the largest group of poor people in the country. A Congressional Budget Office analysis reveals that the poverty rate for minority children is 40 percent compared to 14 for the white majority. But in female-headed
families, the poverty rate is a whopping 50 percent for school-age children
compared to 12 percent for families with two parents or a single father.

Virginia Agosto heads one such family. In 1985, pregnant with her sixth
child, she had no steady housing in which to stay. Every day, she shuttled back
and forth between an emergency shelter and a Bronx welfare office in search of

the night's lodgings. With five children in tow, all aged under ten, and no support from their father, her exile was draining and futile. By some miracle, life may turn out fine for people like the Agosto children, but the odds dictate that they will drop out of school and become the street predators of the future.

Almost half of New York's young people drop out of school; the percentage for minorities is much higher. The unskilled manufacturing jobs they might have filled are drying up. The 141,000 mostly white-collar jobs that have replaced these jobs aren't available to high-school dropouts, nor do they benefit the dropouts' inner-city mothers, who cannot get to the new banking, insurance, and high-tech jobs being created in the suburbs. The cycle of poverty simply gets passed on to the next generation.

The proportion of female household heads who, like Virginia Agosto, are thirty-five years old and younger, has just about doubled since 1960. The trend is clear—growing numbers of young nonwhite families headed by women who are outside the labor market and living in poverty. In 1983, the poverty rate reached its highest level in eighteen years: 15.2 percent. It is against this backdrop that the female economic crime explosion takes place.

CRIME AND THE WORKING WOMAN

It would be misleading to restrict a discussion of female crime trends to welfare mothers and mistreated women. Impoverishment also embraces masses of women who hold jobs but are consistently paid less than men.

Two thirds of the women age fifteen and over, whether employed or not, have incomes of less than $10,000 a year. That compares to one third of adult men. Fewer than a third of adult women have incomes between $10,000 and $25,000 a year as opposed to nearly two fifths of men. Only 5.2 percent have incomes exceeding $25,000 while the percentage of men in the highest income category is nearly 26.

The women whose incomes are derived primarily from wages rather than welfare are concentrated in job ghettos that have come to be classified as low-paying "woman's work": a salesclerk at Neiman Marcus, a dental hygienist on Fifth Avenue, a secretary for a TV station in Boston, a bookkeeper in Los Angeles. In these jobs, as well as the higher-paying ones, they earn from 51¢ to 90¢ for every dollar earned by a man in the same position. That leaves droves of women—especially single heads of households—living below the federal poverty threshold of about $11,000 for a family of four. But there are some programs that help offset the temptation of crime: WEDCO is one.

Kitt Taft, a single welfare mother in Minneapolis, had been jobless for three years. One day, in the spring of 1984, she marched into First Bank Minneapolis and applied for a loan to set up a massage business. Many bank officers might have snickered and thought, "Massages, eh? I know what kind of business you mean!" Not James Hetland. He said yes. Taft had no collateral, but she did have a reference from the Women's Economic Development Corporation (WEDCO), one of a consortium of private agencies trying to fight poverty among women by helping them start their own businesses. Today Kitt is running a legitimate massage business in the physical fitness center of the Amfac Hotel. Other former welfare mothers are running businesses that range from selling Afghan bread to typesetting services.

A recent Wisconsin study gives the lie to the stereotype of welfare mothers as chronic spongers. Sociologist Sandra Danziger examined women whose AFDC (Aid for Dependent Children) payments were reduced because their work incomes had exceeded allowable amounts. "Economists thought that when these women had to choose between work and welfare, they would quit working and return to the rolls. That didn't happen." Despite the fact that the cut caused their overall incomes to decline by an eighth, and 20 percent of them were forced to live below the poverty line, the women kept working.

□ □ □

Welfare mothers are only some of the women who are making inroads in the work world. More than half of all married-couple families now have a wife in the labor force. Married or single, poor or affluent, female workers have swelled all Bureau of Labor Statistics work categories—except for farming/forestry/fishing and operators/fabricators/laborers—by huge percentages, bringing the distaff work force to over 50 million.

Women now make up nearly half the work force. By contrast, in 1950 they were only a third. While many of them hold only part-time jobs, their earnings are essential. A *McCall's* magazine survey found that their readers' incomes contribute 44 percent of their family's subsistence. Ironically, new job markets are opening up new criminal markets.

Many of the assembly and manufacturing jobs traditionally held by women in the textile, clothing, toy, and shoe industries are going to the people of Taiwan, Hong Kong, and the Philippines, where human labor is cheaper. But such losses are being offset by gains in the service sector. In July 1982, for the first time, the number of people working in service jobs surpassed those in manufacturing. Between the end of 1979 and 1984, 5.5 million new jobs were created in the service sector. The largest growth areas were those in which the majority of jobs are "pink-collar" positions held mostly by women: business services; health services; eating and drinking establishments; finance, insurance and real estate; hotels and motels. Most are low-paying, dead-end jobs—a problem for the nearly 10 million families who depend on women for their support, and also the reason that this fastest-growing segment of the economy is the most vulnerable to employee theft.

Financial institutions, for example, lose eight times the amount of money to employees and swindlers that they do to robbers. With the advent of automated banking, any workers with access to the bank's mainframe can manipulate money into their own pockets. Tellers and bookkeepers, 92 percent of whom are women, are among those who have access.

Hospitals stock an extraordinary number of inventory items that carry high resale prices on the outside: narcotics, medical machines, stethoscopes, X-ray film. Most such losses are caused by staff doctors, nurses, orderlies, and technicians. The majority of registered nurses and medical paraprofessionals are women.

Hotels and motels are cornucopias of consumer goods—liquor, silver, blankets, television sets, all things that you can use in your own home. The lodging industry's vulnerability to loss permeates every aspect of service—the valet and catering office, front desk, guest rooms, and dining areas. The major culprits are not guests who swipe towels but employees with access to stealable goods. Ninety-six percent of housecleaners, 87 percent of cashiers, and 75 percent of food service workers are women.

In the property and casualty insurance industry, most thefts are due to frauds perpetrated by outsiders rather than employees; however, there is great potential for collusion in claims and adjustments fraud. Women constitute the majority of insurance adjusters and 26 percent of insurance agents.

Retail stores have the greatest woes of all. Employee pilfering is estimated to eat up half the slim profit margin on which these businesses operate. Retailers claim the majority of thefts occur in sales, stock, and the cashroom. Seventy percent of retail clerks are women, as are the preponderance of cashiers.

Various studies estimate that between 40 and 75 percent of employees steal. Most steal a little; a few steal a lot. The greatest part of these crimes occur in areas in which women hold the majority of jobs. These acts don't show up in official crime counts because employers rarely prosecute insiders, but it's a safe bet that women are doing their share of pilfering and embezzling.

Women have been hired for two thirds of all new jobs created since 1979. That percentage is expected to shoot up to 70 by the end of this decade. Because most of these jobs will be formed in the theft-prone service sector, it's likely that female participation in crime will spiral accordingly.

Economic need is the driving force behind most workers who steal from their companies. An early study of embezzlers showed that close to three quarters of them were in debt and had heavy family responsibilities. In 1939, when this study was done, it was mostly men who found themselves in that bind; now women find themselves increasingly in the same position. More recent research indicates that low job satisfaction can tip a needy employee toward dishonesty. Dissatisfaction is endemic to the low-level, routine jobs that dominate the service sector of the economy.

□ □ □

However, ambition and a strong push from the feminist movement have propelled 11 million women into the more rewarding professional, technical, and managerial job categories. These, too, bring with them an array of criminal opportunities. Sandra Brown, who allegedly stole federal funds entrusted to her for the establishment of women's businesses, is part of a new breed of upscale female criminal.

Embezzlement arrests of women have exhibited a strange pattern; between 1960 and 1972, they skyrocketed by 280 percent compared to a mere 50 percent for men. But the period since 1972 is the one in which women really expanded their presence in higher-level jobs. With greater access to the company books, you'd think there would have been another major spurt in embezzlements; yet, these arrests have actually declined by about 10 percent. For men, the deceleration was twice as fast. This development is inexplicable, except as an artifact of recording procedures.

There is a thin line between forgery, fraud, theft, and embezzlement. Although Sandra Brown had supposedly embezzled government funds, the crime was not called by that name in her 437-count indictment. In looking at arrest statistics for 1971 to 1986, it appears that a slew of such thefts must be buried in the numbers for forgery/counterfeiting and fraud. For women, these arrests increased by about 37 percent for the first category and 146 percent for the second. For men, the rise was only one third that amount.

Murky crime classifications are one more reason to be leery of basing conclusions about crime patterns on arrest statistics. But examples of female white-collar criminals make one thing clear: Crimes are restricted by circumstances. You have to be in a position of trust before you can embezzle money from business accounts; a welfare mother in Detroit has no such access. As women scale the career ladder, their criminal opportunities will expand accordingly.

According to sociologist Rita Simon in the *Journal of Criminal Justice,* "If this trend continues approximately equal numbers of men and women will be arrested for fraud and embezzlement by the 1990's and for forgery and counterfeiting the proportions should be equal by the 2020's." Access to upscale jobs may add to the rate of white-collar crimes, but it can also act as an offset to violent crimes. Simon, an authority on female crime, explains, "Some women committed violent offenses because they were dependent on men and felt trapped or abused. As women have made economic gains, those feelings have diminished."

That brings us full circle in linking the low sex ratio, feminization of poverty, and access to new work opportunities with future female crime patterns. The new female criminal is neither a "moll," like Ma Barker nor a "doll," like the repressed Nora of Ibsen's play. Most of her violent and economic crimes are traceable to her disadvantaged position in the sex ratio. It is only those who have attained the same white-collar opportunities as men whose criminal motives have transcended the sexual barrier.

But the key to the executive washroom or the company stockroom isn't opening the door to happiness. The dearth of dependable mates is leaving women in a state of drift, without crucial anchors and restraints. Some bury their pain in work, while others shy away from men. Still others lose themselves in booze and drugs. Scratch a female criminal, and you'll find one or more of these conditions.

The promises of the women's movement—equality, self-actualization, and freedom—have created rising expectations and an inevitable bipolar set of frustrations: for those in traditional roles, a sense of being trapped in the pressure cooker of the family with no safety valves to vent their steam; for "liberated" women, the anomie that comes from an absence of structure and limits. The growing underclasses of homeless, addicted, and impoverished women, as well as their upscale, professionally active sisters, are at a crossroad where crime is perceived as a tempting and sometimes necessary route to follow.

CRIMEWARPS

· The population is aging. *Because violence against family members and friends is committed mostly by younger women, such violence will decrease as more women get older.*

· The divorce rate will continue to drop. *Because a large part of domestic violence occurs between divorced or separated spouses, these assaults will decrease.*

· There has been a downward trend in the birthrate from 1910 to 1977. From 1977 to 1982, the rate increased slightly, mostly due to rises in the white birthrate. The birthrate for blacks continued to drop. Since 1982, overall rates have decreased again. Because more female than male babies survive, those women born during the five years of increased birthrate will find themselves in a tighter marriage squeeze when they come of age between 1991 and 2000. A larger proportion of those will be white, and they will contribute a growing share to illegitimacy, singleness, and poverty. The black share will decrease in those years. *We will see proportionately less family violence among blacks and more among whites.*

· New police practices will not overcome deeply engrained cultural norms that say it's okay to use force against someone just because they're family or friends. However, police will use the knowledge they have gained about the predictability and preventability of violence to remove assailants from the scene before a domestic squabble turns into a homicide. Therefore, *fewer people will die at the hands of an enraged woman.*

· Potential solutions to rising illegitimacy, like school-based birth control clinics, will be offset by fundamentalist-inspired public policies that obstruct the dissemination of contraceptive information and devices, sex education, and payments of abortions for poor women. Out-of-wedlock births will continue to proliferate among underaged, poor women. Their frustration, ignorance, and isolation will lead to massive increases in child abuse. There is a caveat here: The tipping point for abusive mothers occurs when they have two children. *If birthrates drop to the point where disadvantaged women have fewer than two children, the incidence of violence against children should drop proportionately.*

· As of 1984, half of U.S. couples could not have babies due to surgical sterilizations and fertility problems, a 25-percent rise since 1965. *Fewer children will mean less family tension and proportionately less family violence.*

· The growing singleness of women will perpetuate the growing poverty of women. Innovative programs such as WEDCO will create new, legitimate sources of income for poor women, as will enlarged job markets.

However, WEDCO–type programs will not expand fast enough to outpace the cuts that will take place in the social services—food stamps, medical payments, battered-wife shelters, abused children's programs, Aid for Dependent Children—on which poor people rely. While new jobs will be plentiful, they will be geographically or educationally out of reach of the neediest women. Therefore, *economic crimes by women will remain at current levels.*

· For more affluent women, upscale jobs will continue to open up. Of employed women, more than 25 percent are now found in the professional, technical, managerial, and administrative category. However, the proportion of the total female work force in that area has grown more slowly than in any other since 1978. The crimes that attach to these positions, embezzlement and fraud, will be committed more and more by women. However, the rate of increase will be much slower than the thefts that go with lower-level jobs in the service sector. Overall, *the rate of increase in all economic crimes by women will be much slower than it has been in the past two decades.*

2

Terrible Teens

On an autumn evening in 1974, a powerful, six foot two inch, fourteen-year-old, pseudonymously called George Clancy, got together with two comrades and committed a crime that horrified the city of Indianapolis. Shotgun in hand, the three made a foray into a middle-class white neighborhood and robbed three retail stores. In order to inhibit the sounding of an alarm, they forced the proprietors and patrons to undress. The strategy worked fine in the first store; in the second, however, the fourteen-year-old became aroused and raped one of the female victims. In the third store, he tried to force a male victim to rape a woman. When the man resisted, Clancy clubbed him and proceeded to insert the barrel of his gun into the woman's vagina. The brutality of his crimes led the press to dub George a "monster man."

The monster man had been a well-known problem in his community for three years. He had been born to a white couple, but was fathered by a black. When his true parentage became evident, his legal father deserted the family and his mother dispersed her children to foster homes. George was raised by an older black couple. By the time he was twelve, his criminal and violent tendencies were obvious. He fought, smoked "weed," shoplifted, robbed filling stations, and burglarized a neighbor's home. He was out of control and everyone knew it.

The youth was placed in group homes, given psychiatric evaluations, placed in secure custody, sent out of state. Nothing helped. John Conrad, who wrote about the youth for the book *In Fear of Each Other*, explains: "Irresponsibility occasioned his begetting; more irresponsibility cast him into a ruinous childhood from which a good outcome was improbable. . . . Indianapolis had neither the professional resources nor the institutional facilities to meet the serious need that the juvenile court saw at least a year before George's delinquent career reached its grotesque climax."

George Clancy illustrates the eclectic criminal career of a new breed of psychopath emerging from the nation's growing poverty. However, poverty alone does not explain him. His crimes are the spawn of an expanding pool of unwanted, malnurtured children who are unsuited to civil life.

□ □ □

In July 1984, Gary Lauwers, a seventeen-year-old Northport, New York, youth, had his eyes gouged out and body mutilated by another seventeen-year-old from whom he had allegedly stolen ten bags of "angel dust." The mescaline-crazed killer, Richard Kasso, hung himself in his jail cell, but his eighteen-year-old alleged accomplice, James Troiano, lived to be arraigned for second-degree murder. A fourth member of the group testified that Troiano had handed Kasso the knife and pressed him to slash Lauwers' throat. (However, perceptual distortions caused by heavy drug use rendered both Troiano's confession and the witness's testimony unreliable, and the boy was cleared of murder charges.)

For crazed Ricky Kasso, who lived in cars and dug up graves, killing Gary Lauwers wasn't just a simple act of drug-buddy revenge. He reportedly climaxed the murder by making his victim cry, "I love you Satan!" It was revealed that these youths, who seemed to be as addicted to the heavy metal of The Grateful Dead and Ozzy Osbourne as they were to powerful hallucinogens, were practicing satanists—a phenomenon reemerging in various parts of the country.

Ricky's parents knew he was terribly sick long before he butchered Gary Lauwers. They tried desperately to have Ricky hospitalized, but a staff psychiatrist concluded he was no danger to himself or others. Another hospital refused Ricky for a different reason. The psychiatrist warned that the Kassos were in a desperately dangerous situation, which Huntington Hospital was not equipped to handle. Ricky's mother, Lynn, then reached out to the district attorney who was prosecuting the boy for grave robbery. Mrs. Kasso claims she was told there wasn't anything the D.A. could do. "We didn't know where else to turn. . . . We had come to the end of our road." Ricky Kasso was a time bomb, but there was no place to defuse him.

Flip Wilson was on to something in the early 1970s, when his "the devil made me do it" routine had us roaring with laughter. In a high-tech age, satanism provides a perverse kind of spirituality. For alienated, identity-less youngsters, a devil cult is just another form of retreatest gang—the perfect vehicle for abdicating responsibility.

Kasso's crime is an extreme manifestation of peer culture and teenage "gangism" gone wild. Youth gangs of all sorts are making a comeback. Although it's not clear that they're increasing in number, some are growing in viciousness. Parents and teachers stand very little chance of combating the street lessons taught by hip peers. If current trends continue, the future will hold many Ricky Kassos in a variety of guises.

□ □ □

In 1980, the State of Kentucky condemned sixteen-year-old Todd Ice to die. At the time, he was the youngest death-row inmate in the nation. Todd seemed an unlikely culprit. This soft-spoken, scholarly looking white boy wrote poetry, got straight A's in school, went to church, and came from an intact family. He had nothing in common with the prototypical violent juvenile delinquent. Yet, in a number of ways this so-called "Jekyll and Hyde" killer presaged our response to the juvenile criminals of the future.

The Ice and the Knox families were next-door neighbors in rural Powell County for six years. Their adjoining trailers nestled in the foothills between bluegrass and Appalachia mountain country. The Knoxes were old-timers in the town of Stanton, while the Ices had recently migrated from Indiana. Syl Knox and his service station were community institutions. The Ices, by contrast, were scorned as outsiders in that conservative backwoods. Syl Knox said they were "odd . . . not reg'lar." The Ices didn't have much to do with the local folk. Nor did they, in this fundamentalist community, attend the same church. They just didn't fit in.

Todd Ice's family was large: mother Dana and father Dean; three natural and three adopted children, including an oriental child. Dean worked second shift at Rockwell International ("the best job you can get around here," according to Syl Knox). At home he kept livestock and barking dogs, which disturbed the Knoxes' sleep.

During the years that the Ices and Knoxes lived next door to each other, there was tension between them. Not enough to amount to a "Hatfields and Mc-Coys" mountain family feud, but enough to cause bad blood. The barking dogs were one issue. More important, Sheila Knox was convinced that Todd Ice had been breaking into her trailer and stealing small items—a gun, for example, with which Todd was reported to have been seen at school; also liquor, which a classmate said Todd boasted of stealing from Syl Knox's truck.

When Sheila Knox tried to get the state police to do something about the thefts, they allegedly replied that they couldn't take action: Todd was too young and there was no hard evidence. Sheila, who held on to the shattered glass from a broken-into door, said no fingerprint tests were ever done. Sheila also went to Sebert Gilbert, Todd's principal at Powell County High School, to report the boy's misdeeds. Gilbert was incredulous. After all, Todd Ice was a model student: good grades, exceptionally high IQ, 4-H member, church camp counselor.

People involved with the case claimed the Knoxes scorned Todd's family as white trash, and the boy came to regard himself as the standard bearer in defending his family's honor.

According to a jury's verdict, on the evening of December 5, 1978, Todd Ice, then fifteen years old, exacted the ultimate revenge: he savagely attacked Donna Knox and her mother.

That night, alleged the surviving victim, Todd lay in wait for the Knoxes to come home. When Sheila and her seven-year-old daughter, Donna, arrived, he stabbed Sheila in the back, dragged her into Donna's bedroom, tied her up, and repeatedly hit her with a hard object. All the while, claimed the mother, Sheila pleaded with him to leave and asked why he was doing this. Ice purportedly replied: "I like you, Sheila, but I don't like Syl." Finally Sheila passed out. Then, seven-year-old Donna was taken into the bathroom and held in front of a mirror and made to watch as her throat was slit and the life bled out of her. After she expired, Ice returned to Sheila and slashed her throat as well, leaving her for dead.

Ice never confessed to the crime, and the only evidence linking him to it was Sheila's eyewitness testimony. Bloodstains found on his clothes couldn't be typed, and local police couldn't recall any other forensic tests being done to establish his presence at the scene. An inmate of a local mental health program repeatedly confessed to the crime, but later recanted. Sheila attested that Todd seemed perfectly sane. His arresting officers concurred, but numerous experts testified that Todd was a chronic psychotic and probably insane at the time of the crime. Ice averred that he was never at the scene, having been waylaid in the woods by a bearded man with a gun. That man was never found.

None of these points was compelling enough to introduce an element of doubt about Todd's guilt. It took a jury only thirty minutes to convict. Of the three sentencing options that were available, two were considered "too liberal." The jury voted for execution. Todd Ice became one among thirty American death-row inmates that year who were seventeen or younger at the time they were sentenced to die. (A few years later, he was temporarily removed from death row while awaiting a new trial. Ice admitted to the killing and was re-tried in February 1986. After an unsuccessful attempt to plead insanity, Ice was convicted of manslaughter and sentenced to twenty years in prison.)

Thirty out of twelve hundred capital convicts may not seem like much—a mere 2.5 percent—but the issue confronts us with our confused concept of criminal responsibility. Because of their youth, juveniles are not deemed criminally or civilly liable for their actions. Too immature to vote, do military service, drink, or attend X-rated movies, these children are not considered too young to die in an electric chair.

"If he's old enough to murder my daughter, he's old enough to die," Syl Knox insists. "I'd kill the sonofabitch in a moment, but they won't let me near him."

Crimes like Todd Ice's are so heinous that many states now remove them from the benign ambit of the family courts and try them in the adversarial adult criminal justice system. It is the beginning of a trend that will allow the ultimate sanction to be applied with growing frequency to our increasingly violent teens.

George Clancy. Richard Kasso. Todd Ice. Three teenage boys, from different parts of the country, with diverse socioeconomic backgrounds and criminal styles. They have one thing in common: violence.

Youths account for less than one fifth of those arrested for violent crimes. Additionally, the overall percentage of violent crimes committed by the young has declined 5 to 6 percent since 1973. However, recent studies tell us that *individual juveniles are committing five to six times more violent crimes* than the previous generation. There's nothing new about raging teenagers. What is new is that while there are fewer of them, they are individually more assaultive.

Arrest statistics show that the bulk of today's criminals are young—fourteen to twenty-four years of age. While teenagers make up only about 10 percent of the population, they account for nearly a quarter of all arrests. The remaining nineteen- to twenty-four-year-old age group accounts for another 11 percent of the population and an additional third of the arrests.

By the time they have reached their mid-twenties, most youths have matured out of crime, settled down, and become less violent. The opportunistic crimes they commit to impress their peers lose their appeal and drop off. A small minority move on to become professional criminals. In the interim, however, a tiny percentage of teenagers are responsible for at least half the crimes that are reported.

The oft-proclaimed crime explosion of the 1960s paralleled the onset of puberty for the baby boom generation. As they grew into young adulthood, the crime rate leveled off. With their impending middle age, the crime rate has been sinking. Experts differ on just how much crime is accounted for by birthrates, but no one disputes that there is some relationship. Therefore, as the population continues to gray, we will see steep decreases in crime committed by the young.

By the year 2000, the critical crime-prone age group will make up less than one fifth of the population. That's 5 million fewer youths than today. But that doesn't mean our crime woes will be over. Marvin Wolfgang, a longtime student of delinquency, speculates: "The number of juveniles who get into trouble may become reduced, but the number of offenses committed by that nasty few may increase." A substantial (though slightly decreasing) percentage of these crimes —like George Clancy's—victimize innocent strangers in the course of a robbery or, as in the case of Ricky Kasso, a drug feud.

When people think of teenage crime, it is not usually people like the Kassos, from affluent, white, harborside communities who come to mind. It is the specter of a group of tough-looking ghetto blacks demanding money or worse that evokes our deepest fears. That's why so many cheered when Bernhard Goetz opened fire on the quartet that approached him in a subway car in December 1984. The sense of vindication was palpable when his antagonists' criminal histories were revealed.

Darrell Cabey, Troy Canty, and Barry Allen—nineteen years old—and James Ramseur—eighteen—all had several arrests and/or had done time for crimes ranging from fare beating to armed robbery. Subsequent to the shooting, Ramseur was picked up for rape, robbery, assault, and criminal possession of a gun. The four youths hailed from the Morrisania section of the Bronx, where I had done research nearly fifteen years earlier; the teenagers I worked with then could easily have been their older siblings.

IMPOVERISHED DELINQUENTS

The kids I came to know in the Bronx were walking a battleground between mainstream values and a street-based life-style. Entirely "straight" sentiments were revealed in student compositions: "I am in school to study . . . to grow up to be something in this world instead of a dropout"; "We should respect our teachers and our classmates, but your teacher and classmates should respect you"; "We suppose to go to school to learn not to throw paper around. We should behave like young ladies and gentlemen." Perpetual fighting, boisterousness, and class cutting belied these sentiments. As one teacher said, "They know the stock answers and give me what they think I want to hear."

The students paid equal lip service to injunctions against drug use. Yet, I was told by one, "Everyone fools around with it." Some of the boys were quite proud of their involvement with drugs. This may have been just bravado, but their interest in the subject demonstrated that they held drugs in high esteem. Some talked about their preference for cocaine and disdain for soft drugs. A local tough, one of an elite group of school discipline aides, would stride into squad meetings and greet the faculty supervisor with, "Whatcha got to get high on?"

In talking about the things that were most important to them, students consistently cited school and family. In fact, a mutual disdain existed between them and their teachers, parents, and the white world. Students would talk about blacks and whites in harmony, but in their predominantly black and Puerto Rican school, the only whites to speak of were the teachers. A deep cultural chasm separated those two universes. I still have some sketches in which a student depicted a karate fight called "Blackman vs. Whiteman." The series closed with Whiteman laid out in a coffin and Blackman spitting on him.

Despite such fantasies, I never witnessed an interracial fight in that neighborhood. The fights, such an important part of the status system, were intraracial. Brawls with enormous numbers of spectators often took place just outside the school. When a police whistle would sound to break it up, the crowd would merely regroup across the street or up the block. Melees took place inside the school as well. The stimulus, viewed through my eyes, often seemed paltry. One day, for example, I came across a girl teasing a boy who was hanging around the general office. With his eyes full of disdain, he kept repeating, "I gon' fight you right here, bitch!" This world was peppered with landmines that could explode into violence.

Fighting incurred the wrath of the middle-class school faculty, but it also brought powerful rewards within the peer culture. For many students, misbehavior was a form of machismo and status. One student boasted to me that his misconduct record was worse than another boy's who was also a discipline problem. When his friend challenged this assertion, he vigorously defended it. He had failed to be promoted several times. I asked him, "So why do you do make trouble?" He replied, "I run with my friends and they want to do something and I'm always the first one to get caught." There was no hint that he should stop "running with his friends," only that he should not get caught.

Sexual adventures were an equal source of pride. Even though stated sexual norms were conservative, boys loved to brag about their sexual exploits. Sharing a girl could be a solidifying bond between friends. If she was ugly, it didn't matter. They concurred it was her body and not her face that interested them. Girls were defined by lips, "knobs," and their capacity to make trouble. One youth talking about his girl crowed, "She ain't missed a period yet!" Another, noticing a buddy wearing a buttoned shirt, said, "I'll never wear one of those 'cause the girls start unbuttoning it." Such callous dehumanization of women marks the beginning of the violence-inducing exploitation described in the previous chapter.

Yet, paradoxically, a rigid traditionalism invoked violent responses whenever mama's morals were questioned or private sexual matters were raised. Sex was not something to be discussed in front of just anyone, especially authority figures.

In sum, interactions between girls and boys were focused on sexual encounters and fights. In other spheres, they ignored each other. "Hanging out" and most group activities were more fun when each sex kept to itself.

The fun seemed to end at the schoolroom door. "I'm sick of this place," said a chronic cutter. "I just want to get out. It's their fault I was left back twice." Although he consistently received failing grades in conduct, he felt his schoolwork was "really together." He flunked "only" one or two major subjects each semester.

Even for those who wanted to study, school had little credibility. One girl stood up at a field trip meeting with the Black Alliance at an Ivy League university and declared, "Everytime I open up a social studies book, I read about how we were slaves. We were more than that!" Another girl asked how black studies can "fight the influence of the white establishment."

Students' classroom behavior often reflected how they perceived their teachers. Those teachers who were seen as caring, authoritative, and well-prepared had little difficulty disciplining their classes. Where teachers were perceived as weak, uncool, or phony, students completely took over—if, that is, they showed up at all. One day I came across a group of black students hovering outside a classroom door, debating whether or not to cut. Peering inside, they exclaimed, "Hey, there's a colored lady in there!" That clinched it. They cut. The fact that an "uncool" black teacher was treated with equal contempt as a white one shows that the real barrier wasn't race, but a value gap that could rarely be bridged. One student summed it up when he said to me, "I'm hipper than most of these teachers."

Teachers were only part of the context in which student peer groups functioned. Parents and the wider neighborhood comprised the rest of their world—and both were found wanting: "There's nothing to do in this place; people just hanging around looking out windows, looking at something that isn't there"; "Wouldn't you be embarrassed if it were your street?"

The parents who populated those streets were more feared than loved. Mothers were seen in terms of scolding, complaining, and giving birth. Fathers, if they were around at all, were tolerated only if they were passive: "My father's okay. He don't say nothin'." When fathers took an active part in disciplining their children, they were viewed in the same harsh terms as mothers. "He thought I was cutting classes. . . . My father always accuses me of untrue things. He yells at me, and I don't like being yelled at. He yelled before he came to school but he said he was sorry afterward. . . . I didn't feel anything about it," one student asserted.

Often the relationship between parents compounded the problem. A Hispanic girl grumbled: "My parents have been married twenty-seven years. . . . My little brother's birthday was last Saturday and my mother was sick. My father stayed out late anyway. And now my mother's really yelling at him. . . . During my father's last trip to Puerto Rico, he was only supposed to stay two weeks and he stayed for four instead. He didn't write except for a few lines to say he was very sick. My mother flew down, emergency, and he wasn't sick. She was very angry."

The outcome of these emotional wranglings was captured for me by a black girl: "I only trust my best girlfriend. You can't trust nobody else. . . . I don't like my teachers either."

□   □   □

It is from such a world that four young hoodlums emerged one day to approach Bernhard Goetz in a subway car.

"All street kids," observes author Claude Brown, in a follow-up to *Manchild in the Promised Land,* "are at least semiabandoned. . . . They are at the mercy of a coldblooded and ruthless environment; survival is a matter of fortuity, instinct, ingenuity and unavoidable conditioning. Consequently, the manchild who survives is usually more cunning, more devious and often more vicious than his middle-class counterpart."

In taking a fresh look at the Harlem he brought to our consciousness in his 1965 book, Brown contrasts his peers with the ones who inhabit the streets today. He finds the younger generation to be "persistently violent . . . driven by . . . a desperate need for pocket money that they cannot possibly obtain legally." The money is used in the service of "being somebody"—owning at least one pair of designer jeans, Nikes, Adidas, or Pumas; partying; copping drugs. But money alone is not enough. "Today's manchild," writes Brown, "obtains the biggest gun he can find . . . sticks it in the face of some poor working person and takes all of $5 or $10 and his life."

Life doesn't have much meaning to these young malefactors—not their own,

not anybody's else's. "Many of them were witnesses, at a very tender age, to
. . . shoot-outs and the broad-daylight slayings so typical of the urban drug wars
of the 1970's," explains Brown. "When they were 6, 7, 8 or so, they saw friends,
neighbors, relatives and total strangers brutally murdered, and seldom heard of
anyone even being arrested."

Killing, which is part of the world they take for granted, reaps instant benefits. Not only is a potential witness eliminated, but the slayer is given a forum for
displaying his manhood and "being somebody." All his street friends can marvel
as he gains instant celebrity on the six o'clock news.

UNWANTED . . . UN-NURTURED

Ricky Kasso's and George Clancy's bizarre crimes show that even when we
can identify dangerous criminals in the making, we have no reliable way to deter
them from their course. In a more liberal age it was fashionable to speculate that
such mutants were an inevitable outcome of welfare dependence and racism.
(Ricky Kasso, who was neither black nor poor, casts immediate doubt on that
theory.) In recent years, however, a number of prominent scholars have grown
impatient with such explanations. Some, like James Q. Wilson, in *Thinking
About Crime,* insist that we can't control the social conditions that breed crime.
Therefore, we must concentrate on what we *can* do—namely, locking up the
offender where he can't hurt us. Gwynn Nettler, another crime expert, dis-
counts poverty and racial bigotry as sufficient explanations for violent behavior.
If they were, says the sociologist, Jews would have the highest crime rate of all
ethnic groups since "No people in history has suffered as much hostility, expro-
priation, and murderous attack. . . ." Yet, it is not Jews who dominate the
police blotters.

Nor is it Puerto Ricans or Chicanos. Even in states like Texas, where blacks
make up a smaller proportion of the population than other minorities, they are
overrepresented as both victims and criminals. The same pattern is repeated in
Arizona, Utah, Colorado, California, and New Mexico. Why?

The crowding of urban slums isn't the reason, says Nettler. Writing of the
dense living conditions in Japan as well as the unconscionable and unprecedented internment of the nisei in American concentration camps, Nettler avers
that the relatively pacific behavior of the Japanese demonstrates that "segregation, discrimination, and exploitation . . . do not describe a clear path to robbery, rape, and murder." Nettler finds the missing piece of the puzzle in reproductive practices. "Large, heterogeneous, and free societies have the peculiar
'problem' of civilizing numbers of *unwanted* and *un-nurtured* children . . . and
their indoctrination is left to hazard." (Italics mine.)

This is *not* to say that blacks have an inherent incapacity to teach children
civility. Rather, the preponderance among blacks of early sexuality and childbirth, rampant illegitimacy, and disrupted homes increases the odds that a large
proportion of children will not be properly nurtured.

Such conditions are growing among whites, too; however, the proportions are
much smaller. Nettler cites data from the Alan Guttmacher Institute that dem-

onstrate sharp cultural differences between a cross-section of blacks and whites. Black women report that they have had intercourse in greater numbers and at earlier ages than whites. Ten times more unmarried black teenagers have been pregnant than whites. Of those who have been pregnant, black teenagers are twice as likely as whites to bear their children. There are 505 black babies born out of wedlock for every 1,000 born in wedlock, a ratio more than five times higher than whites, and the span between the mid-1950s and late 1960s saw an increase in fatherless black households that was almost twice that of whites.

Nettler goes on to describe the results of the National Survey of Family Growth and other studies showing that large percentages of births are unintended and unwanted. "Mothers' statements that they or their husbands had not wanted some of their children are more frequently made by poor women, by black women, and by those who had many children. . . . These increases in the proportions of questionably nurtured children have occurred in parallel with increases in violent crime."

Many a ghetto mother guides her family with love, diligence, and a firm hand. But rearing children who are ruled by street peers and whose consciences are numbed by violence, drugs, and alcohol is often too much for even the most well-meaning caretaker.

The outcome can be the monsterlike violence of a George Clancy and a Ricky Kasso or the callous disregard of life that Claude Brown finds in today's Harlems. "My generation," contrasts Brown, "was instructed never to carry a weapon larger than a .38, to always know what's in the till; firing a gun during a take-off was a sign of gross incompetence. A gun was merely to ensure that the take-off artist would not hurt anyone."

What Brown is describing is the hallmark of the professional robber, who is carefully trained and uses violence only as a last resort. Today's young thugs are not professionals; most are careless opportunists for whom violence is mundane. Except for loose loyalty to their peers, they are affectively and morally neutral. Many are, in short, psychopaths.

"Persons diagnosed as psychopathic begin as rejected, cruelly or indifferently treated children," writes Alan Harrington in his prophetic book, *Psychopaths*. "They strike back at the world with aggressive, unrestrained, attention-drawing behavior. . . . Since conscience is instilled by early love, faith in adults close by, and desire to hold their affection by being good, the child unrewarded with love grows up experiencing no conscience. Uncared for, he doesn't care, can't really love, feels no anxiety to speak of, does not worry about whether he's good or bad, and literally has no idea of guilt."

As shown in the last chapter, individuals who are exposed to violence often become violent themselves. My research subjects in Morrisania saw violence in their homes and carried it into their school. Violence became redefined as a virtue, a matter of honor. When you add the disinhibitors, like drugs and alcohol, that are so often linked with crime, it's not surprising that a number of such teenagers evolve into "monster men."

It is this small percentage that we will have to watch in the future. The reproductive practices that create them remain problematic. Overall birthrates are dropping but illegitimate births are not, and births to women under the age of nineteen remain high. The low sex ratio described in the last chapter helps perpetuate the cycle of violence. So, while the ranks of these unnurtured youths is not increasing, their viciousness is. They are unsuited to what Nettler defines as the civil life, "an orderly life among strangers." Their "hatred is diffuse and victims may be innocents. . . . Affluent economies . . . seem to breed a high proportion of such deracinated individuals, people who have no altruistic connection to anyone."

□ □ □

The ones who suffer at the hands of these terrible teens are usually their own people. In crimes of violence, blacks prey on whites about as often as whites prey on blacks. The proportions are, in any case, low. Eighty-one percent of the robberies, rapes, and assaults on blacks are committed by other blacks. Burglaries and serious assaults take place disproportionately in the deteriorated neighborhoods where most blacks live. Homicide is the leading cause of death among black males fifteen to thirty-four years old. It appears that blacks are turning their pain and anger against themselves.

□ □ □

Prison is no deterrent; middle-class policymakers who are appalled by the thought of being locked up themselves don't seem to understand that. Hardened criminals I've encountered have repeatedly told me that life in the can is easier than life outside. At least they know where they're sleeping each night, and they're assured of three square meals a day. Prisons are violent, but so are the streets.

In 1976, a program called "Scared Straight" was launched at Rahway State Prison in New Jersey. Teenagers were invited into the prison for encounters with "lifers." Using raw language and graphic descriptions, the convicts would harangue the kids about the horrors of prison life. Everyone had high hopes for the program. They thought exposure to the truth of life behind bars would frighten the youngsters away from criminal leanings. Similar programs were implemented all over the country, and two years later the gritty *Scared Straight* film was even shown on television.

It backfired. Subsequent evaluation showed that those who went through the program had a slightly *higher* incidence of delinquent behavior than those who didn't. Those who understand peer culture weren't surprised: Prison is a rite of passage into manhood, a mark of status, of being somebody.

GANGS

The ultimate expression of peer culture is the youth gang. Criminologists have spent decades trying to figure out exactly what the word "gang" means. Does it include a drug clique like the one that Ricky Kasso and his satanists formed? A bunch of neighborhood kids making trouble together on a subway like Bernhard Goetz's victims? Three guys going on a joint robbery spree like

George Clancy's cronies? Or must it be a structured organization complete with leaders, colors, turf, and crash pads?

Whatever youth gangs are, the 1981 *U.S. Attorney General's Task Force Report on Violent Crime* concluded that 71 percent of all serious crimes by youths are committed by street gangs. While the meaning of that statistic is open to question, the existence of gang crime cannot be denied. The issue is how it's changing and whether it will get worse.

Gangs have been a part of the urban streetscape for the better part of the twentieth century. They've provided their members with a sense of identity, belonging, and protection. Traditionally, to the extent that gangs have engaged in crime at all, the crimes have been petty property offenses and internecine squabbles. There was a limit to the damage rival gangs armed with only chains or knives could do to one another in the course of a turf fight.

Today's gangs are different. According to the Attorney General's Task Force report, there are about 2,200 gangs with 96,000 members in 300 cities and towns. Killings are a major part of their activities, and their MO's more closely resemble those of organized crime than they do kids hanging out on a corner.

The reemergence of gangs is a shock for those who thought the *West Side Story*–type of youth group had gone the way of bobby socks. In the 1960s and 1970s kids were too doped up to form gangs, but in the 1980s gangs came back armed with Targa .22-caliber pistols and Uzi 9-millimeter semiautomatics.

Frightening stories have come out of large and small cities all over the country. In New York, roving street gangs terrorized audiences at a 1984 outdoor Diana Ross concert and viciously attacked hikers participating in a 1985 charity event for the March of Dimes. In 1984, Los Angeles, which has the worst gang problem of any city, reported 420 gangs, most of them based in the black and Hispanic neighborhoods that cut a forty-square-mile swath east of Los Angeles International Airport. Narcotics syndicates hire gang members as young as thirteen to act as runners, dealers, bodyguards, and executioners. It's made life very iffy for the locals. Says one L.A. school official: "I've dealt with gangs every single day for eleven years. I see kids every day that are afraid to walk home unless they have their gangs."

That fear has been cited as one cause of the 70-percent school dropout rate among Hispanics in Chicago. In the Humboldt Park district on the Near Northwest Side of the city, two rival gangs, the Folks and the People, rule the streets. Sometimes a child is assigned to a school in the rival gang's territory. Rather than risk taunts or death, that child will simply stop going to school. Chicago's black neighborhoods suffer equally. At the end of 1984, a youth gang, the Black Gangster Disciples, was implicated in the shooting death of one of the nation's most sought after high school basketball players.

Gangs in Chicago or New York are yesterday's news. But those cities reporting problems with gang activities *today* are mainly in the West and South. Black, Hispanic, and Asian gangs have sprung up where the Sunbelt migration has taken them. It's pretty intimidating to see a procession of hip dudes bopping down graffiti-covered streets in "fierce" bomber jackets. Yet, that sight is evident in all kinds of places that you wouldn't expect—smaller, once-quiet cities like Portsmouth, VA.; Peoria, IL.; and Hayward, CA.

□ □ □

If you follow media accounts, the youth gang phenomenon sounds ubiquitous. But a close look at the data paints a different picture.

Gang crimes, by definition, involve more than one offender, and the plurality of multiple-offender violent crimes involve youths under the age of twenty. I compared government surveys over a twelve-year period starting in 1973 and found the proportion of violent crime committed by youthful groups had actually *dropped* by more than 8 percent. For other age groups, the numbers increased and then dropped off. During that same time period, group crimes for blacks of all ages decreased, while those of whites increased.

There's no reliable way to determine the extent of gang crime because few police departments keep systematic records of gang activities. But of sixty departments responding to a national survey, fewer than a third reported having problems with youth gangs. Where youth gangs were a problem, half were engaged in minor crimes like vandalism, chain snatching, school disturbances, and harassment. Less than two fifths of the gangs were killing, raping, or otherwise brutalizing people, and only an eighth were involved in serious stealing.

Zeroing in on those crimes committed by the young against the young (which is the case in most gang violence), I found that there had been a small drop in group crimes involving twelve- to nineteen-year-old victims. These numbers indicate that youth gangs are not a growing problem.

News reports create the impression that gangs are taking over the areas in and around schools. Again, the numbers tell a different story. Since 1973, violent crimes inside schools have diminished by nearly two fifths while thefts have dropped by half. Even in the streets, parking lots, schoolyards, and parks, where you'd expect gangs to hang out, crime has dropped by a few points.

THE NEW INTOLERANCE

This brings us back to the nasty few who will haunt us in the future—the deracinated youths who gouge out friends' eyes in the woods, or rape women while robbing a store, or butcher little girls in front of a mirror. The numbing horror of such atrocities has ushered in a new era of intolerance toward juvenile delinquency. The rehabilitation ideal has been forsworn for a "lock 'em up and throw away the key" mentality.

As of January 1983, forty-eight states and the District of Columbia had taken away much of judges' discretion in meting out punishments (New York's drug law and Massachusetts' gun law are examples). Mandated prison sentences have displaced a host of indeterminate sentences and unreliable parole board decisions. Where prison terms are not mandated, an array of sentencing guidelines and fixed and presumptive sentences stand ready to check the vagrant "bleeding heart" impulse that might afflict a liberal on the bench.

As early as 1978, the public's quest for more severe punishment had induced all fifty states and the federal government to enact statutes under which juveniles could be tried in adult courts. Ironically, the public's rebellion against "coddling criminals" has not worked out as planned. Of the juvenile cases waived to criminal courts, the majority are traffic, fishing, boating, drinking, and other minor violations. Most juveniles tried in adult courts don't see the inside of a jail cell. The very mandated sentences that are supposed to make life harder for criminals make it much more difficult to prosecute a youngster.

Nevertheless, the appalling implications of the Todd Ice case cannot be ignored. Had he not been "waived" to adult court, he could never have been given the death sentence. For most of his stay on Eddyville State prison's death row, Todd was the only juvenile. "I had no support," he laments, "no peer group, no nothing. . . . I just tried to stay alive." Because of sterner sentences and widespread referrals to adult court, youths like Todd Ice will have much company in the future.

CRIMEWARPS

- The size of the crime-prone teenage population will shrink—and along with it, the crime rate.
- Most teenagers who commit offenses will outgrow criminal behavior by their mid-twenties. As the offspring of the "baby boom" generation mature between 2015 and 2025, we will experience another decline in crime.
- When, according to Census Bureau projections, zero population growth is attained in 2050, the crime rate will enter a stage of permanent stability or decline.
- A small proportion of teen offenders, probably no more than 20 percent, will become career criminals.
- A growing number of these teen offenders will be *chronically violent*. Marvin Wolfgang's comparison of two birth cohorts found that the rate of violent crime among delinquents increased threefold in a generation.
- The overall rate of violence will decrease, but acts of violence by a small percentage of individual youths will increase. Peer pressure, psychic numbing, and ready availability of guns will sustain an environment conducive to violence. Blacks will be the most frequent victims. However, as the proportion of illegitimate births by whites shifts upward, so will the proportion of violence against whites by whites.
- Increased domestic violence, low sex ratios, and continued high rates of illegitimacy among underaged women will perpetuate the family conditions that breed deracinated youths.
- Intractable poverty and television-inspired materialism will leave deracinated youths with no other means of "being somebody" than to commit crimes, and no other source of affirmation than their peer group or gang.
- Serious gang crime will be concentrated among those gangs that are tied in with organized crime groups or narcotics syndicates. Other gangs will become increasingly more benign, and many will devote themselves to

"cleaning up" rather than destroying their neighborhoods. Most of the new gangs, both violent and benign, will be white.

• "Get tough" policies, which focus on incarceration, will contribute to teenage crime. Research shows that jailing juveniles simply speeds the commission of subsequent crimes. To the extent that alternatives will be developed in the future (see chapter 18), this stimulus to crime will be removed.

3

Geriatric Delinquents

An elderly couple, married for fifty years and living in a retirement home, had only each other on whom to take out their frustrations. One morning the husband sent his wife out for bagels: in old age she'd become somewhat forgetful, and brought back onion rolls instead. Her husband flew into a rage and killed her with a Boy Scout ax.

It was a domestic homicide, the kind that accounts for almost half the murders committed by older people (but only about a quarter of those committed by younger ones). As in this ax murder, elderly assailants know their victims in 92 percent of the cases (as opposed to 83 percent for younger ones). An increase in domestic violence among the elderly will be one of the hallmarks of crime in the future.

☐ ☐ ☐

An older woman was arrested as she was entering her late-model Mercedes with stolen over-the-counter pills. She had just come out of a Drug World store in Hallendale, where she was seen taking boxes of tablets off the shelf. Opening one box, she poured pills from two others into it. At the cashier, she paid for only the one box. The venerable lady claimed to have done nothing wrong, and her lawyer based her defense on the fact that a woman of her wealth could not possibly steal a few pills. The judge disagreed and slapped her with a $500 fine.

Larceny is by far the most prevalent crime of old age. Many of the oldsters doing the stealing are not among the needy ones that you'd expect to pilfer; most are financially self-sufficient and committing the first crimes of their lives.

☐ ☐ ☐

In February 1985, Rudolph Giuliani, the go-go U.S. Attorney of New York's Southern District, announced an indictment of nine men that read like a "Who's Who" of organized crime: Anthony "Fat Tony" Salerno, Boss of the Genovese Family; Paul "Big Paul" Castellano, Boss of the Gambino Family; Anthony "Tony Ducks" Corallo, Boss of the Lucchese Family; Philip "Rusty" Rastelli, Boss of the Bonanno Family; Gennaro "Gerry Lang" Langella, Acting Boss of the Colombo Family. Four others included underbosses, a *consigliere*, and a high ranking member.

These nine men were said to encompass the ruling council of the Mafia's Five Families in New York and other American cities, which, since 1931, had regulated organized loan-sharking, drug-trafficking, labor-racketeering, extortion, and murder. FBI Director William Webster called it a "historic" indictment. "It exposes the structure and leadership of organized crime on a scale never done before." One of the things it exposed was a fact known by everyone who has ever seen *The Godfather:* Mafia dons are *old.* With the exception of Acting Boss Langella, who, at age forty-six was the baby of the group, this social register of the underworld ranged in age from fifty-six to seventy-three.

Old folks have never been and will never be a major factor in street crime (they account for only 4 percent of all arrests), but they have long dominated the kinds of illegal enterprises that call for experience and being in a position of trust. Organized crime is one.

☐ ☐ ☐

In March 1984, police uncovered a plot to help Forrest Silva Tucker escape from a federal prison. It would have been his fifth prison break in the course of a long criminal career. Tucker, at age sixty-three, was leader of the Miami-based "Over-the-Hill" Gang, a group of middle-aged robbers who were reported to be the scourge of banks, jewelry stores, and supermarkets from Florida to Massachusetts.

It sounds like the movie *The Grey Fox,* but it's real. Police say the group had been active in South Florida since 1974. Detective Fred Taylor, who arrested the gang members, has a grudging admiration for the Over-the-Hill Gang's ability to melt into its surroundings: "They picked an excellent locale because South Florida has always been big on retirees."

Few law officers would give a second thought to a group of older men riding around in a car. Nor, asserts Taylor, does paying the rent in cash arouse the same suspicions about older people as it does about younger ones. When Dan

Dalton, fifty-two, and Dick Biller, fifty-eight, plied their trade, they were dressed up and neat. Nothing about them said "robber." Except to Fred Taylor. To him, Dan Dalton "was just one of those guys you wouldn't want to run into— even with his age."

In short, the Over-the-Hill Gang wasn't over-the-hill at all. They had style; they were tough; they were violent. Age and experience enabled them to operate successfully for as long as they did. It took a shoot-out for the FBI to finally capture their leader on a West Palm Beach street in 1984.

"Armed robbery," asserts Fred Taylor, "is usually a young guy's game. Very rarely do you find anyone over forty." But these over-forty robbers struck terror in the hearts of Floridians with their old style "bang-bang-shoot-'em-up" approach.

Forrest Silva Tucker is representative of a kind of older crook who is, and will remain, an oddity: the chronic street criminal. While there has been great growth in robbery arrests for old people, it hasn't kept up with the rate of increase in overall elderly population. The physical stamina a life of armed robbery requires is too demanding for many sixty-three-year-olds to muster.

The FBI reports that arrests of old people (in the Uniform Crime Reports, "old" starts at age fifty-five) doubled between 1970 and 1980. While old people have been a growing force in serious crime, their arrests for minor crimes have dropped by half since 1964. That isn't necessarily because they are committing fewer petty offenses, but because we now have alternate ways of dealing with traditional old people's nuisance crimes—drunkenness, vagrancy, and disorderly conduct. The people we call "homeless," for example, are now taken to shelters rather than jailed as derelicts.

FBI statistics mask multiple arrests of the same person as well as changes in law enforcement policies. So, while arrest rates are a poor measure, they're the best indicator we've got. They show that the increase in criminal behavior among the elderly is far outstripping their rate of growth in the population.

The groundswell in geriatric crime will stay with us well into the future. The Census Bureau projects that *more than a quarter of the population will be aged sixty years and older by the year 2025.* Their numbers will more than double those of 1980.

In trying to explain geriatric crime, one striking feature emerges. Old people live in a state of "drift," relatively free of the social controls and responsibilities that keep the rest of us in line. The drift is induced by old age economics, health, and life-style.

There are myriad life changes that set old people adrift: loss of mates, changes in residence, biochemical alterations, side effects from drugs, deaths and departures of good friends, absence of meaningful work. The elderly must learn new life-styles to accommodate new circumstances. Consider the sixty-eight-year-old widow who meets a seventy-year-old widower. They grow fond of each other and enjoy the comfort of each other's companionship. They want to marry, but they can't afford to give up the survivor's benefit she gets from her late husband's social security pension. So they live together—a shocking decision for a widow who, a few years ago, disowned her granddaughter for moving in with a man.

Sociologist Gary Feinberg, who specializes in studying old-age crime, commiserates with the dilemma: "They're redefining morality with very few standards to guide them." In this context, masses of old people are left without accountabilities. The result is a state of anomie in which a person is free of the most powerful social controls. Some are pushed willy-nilly into criminal behavior. To make sense of the crimes, it's important to understand the demographics of drift.

THE DEMOGRAPHICS OF DRIFT

If you're celebrating your sixty-fifth birthday as you read this, you can probably look forward to living at least another sixteen years. Whether you say your last farewells earlier or later has a lot to do with gender and race. White women hold the clear edge up until age eighty-five; then black women take over, dying at a slower rate than other octogenarians. Black and Hispanic men have the poorest outlook of all.

Jeb, a wizened black man, personifies youth's image of old age. I met him some years ago in the South Bronx. It was winter. He and a group of men were huddled on the sidewalk around a trash barrel fire, trying to keep warm. He'd been living on this street for ten years and in the neighborhood for twenty-five. Due to an operation, he hadn't worked in almost that long. At age fifty-five, Jeb was on the threshold of what various statistical tables call "old."

"Me and my family been separated since '65," he told me. "I got a daughter downtown. [He also had a son in college.] So I live alone now.

"Now and again I come upstairs to get somethin' to eat and then I go down again. I got nowhere to go. I take a rest every day of the week."

Jeb is everyone's secret nightmare of what old age holds in store: Trapped in a high-crime, deteriorating neighborhood, abandoned, ailing, isolated, destitute, idle. But the findings of a 1981 Louis Harris poll reveal that the gray years aren't so bleak after all. It turns out that older people are coping with today's problems better than younger ones. They're less concerned about crime, money, housing, and jobs than most of us think. They're less likely to have dipped into savings in the past year. Even the elderly poor do much better on their small incomes than do younger people of like means. Senior citizens report that getting around, loneliness, energy costs, poor health, and medical care are not the problems for them that younger people believe them to be. On the contrary, a 1982 Roper survey showed that three quarters of its sample of old people claimed to be in good or excellent health. Finally, the National Crime Survey makes it clear that old people are the *least* frequent victims of street crime.

Doesn't sound much like the popular TV image of old people living on dog food and cowering in fear behind barricaded doors. It may be that Harris' picture of the "wellderly" is simply a reflection of lowered expectations and stubborn pride. But if the pollster is to be believed, almost half the elderly feel they have more income than they need; more than half own homes with paid up mortgages; and while most rely on social security as their main source of income, close to 90 percent have savings on which to draw. The vast majority are independent. Fewer than 5 percent are institutionalized. Of those who are, most return to their own homes after a time and only a tiny percentage are shut in indefinitely.

Elliot Stern, a septuagenarian resident of Long Island, New York, prides himself on being one of the "wellderly." He feels "very good" about retirement: "I'm more relaxed. I enjoy myself. I take walks. I have a puppy who's keeping me very busy." Elliot has a working wife, a married daughter living nearby, a handicapped daughter living at home, and a one-day-a-week job as a picture researcher for the *National Enquirer*. It's true that he has medical expenses, but they're more for his daughter's many knee operations than for his own diverticulitis ("It doesn't bother me"), his gall-bladder operation ("That helped me"), or any problems his sixty-two-year-old wife may have. And there are several sources of income to cover those expenses—savings, investments, social security, wages —well over $30,000 a year.

All in all, this former picture agency executive doesn't feel old age has done much to change his standard of living. He's been living in the house he owns for twenty years, and he's not planning to leave it for warmer climes. He enjoys his home more than ever without the daily commute into Manhattan and the expensive business lunches that went with it. Now he spends comfortable time with friends who live nearby and meets regularly with his card club. Elliot explains, "The money that's won gets put into a kitty. When the kitty is full, the money is used to go on vacation together."

Stern's life—composed as it is of family and work responsibilities, strong social ties, and comfortable income—contains all the anchors that will sustain him in the law-abiding life he has always lived. But his good fortune doesn't negate the fact that a significant minority of old people live more like Jeb. Without Medicare, Medicaid, food stamps, and other supports, that number would swell.

Now we come to the flip side of the "wellderly" Harris poll: a graphic picture of geriatric inequality. Consider these median incomes for various groups of old folks:

White men	$11,000
Women	6,000
Hispanics	5,300
Blacks	4,800

On the whole, the median household income of older Americans is less than half that of their younger counterparts. Clearly, men like Jeb are at the bottom of the ladder. Women run a close third. While only 14 percent of the aged fall below the poverty line, women make up more than three quarters of that group.

□   □   □

But again, it isn't lack of income that leads old people to crime; it's lack of responsibilities and controls.

A paying job provides a senior citizen with accountabilities at the same time that it helps beat old-age indigence. When it comes to being healthy enough to work, most old people are more like Elliot Stern than Jeb. Yet, census figures show that labor force participation by the elderly has plummeted as their longevity has skyrocketed.

In 1900, two thirds of men and 8 percent of women over sixty-five were actively working. By the 1980s, widely promoted early retirement incentives had shrunk those percentages to 17 for men and 7.6 for women. Unless there's a dramatic change in retirement policies, old-age unemployment will continue to grow well beyond the year 2000.

Old people are and will continue to be left with vast amounts of drift-inducing leisure time. The problem is finding people to fill it with. Some, like Jeb, find strangers in the street; others, like Elliot, play cards with neighbors and raise a puppy. For still others, it's more difficult. You can find them in places like the First Moravian Coffeepot Community Center on Lexington Avenue in New York City. That's where destitute aged women like Dorothy Robinson must seek shelter and comfort. She has six grown children, but she's alone.

More than two fifths of older women live alone, a 6-percent rise since 1970. Only one third that number applies to older men, and this figure has held fairly steady since 1970. Life expectancies at birth are eight years shorter for men than for women. The life-span gap will continue to grow in the future. Not only are men's death rates higher, but their birthrates are dropping. All this makes for a lot of widowed and unmarried women facing old age alone—a condition that contributes to drift.

□   □   □

There is a stereotyped notion that droves of the elderly are heading south to live in mah-jongg heaven. In fact, most don't head for the sun. Like Elliot Stern, over four fifths live in the same house they occupied prior to retirement. Those who do leave their homes generally move a short distance to smaller quarters. Fewer than 4 percent actually pull up stakes and move to another state; of these, about half—those who are more affluent and better educated—go to Florida, Arizona, or California. Another part of this group moves back from their preretirement locations to their home state.

Of the nine states with the largest geriatric populations, only three—California, Florida, and Texas—are in the Sunbelt. All the others are in the decidedly chillier East Coast and Midwest. But for those three Sunbelt states, the explosion in elderly residents ranged from 190 to 338 percent between 1960 and 1983. Because this is where the growth is likely to continue, the Sunbelt experience with elderly criminals provides a glimpse into the future.

Florida, which is home to almost 7 percent of the nation's old people, accounts for 13 percent of the country's larcenies. Elderly larceny arrest rates have increased by a quarter since 1971, beating out the national rate by a factor of two-to-one. In Dade County, seat of the Miami retirement mecca, one fifth of the residents are senior citizens. In just one year, 1980 to 1981, arrests among them rose by 29 percent.

Unlike the terrifying shoot-outs of the Over-the-Hill Gang, most of Florida's geriatric crimes strike terror in no one's heart. The majority of them are garden-variety petty larcenies like shoplifting. I never got to know Jeb well enough to learn if he committed crimes, but Florida's elderly thieves demonstrate that he would have been an unlikely larcenist. Most are middle-class white-collar types and homeowners with multiple sources of income. They're not stealing to survive—steaks, cosmetics, gourmet cheeses, and clothing are the objects of their pilfering.

A yen for luxury is understandable. But often the thefts are entirely senseless. A bald eighty-year-old man was caught with an armload of hairbrushes; an eighty-two-year-old woman was intercepted stealing contraceptives. Sociologist Feinberg notes that because Miami's elderly population is more affluent than most, their motivation for stealing may not be typical. But since there are so many old people in Florida, their behavior anticipates what we might expect from concentrations of the elderly in other places.

Data from Broward County indicate that geriatric shoplifters are often first-time offenders who have spent their lives as law-abiding citizens. When they explain their criminal behavior, they cite fears about future financial security, a need for attention, boredom, impatience, irritability, forgetfulness, or physical and emotional changes of aging.

Sounds plausible. But Feinberg's research shows that in addition to being relatively affluent, these shoplifters give lie to a host of stereotypes about older larcenists. For instance, you might expect that women are the main culprits. But older men are just as likely to steal as older women are. As for loneliness and a need for attention, most geriatric shoplifters are married and claim to "really feel a part" of their families. Then there's the forgetfulness hypothesis. In almost half the cases studied, shoplifters walked off with two or three items. It's easy to forget *one* item. But *three?*

The standard explanations for elderly stealing just don't fit. There's something else at work. In a pointed insight, Feinberg compares the status of the elderly with that of juveniles. The similar conditions he cites can lead to delinquency in both groups.

Like youngsters, old people are exempt from work and family obligations. Both groups have relatively unstructured schedules, with an emphasis on play and leisure. Both function more as consumers than producers. With young people, the elderly share a low, segregated position in the social and financial pecking order. It's not a matter of being without social ties; it's a matter of being without responsibilities.

Of course, there is one critical difference between juveniles and geriatrics: Youngsters can look forward to moving into the mainstream; oldsters can look forward only to further disengagement. And that can lead to drift. For a large minority, that means violence.

VIOLENT OLDSTERS

While most elderly crime is concentrated in the larceny category, drift sets the stage for more serious crimes as well. A nationwide survey of elderly state-prison inmates revealed that they were more likely than younger inmates to be in prison for violent crimes. But they were less likely to have a history of juvenile crime: almost half were incarcerated for the first time after age fifty-five. The aged were more likely to have been married, and had more children and less schooling than their younger counterparts. Except for these distinctions, which are products of having lived longer more than anything else, the profile of elderly inmates was virtually identical to that of young inmates.

The most violent of violent crimes is murder. Old people commit their share of those—often senselessly. On a Monday afternoon in February 1984, Martha Tozer, eighty-one, of Maurice River Township, New Jersey, died at Millville Hospital. The cause of death was severe skull fractures and brain damage. The next day her eighty-one-year-old tenant, Joseph Bowman, was arrested and charged with killing her. He pleaded guilty to aggravated manslaughter.

There are abundant theories about why the aged kill: frustration, brain impairment, ingestion of conflicting prescription drugs (people aged sixty and older fill an average of 10.5 to 13 prescriptions a year). If these were sufficient explanations, you'd expect that geriatric homicides would be concentrated in those states where you find the most old people.

Not so. None of the places that have the highest arrest rates for older murder suspects—Washington, D.C., Alabama, South Carolina, Arkansas, Hawaii, and Tennessee—are among the nine states with the largest populations of old folks. Three of the nine, however—California, Florida, and Texas—are among the states that have the highest overall homicide rates.

In these Sunbelt states the percent of elderly in the population ranges from 10 (Texas) to 19 (Florida). While Florida has the highest old-young ratio in the country and the second-highest homicide rate, don't conclude that its killings are perpetrated by its geriatric citizens. In the other states on that list, there is no connection between the presence of old people and the homicide rate. Texas, for example, which has the fourth-highest homicide rate in the country, is ninth on the list of states with the largest proportion of senior citizens. Washington, D.C., which ranks first in homicides and arrests of elderly killers, doesn't even show on the roster of places with a high ratio of old people. The Sunbelt has emerged as the homicide capital of the country. That, however, is not where *most* of the elderly live. Again, most reside in the East and Midwest—but they're doing their largest share of killing in the South.

I tried to resolve this paradox by comparing the states with the highest homicide rates to those with the lowest, and those with the highest elderly killer arrest rates to those with the lowest. In looking at a number of variables— population size, density, per-capita income, minority groups, and urbanization— I found only two that seemed to correlate with killings by old people. One was a high level of urbanization (expressed as the percent of the population living in Standard Metropolitan Statistical Areas—SMSA's) and a high proportion of blacks. Others have concluded that poverty is a factor as well.

The homicide offender rate among elderly black males is nearly 10 times that of elderly white males and 175 times that of elderly white females. (If these numbers sound extraordinarily high, keep in mind that old people, as a whole, account for only 1 out of 22 homicide arrests.) Statistically, if someone like Jeb were living in a Birmingham, Alabama, slum, he would be a more likely contender for frustration-induced violence than petty larceny.

It's not race that makes elderly killers—it's fear. Male blacks are the ones most often victimized by street crime. By the time they grow old, there has been plenty of time for a healthy paranoia to set in. When they feel threatened, the aged may strike back—sometimes inappropriately.

Fear can distort perceptions. In 1984, Eleanor Bumpurs, sixty-six, a welfare recipient who hadn't paid her rent for three months, was threatened with eviction from her Bronx housing project. She had a history of physical and psychiatric problems. When a police Emergency Services team arrived to remove her from her home, she became frightened and lunged at them with a knife. In this case, the guns were on the officers' side and she ended up dead.

The outcome was different for a seventy-two-year-old Connecticut woman. For two years, she had been harassed by neighborhood toughs who threw rocks and called her a "witch." One day she picked up a shotgun in what, a jury agreed, was self-defense. This time it was not the oldster who ended up dead, but one of the boys.

Proportionately, guns are used more often by older assailants than by younger ones. Firearms are more likely than knives, fists, or hammers to turn assaults into homicides. That may be one reason that murders by old people are growing at a faster rate than those by the general population, while aggravated assaults are growing at a slower rate.

SEX CRIMES

Sexual assaults are a different story. The numbers are miniscule, but for twenty years they've been rising more steeply for older people than the general population. Our inconsistent stereotypes of geriatric sexuality make it hard to think of old people as rapists. Until Masters and Johnson came along, many of us assumed that sex ended at sixty. The image of the "dirty old man" and the "sexy senior citizen" made elderly eroticism the butt of innumerable racy jokes.

In fact, old people have varying levels of physical prowess, agility, and appetite. The vagaries of geriatric sexuality are reflected in the nature of their sexual crimes. There *are* old men who commit forcible rape, but more often the elderly sex offender engages in passive behavior. Eugene Gold, Brooklyn's feisty district attorney—whose brilliant career had been devoted to public service and social justice—made headlines in 1983 when he admitted fondling an associate's young daughter at a convention in Nashville.

Most elderly sex offenders follow Gold's pattern. Fondling is more prevelant than intercourse—and children are the usual victims. The New Jersey State Adult Treatment and Diagnostic Center at Avanel, which specializes in working with sex offenders, reports that they have recently been seeing more elderly patients—partly due to the publicity surrounding child abuse, but also because economic pressures are inducing a sense of failure among older men.

One Avanel staffer avers that old-age sex crimes tend to be "one-shot deals" committed by men who are feeling "less potent, less active, and less in control." Victimizing someone less powerful may seem to restore some of the declining male's lost self-esteem: Such men are programmed for pedophilia. According to the center's director, William Prendergast, 90 percent of his elderly child abusers were themselves seduced or molested as children. Other experts, however, report that organic brain disease and psychosis have been found in a large percentage of older sex offenders.

BRAIN IMPAIRMENT AND ELDERLY CRIME

Brain disorders are an important source of more conventional forms of assault as well. Writer Joan Gage has sorrowfully recorded the increasingly bizarre and aggressive behavior of her aging father. He suffered from Parkinson's disease and hallucinations, and became totally disoriented when his wife was hospitalized after a stroke. "My father, at home alone," recalls Gage, "began to forget where she was and to wander around the neighborhood looking for her." His wife returned after a month. But she was too weak to pick up Joan's father when his neurological problems would cause him to fall. The couple was forced to move out of their house to a retirement apartment with a medical staff on call. "But," continues Gage, "Mother was hospitalized again and my father kept trying to get back to his old house, where he thought he'd find his wife. If the nurses sought to stop him, he'd attack them with his cane." It's precisely this kind of upset that so often turns frail and mentally impaired old people into hostile assailants. If the weapon in their hands is a gun or an ax rather than a cane, their assaults can become lethal.

Many people who, at one time, would have been committed to mental institutions, are now committed to prisons instead. Combat experience in World War II demonstrated that shell-shocked soldiers recovered better if they were released from hospitals and put right back into action. Other research showed that civilian patients also did better with shorter hospital stays. Landmark patients' rights cases brought a halt to most involuntary commitments. A sole standard emerged for committing patients against their will: They had to be a proven danger to themselves or others. In the absence of meeting this difficult test, they had to be released as quickly as possible. Mental health professionals believed the release policy was good for the patients and could do no harm to the community.

The ensuing two decades have proved they were wrong. Community supports failed to keep pace with the rate of dismissals from institutions. The rate of violence among released mental patients is nearly twice that of the general population, according to Dr. Henry Steadman of the New York State Bureau of Mental Hygiene. But, claims Steadman, the news isn't all bad. Released mental patients may be more crime-prone than the general public, but they are less so than ex-prisoners. Nor are released patients as likely to repeat their crimes as ex-prisoners.

In one of the few studies of psychiatric aspects of older sex offenders and violent criminals, forensic psychiatrist Stephen Hucker found that three quarters of his sample suffered from either organic or functional mental disabilities, including a high incidence of paranoia. If Hucker's findings can be generalized, the increased arrests of old people may merely reflect a lot of elderly clients who more properly belong in the mental health system.

OLD PROS

But let's return to our shoot-'em-up robber, Forrest Silva Tucker, and his gang. He isn't just an old eccentric, nor does he seem to suffer from Alzheimer's Disease. We criminal justice scientists regard robbery as the bellwether crime that tells us which way the felonious winds are blowing. Thus, the fact that Tucker appears to be in full possession of his faculties makes his crimes particularly significant.

Tucker, however, is an anomaly. As his gang's arresting detective told us, older criminals don't go in much for robbery. Their arrests for stickups have been increasing at a slower rate than for the rest of the population. Of all those arrested for robbery, only one half of 1 percent are older offenders. Combining this statistic with those for other property crimes, it's clear that the future crime threat posed by older people is *not* in the area of premeditated crimes with rational motives. Rather, the danger lies in the spontaneous crimes spawned from frustration, boredom, and lowered inhibitions: the violent crimes that take place between people who know each other and the petty property crimes that seem to make no sense. Such crimes tend to be committed by newcomers to the crime scene.

But there's a class of older criminal who has always been around—the con man, the swindler, the crooked businessperson, the Mafia don. Many underworld legends were old: Meyer Lansky, Willy Sutton, Joe Colombo, "Lucky" Luciano, Vito Genovese, Patrick Lennon, Joseph Weil, Victor Lustig, and now the indicted bosses of La Cosa Nostra's "Commission." Between them, they pulled off some of the world's best-known stock swindles, bank robberies, stings, and rackets.

One legendary racketeer, Matthew "Matty the Horse" Ianiello (reputedly a big wheel in the Genovese crime family), had his career aborted late in 1985. That's when he was convicted on charges of skimming millions of dollars from five New York restaurants, including a well known Little Italy landmark called Umberto's Clam House. He and an unsavory crew of eighteen were caught cheating on income taxes, evading New York State Liquor Authority regulations, and obtaining illegal waste removal licenses. Most of the defendants were in their early to late sixties and hailed from such prosperous, respectable Long Island and Westchester communities as Old Westbury, North Hills, Great Neck, Hewlett Harbor, Woodmere, Scarsdale, Roslyn, and Tarrytown. To their neighbors in these old-line suburbs, each man probably seemed like just another hard-driving businessperson. Their crimes blended right in with legitimate activities run by people old enough to have secured the good life. That aura of respectability and success is what makes white-collar crime so insidious—and why older people are the most skilled at perpetrating it.

Plenty of benign looking old people are quietly leading criminal lives. The U.S. attorney for the Southern District of New York scored a big coup with the conviction of an eighty-two-year-old insurance adjuster in 1984. Bernard Gold, who suffers from heart disease and diabetes, was not too ill to lead an arson-for-profit ring that wiped out seventeen occupied tenement apartment buildings between 1976 and 1984.

Gold started his criminal career at age 74. By then he had for a long time been doing business in a firm started by his father. He was in a position of trust, with close ties to New York real estate people and international insurance underwriters. As a public adjuster, his job was to negotiate claim settlements for insureds. Long-standing contacts enabled Gold to corrupt everyone from landlords to an underwriter at Lloyd's of London (to whom he paid a $25,000 bribe for reinstating a lapsed policy).

As the ringleader, explains prosecutor Ruth Wedgewood, Gold would advance money to buy buildings, give advice on how to set fires, falsify insurance claims, and bribe people at insurance companies to pay off. "His most chilling piece of advice was when he told them they'd better have fires in occupied buildings because unoccupied buildings wouldn't pay insurance," says Wedgewood. Despite his age, he was "astonishingly acute mentally." He could recall every fire and every settlement in which his ring had been involved.

It took the sophisticated Racketeering Influenced and Corrupt Organizations (RICO) statute and the testimony of an eighty-seven-year-old accountant who described a special checking account in which Gold kept his illegal profits to nab Gold. The court sentenced the octogenarian to ten years in prison. Said the judge, "If he were a younger man and a healthier man, I would impose a much larger sentence." As it is, ten years probably means "life" to Bernard Gold. He won't have much use for the $25,000 he had to pay in fines nor will he miss the $25,000 in illegal profits he had to forfeit.

The real growth industry for elderly criminals will be white-collar crimes like those of "Matty the Horse" and Bernard Gold. The more the population ages, the more we'll be seeing of them.

CONSTRAINT

Patricians of the underworld are being pursued with powerful prosecutorial ammunition: wiretaps, "stings," the RICO statute. But the more plebeian crimes of the aged are very much underreported and underprosecuted. Police are reluctant to arrest grandmotherly types caught stealing condoms or grandfatherly types who hit their nurses with a cane. But when police are called to the scene, new policies limit their discretion in deciding whether to haul in a white-haired offender. Retail stores, for example, used to be unwilling to prosecute shoplifters. The spectacle of a disoriented oldster being dragged off in handcuffs is bad public relations for your local Bloomingdale's or Saks.

But shoplifting has become a major source of loss for stores. In 1983, police knew of more than three quarters of a million shoplifting incidents with an average loss of $72 per theft. Those thefts cost stores $58 million, a figure that doesn't even include the price of hiring detectives, buying magnetic tags, and installing hidden TV cameras. Because retailers pass these costs on to innocent customers, no one can afford to turn a benign other cheek to petty thieves.

It's now possible to take the offensive against shoplifters without stirring up public sympathy for the little old lady who is about to be arrested. Citizen's arrests by store security guards remove the culprits from public view while they wait for the law to arrive. Since shoplifting is the crime most commonly committed by old people, aggressive prosecution policies portend a vast increase in arrests of geriatric boosters. This alone will create the appearance of a gray crime wave.

The same is true for domestic violence, the kind of serious crime that oldsters most often commit. All through the 1970s, progressive police administrators were promoting mediation as the way to deal with husbands who punched their wives or grandmothers who attacked their daughters. Arrests were a no-no. But by the 1980s women's groups began raising legitimate objections to the "family crisis intervention" approach. Follow-up research in Minneapolis, sponsored by the influential Police Foundation, showed that arrested wife-beaters were much less likely to repeat their assaults than those who are merely calmed down at the scene. Now many police departments are mandating the arrest of the aggressor in domestic squabbles. This, too, bodes for a large increase in arrests of old people.

☐ ☐ ☐

The question is what to do with oldsters once they're arrested. The prosecutor in the "onion roll" ax murder case described earlier, understood the problem: "What do we do now? Set high bail? Prosecute? Get a conviction and send the fellow to prison? You tell me! We did nothing. The media dropped it quickly and, I hope, that's it."

Whether oldsters are first-time criminals, professional robbers, Mafia dons, or con artists, they pose special problems to a criminal justice system that is designed to deal only with young, violent, escape-prone offenders. What to do, for example, with a Bernard Gold? According to his attorney: "Mr. Gold . . . is basically incarcerated by his own illness. He cannot walk without assistance; he cannot drive a car; he cannot venture out of his house or apartment. . . . He cannot tolerate the slightest stress."

It's hard to think of anything more stressful than living in a cell surrounded by noisy, aggressive young thugs. With Gold's need for constant medication and nursing, one must ask whether the Metropolitan Correctional Center is in a position to take care of this octogenarian inmate. Forty-seven states as well as the federal prison system have no special facilities or formal programs for aged convicts.

Yet, the narrowed range of police discretion, along with a proliferation of sentencing guidelines and mandatory sentences, will produce a sharp rise in old-age prison inmates. Most of the prison elderly are there for violent crimes. A high percentage of these are first-time offenders. Their crimes of passion are not likely to be deterred, and an old person is not a good candidate for "rehabilitation."

Nevertheless, the elderly tend to be docile in prison—a stabilizing force on the younger inmates. Old prisoners spend most of their time in their cells—they haven't got the stamina to join their younger counterparts playing ball in the exercise yard or jogging down the cellblock corridor. They read less, go to fewer movies, play cards less, and do less prison work. Nor are they inclined to participate in riots or, like Forrest Silva Tucker, attempt an escape. Maximum security is a waste of resources for the incarcerated elderly.

On the whole, old inmates violate prison rules far less often than young ones. Their curtailed activities reduce their opportunities to run athwart the prison staff. The incarcerated elderly are just as isolated behind prison walls as are their free brothers and sisters on the outside.

□ □ □

The upward crush of elderly crime is triggering debates on whether geriatric delinquents should be processed through a separate justice system (in much the same way as juvenile delinquents are) and incarcerated in segregated prison facilities. As the ranks of elderly criminals swell, it's probable that both these options will be tested. What we're likely to find is that a geriatric justice system will have the same weaknesses as the juvenile justice system. And segregated prisons, built at great cost for relatively few criminals (as of 1981, only 8,853 oldsters out of more than 353,000 inmates), don't make financial sense. A public unwilling to cough up the money to build more prisons for the masses of criminals who really scare them is not likely to do so for the 2.5 percent of whom they aren't even aware.

The wave of the future is not likely to be anything as conventional as new prisons or parallel court systems. The future has arrived in Florida, where the Broward Senior Intervention and Education Program is having great success dealing with elderly shoplifters: Only 1.5 percent of its graduates commit new crimes. That's a lower recidivism rate than any community program I know.

Because BSIE is working in a state with such a high concentration of old people, it's the model for the burgeoning geriatric delinquents in the rest of the country.

The Broward County program got its start in 1978, when a seventy-nine-year-old woman received a summons to appear in court for shoplifting. Confused and frightened, she went to Herb Weiss, the Outreach supervisor at the Jewish community center where she spent much of her time. Weiss decided to accompany her to her arraignment in order to help her through the ordeal. Presiding judge John King was no more comfortable with the long parade of elderly suspects he was seeing than was Weiss. Nor were other Broward County judges. So the judges and the Jewish community center got together to create a diversion program that might make more sense for aged shoplifters than criminal prosecution.

BSIE accepts into the program only those who are at least sixty years old and first-time offenders. Once in the program, clients experience little sense of being in a program for criminals; instead, they receive extensive counseling to get to the roots of their shoplifting and warm support in coping with the humiliation of their exposure. The cure comes in the form of activities at various senior centers and responsibility for a community service: working for "meals-on-wheels," or as a library aide, or helping other senior citizens deal with grief, illness, or loneliness. BSIE takes direct aim at the drift that drives old people to crime and anchors them in a solid range of group activities and obligations. It works for shoplifting; it could work for more serious crimes as well.

AMELIORATING DRIFT

It has been the thesis of this chapter that an absence of structure and responsibilities is the source of elderly drift into crime. Nascent developments will go a long way toward ameliorating that condition in the future. The growing number of old people living alone and close to the poverty level is giving rise to new kinds of living arrangements. Dorothy Robinson, for example, a destitute aged woman who had long sought refuge in a New York shelter for the homeless, has found a companion in Frederick Edwards. A recovering alcoholic twenty years Dorothy's junior, Edwards used to work at a job on the Bowery that paid $50 a week. That was enough to pay for his room at the Blue Jay Hotel. But he lost his job. That's when he, too, joined the ranks of the homeless. Now, he is quoted as saying of Dorothy, "She and I are going to run away and get married. We can't afford to live alone on welfare and social security, but we're planning on getting an apartment together." You don't have to be homeless and broke to share a place to live. Lots of older people are doing it—as married couples, as lovers, or as friends.

At the same time, the business world has discovered the profits in the geriatric market. Cruises, lectures, sports, and shows are all being tailored to the needs and tastes of the elderly. Such enterprises provide the companionship and anchors that help offset old age drift.

The critical factor in providing accountability and structure will be the labor market. Long-standing incentives for early retirement have become too expensive for the economy to sustain. The slowed productivity and high inflation rates of the 1970s forced large cost-of-living adjustments to social security payments. The contributor base is beginning to shrink but, because of increases in life expectancy, the recipient pool is enlarging. Both public and private employers are realizing that it has become more costly to pay pensions to unproductive retired workers than to keep them on the job and find meaningful things for them to do.

Soon, the once popular argument that older workers need to be moved out to make room for the young will no longer hold. Labor shortages are anticipated by the year 2000. Even in the present, while we have relatively high regional unemployment rates, jobs are being created in record numbers. These jobs often go begging because of an absence of skilled workers to fill them. Older Americans, will, in the future, be a valuable repository of those skills.

Community-service jobs are a fertile area for expansion of old-age work roles. Local businesses and major corporations frequently loan out their personnel to government and community organizations. Older workers, often denied promotions within their companies, are ideally suited for such loans. When problems such as crime, drug addiction, illiteracy, and beautification are tackled by skilled corporate problem-solvers, they pay off in both job enrichment and enhanced community life.

Pat Choate, a senior policy analyst at TRW, asserts: "Old people are the fastest growing cohort in our society . . . how well we harness the productivity of older workers will in large measure determine how well we rebuild our economy."

The importance of retaining the productive capacity of older workers has prompted the Administration on Aging (part of the U.S. Department of Health and Human Services) to explore ways of making older people self-sufficient. Its twin goals: to encourage older welfare and social security recipients to work while finding ways to finance job training and entrepreneurship.

Access to the labor force, for those who want it, provides a mooring that discourages the crimes of old age. While it also creates opportunities for employee theft of goods and services, there's good evidence that older workers are more loyal to their employers and engage in less turnover than younger workers. Loyalty and job satisfaction are the two best forms of honesty insurance an employer can have.

If structures are created that enable old people to work, present and future cohorts will be in a good position to take advantage of the opportunities. Unlike those who entered old age in the first half of this century, more than 90 percent of today's oldsters are native-born. They've been raised and educated in the United States, and most have lived their lives in urban settings. In contrast to the turn of the century, when only a tenth of the elderly population had completed high school, almost three quarters of today's old people have a high school diploma. Today's old people know this country and how it works; by mooring them to the world of responsibility, we will incite fewer of them to drift into the sea of crime.

CRIMEWARPS

· As growing numbers of people live to reach the ages at which they are at risk for brain impairments and social as well as physical limitations, there will be an increase in unpremeditated domestic violence and senseless petty property crimes.

· Between the years 1995 and 2050, the numbers of elderly aged eighty and over will nearly triple. Within that group, the numbers of female blacks will have quadrupled, male blacks quintupled, female and male whites nearly tripled. Therefore, it is among blacks that we will see the largest relative increase in crimes of the feeble.

· Crimes of the feeble will be offset by advances in the treatment of Alzheimer's Disease and other organic disorders of old age. These advances, however, will favor mostly the affluent, as reductions in Medicaid and Medicare benefits make quality care less accessible to those without private insurance.

· Domestic violence among the elderly will increase in those Southern states with a high percentage of blacks, urbanization, and gun ownership.

· Crimes such as larceny, which are caused by drift, will decrease as retirement policies shift to keep old people in the work force. Those states with the largest proportions of nonretired elderly will show the most dramatic changes in crime patterns.

· Those businesses with a preponderance of older workers will experience lower rates of theft and other counterproductive behaviors—such as extralong lunch breaks, excessive sick leave, and drug and alcohol abuse—than those with younger workers.

· Sex crimes by the elderly will increase between the years 2000 and 2025 as the molested children of the "baby boom" generation reach old age.

· White-collar crimes will increase as the proportions of old people in the population grows. This trend will be fed by the lengthening of the working years through legislative erosion of mandatory retirement.

· The elderly white-collar explosion will peak in 2025. That is the year in which the proportion of white males and females aged sixty to seventy-nine will drop off. Because they are the ones who are most likely to be in jobs that create white-collar-crime opportunities, their reductions in the population will lead to a proportional decline in these offenses.

· Those now working, who have moved from their home states to pursue job opportunities, will create a tidal wave of migration when they retire in twenty to thirty years. As members of the mammoth baby boom generation, the 4 percent who move will make up a cohort of nearly 2 million elderly migrants between 2000 and 2025. If today's trends persist and half of these go to the Sunshine States, it will mean a gain of about 1 million elderly inhabitants and a massive increase in elderly crime in those states.

· Extending the work years will stem the flow of elderly migration to the

Sunshine States; so will the continued proliferation of two-career families (nonmigration among the elderly is tied to the continued presence of one spouse in the job market). These developments will dilute the impact of the crimes of old age on Florida, Arizona, and California.

• Organized-crime enterprises will be unaffected by old-age demographics. Such organizations will have a constant number of high-level positions and supporting roles to fill with senior members, regardless of how many old people there are in the overall population. The majority of lower-level jobs—runners, executioners—have been and will continue to be filled by younger recruits.

• Except for old pros in the white-collar and organized-crime category, most elderly criminals will commit their first crimes after the age of fifty-five.

Crimewarp II

The March of Crime

Lafayette, Louisiana, is one of the ten fastest growing cities in the United States. Its population has jumped by more than 53 percent since 1970, and its crime rate has bounded up along with it.

Lafayette's gain is New York's loss. In the same period the Big Apple has lost nearly 1 million of its residents. But of late, it has lost some of its crime as well. The crime rate in what has long been known as "Fear City" has dropped by about as much as Lafayette's has increased.

Hundreds of thousands of workers and hopefuls are making the trek from the decaying cities of the Frost Belt to the boomtowns of the Sunbelt. But their path is scarred: Crime marches along the same route. In the future, crime will not settle equally across the landscape—its volume and form will be molded by the economy, migration patterns, and population characteristics that infuse each location. Though crime will display a general downward trend nationwide, much of it will be displaced to the new *megatropolises* that will arise by the year 2000 as well as the promised lands of *the suburbs* and *rural areas*.

The decade of the 1970s turned American migration—and crime patterns—

on its head. For most of this century, people have been moving from the farm to the city and from the South to the North—where we thought most of the crime was, too. Now all that has changed.

City slickers and suburban commuters are heading for the country in droves. Much of the land they're occupying has been vacated by farmers. Thefts have moved in with them. For many of the farmers who remain as their neighbors, rural loan frauds and family violence loom large on the vast horizon.

Northerners, who used to look down their noses at "redneck" neighbors south of the Mason-Dixon line, are now scrambling for their place in the sun. Their adopted regions have some of the highest violent crime rates in the country.

The streams of Poles, Italians, and Irish who once flooded our Northern and Eastern cities to build the American smokestack economy have slowed to a trickle. In their stead have come a torrent of Asians and Hispanics who provide brain power and muscle for the high-tech medinas of the South and West. Barroom brawls, drug wars, and organized-crime triads have taken root, too.

Young working husbands and wives-in-waiting—whose dream was a house in the suburbs and lots of open space in which to raise their kids—are being displaced by two-earner families for whom child-rearing is a lower, long-delayed priority and for whom the "action" of the city has much greater appeal. They have become part of the robbery and assault statistics that haunt large cities.

Middle-class blacks, who were once excluded from the suburbs, are escaping central cities and taking their place in the urban fringes that used to be the sole province of whites. Teenage vandalism and ethnic conflict are waiting to greet them.

Old people, who aged in the jobs that took them away from their hometowns, are migrating back to their roots. If they're affluent enough, they're heading for Florida, Arizona, or California. They are adding to the ranks of victims who lure con artists to the places where old people are found.

America is redistributing itself: black and white, rich and poor, old and young. Because crime is committed by people, it is redistributing itself along with them.

4

New Megatropolises

Between 1970 and 1980, the population of Houston soared by more than 900,000—an increase of over 45 percent. Fifty years from now, Houston is projected to be the fourth-ranking metropolitan area in the country, with a population of over 8 million. To get there, Houston will have to expand its present numbers by 260 percent. It, and its environs, will become a new megatropolis.

In the 1970 census, Houston didn't even make the top ten list of American metropolises; by 1980, it had jumped from number 16 to number 9. In the interim, Houston—along with Dallas, Brownsville, and McAllen, as well as parts of Louisiana and Oklahoma—became part of a regional oil rush that turned this dusty stretch of American outback into one of the most desirable tracts in the country. Even Austin became a boom town—not because of oil, but because of technology.

Austin is still thriving, but Houston is in trouble. A worldwide oil glut killed the golden derrick. Steel and glass office spires rising out of the Texas flatland are one-quarter to one-half vacant. Rents on apartments have plummeted, and condominiums are selling at a sharp discount. Hotels scramble for guests. The oil barons and roustabouts who used to swell the population at the rate of two thousand a week don't go there anymore. Of those who went earlier, hoards are unemployed.

Texas, Louisiana, and Oklahoma are struggling to find a post-oil economy for themselves. For Texas, it's especially tough. One of the lowest tax rates in the nation combined with right-wing fundamentalist educational domination have damaged the school system's ability to provide the high-tech sophistication that the industries of the future require. (Governor Mark White tried to change the latter problem by abolishing the elected school board, giving teachers competency tests, and bringing textbooks back in line with scholarly standards.)

The only groups that still come to Houston in droves are illegal aliens from Mexico and Central America. Young, single, day workers, they take whatever jobs they can find. With no bank accounts and no local ties, they have nothing to do after work and on weekends but spend their money in places like the El Rio Grande bar on Houston Avenue. They drink, get into fights, defend their manhood with a gun, and die. Hispanics, who make up less than one fifth of Houston's population, account for over one third of its homicides. The macho culture they import dovetails with the tradition of violence that has long prevailed in the South and the West—*a tradition which in the future will undergo a subtle transformation.*

□   □   □

Three days after President Ronald Reagan unveiled his revolutionary tax proposals in 1985, he dropped in on Malvern, Pennsylvania, to sell his reforms to its inhabitants. Just eight years before, the Route 202 Corridor was nothing but farmland—not the kind of place to which a President would go to promote a tax package. Today it is a thriving complex of over two hundred computer-related industries, biotechnical research centers, and business service companies.

This burgeoning high-tech gateway nestles in the ambit of the Philadelphia metropolitan area. Plagued with a large proportion of needy minorities and the elderly, low median income, and a substantial loss of population, it is one of those Northern cities that pundits used to predict was scheduled for extinction. But the metamorphosis of nearby Chester County signals a revival of the very urban centers which the Sunbelt is supposedly eclipsing. Philadelphia, some now say, will displace Houston and Atlanta as the city of the future.

Philadelphia—along with Boston, New York, Troy, and other "decaying" cities of the Northeast—is becoming an incubator of new industries. Such cities, major research centers with great universities, are breeding the knowledge on which the future Information Age depends. The Northeast is becoming a magnet for upscale, law-abiding migrants who are changing the face of the Frost Belt.

A 1985 analysis of selected metropolitan regions by the National Association of Realtors showed that home prices in the old cities of the North and East surged by an average of over 12 percent, three times the national average. The

Philadelphia vicinity registered a gain of 8.7 percent. By contrast, Sunbelt homes appreciated an average of only 1.2 percent.

While home values in Philadelphia were going up, the crime rate was going down. Between 1981 and 1984, the number of reported crimes dropped by 18 percent, although the population decreased by a much smaller percentage.

Surrounding Chester County's population has grown by as much as Philadelphia's has shrunk. Whereas most suburbs used to be dormitory communities that fed central cities like Philadelphia, they are rapidly becoming employment centers in their own right. Coincidentally, *suburbs are taking on the characteristics that used to belong only to urban places.*

Projections based on 1975–80 migration rates show that, by the year 2020, the City of Brotherly Love will have lost nearly half its white population while its black population will remain constant. Its suburbs, on the other hand, will have expanded by half—and more than quadrupled their black population— since 1970. The phenomenon of black suburbanization is a new and growing one that will substantially integrate the country's minorities.

For some areas, that means an increase in crime; but for Chester County, it has meant the opposite. The number of crimes reported between 1980 and 1982 dropped by one third, despite a huge jump in the overall population. In fact, according to FBI tables, the crime rate for the entire Philadelphia metropolitan area is far below that of every major growth zone in the country except Florida's Fort Myers–Cape Coral area and Texas's McAllen–Pharr–Edinburg.

The FBI's reports cover mostly street crimes, *but the real crime threat in an upscale, technologically based employment suburb is white-collar crime.* Houston's police chief Lee Brown, whose city used to be in the same growth mode that the Philadelphia metropolitan area now enjoys, warns: "As things change, the nature of crime also changes. To the extent we have increased the government of technology—particularly the use of computers—we can expect that technology will find its way into the criminal arena." High-tech suburbanites may not steal your car, but some of them could well steal your credit.

Development, and its criminal consequences, is not taking place uniformly across all regions. When it comes to crime, the desertion of a farm in rural Iowa means one thing, while the building of a power plant in rural Wyoming or the creation of a high-tech corridor in rural Pennsylvania means another.

Agrarian Iowa is losing its youth and being left with a growing body of old people who will drain its social services, while Wyoming and parts of Texas are being inundated with young, single men who get into trouble. Conversely, Pennsylvania is attracting white-collar workers who are upscale, highly educated, family-oriented—traits that generally signal law-abiding behavior. But like their counterparts in Iowa, Wyoming, and Texas, they are highly mobile—a trait that often leads to the weakened community ties and social controls that promote crime.

Which communities end up with crime booms and which with crime busts will be a function of migration patterns and regional cultures.

When people migrate domestically, it is usually for one or both of two reasons: work and life-style. For those who migrate across international borders, there's a third factor: escape from repression or persecution. All three elements are operative in the population shifts that will determine the landscape of crime in America.

MIDDLE-CLASS MIGRANTS

Those who migrate for economic reasons are generally under thirty-five. In recent years, they have been well-educated, affluent elites who, spouse and children in tow, circulate from one metropolis to another as improved job offers beckon them. Such people have been following the lure of oil and the microchip to Sunbelt locales like the Gulf States and Silicon Valley.

Jerry Sanders, for example, grew up in Chicago. He had just graduated with a degree in electrical engineering from the University of Illinois when he heard the call in the late 1950s. Pulling up stakes, he headed west and went to work as an applications design engineer for McDonnell Douglas. In 1969, after stints with Motorola and Fairchild Camera, he teamed up with seven other computer wizards and founded Advanced Micro Devices. The company rapidly grew into one of the most profitable semiconductor companies in the country. The blue-eyed, silver-haired mogul became one of Silicon Valley's star residents. "This is the place of the American dream," exulted Elliot Sopkin, AMD's vice president for communications. "We're the crude oil of the 1980s!"

That was early 1984, when life in Silicon Valley's fast lane meant a lobster in every pot, a Mercedes in every garage, and a Brioni suit in every closet. Venture capitalists descended on hot young engineers and tripped all over themselves trying to set them up in their own businesses. Some of IBM's and Atari's finest wanted to do the same thing as the former Fairchild Camera employees who had spun off AMD and Intel. But along with the pressures of building multinational corporations—from businesses run out of garages—came drug abuse, trade secrets thefts, and a "gray market" in electronic components. By mid-1985, the dazzling balloon floating over Silicon Valley started leaking air.

The computer market became oversaturated. Japan had won the 256K RAM war, and Korea followed hard on its heels. Undercut and overproduced, Texas Instruments, Intel, National Semiconductor, Apple, and Mostek laid off thousands of workers. IBM, the company with the blue chip on its shoulder, had to own up to a major slump in profits. Even Advanced Micro Devices was hurting. When I chatted with Elliot Sopkin that year, I caught him in the middle of a two-week furlough during which the entire company was shut down. When it reopened, management put employees on a four-day workweek, gave executives a 15-percent cut in salary, and canceled the annual $700,000 Christmas bash.

Excess workers have to go somewhere. The westward migration stream, of which Jerry Sanders was an important part, will soon be diverted from San Jose and its silicon neighbors just as it was from Houston after the oil crash. Engineers, designers, and fabricators will leave Sunnyvale and disperse to electronics centers emerging in places as diverse as Austin, Boston, Seattle and Denver. Until *those* cities' booms also go bust.

THE HISPANIC DIASPORA

Meanwhile, back in the Sunbelt, there's a less-glamorous class of working migrant: the Mexican "wetbacks" who daily stream across porous borders near San Diego, El Paso, Nogales, and Las Cruces. Most come to find day work in the fields of the farm belt or the kitchens of affluent Americans and the restaurants they frequent. Unlike their wealthier white-collar counterparts, they often arrive singly, unattached young men who hope to earn enough to go back to Mexico and help their families.

Between the 1970s and 1980s, Immigration and Naturalization Service records show that the inflow of Mexicans and South and Central Americans far outstripped that of previous decades. The largest concentrations of Hispanic settlers (75 percent) are found in the South and West. Just under half of Hispanic families live in central cities, where, more than other groups, they are the victims of theft. But when they commit crimes, they are more likely to be arrested and imprisoned for violence.

What looks like a propensity for violence may be a reflection of the relative youthfulness of the Hispanic population—the median age, 22.6 for males and 23.8 for females, is lower than that of whites, blacks, or other race groups, but it is rising. According to the National Center for Health Statistics, Hispanic women have a birthrate nearly 50 percent higher than other Americans. More than one fifth are teenaged mothers; one quarter are unmarried, and fewer than half complete high school. The 1980 census counted a large jump in the number of Hispanic toddlers. As young Latinos shed the deeply ingrained deference to authority that forms a key part of their culture, their violence will increase. By 1990 to 1995, when they enter their mid-teens, they will become a major source of trouble in those states where Hispanics make up a significant minority: California, Texas, Arizona, Colorado, and New Mexico.

The killings in and around the El Rio Grande bar in Houston are a foretaste of what is to come. Houston's older, more established Hispanic families look on in horror as they see their newly arrived brethren abusing the cherished ideal of machismo. Roman Martínez, a Houston advertising man who also serves as the State Representative for the *barrio*, has tried to close down the bars where young immigrant toughs hang out and killing has become a way of life.

Raul Correa, a Mexican-American spokesperson for the Houston Police Department, attributes the spontaneous murders to the ubiquitous pistol: "They feel if they are going to be victimized they are going to have some protection." In the countries they left behind—El Salvador, Guatemala—these immigrants knew they could never count on the police for protection. On crossing into "El Norte," the illegal alien's first hurdle is to evade the bandits waiting on both sides of the border to prey on him—and "la migra," the U.S. immigration police. It's hard for them to believe that the Houston Police Department will be on their side.

Although the gap is closing, once settled in, Hispanics tend to fare better economically than do blacks. Almost half of Hispanic families live outside central cities in affluent suburbs and rural areas. Unlike the Northeast, in the Sunbelt, where Hispanic families are concentrated, city dwellers' median incomes are almost as high as the suburbs. But rapid success has its price.

□ □ □

In May 1980, the infamous Liberty City (Florida) riots showed just how high a price. The manifest cause was the exoneration of four white police officers in the bludgeoning death of a black insurance executive. But that was just the final ingredient in a long simmering brew of humiliation and ethnic rivalry.

Dade County's blacks have always been low men on the economic totem pole, and the government hasn't been much help. But when an influx of Cuban refugees poured into Miami in the 1960s, the government came through for the newcomers. Largely middle-class storekeepers, professionals, and financiers, the Cubans rose quickly and took Miami with them while the blacks stayed in the gutter, seemingly forgotten. Four days, eighteen deaths, and $100 million later, the whole country became aware of the fire-scarred battle zone called Liberty City.

The previous month, a second wave of Cubans had arrived in Miami via the "Freedom Flotilla." The *Marielitos*, as they came to be known, bore the stigma of a particularly high rate of criminality. In Hialeah, for example, Mariel refugees made up nearly a quarter of the arrests in the first six months of 1981. Most of their crimes were minor, but an 80-percent surge in Miami murders the year before is also attributed to them. Mariel violence has been linked to the drug trade and revenge killings carried over from Cuba.

Clearly, the Marielitos were a different breed of Cuban than the doctors and businessmen who had come a generation before. Those employed at all were typically working as waitresses, security guards, orderlies, punch press operators. A large percentage were collecting welfare or unemployment. But worse, Fidel Castro had peppered his refugee flotilla with generous quantities of convicts and psychotics. Miami, once the sun capital of the country, became the gun capital instead.

Of those Hispanics who end up behind bars here, the greatest proportion are doing time not in state and local lock-ups, but in federal prisons where drug violators, interstate robbers, and larcenists make up the largest part of the confined. Their presence in the "elite" federal prisons indicates that Hispanic criminals—some Marielitos among them—are involved in more serious or highly organized crimes than the average offender.

ASIAN MIGRATION

Orientals, the immigrant group associated with the lowest levels of criminality, currently make up one of the largest waves of legal migration into this country. The Koreans, Cambodians, Vietnamese, and Laotians who have escaped persecution in their countries, or rape and looting on hostile seas, are converging not only on the same states as Hispanics—California and Texas—but also on places like Minnesota and Louisiana.

The first waves of Asian migrants tended to be disproportionately well educated, professional, and socially active. Though they started humbly, they quickly became absorbed into the middle class mainstream. Like Cubans in Florida, Asian success has been the cause of violent resentments among those who feel scarce jobs and government aid have been monopolized. In 1981, for example, gangs of Denver Chicanos rioted in an oriental refugee community in protest against the preferential treatment they felt the Asians were getting in housing and welfare. The Asians have likewise been preyed on by Texas fishermen and California street gangs. But the most vicious treatment seems to take place at the hands of oriental tongs (benevolent societies), with their young "enforcers" and triads (crime syndicates).

Oriental neighborhoods are suffused with highly organized extortion, loan-sharking, illegal gambling, prostitution, and protection rackets:

ITEM. New York: In 1985, a fifteen-year-old Hong Kong immigrant was arrested and charged with shooting seven people in a Chinatown restaurant during a dispute with fellow gang members over the division of money from their extortion racket. Tung On, the tong for which they worked, extorted money from massage parlors, restaurants, and illegal gambling dens. If any of their victims didn't pay up, it was the job of the younger gang members to beat them into compliance.

ITEM. Los Angeles: A Vietnamese gang tried to extort money from Che Linh, a popular singer known as the "Vietnamese Elvis Presley." They threatened to set off a bomb during his performance at the Hollywood Palladium unless he paid them $3,000. Contrary to custom, Che did not capitulate in frightened silence; he went public and urged all his fellow countrymen to "stand up to the gangs."

ITEM. San Francisco: Three top leaders of a Taiwanese criminal syndicate were sought in the murder of Henry Liu, the author of a biography critical of Taiwan's President Chiang Ching-kuo.

Gangs are a pervasive part of oriental culture—a long-established way of doing business. Unlike black and Hispanic gangs, they maintain a low profile: no flashy clothes, no graffiti, no chains, whistles, or Harley-Davidsons. The only colorful thing about them is their names: Pink Knights, Frogmen, Yakuza, Bamboo, Four Seas, Paratroopers. Secrecy, discreetly veiled threats, and chilling retaliation for noncompliance are their stock-in-trade. So nuanced are the threats that the most innocuous conversation can conceal layers of meaning. A police sergeant in Westminster, a Los Angeles suburb that is about 15-percent Vietnamese, gave this example:

"Someone may call you up and say, 'It's a beautiful day today, but the weatherman said it might rain tomorrow. If it rains, it will water the flowers. You might be around to enjoy the flowers, or perhaps you will fertilize them.' To the

Vietnamese, that's an absolute death threat. But you have a helluva time convincing twelve jurors of that."

Getting a case to a jury is a rarity—cultural and language barriers militate against reporting crime—but the strong likelihood of lethal retaliation is an even more powerful deterrent. From the outside, oriental neighborhoods convey an appearance of tranquillity and safety. In a sense, that appearance is real. The crime and violence that occur tend not to be random, but highly ritualized and codified. The gangs work a circumscribed circuit—encompassing New Orleans, Houston, Los Angeles, San Jose, Portland, and Honolulu—sheltered by extended families and attending to the internal affairs of their fellow ethnics.

As orientals learn to trust American police, some experts report that the gangs are losing their grip. In their stead, the offspring of the latest wave of Asian migrants—who arrived here poorer, less-educated, less-Westernized, and with greater adjustment problems than their predecessors—are engaging in traditional juvenile crimes like robbery and murder. However, despite widespread fears of a growth in oriental organized crime, most police professionals agree that Asian immigrants are among the most law-abiding of all Americans—and they are likely to remain so.

BLACK MOVEMENT

Finally, there are migrants who make a geographic shift for life-style purposes. Among these are middle class blacks. The interval between 1975 and 1980 saw the rise of a new phenomenon in black migration. In contrast to the traditional Southern-rural-to-Northern-urban flow, increasing numbers of middle-class blacks moved from central cities to suburbs. The average annual net urban to suburban movement of blacks increased from 88,000 in the 1970s to 220,000 in the early 1980s.

James Brower, a soft-spoken, strapping six-foot New York City police officer with an elegant profile, was one such migrant. At the end of 1971, he moved his family of five from a lower-income black ghetto near Kennedy Airport to a mixed neighborhood in Suffolk County, some fifty miles from the inner city.

Brower is a member of the first postwar generation of blacks—a group that made gains in education, status, and occupation that had been denied their predecessors. His grandmother raised chickens and grew vegetables in North Carolina. His father, a factory worker, could never earn enough to get his five children out of the Brooklyn tenements in Bedford-Stuyvesant, Brownsville, and East New York. "I came from the streets," Brower says baldly.

In high school, Brower was a star basketball player in a slum where "you were either an athlete or a gangster." A tournament he played for Thomas Jefferson High School took him to St. Albans, Queens—his first taste of what life was like on the other side of the tracks: "I'd never seen trees before. It was a whole different world for me, coming from Brooklyn and tenements, to see one-family homes. At that time St. Albans was beautiful. It was like Beverly Hills."

Brower liked it so well, he decided to stay. At the age of sixteen, a senior in high school, he moved in with the brother and mother of Leroy Ellis, a professional basketball player for the Los Angeles Lakers. He commuted to Thomas Jefferson in Brooklyn until graduation. But evenings and weekends were spent in the comfortable black enclave of St. Albans, where he met his wife, Erlinda. Her father's chain of beauty shops allowed the family to share in the prosperity of St. Albans. When Brower turned seventeen, he and Erlinda married.

Married life and a new baby forced Brower to turn down a basketball scholarship and college. He became a meter reader for the Brooklyn Union Gas Company. But two years later, on a lark, he accompanied a buddy and took the police exam. He was sworn in in 1968 and "felt it was an upward movement." Two more children came, and the two-family house in South Ozone Park became cramped.

Like middle-class whites, the Browers wanted more space and better schools in which to raise their children. They looked to the suburbs, following behind whites by a full generation. It took that long for the racial barriers to drop and for local inhabitants to realize that the presence of a black face was not going to destroy their real estate values.

"I didn't go looking for a black neighborhood," Brower explains. "I went looking for a neighborhood. I wanted a school that wasn't run down. . . . I wanted the most I could get for my money. In the areas in which I looked for a home, people were very nice. I didn't get the feeling I wasn't welcome." Brower settled for a nine-room high ranch-style house in North Babylon, where his family could work and play among dogwoods, shrubs, and vast expanses of lawn. Erlinda has been lobbying to fill some of that lawn with a swimming pool.

Families like the Browers are a stabilizing force on their new communities. "[Black] people who have moved out from the city are generally civil service workers. They take care of their property. They are interested in their children. They do go to PTA meetings. They do take part in community things," avers Brower. The stability is reflected in crime statistics. Between 1973 and 1982, suburban blacks experienced the largest drops in victimization rates for violent crimes, home break-ins, and household thefts.

Because of blacks' long-denied entry to the suburbs, the communities that admit them are often older, working-class enclaves whose status is inferior to that of the middle-class minorities who are coming in. But the movement of industry out of the urban core rejuvenates the older suburbs in its path. Increased revenues, boosted by factories and businesses, reduce taxes for residents while expanding services to support the elderly, treat the troubled, and educate the young.

The influx of families is making the suburbs more dense. Structural density— the number of multiple dwellings in an area—will profoundly influence crime patterns. By reducing residents' sense of turf as well as the open space necessary for surveillance, the suburbs will be more vulnerable to robberies and burglaries, crimes which depend on a degree of anonymity. The Brower home in North Babylon was burglarized twice—something that never happened to young James in Bedford-Stuyvesant. Nor did he ever get chains ripped off his neck by passing carloads of kids from the next town, as do Babylon youngsters on weekends.

On the other hand, internal density—the number of people per room—which is thought to influence delinquency, will decrease as family size shrinks and the number of people living alone grows. The pathologies caused by crowding will be reduced. Brower's sons grew up with their own rooms; there is no sign of delinquency, drugs, or drunkenness among the three of them. It is a source of special pride that Brower and his wife were able to provide their sons with material comforts without spoiling them. All three turned out to be "good kids," with one being both a prelaw major and "one of the most highly recruited basketball players in America."

That's not to say that their sojourn in the suburbs has been without pain. The Brower boys miss the sense of neighborhood closeness they hear their father describe when he reminisces about his own childhood. They feel some anger about the racial fights they've seen at North Babylon High School and the discrimination they experienced toward its all-black championship basketball team. Derek, away at school now, says he wouldn't come back to Babylon at all, if it weren't for his family.

□ □ □

The Brower boys were caught in the backwash of an ethnic warfare that has come to the suburbs. Instead of flashing knives and guns, the warriors sling words and paint. National studies conducted in the 1980s by the American Jewish Committee, the National Association for the Advancement of Colored People, and the Anti-Defamation League of B'nai B'rith show that, for the first time in twenty years, the teenage bigotry quotient is rising.

For Derek and Christopher Brower, it took the form of a black basketball team and white soccer team. In other schools, like Roslyn High in Nassau County, Long Island, it was a separate black lounge. At Schreiber High School in Port Washington, the rise of a full-scale student Nazi party. In Staten Island, a terrifying attack with chains and sticks on a New Dorp high school bus. In the North Shore suburbs of Chicago, a vicious anti-Semitic student mail campaign against a Jewish businessman. Elsewhere, defaced walls, ethnic slurs, human beings reduced to labels like "greaser," "JAP," "nerd," and "nigger." The new bigotry thrives in the culture of *Animal House* and "Saturday Night Live," which promotes ethnic typecasting and says it's okay to hate.

Ethnic barbs combined with teenage bravado can leave long-lasting scars in a community. "A new rash of cross burnings, swastika paintings, desecration of religious institutions . . . in suburban areas on the East and West Coasts represents a serious threat to the peace and stability of our communities," assert Irving Levine and Joe Giordano of the American Jewish Committee's Institute on Pluralism and Group Identity. Bigoted teens grow up to be bigoted adults, often leaving a trail of vile crimes in their wake. Levine and Giordano have found a way to intervene. "Ethnic sharing," in which teens role play and discuss their way to mutual understanding, has aborted physical and symbolic assaults on participants. It is a powerful weapon against ethnic crime, especially when combined with newly formed police "ethnic crimes" squads and toughened laws against acts in which bigotry is a motive.

Given the nation's prevailing migration flows, Levine and Giordano's findings are chillingly relevant. "Teenage violence tended to spread in areas of rising unemployment, tense relations between groups, intense gang conflicts, and rapid movements of new types of people into older, changing neighborhoods. Bitter competition for jobs, wealth and prestige . . . produced social conflict."

It's no coincidence that the suburbs I've cited are all in the North. The new and roomy Sunbelt suburbs are more accessible to, and contain a higher proportion of, minorities than Frost Belt suburbs.

□ □ □

In the metropolises of the Frost Belt, a new segregation is gelling. While more-affluent whites and blacks escape to the urban fringes, a black underclass is becoming intensely concentrated in the pressure cookers of inner cities. As of the 1980 census, 58 percent of black families lived inside central cities, compared to less than one quarter of white families.

Percy Whitaker's family in Detroit, a case in point, stands in stark contrast to James Brower's of Long Island. When I found Whitaker in 1983, he hadn't worked for three years—not since a relative brother had pawned his radio and reacted to Percy's protests by bashing him in the face with a brick and cracking his skull. Seizures started soon after that, and he could no longer function in his job jockeying cars at the Ford plant's parking lot. Whitaker had to undergo surgery and was left disabled.

Yet, his encounters with crime weren't over. In early May 1983, a yen for chips and candy took Whitaker from his home on Humboldt and Buchanan to the drugstore on the corner of Eighteenth Street. He pulled out a handful of food stamps to pay for his snacks. But before he had a chance to put them back in his pocket, Whitaker says a neighbor grabbed $50 worth of stamps and took off.

It wasn't the first time that there had been charges against the husky black man. Like Whitaker, he wasn't working or married. He just spent his time hanging around the neighborhood. The small-time thief was trouble, but somehow the charges against him were always dropped. Whitaker dropped his charges, too, after a mutual friend arranged to get his money back for him. Though they have lots of acquaintances in common—"mostly lady friends," according to Whitaker—the presence of predators like his neighbor makes the ghetto an uneasy place for Whitaker. "I don't trust him. I don't feel comfortable in his company." But for millions of blacks like Whitaker, there is no escape.

The major metropolises of the North and East are projected by the year 2020 to undergo population transfers in which large percentages of whites will have evacuated cities like Detroit along with Chicago, Philadelphia, Boston, and Washington, D.C. They will be succeeded by equally high percentages of blacks —mostly poor ones.

The more-affluent blacks will leave. A partial offset to migrating blacks will be whites who return to "gentrify" the central city. Although supported by a deemphasis on childrearing and a growth in two-earner households, the gentrification movement will not be sufficient to balance out the emigrating black population.

Which blacks go where will impact on crime rates. More than half of all black families live in the South. When blacks born in the South migrate, they are less likely to remain on welfare than blacks born in the North. They are also less likely, according to a Milwaukee study, to be involved in assaultive crimes, like breaking a brother's skull. Southern blacks, however, are no longer heading North as they once did, leaving an unmoderated concentration of angry blacks in central cities of the North and East—a potentially explosive crime situation.

Eleanor Holmes Norton, the great black lawyer and civil rights activist, corroborates the thinking of many analysts in describing the consolidation of a new black underclass of Percy Whitakers in the nation's ghettos:

"In the booming post–World War I economy, black men with few skills could find work. . . . As refugees from the South . . . the World War I arrivals were enthusiastic voluntary migrants, poor in resources but frequently middle class in aspirations. . . . A small middle class emerged, later augmented by the jobs generated by World War II, service in the armed forces and the postwar prosperity. . . .

"Today's inner city blacks were not part of these historical processes. Some are victims of the flight of manufacturing jobs. Others were part of the last wave of Southern migrants. . . . They often migrated not because of new opportunities but because of the evaporation of old ones. Mechanized farming made their labor superfluous in agriculture . . . also in the postwar cities as manufacturing work for the less-skilled and poorly educated declined." Such blacks, argues Norton, are cut off from the values of the black working and middle classes who, along with whites, have fled the central city. Left behind, they have no recourse but to survive, like Whitaker's thief, in the plundering life of the streets.

Anthony Bouza, gentleman-scholar police chief of Minneapolis, concurs: "We're replacing humans with robots—maximizing our profit, increasing the volume with fewer people. What happens to these people? They're excluded from the system. Street crime is going to become a kind of class struggle. Police are going to be under heavy pressure to repress and make the problem invisible."

In the North, burdened as it is with the vestiges of a blue-collar economy, an underclass is indeed being created. But it needn't be permanent. The fecundity of the service sector, with its masses of entry level, low-skill jobs, will provide an alternative for many. The greater those numbers, the larger the mass with a stake in the system and its laws.

To sum up, three major migration streams are converging on the Sunbelt: elderly, Hispanic, and Asian. Another major flow of middle-class whites and blacks is altering the ecology of city and suburb. Each movement brings with it a unique pattern of crime.

Migrating Hispanics are likely to be on the receiving end of household and personal thefts *and*—if young, single, and newly arrived—on the giving end of violent personal disputes.

Asian victims are apt to run into bigotry-inspired violence from other ethnic groups as well as highly organized extortion, gambling, and loan-sharking operations among themselves.

Middle-class migrants to the suburbs are most likely to find themselves victims of larcenies and simple assaults. But when they're the offenders, it's liable to be for a white-collar crime.

But cultural and class patterns don't operate in a vacuum. Migrants are molded by their destinations, too.

REGIONAL CULTURE

Historically, the Sunbelt states, where our major population growth is occurring, have had the highest crime rates in the country. The South takes precedence for violent crimes, while the West prevails in property crimes. As of 1982, the places with the highest overall crime rates in the country—Washington, D.C., Nevada, Florida, California, Arizona, and Colorado—were all in the South and West. Even in 1984, when crime continued its national downward trend, the overall declines were smallest in the South and West, while reports of violence actually increased.

There are long-standing debates as to whether there is a Southern "culture of violence." The South has a higher rate of firearms use in crimes than other regions. The number of law enforcement officers killed there outstrips the rest of the country, despite a decrease in police personnel in many Southern cities. Reports of child abuse are highest in the South. People in Southern states are more likely to own a gun and disapprove of gun control than others in the nation. Yet, those who own guns are most likely to be middle-class, rural whites who keep firearms for sport and have lifelong experience in their care.

Even in this gun-toting culture, however, National Opinion Research Center and Roper poll findings indicate a subtle change in Southern attitudes. The percent who reported owning guns decreased by 10 percent between 1973 and 1982. Similarly, opposition to gun control was led by a smaller margin in 1981 than in 1975. The change could have something to do with the masses of Northern immigrants who are leaving their own stamp on Southern culture.

Regardless of regional culture, low income and unemployment are key variables in predicting crimes—especially violent ones. The industries responsible for enriching the Sunbelt have come upon hard times. Despite the widely touted image of the South and West as a land of gold-paved streets, the streets are paved instead with the country's longest average unemployment lines.

The transfer of employment opportunities in the Southwest to the Northeast high-tech corridors will be partially offset by the retirement of the current crop of Sunbelt baby boomers in the early 2000s. As they leave the work force, they will open up job opportunities for the generation behind them—the children of Hispanic and Asian migrants who settled there during the 1980s. The South Atlantic states (but not the West South Central states) have some of the lowest fertility rates in the country. The shrinking native population will reduce the competition for jobs and open up opportunities for migrants who might otherwise be left to the streets and crime.

While North and South develop more economic symmetry, urbs and suburbs will become more unequal. Central cities will host concentrations of new migrants, disenfranchised minorities, and the aged, while armies of transient white-collar workers troop home to their suburbs at night.

If, that is, they're not already working in the suburbs. Telecommunications will reduce the need to commute to the office, as work gets done on a personal home computer electronically linked to a distant base. For those who still punch in at a plant, there won't be far to travel. Today's bedroom communities will be tomorrow's employment suburbs.

Los Angeles, New York, Chicago, Houston, Dallas, Atlanta, Washington, D.C., San Diego, Phoenix, and Denver will graduate from metropolises to megatropolises by the year 2033. Their reach, made up of interlocking suburbs and cities, will extend across county lines and even state lines to the adjoining megatropolis. City and suburb will become less distinguishable in terms of amenities, employment, and crime patterns. The critical remaining difference will be prosperity. While cities like Phoenix and Houston find their services overwhelmed by the needs of the poor, their suburbs will bask in relative affluence. Not a lily-white affluence, but one shared by the Hispanics, Asians, blacks, and elderly who will reap the benefits of the massive population transfers taking place today.

CRIMEWARPS

- As rapid growth in the Sunbelt becomes moderated by reverse migration, crime will continue to decrease and spread more evenly across all regions. However, with the exception of Florida, birthrates at or above the national average and relatively high birth/death ratios, will sustain large crime-prone youthful populations in the Sunbelt states.
- Nevada, Wyoming, Arizona, and Utah are projected by the Census Bureau to experience population increases ranging from 90 to 140 percent by the year 2000. In Nevada, where birthrates are low, most of the increase will be supported by working migrants who are older than the critical crime-prone age group. In the three other states, much of the growth will be created by higher-than-average birthrates and birth/death ratios. Therefore, a large part of the population will be in the crime-prone age group.
- In the New England and Mid-Atlantic states, birthrates are far below the national average and birth/death ratios are among the lowest in the nation, thus ensuring a shrinking crime-prone population. This, combined with an expected decline of 2.7 million residents by the year 2000, will provide the Northeast with one of the most dramatic crime drops in the country. The upscale, small families that migrate to the region's industrial incubators will help keep rates low.

· Those regions in which illegal Latin-American aliens concentrate—the South and the West—will experience increases in violence among those groups. The violence will peak between 1990 and 2005, when the current Hispanic baby boom passes through the crime-prone ages of fourteen to twenty-four. California, Arizona, Texas, and Colorado will feel the crime surge most intensely.

· The violence of unattached, young male Hispanic migrants in the South and West will be offset by the aging of the other populations in those regions.

· Racial and ethnic crimes will increase as the unskilled jobs traditionally available to minorities vanish and competition for scarce work is heightened.

· The opportunities created for the educated and privileged in the technology sector will increase the sense of relative deprivation among the unskilled. The danger of riots will grow.

· The disproportionately educated and socially active oriental community will grow in size and influence. As it enters the mainstream, the domination of tongs and triads will diminish.

· High fertility and migration rates will make Hispanics the largest minority group in America. As they rise up the socioeconomic ladder, they will gain political muscle. Hispanic voting power, which National Opinion Research Center surveys identify as 74 percent moderate or liberal and 56 percent Democratic, will be used to garner educational and social service resources that will benefit newcomers. Within the next twenty years, fewer Hispanics will resort to crime.

· As elderly migration and aging-in-place continue to swell the populations of California, Arizona, and Florida, the serious crimes of youth will be displaced by white-collar crimes, larcenies, and domestic violence committed by the elderly. Assaults and robberies, of which the elderly are the least frequently victimized of all age groups, will decline. Purse snatchings, pocket pickings, and confidence games, which victimize the elderly more than other age groups, will abound in these same states. However, since the elderly have the lowest composite rate of victimization, the overall crime rates will decline.

· The shrinking of central cities and swelling of suburbs will lead to an increase in the property crimes that dominate suburban police blotters.

· For those trapped in the central cities, life will become more violent, especially in the Northeast, where income differentials are the greatest. But because the overall and youthful population of central cities will decrease, the overall rate of violence will lessen.

· The South and West will become less violent as they become more permeated with the more peaceful cultures of some outside migration streams.

5

Promised Lands

November was a bad month for two Iowa families hit by the farm crisis. Each reacted in different ways—both of which were criminal.

One family, whom I'll call the Brevorts, had spent their lives raising livestock and grain along with five children. In mid-life, their children grown and gone, high-interest bank loans and low-profit produce caught up with them and they had to sell out. But three years of trying to hang on had driven Dutch Brevort to drink. In almost a quarter century of marriage, Mary Brevort had never known her husband to drink more than one beer a night. Now she stood by helplessly as she saw him drink eight to ten cans a day, a habit that was gradually supplanted by hard liquor. Dutch was so afraid of neighbors finding out how bad off they were that he kept Mary a prisoner in their home. She was forbidden to use the phone or to maintain contact with anyone they knew. The only visitors were their children, who continued to come for Sunday dinner. They had no inkling that anything was amiss between their parents. Both on their best behavior for those occasions, Dutch would sober up and Mary would keep the peace.

But things continued to deteriorate. Unrelenting financial pressure led Dutch to rail against his wife. Then, in November of 1984, he unleashed a frenzy of physical violence. Trapping Mary in the living room, he grabbed the couch and the chairs, smashed them on her back, and hurtled them against the wall.

Mary was shell-shocked. Dutch had never before laid a hostile hand on her. Until this incident, she felt his aberrant behavior was just a reaction to an abnormal situation. Now she knew she'd have to leave everything that was familiar. She didn't have much in the way of education and work experience: The only life she ever knew or wanted was the farm. That would all have to change.

But where to go? The nearest neighbor lived six miles away, and the nearest mental health center was sixty-five miles away. Besides, good stoic Iowa farm families keep their problems to themselves. The hospital was out of the question: Too many questions to answer. Maybe even a criminal prosecution of Dutch—and she didn't want that. So she went to her friend, a nurse, to have her injuries treated. Her next stop was to a clergyman, who arranged to commit Dutch to an alcohol treatment center.

Today Mary is working to sustain herself in a small room in a strange town and Dutch—who was spared arrest and prosecution—is in an institution somewhere across the state. Mary isn't ready to close the book on her marriage, but she has no idea if and when life will ever be the same.

□ □ □

One year before Mary Brevort was battered by her stressed husband, Morgan Jensen (his name has been changed to protect him) found out that his bank garnisheed a deposit from his checking account to cover past-due payments on his loans. That act set off a chain of events which, a year and a half later, would earn him a criminal conviction and a month in jail.

Morgan and Ruta Jensen farmed two hundred eighty acres in northwest Iowa, where they raised hogs, corn, and soybeans. They inherited much of their land from Morgan's father and bought the rest in 1963, when it was cheap. Their two sons, aged twenty-four and twenty-eight, were already farming their own subdivisions on the land. "This has been the only thing our two sons have ever wanted to do, but it doesn't look very hopeful now," confides Ruta. Farming is an expensive vocation, which so far hasn't even allowed money for marriage.

As with so many of their neighbors, the early 1980s turned the Jensens' world upside down. Interest rates settled at stratospheric levels; the costs of production began outrunning the profits; fresh infusions of bridge funds were a constant need, but banks changed their practices in midstream. The value of Iowa farmland tumbled by nearly a third in 1984. While banks had previously accepted land as collateral, they would now accept only cash flow. "And," laments Ruta, "there's no way anybody around here can cash flow when prices are so variable."

By 1983, the bank was taking all the proceeds from the Jensens' hog sales and leaving them nothing on which to live. Morgan needed money to cover a government debt. He resorted to a ploy that seemed harmless enough but was illegal.

The Jensens have grain storage on their spread. Every year the Federal Commodity Credit Corporation pays them a set rate per bushel to keep their corn off the market for a period of time. When the maturity date comes, they have a choice of either selling the grain and returning the government's check or keeping the grain sealed and holding on to the money.

For tax purposes, the Jensens always chose to sell their sealed grain. The proceeds were used to repay the government. But in 1983, the bank seized the deposit intended for the CCC and bounced Morgan's check. Jensen raced around frantically trying to cover the draft, all the while assuring the CCC it would be taken care of, but money was hard to come by and it remained unpaid. Morgan was charged with using government commodities for his own profit. In April 1985, he went to jail.

Ruta finds the whole thing ironic. In his own mind, her husband didn't do anything illegal; and, she muses, "We don't have a penny to show for it." The Jensens have been living by borrowing against life insurance and accepting their sons' support. She doesn't know how long they can go on this way, but somehow, she says, "We will survive. There may be a lot less farmers, but with that they're going to take a lot of small towns with them. The entire way of life is going to change."

The nation's rural areas are undergoing dramatic transformations. While rural land values plummet in Iowa, Illinois, Nebraska, and South Dakota, they're skyrocketing in Maine, New Hampshire, Vermont, Massachusetts, Rhode Island, and Connecticut. The wildly variable worth of farmland signals an exchange of rural populations in which farmers are leaving, clearing the way for industry and ex-urbanites to move in. Both the desperation and the big business of farming leave it highly vulnerable to crime, and the new rustic sojourners bring with them their own repertory of offenses.

SOUL EROSION

Americans have always romanticized the country: open spaces, fresh air, bucolic scenes, stability, traditional values, fertile farms, fatted calves, the simple virtues of working the land. *Suicide, child abuse, spouse beating, drug addiction, and alcoholism* are not part of that pastoral image; neither are rustling, vandalism, stealing, and swindling. Yet, these are an expanding part of the rural scene —the inevitable fallout of intersecting tides that are transforming America's last frontiers.

Recent movies—*Country, Places in the Heart, The River*—warn us that the small farmer is facing eradication. As of the mid-1980s, the average young farmer owed $63 for every $100 in land and equipment that he owned. Thousands are losing their farms to creditors and, predicts the Food and Agricultural Policy Research Institute, at least 20 percent will go bankrupt over the next few years. In order to survive, an agricultural family must diversify its income sources or be fortunate enough to own an automated superfarm that churns out produce at a megaprofit. Many, like Mary and Dutch Brevort, have no choice but to leave the land and find some other way to make a living.

Farming has always been a hard life, but the hardship has shifted from soil erosion to soul erosion. Father Norman White, director of rural life for the archdiocese of Dubuque, sees it in weekly retreats, held from end of harvesting to beginning of planting, where farm families exorcise their stress. Sit in on any gathering in the thirty counties over which he presides and you're likely to hear any of these anguished voices:

"As the years went on, we had quite a large assignment taken out of our milk income, and the point got to where it was takin' just about everything we had. I went and talked to the lender. He would not budge. There wasn't money to buy groceries. There wasn't money to buy feed. It's a sad thing when a father has to go to his oldest son and say, 'Well, maybe you can help buy some groceries or something.' And the lender, we talked to him. 'Well,' he says, 'you can qualify for food stamps.' "

"One of the first things a guy has to do is throw pride out. But when you have no funds, you've exhausted all your savings an' everything and cannot get money to feed your family, you'll do something."

"After you get down so low, you just kind of don't care if you get up in the morning. I'm a fourth generation on this family farm, and I got a lot of pride. It's gonna take a hell of a lot of pride to get me out of there. We're in Chapter Eleven bankruptcy now."

"You feel that you're the provider. The sacred trust of the land has been entrusted to you. You feel that your parents provided from that land. That it should be your job to turn around and provide for your family. When this plan doesn't work, you feel like you've been a great failure."

Sometimes the despair stops just a breath short of death. Father White recalls a phone call one of his lay counselors received from a desperate farmer. The granger had been holding a loaded .45 in his mouth. He couldn't pull the trigger, but a frightening number of farmers have.

Some turn their rage against others. White tells of a farmer who, having reached the end of his rope, grabbed $300 and picked up and left. He came back. But he started doing things he'd never done before—beating his kids and being "real rough on his wife."

The families being seen by Father White are similar to the Brevorts. So are the ones counseled by Joan Blundall, the consultation and education coordinator at a mental health center in Spencer. She cites one rural Iowa county in which reports of family violence increased 200 percent in just one year. "Grief overload," says the social worker, is turning otherwise good people into criminals.

The means are at hand. Of the four major occupational categories, farmers are the ones who most frequently own guns, and those guns are usually powerful rifles. Traditional rural norms, which define seeking help outside the family as a sign of weakness, don't provide the tools for dealing with crises that relatives can't control. When a thirteen-year-old sees his father pacing in the shed with a gun, he can sense that something is wrong, but he doesn't know where to turn to deflect the impending act of violence.

"Our greatest sin out here is the sin of silence," Blundall maintains. The Dutch Reformed and Swedish ethnics who dominate Iowa's vast plains are a stoic lot who frown on displaying emotions or woes outside the family. But, explains Blundall, "any family that's been in crisis for a long period of time breaks down. You either commit suicide or you begin to turn that anger outward to your neighbor or your family."

Anger toward the bank that's calling a loan is displaced onto the family, where it can be vented more safely. "For the first time," observes Blundall, "parents feel out of control. Many have raised two or three children successfully, but now they're not talking to them the same way. They're ready to strike out rather than talk out some of their difficulties."

FRAUD ON THE FARM

The self-help ethic is not the only one that's being distorted into criminal acts. A strong work ethic, rigid injunctions against breaking the law, and intolerance of cheating are also exacting a price. The rural code of honor is at war with the need to survive. The guilt often becomes too much to bear as farmers choose between clinging to their moral heritage and clinging to their land.

Says Blundall, "People in this area have functioned for decades on handshakes and trust. Now they perceive themselves as having to do the illegal to survive. We're now seeing families who are teaching their kids to get by even if it means they have to be crooked."

The economic motives are clear. Morgan Jensen went to jail for selling sealed government grain; another farmer was charged with cruelty to animals when his livestock starved to death. Some are lying to banks about their assets. And many, instead of making payments to the banks which by law hold primary liens on their property, are allocating scarce funds to long time friends who give them unsecured feed loans.

The stakes for farmers are terrifyingly high. They stand to lose everything— not only their job, their land, and their home, but their whole way of life. In the end, many become refugees within their own nation.

When they get desperate enough, these families fall prey to con men who pour into town selling them on schemes for holding onto their land and end up stealing it instead. Evelyne Burger and her husband Clifford almost lost their Unionville, Iowa, farm to two such swindles.

"We were looking for some help," she explained in an affidavit. "I telephoned Mr. Wright in Noti, Oregon."

☐ ☐ ☐

According to court records, in 1985, Robert J. Wright solicited Iowa farmers to trade their land for shares in the Evangelical Oregon Trust, of which he claimed to be trustee. The fund claimed assets of $6 billion, including $700 million allegedly owed it by the federal government for excavations of uranium and gold from Trust lands in Utah, Oregon, and Nevada. This huge government debt was asserted to date back to an arcane agreement with Presidents John Kennedy and Lyndon Johnson. But the federal government, insisted Wright, had reneged on the deal.

Wright, however, had come up with a way to use farmers to recoup his "losses." The church wanted to help farmers, his prosecuting attorney reports Wright to have said; keep them on their land, keep them producing food for famine-stricken African countries. Trading their land for his shares would benefit farmers and the Trust. The farmers could use the shares, negotiable through the U.S. Treasury, to pay their debts and the Trust would use those debts to pry its money loose from the federal government. Farmers were allowed to lease their traded land and work it for $300 a month. Anytime during the next fifty years, the farmers had the option of buying back their land from Wright for 25 percent of the original purchase price. It sounded terrific.

Wright did omit a small detail in selling his package to farmers: a court of claims trial and subsequent appeal, in which Wright acted as his own lawyer, failed to establish his suit. The Evangelical Oregon Trust didn't exist, except on "indecipherable" pieces of paper, which the appeals judge said carried "strong inferences of fraud and forgery." The shares for which the farmers had traded their land were worthless.

As of this writing, while prosecution has not been completed, five farms were known to have been lost to this scam. Tam Ormiston, the Iowa assistant attorney general prosecuting the case, is certain more will surface: "What is happening is that the people who perpetuate the frauds are using the traditional strengths of the farming community against the farmer. The desire to do things better and more cheaply. The risks they take. The sense of individuality. These are the people who rely on themselves to solve their own problems. Once having made a commitment to a program or strategy, a farmer will work like heck to make it succeed. Finally, a farmer can be stoic, a proud person who doesn't want to admit that he was boondoggled. He's the perfect con. There's a highly sophisticated high dollar industry here that has gone unregulated."

Most rustic crimes are economic. With over $660 billion in net assets, agriculture is the nation's largest industry. A $148 billion farm output in 1985 accounted for more than one seventh of our export trade that year, according to the Department of Agriculture. Geographic isolation, a wealth of produce and machines, and the low risk of detection make the country highly vulnerable to crime.

- Stockport, Iowa: The embezzlement of soybeans, corn, and grain from the Prairie Grain Company elevator left this town of 334 people with a loss of $10 million and led to its being declared a disaster relief area.
- Plainfield, Wisconsin: A farmer's portable irrigation system was spirited away at a replacement cost of $10,500.
- Jasper County, Ohio: A single incident of vandalism destroyed $10,000 worth of property.

The big business of farming has seduced even organized crime.

• Colorado: A multistate grain fraud deal.
• Alabama, Florida, Kentucky, and Tennessee: The pirating of $400,000 worth of farm equipment in a two-year period.
• Indiana and Wisconsin: The alleged default by associates of Carlo Gambino on well over a million dollars in payments to dairy farmers.

Tam Ormiston, who's seen scores of such crimes, points out: "There are not a great many small businesses that have values that exceed the millions of dollars." But farming is one. "It's not an ostentatious kind of thing because the money is tied up in equipment. A farmer can literally pull out a beat up old checkbook and write a check for tens of thousands of dollars. When you have that kind of major expenditure there's an open invitation to defraud the buyer." The high-stakes business of farming is a tempting target for sophisticated economic crime. Whether our grangers prosper or languish, a great deal of money is at stake.

□ □ □

The small-time, "salt of the earth" farmer is vanishing; in his stead are vast anonymous farms that displace people with machines. Where humans are necessary, some enterprises bring in workers who have no investment in the land. Some have criminal records; others act as advance scouts for organized crime groups.

As the stable, solidly rooted, law-abiding farm family passes into folklore, most rural land is, in fact, not used for farming at all. Fewer than one tenth of today's rural inhabitants call themselves farmers.

Small and medium-sized farms are being scooped up by outside interests. Joan Blundall points to the recent purchase of 3,000 Iowa acres bought by the Mormon Church. She worries about the defaulted farms being bought as tax write-offs. "We're seeing a transfer of land that may be dangerous for the total population—a danger to a cheap, sustainable, safe food supply."

Father Norman White's fears are more graphic. He sees "large outfits coming in and gobbling up the land," turning the country into a food OPEC. He predicts a "Central Americanization of the United States by the aristocracy having control of huge expanses of land, with the rest working as peons or peasants at starvation wages." In another twenty years, he foresees parents pulling guns to get food for their kids; wholesome farm families driven from the land into the city, where there is already vast joblessness. "Land does give power. When just a few get control of the food supply, that will lead to more crime," cautions Father White.

Chronic world hunger and famine combined with ballooning third-world populations make food the globe's most precious commodity. The struggle to meet the demand will render American agribusiness an increasingly attractive target to professional criminals and unscrupulous corporations.

Nasib Ed Kalliel, North Dakota–born with an Arabic name, was reportedly ready to use international food politics to make a fast buck off farmers. As principal of the Texas-based First Financial Guarantee, he claimed to have holdings of farms and construction companies totaling hundreds of millions of dollars. He came to Iowa seeking to pick up farms that were in serious financial trouble; he found at least eighteen farmers who were willing to bail themselves out through him.

Kalliel made an offer that was hard to refuse: He would take joint ownership of the property, paying all debts, allowing the farmer to stay on the land, giving him a $2,000 a month stipend, and taking 50 percent of the profits. The magnate was going to ensure that those profits would be considerable. He would use his alleged position as trade counselor to Jordan, Saudi Arabia, and Mexico; a large landowner in Saudi Arabia; and brother-in-law to King Hussein of Jordan, to secure good export prices for the produce.

Some farmers believed him. Evelyne Burger, who had lost only $300 to the lure of Robert Wright and his Evangelical Oregon Trust, was not as successful when it came to Ed Kalliel. After paying a substantial up-front fee, she and her husband turned their property over and called on Kalliel to arrange loans for them. They say he obtained $100,000 on their behalf, but turned over only $40,530. Kalliel kept the rest, leaving the farmers liable for the whole amount. When the bank demanded repayment of the full $100,000 from the Burgers, they, like other hapless victims, were left in worse trouble than before.

So was the bank. Kalliel's lender, the Rexford State Bank in Kansas, was eventually drained of all its assets. The draw for the bank, explains the prosecutor, was the prospect of bringing oil money into the United States via the Iowa farmer. Kalliel's Arabic name and his active membership in several Arab organizations lent credence to the alleged scam.

There was one hitch: Foreigners are not allowed to own land in the state of Iowa. Nor are loan-finding services entitled to collect fees in advance of closing a loan—especially when those fees involve fraudulent transfer of grain or livestock that is part of a current bankruptcy proceeding. Kalliel's prosecution is ongoing at this time.

In 1982, another con man, Eugene Pietsch, Jr., looking to cash in on the international food shortage, offered to set up an export trade company through which farmers could send their produce directly overseas. Describing himself as having connections in the African market, he promised corn sales at a large profit. Well, farmers sure weren't making much money selling corn at home, so at least 297 of them thought the 24-percent annual return promised by Iowa Farmers International sounded very good. They thought well enough of it to put up the $1,200 front money that the investment required.

However, their benefactor neglected to tell them that he had recently filed for personal bankruptcy and was a sentenced felon out of prison on an appeal bond. Nor did he bother with other small details: Both the IFI securities and its brokers were unregistered, and the proceeds were used not to sell grain overseas, but to buy life's comforts for Pietsch, who subsequently pleaded guilty to fraud.

The world needs food and farmers need trade. The nexus of those needs will continue to be fertile soil for a wide variety of farm frauds.

THE URBANIZATION OF RURAL CRIME

The transformation of American farming is being hastened by small towns—some dying, some healthy—that compete to attract industry. The wide open spaces of the country provide more flexibility in building, greater access to skilled—and often less expensive—female labor pools, and more favorable tax and rent structures than the city. As industry moves out to the country, it brings with it a transient daily work force, impersonal relationships, congestion, and stealable goods. As a result, rural crime patterns have come to resemble urban ones.

Urban property crime rates are three times higher, and violent crime rates four times higher, than rural ones. Nevertheless, where crime rates have grown in recent years, they've done so more slowly in urban than other areas. But the people who commit crimes have the same characteristics in the city and the country. Young males and blacks are the highest-rate offenders. In the backwoods, however, they are much more likely to act individually than in groups.

Their crimes include the same thefts from unlocked cars, home and business burglaries, and vandalizations that plague big cities—but on a far smaller scale. These are young people's crimes. While such acts decreased nationwide between the 1970s and 1980s, the largest percent drop in the rates took place in rural areas. As more young people leave the land to go off in search of a livelihood, the youth drain will perpetuate the decline in rural property offenses.

Racial patterns of victimization, on the other hand, diverge in city and country. Where property crimes decreased between 1973 and 1982, they did so by a greater percentage for rural and suburban blacks than for whites. White females, who in central cities tend to have the lowest victimization rate for violent crimes, had the largest increase (up 32 percent) when they lived in a rural area. Part of that increase, chronicled by the FBI, was a 10-percent climb in reports of forcible rape between 1983 and 1984—twice the increase that took place in cities.

The country has experienced a disproportionate rise in violent crime. (Meanwhile, property crimes dipped by 6 percent.) Joan Blundall has little doubt that this anomaly is a reflection of the family and economic dissolution that is occurring in our hinterlands.

"The whole social fabric of Iowa is at risk," warns Blundall. "We're at a critical point now. With farm families not knowing if there's going to be money to plant. With small-business owners not knowing if there's going to be enough money to pay the electric bill. With people coming into shops feeling guilty about only buying a spool of thread. With bank presidents concerned about the health of their employees because they are having to confront stresses that they've never had in the past. There is no one that is not touched by the pain out here." Blundall is describing a state of anomie, a breakdown in traditional norms and controls, the fecund earth in which crime and deviance take root.

THE GENTRIFICATION OF THE HINTERLANDS

The rustification of America is under way. During the 1970s rural America registered a population gain of almost 14 percent, while metropolitan county growth was just under 10 percent. The surprising spurt in rural growth has nothing to do with prolific reproduction. On the contrary, rural areas are mired in aging townfolk. Combined with the trend toward small families, they produced a 10-percent decline in the natural population between 1965 and 1970. Newcomers more than made up for that loss. The latest census tells us that one sixth of the U.S. population now lives in rural areas and 40 percent of all new housing in the 1970s was built on rural land. The country is growing faster than the city for the first time since the early 1800s.

While the farm and youth drain takes one group of migrants out of the backwoods, another is plugging the dam—ex-urbanites and ex-suburbanites—who come not in search of employment, but for a life-style that gives them ready access to nature, open spaces, a slower pace of living. It is the same drive that impelled them to the suburbs in the 1950s and 1960s. Those suburbs have now matured. As commerce and middle-class blacks move in, many whites escape by pushing ever further into the wilderness. With the relentless suburbanization of industry, commuting is no obstacle. Jobs have followed the migrants beyond the urban ring.

The newcomers don't have the same commitment to land and community as old-timers. While many harbor idealized notions of neighborliness, they are, in fact, isolated by vast spatial distances and buffered by television, telephones, and cars. You can make a case that rural ranch dwellers are even more socially atomized than urban high-rise dwellers.

The new landed gentry brings alien values that tolerate a broader range of behaviors and beliefs than do the rustic neighbors whose families have occupied the farms next door for more than a century. The clash of life-styles further erodes the social controls built into the traditional community.

□ □ □

The erosion is nowhere more evident than in the boomtown-doomtown cycles that have taken place in the West. When you think of states that have had the largest percentage of population increases since the 1970 census, it's probably California, Texas, and Florida that come to mind. Of those, only Florida is near the top of the list. But number four, right after Florida, is Wyoming.

Yes, *Wyoming*.

The residents of this remote Rocky Mountain enclave multiplied by 41 percent between 1970 and 1980. The growth has not been concentrated in its largest cities, Casper and Cheyenne, as you might think. Instead, migrants have gravitated to towns with names like Gillette, Evanston, Rock Springs, and LaBarge—towns so small that they don't even appear in the Census Bureau's roster of incorporated places of 25,000 or more.

Wyoming's metamorphosis is shared by the eight states that encompass the

Rockies. Their wealth of oil, natural gas, uranium, and coal have drawn tens of thousands of workers every year to dig, build, and process the states' ecological resources. The Jim Bridger power plant, Power River Basin coal mines, and Pineview oil field have transformed rural hamlets into boisterous, brawling boomtowns. Wyoming is the breeding place of what has come to be known as the "Rock Springs Syndrome" or the "Gillette Syndrome."

These syndromes denote what happens when a small, quiet town is besieged by transient, often single young men who come to work on big energy projects. For these villages, the doublings, triplings, and quadruplings of population bring with them unprecedented wealth, traffic, congestion, and social problems.

Wildcatters, construction workers, and "oil field trash" come to places like Evanston to work hard and make a fast buck. With no community ties, liquor is the focus of leisure life. Guns are legal and easy to come by; combined with liquor, they make a lethal mix. As one resident explained, "There's nothing to do in this town except drink, fight, and go home to bed." In Gillette—where the population grew by half in the five years beginning in 1978—the incidence of major crimes doubled in only three years.

Research shows that boomtowns' indigenous youth are especially hard hit by the dislocations of rapid growth. They complain of feeling alienated, insecure, and physically threatened. Unlike their old-timer parents, they can't insulate themselves from the newcomers. Each day spent in school surrounds them with the minions of an alien culture. With the collapse of the small town world in which everyone knows everyone else, a crucial form of social control over teenagers is lost. With increasing anonymity comes growing delinquency.

Today, the oil and coal rush is waning; Wyoming's economy is in a slump. The unemployment rate is well below the national average—not because the state is generating jobs, but because boomtowns are hemorrhaging workers going elsewhere to seek their fortunes. In their wake, they leave a legacy of drunkenness, wife beating, drug addiction, suicide, prostitution, child abuse, assault, and murder.

As minibooms recur, a new Wyoming state law requires companies like Exxon to finance the burden that their projects impose on small towns. Lincoln, Sweetwater, and Uinta counties will be playing host to thousands of workers who are coming to build Exxon's new gas-treatment plant and other facilities. This time, however, Exxon is paying for additional police, fire, and other municipal services in a struggle to keep Wyoming's boomtowns on an even keel. In many cases, police have to be imported from the outside, their big-city ways often fueling local resentments.

Wyoming's transmutation presages the fortunes of developing areas all over the country as agrarian America becomes a growing target for industry. The old rural-urban dichotomy is fading. Even concepts like "density" are losing their meaning in the face of rapid transportation, increased mobility, and easy access to the excess of the city. (Oddly enough, structural density seems to be even more strongly related to crime in rural areas than in urban ones.) The melding of urban and rural life-styles has created a greater parity in crime victimization and a remarkable consistency in crime patterns.

CRIMEWARPS

· Crimes of stress—domestic violence, drunken brawls, substance abuse—will increase among the large percentage of farm owners who have incurred unmanageable debts and are threatened with the loss of their land and livelihood.
· As agriculture continues to become more technologically advanced, and therefore more expensive to operate, the majority of farmers will be forced out of business. Food monopolies will form with attendant price-fixing schemes, land frauds, and export-import swindles.
· Among those working in the private sector, self-employed agricultural workers have the lowest rate of victimization for crimes of both violence and theft. Salaried farm workers, on the other hand, have the highest rate of victimization for violent crimes. As independent farmers are gradually displaced by large agribusinesses that hire workers for wages, a low-victimization group will be replaced with a high-victimization group and crime in rural areas will increase.
· The proportion of young people living in rural areas will decline. Crimes of the young—vandalism, petty theft, assault—will decline with them. Of those who remain and find themselves in the path of industrial development, delinquency will increase in seriousness and frequency.

Crimewarp III

Ring Around
the White Collar

His friends call him "quite a guy," "magnanimous," "generous to a fault."
There's only one problem with Albert F. Arbury: By age forty-one, he was an
admitted embezzler.

Arbury used his position as assistant vice president and trust officer of the
National Bank of Detroit to loot $1.1 million from wealthy clients' accounts
from 1975 to 1982. He had been working at the bank for only a year or so when
he initiated the first of sixty-one questionable transactions.

He was *not* desperate for money. Arbury lived with his wife and two children
in elegant Grosse Pointe Farms and had a wealthy mother whose estate was his
to manage. His brother was a top aide to Michigan's Democratic senator, Donald Riegle. Of the $1,150,065 his bank claims he stole, Albert kept only about
$100,000 for himself. Most went to companies that were in financial trouble,
companies in which he was heavily invested; the rest was donated to charity—
Wayne State University, the Old Newsboys-Goodfellows. How much more respectable can you be?

Talk about respectable, what about the infamous $30 million Jake Butcher admittedly misappropriated from his own banks? The former Democratic candidate for governor of Tennessee and chair of the 1982 Knoxville World's Fair was charged with having diverted his banks' assets "to cover expenses of enterprises he controlled . . . and using some of the funds to finance his lavish lifestyle." Then, too, there is the notorious Georgia banker Jack Donnelly Gray, who pleaded guilty to making an unauthorized loan to finance an insurance company he had founded. All were entrepreneurs using illegally obtained bank money to support their investments.

Despite the derring-do celluloid image of the mysterious masked robber, banks lose eight times more money to humdrum employees, executives in gray-flannel suits, and slick swindlers than they do to street criminals. White-collar crimes like those of Arbury, Butcher, and Gray almost always involve deception by those in a position of trust, power, or influence. Perpetrators must be of an age and skill level that gives them access to such positions. In other words, they must be *mature, experienced, and educated*—the kind of person who dominates the burgeoning managerial, administrative, and professional segment of the labor market.

The bulk of criminals arrested for fraud, embezzlement, counterfeiting, and forgery are between the ages of twenty-five and forty-four. Within the next fifty years, the median age of the population will float within that range. The majority of this cohort will have exposure to the education and technology that equips it to commit these crimes. "White collar crime is definitely the wave of the future," proclaims Leo Callahan, former head of the International Association of Chiefs of Police.

White-collar arrests have surged between 10 and 90 percent just since 1972. They account for nearly 30 percent of case filings in U.S. District Courts—more than any other category of crime. The combined burglary, mugging, and other property losses induced by the country's street punks come to about $4 billion a year. However, the seemingly upstanding citizens in our corporate boardrooms and the humble clerks in our retail stores bilk us out of between $40 and $200 billion a year!

If you think it's only property that's at stake, note what criminologists Harold Pepinsky and Paul Jesilow assert in an award-winning monograph: "white collar and organizational crimes kill far more people than do street criminals . . . well over 100,000 criminal homicides are committed annually by respected professionals." That's five times the number of deaths caused by street criminals in an average year.

When Ford Motor Company knowingly puts defective Pintos on the road, your life is at stake. When Eli Lilly plies you with Oraflex without warning of its potential lethal effects, your health is on the line. The regulatory agencies on which we count to shield us from dangerous drugs, toxic wastes, carcinogenic building materials, noxious airplane cabin fumes, terrorist bombs, and flammable children's toys are under attack. Even in a political environment that supports regulation, agencies tend to be co-opted by the very groups they are charged with overseeing. We can't depend on the FAA, ICC, EPA, or any of our alphabet soup of protector agencies to save us.

Finally, the ring around the white collar can separate us from our livelihoods. Even after years of supply-side economics, with an attendant recession and recovery, the rate of business flops has more than tripled since 1979, according to Dun & Bradstreet. The U.S. Chamber of Commerce reports that 30 percent of all business failures each year result from the embezzlements, pilfering, and swindles of trusted employees. That number seems high, but there's a more defensible figure of 5 percent, which is cited by the National Council on Crime and Delinquency. Even so, that's a lot of crime-induced collapses when you consider that we've had several hundred thousand failures and bankruptcies in recent years. The Reagan administration, in an attempt to reverse a trend in which our economy is cannibalizing itself through mergers, gave pep talks to would-be entrepreneurs. In 1983, they responded and new business formations began to pick up. But if you want to heed that call, be mindful that crimes of "respectable" people could very well force you to go under.

The 1973 bankruptcy of a Washington trucking firm is a good example. The company could no longer sustain the 30-percent workplace crime losses it was experiencing. When it went out of business, 260 employees found themselves without jobs, more than $400,000 in capital investment was lost, and $1.2 million in loans was defaulted. This firm was just one of nearly 11,000 which collapsed that year. Ten years later, there were more than 31,000. The nearly 3 million businesses that make up our economy are all susceptible to the same corrosion. The exploding theft-prone service sector is the most susceptible of all.

Small businesses, which account for 40 percent of the gross national product and 57 percent of private sector non-farm jobs, are particularly vulnerable. According to the Small Business Administration, when a minimerchant is stolen from by his workers, it eats up a percentage of his receipts that is 24 times greater than that of a firm grossing $5 million or more a year. One expert alleges that three quarters of all workers become thieves within five years of their employment and up to 8 percent steal in volume.

Despite the threat to our economy, health, and safety, we worry much more about street crime than we do about white-collar crime. And as followers of public opinion, so do the police. Lee Brown, Houston's much-admired police chief, admitted: "Police do not devote their efforts to get the white collar criminal. The crimes we devote our efforts to are the ones the public is more concerned about—street crimes. I don't foresee that changing."

The Carter administration identified white-collar crime as a national priority which the FBI was charged with pursuing. Devout Republicans—such as superstar U.S. Attorney Rudolph Giuliani, who has personally indicted a slew of executive suite criminals—contend that the Reagan administration sustained that focus. Ralph Nader, for one, hotly contests that assertion: "Serious law enforcement activity in virtually every government regulatory agency is down dramatically from the modest levels of the Carter Administration. In 1980,

Ronald Reagan promised to get Government off the backs of business; few voters suspected that less regulation would mean more corporate crime."

Antiregulatory zeal seeks to return us to Adam Smith's laissez-faire capitalism. In his book *The Acquisitive Society*, R. H. Tawney paints a grim portrait of what the nineteenth-century triumph of free market economics means: "It assures men that there are no ends other than their own ends, no law other than their desires. . . . It relieves communities of the necessity of discriminating between enterprise and avarice, energy and unscrupulous greed, property which is legitimate and property which is theft."

In the 1920s, when Tawney's book was published, we had the muckrakers— Lincoln Steffens, Ida Tarbell, Upton Sinclair—to balance things out. Today we have the consumer advocates epitomized in the person of Ralph Nader. His "raiders" notwithstanding, an orgy of white-collar wrongdoing seems to be an inevitable part of our prospects. Its growth is reflected in the activities of those agencies charged with controlling economic crimes:

- The U.S. Secret Service, which handles all manner of forgery and counterfeiting, investigated almost 40,000 more cases in 1982 than it did in 1972.
- The Securities and Exchange Commission oversees the stocks-and-bonds business. In 1981, it referred twice the number of cases to the U.S. Department of Justice than it did in 1968.
- In 1982, post-Watergate federal courts convicted 671 national, state, and local officials of bribery, extortion, or conflict of interest while in public office. The convictions in 1970 numbered 44.
- The number of federal criminal antitrust suits filed in U.S. district courts tripled between 1960 and 1982.
- Mail fraud complaints handled by the U.S. Postal Service more than doubled in the same time period.

The ring around the white collar will encircle all our necks. Our money, credit, consumer prices, and trust will be vulnerable to the manipulations of older, more sophisticated wrongdoers. We will be playing an adult game of *minders, keepers* in which some of those charged with *minding* our property will end up *keeping* it instead. Our physical well-being is in the hands of inert, underfunded, corrupt, or co-opted bureaucracies.

The ring around the white collar is becoming very dark indeed.

6

The Computer Catastrophe

In 1982, a government survey uncovered a portentous 172 cases of computer fraud in twelve federal agencies. Among the reported fraud cases was that of a federal employee who had embezzled over $100,000 in an eighteen-month period. He had simply reactivated the names of dead beneficiaries to create fictitious accounts through which he pocketed monthly checks spit out by the computer. It was easy; anyone with rudimentary knowledge can do it. Just keypunch a few names and numbers into the system and you're rich!

A year earlier, Janet Blair, a Baltimore social security clerk supervisor, had pleaded guilty to adding a number of false names to her branch office's disability rolls. But the claim money wasn't going to anyone who was crippled or ill; it was being siphoned off by Blair and her confederates in a California prison.

Nearly 3 million workers specialize in various aspects of computer programming, engineering, systems analysis, and data entry. Countless others are involved peripherally. As the electronic labor force dilates, the opportunities for megabite mischief will multiply.

□ □ □

In 1981, Robert Marr, treasurer of his family's business, National Bonded Money Company of Shreveport, Louisiana, was puzzled. His bank told him the firm's account was overdrawn by $141,000—a negative balance costing $2,000 a month to maintain. But for five months, his computer insisted the money was there.

A savvy dealer tracked down the problem: a "Trojan horse" had been buried in the software, bearing gifts of $1,000 a day to Michael Murray, a prodigal programmer who was bleeding the company. Murray's crime forced the Marrs to sell a family tobacco business to cover their losses. Within three years of the discovery of the theft, they had to give up their twenty-year ownership of National Bonded, too. By internally modifying the computer program to corrupt all the data it processed, Murray cost the Marrs two businesses and over $200,000 in cash.

The Trojan horse and related "logic bomb" (a program alteration activated by some specific event or a preset time in the future) are highly sophisticated forms of crime tailored specifically to a computer. Unlike Janet Blair's social security scam, they require great expertise. Those who have it are in a position to do great damage—not only to business, but to national security.

Fortunately, large mainframe installations are compatible with security devices that can protect their programming level and help detect unauthorized entries. But the 1 million minicomputer and 10 million personal computer systems on which small and medium-sized businesses rely, are much more vulnerable—and they outnumber the large systems by a factor of two-to-one and twenty-to-one respectively.

□ □ □

In mid-August 1983, a group of rosy-cheeked Wisconsin youths sat at a personal computer and scrambled the radiation therapy records of New York's Sloan-Kettering Institute for Cancer Research. Had they been of a mind to, the computer "hackers" could have spirited away millions of dollars. But they weren't and they didn't. The voltaic vandals broke in just for the fun of wreaking long-distance havoc on one of the country's premier cancer treatment centers.

"Data diddling" is the compuspeak name given to their crime. Rather than messing with the processing program, they simply altered the information that goes into it and manipulated it for their own ends. Data diddlers can operate on site, as did the federal clerk who created phony accounts through which to collect monthly booty. They may be remote control crooks, like a band of mischievous Los Angeles teenagers who meddled with the files of a Lexington, Kentucky, thoroughbred-listing service. Or, they may operate both on and off site, like the ring of thirty students who were accused of working with an accomplice in the records office of UCLA to alter grades and issue fraudulent degrees.

Anyone with access to, and minimal knowledge of, a personal computer can diddle their data. PC's are designed for easy use by anyone from a secretary to a chief operating officer, a pupil to a principal. This form of abuse will escalate in direct proportion to the expanding computer population in the classroom, the home, and the office.

☐ ☐ ☐

IBM learned in the 1960s that neither the program nor the data need be jumbled for a computer to be the scene of a crime. When thieves stole a tape-stored "on-order" list from the back of a truck in New Jersey, it was a computer "output" that was targeted. In this case, the output contained a valuable trade secret: It spelled out exactly which customers had ordered what kinds of equipment. Imagine what the competition could have done with that! IBM has since been storing all its valuable data in code.

Computers are electronic, paperless safes that have become the repositories of our knowledge and our secrets. Anyone who can crack them will have found a gold mine for industrial espionage, theft of trade secrets, unfair competition, blackmail, terrorism, or political spying.

☐ ☐ ☐

On New Year's weekend 1983, someone broke into the offices of Paychex Incorporated in Paramus, New Jersey. The intruder destroyed all the source and backup disks that contained payroll orders for 95,000 employees in 1,300 companies. Without those data, Paychex was immobilized. Had the crime occurred one week earlier, the company would have gone down the tubes. However, the company had just printed its year-end reports, so it was able to punch the necessary information back into the computer. Even so, it cost the company $100,000 and the loss of 10 percent of its customers to start up again.

The crime was sabotage. But were it not for the highly concentrated nature of the Paychex records, the damage would probably not have been as extensive. Computer dependency will make companies increasingly vulnerable to disgruntled employees and high-tech vandals.

Computers can be violated at four levels to commit a wide range of crimes: *data, processing program, output, and as an accessory for traditional crimes.* The threat of computer crime is magnified by the phenomenal growth in computer uses, users, and hardware. By 1990, our computer census is projected to graze the 5 million mark—1 for every 50 people in America. Yet as of this writing, twenty-nine states have no laws proscribing the use of computers for crime. Ace criminologist Marvin Wolfgang predicts that this situation will change: "By the turn of the century, the main concern of criminal justice will be information crime."

Government will be among the most fertile criminal justice system targets. The federal government is the country's most voracious consumer of computer services, and its appetite will grow at least tenfold by the end of this decade. The IRS, Social Security Administration, Department of Health and Human Services, and Department of Defense all maintain computerized records with which nearly 3 million civilian employees can create felonious boondoggles. State and local governments employ a total of almost 14 million workers. While the numbers of employees have held fairly steady in the 1980s, the number of computers has not.

A nationwide survey conducted in 1975 found that about one quarter of this country's 20,000 city and county governments had converted to electronic data processing and information systems. The vast majority of larger cities and counties used computers, but fewer than half of the smaller ones did. A few years later, a silicon revolution took place that reduced the price and complexity of computers and made them accessible to any size government. When another survey was taken in 1983, cities were using computers about twice as much as counties. But computer usage by small government had increased by less than one fifth.

The computer conversion was not as dramatic as expected. We've now learned that it takes about ten years after the introduction of a technology for it to be adopted by a large government, fifteen for it to take hold in a small one. In local government, the revolution triggered by the low-price silicon chip is still ahead of us. It will peak between 1990 and 1995. That proliferation will in itself produce criminal opportunities. The functions to which computers are dedicated will be the lure.

Most in-house government computers are used to perform financial management tasks. A whopping 85 percent handle payrolls. Accounting, budgeting, and utility billing follow close behind. The potential for data diddling and salami slicing (a form of embezzlement in which small amounts of money are diverted from large numbers of accounts) is enormous. Because most official computers are administered by city or county clerks, these offices will be the ones to watch for binary bandits.

The criminal possibilities will be somewhat limited by the fact that about two thirds of government users buy prepackaged software rather than hiring programmers. Therefore, those forms of computer abuse that require a high degree of expertise—Trojan horse, logic bomb, and trapdoor (a device for bypassing a computer's security system)—will be unlikely to show great increases in government systems.

While assembly line software packages may reduce the need for custom-tailored programming, the diversity of government computer *applications* will create a need for specialists: police workers skilled in using a modem to interact with the FBI's criminal files, or in sending electronic mail to a Canadian Mountie about a fugitive crossing the border; social security data base managers who can crosstab disability payments with IRS returns; military security workers adept at encrypting classified data to protect computer installations against infiltration.

The emergence of myriad specialties raises the specter of reduced control over computer systems. Nonexperts charged with overseeing the adepts' activities simply won't have the knowledge to monitor them effectively. Unscrupulous tinkerers will run less risk than they now do of being caught in a computer caper.

DECENTRALIZED DATA SYSTEMS

Another aspect of reduced control is decentralization of facilities. In the early days of computers—the 1950s and 1960s—big, expensive clunkers were the only technology you could get. Costs made it impractical to scatter them around, so all record-keeping and data processing took place in a central location. It was clumsy, but the span of control was extensive. Everything could be overseen and approved by a central command.

By contrast, the earlier paper-and-pencil era required decentralization. Each department kept its own records and operated with a relative degree of autonomy. The invention of the inexpensive microchip has inverted the economics of computing and brought us back to that earlier era. Terminals and displays are now strewn about offices like so many leaves. The personal computer has freed managers to develop their own priorities and methods for basic data-processing functions and given them a tool to enhance productivity and provide better service. The price has been weakened control over who has access to computers and how they are used.

In 1982, the New York City Board of Education found that its computers were being used for purposes very remote from the schooling of young minds. An errant system manager, Ted Weg, was helping himself to BOE facilities to pursue his own interests. Smuggled into the computer were Weg's data on geneologies of racehorses he owned; a mailing list and label program for his Pennsylvania landowners association; and a program for the production of purchase orders bearing the imprint "Ted Weg, Data Processing Consultant." Weg was charged with theft of services, but the judge dismissed the case: New York State had no law barring such abuse of an employer's computer. Nevertheless, Weg demonstrated yet another way in which computers are subject to tampering.

INTEGRATED SOFTWARE

The ports of entry into galvanic forbidden zones have grown significantly. Integrated programs—with evocative names like Lotus, Jazz, Symphony, and Samna + —perform word processing, data base management, subject searches, and spreadsheet (bookkeeping and accounting) functions all in the same software package. Theoretically, any typing pool clerk can now have access to an agency's most important data. Control has been reduced even further.

Of course, everything I've said about the vulnerability of government computers also applies to businesses and individuals. Any hacker could break into my computer and get all kinds of information via the integrated software I use. By typing in the name of a known client, for instance, my processor would search all stored data and tell the intruder exactly in which file and on what line to find what I had done for that client and on what dates. Alternately, a high-tech con man could use my silicon safe to determine if I would make a worthwhile bunco target. He could easily "case" my electronic records and find out my net worth, where I keep my money, and how much insurance my husband carries. Were I to do my banking through programs that allow my PC to interact with a bank's mainframe, the marauder could confound my commands and throw my finances into disarray. (Others must share my fears, because the response to PC banking has been slow.) Or a competitor might want to gain some advantage in pitching a client. All he'd need do is display my root directory to find where my work history is located. Then he could do a line by line analysis of my curriculum vitae and design his pitch in a way that takes account of my strengths and my weaknesses. Worst of all, a disgruntled assistant could enter my research files and destroy all the notes for this book along with my backup floppy disks.

Armed with a Hayes Smartcom, my hypothetical intruders could do all this without ever leaving the safety of their homes. That's why I never keep my modem connected unless I'm using it. By keeping my system electronically isolated, I can, at the very least, protect myself against long-distance banditry.

My hot-rod IBM, for all I've done to soup it up, is nevertheless only a lowly PC: It's not designed for sophisticated security programs. If I were very concerned, I could always invest $225 in Super Encryptor II software or buy a bunch of Filelok diskettes. But for work like mine, it doesn't seem necessary. So like most PC owners and operators, I am vulnerable.

INTERLOCKING SYSTEMS

The proliferation of "distributed" systems will make computing even more precarious in the future. Discrete computers will be linked together by telecommunications devices that allow exchanges and sharing of data. The only such system that now exists in national government is the linkage of the FBI's National Criminal Information Center with local police departments. Similar systems for welfare and court activities are in the conceptual stage. In a 1983 New York *Times* article, a spokesperson for the Office of Management and Budget projected that 1990 would see between 250,000 and 500,000 personal computers operating in federal agencies, many of them integrated into larger information processing systems. In the Department of Health and Human Services alone, there were 41,000 employees working with computers in 1985. Forty-six were convicted of computer crimes that year. One quarter of those were found to have had previous felony convictions, and three quarters admitted to having worked with other government employees in committing their crimes.

Interlocking computers are not restricted to government operations. Private "bulletin board" services allow subscribers to link their systems and use the host as an electronic message center. Such centers are part high-tech pamphleteering, part church bulletin board—and part criminal.

In May 1984, police raided the home of Thomas Tcimpidis and arrested his computer. Someone had posted a stolen telephone-credit-card number on his bulletin board and "phreaks" (specialists in making calls with stolen credit cards) all over the country were ripping off Pacific Bell. Tcimpidis, a Los Angeles television engineer, had unwittingly become an accessory to his computer's crime.

In the same year, a neo-Nazi group in Idaho was reported to have been using its bulletin board to "export" fascist literature to Canada, where it is illegal to distribute such material in printed form. No one could determine whether electronic blips constitute "printing" and who should be responsible for its contents.

More comprehensive are the private packet-switching networks (systems for electronically linking diverse computers) that crisscross the country like great arteries, carrying digital pulses among thousands of computers. Legendary "hacker" break-ins, of such institutions as Sloan-Kettering and Los Alamos National Laboratory (a vital military installation), were achieved through networks.

By 1983, Telenet, for example, had given users access to 1,200 business and military computers and facilitated functions as diverse as airline reservations and exchanges of scientific information. If you're a subscriber, you too can be a "hacker." To target your destination, just type in a standard three-digit area code. Once there, trial and error typing of two-digit computer codes will eventually get you into someone's system. If a computer answers, don't hang up: You need a password to start interacting with it. If your victim is lucky, you won't have it. But one group of clever hackers simply entered the word "test." They rightly assumed that the operators of the host system had neglected to wipe out that standard factory-installed password after creating their own customized one.

Raping a computer is easy. For a terrorist, blackmailer, or psychopath, it's terrifyingly easy. Distributed networks have made painful questions of security and privacy more acute than ever before.

DETERRENCE

A computer crime takes as little as three milliseconds to commit. Estimates of annual losses are just guesswork, but a recent American Bar Association study revealed that half of its respondents suffered computer crimes in the previous year.

The problem is not being ignored.

A flurry of laws oversee the use of computer data and provide devices to prosecute computer crime. However, they are plagued by overlaps with existing wire fraud, mail fraud, embezzlement, and other statutes. The intangible nature of digital pulses makes it difficult to define the nature of the "property" being violated. Nevertheless, more local legislation is enacted with each passing year.

In 1985, Congress passed the first federal law making unauthorized disclosure of information from government computers a crime. But the Counterfeit Access Device and Computer Fraud and Abuse Act is a two-edged sword. Many fear that, rather than deter felons who use computers to steal money or blackmail people, it will promote government secrecy and discourage "whistleblowers."

Changes in law have been supported by changes in security procedures and public education:

- Volumes have been published on protecting computers and the secrets they contain.
- Computer security courses are springing up across the country. An ad for a 1985 class, held at New York's World Trade Center, read: "Thieves used to get their education on the streets. Today, it might be the classroom. Computer Crime. A Seminar for the Vulnerable."
- The FBI is conducting thorough background checks on government employees entrusted with private information or inputting payroll commands.
- A bevy of encrypting programs are available to keep vital information out of the wrong hands.
- Dial-back mechanisms, in which a computer won't respond to certain requests before calling an authorized user's phone, are being installed to discourage electronic snoopers.
- Some large computer systems reject callers who input more than two false passwords.
- Data networks are experimenting with delaying entry into the system until the caller's password can be checked against a list of authorized phone numbers.
- Large organizations are separating programming, output, and storage functions in order to minimize the possibility of embezzlement.

The very technology of the microchip will be altered to make it more secure. Coming soon is the "biochip," a protein-based, organic processor that, like the human body, has the capacity to assemble, repair, and replicate itself. The computers that house biochips will be far less vulnerable to high-tech vandals than the present generation of hardware. Silicon chips, for example, are susceptible to heat. When melted, they can take with them millions of bits of information. Just turn off the air-conditioning in a poorly designed computer room on a sweltering day—and see what happens.

Above- and below-ground computer backup facilities—The Iron Mountain Group, Dataguard, Vital Records, Incorporated, Comdisco Disaster Recovery Services, Sungard Services—are providing disaster-proof remote housing for computer tapes and hardware. In the event of nuclear war, floods, earthquakes, thefts, sabotage, or power blackouts, these facilities protect an organization's vital data and give it the ability to resume computer operations within a few days, if not immediately.

We are learning to defend our computers. But with silicon vaults, as with mechanical ones, high-tech safecrackers will learn to defeat each new generation of security technology that comes along. However, each refinement screens out those who don't have the technical expertise to overpower it, thereby reducing the pool that can do us harm. Criminal entry will be restricted to the most professional who, unlike amateurs, tend to be selective rather than casual about their targets. Since at present computers give everyone the tools to do great damage, I'm glad to settle for porous security that admits a few pros but bars the masses.

We are becoming a computer-addicted society. You name it, there's an electronic brain behind it: transportation, military installations, hospitals, businesses, schools, leisure activities, cars, money, factories, power grids. We are vulnerable to crime at almost every level.

CRIMEWARPS

- There will be a surge in computer crime against government after 1995, when both computers and the number of employees with access to them will increase dramatically. Much of the leap will take place in smaller local governments which, until then, will have lagged behind in the microchip revolution.
- The greatest part of computer crimes will involve manipulations of data rather than programs.
- The proliferation of system specialists will reduce the odds of computer crimes being detected.
- Future computerization will be decentralized, integrated, and distributed, leading to breakdowns in control over, access to, and use of the system. Geographically remote abuses will rise as a proportion of on-site crimes.
- A variety of devices will restrict access to currently unfettered electronic bulletin boards. But they will remain a private means of distributing contraband forms of information.
- Enhanced computer security will eliminate hordes of amateurs from criminal ranks. Computer crimes by professionals who can bypass security will become more far reaching and expensive.
- Computer facilities will become favorite targets of terrorists.
- Backup data storage and computer facilities will be a growth industry and will reduce the vulnerability of businesses to sabotage and theft.

The Cashless Crisis

At the age of thirty-two, Stanley Rifkin, a private computer consultant with a cherubic face and receding hairline, had it made. The year was 1978, and he had just committed one of the biggest one-man thefts on record. With a telephone, he transferred $10.3 million from its home at Security Pacific Bank in Los Angeles to a merchant's bank account controlled by him in Switzerland. Soon afterward, he flew to Europe, converted his booty into diamonds, then came back to Los Angeles. He probably would never have been caught, but he couldn't resist bragging about his feat to a local diamond dealer who turned him in to the FBI.

Crimes like Rifkin's are disarmingly simple to commit. In this case, Rifkin had been a consultant to the bank he embezzled. Although no longer on its payroll, he returned to the bank, posing as an employee, and went to the wire room, where he knew he would find the computer access code for making electronic money transfers. Although such passwords should be a bank's most carefully guarded secret, the workers at Security Pacific had left it posted on a bulletin board. All Stanley had to do was get a quick peek and his existence would be transformed from the life of Rifkin to the life of Riley.

With the code in hand, a quick call from a pay phone is all it took to make the plumpish man with the toothy smile an instant multimillionaire. Except for the brief stop in the wire transfer room, there wasn't a single clue to connect the crook to the crime.

A bank bandit nets less than $10,000 in an average robbery. To get at that money, he must be on the scene, exposing himself to witnesses, and often carry a gun. By contrast, a *binary bandit,* armed only with a phone, can loot an estimated average of $25,000 to $430,000 across miles in an almost risk-free caper.

Rifkin's offense was a computer-assisted wire fraud. In 1980, approximately 60 million wire transfers amounting to $117 trillion were completed. Few banks confess to hijacked electronic funds, so there's no way to know how much of that amount was stolen. But losses such as that caused by Stanley Rifkin are expected to increase by 70 percent by the end of the 1980s.

Interbank wire transfers, along with automatic teller machines and point-of-sale terminals, are spearheading an electronic revolution that is propelling us toward a cashless society. Far greater sums are available for theft than paper money ever provided.

□ □ □

In March 1985, four men were indicted for running a credit card counterfeiting operation out of the Staten Island home of Salvatore Golinello. Ranging in age from thirty-four to fifty-two, they had come up with a true crime of the times. Working with an embossing machine, computer, and printer, the group allegedly turned out phony American Express, Visa, and MasterCard credit cards embossed with real names and account numbers. They found the names and numbers by mining "black gold"—carbon copies of valid credit card transactions—provided by crooked clerks and careless customers. Theirs was a full-service operation, right down to the driver's licenses and other ID's they printed to back up the bogus credit cards. Cards they didn't sell, they used themselves.

After fabricating over 50 cards and buying close to $100,000 worth of merchandise in less than a year, the foursome were caught and convicted of charges ranging from conspiracy to wire fraud.

Since 1977, credit-buying power has more than doubled and credit purchases have nearly tripled. Losses from counterfeiting have skyrocketed from $66,000 to an estimated $40 million worldwide. Fiorentino Zambrano, Salvatore Golinello, Nicholas D'Angelo, and Gerard Chilli, in the vanguard of a growth area for organized crime, had found a fruitful incubator in which to cultivate a plastic pox.

□ □ □

In a 1974 pamphlet on white-collar crime, the U.S. Chamber of Commerce told of a wily check scam. A man claiming to be an executive of a local company called a bank to say that he had dispatched an assistant to cash a check and asked that the aide be told to call him upon arriving. Having used this ploy to establish his identity, the pseudo-executive's check was cashed by the bank. The draft, though imprinted with the name of a legitimate local company, turned out to be counterfeit.

A later study by the Chamber of Commerce declared that as of 1977, 90 percent of the volume of American business was done via 29 billion checks drawn on any of 100 million checking accounts. Our erstwhile executive's bad check was a mote in an avalanche of check fraud losses that amount to over $1 billion a year.

The losses from check fraud are about twice that from credit fraud. But the halcyon days of bum checks will expire by the end of this century. Paper, as a preferred medium of exchange, will become an anachronism.

□ □ □

Digital money is providing vast new opportunities for electronic pickpockets to reach into our remote control wallets and steal our credit, savings, and investments. Home banking and interactive television have ushered in an era in which paper money and physical mobility have lost much of their meaning. Electronic bleeps are progressively replacing cash and paper as specie of the realm.

Warner Amex foreshadowed home banking when it put Columbus, Ohio, on the high-tech map with the first experiment in two-way interactive television. "Qube," as it is called, allows viewers to become doers. They can instantly register their responses to a television show; contribute their opinions to a poll; hook up to a security system that monitors them for heart attacks, fires, or burglaries; buy a new wardrobe without ever leaving their favorite recliner.

Several years ago, two financial giants introduced home banking to the computing public. Anyone with a PC can now subscribe to Chemical Bank's "Pronto" or Citibank's "Direct Access" and perform instant financial transactions. For a monthly fee, you can command the computer to pay your Southwestern Bell telephone bill, call up check clearance and balance information, look in on the Dow Jones data bank, and transfer money from a revolving credit line into your overdrawn checking account. In the future, you'll be able to bring Smith Barney into your den and earn money the new-fashioned way: through electronic trading of stocks. To work this magic, all you need is a floppy disk and a few strokes on your Keytronic keyboard.

Today, no more than 100,000 homes are equipped with the telecommunications equipment needed to conduct long-distance money transfers. But one estimate holds that the next 50 years will see 80 percent of the nation's households capable of conducting armchair finance. Punching up your net worth in iridescent green on an Amdek monitor is not the same as sleeping on it night after night with its reassuring bulk under the mattress. As hands-on control of one's assets disappears, the cashless society is giving rise to mutations in the traditional white collar crimes of embezzlement, counterfeiting, fraud, and forgery.

HOT WIRES

As the costly Rifkin ruse shows, interbank wire transfers are the biggest threat. A 1983 study of 16 banks showed that their average exposure to loss in each of 139 suspicious transfers was over $833,000.

Bank-to-bank exchanges are the wholesale end of the electronic funds transfer business. The retail end is conducted by over 40,000 bank branch automatic-teller machines. In 1983, the wonderful convenience of being able to withdraw money, make deposits, transfer funds, and get balance information twenty-four hours a day led to ATMs being used 2.7 billion times to process transactions worth $262 billion. Of this figure, banks are estimated to have lost between $70 million and $100 million to fraud.

Compared to credit card crimes, this figure is low. When a California crook used a stolen bank card to make ATM withdrawals of $2,079, it was a small amount compared to the $100,000 in losses caused by the Staten Island counterfeiters. Visa, whose losses are slightly greater than MasterCard's, reports giving up $1.59 to fraud for every $1,000 transacted. For ATMs, the estimated ratio ranges between $0.12 and $1.12.

More than half of lost ATM cards are spirited away from homes, stores, and cars. You'd be amazed at how many owners abet thieves by keeping their PIN on or near the card. That's like handing someone the combination to a safe and saying, "Here, take my money."

Three quarters of ATM frauds involve withdrawals. Unlike credit cards, ATMs restrict the amount of money that can be withdrawn per day. By the time enough days elapse to make the money add up, the purloined plastic will long have been "hotcarded" and rendered useless. Nor can a con artist charm an electronic teller into accepting his calling card without a PIN (Personal Identification Number). If he tries to fake it, some machines will simply "eat" the card after he enters several incorrect access codes. To the extent that financial dealings shift away from checks and cards to ATMs and point-of-sale terminals, fraud losses will remain relatively low.

Counterfeiters don't seem to have much interest in bank cards. When a Dominican cocaine ring that sold sham credit cards as a premium to its customers was broken up in the Bronx in 1985, there wasn't a single ATM card to be found on the varied menu.

PLUNDERED CREDIT

There are some 600-million credit cards now in circulation. Each one is a potential target of fraud which, in 1984, cost banks and consumers an estimated $302 million. Even when you consider that as recently as 1977 credit fraud losses totaled about one tenth that amount and ranked last among nonviolent crimes against business, it's an extraordinary figure.

Peter Herrick, of the Bank of New York, avers that 65 percent of credit frauds occur in New York City. Visa claims a lower figure, 25 percent, but adds that one third occur in Brooklyn. In 1984, Brooklyn's district attorney, Elizabeth

Holtzman, responded to this dubious distinction by "stinging" 85 businesses that ranged from neighborhood stores to national chains. One fourth were willing to admit they knowingly accept stolen or fake credit cards in exchange for a fee or double billing. Merchant collusion is the single greatest cause of major credit card frauds and accounts for one quarter of all incidents.

The reason credit cards are so appealing as a medium for fraud is that they're simple to steal, make, and pass off. The Dominican cocaine ring, like the Staten Island Four, used throwaway carbons as a source of names for their plastic lookalikes. Those carbons are easily retrieved from waste baskets, waiters, and retailers.

Phony IDs can be solicited through a variety of dial-up scams as well. In one of the most frequently used ploys, cons call dupes and tell them they have just won a vacation, a car, or big cash prize. But in order to confirm their identity, the caller says, he must get a credit card number. In the flush of good news, many people succumb. They give information that will surface one or two months later in the form of fraudulent charges on their American Express statement.

Dial-up stolen credit information can also be used to get real credit cards. Up to 120 million of us whose credit reports are stored in the computers of TRW, one of the country's largest information services, are at risk right now. A two-year FBI probe, which ended in 1984, revealed that 30,000 credit reports had been stolen from TRW's computers by rogue collection agencies. While these agencies used the private information to track down the assets of debtors they had a stake in dunning, they could just as easily have used the reports to steal their credit. In theory, anyone ever employed by a client of TRW, and in possession of its access code, has the capacity to steal information. It's a simple matter of dialing up the TRW computer and taking the data that will give them access to your credit and mine.

That, in fact, is what happened to Robert Nascimben of Houston, whom we met in the introduction to this book. The gang that victimized him had gotten hold of a remote terminal that was connected by phone lines to the Credit Bureau of Greater Houston. All they needed were names and they could get complete credit information on anyone in the area. Nascimben's name surfaced because he had been a customer at First America, where one of the confessed con men, Timothy Leighton, worked as a mobile-home salesman. From then on it was easy. All they had to do was punch in his name and look up the credit cards and bank accounts Nascimben already held. Then, they used his perfectly good credit information to open new accounts, in his name, for their own use.

The con men then used Nascimben's credit to buy merchandise and draw cash. They never paid for any of it, and neither did Nascimben because he never got a bill. Monthly statements languished, unclaimed, in a private postal box. If it hadn't been for an independent investigation, Nascimben would never have known about his victimization. But next time he applied for credit, it would have been denied, his credit rating wrecked by unseen looters.

Because he was the victim of fraud, Nascimben was not liable for any of the bank losses that were incurred. Even if he were, the limit would have been $50 per card. That limit, established by Federal Regulation E, is one in which you probably take comfort. Don't—even if nothing is stolen directly from you, we all pay our banks' losses through high annual card fees and exorbitant interest rates that don't float downward with the prime rate.

New credit card technology will depress the fraud industry. Three-dimensional holograms, ultraviolet ink, fine-line printing, and two-sided embossing will deter counterfeiting. Carbonless sales slips will protect holder identification. Point-of-sale scanners will read magnetic stripes and provide instant feedback on whether a card is legitimate. Voice, retinal, and palm print identification will make a stolen card useless to a thief.

RUBBER CHECKS

But that won't stop other forms of fraud. The crimes of Leighton and company, for example, were not restricted to credit. Nascimben's financial information was used to open fraudulent bank accounts against which were drawn five checks totaling $5,100. A 1977 study by the American Management Association estimates that check chicanery costs up to four times more than credit fraud. The Chamber of Commerce asserts the problem is growing. That's only partly true.

Generally, it's the young and the poor who have no checking accounts. The young population is diminishing at a faster rate than the poor is expanding, leaving us with a net gain in potential check writers. Since check writers as well as forgers and counterfeiters tend to be older, we can expect to see short term increases in check crimes.

Secret Service records indicate that the number of forgeries is, in fact, increasing. In 1973, the agency investigated 91 forged checks for every million Veteran's Administration, social security, IRS, and government payroll check issued. After bouncing up and down in the intervening years, the rate settled at 150 per million in 1982.

In 1985, investigators busted a Filipino forgery ring that had stolen bulk check mailings worth $75 million from San Francisco International Airport. Stateside thieves sent the checks to middlemen in the Philippines, who sold them at a great discount—as low as 1 percent of face value—to locals who would cash them. The group was well financed, highly organized, and sophisticated.

By contrast, observes a Secret Service spokesperson, most check forgers are small-time bandits who follow the mailman around and learn when their neighbor's disability check is due. On that day, they dip into the mailbox, grab the check, and cash it at the local delicatessen. It's easy to arrest these thieves: They operate close to home, and the neighborhood merchants know which faces belong to which checks.

The pickings for check thieves are becoming slimmer. The familiar green drafts—now transformed into hard-to-counterfeit rainbow-colored notes—issued by the U.S. Treasury have been declining steadily from a high of over 800 million in 1976 to a low of 615 million in 1985. Electronic transfers of social security payments account for much of that drop. The federal government's lead will sweep the private sector as well, and we will have gone a long way toward eliminating a prolific source of crime.

Treasury bonds, another form of negotiable paper, suffer the same weaknesses as checks but are a less frequent source of crime. Bond forgeries, which dipped by one third between 1973 and 1982, increased by 33 percent in 1985. Jack Thayer of the U.S. Secret Service notes that forgery statistics tend to follow interest rates. During the high rate years, U.S. Savings Bonds were simply not competitive with money market funds. In 1984–85, overall interest rates dropped and Savings Bonds once again became attractive targets—for both investors and forgers.

Some brokerage houses are now storing bonds, along with stocks, in their computers. By transferring them electronically, rather than physically carrying them from vault to vault, the chances for theft are reduced. When all paper transactions go digital with "Direct Deposit," check and bond forgeries will fade away.

DETERRENTS

The good guys have one more ace up their sleeves. It's *floating credit,* a whole new concept in money. Developed in France, the first American licensee is Smart Card International, Incorporated. The card contains a computer microchip that stores current holder information such as credit limits and unpaid balances. It could just as easily include bank balances. The card is read by a point-of-sale terminal. Scanners instantly verify the holder's signature or fingerprint. If everything checks out, the "Smart Card" automatically debits the buyer's account and transfers funds to the merchant's.

Without the scanner's approval, the merchant gets no money. In the absence of a legitimate signature or print, the scanner won't accept the transaction. The automatic debit means no carbons, and electronic fund transfers mean no paper. So much for the crooked retailer, the card thief, the counterfeiter, and the check forger.

Wire transfers, such as Direct Deposit, ATMs, home banking, and Smart Cards, will help plug the leaks in our cashless money supply. But, as you saw in the last chapter, without diligent security measures, electronic funds will remain susceptible to binary bandits who manipulate the microwaves to divert your money into their accounts.

CRIMEWARPS

• Today there are approximately 52.6 million people in the white-collar crime-prone ages of twenty-five to thirty-nine. Those now ten to twenty-four years old number closer to 58.4 million. As they enter the twenty-five-to-thirty-nine age group over the next fifteen years, the additional 6 million will create a surge in cashless money crimes. However, the youngest co-

horts, following behind today's ten-to-twenty-four-year-old group, are
much smaller than their predecessors. By the time the youngest group
reaches age twenty-five in the year 2010, white-collar crime rates will
begin to drop off.

· The lagging home computer market, which all but collapsed in 1984–85,
will retard the acceptance of home banking. Smart Cards, however, will
eventually be able to perform some of the same bill-paying functions as
banking software. Both technologies will eliminate the need for paper
checks and greatly reduce opportunities for forgery and counterfeiting.

· While the dollar remains relatively strong against other currencies, counterfeiting of all American exchange media will increase. When the budget
and trade deficits eat into its value, counterfeiting will decline. During
periods of elevated interest rates, however, corporate, municipal, and
some government bond forgeries will grow. New security technology will
offset these trends.

· As enhanced security technology reduces opportunities for forgery, counterfeiting, and fraud, fewer credit, check, and ATM thefts will occur. Crime
will be concentrated in the spectacularly lucrative wire transfer arena.

8

Stealing Technological Secrets

In September 1981, William Klein was the manager of advanced head technology for IBM. In a typical Frost Belt–to–Sunbelt career move, he was transferred to San Jose, California. But after nineteen years with Big Blue, Klein was bitten by Silicon Valley's entrepreneurial bug. He left IBM, and four key employees followed within twelve days. The five reemerged on the scene as Cybernex, a fledgling firm making thin-film read/write heads for computers.

Klein calls it fulfillment of the American dream.

IBM calls it theft.

IBM spent more than fourteen years and $200 million developing its own thin-film read/write technology, a manufacturing process involving over one hundred steps. Cybernex, whose principals had had access to the process, developed what IBM claims is an identical product in only a few months. In March 1983, IBM squared off against Cybernex for stealing proprietary information. It was the fourth time in six months that IBM had sued former employees. In this high-tech version of David and Goliath, the ammunition in the slingshot is a trade secret that can make or break a company's edge in the electronic jungle.

"IBM will take whatever actions are appropriate to protect trade secrets and proprietary information," averred a spokesperson for the company. "We have an enormous investment in R&D, which represents the future of this corporation." Klein, of Cybernex, denies any wrongdoing and contends IBM is merely using its legal muscle to thwart competition. "It's one thing for IBM to claim. It's another for them to be right."

The suit has cost the newcomers "millions of dollars in licensing agreements and we've had to walk away from business opportunities involving technology transfer," asserts Klein. "The company is almost at a break-even point and sales have grown, but not as fast as they would have. Certain customers won't do business with us because they're afraid of a backlash from IBM. Others won't because they feel we won't be viable in the long run."

Cybernex has done what many companies in similar situations do: They have countered with an antitrust suit that charges IBM with restraint of trade. Years will have passed by the time it's all sorted out.

Suits like IBM vs. Cybernex—and Cybernex vs. IBM—will become commonplace in the Information Age. *Ideas, more than tangible assets, will fuel the industries and the crimes of the future.* Like tractors, mink coats, and electronic typewriters, they will be protected under the laws of theft.

□ □ □

Neighbors in Cerritos, California, didn't know very much about the family that had been living in the stucco-and-frame house next door for the past four years. But when the smoke lifted in late 1984, it was revealed that Thomas Patrick Cavanagh, age forty, had just become the fourth American to be charged with espionage in the United States that year. In March 1985, Cavanagh admitted his guilt. The Northrop Corporation engineer with security clearance had been caught red-handed trying to sell our air force "Stealth" technology to the Soviets.

He wasn't a communist; in fact, ideology had nothing to do with his crime. He was, quite simply, broke.

Cavanagh had moved out of the big house in Cerritos in 1982. His marriage, unable to survive the two-earner stresses of life on the fast track, had crumbled. He was sodden with debt and desperate for cash. The Soviet Consulate in San Francisco offered him relief. In exchange for $55,000, he was ready to hand them the secret to building planes that can fly undetected by radar.

There were no red flags in his past to warn that he would sell out his country. He was a clean-cut kid born in Brooklyn, New York, and raised on Long Island. The years after his mid-1960s graduation from Uniondale High School led him to a twelve-year stint with Hughes Aircraft. When he left Hughes in 1981, he joined the ranks of experienced engineers who are lured to competing companies by more money and bigger titles. In Cavanagh's case, it was Northrop Corporation in Los Angeles. Three years after joining them, he was poised to sell the secret technology to which his employer had given him access.

Experts say Cavanagh is one of a new breed of spy. Unlike Ethel and Julius

Rosenberg, whose alleged betrayals were motivated by an idealistic commitment to a utopian vision with clay feet, the new spies are out for themselves. Products of the "me" era that sprang from Vietnam protest and Watergate disillusionment, they have decided that loyalty to one's government is no longer de rigueur. William Webster, director of the FBI, says: "We have more people charged with espionage right now than ever before in our history." *The social pressures creating the new breed of opportunistic spy will intensify.*

Theft of technology has escalated. Secretary of Defense Caspar Weinberger sounded the alarm a few years ago: "Businessmen, engineers, scientists and workers have been bribed. Innocent-looking corporations have been created to buy equipment later sent to the USSR." Roger Milgram, a prominent East Coast lawyer, adds: "I'd say there's five to eight times as many trade secrets cases now as there were ten years ago." Giving the West Coast perspective, James Pooley, who wrote *Trade Secrets*, maintains: "We have had many more of these kinds of cases now than we had three years ago. They've more than doubled." Phoenix-based Jack Brown, considered by some to be the dean of trade secrets litigators, is IBM's counsel in the Cybernex suit. He insists, "I don't have any doubt in my mind we're talking about a very significant societal problem."

"ENTREPRENEURIALISM RUN AMUCK"

It's no coincidence that so many technology thefts have originated on the West Coast, where our biggest defense contractors and electronics companies are found. The highly charged atmosphere created by technological warfare has bred a dangerous mix of mobility and materialism that bodes badly for the protection of secrets.

High-tech companies live on ideas. The state of the art has turned over so rapidly that a long-term investment can be rendered obsolete before its product ever gets to market. The cutting edge of technology is so fine that if companies don't stay one step ahead of the competition, they can go under.

Whether a critical idea falls into a competitor's hands—foreign or domestic —is largely a matter of employee scruples. And that is where the current work ethic will get us into trouble. "Everyone wants to be their own entrepreneur here," explains Dr. Bruce Abt, a Silicon Valley industrial psychologist. "They may be working for one company but really, on the side, planning to open up their own corporation."

Wayne Brown, a private investigator who claims to have handled over one hundred trade secrets cases in the last few years, put it this way: "Say you're a large manufacturer with a research team of engineers. These research people understand they have just invented something that will blow the industry wide open. Why should they let the mother company get all the benefits? They become their own company."

That is precisely what happened in March 1982, when Lewis Eggebrecht defected from IBM. It's hard to imagine a more honored employee than Eggebrecht. He had personally designed the IBM PC, which became the industry standard and gave the company its preeminence in a highly lucrative market. Yet, while still on IBM's payroll, Eggebrecht and a small group of key employees formed Bridge Technology and went into direct competition with the mother company by peddling her insider communications advances. But a permanent injunction coming from an out-of-court settlement eventually stopped them dead in their tracks.

A potential client had blown the whistle. When he asked the renegades why they were betraying their company, they indicated, "IBM was a great company, the best company to work for, but they wanted to do things on their own. They wanted to be rich; to get one of the fortunes others were making all around them. Here's Eggebrecht, who designed the PC, which is incredibly successful, and in his mind, he's only got X dollars to show for that. . . . And he was dissatisfied."

High-tech ambition breeds dissatisfaction and has turned the notion of loyalty on its head. What was once regarded as a virtue—making a career out of staying with one company and spending thirty years moving up through the ranks—is now viewed with suspicion. Management consulting firms—such as Rohrer, Hibler, Replogle—regard the overly loyal employee as "someone who is averse to taking risks, is a task-oriented rather than strategic thinker, requires structure, defers to leadership, refrains from expressing himself for fear of losing his job." Such a worker is the antithesis of the high-tech opportunist whose career is made up of multiple job moves to the highest bidder, often with an eye toward starting his own company.

T. J. Rogers, for instance, quit a $100,000 job at AMD to start his own firm. Even though he was sued by them, Rogers calls AMD "the most entrepreneurial of the semiconductor companies." But as their hired hand, he missed the freedom of determining his own destiny. "There's a difference between being a good manager and a president. The main attraction of start-up is a chance to own part of what you're building."

Of careers like T. J.'s, New York *Times* reporter Andrew Pollack observes: "Too many companies specializing in the same things have been formed, each lured by potential riches and each believing in its own success." It's a case of "entrepreneurialism run amuck." Jerry Sanders, Rogers' charismatic former boss, puts it more kindly: "We're in a very competitive industry and we attract a class of overachievers."

But not everyone makes it big. James Harper was among the first fortune hunters to come to Silicon Valley in the late 1950s and early 1960s. He watched contemporaries like Jerry Sanders and Robert Noyce found blockbuster businesses like AMD and Intel. By contrast, his own company went bankrupt in 1975. That same year, Harper, now a middle-aged failed entrepreneur, started passing military secrets to Polish agents. Using the security clearance of his wife (who later died of cirrhosis of the liver at age thirty-nine), he stole ballistic missile research from Systems Control Incorporated and sold it over an eight-year period for accumulated fees of $250,000. He had found a way to strike it rich after all.

Stars like Sanders and sellouts like Cavanagh and Harper live on opposite sides of the fast track. The unrelenting drive to achieve and the professional crapshoots that go with it, as well as the insecurity that comes with chronic change, can exact a high emotional and ethical toll. Psychologist Bruce Abt, who has counseled many casualties of the high-tech career path, explains: "Here someone can be employed for six months as an employee and then become a manager. They'll come into my office saying, 'Gee, I really don't know what I'm doing. I'm uncomfortable with my position and my job. But also, the insecurity is in my company. Is it going to be successful? Is it going to be here in two or three years?' "

The nightmare buried in that question has come true. The industry that couldn't fail is in deep trouble. Profits have fallen short of goals, workweeks have been shortened, and thousands of high-tech workers have been pink-slipped. Industry giants as well as small companies are going through a brutal shakedown period.

"Loyalty has always centered around the notion that 'the company will take care of me,' " says James Cabrera, head of an outplacement firm. But companies now can't or won't take care of their employees and looking out for number one has become more prevalent.

"What's happening in Silicon Valley is going to be happening in the rest of the United States," warns Dr. Abt. "More technology. More isolation of employees. More emphasis on individualism. Fast pace.

"When you're looking at Silicon Valley, you're looking at an area that doesn't have real roots. People are coming from all over the United States. There's not a lot of sense of community." Abt is describing a breakdown of the social controls that keep people from committing crimes and engaging in self-destructive behavior.

Ironically, the shakedown will reduce the incentive to steal technological secrets. The current buyer's market offers fewer options to wayward employees, making the job in hand more valuable. The madcap years of unbridled venture capital investment, which prompted some high-tech entrepreneurs to plunder their mother companies, are over. "There's a mathematical relationship between a decrease in start-ups and a decrease in trade-secrets suits," explains venture capitalist Roger Borovoy. With fewer places to go, more people will stay put—perhaps even sinking roots in a community and rebuilding the ties that keep people loyal to their companies, their families, and their country.

REBUILDING COMPANY LOYALTY

According to private investigator Wayne Brown, most of the giants of the electronics industry—IBM, Intel, Memorex, Atari, Amdahl—were founded with a technological secret fueled by ambition. Whether or not the founding secrets were "stolen," it's clear that the electronics industry is an incestuous one. Compaq was spun off from Texas Instruments; Intel and AMD from Fairchild

Instrument and Camera; Seeq Technology from Intel; Cypress Semiconductor from AMD; Trilogy from Amdahl; Trimedia from IBM; and so on, ad infinitum.

In the early days, the electronics companies were more tolerant of their prodigal employees. They could afford to be. A study sponsored by IBM reveals that in 1955 there were only 5 firms identified as information-processing companies. Thirty years later, the count was 15,000. In the intervening years, fortunes were being made by engineers like An Wang, who started multinational Wang Laboratories in his Roxbury garage.

"There's no way in the world you can stop a dishonest engineer from getting something out," proclaims Borovoy, a former Intel executive now with Sevin Rosen Management. T. J. Rogers, who left AMD to found Cypress Semiconductor, emphatically states: "Trade secrets don't mean a damn thing. Making a technology work requires so many people and so much management, it can't be executed alone. You can't have good security with the kind of job mobility here and the types of people. You have to trust employees not to violate trade secrets."

Some companies, like IBM and AMD, now work hard at building trust and loyalty. They lavish employees with bonuses, profit sharing, stock plans, recognition, promotions, job security, houses, expense-paid vacations, counseling programs, gyms. Jerry Sanders of AMD muses: "I look on the corporation as the most important societal unit we have in the twentieth century. In the high-tech businesses, we tend to be enlightened employers. We're prepared to make an investment in people. And if this means helping them solve their problems, we're prepared to do that. I see us as quite paternal." IBM, the big daddy of them all, sees such policies paying off in an unexpected way: It keeps them out of the defendant's seat in trade secrets suits.

Lyle McGuire, one of IBM's army of public information specialists, explains it this way: "At IBM, most of the promotions are made from within and most of the recruitment takes place early in people's careers. We don't usually hire people who have proprietary information from other companies." However, as the Bridge Technology suit attests, even the most enlightened personnel policies can be defeated by unbridled ambition.

PROTECTING "IDEAS"

Ambition can, however, be significantly curtailed by sound security. A number of companies have started tinkering with various devices to keep track of their technology and secrets:

- Monitoring copying machines. (That wouldn't help in a case like James Harper's; he bought his own copier and reproduced documents in his home.)
- Briefcase checks. ("A waste of time," exclaims Roger Borovoy.)
- Wiretaps. (A big civil liberties problem.)
- Anti-bugging sweeps. (Cost a fortune!)

• Lie-detector tests. (Notoriously unreliable, especially with professional moles who are trained to beat them.)

The list could go on and on. The right security consultant might be able to determine the relationship between the length of the list and its deterrence and detection potential, but the cost in creativity isn't worth it.

"You can't run a high-tech company like an armed camp," warns Borovoy. "It destroys morale." So most companies concentrate instead on controlling who has access to technological secrets. For the 14,000 contractors who do government work and the 4.2 million people who are allowed to work with classified material, the screening is not very efficient. Only 1 percent of security clearance applications are denied. Even fewer are revoked once granted. It's no wonder: Most of the checks consist of little more than a fingerprint query.

The Defense Intelligence Service is charged with inspecting all contractors with classified ratings at least once a year, although only 200 of them actually house classified material. The DIS field staff of 225 investigators, however, isn't much competition for the U.S.–based KGB agents who reportedly outnumber them by a factor of six to one. As if that weren't enough, the service now conducts twice the number of espionage investigations that it did ten years ago.

These facts tumbled out on the heels of the shocking spying arrests of several all-American types: an FBI agent, a young TRW genius, a family of navy men, and assorted others whom I've already discussed. In a flurry of outrage, officials started calling for strapping thousands of workers into polygraph machines and reinstituting the peacetime death penalty for treason. However, these measures will not solve the problem. In a well-reasoned editorial, Morton Halperin, a former Defense Department official, proposes a more practical, less-repressive solution: "We should begin by reducing the amount of classified material and the number of clearances. When everything is classified, nothing is; when everyone has a clearance, no one has been adequately cleared." With streamlining, the 225 DIS investigators should be more than enough to effectively police the dissemination of technological secrets.

Halperin goes a step further. He points out that our security clearance procedures are out of date. Put in place during the post–World War II years, they were designed to ferret out "subversives." As such, they focused on searching out applicants' political beliefs. But today's technology peddlers aren't political; they're mercenary. And they get sucked into espionage after they've been cleared, not before. In short, says Halperin, our criteria for assigning secrecy ratings gauge the wrong traits. He argues that we should be "doing periodic reviews of those who have been cleared and examining their finances rather than their politics." The press of necessity will bring policymakers around to Halperin's way of thinking and our spy threat will take a plunge.

TRADE SECRETS LITIGATION

That takes care of our defense secrets, but it doesn't plug the domestic leaks of our trade secrets. Trade secrets litigation, pioneered in California, has opened up a whole new area of law. It picks up where patent and copyright law leave off. For the first time, ideas are being treated as corporate assets. The multitude of suits that have sprung up are both a threat and a promise.

The threat? Using trade secrets litigation unfairly to restrain competition and chill the creation of new businesses; making employees so security conscious that their creativity is smothered; filing frivolous suits to destroy a business. When a company is in the throes of defending itself in such an action, almost all its resources are devoted to the suit rather than to business. Assets and productivity are drained in the service of a court fight. Customers become gun shy. Aggressive marketing is inhibited. Embryonic businesses, like Cybernex, must struggle to stay afloat in such turmoil. If they truly believe they have a right to the idea or process they are using, their only recourse is to countersue.

The promise? Companies can now use criminal and civil courts to protect the ideas they invest so much time and money to develop. Ambitious, but unscrupulous, employees can be deterred from using what rightfully belongs to a present or former employer against him.

Even so, nobody likes trade secrets suits. They can be a catch-22 that makes public the very secrets a company wants to protect. For this reason, they are seldom treated as criminal matters and police are almost always kept out of the investigations. Often, as in AMD v. Cypress Semiconductor, an independent inspector or monitor is assigned to determine whether violations have taken place.

If there seem to be grounds for a suit, civil court is the forum of choice. As of this writing, Cybernex and IBM expect to have their day in court. But such cases seldom go to trial: The usual procedure is to obtain a temporary restraining order that bars alleged offenders from using the secrets in question pending further investigation. If the suit persists, litigants are apt to try to avoid a public trial and arrange a confidential settlement instead. That's how IBM resolved its grievances with competing computer companies like Bridge Technology, Trimedia, and others. Its alleged secrets were thus kept out of the public record and everybody was able to save face.

The conundrum of trade secrets litigation is illustrated in two recent cases involving someone who ought to know better. Jim Pooley, who wrote the classic text on trade secrets law, found his firm on the receiving end of two suits charging trade secrets violations:

CASE 1: Mosher, Pooley, Sullivan, & Anderson were representing National Semiconductor in a trade secrets suit against Linear Technology. However, a busy lawyer making a routine filing for the client forgot to ask the judge to seal a twelve-page document describing the secrets in dispute. A short time later, National Semiconductor read about its precious trade secrets in *Microelectronic News*, an industry publication with several thousand subscribers. Once in the public domain, they were technically *no longer secret.* National's case against Linear was almost wrecked.

CASE 2: Jim Pooley defended two IBM employees who had departed the company to found Trimedia. As per the norm, the case was settled. But Pooley still had in his files some IBM secrets that had been disclosed during negotiations. The lawyer mistakenly showed those documents to a Control Data executive while trying to get some financing for his client. IBM sued Pooley—and settled.

Trade secrets suits can be as destructive as they are beneficial. While lawyers like Jack Brown feel that actual "stealing" is rare, the new laws are vital to our national defense and economy.

Since the first statute was enacted in 1967, a growing number of states have been struggling with the problem of protecting proprietary properties that range from customer lists to key employees to manufacturing processes. The federal government is belatedly moving to enact legislation to safeguard the chips that drive our high tech industries.

However, the need for such laws is grounded in the values that dominate the workplace: money, individualism, and ambition. As the outlets for expressing those values diminish, so will the crimes that they induce.

CRIMEWARPS

- American society is entering a time of lowered expectations. The shakedown in the electronics industry, which is regarded by some experts as permanent, will reduce job mobility and the domestic theft of secrets that often goes with it. Reduced geographical mobility in other industries will have the same effect.
- The growing materialism that will characterize American society for the life of the "yuppie" generation will partially offset the anticrime benefits of reduced mobility.
- The heating up of the weapons race, especially the sophisticated "Star Wars" technology, and the subsequent increased value placed on defense secrets, will combine with increased materialism to induce greater espionage in the military area by Americans.
- The reawakening of American patriotism, initiated by conservative politics, will reduce inducements to spying among those growing up in the post-Vietnam and Watergate era.
- Greater selectivity in assigning "classified" ratings to materials, and security clearances to individuals, will heighten the protection of national and trade secrets. Violations will decrease.
- Trade secrets litigation will warn off potential violators and ensure that more employees leave a company "clean." Employment contracts specifying a company's rights over intellectual property and employee inventions will further reduce violations. Entire legal practices will be built on clarifying these issues.

Caveat Emptor

In 1983, a federal jury in Georgia awarded a man $6 million for the wrongful death of his mother. She had been taking a widely hailed arthritis drug, Oraflex, which Eli Lilly and Company had neglected to tell consumers was killing people.

Oraflex had been removed from the American market in August 1982, three months after its introduction here. Too late for the man's mother and more than 100 other victims elsewhere in the world. The pharmaceutical company knew that the drug was inducing liver and kidney failure in users, but it had failed to submit the new information to the Food and Drug Administration, as required. The U.S. attorney prosecuting the case found no intent to break the law, but that didn't absolve the deaths. In 1985, the company pleaded guilty to criminal charges and was fined $25,000. Its former chief medical officer, Dr. William Shedden, was personally fined $15,000.

In the same year, SmithKline Beckman Corporation was placed on two years' probation and ordered to donate $100,000 to a child abuse program. The company, and three of its principal doctors, pleaded guilty to thirty-four charges filed in connection with their failure to promptly report lethal liver damage caused by the blood pressure medication, Selacryn.

The Eli Lilly and SmithKline cases were noteworthy in two respects: as being among the few instances in which criminal charges were brought against drug companies, and as part of a new trend in which principals are held personally liable for corporate wrongdoing. For the future, however, they hold an entirely different significance: They are among a host of medical frauds and other white-collar crimes that will derive from the needs of an aging population.

□ □ □

At the end of 1984, an attractive woman wearing sunglasses and a white suit was arrested in New York City. Carmen Torres (also known as Carmen Bayne), in her late thirties, was charged with cheating about 50 poor Hispanics out of amounts ranging from $200 to $600. All her victims thought they were paying an advance fee for an apartment.

The bilingual Ms. Torres was systematic. She reportedly made the rounds of dilapidated tenements to query superintendents and neighbors about which tenants were on the waiting list for public housing. Upon finding a prospect, she was said to show up at their door armed with official-looking forms and documents. Presenting herself as a Housing Authority employee, she offered to assign them an apartment in exchange for a fee or rent advance. Of course, she had no apartments and her dupes lost their money.

The swindler, who pleaded guilty to grand larceny, had developed a timely specialty. Disenfranchised minorities, trapped with tattered armies of the homeless in the core of expanding megatropolises, put pressure on housing markets. Their swelling ranks compound the influx of affluent urban- and suburbanites who need shelter and office space. Housing starts, which ebbed steadily from a high in 1978, started to rebound in 1983. Carmen Torres' gambit is one of many cons that will invade the real estate, construction, mortgage, moving, and allied industries.

□ □ □

Crimes of deceit by those in positions of trust are, like street crimes, being reconfigured by demographic shifts in age, migration, and economics. Our changing needs in basic health care, housing, and leisure are leaving us wide open to new forms of old frauds. Consumers will get taken accordingly.

BAD MEDICINE

The population is aging and life expectancies increasing. In living longer, we will be exposed to more dangers in the environment, at work, and in travel. We will contract more diseases of old age and invest more time and money in staying healthy. Questionable drugs, medical quackery, Medicare rip-offs, and corporate irresponsibility are four forms of fraud that will flourish in the future.

Let's start with pills. An FDA report on "Drug Utilization in the United States" shows that between the ages of nineteen and fifty, use of prescription medicine more than doubles. After age sixty, it more than triples. Cardiovascular and arthritis drug consumption, in particular, have gone up, just as you'd expect in an aging population. (Valium, the long-reigning queen for fighting angst, dropped from first rank to fourth between 1981 and 1983.)

It's no wonder that companies like Eli Lilly and SmithKline have rushed in to fill the need. To their credit, they came up with answers to old-age suffering. To their discredit, they knew that some of the answers were dangerous. I can only speculate that they were lured into corporate criminality by the vast profits to be wrested from the expanding older market.

Pressure on investigators to show results may have had something to do with it, too. It's a problem shared by all medical inquiry. The big business of research has birthed a relentless struggle for funds; competition to be first with a breakthrough; urgency to beef up academic credentials with publications. The unintended consequence is a spate of plagiarized, fudged, and erroneous data, often at the expense of consumers. The drive to relieve cancer, arthritis, and other diseases of aging will sustain the impetus for fraudulent studies.

No one, not even their prosecutors, would accuse two such reputable pharmaceutical companies as Eli Lilly and SmithKline of quackery. However, there are plenty of pharmaceutical charlatans around, and they drain the elderly of more than $10 million a year, according to a House Select Committee on Aging report. Most of the money goes to bogus cancer remedies. One fifth is spent on illusory arthritis remedies; the rest is wasted on useless rejuvenators. As of 1984, when those over sixty-five made up only one eighth of the population, the elderly accounted for 60 percent of these fraud victims; imagine what will happen in 2025, when they climb to about one quarter of the population!

We will certainly see a profusion of pseudomedical facilities. Bio Health, for one, a California-based mail order laboratory, was recently sued by the New York State attorney general for fraud. For a fee of $350, the firm used Cytotoxic III— a process discredited by the FDA—to test blood for food allergies. When a sample of cow's blood was sent in, the lab reportedly failed to question its source and identified the donor as being allergic to milk, cottage cheese, and yogurt. There is now an injunction in force prohibiting Bio Health from doing business in New York.

A criminal investigator for the postal service tells the story of Midwest Health Research Clinic in Kansas City, which neither ran a clinic nor did medical research. What they did do was advertise a "Health Bible Handbook," which allegedly contained the panacea for manifold ailments. The cure? "Colonic irrigation," otherwise known as an enema. For an additional fee of $29.95, the hucksters were willing to provide a kit to do the recommended purging. The wonderfully flexible mail fraud statute eventually allowed postal inspectors to catch up with them and see the owner convicted.

So where are the FDA and the FTC? The congressional health fraud report has this answer: "The Food and Drug Administration, once a formidable force in controlling quackery, now directs less than 1 percent of its budget to control of quackery. . . . The Federal Trade Commission's efforts to control misleading advertising are even less significant and have diminished in recent years to the point where they are almost nonexistent." (The postal inspectors, on the other hand, were left unscathed. In fact, the report praised their aggressive pursuit of charlatans.)

□ □ □

If, as many contend, the regulatory agencies are falling down on the job, we must count on our doctors to guide us through the labyrinth of palliatives that beckon from ads in every magazine. But even here, we're less than safe. A congressional investigation has revealed that more than 10,000 practicing physicians are impostors. A 1984 New York *Times* editorial by Nicholas Wade summed it up well: "Today's snake oil vendors don't peddle snake oil. They profess real medicine and have diplomas to prove it."

One of these "vendors" was a Ghanaian immigrant, Abraham Asante, who worked as an anesthesiologist at Walson Army Hospital at Fort Dix. The "doctor" had practiced in various medical facilities for fifteen years. Then, the unthinkable happened: a forty-seven-year-old retired naval officer was undergoing bladder surgery when his heart stopped. It was four minutes before Asante noticed. By the time the real doctors got the patient's heart started again, it was too late. His brain destroyed, he had become a human vegetable. Asante was convicted of aggravated assault.

My almanac tells me that in 1975 we reached our highest ratio of doctors to U.S. population since 1900. The ratio continued to climb in 1980. Yet, we still seem to have a surplus of aspirants trying to break into the profession.

Dale Shaller, head of the Center for Policy Studies in Minneapolis, feels the doctor glut will ultimately erode medical incomes as well as quality medical care. On a recent radio interview, Shaller foresaw "a lot more doctors competing for a lot fewer patients. . . . If the physician glut severely shatters physician income, we'll have the potential to see a decline in the caliber of people who are in the medical profession."

There are plenty of suppliers—as many as two hundred rings—willing to provide phony degrees to those willing to make an end run around legitimate certification procedures. Some foreign medical schools, which lack even the most basic equipment, are among them. As long as the obstacles against, and the rewards for, entering the medical profession remain high, there will be a ready market of gate crashers.

□ □ □

Large amounts of Medicare and Medicaid payments are falling into the hands of these frauds. But bona fide facilities cheat, too. A 1985 General Accounting Office survey found that Medicare had been cheated of over $900 million by many of its 5,500 member hospitals. Apparently, a number of facilities thought that hockey passes, liquor, country club dues, color televisions, phones, and plane tickets for administrators' wives were part of rendering a reimbursible medical service.

Individual doctors and clinics have their own gimmicks. "Ganging" (treating only one member of a family, but billing all present), "ping-ponging" (a form of fee-splitting), and "upgrading" (performing one service, but charging for a slightly more expensive one) are common ways of stealing an estimated 10 percent of all health care dollars paid by third-party programs. A fourth form of abuse, performing unnecessary procedures, is more ambiguous: Where do you draw the line between fraud and defensive medicine?

Private insurers, reeling from health care costs that more than tripled between 1972 and 1983, have launched their own audit offensive. Aetna Life & Casualty's Fraud Squad calculates that more than $1 million a day is paid out in fraudulent health claims. Writing in 1984, Harold Pepinsky and Paul Jesilow assert: "Physicians and other health care providers stole more money last year than all the robbers, burglars, and other assorted thieves responsible for crime on the streets."

The older our population becomes, the more time we will spend in doctors offices, hospitals, and long-term nursing care. Medicare enrollments expanded by 40 percent in just one decade, 1970 to 1980. As we lean ever more heavily on private and public medical insurance, the opportunities for fraud will be legion.

□ □ □

However, two new developments promise to temper the larceny in medical administrators' hearts. The first is the judicious use of audits. According to one report, the federal government saves $5 for every $1 it spends auditing hospitals nationwide. In Texas, the rate of return is even better: 27 to 1.

The second development is the advent of Health Maintenance Organizations. By providing medical services for a flat fee, fiscal incentives to overtreat or overcharge are removed. Family physician Dr. Steven Lamm is executive vice president of Life Extension, Incorporated. Recently, he also became vice president of Oxford Health Plans, Incorporated, an HMO in the New York tri-state area. Between patients, he explained to me how this form of service reduces fraud:

> Because their margins of profitability are relatively low, there are important built-in measures that permit HMOs to evaluate services on a day-to-day and month-to-month basis. Computers do ongoing reviews. They can tell when a patient who has hypertension sees a physician every couple of weeks even after being stabilized. It's very clear when a physician overutilizes a service. This is true also of drug overuse and hospital overuse.
>
> HMOs will not entirely replace a private relationship with physicians. There will always be a group of people who are willing to pay a premium to get that. But economic pressures will force HMOs to increase.

Demographics support Dr. Lamm's prophecy. As the population ages and contains more female-headed households, it will become less affluent. HMOs will be medicine's answer to tight dollars.

□ □ □

While HMOs provide us with maximum medical service for the money, consumers will be threatened from another quarter: the breakup of the regulatory agencies that protect our health and life at work, in the general environment, and in our travels. Among the deregulators' pet quarries are OSHA (Occupational Safety and Health Administration), with 3,000 employees and a $187 million budget; and the EPA (Environmental Protection Agency), some 11,000 strong with a bankroll of over $4.5 billion.

When OSHA was founded in 1970, it adopted standards so far-reaching and precise, that they took up two hundred and fifty pages of the federal registry. After evoking the ire of business and Congress alike, the gadfly agency pulled back some of its more arcane standards. However, issuing the standards turned out to be much easier than trying to revoke them. All kinds of foul things keep happening that convince the public of a need for tight regulations.

• Twenty-one workers were killed in Hallett, Oklahoma, when their fireworks factory exploded.
• An employee in a fast-food restaurant was left partially paralyzed. Her brain had been penetrated by a three-inch nail fired from a nail gun being used to do carpentry on the other side of a common wall.
• Stefan Golab, a Polish immigrant working for Film Recovery Systems near Chicago, lost his life when he was unknowingly exposed to cyanide poisoning.
• A driver for General Dynamics in Michigan died when he inhaled fumes from a solvent used to clean his vehicle.
• Seventeen employees were killed and twenty-two injured when two explosions rocked the Union Oil refinery at Romeoville, Illinois.

Work can be hazardous to your health, but it's not as dangerous as it used to be. In the ten years prior to OSHA's founding, the worker fatality rate dropped by 16 percent; the injury rate, 5 percent. The decade following OSHA's arrival saw fatality rates drop another 25 percent, and injuries 21 percent. We didn't need OSHA for workplaces to become safer: It was happening anyway. But workplaces became safer at a much faster rate after OSHA made its debut. Still, if cost-effectiveness interests you more than lives, you'd be justified in asking: Is the extra margin of safety worth the cost of producing it?

The answer seems to be yes. Aggregate costs of work accidents have grown sevenfold since 1960. Factoring in inflation and the expansion in the work force, we're still left with a 37-percent dollar increase per worker. (However, the average cost per worker has been dropping since it peaked in 1979, probably due to expansion of the labor force.)

The new entry into the workplace safety fray is occupational disease. Between 1979 and 1982, breathing ailments dominated the charts. But chemical poisoning—like Golab's—and asbestos contaminants made a strong showing, too. Exotic-sounding travails—byssinosis, silicosis, black lung—and cancer round out the picture.

Occupational diseases account for only 1 percent of workmen's compensation claims, but they're twice as costly as the more common broken legs and wrenched backs. But worse, they're slow in brewing, taking as long as forty years to display symptoms. At an average insurance payment of $12,500 per case, the toxic exposure of today's baby boom workers will cost us dearly in the next half century. If we exercise enough caution, we'll be able to reduce those costs for the baby boom "echo" generation that enters the labor force in the 1990s and early 2000s.

Cost/benefits notwithstanding, OSHA has not escaped the ax. Stripped of its teeth and committed leadership, workplace injuries and health problems rose a hefty 12 percent between 1983 and 1984. But don't expect to see an epidemic of poisoned and maimed workers: The courts are stepping in to fill the breach. As with bad drugs from pharmaceutical companies, for the first time corporate executives are being held criminally responsible for negligent deaths and injuries at the workplace.

Film Recovery Systems' president, plant manager, and foreman were well aware of hazardous plant conditions, said their judge. But they made little effort to warn their employees, many of whom spoke poor English. When Stefan Golab died of cyanide poisoning, the defendants were found guilty of murder.

At General Dynamics Corporation, managers were deemed responsible when one of their drivers was overcome by toxic fumes in his work vehicle. The charge was involuntary manslaughter.

In commenting on the new trend, John Coffee of Columbia University Law School dryly observed: "When you threaten the principal adequately, he will monitor the behavior of his agent." It boils down to regulation by court action rather than rulemaking. Quite effective, actually. The problem is, it's reactive rather than preventive.

□ □ □

In the meantime, new technologies—in which lethal chemicals are the catalyst or product of manufacturing processes—are creating increasingly hazardous work and environmental conditions. Love Canal has become synonymous with chemical contamination. That horrendous experience has been repeated at least 10,000 times across the country.

In 1984, the new owners of Circuitron Corporation, a Long Island electronics company, were shocked to discover that their factory was sitting on top of an eight-foot-wide well filled with highly toxic wastes. The previous owner had allegedly dumped millions of gallons of TCA, a solvent used in the semiconductor industry, into the ground. The toxin, which caused widespread water pollution in Silicon Valley, had now become one of New York's largest industrial pollution cases. In exchange for being relieved of the bureaucratic tangle of dumping wastes legally, corporate violators jeopardize our air, our water, our soil, and our lives.

In their book *Poisoning for Profit,* Alan Block and Frank Scarpitti disclose that organized crime has stepped in to capitalize on the crisis. The toxic waste industry evolved from the solid waste industry. Having taken over private garbage collection, it was easy for the mob to move into toxic dumping. As with so

many other white-collar crimes, this one could not persist without the cooperation of "law-abiding" people.

Enter the EPA. When the agency was first established, it had a tough, adversarial image: clear objectives, specific timetables, instructions for implementation. Everything possible was done to keep the agency "clean." Everyone knew
the deadlines and procedures for getting dioxin out of our rivers and carbon-
monoxide emissions out of our sky. But as one critic points out, the goals were
neither technologically nor economically feasible. As the economy worsened,
industry and workers were up in arms. Protecting the environment was costing
too much and achieving too little. Countless dollars were tied up in litigation,
and that seemed a highly unproductive use of capital.

The Reagan years witnessed the taming of the EPA. Managers who seemed
basically hostile to the mission of their agency were installed. At times, hostility
degenerated to downright conflict of interest. Clear violators were often not
investigated because of former business ties between EPA honchos and the
offending companies. What happened to the EPA is not unusual. Jack Douglas
and John Johnson, in their book *Official Deviance*, put it in no uncertain terms:
"The magnitude and significance of official deviance within regulatory and planning agencies is very great and will become even greater in the future. . . .
Bureaucratic agencies tend toward autonomy over time" and "become 'captured' by the very interests . . . they are supposed to regulate."

In *Myths That Cause Crime*, criminologists Harold Pepinsky and Paul Jesilow
argue that corporations lobby their regulators to pass rules that benefit them.
Indeed, the regulators often end up working for the companies they once regulated. In a separate article, Jesilow asserts: "The greater the number and complexity of legal enactments, the more these favor corporate giants, since litigation and the search for loopholes is the forte of big business." If we are to
believe the critics, regulatory agencies not only fail to stop crime against consumers; they may actually *provoke* it.

REAL ESTATE CRIME

Housing is another area in which consumers are ripe for shady dealings. An
older population means more households. Driven by divorce, death, low sex
ratios, and career, the average size of each household has steadily waned since
1900 while the number of households has surged, far outpacing the expansion of
our population. Since the dawn of the twentieth century, the population has
tripled but the number of households has quintupled. By 2025, projects the
Census Bureau, the population will have reached the 300-million mark, a near
doubling since just 1950. As our families shrink and disperse, we will need to
find new places to live and work in the far-flung megatropolises of the next
decades. We will be ready cat's-paws for real estate and construction swindles of
every ilk.

It is a truism that the amount of land remains constant while the population
keeps growing. But even when we reach zero population growth in 2050, sentiment will perpetuate an economy of scarcity, making some places more desirable

than others. It is in those desirable places that we will see land frauds. The retiree's fantasy of "a place in the sun," for example, has been the root of many worthless land sales. Since the early 1960s, Americans are purported to have lost some $100 million in the proverbial desert land scheme.

In choice locales we will see space shortages, especially among the poor. Carmen Torres' subsidized apartment scam is one outgrowth of a chronic housing deficit. But while she was swindling New York's poor, hordes of real estate agents, superintendents, and tenants were bleeding the middle class for a leg up on a rent-stabilized "4 rms, rv vu."

The Northeast, according to Department of Housing and Urban Development analyst Doug McGough, is historically the lowest producer of new housing starts in the country. Compounding the problem, New York's rental market had been squeezed to a pulp by the same conversion fever that had earlier swept cities like Chicago. Co-ops and condominiums became a highly lucrative area for plunder; and some of the city's most noted citizens were involved in real estate scandals.

Evangeline Gouletas, wife of the New York State's former governor, Hugh Carey, was viewed with suspicion when she married into New York's First Ladyhood. Her family owns American Invsco Corporation, a controversial real estate converter that controls some prime New York City property. Given the complaints that were later lodged with his office, the state attorney general, who must approve all conversions, would have been placed in an awkward position in ruling on Gouletas's transactions while her husband was still governor. Donald Trump, the city's enfant terrible of developers, was reamed in the press for allegedly trying to oust little old ladies from their homes in a Central Park South property he wanted to develop. John Zaccaro, husband of former vice presidential candidate Geraldine Ferraro, was sentenced to one hundred and fifty hours of community service for a fraudulent real estate transaction involving five Queens apartment buildings he wanted to buy and convert.

□ □ □

When supply is low and demand is high, the logical antidote is to increase the supply—and that takes money. Mortgages are the heart of the building industry. When lending rates are high, the industry languishes; when they drop, it revives. Rates peaked at over 15 percent in 1982 before inching downward. Meanwhile, the savings and loan institutions, whose bedrock was mortgage loans, ran into trouble: They found themselves stuck with reams of old paper on which they were taking in less in loan interest than they were paying out on deposits. You'd think they would have collapsed. Some of them did, but most have been buoyed by the federal government.

Today, according to Michael Rakosi, one of New York's smart, young, independent real estate entrepreneurs, these "bankrupt" financial institutions are racing to give out money: "Loans are becoming more and more liberal. Banks want to close loans because it's free money for them. They take their points and sell off the paper."

That helps explain what happened in early 1985, when Texas insurance officials brought suit against West Pac, a California mortgage brokerage company, for allegedly conspiring to sell mortgage-backed securities based on fraudulent loans. The securities deal fell apart when one of the principals defaulted on mortgage payments for Oxford Court apartments, a Houston area project slated for improvements and condominium conversion. Now the apartment complex stands abandoned and decaying; and BankAmerica, which acted as escrow agent for the deal, is out $37 million.

According to Rakosi, the old days when you and your neighborhood savings and loan became thirty-year partners on your house, are gone forever. Today, "Banks are acting as brokers." They turn right around and sell your mortgage to the government as part of a Fannie Mae or Ginnie Mae. "It becomes risk-free new capital," explains the real estate expert. With this incentive, "banks may fudge on applications." Rakosi chortles over a deal he was offered by a major commercial bank in which, for 25 percent down, no income verification was required. An applicant could pick a number out of the air and use it to leverage a huge loan for himself. "It's a license to steal!" Rakosi exclaims.

Sloppy verification may have encouraged John Zaccaro to doctor his loan application. In pitching Prudential-Bache, he inflated his net worth fivefold to $21 million and submitted a falsified sales contract for the buildings he wanted to finance.

Title companies are the key to determining who owns what property. Rakosi, who also teaches real estate, speaks of them with contempt and contends that their practices encourage fraud: "Title companies are slow, poorly run, and basically the collectors of premiums. If they make a mistake, they're not likely to own up to it. They have almost no verification procedures."

Charged with ensuring that the person claiming a piece of property is indeed its rightful owner, title companies must be part of every closing. As Rakosi explains it:

> Of all the closings I've been to, there's been only one verification of a person's name as it related to the ownership of the property. And that was done by producing a MasterCard. Why, that's hardly proof of anything except that he has the same last name as the owner of the house! Anybody can pretend they're anybody.
>
> Because of the tremendous money in the banking system, it would be easy to finance the same property three or four times within a very short time. Slow checks made by title companies mean information doesn't come up in the system for several weeks. You could get a couple of million dollars and disappear.

☐ ☐ ☐

Assuming a developer doesn't take the money and run, construction can begin. And begin it did in New York City. After a long lull, the mid-1980s saw the Big Apple's streets aswarm with cranes, rigs, cement mixers, and scaffolding. Construction workers, whose ranks had been dwindling nationwide since 1979, were going back to work. In many cases that only encouraged more dirty practices.

George Morrison is an operating engineer. In 1984, his base pay of about $60,000 had ballooned to more than six times that amount, making him the highest-paid construction worker in the city. Investigators felt something was amiss. Here's what they learned: Under a collective bargaining agreement, unions are allowed to designate workers like George as supervisors with the title of master mechanic or working foreman. Major construction sites, like the sprawling Jacob K. Javits Convention Center and the landfill known as Battery Park City, employ operating engineers around the clock to run heavy equipment. The master mechanics who supervise them are theoretically on call as long as any member of their union is working on overtime. This arrangement assures Morrison and one hundred and fifty of his colleagues of thousands of hours of double and triple overtime pay each year, whether they're on site or not. George, for example, was reportedly paid overtime while vacationing in Acapulco, St. Martin, Europe, and South Carolina. Irregular? Yes. But not illegal.

However, scratch the surface and you'll find a crime for which consumers pay. Construction supervisors are members of the powerful Teamsters Union. Contracts such as Morrison's are enforced by organized crime through its influence on the Union. Building is a multibillion-dollar game, and the Teamsters have the muscle to slow down, expedite, or wreck any construction project. At New York State hearings, real estate developers testified that extortionate collective-bargaining agreements were the price they had to pay for labor peace. Edward McDonald, an Organized Crime Task Force official, is quoted as saying, "Corrupt labor leaders, who are often tied in with organized crime, have these people over a barrel." State investigators disclosed that featherbedding like George Morrison's had boosted New York's construction costs by more than $11 million in 1984. In a separate investigation, bid-rigging and overcharges in the mob-linked concrete industry were alleged to cost the construction trade an additional $40 million to $50 million a year. The price tag landed squarely on the leases of the consumers who pay Gotham's fabled rents.

☐ ☐ ☐

Once a building is ready for occupancy, it invites still more crooked dealings in lease negotiations and moving costs. While the State Commission of Investigation was holding featherbedding hearings in Manhattan, a second group was being indicted across the river in Brooklyn. The mob tocsin was sounded again, this time involving racketeering in the moving and storage industry. Charges were leveled against seventeen people, including some top officials of a Teamsters local and the reputed head of the Bonanno crime family. Here, too, the carrot had been "labor peace"—and consumers paid.

At the same time that racketeering charges were crisscrossing the city, New York City sued its convicted former chief negotiator of leases for extorting $1.5 million from landlords eager to have municipal agencies as tenants. During a four-year period, starting in 1979, Alex Liberman was alleged to have taken individual bribes of $5,000 to more than $400,000. Bribes of that size are ultimately amortized through higher rents.

A similar scenario can be played for residential housing. A HUD insider amazed me with the news that, nationally, the home vacancy rate is at a twenty-year high. While the market is tight in the Northeast (partly due to migration back to the Frost Belt), almost everywhere else there's a glut.

□ □ □

Once we've moved into a building, we expect it to protect us from the elements. Construction standards determine if it will. In 1985 the federal government began to dismantle a system of mandated building codes that dates back to 1934. Embodied in a five-volume tome, *Minimum Property Standards,* they specified health, safety, livability, and marketability criteria to which builders had to conform if they wanted to be eligible for VA and FHA loans. A HUD spokesperson assured me that a core of general health and safety standards from *M.P.S.* have been preserved, but the details are being left to the states and the free market. However, if local standards are nonexistent or unacceptable, the federal government retains the power to impose one of three nationally recognized codes.

The HUD specialist explained, "This is deregulation that is not deregulation." Nevertheless, he added, "It's an effort to put more responsibility into the private sector." Citing the "wonderful set of checks and balances" in the building industry, he was certain the experiment would cause no serious damage. "Anything that we undo legislatively can be recast if it doesn't work."

The federal code specifies some minimum requirements that address security: locks on doors and windows, durable exterior locks with at least a half-inch throw. These paltry guidelines have been retained for multifamily dwellings but deleted for single family houses. *Minimum Property Standards* doesn't deal with commercial structures at all.

Unless local regulations take up the slack, we can't be assured of even a modicum of protection. Those locales least able to afford building in their own standards will be the ones in greatest danger. Northeastern cities and states, which have a long history of their own detailed building codes, won't feel the absence of the federal standards. But, in the developing areas of the South and West, codes are less strict. Without rudimentary security provisions, consumers could be killed, injured, or robbed because of negligent construction.

And don't attorneys know it! The size and number of personal injury lawsuits have skyrocketed since 1962, when the first historic million-dollar verdict was rendered. To indemnify ourselves against such judgements, we are spending seven times more premium dollars now than we did then.

Most of the action is in liability claims. Submerged in those is a new type of prosecution: failure to protect against crime and trespassing. Since 1958, landlords, retailers, hotels, hospitals, private schools, government agencies, and others have been sued nearly 200 times for "inadequate security." Damage awards have catapulted to a rate 17 times higher than inflation. Most of the incidents took place in apartments, parking lots, hallways, and hotel/motel rooms, making landlords—whose liability has swelled by 1,000 percent—the greatest losers.

Transitions in our need for shelter and work space are opening new crime markets. Every aspect of the real estate industry is up for grabs and we, the consumers, are its fair game.

LEISURE SERVICE CRIMES

After health and shelter, leisure is the new growth area for fraud. Since 1850, our stock of time-off from jobs has increased by 34.6 hours a week. Even after you factor in moonlighting, part-time jobs, and commuting, we come up with a net gain of 18 hours. Although in the past two decades, the average workweek for manufacturing workers has tended to stay high, it has decreased by four hours for other workers. Manufacturing jobs are dwindling, the service sector skyrocketing—making a somewhat shorter workweek the norm for the future.

The steady upward creep of the "compressed" workweek (4½ days or less) will augment our free time. Add the swelling masses of people who stay at home —retirees, single mothers with young children—and you can see that leisure industries face a bright future. But one stands to inherit the windfall more than others: television. Most of the leisure activities that people used to pursue outside their home—sports, theater, music, shopping—are now available in their living room with the push of a remote control button.

A 1983 National Opinion Research Center poll revealed that three quarters of its respondents spend between two and nine hours in front of a television screen on an average day. Neilson figures show that people over fifty-five, the most prolific tube-gazers, spend the equivalent of a 35- to 41-hour workweek in front of their sets. Vying for preeminence in filling those hours are a multitude of providers:

- Video cassette recorders, now numbering about 25 million and selling at the rate of 20,000 a day, are gobbling up network audience shares.
- Backyard earth stations, 750,000 of them propagating at the rate of 30,000 to 40,000 a month, are hijacking the cable and broadcast signals that were supposed to be the lucrative province of direct broadcast satellites.
- Pay television, which peaked at 1.4 million subscribers in 1982, has dwindled to 560,000 homes, bested by the lure of low-cost movie rentals for VCRs.
- Low-power TV stations are stuck in a regulatory logjam of thousands of FCC applications, and a proviso that prohibits them from encroaching on full-power TV markets.
- Cable systems, which whipped through the top of the graphs for their first few years, have now exhibited some spectacular failures. Today their growth is slower, but still steady. Deregulation promises to remove obstacles to wiring large cities, and subscriber revenues are expected to double by 1993.

Among these, three gainers emerge for the future: home VCRs, backyard earth stations, and cable systems—precisely those technologies that are most susceptible to theft. In the war for viewer attention, they have spawned a new breed of bandit; the video pirate. Cable systems provide the booty that VCRs and home satellite dishes plunder. Home Box Office and other major operators are fighting looters with scrambling and decoding devices. The spoils, however, will be too rich for privateers to resist.

In 1984, the deputy attorney general of Pennsylvania made a speech to the National Cable Television Association. He described how pirates in the Scranton area had been ripping off HBO signals by making illegal cable hookups. State agents caught them climbing telephone poles and dropping lines into clients' homes. Search warrants later surfaced a stash of illegal decoders as well. The cable marauders had stolen HBO services on behalf of 1,800 residents. Similar accounts were echoed in Florida, California, and elsewhere in the country. It was estimated that in 1983 alone, theft cost the cable industry close to $400 million in revenues.

By 1985, a landmark measure was introduced in California meting out tough penalties for buying or selling illegal decoders. Consumers could be fined $1,000 or jailed for ninety days; pirates, held liable for treble damages to cable operators plus additional damages of up to $5,000. "Pay TV pirates are no different from any other criminal who sells fraudulent, counterfeit merchandise," announced California State Senator Joseph Montoya.

Some of us like to spend our leisure time traveling around the world. Planes are the most efficient means for doing so. Yet, 1985 was the worst year ever for commercial aviation, with 16 accidents and more than 1,400 deaths as of early September. A Delta flight crashed in Dallas. A Midwest Express plane plummeted earthward in Milwaukee. A commuter plane carrying Samantha Smith, our goodwill ambassador to the Soviet Union, crashed in New England. A Pratt & Whitney engine broke up in a British Airtours jet. The airframe in a Japan Airlines 747 failed. An Air India 747 exploded in midair. Later in the year, an Arrow Air charter plane carrying our troops home from the Middle East disintegrated near Gander Air Force Base in Iceland. American-built parts and planes were going down everywhere. Some of these catastrophes were preventable.

The FAA responded by ordering a broad inspection of jet engines and slapping heavy fines on airlines. That may take care of errant Pratt & Whitneys, but it doesn't address the problem of wind shears, which dropped the Delta plane in Dallas. "Unlike most air disasters," said a New York *Times* editorial, "the Delta crash . . . was the result of a serious problem with a clear solution." The article then went on to accuse the FAA of dragging its feet on installing Doppler-effect radar, which was known to pinpoint wind shears. The reason? Jurisdiction fights and money. The *Times* diatribe went on to quote a budget official who callously said, "More people were killed on motorcycles last week. How safe is safe?" In other words, the airline industry has such a good record overall that it doesn't find it cost effective to add an extra margin of surety.

That's hard to fathom. I was a network correspondent for NBC News at the time that an American DC-10 crashed near Chicago's O'Hare Airport. An improperly maintained engine that fell off after takeoff caused the calamity. A dear friend of mine was on that plane. In the newsroom when the first live scenes of the crash site came in on our closed circuit monitors, I scanned the footage for some sign of her. There was nothing but rubble. People can survive motorcycle accidents, but nobody could have survived this. Judy's sparkle, beauty, and talent were stolen by a wayward engine and inadequate inspections. We have the means to save future Judys, but the powers charged with doing so have put a cost/benefit ratio on her life. Once again, the cleanup is left to litigators.

In his article "Lethal Smokescreen," writer Dan Berger charges that the FAA has allowed the airline industry to regulate itself. He cites a 1975 congressional subcommittee that condemned the FAA as having an action record so abysmal that it "may actually endanger human life." The FAA has the power to do better. It can issue various levels of rulings that range from wishy-washy service bulletins to intimidating Airworthiness Directives. When an AD comes down, writes Berger, it means "act and act now." "Action," however, can be expensive to airlines, so the FAA is often reluctant to use its ace in the hole. Its hesitation has lost lives.

"So," concludes Berger, "for the moment, airline passengers concerned with their safety can only continue to do what they have always done: sit near an exit, read the directions in the pocket in front of them, not drink or smoke and pray. The laws that protect them have not yet been passed."

□ □ □

Some of us find it safer to spend free hours on the ground tooling around in our cars. But even there—especially there—we're subject to fraud. An ingenious analysis of criminogenic market forces by William Leonard and Marvin Weber, contributors to a 1977 book, *White Collar Crime,* shows why the automobile industry is prone to cheat consumers. Concentrated market conditions and heightened barriers to entering the industry are the causes.

In 1921, there were 81 American car manufacturers; today, there are only four. There has not been a single successful contender since Chrysler entered the fray in 1925. (If it weren't for Lee Iacocca and his Uncle Sam, Chrysler might not have survived either.) These manufacturers pour millions into annual design changes and extravagant advertising campaigns in an attempt to whet our appetites for the latest in aerodynamic motoring. To be profitable, a car maker must have a titanic sales volume—at least 250,000 autos a year. A small company can't compete. That's what Leonard and Weber mean by "heightened barriers."

The Big Three and the little Fourth have managed to sew up the domestic car market for themselves. They don't sell by direct marketing, but through dealers. A dealer doesn't get an exclusive franchise in a territory. All he gets is a location, which is largely owned by the manufacturer. In order to keep it, he has to meet a sales quota. Many don't make it. According to Leonard and Weber, the number of franchised domestic car dealers shrunk by 35 percent between

1954 and 1968. The ones that survived got fatter, while the demise of others enhanced the manufacturers' span of control. That's an example of "concentrated market conditions."

What's a dealer to do? He's hog-tied. If he wants to sell Ford cars, he has to go along with Ford's terms. And Ford wants sales. So he becomes sales-oriented. Crooked dealers, eager to increase sales, have their own specialties: jacking up used-car prices, turning back odometers, selling fleet cars as executive cars, and forcing unwanted accessories on buyers. Maintenance and repairs get downgraded to nuisance status.

Meanwhile, the shrinkage in franchises has left a host of orphan cars in need of service. In the absence of dealer outlets, owners go to independent shops and garages. What they find there is a shortage of mechanics. In the 1950s, there was 1 mechanic for every 80 cars on the road; by 1968, it was 1 per 130. Dishonest service departments and independents overcharge for services, sell rebuilt parts for new, do unnecessary repairs, and bill for repairs that were never done. According to one study, we spend more than $40 billion a year to maintain our cars; about $2 billion of it is siphoned off by cheats. When it comes to service, it's been a seller's market and we've been getting hoodwinked ever since.

□ □ □

The trend in corporate mergers will replicate these conditions in other industries. Bolstered by a deregulatory climate that enables large corporations to relax consumer protection standards, white-collar criminals will have a field day.

Adam Smith disapproved of corporations, believing that management should be personally liable for the outcomes of their actions. He relied on pure economic self-interest to keep them honest. Like his antithesis, Karl Marx, Smith believed that legislation (read regulation) simply pandered to the interests of the powerful. Unlike Marx, he believed that business crime would not exist were it not for restraints on the free market. Commerce is no longer dominated by the intimate entities that fueled Adam Smith's theories. Today's corporate behemoths find regulatory agencies a convenient, if pesky, foil. They satisfy public clamor while ensuring that supervision will be minimal.

Effective regulation seems to have been dumped in the laps of negligence lawyers and federal prosecutors. By striking fear into the hearts of white-collar wearers of black hats, they whip us into responsible behavior. It's not the best way, but it is one way, to stop consumers from getting taken.

CRIMEWARPS

- Starting in about 1995, the baby boom generation will begin to acquire the diseases of aging. Medical quackery will increase.
- Due to increased longevity and environmental hazards, the death rate from cancer has risen steadily since 1900, despite dramatic advances in treatment. Bogus cancer remedies will continue to dominate quack medicine.
- As HMOs proliferate, medical insurance fraud will diminish and doctors'

fees will rise more slowly. Lower real income combined with escalating malpractice insurance rates will render medicine a less-attractive career option. Ensuing shortages of highly qualified physicians will create openings for impostors.

· The number of households being formed will continue to outpace population growth, but at a slower rate. Decreased divorce and increased marriage rates are putting the brakes on household formation. But so is a tight economy that discourages youngsters from forming premarriage independent households or buying homes. The smaller size of the baby boom "echo" also presages slower household formation.

All this adds up to a housing glut. The regions with the largest surplus will be those with the highest rate of housing starts—for example, the Sunbelt. In this buyer's market, high pressure and/or dishonest sales practices will prevail. Corruption hazards and dishonest financing schemes will multiply as speculators and developers try to make good on their investments. Inferior building standards, relative to the Northeast, will generate high rates of liability suits.

· In the Northeast, where housing starts are the lowest in the country, vacancy rates will remain extremely low. The resulting seller's market will stimulate price gouging, graft, tenant harassment and labor irregularities.

· Inadequate verification procedures will encourage mortgage fraud—especially in the Northeast, where real estate values are highest.

· Federal deregulation will be replaced by state regulation. However, reduced federal, state, and municipal budgets will reduce the resources regulatory agencies have available to monitor their charges. Enforcement will suffer and criminal violations will increase.

· Litigation will impose far more severe penalties on violators than do regulatory agencies. Therefore, the courts will be the prime deterrents against large-scale white-collar crime.

Cheating

Late in 1984, a decommissioned stockbroker joined the "respectable" rogues gallery. Federal authorities charged that James Masiello, 37, swindled about $1 million from friends, neighbors, and even his own mother. Although the Securities and Exchange Commission had barred him from working as a stockbroker years earlier, Masiello continued to lure his victims into bogus stock partnerships.

He baited the hook by creating an aura of wealth and class about himself. Posing as a successful investor, he moved into a rented house on "Millionaire's Row" in Greenwich, Connecticut. He polished up his pedigree by falsely claiming a Harvard education and an army commission.

Masiello was sentenced to fifteen years in prison and made to pay a hefty fine. He joins other convicted white-collar crime notables whose schemes are responses to economic exigencies.

Inflation-adjusted per capita income has risen 75 percent since 1960, leaving a net gain in disposable income to be spent, invested, sheltered, and insured. For those who have assets, efforts to enlarge and protect them leave us open to a vast array of financial frauds.

Banker Jake Butcher, tax shelter promoter Edward Markowitz, the check-kiters at E. F. Hutton, bill-padders at General Electric and General Dynamics have all taken advantage of our vulnerability as individuals and a nation. But victims of perceived and actual fraud can revolt. Using cunning and the courts, they're getting even by cheating the faceless institutions that permeate our lives.

Most of these "criminals" are otherwise honest citizens, yet they gouge organizations with finely honed weapons: theft of services, insurance fraud, pension fraud, tax evasion. As our lives become ever more entwined with massive, impersonal bureaucracies, the inhibitions against defrauding the systems that provide, invest, insure, and tax our assets will diminish.

INVESTMENT FRAUD

James Masiello, the "Greenwich swindler," was more than ready to help his prosperous neighbors dispose of their excess income with phony investment deals. But even "safe" government bonds are prone to shady practices. In 1985, the back-to-back failures of E.S.M. Government Securities, Inc. and Bevill, Bresler Schulman Management caused worldwide reverberations. The two unregulated dealers were accused, among other things, "of using the same collateral for multiple transactions." When you think about it, that's not much different than kiting checks. By the time the dust settled, banks and municipalities had allegedly lost $600 million.

No sooner had the E.S.M. and Bevill frauds been discovered, than the headlines exploded with E. F. Hutton's multimillion-dollar cash "float" extravaganza. By juggling billions of dollars among a galaxy of bank accounts, the brokerage firm was able to write more checks than its balances could cover. In the process, Hutton garnered an $8-million bonanza of extra interest in a twenty-month period. When caught, E. F. Hutton talked and the government listened: The company pleaded guilty to 2,000 felony counts of wire and mail fraud.

In July 1985, William Safire wrote a column in which he broke the story of some doings at Prudential-Bache. A compliance officer had observed that the company's in-house mutual fund—which was "supposedly following recommendations of the firm's research department"—had been "improperly handled." In about twenty trades, noted the officer, the fund actually moved *against* the firm's recommendations. In a score of others, it used the firm's information before recommendations were released to other Prudential-Bache customers. (In the case of one advance buy, the research department subsequently raised its earnings estimate of the stock.) Finally, there were instances of violations of the firm's forty-eight-hour-rule against trading stocks that might pose a conflict of interest.

Prudential-Bache explained to Safire that the mutual fund's trades were proper. You can't manage a portfolio, paraphrased the columnist, "by slavishly following all research recommendations." But it's hard to argue wth Safire's rejoinder: "At the least, investors are entitled to fuller disclosure of the interests and activities of Pru-Bache's advisers, especially when the firm's fund is unloading a stock it is encouraging its customers to buy."

In 1986, Wall Street's crime-of-the-year award went to a managing director at Drexel Burnham, who had masterminded a vast insider trading scheme. His sparkling career, along with that of a host of his fellow "yuppies" at other firms, came to an abrupt halt when the shady dealings were revealed.

Scandals like these evoke the ire of the Securities and Exchange Commission, which monitors a host of misdeeds. The preceding paragraphs have illustrated most of them—misrepresentation, misappropriation, self-dealing, manipulation, investment schemes, registration violations, improper sales techniques—in several combinations. As a rule, the SEC prefers to respond to confirmed illegality with administrative rather than criminal sanctions. However, when violations are vast, complex, ongoing, and extremely damaging, the SEC turns them over to the courts. Those referrals have doubled since 1968, indicating that investment crimes are getting more serious.

TAX FRAUD

Taxes, along with death, are the proverbial inescapable facts of life. Yet, thousands of us try to escape them through sheltering money and/or underreporting income. The government has been kind enough to help us out with the former. We've been granted IRAs, Keoghs, profit-sharing plans, and annuities that defer taxes until we get closer to death. But the well of legitimate nonretirement tax shelters has steadily dried up.

Nevertheless, there are plenty of illicit schemes for keeping your money out of the government's pockets. One of the biggest scammers to get caught in 1985 was Edward Markowitz, a thirty-five-year-old financial promoter. More than one hundred investors are reported to have turned some $20 million over to Markowitz for trading in government securities. *That* part was legitimate. Later, however, the promoter admitted to creating sham transactions to make it look as if his partnerships had taken whopping losses. Those losses were translated into $445 million in fraudulent income tax deductions. His clients—who, among others, included Woody Allen, Dick Cavett, Erica Jong, Bill Murray, Frank Langella, and Alexander Cohen—not only lost most of their investments but had to cough up fortunes in back taxes.

In the sweeping tax reforms of 1986, the stream of deductible items evaporated along with potential tax shelters, leaving us with the traditional evasion of underreporting income.

Edmund Wilson, a former intelligence agent who allegedly sold $50 million worth of arms to Libya, apparently never shared his ill-gotten gains with the government. In 1983, however, the IRS stepped in to claim $21 million in back taxes and penalties.

Two years later, high-fashion clothing designer Albert Nipon was tripped up by the government. He pleaded guilty after he bribed two mercenary IRS agents to overlook his falsified 1978 tax returns. Those returns declared that Nipon had personally earned only $32,000 in taxable income when he had, in fact, netted

$884,000. The difference between taxes paid and taxes owed came to nearly a half million dollars. His corporate tax discrepancies were even greater.

Wilson and Nipon are not unique. Underreporting has long been a favorite maneuver of mobsters, drug dealers, barterers, prostitutes, independent contractors, taxi drivers, waiters, free-lancers, cash-only physicians, and mom-and-pop store proprietors—in short, just about anyone who is privy to some source of income that doesn't show up on a W-2 or 1099 tax form. In New York State alone, cheating on taxes is said to be a billion-dollar racket. In announcing a crackdown, the head of the state tax commission pointed to some telling illustrations: 91 doctors, who had not filed returns, owed an estimated $17.6 million; 1,800 other underreporters owed more than $70 million.

The Lipman Report averred in 1983, "as much as 40% of self-employed income goes unreported." A recent recession left many people jobless. Necessity spurred the invention of a cacophony of new small businesses. Unemployment rates have dropped, but cottage industry and sole proprietorship formation has persisted. An increase in old people and female-headed households has created a vast market for work-at-home enterprises, and the democratization of the computer has provided the means to start new businesses. With their low visibility and informality, it's easy for small businesses to fall below the radar range of regulatory agencies and tax collectors.

Since the latest recession subsided, job growth has been phenomenal. Temporary employees—one solution to the multitudes of low-level jobs crying to be filled—will be a source of criminal innovation. Newsman Mark Monsky cites cases in which "temps" use their real social security numbers only so long as their wages remain below taxable levels. After that, they use phony numbers and names for other jobs. As each identity reaches the tax breakpoint, it is discarded and a new one assumed. Accumulated earnings may be substantial, but divided as they are among a series of low income identities, no taxes are paid.

Nationally, since 1973 the growth in unreported income from all sources has increased slightly, with the tax gap in illegal activities being larger and spreading faster than in legal ones. While the IRS no longer estimates revenues lost from crime, it continues to track the ways in which "honest" people cheat and it has concluded that we cheat plenty. Congress has taken corrective steps. The Tax Equity and Fiscal Responsibility Act of 1982 is directed at those who hide their income from tips, bury the interest and dividends from their stocks and bonds, and just plain lie about their regular income. The Tax Reform Act of 1984 tries to keep us honest about our business deductions and protect us—and the IRS— from crooked shelters like Ed Markowitz's. The latest round of tax legislation cuts overall tax rates, thereby reducing the incentive to cheat. The data are not yet in on how TEFRA and the Tax Reform Acts have affected tax evasion, but we do know that levies collected on tips have risen by about $1 billion. However, given the ingenious ability of people to get around all tax regulations, increases are likely to be temporary.

But there are two big guns in reserve: the Bank Secrecy Act of 1970, which requires banks to report large deposits of cash along with its movement in or out of the country, and the 1970 RICO statute, which allows the government to go after the assets of those who engage in patterns of racketeering. RICO and the Bank Secrecy Act are often our best weapons against major offenders.

The Bank Secrecy Act has been sufficiently porous that even so grand an institution as the Bank of Boston saw fit to become a money laundry. In 1985 it pleaded guilty to a felony for failing to report $1.22 billion in cash swaps with Swiss banks. Some Florida banks, eager to cash in on drug millions, are notorious for unblinking acceptance of wrinkled street bills brought in by the suitcase- and shopping bag-full. According to *The Lipman Report*, "Syndicate gangsters are the most experienced of the users of money laundries. The use of average citizens . . . is quite small. Similarly, large corporations are probably not heavy users, because they would have too much to lose if caught. Nevertheless, available evidence indicates that laundering of money, by all types of users, is increasing."

RICO, on the other hand, has become the sweetheart of federal prosecutors. Created as a tool to pursue organized crime, this fissionable legislation has far surpassed its initial scope. With the blessings of the Supreme Court, RICO is now invoked to cover everything from the grubby Hell's Angels to straight-laced Coopers & Lybrands. There's no good way to tell how many would-be frauds RICO stops dead in their tracks, but one thing is clear: RICO has both the underworld and upperworld running scared.

PENSION FRAUD

Medical advances have assured many of us of a long life, and we will require longer lasting income sources in order to subsist. The line at the annuity window will lengthen steadily through 2050. Standing in the shadows will be a motley array of pension abuses.

Uniformed services are a case in point. According to the Better Government Association, one out of every four American fire and police officers retires on a disability. Of the $200 million in claims paid to them each year, BGA contends that at least 10 percent is undeserved. The implications of such fraud for cities like New York and Seattle are mind-boggling. Between 1970 and 1980, 70 percent and 86 percent, respectively, of those two cities' firefighters left work on a disability.

Asserting that similar pension abuse is rife in the social security disability program, the Reagan administration slashed the recipient rolls. Critics cried "Overkill!" and, with the help of the courts, many deserving pensioners fought their way back. In the future, as people work longer and health and safety regulations grow weaker, the propensity for making disability claims will increase. A proportionate number of claims will be fraudulent.

Nondisability pensions are equally subject to abuse. Some civil service systems compute retirement allotments on total salary earned in the last few years on the job. For those occupations, like uniformed services, which pay employees for overtime, this is a real boondoggle.

During my years in government, colleagues who were winding down their careers would often boast of putting in as much overtime as possible in order to inflate their pensions. The practice may have been sly, but it wasn't criminal. In the future, however, supervisors' power to assign overtime may well be a temptation for bribery.

While some beneficiaries rip off government or private pensions, others become *victims* of pension abuse. Prior to the enactment of ERISA (Employee Retirement Income Security Act) and the PBGC (Pension Benefit Guarantee Corporation), many retirees found themselves high and dry just when a lifelong pension was due to pay off; now, their assets are protected. However, an expanding range of private retirement options—IRA, Keogh, profit-sharing—is creating huge pools of money ripe for embezzling and tax evasion.

Parity plans, in particular, provide opportunities for pillage. Operationalized in 1984, the plans put sole proprietors on a par with corporations. By allowing participants to self-administer their retirement income and act as their own trustee, the middleman—often a large bank or brokerage house—is removed and a measure of oversight is lost. Most owners of parity plans are self-employed. According to *The Lipman Report*, a security newsletter, "The IRS estimates that self-employed persons are among the worst offenders with regard to evasion of taxes."

INSURANCE FRAUD

Investments, tax shelters, and pension plans are three of the ways we protect and build our capital. But the reverse side of having money is spending it—on cars, houses, jewelry, office equipment, hired help, and an infinite array of other goods and services. We invest so much in our material well-being, that most of us can't afford to replace it. Nor can we afford the loss of income and unplanned expenses that come with falling off a ladder, getting pinned under a car, or falling prey to terminal cancer. We buy peace of mind with insurance.

Businesses and individuals reassure themselves with $100 billion in property and casualty premiums and $5 billion in life insurance—a six- and eight-fold increase since 1960. The cost of the things we insure has only tripled since that time, so inflation alone doesn't explain our insurance glut. Rather, we earn more and own more. Our lives are longer and therefore worth more.

We have a love-hate relationship with our insurers. We count on them to bail us out of crisis and loss, but in our heart of hearts, we believe they're fleecing us. Andrew Tobias, in his book *The Invisible Bankers*, gave eloquent voice to all the resentments we feel when that $900 premium falls due. In his blistering attack on the industry, he accused them of being too big, too profitable, both too fast and too slow to pay.

As a consultant and an insured, my experiences with the industry have, for the most part, been good. Harboring an initial distrust of them, I've been astounded at how many honest agents I've met. There was one who bailed me out of a dumb real estate investment. Another talked me out of buying one of his own lines because he felt it wasn't a good deal. A third showed me exactly where I was wasting money. I also have only good things to say about the upright corporate citizens with whom I've worked in the industry's executive suites.

But that much-maligned industry is in trouble. For the past thirty years, the profitability of the property and casualty industry has held below the average for all American industries. In 1984, it hit rock bottom. I've worked with a number of insurance concerns. What happened to them illustrates what's going on in the industry: Commercial Union Insurance laid off 3,000 workers; the Insurance Information Institute shed 10 percent of its employees; Independent Insurance Agents of America, which held its own through most of the crisis years, found itself tightening its belt for the 1986 fiscal year. The major source of these woes is the white-collar cheating you've been reading about in this book.

For years, the industry's combined ratio (the figure used to measure its profitability) has been colored bright red. The biggest losses have been in the liability lines that cover people for asbestos poisoning, environmental pollution, malpractice, car accidents, and the like. In 1984, underwriters paid out $150 in claims for every $100 they took in. But as Tobias correctly points out, investment income more than offsets their underwriting losses.

Leaning on investments leaves the industry in a no-growth situation in which it must, at times, invade the reserves set aside to cover claims. Thanks to the rash of liability suits, those claims have become almost impossible to predict and plan for. "Courts, in the past several years, have been extending areas of liability," explains Charles "Bud" Clark of the Insurance Information Institute. "Awards are getting higher and higher and more and more liabilities are being found. Courts are finding ways to construe insurance policies [to pay for damages they were never intended to cover] so that the victim can get compensation."

Asbestos suits drove the Manville Corporation into bankruptcy. Dalkon Shield claims pushed A. H. Robbins Co. into Chapter Eleven. Wide-scale litigation is threatening to do the same to other companies and the insurers who indemnify them. The problem has gotten so bad, says Clark, that Lloyd's of London has threatened to pull out of the American reinsurance market.

Gargantuan liability awards are threatening to kill the goose that laid the golden egg, but it is automobile insurance (which also includes liability coverage) that generates the major volume of claims. Commercial and personal auto lines together account for nearly half of property and casualty premiums. The P&C industry is divided into commercial and personal insurance lines. Commercial policies—comprised of auto, general liability, workers' compensation, and multi-peril packages—produce slightly less than half the premiums received. Personal policies—homeowners, auto, and a sprinkling of "other" coverage—bring in 51 percent of the premiums paid.

The combined ratio for commercial markets has remained depressed despite higher liability premiums, but it has started to break even in the personal ones. The reason is that, for the first time in years, premium rates for cars and homes have begun to catch up with and surpass the consumer price index. While that's good for the industry in one sense, it's bad in another. "My personal belief," comments Clark, "is that increased premiums cause people to make more fraudulent and inflated claims."

Phony claims are a major problem for the industry. The number generally bandied about is that 15 to 20 percent of all claims are frauds. Fraud is rare in the commercial lines, declares Clark; the size of those claims exposes them to careful scrutiny. Most of the false claims come from personal lines—where rigged car crashes, auto thefts, slip-and-fall scams, and inflated burglary claims are rife. Because homeowners and noncommercial auto claims are relatively small, it's often more economical to pay them off than investigate them.

Clark feels that giving out easy money encourages litigiousness. "Say it's going to cost $5,000 to defend against this claim. I can avoid high court costs by offering the guy $1,000 to let it go. He takes $600 and his lawyer takes $400." He condemns such practices as the single biggest drain on the insurance business. "In the long run, it will cost companies a hell of a lot more. But, in terms of this year's bottom line, it's going to cost them less. And people's jobs and salaries are based on this year's bottom line."

Despite taking the low road to settling often phony claims, many insurance companies have set up in-house fraud units. These are backed up by five industry-wide investigative bodies. Most states have joined the fraud hunt by enacting immunity laws that allow insurers to prosecute fraud suspects without being exposed to lawsuits if there's no conviction.

The first line of defense is a computer that cross-checks claims:

- Has the same person made several claims?
- Has the same item been the subject of multiple claims?
- Does the claimant hold similar policies with several companies?
- Is the policy recently written?
- Are the claimants in an accident all being treated by the same doctor?
- Is the item being claimed very expensive compared to the face amount of the policy?
- Did the reported burglary take place while the claimant was on vacation?
- Would a person really have lost a sable coat on a plane bound for Hawaii?
- Can a person be suffering from an injured back if he was seen playing two hours of tennis?
- Was business bad for the two years prior to the fire that destroyed a claimant's restaurant?

Any of these queries can signal a fraud, and the industry has become pretty sophisticated in detecting deceit. Insurance fraud is now a felony in many states. The following gleanings from the New York *Times* show that some startling arrests have ensued.

- Los Angeles: A ring of Hungarian immigrants—including lawyers, an actor, and a bank executive—were caught in auto insurance swindles totaling as much as $400 million.

- Greenville, Texas: Two former cops were reported to have been part of a ring that rigged fake accidents.
- Columbia, South Carolina: A doctor and a lawyer, both members of their county council, were found guilty of falsifying medical reports in an insurance swindle.
- Chicago: The owner of a driving school pleaded guilty to cheating eight insurance companies out of $1 million in inflated accident claims.
- Charles City, Iowa: The head of a ten-member ring took out 455 insurance policies to cover phony accidents. Another member beat up the "victims" (with their prior consent) in order to make their claims look convincing.
- New York City: One hundred and twenty-two people, including 96 "law-abiding citizens" were netted in an auto ring that disposed of unwanted autos. Middlemen would "steal" the cars, cannibalize them, and reap huge profits from selling off the parts. Their clients were content to sit back and collect checks from their insurance companies.

Insurance companies are fair game for middle-class cheats who wouldn't dream of committing a "real" crime. Often, they believe that no one is really hurt. After all, insurance companies are rich; they've been taking our money all these years. Why not cash in on some of it? This kind of thinking is especially tempting when people hold policies that are more valuable than the property they cover.

But the raw truth is that people *do* get hurt. People die in arsons and get injured in staged accidents. Insurers build their losses right into our premiums and honest policy holders end up subsidizing crooked ones. We all pay, one way or the other.

CRIMEWARPS

- The swelling proportion of older, more affluent people requiring financial services will enhance the market for investment fraud.
- Income tax evasion will increase at times of high un- and underemployment when people are forced to turn to cottage industries and sole proprietorships.
- Income tax evasion will increase as legitimate opportunities to shelter and deduct income dwindle.
- Pension abuse will peak in 2010 to 2020, when the baby boom generation approaches retirement.
- Successful insurance fraud will decrease as antifraud units proliferate. With the advent of centralized computerized records, fraudulent claims are relatively easy to detect.
- Liability claims will increase. The kinds of "crimes"—for example, health and safety hazards, or professional malpractice—that might be adjudicated through the criminal courts will be resolved through personal injury and product safety litigation instead.

• Conversely, some areas of liability underwriting will become unprofitable and these will have to be adjudicated through other means. Pollution risks, liquor liability exposures, day-care center exposures, medical malpractice, high limit coverage for industrial concerns, asbestos removal from schools, commercial fishing boats, and municipal liability are areas in which many insurance companies are leaving the marketplace. This will force many industries to self-insure. If claims against them outstrip their coverage, they will be forced into bankruptcy, thus reducing the civil remedies available to plaintiffs. Criminal sanctions will become more common and contribute to deterring corporate criminality.

Crimewarp IV

The Politics of Pleasure

Times Square, New York. A pulsating microcosm of America's illicit pleasures. Walk around Broadway and Forty-fourth Street any night, at about ten o'clock. You'll enter a half-lit, furtive world of tough streetwalkers soliciting "johns," middle-aged gays cruising young "fruit hustlers," porno shops hawking X-rated peep shows, three-card monte players suckering small-time gamblers, drug dealers pushing glassine envelopes. And wearily stalking them, the police. Arrayed in special squads—"narcs," "pussy posse," Manhattan South Task Force—they have the unending job of trying to keep the lid on it all.

There, in stark relief, is the intrinsic tension between what adults do in pursuit of pleasure and the laws that define their behavior as criminal. Prostitution, homosexuality, pornography, gambling, drugs. Are they sins? Vices? Or personal preferences?

The so-called "consensual" crimes are the product of conflicting value systems—on the one hand, the various ethics of our myriad subcultures; on the other, an absolutist standard enshrined in our legal codes. Those codes, enacted through the political process, may or may not reflect a broad consensus on good and evil. But they definitely represent the values of those who have the power to influence law making. In America, our potentates were the Puritans and their descendants. Under the laws they bequeathed us, we're less free to pursue some pleasures than were the slaves of ancient Greece.

Sigmund Freud would have approved. He theorized that repression is the sine qua non of civilized life. The great analyst identified two basic human drives that lure us from work, higher thinking, and responsibility. In his early work, he introduced us to eros—the "pleasure principle"—which propels us to maximize good feelings and avoid pain. In his later work, after witnessing the ravages of world war, Freud reluctantly postulated a second drive, thanatos—the death wish that impels us toward self-destruction. Given full rein, both eros and thanatos are antisocial. For society to function, our most extreme impulses have to be kept in check. The practical question is: *How?*

From the earliest taboos against tribal sons raping their fathers' women, that question has been answered in the form of moral codes. Our own moral lineage weaves its way from the ancient Hebrews to the early Christians through Elizabethan England via American Puritans to today's New Right. The consistent thread in this tapestry has been the Bible.

The Bible, whom believers accept as the Word of God, informs our concept of right and wrong. However, the Word is binding only on those to whom it is revealed and many alternate "truths" vie with the Judeo-Christian ethic for a monopoly on righteousness. In his *Notes on Religion*, Thomas Jefferson wrote in 1776: "Every church is to itself orthodox; to others erroneous and heretical."

In a heterogeneous society, moral schisms are inevitable—and so are the consensual crimes that reflect them. Our Puritan forbears, however, recognized no such pluralism. Guided in all matters by a literal interpretation of the Bible, they equated idle pleasures with sin and worked hard to repress all ungodly desires. They sublimated their baser energies to tame a wilderness and build a great nation. A brilliant, passionate people—with much more zest than the grim, steeple-hatted cartoon characters convey—they nonetheless paid a price for suppressing the libido.

In analyzing the ravages of repression on the human psyche, Freud found hysteria, anger, hatred—all of which can lead to breaking the law. Puritan restraints erupted into witch trials, snooping, and intolerance.

Absent safety valves for repressed urges, a society can hemorrhage from its own pressures. Sometimes, we substitute one "bad" thing with another more acceptable one, like watching men tackle each other on a football field instead of in a bed. Or we become fanatical about destroying anything that can tempt us or anyone else; observe the delirium of book burnings. Or, we get so frustrated that we burst into an orgy of violence. Take the rapist who assaults the first woman to walk into the elevator each time he remembers being humiliated by his mother for having touched his penis. More often the violence is directed against ourselves instead of others—in depression, diets of alcohol and Seconal, and suicide. Some of us release our pent-up passions in the purified ecstasy of religious ritual—witness the frenzies of a revival meeting.

The warring drives, eros and thanatos, are evident in many consensual behaviors that have been defined as criminal. Because the drives are instinctual, the need to fulfill them will always be there. So will the black markets that stand ready to service them.

Religiosity, frontier living, and capitalism have combined to make us a people at once intensely individualistic, hedonistic, and morally conservative. This mix has created an absurdity. In an unpublished paper, "The Law Is a Busybody," University of Chicago Law School dean Norval Morris writes: "Half of all arrests are for crimes without direct victims, crimes which bring no complainant to the stationhouse, no call to the police switchboard."

As the New Right brings religion into the realm of contemporary coalition politics—with all its attendant accommodations and compromises—it will lose some moral authority. Subsequently, the absurdity will be corrected. Only in those cases—such as the drive to ban pornography—where the New Right finds allies outside its own precincts, will attempts to further legislate morality succeed. Elsewhere, they will backfire. Criminologists Jerome Skolnick and John Dombrink predict a number of consensual crimes will be legalized and we will find ourselves "shifting from the relative conceptual simplicity of criminal prohibition to the subtlety and complexity of administrative regulation."

11

Upscale Hookers

Linda hurries out of her office to catch a cab across the East River. She has a five-thirty appointment at the Westbury Hotel. When she gets to room 102, she adjusts her rose-tinted glasses and knocks on the door. A portly businessman answers. They exchange a few quick civilities and share a drink. Then, mechanically, she takes off her beige wool suit and strips down to a red elastic bikini. She coaxes the man to undress too. Having other things on her mind, she does what she must to bring him to orgasm as quickly as possible. After ten minutes, he hands her fifty dollars and she rushes out. Not to another client, but home to her husband so she can cook him dinner before he leaves for work. Linda is a part-time prostitute—a growing breed who don't think of themselves as prostitutes at all.

Linda's not the kind of woman you'd pick out in a crowd. Her life is outwardly conventional: wife, mother, office worker. She lives in the kind of humdrum working-class neighborhood that Archie Bunker made famous.

In this chapter, all characters are real people. However, biographical facts have been altered to protect their identities.

When I met Linda, she had been tricking for more than twenty years. So well concealed was her doppelgänger existence that it took weeks to surface her for my research. But one contact led to another, and I found myself with an ad hoc network of part-time pros that spanned from Florida to New York.

Seven years after she married him, Linda's husband lost his electrician's job. As the father of three children, he couldn't take the blow to his pride. He got sick, started drinking, and lost his drive. Eventually he went back to work, but never back to loving Linda. He hasn't touched his wife in years.

Now Linda understands his despair, but in the early years her young ego was shattered. Poverty and her deflated sense of femininity left her primed for prostitution. "One day I had a nickel to my name," she recalls. "I wanted to look for a job. I went to the bus stop, but I didn't have enough to get on. So I just stood at the bus stop and cried." That was the instant in which a married woman with three kids decided she'd never be broke again.

Linda found work in a Brooklyn tool shop. But that job turned into two jobs. One day, she was asked by her boss to work late. After everybody left, he propositioned her. Linda turned him down. Then he offered her money and Linda made an appointment to see him the following week.

On their maiden voyage, Linda says, "He petted me. He tried using his tongue on me. And I liked it." She walked out with $25. Soon, Linda's employer introduced her to other people in downtown Brooklyn, and she would spend lunch hours servicing them. A quarter of a century later, Linda is paid $50 to $100 each time for the services her husband rejected. And there are "perks"— hobnobbing with lawyers, doctors, show business luminaries; access to restaurants and clubs that don't usually cater to second-generation Italian shipping clerks from Brooklyn. Several hundred clients have given her children the good life their own father couldn't provide: college, trips to Europe, furniture for their apartments, expensive surgery.

In her own view, Linda is damaged, "being very immoral and not caring about myself as a person . . . abusing the privilege of being a woman, using myself for other people's purposes. Money could never be that important." Linda, a staunch Catholic, is convinced she is doomed to burn in hell. Yet, for all her "sins," Linda regards herself as a faithful wife: "I never had boyfriends. I never had the urge to go out with them just to go out. I'm home every night. I cook him dinner. I take care of everything—the cleaning, the washing, the ironing." Her prostitution is a world apart from her domestic life. "I can separate the two. I'm married and I need to earn money. One has nothing to do with the other."

Part-time prostitutes like Linda, observes criminologist Freda Adler, "are in the vanguard of a more mobile, less regimented group of female entrepreneurs who are beginning to dominate the field." Such working girls represent the climax of an evolution in which prostitution has moved from the sacred to the profane to the almost respectable. Their presence on the scene will ease the way toward legalization.

Prostitution has not always been illegal. Religious tenets and historical circumstance have determined our responses to prostitution over time and will continue to do so in the future.

Right through the Middle Ages, prostitution was condoned as a necessary evil that prevented seductions and rapes and kept the family intact. The Catholic Church even went so far as to maintain its own houses of ill repute. But by the end of the fifteenth century, Europe was swept by two fevers: syphilis and the Protestant Reformation. The battle against "sins of the flesh" began in earnest. Our Puritan forbears brought to the New World the legacy of Protestantism. In their eyes, the most important issue of the day was the tug-of-war between Protestantism and Catholicism. Catholicism was their pornography. Midst visions of whoring priests and fornicating nuns, prostitution symbolized the ecclesiastic corruption against which the ascetic Puritan spirit had rebelled.

The doctrine of biblical inerrancy required that Puritans—and today, fundamentalists—shun the harlot, their image of her shaped by terrifying admonishments such as those in Proverbs: "And, behold there met him a woman with the attire of a harlot. . . . Now is she without, now in the streets, and lieth in wait at every corner. . . . With her fair speech she caused him to yield. . . . He goeth after her straightaway, as an ox goeth to the slaughter. . . . Her house is the way to hell, going down to the chambers of death" (7:10–27). To a literalist, the message is unmistakable: The adulterer and the debaucher will smolder in the eternal inferno. And his guide to the depths is the "whorish woman."

In the North, where Puritan rule held sway, stringent laws were enacted against fornicators, "bawdy houses," and "nightwalkers." But in the South, where religious and secular law were disjoined, prostitution was more common. Because wealthier men had easy access to live-in carnal servants, it was mostly lower-class men who had to resort to the corner tart. That class distinction helped seal the fate of the prostitute as an outlaw.

But criminalization didn't mean the end of prostitution. In *The Lost Sisterhood,* Ruth Rosen points out that women were simply ejected from the safety of the bordello into the precarious life of the streetwalker. Rather than basking in the relatively benign ambit of a solicitous madam, they were cast onto the savage mercies of pimps, pushers, and mobsters.

Individual entrepreneurs like Linda made their debut during the Depression, when ordinary sources of income dried up. Starting in the 1930s, observes Freda Adler, "commercial prostitution has shown the steady decline characteristic of a dying business." By 1967, commercialized prostitution had dropped to about one third its 1920s level. Young single men in 1972 patronized prostitutes only about half as much as their predecessors in the 1940s, when Alfred Kinsey burst on the scene with his revelations about American sexual habits. "That is not to say that prostitution is a declining activity," adds Adler, "but simply that as an organized enterprise it is languishing." The future of the oldest profession belongs to the independent entrepreneur.

THE DEMISE OF THE STREETWALKER

Today between 117,000 and 690,000 prostitutes are turning 1 to 6 tricks per day. Of these, streetwalkers are among the least active, lowest paid, and most harassed. Theirs is a dying sector of the skin trade, but the junkies among them are stuck.

In his book *The Lively Commerce*, Charles Winick estimates that about half of all prostitutes are drug-addicted. However, an earlier study found that only 9 percent had experimented with drugs and only half of those had actually become hooked. For the unlucky ones, the heroin habit instigates a chaotic lifestyle organized around getting a "fix." Needing to be near her "connection" at all times, the hooked prostitute starts working his streets and attracting only the lowest-paying johns. If she's strung out and desperate for money, her fee slides even further. Before long, she becomes slovenly and careless—easy vice squad bait.

Her fellow prostitutes look down on her. Dana, a part-time call girl, insists: "I don't feel what I'm doing is wrong. What's wrong is walking the streets, being on drugs, paying a pimp." So strong is her outrage that she is active in civic campaigns to shoo streetwalkers off the sidewalks of her neighborhood.

But the addict-prostitute has very little choice. Instead of working her way up from the street, she has generally mainlined her way down from a massage parlor or a house. Today, she carries the additional taint of acquired immune deficiency syndrome (AIDS). Any "respectable" madam, agency, or hotel will screen her out before she gets anywhere near their clientele.

The addicted hooker is likely to be a diminishing presence. According to Winick, 53 percent of prostitutes are twenty-two to twenty-nine years old. Self-reports show that, among young adults, heroin use was almost four times higher in 1972 than in 1982. For those twenty-six and older, the percent who have ever used heroin has about doubled in that time. But even so, we're talking about only 1.1 percent of the sample—and most people who try heroin don't get hooked. Where there is an increase, it's more likely to be among men.

FBI statistics show that total "pross" arrests have quadrupled since 1971. Being the most visible of their profession, streetwalkers are the first to be arrested whenever anyone calls for a crackdown on prostitution. Most don't go to jail. But time is money, and it's costly to lose all those hours hanging around a courtroom. Many who are off drugs have left the streets to try the safer precincts of house, massage parlor, or bar.

THE RISE OF THE PART-TIME PROSTITUTE

Sophisticated analyses based on shaky assumptions estimate that about 1 in every 200 American women has been involved in prostitution at any given time in the last decade. Somewhere in that number are buried the part-timers—independent entrepreneurs who have been on the rise since the decline of the red-flocked, gaslit bordello. They rarely have run-ins with the law, so it's impossible to estimate how many there are.

You're not likely to see "working girls" like Linda cruising Times Square or soliciting hurried oral sex in passing trucks. As a rule, she and her colleagues are not junkies. Nor do they have pimps. Nor are they part of an organized crime syndicate. Unlike streetwalkers, who account for about one fifth of all prostitutes, part-timers are an invisible group who work mostly through referrals, bars, hotels, or massage parlors. Middle-class women who service middle-class men, they pride themselves on sustaining an ongoing relationship with their clients—even a friendship.

"A lot of them are still friends of mine from ten years ago," boasts a demure-looking former massage parlor madam. "I even went to work for one as a straight receptionist in his real estate office. And some of them are such good friends that if I ever needed anything, I could just get on the phone and they would help me out."

Such good client relations are the product of trust. Part-timers, because they look for repeat business, don't roll their johns or cheat them. Nor do the johns cheat or abuse their prostitutes. If there's such a thing as a safe, upscale form of hustling, this is it.

While zealous vice cops shrink the streetwalker population, the ascendancy of the half-time harlot is abetted by a triune trend: the women's movement, economic shifts, and the sexual revolution.

□ □ □

For the women's movement, prostitution poses a dilemma. On the one hand, it represents the ultimate debasement and exploitation of females—the hallmark of a male supremacist culture. On the other hand, prostitution is one option that women exercise in laying claim to control over their own bodies. By being paid for services rendered, they avoid being exploited in the same way as a woman who just "gives it away" and ends up with nothing but a broken heart.

The women's movement helped liberate prostitutes from pimps who ran them ragged and took all their money. The independent—whether part-time or full-time—works through agencies, word of mouth, and advertisements. Because she is invisible, she has no need for a pimp to spring her from jail or protect her on the street. She pays her own debts and keeps her own profits.

Marlene, a nineteen-year-old blonde, carries an eighteen-credit course load at the University of Maryland. She supplements her senatorial scholarship with an occasional $150-a-night stand. But the feminist in her bridles at the position in which she is placed: "It's wrong that the only easy avenues of power open to women are vicarious ones using your sexuality. I think it's a shame that I have to be witty when I'm out with these men, but not too intelligent. I have to be on my guard not to intimidate them or I won't be fun anymore." She derides her clients for having "to use power to buy sex," but puts up with it in order to pay her tuition. "What I'm doing to get where I want to get is a lot less offensive than stealing, selling heroin, or stepping on everybody so that I can get to the top."

□ □ □

Most of the part-timers I met were not, like Marlene, carefree coeds. Rather, they hail from the ranks of two-earner and female-headed households that have been proliferating since 1960. The women's movement helped catapult them into the labor market. What they found when they got there were, more often than not, dead end jobs. While the well-paid industrial jobs they might have filled are being displaced by low-pay work in the expanding service sector, some eke out extra funds in the high-pay vice world.

Dana, thirty-eight-year-old divorced mother of a handicapped child, gets no money from her estranged husband. Sporadic work as an investigator and courier doesn't begin to cover her daughter's medical and psychiatric bills. But welfare didn't sit well with Dana, so she used her limited hours away from home to turn tricks. "I need the money," Dana asserts. "But I'm always home for dinner and the evening news."

The galloping inflation of the 1970s eroded the value of everyone's salary. Sexual moonlighting enabled many women to earn extra cash and control their own schedules without running afoul of the law. Judy, a grandmother in her late forties, was one of those who used her body to supplement her family's dwindling income. While her husband Joe was working nights, Judy worked too. When she first told him, Joe was crushed. Not knowing how to handle it, he packed up and left for six months. But he came back. "She's a good wife, she takes care of the kids," volunteers Joe. "But when it comes to holding a job, she hasn't got much education. She tried waitressing but she couldn't do it. There are some things people are not capable of. But she's capable of taking care of men." Judy was earning much more providing a specified number of orgasms to a police sergeant (her best customer), at $600 a full night, than she could earn in any other job for which she was qualified.

□ □ □

In this age of conspicuous carnal consumption, you'd think there'd be very little call for a prostitute's services. Why pay for what you can get for free at any singles bar? Oddly enough, the "sexual revolution" has not dampened demand. The popular appetite for "swinging," "swapping," "orgies," and other experiments has created a market for boutique sex—the kind you don't usually get at home. The part-time professional, who is not far removed from the promiscuous housewife, fills the bill.

Janine, a fragile, but buxom forty-year-old transplant from Atlanta, was playing musical beds long before she turned professional. Peeking out from behind her granny glasses, she recalls the workaholic businessman to whom she was married for ten years: "I wasn't getting any affection from my husband because he was too busy. He would come home, eat dinner, and go back to the office and stay until midnight." After a prodigious spree of extramarital sex, Janine left Peachtree Street and headed for Broadway. Left behind were her son, her husband, the swimming pool, the rose garden, two cars, and the presidency of the local Jaycettes.

Janine never did make her Broadway stage debut. All her acting was done in a massage parlor. "I was like a piece of meat," she remembers, "sitting on a sofa and the guys came in off the street and said, 'I'll take that one.' And they weren't all such nice guys."

As one among an estimated 50,000 massage girls in the early 1970s, there was still enough demand to net Janine $1,000 a week. But finding it all a bit gamy, she allowed a benefactor to set her up in business for herself. From then on, she chose her clients and catered to them in her own good time.

For the man intimidated by the orgasmic demands of the so-called New Woman, someone like Janine provides an uncomplicated transaction. He needn't feel threatened by sexual expectations he can't fulfill, nor need he be daunted by glamour he can't handle. Janine is a wan-looking, girl-next-door type. Solicitous, she loves to parade her pale body before her clients. She savors the lusty appreciation she never got in her marriage. Her johns are rewarded without intimidation or strings.

Reverend Jerry Falwell calls this attitude the "cult of the playboy"—a philosophy that tells a man he doesn't have to be committed to his wife and children. "Men are satisfying their lustful desires at the expense of the family." Prostitutes remain the biblical temptresses who seduce weak males from their godly duty.

But Marlene, who comes from a Pentecostal family, can thump a Bible as hard as Falwell. "I don't see where it is considered an abomination in the New Testament. The only laws I ever heard by Jesus or the Ten Commandments were against adultery. And I'm not married." She laughs and adds: "If I'm not hurting anyone, or destroying God's temple—which is my body—I'm not sinning. I am a good person—a morally upright, truthful, and compassionate person." Falwell and his co-religionists would surely quarrel with Marlene's interpretation of scripture as well as her definition of goodness. They recognize the threat she represents.

So do women's libbers.

In her excursus, *Sexual Politics*, feminist Kate Millett addresses the paradox of sexual revolution fomenting a demand for prostitutes: "Men who might be sexually accommodated by casual pickups without expense still provide a demand for prostitution. . . . In the case of each partner to such prostitution, some need to . . . affirm male supremacy through humiliation of woman seems to play a leading role."

Marlene sees Millett's point. "Some men approach you with this superiority thing. It's a real thrill for them to be able to buy a service; I am like a servant, and not an equal.

"My customers are turning to me for approval and acceptance of something they don't approve and accept. I am the bad person, bringing them down and tempting them in this evil thing. And yet I am the only person that they can turn to to sanctify what they are doing."

The Fundamentalist Right is fighting back with a sexual revolution of its own —the hyping of married Christian sex. A barrage of Christian marriage manuals, family seminars, and *Total Woman*–type books have introduced the pious to the inner sanctum of black lace and garter belts. In the battle for the family, wives are being encouraged to keep their husbands at home by bringing just a touch of the whore into the conjugal bed. According to New Right watcher Carol Flake, Christians are wresting "the joys of sex from the exclusive possession of secular humanists."

In a backlash against the 1970s' sexual free-for-all, fewer Americans "welcome more acceptance of sexual freedom." Among college students, says a 1984 study conducted by Northern Iowa University, there is less casual sex and more guilt about sex than there was in the last decade. Today, sex before marriage is "in" but infidelity after marriage is "out." Marilyn Story, a family studies professor, attributes the change to a rightward shift in our values. "Sexual guilt correlates with being religious and a more conservative political orientation." The New Right's sage, Richard Viguerie, is cheering: "I would like to see . . . a greater interest in opposing premarital sex and adultery. . . . They lead to over half a million illegitimate births a year and the break up of millions of marriages and broken homes for tens of millions of children." Viguerie is getting at least part of his wish.

On the face of it, these developments could seriously cut into Marlene, Linda, Dana, and Judy's business. But traditional theories of prostitution posit that demand for paid sex increases as other sexual outlets dry up. The new conservative mood may actually improve market conditions.

The clientele serviced by Linda and her colleagues is mostly middle aged and older. With the aging of the population, the pool of potential clients for part-timers is increasing. But the conservative swing in matters sexual could add younger people to that pool as well.

THE DECRIMINALIZATION OF PROSTITUTION

In a free market the sexual competition is strong. As early as the late 1800s, the nation's burgeoning cities were awash with red-light districts. By 1901, Social Darwinists and concerned civic groups decried prostitution as "the social evil," while pseudoscientific "family studies" denounced the "loose woman" as the "mother of criminals." Venereal disease was on the rise at the same time that a Great War was brewing across the sea, just when we could ill afford to have our boys cut down by syphilitic dementia. Patriotism and hygiene joined moralism to make the hapless hooker everyone's scapegoat. By 1918, most cities had enacted ordinances banning brothels and making prostitution a crime. History is repeating itself today. Much like the crusaders at the turn of the century, the New Right proposes to turn the nation around with laws that prohibit permissiveness. As the criminalizing of prostitution and other "vices" has shown, this is one area where statutes don't work. Even those that exist are not likely to stand up much longer.

Public opinion favors, by a small majority, laws that "enforce community standards of right and wrong." But when it comes to specific applications, polls come down squarely on the side of decriminalizing prostitution. Respondents favor either a hands-off or licensing and regulation approach to prostitution. "Although it is scarcely a socially approved form of conduct," say survey researchers Herbert McClosky and Alida Brill, "neither does it strike the majority as especially dangerous." "Eventually court decisions are bound to reflect reality and practice," they continue, "and thus transform prohibited forms of behavior into protected forms of behavior." Prostitution is already legal in certain counties, and there seem to be no dire consequences.

When the Star Ranch, a brothel in Beatty, Nevada, burned down in 1980, 200 of the town's 670 residents threw a benefit dance to rebuild it. The madam, Fran York, was a civic-minded, "very nice woman," and the townfolk felt she deserved help in her hour of need. She had always done things like buy uniforms for the high school band, take out ads in the school yearbook, and make donations to the volunteer fire department. Now it was time to reciprocate.

The massage parlors in Maricopa County, Arizona, didn't fare quite as well, but at least they weren't subject to any criminal charges. When these pleasure palaces started to proliferate in the mid-1970s, the sheriff decided to invoke the 1916 Bawdy House Abatement Act—a civil statute forbidding the operation of bordellos. He needed witnesses to testify against the parlors. The deputies, all married family men, were considered unsuitable for the undercover work that was required. Local singles were recruited instead. "There's been no end of volunteers," said the deputy county attorney in 1981. These upstanding citizens helped to whittle Maricopa County's massage parlors from 60 to about 15.

Free-lancers would probably not have evoked the ire of the sheriff in the same way that the organized massage girls did. No doubt, the middle-class respectability of the new crop of part-timers will hasten acceptance of legalized prostitution in other states as well.

Precedents in other Western democracies are instructive. In England the 1957 Wolfenden Report inspired decriminalization of prostitution between consenting adults. Among its contributors was a committee of Catholic priests. The report advised: "It is not the business of the State to intervene in the purely private sphere but to act solely as the defender of the common good. . . . Sin as such is not the concern of the State but affects the relations between the soul and God." A government committee in another Commonwealth country, Canada, has recently recommended that prostitution be decriminalized if it takes place in a home.

In the United States, prostitution has long been on the legal agenda. The American Law Institute deleted adultery and fornication from its model legal code in 1955. In 1984, Margo St. James, a former prostitute, and one of her clients filed suit in New York to legalize private sexual contacts between consenting adults. (Once again, street solicitation was excluded.) The sexual-rights activist explained, "The suit is intended to legitimate my work as a provider of a service."

Prostitute unions such as Coyote (Call Off Your Old Tired Ethics) and its chapters, ASP (Associated Seattle Prostitutes) and PONY (Prostitutes of New York), now constitute a lobby for speeding along the process. The lobby has a powerful economic argument going for it. The estimated unreported illegal income generated by prostitutes has quadrupled since 1973. Ninety percent of it is generated in those sectors in which part-timers operate. Should that income emerge from the underground economy, government could tap a new pool of up to $11.6 billion in taxable revenue.

CRIMEWARPS

- The shift from smokestack to service economy will have the strongest impact on the working class and lower middle-class sectors from which prostitutes are most often recruited. The need for economic supplements will induce more women to turn to part-time prostitution.
- Unabated growth in female-headed households will add to the prostitute population.
- Young people will grow sexually more conservative, thus restricting the pool of legitimate sexual outlets.
- At the same time that young people grow more sexually conservative, increasing percentages of them are acquiring college educations. Research confirms a direct relationship between increased education and civil libertarianism, thereby setting the stage for legalization of private acts between consenting adults.
- As part-timers infuse the indoor prostitution trade with middle-class workers and clients, private transactions between consenting adults will be decriminalized.
- Both streetwalkers and their clients will be on the lower end of the social spectrum. Therefore, public solicitation will remain illegal and/or subject to penalties.
- Zealous street-level enforcement as well as public protests will diminish the role of streetwalking in prostitution.
- Fear of AIDS will reduce the demand for streetwalkers' services.
- Chronic budget deficits will force the government to find new sources of revenues. The underground economy will be one of these. In order to encourage reporting of income, many states will legalize some of its sources. Benign public attitudes will allow prostitution to be one of the first underground sources to be legitimated.
- The legalization of prostitution will take two forms: nullification (in which the law withdraws entirely, leaving private sexual relations between consenting adults totally unregulated) and a commercial service model (in which prostitution is treated as any other personal service).
- As part-timers and other independents proliferate, prostitution will become increasingly difficult to control and profits to organized crime will decline. The mob will lose interest and turn to more lucrative areas of exploitation —a trend which has been ongoing for quite some time.
- Because of the low organization potential for prostitution, no significant financial interests will be threatened by its legalization. The only strong

opposition will be on moral grounds and come from the Fundamentalist Right.

· Legalization of prostitution will occur first in those regions of the country where Protestants do not comprise a wide majority: New England, Middle Atlantic, Pacific.

Homosexuals: The Road from Sodom and Gomorrah to the National Democratic Convention

In the summer of 1979, Hollywood's money moguls and local gays collided in New York, and the city exploded in a storm of protest. Director William Friedkin and company were camped out in Greenwich Village to do a movie about a psychopathic killer who was decapitating and castrating homosexuals. Shot against a backdrop of S&M bars, sleazy West Side movie theaters, and third-rate hotels, it portrayed a narrow but grisly sector of the gay community.

The timing could not have been worse. Anita Bryant had just finished her Dade County, Florida, gay-baiting campaign. A gay man in San Francisco had been stabbed to death by a gang, one of whom exulted, "This one's for Anita!" In the same city, Dan White had avoided the electric chair for shooting Mayor George Moscone and the first openly homosexual supervisor, Harvey Milk. In New York, seven men had been viciously clubbed by "queer bashers" in the Central Park Rambles.

Gay activists perceived this wave of violence as a backlash against their emergent civil rights movement. They reasoned that the movie, *Cruising*, was going to inspire more brutality against a group whose practices are despised and feared to begin with.

They took to the streets by the hundreds. Decked out in the Village uniform of T-shirt and jeans, fists raised in the air, they chanted, "Stop the movie *Cruising!* Stop the movie *Cruising!*" and "Hi, hi! Ho, ho! The movie *Cruising*'s got to go!" Police barricades were overturned as chattering newsroom wires tapped out copy announcing an injured cop here, an assaulted reporter there.

Gays started flexing their political muscle in 1969 when police raided a homosexual hangout, the Stonewall Inn, in Greenwich Village. That improvident foray resulted in three days of rioting against New York's Finest. It was the first time anyone could remember gays fighting back.

From that point on, the gay rights movement steadily gained momentum. But outrage over related events had spurred a parallel movement, the Fundamentalist Right. The two were headed on a collision course that symbolically converged on Billy Friedkin's movie set in the summer of 1979.

I covered the protests for NBC News. With the help of Arthur Bell, who had instigated the anti-*Cruising* protests in a column he wrote for the *Village Voice*, I was able to bring cameras into the leather bars that were shunning Billy Friedkin.

My crew shot the men relaxing on a routine Friday night. The scene they captured was one of loud, driving music and glittering pinball machines; posters of brawny men sporting tight jeans; tinkling key chains; dangling "hot hankies" in red, blue, yellow, green, and brown—shorthand for the kind of sex act being solicited (worn to the left or right, they signaled whether one wanted to give or receive); muscle shirts on sinewy physiques; full-leather regalia for those who could afford it; full vinyl for those who couldn't. In back rooms, away from our view, men were getting high on amyl nitrate—a drug that relaxes muscles sufficiently, especially sphincters, to enable sex acts such as "fist fucking." On the Morton Street pier, anonymous men were making their rounds of unknown bodies in the sweaty dark of the old depot. This tiny, seamy side of the gay life is what the protesters didn't want a hostile public to see.

Most gays, I was told, don't make the leather bar scene—or any bar scene at all—with any regularity. Middle-class, well-educated, well-paid and, except for their sexual preferences, conventional, they're more like Robert Wolff, an architect-artist whom I interviewed.

Wolff, married with a teenage son, was not of the gay ghetto. He lived in a pristine white loft with colorful, cushy chairs and an assorted jumble of paintings and sculpted masks. Work and family, along with his relationships with men, were the most important things in his life.

Robert didn't consider himself a freak. He went to the store, bought coffee, selected art supplies, ate, slept—"like most people. Normal is normal." His lifestyle, he claimed, is more typical of the gay world than the very visible scene on Christopher Street. Yet, even assimilated homosexuals like Robert were afraid of what *Cruising* would mean to them.

Looking back on it, it meant very little. The movie wasn't a box office smash, and its theater run was short. But today, there is a new specter to haunt the gay community, AIDS, which will have more impact on the future of gay rights and decriminalization of sodomy laws than a hundred movies like *Cruising.*

AIDS hit the gay community like a plague. To biblical literalists, it must seem like divine retribution for an act they call "abomination." In centuries past, laws were enacted to rein in prostitutes during periods of rampant syphilis. A parallel pattern is now enveloping gays. The privacy of sexual behavior is being seriously threatened as local mayors monitor bathhouses, "swinging" clubs, and hotel rooms in an attempt to halt the killer disease. In 1977, before AIDS became a household word, 43 percent of respondents favored legalizing homosexual acts between consenting adults. By 1982, that percentage had slipped to 39.

Yet, according to Gay Rights National Lobby estimates, 10 percent of our population defines itself as homosexual. That's some 24 million men and women with an interest in finding shelter under the umbrella of civil rights legislation and decriminalizing what they do between their sheets with other consenting adults. The major obstacle they face is religious teachings that brand them outcasts.

THE BIBLICAL MISINTERPRETATION

"Thou shalt not lie with mankind as with womankind: it is abomination" (Leviticus 18:22).

So reads the first of six biblical condemnations of homosexuality. With so few references in over a thousand pages of text, homosexual sin couldn't have been a high priority to either the ancient Hebrews or the early Christians. Yet it came to pack tremendous emotional wallop—all because of what now seem to be misinterpretations of an early text.

Scholars agree that the injunction against homosexuality is rooted in the story of Sodom and Gomorrah. The story opens with two sinful cities that stand on the brink of destruction. Before acting, God sends two emissaries to find "one just man" who might be saved. Disguised as travelers, the angels come upon the house of Lot. Because a stranger's kindness was often a matter of life and death in the nomadic world of the ancient Middle East, Lot invites the wayfarers to rest and refresh themselves in his home. After some resistance, they accept.

However, the inhospitable men of Sodom throng around Lot's house, demanding: "Where are the men which came in to thee this night? Bring them out unto us, that we may know them" (Genesis 19:5). Lot, ever the gracious host, doesn't want to subject his guests to indignities. Hoping to placate the angry horde, he offers them his daughters instead. But the Sodomites will settle for no less than the newcomers, and nearly break down Lot's door in a frenzy to get at them.

The angels-cum-travelers strike the Sodomites blind and exhort Lot to gather his family and escape from the city. Soon after, "the Lord rained upon Sodom and Gomorrah brimstone and fire from . . . out of heaven" (Genesis 19:29), and the cities were pulverized.

The key to the injunction against homosexuality is found in the final five words of the Sodomites' demand: "that we may know them." In the Bible, the phrase "to know" is usually assumed to mean carnal knowledge. Because the men of Sodom demanded to *know* the men in Lot's house, their words were taken to denote homosexual lust. Sodom and Gomorrah were ravaged on the heels of this alleged lust. Therefore, the Sodomites' sin has come to be known as "sodomy."

The true meaning of these five words, upon which hangs our powerful cultural hatred of homosexuals, is open to question. Nowhere in the text are the sins of the cities actually enumerated, except in the most general way:

"But the men of Sodom were wicked and sinners before the Lord exceedingly" (Genesis 13:13).

". . . the cry of Sodom and Gomorrah is great . . . their sin very grievous" (Genesis 19:20).

Critics of the traditional homophobic interpretation argue that the sins that wrecked the cities were more likely rape, idolatry, and inhospitality than carnal knowledge of men by men.

Original biblical texts, distorted by layers of translations, show no uniform use of the phrases referring to carnal knowledge. For example, in Genesis 16:2, we come upon the story of Sarah's tragic sterility in the face of God's promise to build a great nation from the seed of her husband, Abraham. She offers him her maid, Hagar, as proxy childbearer.

"Behold now," Sarah says, "the Lord has restrained me from bearing. I pray then, go in unto my maid; it may be that I may obtain children by her." The same chapter in Genesis continues: "And he went in unto Hagar and she conceived . . ." (Genesis 16:4). In this context, the meaning of "go in unto" is indisputably sexual.

But later, in the story of Sodom and Gomorrah, a similar phrase is used completely differently. The angels who visit Lot tell him that they will spend the night in the streets. But Lot beseeches them to accept his hospitality.

"And he pressed upon them greatly and they turned in unto him, and entered his house" (Genesis 19:3).

Surely God's own emissaries didn't engage in sexual intercourse with Lot!

The inconsistency that applies to the phrase "go in unto" also applies to the phrase "to know." "To know" is hard to find in the Old Testament. The term most often used to denote sexual intercourse is "to lie with." Even in the Song of Solomon, the most explicitly sensual part of the Bible, the word "know" is not used even once with reference to sex. Why then should we assume that the Sodomites demand, "that we may know them," refers to carnal knowledge?

Here's an important clue: The story of Sodom and Gomorrah is found in Genesis, the first book of the Bible, whereas the two Old Testament condemnations of homosexuality are found in Leviticus, presumed by some theorists to be a later book.

Leviticus, the book of laws, was set up as a code for the fledgling Jewish nation. Moses was concerned that the new state be strong in numbers. Any intercourse that didn't further that end had to be condemned. The severe penalties with which homosexuality has been punished in England and the United States probably originate with that third book of the Bible: ". . . if a man lie with mankind as with womankind both of them have committed abomination. They shall surely be put to death" (Leviticus 20:33).

But the issue was survival, not morality.

Homosexuality was outside the mainstream of early rabbinic thought. It was only with the New Testament and the Palestinian Jewish reinterpretation of Genesis 19 that it became a major theme. Intervening events are believed by some scholars to account for the change.

One factor was a carryover from the apocryphal Book of Jubilees, which alleged that the Sodomites had created a race of giants by cohabiting with gods —the "Watchers"—who lusted after mortal women. For their crime against nature, the Sodomites were punished. Over time, it seems the "Watchers" were forgotten but the notion of "crime against nature" remained.

The critical factor in that selective memory was the antagonism that had developed between the pious Hebrews and their hedonistic Greek conquerors. The reinterpretation of the collapse of Sodom and Gomorrah was, in part, a reaction against the Hellenistic way of life. Homosexuality, one of the hallmarks of Greek civilization, became the symbol for the vices of an alien and hostile culture that offended the devout Jewish spirit.

References to homosexuality became much more explicit as they evolved in the New Testament, where four of them are found. But, in the final analysis, it was not divine ordinance that created the Judeo-Christian injunction against this form of sex; it was the survival needs of a nation and the clash between Hebrew and Greek culture. Those conditions don't exist anymore. Yet, the injunction has remained to mold our laws and attitudes to this day.

THE CRIMINALIZATION OF HOMOSEXUALITY

The model for our sodomy laws is a series of statutes instituted in the 1500s by Henry VIII of England. These enactments forbade, under pain of death, any anal-genital contact with man or beast Somehow oral sex was left out, and that created some problems of prosecution later on.

In 1817, for example, a defendant convicted of fellatio with a child had to be pardoned. Technically, he had not committed sodomy. However, American courts have since corrected this deficiency and, in some states, oral sex enthusiasts of both sexual persuasions—homo and hetero—are subject to criminal prosecution if their partner complains loudly enough.

In 1837, North Carolina adopted the more inclusive version of Henry VIII's buggery statute, death penalty and all. In 1869, the death sanction was charitably deleted and replaced with a maximum sentence of sixty years in prison. That statute was still on the books in 1962, when Max Perkins and Robert McCorkle were convicted for the "abominable and detestable crime against nature." McCorkle pleaded no contest and received a relatively benign five- to seven-year sentence. Perkins, however, decided to plead not guilty and stand trial. He was convicted and slapped with a twenty- to thirty-year sentence. This vast discrepancy in punishments for two men engaged in the same act of mutual fellatio led to a new trial for Perkins. He was set free, but the North Carolina law still stands.

While Illinois was the first state to decriminalize homosexual acts in 1961, "crime against nature" laws are still in effect in more than twenty states and the District of Columbia. Among the sodomy laws being litigated is an 1805 Louisiana statute which forbids "unnatural carnal copulation"—interpreted by that state's supreme court to encompass both oral and anal sex. Even when consenting adults indulge in the privacy of their own bedroom, they can be subject to a fine of $2,000 and/or five years in prison.

In 1985, the Lambda Legal Defense and Education Fund (a gay rights organization) and the American Civil Liberties Union moved to overturn that law. Their suit charged that Louisiana's sodomy law violates gays' privacy rights while its religious nature violates the First Amendment guarantee of separation of church and state.

Similar arguments have been used in most homosexual rights litigation. The results have been uneven. In 1976, the United States Supreme Court summarily upheld a Virginia law making it a crime to engage in private consensual homosexual conduct *(Doe v. Commonwealth Attorney)*. This case is the precedent that is constantly invoked to justify rulings that extend the right to privacy only to heterosexuals.

In the same year, however, the Supreme Court ruled in *Singer v. the U.S. Civil Service Commission*—its first decision, say the experts, to be even remotely favorable to homosexuals. A federal employee, John F. Singer, was working as a probationary clerk/typist at the Seattle office of the Equal Employment Opportunity Commission. Although his job performance was rated "very good," his sexual orientation was unabashedly gay. In 1972, he was fired.

Charges against Singer included kissing another man in the EEOC cafeteria, applying for a marriage license with his male lover, organizing a symposium on civil rights for sexual minorities, and attracting widespread press coverage. Singer appealed his dismissal all the way to the U.S. Supreme Court, which ordered that the case be reopened by the Court of Appeals. Singer was eventually reinstated with back pay. A modest victory, but not a lasting one.

In 1984, a conservative judge appointed by the Reagan administration affirmed the navy's discharge of an admitted homosexual petty officer with "an unblemished service record," ruling that "private, consensual homosexual conduct is not constitutionally protected." Judge Robert Bork's opinion was reflected in a 1985 decision upholding a Texas law that makes the private sexual conduct of that state's estimated 700,000 inverts a crime. Later in that year, a federal judge in Philadelphia maintained the federal government's right to bar homosexuals from the military, even when that stricture conflicted with local antidiscrimination laws.

As dire as 1985 was for gay rights, it did bring gays a narrow federal victory. A deadlocked Supreme Court, ruling without a written opinion, upheld a lower court decision prohibiting Oklahoma from dismissing public school teachers simply because they speak out in favor of homosexual rights. The ruling protects freedom of speech while ducking the issue of freedom of private consensual sex.

That issue was addressed in 1986. A bitterly divided Supreme Court ruled that the Constitution confers no *fundamental* right to homosexuals to engage in sodomy. Such behavior, said the majority opinion—even when practiced at home, between consenting adults—is not protected by the right to privacy.

In his analysis of gay civil liberties litigation, Donald Knutson observes: "Most of the cases that were decided adversely to the gay litigant were handled by courts that viewed the issue from a conventional, moralistic perspective. Relief was denied on the grounds that the government is free to impose restrictions on individual liberty in order to promote 'morality and decency.' . . .

"Positive results for gay persons . . . have come only from judges who have viewed homosexuals as a minority group worthy of . . . protection. . . ."

According to the LLDEF's managing attorney, "Criminalization of the sexual activity of lesbians and gay men is often cited as the legal foundation for the discrimination gays face in employment, child custody, and many other areas."

Erratic decisions in federal courts have led gay activists to try to break down discriminatory barriers at the local level. Indeed, the 1986 Supreme Court decision affirms states' rights in this matter. In New York City, Mayor Edward Koch found himself going head-to-head with John Cardinal O'Connor when he issued an executive order forbidding job bias against gays by City contractors. The state's highest court found that the mayor had exceeded his authority, and he was overruled. Nonetheless, a gay rights ordinance ultimately passed.

In Houston, Mayor Kathy Whitmire battled her electorate with a similar antibias order. She was defeated in a referendum that denied gays legal protection in city hiring. Nonetheless, as of 1985, some 77 state, county, and local governments had invoked ordinances barring discrimination against gays in employment, housing, and public accommodations.

The "widespread belief that homosexuality is wrong" seems to be "counteracted by the widespread belief that discrimination is also wrong," opine poll analysts William Schneider and I. A. Lewis.

THE MAJORITY VIEW ON HOMOSEXUALITY

Six polls taken between 1973 and 1982 showed that 67 to 70 percent of respondents consistently felt that homosexual relations were "always wrong." But there are strong signs that the public is softening. National Opinion Research Center polls taken in the early 1970s and 1980s measured tolerance of gays by asking people whether an admitted homosexual should be allowed to make a speech in their community. In a ten-year period, tolerance increased for each age group except eighteen- to twenty-four-year-olds. Since this group is a shrinking part of the population, tolerance of gays is apt to grow in the future.

Averaging results from 1974–82, another set of NORC findings showed that one of the areas of greatest divergence between conservatives and moderates is the notion that it is wrong to have homosexual relations. Since this nation is overwhelmingly middle-of-the-road, moderates' more sympathetic attitudes toward gay sex are likely to carry.

Schneider and Lewis discern other pro-gay trends. Their assessment shows that education is a key factor in support for legalizing gay sex. Sixty-one percent of the college educated feel it should be legal, while the same percentage of the grade school educated believe it should remain illegal. Because a growing proportion of the population is being exposed to higher education, the battle for gay rights will be fought in a more friendly climate.

Even where religion is an issue, a five-to-three majority feel that being gay doesn't interfere with being a good Christian or a good Jew. Indeed, many of the mainline churches are making room for gay congregations, gay "unions" (same sex marriages), and gay ministers.

However, religion still remains a major stumbling block to full acceptance of homosexuality. Schneider and Lewis find that Protestants are more antigay than are Catholics, and the strongly religious are more antigay than the irreligious. A Lambda spokesperson draws the line, not between Catholics and Protestants but between right-wing fundamentalists and mainline churches. As a nation, we tend to separate scripture from public policy. Therefore, gay rights might well prevail.

THE FUNDAMENTALIST PROTEST

The Fundamentalist Right is fighting hard against such an eventuality and has incorporated all of the most lurid imagery of homophobia: the homosexual as pervert; corrupter of young children; destroyer of families; moral criminal; eroder of our national prestige; harbinger of the collapse of the Holy American Empire. Although none of these assertions have any basis in fact—on the contrary, most rapes, child molesting, family violence, and corruption seem to be the province of heterosexuals—the leaders of the radical right don't hesitate to condemn gays in the most acrid terms.

- "Remember, homosexuals do not reproduce! They recruit! And many of them are out after my children and your children," warns Jerry Falwell in a 1981 fund-raising letter.
- "As far as I'm concerned," proclaims televangelist James Robison in the *Texas Monthly*, "a homosexual is in the same class with a rapist, a bank robber, or a murderer."
- "I agree with capital punishment," declared Dean Wycoff, a former Moral Majority chapter head in a TV interview, "and I believe homosexuality is one of those that could be coupled with murder and other sins. . . . It would be the government that sits upon this land who would be executing homosexuals."
- "Homosexuality is a sin," intones Jerry Falwell. "Homosexuals are people blinded by Satan. . . ."

By targeting sex education in the public schools, the New Right is countering what they regard as a wholesale endorsement of homosexuality. In savaging the

"Gay Rights" bill, H.R. 2074, they tried to block homosexuals from being protected as a bona fide minority like women, blacks, and Hispanics. By attacking the Kennedy criminal code reform bill, they defeated federal attempts to legitimize homosexuality. Through promoting the Family Protection Act, they succeeded in watering down the Legal Services Corporation which, among other things, provided counsel in homosexual rights litigation.

But even among the fundamentalist faithful, gays have made inroads. John (Terry) Dolan, chairman of the powerful National Conservative Political Action Committee (NCPAC), broke ranks with his colleagues in the New Right and declared: "Sexual preference is irrelevant to political philosophy. . . . If we conservatives believe the government has no right to regulate our economic life, then it certainly has no right to regulate our private life, except to the point where we do harm to each other."

Robert Bauman, at one time a consistent leader on pro-life matters and sponsor of a bill condemning homosexuality, was later caught in a homosexual bar. He had offered a sixteen-year-old boy $50 to perform oral sex. Promptly disowned by Jerry Falwell and Paul Weyrich, Bauman turned sharply around and began a new life as an outspoken gay conservative.

THE GAY RIGHTS POWER BLOC

Gays have become a potent force, and many a candidate whirling through the political prom is asking them to dance. The Democratic Party came acourtin' during the 1980 election year. The National Association of Gay and Lesbian Democratic Clubs claimed that there were 77 acknowledged homosexual delegates and alternates from 17 states at that year's Democratic National Convention—a bloc larger than the delegations of 25 states.

The local level, however, is the stronger bastion of gay influence. In Seattle, Police Chief George Tilsch had invoked wrath with what was perceived as harassment of gays. He was forced to resign, and angry homosexuals claim to have been instrumental in his demise. Robert Hanson, Tilsch's replacement, was much friendlier to his gay constituents. He lost no time in lining up speaking engagements before homosexual audiences. Pat Fitzsimons, Hanson's successor, maintained the rapport. Today, according to one writer, "Both police and gays say Seattle is a paragon of police-homosexual relations."

In San Francisco, where 40 percent of single men have been found to be gay, politicians regularly take their interests into account. Gays provided the key margin of victory in George Moscone's mayoral election. Before his assassination, Mayor Moscone had appointed a pro-gay police chief, Charles Gain, who actively recruited homosexual officers and put a stop to harassment of gays. However, some of Gain's eccentricities had proven to be an embarrassment to the police force. Like the time he removed the flags from his office and replaced them with potted plants. Or when he posed with a prostitute who had adorned herself with a dildo and a douche bag. When Diane Feinstein took over after Moscone's assassination, a conservative backlash forced Gain's resignation. But the pro-gay policies continued.

On the other side of San Francisco Bay, Berkeley became the first city in the country to offer employee benefits to homosexual partners. Dubbed the "domestic partners law," it extends insurance, pension, and death benefits to unwed live-ins as well as bona fide spouses of city workers.

In Los Angeles, police used to prey on gays, instigated, some say, by Chief Ed Davis' virulent anti-gay rhetoric. In order to evade his reach, many gays moved into West Hollywood, an unincorporated town in Los Angeles County. The city of West Hollywood has since become L.A.'s gay ghetto.

In 1984, a proposal was successfully put forward to incorporate West Hollywood as a city. Because of its gay majority, it is run by homosexuals and officially free of antigay bias. The new city—the eighty-fourth to be incorporated in Los Angeles County—contains about 35,000 residents and is 1.9 square miles in area. Politically, it hangs together as a coalition of gays and elderly heterosexuals who share an interest in rent control.

Nearby Laguna Beach, a quiet seaside resort, became a focal point for gay politics in that same year when City Councilman Robert Gentry acknowledged his homosexuality—the first municipal official to do so in conservative Orange County. In this city, gays are estimated to make up between 18 and 30 percent of the population. Under Gentry's stewardship the city council unanimously adopted an ordinance prohibiting job and housing discrimination against gays, even though a similar bill failed at the State level. The city has even introduced walk-along programs in which local residents can accompany police on their patrols of gay gathering places.

The West Coast is not the only place where gays have been accepted. In 1980, New York City witnessed an extraordinary public confession. A seventeen-year veteran of the New York City Police Department, Sergeant Charlie Cochrane, stood before TV cameras, tape recorders, and scribbling reporters to declare his homosexuality. The occasion was a city council hearing at which he was testifying on behalf of a gay rights ordinance that had failed to pass in numerous sessions.

The New York City Police Department is the largest in the country, extolled for its "macho" in movies, books, and TV series. You'd think that Charlie's announcement would have caused a tremendous splash. Instead, it landed with a dull thud. No one sought his resignation. The ribbing from his colleagues was friendly. The hate calls and mail were minimal. Charlie went on to organize the Gay Officers Action League (GOAL), three fifths of whose small membership are his fellow cops.

An amazing thing had happened: Charlie was defined not by his sexual behavior but by his occupation. Charlie was a well-liked cop, not a despised gay.

AIDS

Having made inroads in public opinion polls, politics, and religion, the last major hurdle on the path to full rights for gays is the stereotype of their lifestyle. The popular image is one of compulsive, promiscuous, public sex: steamy bathhouses in which private cubicles become the scene of hurried, impersonal trysts; public restrooms in which unsavory sex acts are committed in dirty toilets; "adult" movie houses in which anonymous hands grab at unzipped flies; Boston's "Combat Zone"; San Francisco's "Tenderloin"; New York's Morton Street pier. There's an element of truth in the imagery. To an extent, a mode of life has been forced on a subculture within a subculture because of its rejection by the straight world.

AIDS is changing that life. AIDS is not a disease of homosexuals: It can be caught and transmitted by anyone. It simply happened that gays were among the first to catch the virus in America. (In Africa, the disease strikes mostly heterosexuals.) Today, in New York City, AIDS is the leading cause of death among men aged twenty-five to forty-four. Sexual promiscuity abetted the flashfire of affliction, but that epidemic is now shifting the focus of gay sex from casual encounters to long-term monogamous relationships.

"Is compulsive sexuality freedom?" said a founder of the Gay Liberation Front to a reporter. "I would argue it's not. All we got was a lot more alienated sexually, and a lot more disease."

John Martin, of the Columbia University School of Public Health, collated interviews with one hundred homosexuals. Prior to the AIDS epidemic, he found that gay men had averaged 64 different sexual partners outside the home per year. After, the number dropped to 18. Before learning of the disease, one third visited bathhouses in search of sex. By 1985, that percentage had been halved. At the same time the city health department noted an 80-percent decline in venereal disease among gay men—even though the incidence continued to climb among straights. Martin's data show a 50-percent drop in anal intercourse and oral sex, a somewhat smaller decrease in kissing, and a two-thirds increase in use of condoms.

It's clear that gays have dramatically reduced the range of their partners as well as the scope of the sex in which they engage. The next step is settling down with one partner.

You won't find reliable numbers, but knowledgeable sources say that herpes and AIDS have added stability to the homosexual community. More and more gays are living as couples, their unions reinforced by religious ceremonies, wills, and "marriage" counseling. Jerome Skolnick's admonition, "the acceptability of certain behavior tends to vary positively with the social position of users," applies here.

Our rung on the social ladder is determined by our work, income, marital status, appearance, musical tastes—all the myriad quirks that make up this thing called "life-style." As upscale, monogamous gays become more visible, they will displace the popular—and unrepresentative—image of the effeminate "queen," the promiscuous leather boy, and the "butch dike." AIDS–induced equilibrium in the gay community will go a long way toward promoting its political, theological, and legal agenda.

ADVANCES IN DECRIMINALIZATION

None of this means the New Right will fold up its tent and give up its heartfelt antipathy to full legal and civil rights for gays. However, all its arguments were anticipated more than twenty years ago by the ground-breaking Wolfenden Report—which decriminalized private sexual conduct between consenting adults in England. Its answers are compelling:

> It is not the function of the law to intervene in the private lives of citizens, or to seek to enforce any particular pattern of behavior. . . . It follows that we do not believe it to be a function of the law to attempt to cover all the fields of sexual behavior. Certain forms of sexual behavior are regarded as sinful, morally wrong, or objectionable for reasons of conscience, or of religious or cultural tradition; and such actions may be reprobated on these grounds. But the criminal law does not cover all such actions. . . .

The Wolfenden Report draws a distinction between the private acts of consenting adults and other spheres of behavior. Part of the function of law, argues the report, is to safeguard youths or the mentally defective. Those who molest or seduce the helpless should be treated as criminals. Another function of law: to preserve public order and decency. Public homosexual behavior should continue to be dealt with by law, but acts committed in private by consenting adults should be exempt—even if the behavior makes a person susceptible to blackmail. Gamblers and drunkards are equally susceptible, says the report. Yet, they are not regarded as criminals. Neither should homosexuals be.

As for the damaging effects on family life, the report cites noncommercial adultery and fornication as much bigger threats than homosexuality (here even Richard Viguerie agrees). Yet, for the most part these are not criminal offenses. Why should homosexuality be?

Finally, the report addresses the old bugaboo about liberalization leading to license: "It is highly improbable that the man to whom homosexuality is repugnant would find it any less repugnant because the law permitted it in certain circumstances. . . .

"This is not to condone or encourage private immorality. On the contrary, to emphasize the personal and private nature of moral conduct is to emphasize the personal and private responsibility of the individual for his own actions. . . ."

CRIMEWARPS

- Antidiscrimination statutes will continue to proliferate at the local level, where moderate and/or Democratic administrations are the norm.
- At the federal level, protected status will not be extended to gays in the near future—especially during conservative and/or Republican administrations.
- States with existing sodomy laws are concentrated in the South, West North Central, and Mountain states. (Only Rhode Island falls outside these

three regions.) These three regions all have much larger Protestant majorities than those regions in which all or most states have decriminalized homosexuality. Decriminalization will proceed more rapidly in the West North Central and Mountain states than in the heavily fundamentalist South.

- Decriminalization through federal courts will be stymied due to the preponderance of conservative judges appointed during the Reagan years.
- A more educated and solidly moderate public will become increasingly tolerant of alternate sexual orientations.
- The number of AIDS cases will increase geometrically, thereby further restricting "compulsive" gay sexuality and encouraging gay monogamy. The ensuing "respectability" will ease the way for decriminalizing homosexuality.
- The incidence of homosexuality has remained constant despite liberalization of sodomy laws. There are no trends, demographic or otherwise, to indicate that this will change in the future.

13

Purveying Prurience

A video rental store in my neighborhood is a movie junkie's dream. Row upon row of tantalizing titles in every genre, every theme, every proclivity: Mystery, Adventure, Comedy, Horror, Foreign, Musical, Cartoons, Children's stories.

And in a far corner of the store, the X-rated section.

My neighborhood is a staid area of families, young children, and Park Avenue matrons. When the exclusive private schools let out at three o'clock, I often see youngsters trooping into the video store.

The store is staffed by hospitable, helpful workers, hardly the types you'd associate with purveyors of prurience. It's a nice place to hang out and watch whatever movie happens to be playing on the giant monitors. I've never seen the local students pay any attention to the "adult" corner. But the fact is, the kids and the X-rated tapes are there in the same room.

The friendly local video store has brought pornography uptown. No longer confined to masturbation galleries, dollar peep shows, and sleazy theaters, smut can now be found in better neighborhoods and shopping malls. There's no need to cross the tracks for a furtive exchange of cash for celluloid. Just phone it up and have it delivered along with a take-out pizza.

This newest kink in the sex trade has a lot of people upset. They are making up a new coalition of censors to ban pornography—and to a great extent, they will succeed.

□ □ □

Recently, the citizens of Phoenix prosecuted Arizona Home Video and Arizona Video Cassettes for obscenity in renting sexually explicit films. Similar actions had occurred in Cincinnati, Memphis, Nassau County, and Buffalo.

Such actions were not confined to little boxes labeled "VHS." The State of Utah tried in three separate instances to establish a law barring cable stations from carrying "indecent" programming. Indianapolis had earlier struggled to outlaw pornography on the grounds that it discriminated against women. The Federal Communications Commission attempted to limit the hours during which "dial-a-porn" services could operate. And a Fort Lauderdale, Florida, plumber, claiming to act on behalf of Jesus Christ, stripped copies of *Playboy* from the shelves of the Broward County library. Almost none of these efforts succeeded. But abetted by a powerful team of cheerleaders, the New Right on the one hand and feminists on the other, they might.

"It's time to stop pretending that extreme pornography is a victimless crime," declared the conservative President Ronald Reagan in June 1984.

"Pornography violates the civil rights of women and children," resolved the National Organization of Women at its Annual Meetings, in the same month.

Strange bedfellows, these two. They agree on only one issue: *the need to proscribe smut.* Because of their alliance, pornography will be the only consensual crime to be subject to more, rather than less, government interference in the future.

Pornography, per se, is not illegal. Obscenity is a crime, but it's tough to enforce because no one seems to know what it is. Where is the line between erotica and pornography? Between sexual explicitness and lewdness? Is a picture of an erect penis or vaginal lips more obscene than one of a gun held at the head of a Vietnamese peasant? Is sexual imagery part of free speech protected by the Constitution, or is it presumed harmful and therefore subject to prior restraint?

These questions are unanswerable. After muddling through various obscenity decisions for one hundred years, the Supreme Court threw up its hands in 1973 and dumped the definition of obscenity into the laps of individual communities. According to *Miller v. California,* "obscenity" must meet three tests:

1. The average person, applying "contemporary community standards," would find that the work, taken as a whole, appeals to prurient interests.

2. The work depicts, or describes, in a patently offensive way, sexual conduct specifically defined by the applicable state law.

3. The work, as a whole, lacks serious artistic, political, scientific value or other socially redeeming qualities.

These standards are almost impossible to meet and pornography—whatever it is—has blossomed into a $2-billion-to-$4-billion industry, some of it comprised of sexual exploitation of children.

ENFORCEMENT OF OBSCENITY LAW

The part of the smut trade that is criminal—child pornography, interstate transportation of obscene materials, unlawful mailings of obscene matter—is buried in a statistical category the FBI calls "sex offenses (except for forcible rape and prostitution)." Between 1973 and 1984, arrests for sex offenses increased 134 percent. However, the FBI has no way of telling what proportion of these arrests involve pornography. Nor does the increase in arrests necessarily imply an increase in the crime. Throwing the local sleazeball into the slammer may simply be a response to public pressure or changed police priorities rather than a growth in pornography.

The U.S. Postal Service, on the other hand, does track pornography. Obscenity complaints received by the U.S. Postal Service peaked at over 284,000 in 1970 and plummeted to about 5,000 in 1982. With the exception of a slight bump in 1976, the downward slide has been unbroken.

The number of investigations completed by the U.S. Postal Service in 1982 was about half of what it had been just four years earlier, but the number of convictions more than doubled. In 1977, a change in policy determined that postal inspectors would pursue only major dealers and organized crime networks. The petty operator mailing amateur photos from his basement would be left to pursue his fantasies in peace. By 1982, the number of dealers convicted was only 5. But even prior to the policy change, when small-timers were included convicted dealers never totaled more than 36.

Every once in a while, the federal government makes a sensational bust. A five-month sting completed in 1983 yielded up a New York peep show operator and two associates who had been planning to blanket Canada with American porn. By the time the FBI and Canadian Mounties got through with them, they had pleaded guilty to conspiring to transport hundreds of obscene videotapes across state lines. But for such exceptions, federal enforcement efforts are about as hamstrung as local ones.

THE REBELLION OF THE FUNDAMENTALIST RIGHT

Existing crime statutes don't seem to be the answer to erasing what many regard as a blight on our land. So pornography prohibitionists have elected to take the politico-religious route instead.

This is a good place to point out the class aspects of the fight against pornography. Nobody made much fuss about dirty amusements as long as they were restricted to the upper classes. Until the invention of Johannes Gutenberg's printing press in 1450, books were hand-copied by monks and stored in monasteries. Privately owned books were affordable only by the wealthy. Mass literacy did not arise until the eighteenth century. Up until then, pornography was the exclusive province of the religious and the rich.

As literacy spread, pornography became democratized—and that's when it became worrisome. A rising middle class challenged the power of entrenched aristocracies. A new kind of house, which featured a bedroom separated from the living room, introduced people to the notion of privacy and altered relationships between parents and children. Children, who until this time had been regarded as miniature adults needing no particular care, were now defined as immature creatures in need of protection. The role of mother assumed new importance. She had to become a "good example" for her offspring to follow. Powerful social forces dictated that everyone mind their morals. Pornophobia was born.

The phobia went so far, say sex historians Vern and Bonnie Bullough, that "The Song of Songs from the Jewish Scriptures and the Christian Bible has been banned as pornographic when printed separately from the Bible." Even the Puritans, frowning on lewdness and immodesty as they did, didn't go *that* far!

Today's new Puritans, the Fundamentalist Right, take their cues from the Bible and argue that the moral relativism of secular humanism has led to a pornographic explosion. By violating biblical teachings, they say, pornography enslaves and distorts women, destroys the privacy of sex, and abuses children.

Jerry Falwell brands pornographers "idolators" who worship money and will do anything to get it. Yet, despite the alleged threat these hedonists pose to civilization, Falwell disavows any interest in censorship. He puts his money on economic boycotts as the proper way for the free enterprise system to coax the media back to a "sensible and reasonable moral stand."

Richard Viguerie couldn't agree more. Touting the Reverend Don Wildmon's advertiser boycotts, he unfurls a catechism of television's sexual sins:

- In the fall of 1977, 1978, and 1979, almost all television sex took place outside marriage.
- During an average year of prime time viewing, television viewers are exposed to more than 11,000 sexual innuendos or scenes of implied intercourse. "Skin scenes" add another 7,000 to the total.
- Between 1978 and 1979, broadcast profanities increased by nearly half.

Viguerie grimly concludes: "The trend toward 'soft porn' on TV must and can be stopped. If we don't act, the 'porn' will get a little harder and more explicit each year." As a slavish follower of community standards, television will become sexually more conservative if its viewers do. So while plausible on its face, Viguerie's prediction isn't necessarily sound. In its sex-in-media protest, the New Right is lumping pornography with the quite different issues of chastity and extramarital sex.

Older Southern female Protestants are the New Right's strongest source of support for its position on pornography. Yet, even in the South a "community standard" can be elusive. In an Atlanta metropolitan area study, Georgia social scientists Margaret Herrman and Diane Bordner found an inconsistency between personal standards and perceived community standards. Material involving rape was strongly rejected as unacceptable at both the community and personal level. But media nudity, adultery, or gay sex were taken much more in stride at the personal level.

Young people, males, blacks, the highly educated, and not strongly religious were quite content to say "to each his own" when it came to the sale and distribution of pornography. Yet, when called on to judge a specific item of pornography, respondents transcended their own preferences and opted for what they perceived as the more rigid community standard.

If this is how jurors behave in an obscenity trial, Richard Viguerie and Jerry Falwell should feel quite hopeful about driving smut into the nether regions. Especially with the help they're getting from their unexpected feminist allies.

THE FEMINIST UPRISING

Feminists, who don't share fundamentalists' reverence for the Bible's depiction of women, are more focused in their attacks. Susan Brownmiller, author of *Against Our Will: Men, Women and Rape*, captures the essence of the feminist stance: "Pornography, like rape, is a male invention, designed to dehumanize women, to reduce the female to an object of sexual access, not to free sensuality from moralistic or parental inhibition. . . . Pornography is the undiluted essence of anti-female propaganda."

In supporting her argument, Brownmiller cites findings of the 1970 Report of the President's Commission on Obscenity and Pornography. The report revealed that only a small percentage of pornography is aimed at male homosexuals. The vast majority of consumers are middle-class, middle-aged, married heterosexual men whose self-esteem, attests Brownmiller, is bolstered by group gawks at naked female bodies.

The prevalent fantasies involve innocent virgins turned wanton sex slaves by one administration of a thrusting penis, and ravenous nymphomaniacs who can't get enough of that worthy organ. The report—finding porn to be harmless, if dirty, fun—was strongly denounced by the Nixon administration, which commissioned it.

Brownmiller joins in that denunciation, comparing pornography to "nigger" jokes and the worst anti-Semitic propaganda of the Third Reich. According to her, its contemptible stereotypes deprive women of civil rights as surely as negative imagery damages blacks, Jews, and other minorities.

She also argues that pornography deprives women of safety from sexual attack and takes the President's Commission to task for ignoring police testimony on how pornography causes crime. Sex offenders, say the cops, are avid consumers of pornography. Echoing Brownmiller and the police, the 1986 Attorney General's Commission on Pornography came out squarely on the side of the smut-violence connection. That argument was salient in 1985, when North Carolina got tough and declared distribution of obscenity a felony punishable by three years in prison. The sponsor of the bill, State Representative Richard Wright, had no trouble explaining its rationale: 75 percent of violent sex crime defendants in his state were found with hard-core S&M magazines in their homes or cars.

Diane Russell, a leading thinker in all areas of sexual exploitation, knows why: "pornography appears to foster rape fantasies and desires in the men who view it . . . pornography also plays a role in overcoming internal barriers against acting out these desires." She goes on to describe one study in which 10 percent of a random sample of San Francisco women complained that pornography-provoked partners tried to coerce them into humiliating or upsetting sex acts: urinating in someone's mouth, group sex, fellatio, spankings, bondage. Since pornography almost always depicts women being dominated in demeaning and unconventional situations, it's no wonder, explains Russell, that the red-blooded American boys who partake of it want to come home and try out what they've seen.

Frequently cited laboratory studies by social psychologists Edward Donnerstein, Seymour Feshbach, and Neil Malamuth show a strong link between sadistic pornography and aggression toward women. Sexual desire, like other forms of behavior, is a conditioned response. The linking of genital tingles with images of rape, bondage, and beating can create a response in which violence becomes associated with pleasure. The mechanics of behavioral conditioning are, for these researchers, a powerful argument against pornography.

Attitude surveys show that most of the public shares their perception. In 1980, when NORC asked respondents whether they felt pornographic material leads to rape, 54 percent said "yes"—a response that had inched up steadily since 1973. The conviction is strongest among those who share this profile: black, older, Protestant, female, grade school education, Southern, clerical worker, low income.

But the public doesn't translate a perceived link between pornography and rape into a total ban on smut. The majority believe that laws should forbid distribution only to those under eighteen. Since we now know that most consumers are middle aged, it's hard to see how that addresses the problem of rape.

CRY RAPE!

The rape connection is spurious. Therefore, if sexual assault is the rationale, it would be a mistake to extend pornography bans to adults.

It pains me to oppose Susan Brownmiller and Diane Russell, whose work I greatly admire. Having been an activist for women's rights and an advocate for rape victims, I am sympathetic. However, as a social scientist I cannot in good conscience agree with the feminist position on the link between rape and pornography. The evidence simply does not hold up.

In supporting her claims, Brownmiller cites police experience with sex offenders who are caught with vast caches of pornographic material. But she falls into the trap of generalizing from a self-selected sample. While there may be some rapists who indulge in porn, there are many more pornophiles who never rape.

One indicator of pornography consumption is the circulation of sex magazines. In 1983, according to the Audit Bureau of Circulations, the most popular among these had the following circulation:

Playboy	4,209,324
Penthouse	3,500,275
Hustler	1,083,744

Even assuming that the people who read *Penthouse* and *Hustler* are the same ones who read *Playboy*, rent X-rated videotapes, attend live sex shows, and masturbate to dial-a-porn messages, that still leaves a minimum of 4.2 million consumers of pornography for 1983. Yet, according to the National Crime Survey there were only 162,000 rapes (both reported and unreported) that year. That's, *at most*, 1 rape for every 25 people who consume pornography. This unrealistically high ratio assumes that: There are no more than 4 million consumers of pornography in this country (the likelihood is that there are many times that number); every rape is committed by a consumer of pornography (not true); each rape is committed by a separate offender (wrong—some commit multiple rapes). With less-conservative assumptions, we could easily defend a ratio of 1 to 100 and lower.

But regardless of the ratio, while there seems to be an increase in the consumption of pornography, there has actually been a slight decrease in the rate of rape since 1973. For those rapists who happen to be pornography enthusiasts, who's to say that a sexual assault wouldn't have occurred even without the titillation of a *Playboy* centerfold? In my admittedly few interviews with rapists, I never came across one who said *"Hustler* made me do it." As feminists freely acknowledge, rape is primarily a crime of power, not lust.

Yes, you might reply at this point, but pornography feeds the need for power and dominance just as much as it stimulates lust. And you could be right. But that link has never been firmly established.

Laboratory situations in which unrepresentative samples of college students and children have been tested for a link between pornographic stimulation and aggression have very little in common with the real world. The lab is an abstract setting in which the ordinary forces mediating social intercourse are missing. Most studies test the response to a single violent episode and tell us nothing about the effect of repeated exposure. The aggressive effects they test take place immediately after the viewing and tend to evaporate within twenty minutes. Often the subjects have been angered or frustrated before being exposed to the violent stimulus, creating a condition that does not reflect the circumstances under which most people go to a movie or watch television. Absent are inhibitors such as rejection, fear of reprisals, reality-testing, fondness, criminal sanctions, elapsed time. By diluting social controls, laboratory conditions allow subjects to act out behaviors that they would be unlikely to replicate in real life. Just because an aroused nineteen-year-old administers a mild electric shock to a partner in a simulated situation doesn't mean he'll beat his girlfriend upon leaving the neighborhood screening of *Deep Throat.*

On the contrary, a convincing argument can be made that pornography acts as an institutionalized safety valve which allows the safe release of unsavory sexual appetites and aggressions. According to Shere Hite, less than one third of her *Hite Report* subjects felt that pornography represented "elemental truths about how men and women really are." They were perfectly capable of separating fantasy sex from real sex. While 40 percent thought the pornography they had seen was "good" or "O.K.", most thought it was "poor, disgusting" or had mixed reactions:

"My first hard-core movie made me want to give up sex altogether. . . . I felt degraded to be in the same species as the things on the screen," said one of the men Hite interviewed.

"Most porno turns me off," said another. "There is no feeling, caring, or tenderness in it. A lot of it seems to me to be sexual violence."

A third man was just plain bored by pornography. "How many women in black lacy garter belts do you have to look at before they all look the same? . . . How many pictures of dogs humping fat models before they all look the same . . . even the dogs!"

Only one third of Hite's sample looked at pornography with any regularity. Clearly, men are not without critical faculties when it comes to smut.

Hite's respondents included a subset who had learned of her survey through men's magazines. One of these, *Penthouse*, printed her questionnaire in its entirety. Among the questions she asked was, "Have you ever wanted to rape a woman?" In her anonymous general sample, only 14 percent answered "yes." The highest percentage of positive responses—a terrifying 39—was found in the men's magazines subset.

On the face of it, this seems to support Brownmiller and Russell's claims. But there's a big difference between thinking about rape and doing it. It simply may be that men who are particularly angry toward women vent their spleen in the pages of girlie magazines.

But men who rape are typically between the ages of eighteen and twenty-nine —with twenty-year-olds taking the lead in rape arrests, and Brownmiller cites data showing that pornography is primarily a middle-aged preoccupation. So it can't be sleaze that's driving most of our young rapists.

CIVIL LIBERTIES VERSUS CIVIL RIGHTS

At bottom, the battle raging around pornography is a conflict between civil liberties, which focus on individual freedoms, and civil rights, which emphasize equality.

Russell describes women—a scant one tenth of her San Francisco sample— who have been maneuvered into degrading sexual encounters by men assumed to be overstimulated by dirty reading and lewd movies. But even this small group has a right to be free of unwanted sexual pressures. It is here that free speech rights butt up against women's minority rights.

The civil rights argument holds that pornography damages women as a minority group, both physically and socially. In 1984, this assertion was brought before the Senate Subcommittee on Juvenile Justice, which was examining the effects of smut. The subcommittee heard testimony that pornography acts as a "triggering factor" in a wide range of sexual abuses—incest, pedophilia, wife beating—by implicitly legitimating the behavior it depicts.

On the social level, pornography communicates a message about women that impacts on the way the world responds to them. In the sordid purgatory of X-rated fantasies, women are objects to be probed, prodded, tortured, debased. They are accorded no reality except as hollow vessels for male effluvia of every sort. Porno-women don't exist as mothers, friends, or wives except insofar as these roles provide fodder for mate swaps or a ménage à trois. Women's needs, thoughts, feelings are safely omitted from consideration. Like the protagonist in *The Story of O,* their sole function is to fulfill men's impulses. What depths of contempt such fantasies convey! It is horrifying to think how profoundly the sexes can hate each other.

Women want to seek relief for their defamation through the civil courts. Where they can establish that they have been harmed by specific items of pornography, they propose to sue for injunctions and monetary damages. Rather than relying on the fickle protection of criminal obscenity and child pornography laws, they want recourse to civil sex discrimination statutes.

Yet, just because an idea is ugly doesn't mean that it cannot be expressed. In response to the proposed antismut civil rights legislation, the New York *Times* editorialized: "By casting so wide a net, the sponsors have turned a grievance into an unconstitutional assault on expression." The Supreme Court concurred when, in February 1986, it struck down an Indianapolis ordinance that defined pornography as a form of discrimination against women.

Freedom and equality are at war over smut. Under our Constitution, we have no more right to stop pornographers from exposing women's genitals than we have to ban white supremacists from scorning blacks or to prohibit Louis Farrakhan from villifying Jews. All are part of the baggage that comes with the First Amendment. But freedom of speech is its own remedy. So long as that liberty exists, all groups have a limitless platform through which to struggle for their civil rights and counter the poison of hatemongers.

CHILD PORNOGRAPHY

There is one form of pornography that is reviled by libertarians, conservatives, fundamentalists, and feminists alike: kiddie porn. Children require special protection from adult sexual predations, and courts have ruled that freedom of speech does not extend to that form of expression. Since the passage of the 1977 Protection of Children Against Sexual Exploitation Act, child pornography has become one of the few forms of smut that is unequivocally criminal.

Close to 45,000 children are estimated to be sexually exploited each year. Many of them are runaways who support their lives on the street with prostitution and pornography. Others simply fall victim to the camera of the neighborhood Boy Scout leader.

Pederasty did not always have a bad name. The term derives from the Greek words for "boy" and "love." In ancient Greece, the love of boys was a vehicle for inculcating manly virtues into each generation of free men. The sexual component of such liaisons was incidental and flowed from the Greek ideal of youth and beauty, an ideal in which women had almost no place. The main focus was to train youths in Greek ethics and promote the symmetrical development of mind and body that was the hallmark of Hellenic civilization.

Contemporary pederasts are not so noble in their intent. Like the Greeks, they tend to be male (female pedophilia is virtually unknown), but their quarries are not restricted to boys. Nor do their goals have anything to do with inculcating high ideals and good citizenship.

Their real interests are reflected in the titles of pedophile literary tomes such as: *Lolita Love, Lesbian Lolita, Advanced Young Sex, Little Girl Lovers, Little Boy Homo Come Blow Your Horn, Pre-Teen Girls and Animals, Dad & Auntie Show Them How, Big Daddy's Little Girls, Children in Chains, Kinder Orgy, Baby Sex,* and *Boy Hungry Studs.* The titles sound obviously sordid, their subjects blatantly illegal, but it isn't always easy to confiscate such work. You can't always tell from a picture whether a model is underaged or just young-looking. And some perfectly wholesome "facts of life" books, like *Show Me!,* depict children in some of the same poses as pedophilic smut.

One Los Angeles ring, thought to control 80 percent of the organized kiddie porn trade, grossed $500,000 a year with its 30,000-name mailing list. The ringleader, Catherine "Black Cathy" Wilson, was a middle-class housewife and mother of five. With her conviction and demise, the child pornography business was driven deeper underground where it is harder to ferret out.

Homegrown kiddie porn is now said to make up 90 percent of the child pornography market. Pedophiles are loosely organized into networks that meet to swap children's pictures, recruit victims, and slaver over each other's sexual encounters. A few years ago, an investigation in New Orleans unearthed a web of 25 pederasts in the Boy Scouts, Big Brothers, and a local private school who had seduced and photographed some 100 children.

Lone child molesters also indulge in homemade pornography. In late 1985, a Louisiana priest was sentenced for engaging in oral sex and sodomy with dozens of parish children over a six-year period. The now defrocked priest, Gilbert Gauthe, often commemorated these trysts by photographing them. Among the victims were little girls and altar boys who were molested in the priest's van, the rectory, and even the confessional.

Devout pedophiles have several organizations to lobby for legalizing sex with children: North American Man-Boy Lovers Association, Pedophiles Alliance League, and Rene Guyon Society (whose creed is "Sex before eight, before it's too late"). Legal or not, the pederast's victims often grow up to become pederasts themselves, thus expanding the market for child pornography.

The pedophile's appetite for photographs of spread-eagled, naked children is only partially satisfied with local talent. The rest is fulfilled by professional "chickens"—often young runaways—who get paid for posing. In one study of the interrelationship between child prostitution and pornography, more than one quarter of the "chickens" had been photographed by customers. In another, it was just under one fifth.

The kiddie porn problem has been exacerbated since the passage of the Juvenile Justice and Delinquency Prevention Act of 1974. Prior to the act, tens of thousands of youths had been jailed for minor acts—known as "status" offenses—which, if committed by adults, would not be considered criminal. Running away was one. By 1984, the number of jailed status offenders (and nonoffenders) had dropped by over 88 percent. The intervening years had seen the implementation of a policy of "deinstitutionalization." If runaways ran into a cop, the worst that could happen was that they would be remanded to a voluntary shelter—from which they were free to run away again. Back on the streets, they remained prey for the predators who recruit children for pornographic pictures and other sexual services.

Penny was an eleven-year-old runaway in Los Angeles. In June 1983, she found herself a place to live. It was the kind of place that runaways often find—a "crash pad" in which adults house juveniles for purposes of prostitution and pornography. Although the authorities couldn't legally hold her for running away, she soon gave them reason enough. She became a thief and a streetwalker. How else can an eleven-year-old possibly survive on her own?

Such stories are ghastly. You must be wondering why sexual exploitation of children has grown rather than abated since it was outlawed. Gloria Steinem has a penetrating answer: It's a backlash against the women's movement. Because men can no longer sexually dominate adult women as easily as they once did, many are turning to malleable youngsters instead.

In some cases, the way men are brought up primes them for such a solution. Unlike women, they're often taught to pursue partners who are smaller, weaker, younger—more "childlike" than themselves. Men, more than women, are easily aroused by sex devoid of any prior relationship. Men, unlike women, have trouble distinguishing between affection and sex, adds David Finkelhor, a family violence expert, in a study on sexual abuse of minors.

All of this spells trouble for children. They will remain popular objects of pornography for the generations of older men who grew up in the prefeminist era and must now negotiate its unfamiliar terrain. The younger ones, for whom sexual equality is part of the world they take for granted, will be less attracted to child pornography than their predecessors.

For those inclined to exploit children, the law is a sieve that's easy to slip through. In addition to federal legislation, at least fifteen states have added sexual exploitation to their definitions of prosecutable child abuse and neglect statutes. Some laws aim at the offender while others focus on providing services to the victim. Locating either one is a monumental task, especially when the two must be brought face-to-face in a courtroom. For that reason, more than 90 percent of all child abuse (including sexual exploitation) cases never get prosecuted.

However, a number of innovations are making it easier for victims of child pornographers and others to confront their exploiters. Videotaped and closed-circuit television testimony are among the most publicized but least widely used methods. More popular and less constitutionally troublesome are enhancing the child's ability to communicate through use of dolls, pictures, and simplified vocabulary; making the courtroom more friendly by putting the child in a small witness chair on the same level as the judge; briefing the victim on what goes on in a court and who plays what role; and having the child answer questions in the presence of a supportive person. Techniques such as these require no statutory changes. They will become widespread and help rectify the wrong of child pornography.

THE COMING BAN ON PORNOGRAPHY

When judging pornography—whether child or adult—most people seem willing to transcend their own preferences and defer to what they regard as the greater good. Attitude surveys consistently find that the majority of the public is ban-happy. Rather than seeing pornography as a "victimless" crime, they regard it as actively harmful to community standards. They're ready to censor obscene books and remove them from high school libraries; pull all X-rated movies out of the theaters and clean up sex scenes in television shows. Only the courts stand in their way.

This isn't surprising. Polls of lawyers and judges show them to be vastly more libertarian in their outlook than the mass public. It's not because they're knee-jerk liberals; rather, superior education in law and government and a hands-on understanding of the Bill of Rights make them extremely reluctant censors.

Community leaders also score higher on tolerance and civil liberties than does the mass public. Therefore, the two groups that sit in the driver's seat in terms of banning pornography are not likely to do it without a very strong push from the general population.

Among the mass public, a libertarian ideology prevails most strongly among the liberal left, where 95 percent have a high tolerance of freedom of speech, expression, and privacy. This compares with a scant 10 percent in the conservative right. Most of the public is found at neither of these extremes, but rather defines itself as middle-of-the-road. Even among these moderates, a larger percentage would favor an action like closing down a nude play than those who would protest it as an incursion on freedom of expression.

When it comes to pornography, the libertarians lose.

CRIMEWARPS

· Herpes, AIDS, and other health scares will discourage people from indulging in multiple sexual partners. Pornography will become more popular as an aid to infusing excitement into monogamous relationships and solitary sexual activity.

· As pornography becomes more "private," via the VCR and cable television, it will become more accessible and acceptable to the middle class and use will increase.

· Sexual explicitness will increase on cable television as technology makes it possible for parents to scramble signals or lock out certain programming options for their children.

· As pornography becomes more popular among the middle class, it will become more sanitized. That is, it will be less exploitative of children and less brutal toward women.

· The appeal of child pornography will decline as the current and future generations of men reach adulthood. They will have grown up in an atmosphere of greater female equality and will be less threatened by its sexual consequences than those who grew up in more traditional role assignments.

· The number of pederasts will increase as the baby boom generation of sexually abused children reaches adulthood, thereby expanding the market for child pornography.

· Tolerance of pornography varies directly with the size of the city in which one lived during one's formative years. This and the past several generations of Americans have been raised in or near large cities, but the current urban-rural migration will spread tolerant attitudes toward pornography into the hinterlands.

· Migrations from the more liberal Northeast to the more traditional South will similarly diffuse more tolerant attitudes about pornography to the South.

· As women become a growing force in the labor market, they will become more resentful of obscene material that degrades them. This resentment will not extend to nondegrading sexually explicit material, to which increased educational levels will make them receptive.

· The more religious a person, the more intolerant of pornography. Because religiosity will grow with the aging of the population, pornography will be rejected by an increasingly powerful voting bloc who will promote local bans based on broad community standards of "obscenity." They will be joined by feminists.

· At the federal level, where judicial appointments are more remote from local pressures, courts will remain leaders rather than followers of public opinion, upholding a libertarian interpretation of pornography.

· The New Right's attempt to lump all manner of sexually explicit material into the same category as pornography will be more successful in areas that are heavily fundamentalist, low income, and poorly educated.

14

Upping the Ante on Gambling

A mournful-looking man stood at the podium, his eyes as dark as his suit. On his head was a yarmulke, the skullcap worn at all times by Orthodox Jews as a sign of deference to God. The man, however, wasn't just any Jew. He was a rabbi, heir to a proud calling he shared with his father and three brothers. This gathering at the United Jewish Appeal's headquarters in New York wasn't his usual pulpit. Nor was he about to preach from the Torah. The rabbi's sermon this 1984 Chanukah season dealt with his own hellish descent into uncontrollable gambling, a disease which has been proliferating with the commuter casinos on Atlantic City's glitzy boardwalk.

The speaker's compulsion had begun eleven years earlier, when he was invited to go to a racetrack in the mountains. He was unlucky—he won his first bet. It was the beginning of the end for his family, his honor, and his calling: "I was ready to give up the rabbinate and make a lot of money."

Soon gambling became a "total preoccupation." His life revolved around the OTB (Off Track Betting) parlor and Atlantic City. He gambled away his children's Yeshiva tuition. He neglected his congregation. He even embezzled proceeds from the raffles he had sold on behalf of his brother's dead seven-year-old child.

Horses and gaming tables had become bottomless wells into which the rabbi poured his life. His wife left him. His children rejected him, and his grandchildren were kept away from him. He could sink no lower. He joined Gamblers Anonymous and fought his way back to self-respect and his tradition.

That tradition has had a profound impact on America's love-hate relationship with games of chance. Rabbinic literature regards gambling as a form of theft because winning means taking another person's money for sport. Wagering *is* permissible at designated times: Purim, Chanukah, Succoth, to pass the hours while attending a childbirth, and to ease pain while sick. But the gambler— especially the compulsive one—is viewed as a reprobate. He wastes his time in useless activity when he should be spending it on gaining knowledge and doing community service. As a Jew, he is derelict; gambling interferes with his study of Torah and the keeping of holy observances.

Jewish law levels harsh penalties at gamblers. They are barred from the honor of being called to the Torah. They cannot be married in a synagogue or buried in hallowed ground. Gambling debts, unlike all other obligations, are not collectible through Jewish courts.

Early rabbis tried to ban gambling—with little success. They could not buck the tide of dice, cards, and lotteries that had swept through Europe—including its Jews—by the eighteenth century. Horror of gambling was brought across the Atlantic by the Puritans, whose strictures echo their Hebrew moral roots. Today's fundamentalists have inherited that legacy.

The issues around gambling have not changed for hundreds—perhaps thousands—of years. Gambling is a crime that breeds crime. But that doesn't lessen its appeal. As long as people believe that "everybody's doing it" and there are ready outlets for wagering, we will play the odds. The more gambling becomes available and legal, the more people will be drawn into it.

THE DEMOGRAPHICS OF AMERICAN GAMBLING

The first serious measures of gambling in the United States came out of the 1976 Commission on the Review of National Policy Toward Gambling. A whopping 61 percent of the sample admitted to betting—most of it casual. Nearly half patronized legal commercial games like lotteries and races. Eleven percent dabbled in illegal gambling. Another 3 percent placed more than $200 a year in illicit bets.

Prior to the fiscal crises of the 1970s, the majority of states forbade all forms of gambling. Today, almost all permit some gambling, usually at racetracks. More than one third sponsor lotteries and several allow off-track betting, casinos, and sports wagering.

If you want to bet legally, 42 states also give you the option of charity bingo, and about 170 Indian reservations, where states have no jurisdiction, offer a high-stakes, fast-action variety. In Red Rock, Oklahoma, for example, the Otoe Missouria tribe plays host to bused-in bingo fans from St. Louis. In contrast to the tame $500 grand prize in that city's church basements, the Otoes provide a pot of up to $400,000 for a weekend.

But most of us who gamble lean toward the penny ante, wagering less than $50 in the course of a year. High rollers (defined by the commission as those who bet more than $200 a year) make up only about one seventh of the population. If you're male, under forty-four years of age, Catholic, divorced or separated, of Italian or African descent, have only a high school education but a $15,000 plus income, and live near a large city in the Northeast, the commission's surveys say you're more likely to be a heavy bettor than the rest of us. Big spenders tend to favor betting on football games and other sports. But for others, penny poker with friends absorbs the largest share (16 percent) of all gambling activities, followed by lotteries, bingo, and sports bets.

Despite all the agonizing about the economic costs of gambling, our net outlay for legal wagering is quite small. Once you deduct the "take-out" and winnings from the total taken in of $22.4 billion, the cost in 1974 was $4.4 billion—about the same amount we spent for newspapers and magazines that year. The illegal net was even smaller, coming to about $1 billion. This relatively modest amount is attributable to the demographics of illegal gambling. Black and Hispanic central city males in the Northeast are overrepresented among closet bettors. Numbers, the game they favor, involves light bets and accounts for only 1.5 percent of all gambling in the U.S. Lotteries are another low-income, low-ante favorite.

The Founding Fathers—and even the Puritans—approved of legal public lotteries as a benign, voluntary form of taxation. In the colonial period and the early days of our nation, lotteries financed wars, schools, public buildings, bridges, churches, and municipal services. We have since learned that both overt and covert games can be highly regressive. The most regressive—those with high take-out rates and outrageously unfair odds—are the ones on which the lowest income bettors wager: numbers and state lotteries. The progressive games are the ones favored by higher income gamblers: casinos, sports books, and horses. If every form of gambling were to be legalized in every state, the government's share would add revenues of only 4 percent to our national treasury.

In states that have legalized various forms of gaming, there is a lower percentage of nongamblers than in those few states that remain staunch holdouts. Nongamblers are becoming an endangered species.

But there will always be a pool who cannot be enticed to bet. Two thirds of these think gambling is "a waste of money," or "don't want to lose money," or "don't have the money." One half were brought up to believe that gambling is sinful and wrong. Fundamentalists and other serious churchgoers have put a great distance between themselves and games of chance, but they've been surprisingly mute in terms of formal opposition to legal gambling.

Among the holdouts are those who grew up in rural areas and work as farmers or semiskilled laborers. They spend more of their free time lolling in the house and have less money to spend than the more restless gambling population. Nearly two thirds of nonbettors have incomes under $10,000.

Except for the forms favored by low income groups—numbers and lotteries—gambling is an elite activity. That's why it garners so much social approval. The highest proportion of gamblers are suburbanites. The more degrees they have on their wall and the more money they make, the more likely they are to gamble. As with pornography and prostitution, vice seems acceptable as long as it's upscale.

To a gambler, legal and illegal bets are interchangeable. It's the form that counts:

· Do you like the horses? You're apt to bet on them legally at the track, as well as illegally off-track.
· Is football your game? Odds are you won't stop to think whether you're breaking the law before you call your bookie or organize your friends into a pool.
· Do you bet on state-run lotteries? You're just as likely to play illegal numbers.
· Are you mainly an illegal gambler? Then you're also among the heaviest hitters on legal and informal wagers.

But for the serious gambler, legal games can't begin to compete with the personal service, credit extension, and nontaxable earnings of the clandestine ones.

GAMBLING AND THE MOB

Illegal gambling is an issue, not so much because it eats up taxable revenues but because it is commonly assumed to be controlled by mobsters. By the time Prohibition came and went, gangster-capitalists had secured a foothold in what came to be known as "organized crime." Gambling had become big business—one of the ways that immigrants and blacks could claw their way out of the tenements of New York's Harlem and Lower East Side, and the slums of Chicago, Detroit, and Philadelphia. Policy, poolrooms, private casinos, and sports cards gave impoverished Jews and Irish a leg up in the Anglo-Saxon world that wouldn't accept them. Soon, joined by the Italians, they came to dominate the gambling rackets. They went on to create the gaming meccas that drew high rollers from all over America. Meyer Lansky and Bugsy Siegel developed Las Vegas. Lansky also moved in on Miami and Havana—later, the Bahamas—under the approving, if wary, gaze of Lucky Luciano, Frank Costello, and Vito Genovese. Meanwhile, WASP descendants of riverboat gamblers had established their own gambling empires in the parishes around New Orleans and the Ohio River valley.

More recently, the Justice Department has found the mob's hegemony to be incomplete. Even in the Northeast, where organized crime is most active in gambling, it controls no more than 54 percent of the action. In the Southwest, where its influence is weakest, it directs only about 2 percent. Although we tend to associate organized crime with the glittering Strip in Las Vegas, casinos are the smallest contributors to the mob's gambling revenues. Sources agree that organized crime's richest vein is the sports bookie.

Heavy betting on one team could easily wipe out an independent operator.

The alternative is to spread the risk, just like an insurance company; only in this case, the underwriter is the mob. Next time you place that illegal bet on a Jets or Cardinals game, know that—unless you're playing the odds with your drinking buddies—your money is going straight into the till of a syndicate.

That same kind of laying off of odds takes place in the numbers racket. A Cuban-American syndicate called "the Corporation" allegedly runs a $45-million-a-year gambling cartel in New York and New Jersey. Having discovered high tech, the Corporation runs its numbers by rigging video card game machines. Working in cahoots with the Mafia, the racketeers consolidated their control by killing some twenty competitors—mostly Hispanic owners of bars and bodegas—and burning down their businesses.

"In the tristate New York area alone," estimates Federal Judge Irving Kaufman, "$1.5 billion is spent each year on numbers games, sports, bookmakers and other forms of illegal wagering controlled by organized crime."

Organized crime doesn't limit itself to illegal gambling. Debacles like the 1950 Kefauver Committee and Fidel Castro's 1959 nationalization of Cuba's hotels taught mobsters a lesson: Conduct business where gambling is both legal and safe from Communist revolutions. In the United States, that has usually meant Nevada—where, since 1931, anything goes—and New Jersey.

In Atlantic City, Caesar's World, Bally Manufacturing, and Playboy Enterprises all had licensing problems because of the presence of organized crime figures on their payrolls. Their owners were banished from the casino business in New Jersey and forced to sell their interests in their companies. Hilton, which would have been the eleventh casino to be built on the Boardwalk, was denied a license altogether partly because of its retention of reputed mob lawyer, Sidney Korshak.

There's good reason to believe that organized crime does better with legal than illegal gambling. The highly profitable games are legal, but the skimming, fixes, credit frauds, and payoffs for labor peace aren't. Thanks to the money laundering skills that Meyer Lansky gave vice entrepreneurs, the mob is camouflaged in a veil of corporate respectability. But it's there—on the Strip and the Boardwalk; among the junket operators; in the Teamsters Union; behind the charity games; lurking in the shadows of the superfectas. The only form of gambling that shows no sign of mob infiltration is the state-run lottery.

GAMBLING ADDICTS

The gambling commission's report conservatively estimates that there are about 1 million compulsive gamblers in the United States. It further surmises that slightly more than 2 percent of the adult population is *potentially* compulsive. That means, given the opportunity, some 3 million addicted bettors could be added to the roster of walking catastrophes. Nearly all the states are now providing that opportunity in some form or other. Therefore, we are faced with a potential pool of 4 million gambling addicts. Those who treat them say that each addict causes 10 to 12 other people—family, friends, co-workers—to suffer with his excesses. (I use the pronoun "his" advisedly: Studies show that men are twice as likely to be compulsive gamblers as women.)

Prior to the opening of the first Atlantic City casino on Memorial Day 1978, Americans had to travel to isolated places if they wanted to play legal craps, blackjack, or keno. If you were classy and wealthy, you might have joined the chemin de fer crowd in the black tie casino in Monte Carlo. The casual type? You hopped a plane to Las Vegas and played the one-armed bandits. The Caribbean more convenient? The El San Juan in Puerto Rico might have been your lure. If all else failed, at least they'd send you home with a foil bar of souvenir dice. There were also the sad casinos of Haiti and the garishly festooned tourists of once-elegant Paradise Island. The more subdued might have grabbed their passports and headed for the tightly regulated private clubs of London.

The point is, casino gambling as a means of amusement used to be out of the way. You needed both the time to travel and the money for the airfare. Lots of people had neither. Today, commuter gambling has been plunked in the middle of the most concentrated population center in the country—the New York megatropolis that stretches from Boston to Washington, D.C. Any evening or weekend, 37 million people of gambling age are within an easy drive of the tables in Atlantic City. Visitors amounting to three fifths that number jam into the forty-seven-block resort annually—twice the quantity that go to Las Vegas. The first casino to debut in New Jersey took in more money in its opening year than the four largest Las Vegas casinos combined.

Monsignor Joseph Dunne, President of the National Council on Compulsive Gambling, warns, "Las Vegas has moved East." In 1983, 45 percent of the calls to his organization came from the New York area. Since the Atlantic City casinos have opened, Gamblers Anonymous meetings have burgeoned. The fallen rabbi is in good company.

□   □   □

Gamblers Anonymous says the average age of its members is dropping. Addicts as young as fourteen are showing up at meetings. Dr. Henry LeSieur, a criminologist who has spent years studying compulsive gamblers, found that 5 percent of the New Jersey teenagers he surveyed were diagnosable pathological bettors. LeSieur's survey drew a random sample of students from four middle-class, suburban New Jersey high schools. Their extracurricular activities were not what you'd expect:

• 45 percent played the illegal numbers or the legal lottery—13 percent weekly.
• 46 percent gambled in casinos—3 percent every week.
• 45 percent wagered on illegal football pool tickets—17 percent weekly.

Teenagers are spending their lunch money on lottery tickets, OTB parlors, racetracks, casinos, and illegal sports cards. When they can't finance their gambling legally, LeSieur finds they are shoplifting, stealing from their parents, and selling drugs. Many of them reason that if gambling's okay for their parents, it's okay for them. Five percent of the students define their parents as problem gamblers. The addicted teenage gamblers are, more often than not, their off-spring. Robert Custer, who set up a federal gambling treatment center in Cleveland, observes that all the compulsive gamblers he has treated recently started out with illegal underage betting.

The young are the most vulnerable bettors, and gambling rates decrease with age. But those who are exposed to wagering as children and live in a setting where gambling is readily available, are more likely to become bettors than those for whom gambling is a distant rumor.

State-run and legalized gambling are creating an environment in which children are learning to glorify the crapshoot. Dr. LeSieur deplores this ethic in New Jersey: "The state is the biggest bookie. The state is legitimizing gambling and it's throwing out peanut shells. It has established one treatment center. They're making millions of dollars on racetracks, lotteries, and casinos. And they're not giving back 1/10th of 1 percent to help solve the problems they're creating."

□　□　□

In Atlantic City, ten casinos are currently grossing a total of $2 billion a year. Of this amount, each casino is required to invest 1.25 percent of its revenues in community redevelopment projects for twenty-five years—an estimated $1.6 billion over a quarter century. Another hunk comes off the top to help the aged and handicapped. The casinos have created 35,000 jobs. (The good ones, complain the locals, all go to out-of-towners.) With gambling legalized, the need to bribe cops is removed. That's the up side.

The downside? Along with billions of dollars and millions of visitors come common thieves, prostitutes, con men, and organized crime. Between 1976 and 1981, major crimes soared 170 percent. Just a couple of blocks off the tinsel trappings of the Boardwalk, Atlantic City remains dilapidated and grim. If Monsignor Dunne is right, nearly half the National Council on Compulsive Gambling's constituency is in the New York metro area. That means we have paid for New Jersey's windfall with the well-being of at least 2 million people—addicted gamblers and their families. The issue for us voters is how many compulsive gamblers we're willing to abide for each million dollars in additional revenue the state rakes in.

ENFORCEMENT

Despite the presence of organized crime, illegal games, and a growing hunger for wagering, gambling enforcement has been waning. According to the FBI, gambling arrests have slipped by about 60 percent since 1973. No doubt this has much to do with the wave of legalization that began with the 1963 education sweepstakes in New Hampshire and the 1970 opening of OTB in New York. The roughly 40,000 gambling arrests made in each recent year account for a mere .3 percent of all arrests combined. Most involve small-time crooks: street level numbers runners, local bookies, and floating crap games.

The organized crime honchos are sufficiently well buffered that you won't find them in the Uniform Crime Reports. Look for them instead in the U.S. district courts, where the big guns are tried. In 1983, 118 defendants were sentenced on federal gambling and lottery charges. Only half went to prison. The more telling statistic for organized crime, however, is the one found on the line above "gambling and lottery." This is the one called "extort racketeering threats." Here 574 were convicted and nearly three quarters went to jail.

If these numbers seem low, it's because gambling has been a low priority for police and public alike. Resources devoted to gambling enforcement average only about 1 percent of the police force.

It's tempting to argue that if a gambling law can't be enforced we should get rid of it. Yet, even in states where legal forms of gambling are available, the public expects existing laws to be upheld. Nonwhite residents of Northeast urban areas, in particular, demand not only that police hold the line but that they increase gambling enforcement. Given the popularity of numbers games in those parts, this finding is hard to explain. It may simply reflect the fact that, because they suffer disproportionately from crime in general, low income minorities favor more zealous policing as a matter of course.

THE DECRIMINALIZATION OF GAMBLING

Gambling has always been a favorite target of reform administrations. Throughout our history, we have tread a thin line between permissiveness and prohibition. When abuses got out of hand, the reformers would blow in. But every time gambling was suppressed, it came back stronger than ever. After Prohibition, during the Depression, in the riotous prosperity of the postwar years, and in the freewheeling 1960s and 1970s, America rushed to place its bets. By 1982, we were wagering nearly four times the amount that we had ten years earlier.

If local coffers were ringing empty, all other considerations were set aside and a new push for legalization would ensue. Pari-mutuel betting and lotteries always came up as the odds-on favorites in such drives. When synagogues and churches grappled with the ethical dilemma of sponsoring gambling to fund worthy causes, bingo games and "Las Vegas nights" made a good showing. Gambling gained respectability whenever it was adopted as a revenue raiser for public causes.

Despite zeal to enforce gambling laws, time and again voters have shown a great willingness to change those laws. In the nineteenth century, for example, lottery brokers became bankers of sorts; some went on to found real banks. But the late 1800s saw the development of more conventional means of public finance. By 1930, 45 states had joined the federal government in outlawing lotteries. In the 1960s, they started reversing themselves.

In those states where some form of gambling is already legal, there is a predisposition to favor the legalization of other forms. Ironically, it is our Puritan stronghold, the Northeast—where four fifths of adults gamble—that has been most receptive to legal gambling. The South, fundamentalist heir to the Puritans, where only two fifths of adults indulge, has been the most resistant.

Over 50 gambling referenda representing more than half the states have been held in this century, the majority of them since 1970. All of those dealing with state-run lotteries, bingo games, and charitable Las Vegas nights have garnered clear majorities in favor of legalization. Perhaps because they acquired a bad name in the nineteenth century, private lotteries have been consistently rejected. Only a smattering of referenda dealing with horse or dog races have succeeded. (Because they have been enjoined by state constitutional amendment rather than statute, lotteries must be approved by referendum. Races, on the other hand, are generally legalized by statute.)

Casinos are the clear losers. New Jersey, where it took two tries, is the only state to pass a casino gambling referendum—and then, only with the proviso that it be restricted to Atlantic City. Even Florida, which Meyer Lansky so carefully cultivated as a gambler's paradise, rejected a 1978 bid to legalize casinos. Arkansas, California, and Colorado followed suit.

Voters have an instinctive aversion to casinos. Their gut feeling is well-founded. The atmosphere in a casino is more highly charged than other forms of gambling. Redolent with instant gratification, there's no wait for a payout; the action is fast. Unlike a horse race or a lottery, there's no chance to think between bets. Free drinks, easy credit, plush carpets, and a background symphony of tinkles, clangs, and clicks can entice any susceptible patron to leave his discretion at the door with the half-nude coat check girl.

The first time I went to Paradise Island in 1972, I made a tentative foray to the casino, where I was positioned across from a beefy, bald-headed man at a craps table. My hand held a small heap of chips—the limit I had set for a week's vacation. His held a stack many times higher. But what caught my attention was his anxious perspiration and the fat, unlit cigar in his mouth. As the dice worked their way around the shooters at our table, his cigar became shorter and shorter. So intense was his involvement that he had absentmindedly chewed and swallowed the tobacco. That image never left me: It is my vision of the compulsive gambler.

In 1972, Norval Morris, dean of the University of Chicago law school, predicted: "Gambling is likely to be the first victimless crime fully rationalized." It's simply a matter of who the pit boss will be. Don't count on the government —it can't afford the overhead or deliver the efficiency of the private entrepreneur. The Nevada and New Jersey model of privately run, state-regulated gambling has worked out fairly well as a business enterprise. While the competition has not driven out organized crime, it has certainly created an alternative to illegal gambling.

But for the free marketplace to do its work, Norval Morris recommends that gambling be legalized across the board. Fraud, cheating, and skimming should remain crimes, he argues, but wagering itself—like going to the theater or dining out—must be a matter of free choice.

Morris's utopia won't come to pass unless more states run into severe budget shortfalls. While no unified opposition to gambling as a whole exists, there are strong, persistent pockets of resistance to casino gambling. The residents of Arkansas, for example, have, on repeated tries, staunchly fought bringing casinos to Hot Springs. However, as the Atlantic City and Nevada cases show, when the state treasury is yawning wide or a seedy resort needs help recovering its past splendor, voters have a penchant for overcoming their scruples.

The hope of legalization is that it will raise money for government and cut into the profits of organized crime. In fact, it does very little of either. Newly legalized gambling merely attracts new gamblers. But we've always been a wagering nation. Good causes and bad consequences aside, a majority of Americans argue that gambling is a taste consenting adults are entitled to indulge. Shimmying trends show that we're ready to ante up. Most forms of gambling will be legalized.

CRIMEWARPS

- The proportion of the population that gambles will increase with each state that legalizes gambling and each form that becomes legal. The new gamblers will be drawn from the 30 percent who now refrain from gambling because it is illegal.
- Half of nongamblers refrain for religious reasons. The growth of fundamentalist churches will increase the size of this pool. However, the increase will not be sufficient to offset the growth in the gambling population.
- Those aged sixty-five and older have the lowest rate of gambling. As the baby boom and prior generations age, gambling will decrease proportionately.
- The current younger generation and future generations will show slower declines in gambling as they age because they will have been raised in an environment in which approved gambling is part of the world they take for granted.
- The current urban-rural migration will diminish rural areas as a stronghold of nongamblers.
- Because gambling is primarily a suburban phenomenon, the growth of suburbs will add to the pool of gamblers.
- The population is becoming more educated, and this will contribute to an increase in gambling.
- Military service is related to gambling. Continued elimination of conscription will reduce the role of the armed forces as an introduction to gambling.
- The growing popularity of the VCR is helping to keep people at home. Time spent at home correlates with nongambling. Therefore, the VCR will help to reduce gambling.
- Because gambling is partly a function of disposable income, the amount of money gambled will contract with unemployment and high inflation. More people will turn to low-stakes games such as lotteries.
- Sports books will remain one of the most popular forms of gambling. How-

ever, as tennis and soccer become more widespread, they will join football and baseball as important objects of wagers.

· Organized crime will be aided in its infiltration of legitimate businesses through legalization of gambling.

· The number of compulsive gamblers will continue to escalate as gambling outlets become increasingly available. However, the proportion of addicted bettors in the gambling population will remain constant.

· Gambling enforcement will continue to decline, except for pursuit of high level organized crime figures. These will be prosecuted, not under gambling statutes but under racketeering and tax laws.

· As gambling becomes increasingly legalized, corruption of police and public officials will diminish.

· All forms of gambling, except casinos, will be widely legalized. Except for lotteries, gambling enterprises will be privately run as publicly traded corporations.

· Because of the need to protect the price of stock and be accountable to stockholders, publicly traded corporations will ensure that gambling is a relatively "clean" enterprise.

· Where casinos are legalized, they will be restricted to resort areas in need of revitalization. These might include Pueblo County, Colorado; Coney Island/the Rockaways, New York; Catskill Mountains, New York; Niagara, New York; Miami, Florida. Casinos will also be legalized in those places that experience severe downturns in their economies—the oil-producing states of the South and Southwest, for example. Because opposition has become stronger rather than weaker between referenda, casinos will not come to Hot Springs, Arkansas.

· While the South and Southwest have been resistant to legalizing gambling —especially casino gambling—the resistance will be lowered by the massive influx of workers from the Northeast and Latin America.

· Computer electronics will create new forms of gambling, such as coinless slot machines. Working much like "smart cards" (described in Chapter 7), they will discourage rigging of machines as well as ensure that a player does not gamble beyond his cash limit. Video games of all sorts will be subjects of wagering. When commercially run, they will provide similar controls as coinless slot machines.

15

The Demise of Drugs

An abandoned Hispanic social club on Eldridge and Stanton Streets. Decades ago, when they were growing up, George Burns, Fanny Brice, George Jessel, Irving Berlin, Al Jolson, and Eddie Cantor used to roam these parts. It was the golden age of New York City's Lower East Side, then a Jewish ghetto teeming with talent. By 1980, the once-illustrious intersection had turned sinister. Lookouts were posted out front and on the north and south corners. Steerers directed a continuous flow of traffic. From 7 A.M. to 10 P.M., groups of fifteen people were ushered in and out of the decrepit building. Most were white, decked out in expensive leather and furs. Their license plates checked out to bedroom communities in New Jersey and Nassau and Suffolk counties. Some hailed from as far away as Philadelphia and Buffalo.

Parading into the club with palms up to the ceiling and bills in their hands, they were brought before what might have passed for a bank teller's window. They placed their order, got it filled, and were led out. The object of the exercise was heroin . . . the highest purity junk ever to hit the streets of New York.

This story ends on the decaying streets of the Lower East Side—and similar connection points in cities and suburbs across the country. But it begins in the ancient warrens of Islamabad, Kabul, and Tehran. The Golden Crescent of Southwest Asia is the source of the worst heroin influx ever to reach our shores —one directly related to the collapse of remote governments.

The red tide from Afghanistan, Pakistan, and Iran is lethally pure. In 1980, levels as high as 80 percent retailed on the Lower East Side and the average purity in New York was about 7 percent. A single dose purchased in Harlem used to be just 3 percent pure; the rest was filler like quinine or sugar. Such diluted fixes cause mild addictions—"ice cream habits," as they're called. But the pampered bodies of suburbanites and the battered bodies of ghettoites weren't used to the potent junk that hit the streets a few years ago. It killed and injured users at higher rates than ever before.

Since 1980, the worldwide poppy crop has increased. The quantity and value of heroin seizures have about doubled, and the black market price has stabilized at $2,110 to $2,340 a pure gram—$1,000 more than it cost in 1975. The average purity has risen to 6 percent nationwide and up to 15 percent in New York. Heroin-related injuries have doubled to 12,000.

International politics are impacting on the cocaine, marijuana, and illicit pill trades, too. We've been blatantly unsuccessful in reducing the supply at the source. But significant changes in demand are taking place and will lead to a reduction in use of most drugs.

□   □   □

Lunchtime on a desolate stretch of road near Highway 101 in San Jose, California. Just a short hop from many of the high-tech companies that dot Silicon Valley, there's an assortment of parked cars. Some have lights on; others have their hood or car door open. The drivers are signaling that they want to score cocaine.

The "MacNeil/Lehrer NewsHour" shot this scene from a surveillance van run by an undercover narcotics officer. We were doing a story on cocaine in Silicon Valley. In the van was our guide, Beverly (a pseudonym), a high-tech engineer and former drug dealer who had turned police informant. Beverly told us that eight out of ten people in the companies for which she had worked— some of the largest in Silicon Valley—used drugs. We felt her estimate was high.

"It's around a lot 'cause there's a lot of pressure. Engineers, technicians, supervisors, they work really long hours. In order to keep up with the hours and with all the pressure, they need drugs to keep them going," Beverly explained.

For those who don't make it to the upper reaches of management or design work, the sheer tedium of assembling and inspecting minute circuits is often enough to drive them to drugs. Their motives are understandable, but they endanger the rest of us: The chips that come out of the Valley run everything from our cars and toasters to pacemakers and missile guidance systems. A defective microchip can cost lives and fortunes.

In describing her drug days, Beverly told us:

After a while, doing so much drugs, you don't see mistakes. And the mistake just gets larger and larger until it gets down to where the company has spent, say, $5000 to have these [circuit] boards built up. They spent money and find out they don't work because of an engineer default. And it isn't because the engineer wasn't smart enough. He was just burnt out.

A shift supervisor at another company found similar problems in the quality control areas: "I've watched people test, and they'd be sitting there, and they'd be dancing and humming away and not paying any attention to what they were doing." Dick Hesenflow, a former narcotics detective-turned-consultant, shudders at the implications of this kind of quality control: "If you're testing for military application and you have a hundred thousand pieces you have to test and this person is stoned, his judgement is impaired. . . ."

High-tech executives tend to pooh-pooh the problem, claiming that drug use is no greater in their industry than in any other. It's hard to argue with them, what with recent cocaine exposes in entertainment, government, and baseball circles. But while the latter scandals do no more than reveal our heroes' clay feet, the former, says Hesenflow, "affects all our lives somewhere along the line."

Joe McNamara, San Jose's police chief, thinks "management is asleep at the switch." Not only does the drug-besotted worker affect the competitiveness of the products and expose himself and others to calamitous industrial accidents, but he is a theft hazard as well. Dr. Mark Gold, director of a national cocaine hotline, describes coked-up thieves as "people who are working professionals, driven and goal-directed and drug-naive." In a national sample of callers to his hotline, nearly one quarter of cocaine users admitted that they steal to support their habit. McNamara, however, didn't get his information from a survey: He found it out firsthand when he went into the bartending business. In 1983, the San Jose police opened a tavern for the purpose of conducting a "sting" operation. When the bar opened, the "owners" let out the word that they were ready to "fence" stolen goods. Hoping to catch conventional burglars, the cops-cum-barkeeps were sure they would receive the usual assortment of televisions, silver candlesticks, and gold jewelry. Instead, the back room filled up with purloined computers, disk drives, and microchips. Employees were stealing from their companies to support cocaine habits.

The booty often ends up in the scrap yards that pepper the Valley. Scrappers have a reputation for dirty dealing. In 1984, I had a chance to talk to one—I'll call him Bert—who had been convicted of receiving stolen property.

Bert claimed he did business only with reputable firms. "I got into this business," he mused, "thinking everything was on the up and up. But go to any scrap yard—employees of high-tech companies steal scrap and sell it to buy cocaine." On one occasion the scrapper tried to do business with one of the giants of the industry, but the purchasing agent told him if he wanted the account he'd have to kick back both cash and cocaine. "That," claimed Bert, "is the norm for doing business in the electronics industry."

In 1937, the St. Louis *Post-Dispatch* recorded the prophecy of a physician who scrawled clinical notes on the wall as he watched himself die of cocaine poisoning. Among Dr. Edwin Katakee's final words were: "Cocaine addiction will be a major problem in the U.S.A. in the near future."

Katakee was right, but it took almost fifty years for all hell to break loose. By 1984, another physician, Dr. Arnold Washton, director of substance abuse and research at a New York hospital, estimated that 10 million Americans used cocaine at least once a month.

But the phenomenon of workplace drug use is a recent one. Unlike the unemployed, black street kid nodding out on the stoop, the new generation of drug users is middle class and working. Their recreational and habitual drugs are costing the country nearly $26 billion in lost productivity, medical expenses, and crime.

By taking the drug problem into the boardroom, we are introducing a new element into the politics of legalization. Now it's the powerful rather than the powerless who are using drugs. As a growing segment of the population, they will influence existing drug legislation.

☐ ☐ ☐

In July 1983, a new state law went into effect in Arizona that requires illicit drug dealers to buy a $100 business license and costly tax stamps to affix to their product. The stamps range from $10 an ounce for marijuana to $125 an ounce for heroin and other hard drugs. Those who fail to comply are subject to severe criminal sanctions as well as high tax penalties for any contraband found in their possession. If they do comply, they're prosecuted anyway—for dealing drugs. Talk about being caught between a rock and a hard place!

In some ways, the legislation is a replay of the Marijuana Tax Act, passed by Congress in 1937. But unlike that act, no one has challenged the constitutionality of asking illicit drug dealers to incriminate themselves and punishing them if they don't. However, according to the Arizona attorney general, not many prosecutors have made use of the statute.

Still, Arizona has almost done something extraordinary. Were it not for its tough criminal drug penalties ("I wish they were tougher," grumbles the attorney general), the state might have de facto decriminalized drug offenses while taking the profit—and incentive—out of dealing. But Arizona didn't go that far.

In the future, the rest of the country will borrow Arizona's innovative bill to finish what that state started. Such statutes will be our best means to drive big-time pushers out of business.

Drug use in this country has snaked back and forth between the affluent and impoverished. Today it has gravitated from the lower class back to the middle class. In the 1960s, while the slums mainlined heroin and artistes snorted coke, the scions of the student revolution smoked grass and hash between jolts of LSD. In the 1970s, the upwardly mobile were doing Quaaludes, and by the 1980s heroin gained stature along with increased purity and became more accessible to the weekend "chipper." Cocaine has become the darling of the yuppies and "crack," the sop of the inner city.

We became inundated with cocaine, courtesy of our neighbors in South America. So plentiful was the supply that something unprecedented happened. The price tumbled from a high of $780 a gram in 1979 to a low of $110 in 1983 —still dear compared to every drug other than heroin, but infinitely more accessible than ever before.

But our greatest troublemaker, by far, became the illegal use of legal drugs. In addressing an audience of police chiefs, a deputy director of the Drug Enforcement Administration revealed that drugs of legitimate origin were responsible for 350,000 drug-related deaths and injuries between 1980 and 1982. By contrast, illicit drugs like heroin and cocaine accounted for less than half that number.

During the latter part of this century, doctors appear to be much to blame. "We find that most of the diversion of legitimately produced drugs occurs at what is referred to as the 'practitioner level' . . . physicians, dentists, pharmacists, and other health care professionals," declared DEA's Ronald Buzzeo. "It may occur through unlawful sale of the drug itself or . . . a physician writing prescriptions for which there is no valid medical purpose." During fiscal year 1982, the DEA investigated over 300 such violators. "This number," avers Buzzeo, "represents less than five percent of the total number of practitioners who are believed to have diverted drugs."

On the average, more than 90 percent of us have never used a sedative, tranquilizer, stimulant, or analgesic for purposes of getting high. Yet there has been an across-the-board increase in nonmedical usage in the decade between 1972 and 1982. In the same period, thefts of stimulants and depressants from registered handlers dropped to about one fifth their earlier levels. The tightening supply is evident in the fivefold increase in black-market prices of various "uppers" and "downers" since 1975. The gap between the expanding market and contracting thefts can only be explained by rogue doctors or pharmacists and bootleggers of look-alike drugs.

According to Buzzeo, look-alikes have indeed become a major national problem—one in which the DEA has no specific jurisdiction because the sham pills contain no controlled substances. Most states, however, have attempted to plug the loophole with legislation of their own.

☐ ☐ ☐

Careless bandying of government statistics would lead you to believe that we are a nation of unbridled chemical hedonists, but a closer look at the data reveals that most people who try drugs do not become regular users. In fact, only about 1 in 450 Americans is opiate-addicted, a lower ratio than at the turn of the century.

The government sponsored National Survey on Drug Abuse is the most widely-cited source of information on drug use. You've probably heard that, as of 1982 (the latest available survey), nearly two thirds of young adults aged eighteen to twenty-five had used marijuana, and that more than one quarter had tried cocaine. But you have to read the fine print to realize that those percentages refer only to those who have *"ever* used" a drug to get high. Side by side in those figures are people who get high every day and those who tried a drug once ten years ago and never touched it again.

More telling indicators of regular use are the numbers that deal with usage within the month before the survey. Here we find that of two thirds of young adults who ever tried marijuana, less than half used it recently. Of those who ever tried cocaine, only one quarter used it in the past month. Similar findings accrue to all drugs and all age groups. What this tells us is that lots of people experiment, but relatively few acquire habits.

National surveys dating back to 1972 show significant increases in experimentation with all drugs. Heroin use—which has crept up among adults but dropped dramatically among younger people—accounts for only a tiny fraction of all illegal highs. In the case of cocaine, the percentage of those who have "ever used" has shown a steady rise across the board. However, among those twelve to twenty-five, overall experimentation has tapered off since 1977. Marijuana, hallucinogens, heroin, cigarettes, and alcohol are losing popularity. Among young adults, illicit use of tranquilizers and stimulants is dropping off as well. Youths between the ages of twelve and seventeen, while starting to abandon other drugs, continue to increase their dabbling in pills. For adults, the percentage who have ever used any drug, other than alcohol and cigarettes is growing. But illegal drug use among adults is so minimal, compared to that among youths and young adults, that the rise isn't significant.

The most drug-prone group is young adults of eighteen to twenty-five. In every drug category they outstrip those both older and younger in past as well as recent usage. The next most active drug group is youths of twelve to seventeen. These demographics portend two things:

• First, the aging of the population will bring a tremendous drop-off in drug usage.
• Second, the active drug-using ages will shrink as a proportion of the population between the years 2000 and 2050.

Surveys of high school seniors foreshadow these developments. Recent use of almost all drugs has been dropping off since 1982.

The culture has changed. As a nation we're more health- and fitness-conscious than ever before. We pack our refrigerator with natural foods, flock to holistic doctors, and work out religiously to Jane Fonda's tapes. We keep a sharp eye on the chemicals that pollute our fish or our air, and we're leery of all kinds of toxic substances—including the ones we inject or snort. Mainlining and jogging just don't go together.

But remote predictions are scant comfort to those whose lives are haunted by today's addict-criminals. It seems that by criminalizing dope, the government has created a problem much larger than the one it had intended to solve:

• Forty-seven percent of female inmates in state prisons and 56 percent of male inmates have used an illegal drug within the month previous to the crime for which they were confined.

• One third of all inmates are under the influence of a drug at the actual time of their imprisonable offense.

A dope tour of the country gives flesh to the raw numbers:

• New York City: In 1981, almost one quarter of all homicides were tied to drugs. Most involved the murder of dealers or stemmed from disputes over drugs.

• Dade County, Florida: 1981. The number of murders nearly doubled in five years. Most of the increase was traced to drug dealers killing other drug dealers.

• Monterey County, California: By the late 1970s, it had come to be known as Marijuana County. Homegrown "weed" was estimated to be the fourth-leading cash crop in the United States. Abundant sensimilla fields on private property and national parks were the site of an upsurge of violence. Growers shot at workers, loggers, campers, tourists—and even the law. They booby-trapped illegal fields with eye-level fishhooks, barbed wire, and Punji sticks.

• Washington, D.C.: In 1984, a former New Jersey police officer testified before the President's Commission on Organized Crime. The thirty-year-old witness, a recovering cocaine addict, had indulged his $500-a-day habit while on patrol in his squad car. As his addiction grew, he financed it by extorting protection money and drugs from the dealers and criminals he was sworn to arrest. From cocaine, he graduated to heroin—and he became hooked on that, too.

• Baltimore: Over a nine-and-a-half-year period, 354 known opiate users committed nearly 750,000 crimes. When they reduced their habits, their crime rates dropped. But when they had a strong drug need, their criminality mushroomed. Overall, they averaged 2,000 crime-days per junkie—255 a year while addicted and one quarter that number when not addicted. The crimes per addict included 829 thefts; 581 drug-dealing offenses; 561 gambling, pimping, fencing, and con game violations; and over 200 assorted forgeries, robberies, and assaults.

• Detroit: In the early 1970s, successful enforcement cut down the supply of dope. But clamping down backfired. Every 10-percent increase in the price of heroin led to a 2.2-percent reduction in its use but produced a corresponding 3-percent increase in property crimes. To buy the more expensive stuff, junkies had to do more stealing.

• California: A 1975 study of the Civil Addict Program showed that criminality decreased dramatically during periods of lessened addiction. Methadone maintenance reduced both the cost of heroin and the amount of crime.

• Nationwide: A study of criminal youths disclosed that three quarters of all robberies and one half of all felony assaults were committed by only 3 percent of the sample. Members of this subset had each committed three or more major crimes and were pill, cocaine, or heroin users.

• Nationwide: A Rand Corporation study discovered that most violent predators have a history of heroin use, usually in combination with alcohol and other drugs. Drug abuse was identified as one of the best predictors of serious criminality.

The link between drugs and crime appears to be inexorable. Or is it?

THE POLITICS OF DRUG LAWS

It's clear that crime increases with individual levels of addiction. And crime colors our attitudes toward drugs. But much mythology about drug use has sprung out of the politically motivated hysteria that has accompanied antivice campaigns.

Drug use did not always carry the stigma it does now. Up until the passage of the Harrison Act of 1914, narcotics addiction was pretty much the province of rural, middle-aged, middle-class white women who took legal opium prescribed by well-intentioned doctors. A host of prescription medications, as well as popular over-the-counter nostrums, like Mrs. Winslow's Soothing Syrup and Dr. Bull's Cough Syrup, stood ready to calm female nerves, hysteria, and menstrual cramps. Because of the extreme disrepute into which alcohol had fallen by the end of the nineteenth century, opium became a respectable and benign alternative, worthy of a society matron. By the turn of the twentieth century, it was estimated that America was home to 200,000 opium addicts, with women outnumbering men by a factor of 2 to 1. One out of every 400 Americans was said to be addicted.

For the more adventurous, opium dens were a fashionable pastime. Well-heeled socialites in evening attire traveled to not-so-secret locations where they were awaited with couches, pillows, and opium pipes. A newspaper account of 1899 denounced one such mecca on New York's Upper Broadway, a neighborhood of large and fashionable hotels. "Resort in Shadow of Big Hotels and Notorious in Neighborhood, but Police Are Inactive," proclaimed the headline.

The "low dives" of Chinatown's Mott Street had earlier incurred similar wrath. An 1895 article charged: "Things not appointed for the Sabbath are done down in Chinatown late on Saturday nights, and even until the following Monday mornings. The Chinamen . . . and their friends purchase and drink intoxicants; . . . they play fan-tan; . . . they keep open house to dissolute women, and . . . they smoke opium in large quantities." Opiate addiction was spreading to the poor in immigrant-bloated cities. The association with "the yellow peril," poverty, and moral degeneracy gave drugs a bad name. But it was not until the Harrison Act that drugs became synonymous with crime.

The 1914 Harrison Act sought to control drug distribution by making it a matter of record. Addicts could get drugs only from registered doctors. Subsequent Supreme Court decisions went further. They put a ban on prescribing drugs to addicts and prohibited addicts from possessing drugs. Thousands of pitiful users—mostly women—were left without relief. Because of their confined social roles, women had little opportunity to obtain illegal drugs. But a criminal subculture of more enterprising users—mostly men—was created.

Antivice crusaders blamed narcotics for everything from suicide to white slavery. What had been a middle-class, rural, female proclivity came to be dominated by lower-class, urban males. And so it has remained through this century. Today there are nearly three men for each woman admitted to federally funded drug treatment programs; six men are arrested for each woman on drug violation charges.

In 1982, retail sales of illegal heroin, cocaine, and marijuana generated close to $27 billion, with an unreported illegal income of about $21 billion. Illicit sales of all drugs have been estimated to be as high as $75 billion. Any way you cut it, that's big business. Three groups have a vested interest keeping it that way: organized crime, terrorists, and the Drug Enforcement Administration along with other police agencies. All make their livings off drugs.

If prohibited drugs were made legal, organized crime would lose its largest source of income, the Palestine Liberation Organization would lose a crucial source of financing, and law enforcement agencies would lose a major reason for existing. Illegal drugs and the crimes they generate provide police with much of their rationale for demanding larger budgets and more manpower.

During his tenure as head of the Bureau of Narcotics from 1925 to 1962, Harry Anslinger tormented us with the image of "reefer madness." Seeking to gobble up ever-greater appropriations from Congress for his agency, Anslinger did not hesitate to use every scare tactic in his vast arsenal. In going after marijuana, for example, Anslinger invoked the phrase "assassin of youth." Anslinger's early "crusade against marijuana," wrote John Jay College professor Isadore Silver in 1974, "was undertaken largely to maintain the viability . . . of the Bureau itself . . . the dilemma faced by all law enforcement agencies— they must simultaneously argue their work is effective . . . but that more money is needed to wage the war. Anslinger's answer . . . was simply to find new dangers to combat (while claiming victory . . . over the old ones)."

Later the Nixon administration was charged with impure motives in its effort to set up a powerful antidrug agency. Doctored statistics showed an absurd eightfold increase in heroin addicts in just two years. In his 1977 book, *Agency of Fear,* Edward Jay Epstein wrote: "If Americans could be persuaded that their lives and the lives of their children were being threatened by a rampant epidemic of narcotics addiction, Nixon's advisors presumed that they would not object to decisive government actions such as no-knock warrants, pretrial detention, wiretaps, and unorthodox strike forces."

The drug scare had become an excuse for attacking civil liberties.

□ □ □

That doesn't mean the drug problem is an illusion. Drug abuse wreaks havoc on lives, so I want to go on record as saying I don't advocate drug use. But history—and pragmatism—tells me that criminalization is not the answer. The precise mix of regulation and freedom is elusive. You can't regulate without creating a black market and you can't play laissez-faire without unleashing chaos. Nor can we continue our present counterproductive strategies.

There are only two ways to reduce drug consumption: turn off the supply or limit the demand. We've failed at both.

CONTROLLING SUPPLY

On the supply side, we've been active on the international scene. We've tried to cajole, browbeat, and bribe producer nations to eradicate poppy, coca, and marijuana crops and clamp down on illegal drug labs. We've offered crop substitution programs, drug enforcement advisers, direct payments. It worked for a while.

Up until the late 1970s, heroin addiction seemed pretty much under control. DEA estimates showed the number of junkies declining for four consecutive years until it hit a low of 380,000 in 1978. Drug-related deaths and injuries eased off, too. A drought in Southeast Asia reprieved us from the usual deluge of Golden Triangle heroin. Signed agreements with Turkey and Mexico kept their opiates out of our markets. An enforcement treaty with Afghanistan allowed us to seize drugs moving across its rugged terrain in overland caravans. Stringent martial law and the Islamic revival assured Pakistan's ban on opium production. A friendly Shah welcomed our DEA agents in Iran. Turkish farmers learned how to grow soybeans instead of poppies, and still make a profit. NATO, the United Nations, and the World Bank joined us in fighting the new opium war.

All these successes were predicated on governments that were willing and able to cooperate. They did not anticipate that our influence in key drug-producing nations would shrivel.

Our staunch ally, the Shah of Iran, fell to a fundamentalist Islamic fanatic who executed drug dealers and held our embassy hostage while driving the American "Satan" out of his country. Iranians trying to escape the Ayatollah Khomeini's grip often used opium as currency.

The Soviet Union invaded Afghanistan, removing it from our sphere of influence. Now, as always, border tribesmen conceal themselves in the mysterious western extension of the Himalayas and use its hidden villages and vast valleys to ply their opium trade. The autonomous tribesmen are beyond the reach of the law. Not even the vacuum-sealed borders imposed by Soviet occupiers can tame their tribal smuggling heritage.

In Pakistan, General Muhammad Zia continued to cooperate with our drug programs. But things were touch and go when our embassy in Islamabad was overrun in 1979 and when Zia thumbed his nose at a $4-billion aid package we offered him. Even when the general was his most congenial, he didn't hold all the cards. He was thwarted by the same tribal autonomy that exists across the border in Afghanistan. He dared not risk stirring up the Pathan tribes in the frontier areas.

In 1978, it didn't dawn on us that our neighbors in Latin America would become a bigger nemesis than our enemies in the Golden Crescent. Hostile and corrupt governments, roving insurgents and terrorists, ignorant and destitute peasants ganged up to dump their hellish white powders and homely green weeds on our doorstep.

Peru, the largest producer of coca leaves, was perfectly willing to work with us in eradicating illegal fields, but American-financed antinarcotics workers sent to work in the Cuzco region set off an economic depression. The migrants who had settled there didn't know how to grow anything but coca. Nor was anything else as profitable. Their resentments were exploited by the Shining Path guerrillas who started recruiting in their valleys. On November 17, 1984, nineteen antinarcotics workers were slain and the eradication efforts were derailed—at least for a time.

Bolivia, on the other hand, hadn't even made a dent in its coca crop. Coca, a mainstay of its gross national product, was Bolivia's most important foreign exchange commodity. Bolivia's lack of cooperation had cost it our foreign aid for a while, but that meant little. Our offer of less than $100 million in aid was dwarfed by that country's cocaine profits. In 1986, however, Bolivia's drug-driven economy backfired and local authorities worked with the U.S. Army to clean up Bolivian cocaine processing plants.

Colombia has been a stand-up guy. It valiantly destroys marijuana fields and extradites its drug traffickers, but its abundant marijuana and processed cocaine are cash crops that simply won't die.

In Paraguay, American officials claim to have discovered links between drug traffickers and senior military officers. What can you do when the government itself is the pusher?

Our rapprochement with Mexico has collapsed. Mexican "brown" is back on our streets—especially in the West—and we're inundated with "Acapulco Gold." The pervasive corruption of the Mexican government has offset even the best-intentioned antidrug agreements.

Even tiny Belize has become a sore spot. The spraying of paraquat on its marijuana fields became a political issue that threatened the newly independent nation's first national election. The Prime Minister didn't want to jeopardize his country's ecology or politics with a chemical that we won't spray on our own land.

We didn't predict that insurgents of every stripe would infest Latin America and that its governments would have more important things to do than help solve our drug problem. Nor were we prepared for the fact that drugs would become a critical part of national economies. Nor did we anticipate the intransigence of peasants, whose illegal crops were giving them the only decent living they'd ever known.

Since 1978, when we thought we had things under control, the world has become a less friendly place for America. Third world countries, with whom we once had leverage, are telling us that our junkies are a domestic problem—not one for which they should be expected to sacrifice their substantial narcodollars. Others won't tell us anything at all. We have become lonely warriors in the fight against drugs.

□ □ □

Obstructed at the source, we're struggling to control the supply at home. The coast guard has been recruited to monitor small craft while the customs service searches our ports. Joint narcotics interdiction programs zero in on hot spots like South Florida. FBI, DEA, and other federal agents descend like lemmings on the big-time dealers who are killing our young people. Gallant agents launch "Operation Delta-9" missions in all fifty states, raiding booby-trapped sensimilla fields and destroying hundreds of thousands of marijuana plants. Seizures, deportations, arrests, convictions are all way up. It doesn't seem to make any difference: The borders and wildernesses of a democracy are simply too porous to control.

Major organized crime figures and big-time dealers are being prosecuted under RICO, the Bank Secrecy Act, tax law statutes—anything that will bring them to trial. It doesn't help. They're replaced as quickly as we take them out of the system. And independent third-world dealers "just keep coming like ants," says John Lawn of the DEA.

Local police do what they can. They harass street-level dealers with periodic street sweeps, but the dealers regroup somewhere else. Police try to infiltrate drug-dealing organizations, but they don't have enough buy money and flashy cars to work their way to the top of the hierarchy.

Sterling Johnson, special narcotics prosecutor for New York State, likens it to "turning off a faucet." But it won't shut off.

CONTROLLING DEMAND

We're not having much more luck controlling our domestic supply than we are our foreign sources. That leaves us with the option of tinkering with the demand. Police harassment, treatment, and education have been our methods of choice.

The harassment method is exemplified by a program launched in Sacramento County, California. Unveiled in 1976, it was dubbed "Heroin Impact Program (HIP)." It wasn't new, it wasn't even interesting. All it did was dust off an old California law that allowed a judge to send a heroin user to jail for ninety days if he was caught with the drug in his bloodstream. Unlike ambitious buy-bust efforts, HIP cops settled for the lowest figure on the drug totem pole—the street-level junkie. Economists at the University of California at Santa Barbara had estimated that every addict who cools his heels in jail for 30 days means 22 fewer thefts for the county—and the HIP cops just wanted to get the junkies off their streets. The officers hoped that by hassling them enough, the addicts would leave the HIP communities and find some other shooting gallery.

"In no way, shape or form are we trying to help heroin addicts, or get rid of heroin," said Detective Al Bedrosian of the San Mateo HIP team. "This is a burglary prevention program."

☐ ☐ ☐

Like the HIP officers, Rudolph Giuliani, U.S. attorney for the Southern District of New York, suffers no moral confusion when it comes to hard drugs. Drug addicts, in his view, are parasites. "In our society," says Giuliani, "you can't say any longer that a person can render himself irresponsible and not harm society. We feel a responsibility for supporting people who can't support themselves."

This argument presupposes that addicts are incapable of leading normal lives. However, there is strong evidence that it is the black market life-style and not the addiction that destroys productivity. Doctors, for example, have the highest addiction rate of any group—thirty to one hundred times that of the general population—but you'd never know it. They support their habit without resorting to street crime.

Oakley Ray, who wrote a textbook on drugs, maintains: "The usual medical and vocational problems that are correctly associated with opiate addiction today stem neither from the drug nor its regular use but from the drug delivery system and the subculture that surrounds this illegal drug use."

For those who succeed in developing a habit, the addiction is seldom permanent. Contrary to what most people think, heroin addicts who survive tend to spontaneously mature out of their habits between the ages of thirty-five and forty-five. During the eight to nine years that the average addict is hooked, he weaves in and out of heavy drug use, adjusting his habit to prevailing market conditions. A maintaining addict is perfectly capable of controlling his impulses, working, and leading a normal life.

Giuliani, however, remains a true believer. "If we made it easier to obtain drugs than it is now by either decriminalizing drugs or having the government make them available, we would substantially increase the addict population."

No one can say for sure. The plentiful supply of heroin that has existed in the past few years did not increase the number of addicts. DEA data show that the addict population has stabilized at about 490,000 and has not changed since 1982, when there was a big jump in the statistics.

But most users never get addicted to heroin. Various studies show that there are anywhere from two to ten users for every junkie. The old saw "one shot and you're hooked" is nonsense. You really have to *want* to get hooked—it takes a week or more of three to four injections a day, often accompanied by beginners' bouts of nausea and discomfort. Not so with "crack." "Crack" acts directly on the pleasure centers of the brain and the addiction process is greatly accelerated.

□ □ □

"If you assume that a number of persons are going to become addicted, then the responsibility for supporting them is going to fall on the taxpayers," parries Giuliani. "Morally that's a very bad lesson to teach."

The point is well taken. Who could dispute the fact that the costs of drug use are gargantuan? One study estimates that every daily heroin user costs us $55,000 a year, while sporadic ones cost about $15,000 a year. These figures are conservative. They calculate only the cost of thefts, sponging, and illegal distribution of drugs. They omit the price of lost productivity, treatment, law enforcement ($1.2 billion), crime prevention hardware, the suffering of victims, and the fear that pervades our streets.

But read the list closely. Except for treatment and lost productivity, every one of these costs is the result of criminalization. The Harrison Act period taught us that removing high demand, recreational drugs from legal circulation turns addicts into criminals. We later learned that the dearth of legal supplies creates a highly profitable demand which organized crime groups—ranging from the Mafia to outlaw motorcycle gangs—are only too happy to fill. Such dire consequences are the best argument there is for legalization.

Giuliani counters that it's folly to assume that free access to drugs will automatically mean less crime. According to him, "Not all addicts are going to stop committing crime and go to work for IBM. They'll still steal to obtain disposable income. For a while we might see a decrease in crime if we gave all addicts all the drugs they wanted. But over time, regulation will increase and a new black market will be created. We might end up with a higher crime rate."

Giuliani has a point. Narcotics addicts share a number of traits with property and violent criminals that users of pills and marijuana do not. Junkies and criminals come, for the most part, from the same neighborhoods; their environment breeds both pathologies.

It's no coincidence that the average age for first narcotics addiction is twenty. That's the age at which drug and other vice arrests peak. It's also the midpoint in the critical crime-prone age span of sixteen to twenty-four. Indeed, crime often starts at an earlier age than drug use, indicating that addictive drugs are often part of a criminal life-style.

That crime escalates so rapidly during periods of heavy addiction is more a function of economics than drugs. By making drugs illegal, the price is driven so high that lower class dopers can't afford their habits. Stealing is the least way they make up the shortfall. Dealing and freeloading account for the greatest part.

□ □ □

From an economic point of view, it doesn't make sense for narcotics to be illegal. Occasional users, who make up the vast majority of dopers, are not responsible for the waves of crime that accompany addiction. Neither are affluent addicts. That leaves only the poor. If the cost of drugs was not so outrageously inflated by smuggling, *they* wouldn't have to steal either.

Experience with methadone maintenance supports the point. By reducing the cost of a "fix" and making it accessible, users commit fewer crimes and find more employment—especially if they're over thirty.

As Giuliani points out, this doesn't mean they wouldn't steal for other reasons. There's some evidence that those in the crime-prone years commit even more robberies, thefts, and assaults while in methadone programs. It's only their drug-related crimes that evaporate.

Given such vagaries, Giuliani maintains: "It's a more tolerable price to pay to fight against drugs than to support drugs. Taxpayers then pay their tax dollars to support a moral principle rather than to support heroin or cocaine."

□ □ □

For the liberal, however, treatment rather than jail is the preferable response to drug abuse.

A variety of federally supported and private programs vie for the wayward addict. Phoenix House, Synanon, and Daytop Village are among the more well-known private ones. Some replace the needle with God; others substitute it with "tough love" or "love bombing." But methadone maintenance is the most prevalent treatment for drug habits.

Methadone is not an ideal solution. Local residents bridle at having a drug clinic plunked down in their midst. A minor black market has grown around take-home doses and thefts from methadone clinics. Methadone overdose deaths are being reported, though in decreasing numbers. Most of these problems have proven manageable.

More difficult are the side effects of methadone. The high dosage needed to totally block a user's ability to experience a heroin high also induces spontaneous sleep. That makes it difficult to function as a worker, lover, or parent. Methadone users also complain about perspiration, constipation, memory lapses, sexual dysfunctions, and heart problems. Finally, while heroin addiction tends to occur in spurts of weeks or months, methadone maintenance can last a lifetime.

For the highly motivated addict who wants to be liberated from the daily disruption of visits to a methadone clinic, a new drug has become available. Naltrexone is reported to completely block the craving for heroin and costs about half of annual methadone maintenance. However, it's poison to anyone with liver trouble—a common ailment among junkies.

Because heroin blockers create their own problems, some daring souls have suggested giving out free heroin in drug clinics or leaving it up to doctors to prescribe. That's been tried in England, where addicts are registered and maintained in clinics. While it hasn't contained the demand for drugs—dosage restrictions created a black market for those who wanted more than the clinics were willing to give—it has helped keep users alive. At least they now self-inject with sterile needles and clean water; previously, many used tainted syringes and water from toilet bowls. "Mortality resulting from these methods sometimes reached 10 percent of those treated," observes Dr. Richard Phillipson, who helped organize the British drug program. Nevertheless, he confesses, "The

British themselves recognized that heroin may not be the safest and most appropriate form of treatment for heroin addicts." England is now shifting to methadone maintenance.

As for turning the drug problem over to the medical profession, nineteenth-century ignorance and twentieth-century corruption have shown it to be less than trustworthy. But police have proven to be corruptible and ineffective as well. It is unfair to charge police with control of what is, at base, a medical problem.

□ □ □

Since all else has failed, our last—and I think best—hope for reducing the demand for drugs is education. Rudolph Giuliani maintains that criminalization is one form of education: "Society has only a few ways of teaching. The law is one of them. The simple statement that something is wrong helps control behavior."

Giuliani is right. It helps. But compared to other forces, like peer pressure, it's woefully inadequate. The 1986 anti-"crack" street vigils were a dramatic development in grass-roots drug reform. It's too early to tell, but such peer-driven actions will do more to define "crack" as unacceptable than a hundred laws. In another life as a sociology professor, one of the first concepts I taught introductory classes was the concept of "reference group." My students learned that people model their behavior after those whose approval and acceptance they seek. If "significant others" happen to be law-abiding, they exert a powerful influence toward conformity to the law. If not, the reverse is likely to happen. The key to reducing the demand for drugs, therefore, is to create drug-free heroes with whom we can identify. Let *them* be the messengers who educate people about the consequences of drug use.

Education done right does work. Witness the decline in use of both cigarettes and alcohol across all age groups since 1979. These years witnessed intensive campaigns to teach the public about the hazards of both.

PUBLIC OPINION

The public, however, comes out on the side of outright bans. In contrast to Prohibition's hugely unpopular "dry" law, most of the public does not favor legalization of hard drugs. The response to marijuana is a good barometer of attitudes.

Marijuana is now considered a "soft" drug, one of the more benign of recreational highs. Although trounced by the federal government with the Marijuana Stamp Act of 1937, the drug lost much of its criminal stigma with the Controlled Substances Act of 1970, which reduced the severity of penalties for possessing and selling marijuana. By the time the 1970s ended, eleven states had decriminalized possession of small amounts of the weed. Alaska went so far as to allow people to grow it for personal use in their backyards. But despite the efforts of a lobby group called NORML (National Organization for Reform of Marijuana Laws), attempts to legalize it at the federal level stalled—perhaps because most users were young and powerless, or maybe because older people were once again defining marijuana as the "assassin of youth."

The 1980s blew in on a diminishing cloud of smoke. Young people were trying grass at a lower rate than they had in 1979, but still about 50 percent more than in 1972. Only adults continued to show an increased rate of usage, but that increase turned out to be more a function of past dabbling than present use. In a national survey, only about 7 percent of adults, compared to 27 percent of young adults, had used marijuana in the past month. But even that low percentage represented an increase over the end of the 1970s.

An unexpected thing was happening: Young people were becoming less tolerant of marijuana. In the early 1980s, a smaller percentage of the overall population thought that marijuana should remain illegal than in the early 1970s. The only exceptions were those aged eighteen to twenty-four. In their case, a larger percentage rejected legalization in the more recent period than in the earlier one.

Surveys of high school seniors focus the issue even more sharply. Scanning from the Class of 1976 to the Class of 1983, there is a nearly unbroken rise in the percentage of seniors who believe smoking marijuana (and hashish) both in public and private should be outlawed. (Even though their ranks are growing, only about one third believe that private use should be banned.) Were it to be legalized, nearly half favor selling it only to adults.

In examining the demographics of attitudes toward marijuana, a 1982 Gallup poll turned up no group in which a majority favored legalization. But those with the largest percentage in favor had these traits: nonwhite, male, college-educated, Westerner, income over $25,000, Independent, Catholic, and resident of a large city.

Because the college-educated, nonwhite, high-income drug users, and Western populations are expanding, these demographics bode poorly for legalization in the present, but portend a mushrooming of support in the future.

□ □ □

In the meantime, young people seem more willing to get tough on drug violators. In 1985, Scott Pallito, senior class president at Howell High in New Jersey, sold a gram of cocaine to someone he thought was a transfer student. Unfortunately for him, it was an undercover cop—one of many who have been assigned to New York metropolitan area schools since the mid-1980s. Despite his popularity and broad student support, Pallito was convicted of eight counts of possession and distribution of illegal drugs. Had a campus undercover cop arrested him twenty years ago, it would have occasioned student strikes and riots; the mere thought of the "fuzz" in the students' midst would have induced mass paranoia.

But in 1985, students seemed quite amenable to campus cops. "If they are not openly invading our rights and are not tricking people, then I think it's OK to have them," opined a senior at Teaneck High School. "If that's the only way to catch these people, then that's the way to do it," echoed a sophomore at

Howell High School. "It works—it's cleaning them out," concurred a junior at the same school.

A clue to this radical transformation in attitudes is found in high school seniors' perceptions of the harmfulness of drugs. Recent seniors are much more apt to think that regular, and even occasional, use of marijuana is dangerous than did their predecessors in 1975. The same increases are evident in their perceptions of heavy smoking, drinking, cocaine, and LSD.

Oddly, the Class of 1983 was less convinced than that of 1975 about the dangers of any use of heroin, amphetamines, barbiturates, and a onetime try of cocaine and LSD. In the case of uppers and downers, a shrinking percentage favor prohibition. For all other drugs, however, a growing majority support existing bans.

The newfound antidrug ardor is shared by police and prosecutors. In the ten years between 1974 and 1983, local drug violation arrests for adults increased by almost 13 percent. In that same time, federal prosecutions wavered between all time highs and not-so-highs but ended with a substantial showing in 1983. Most defendants were convicted. But those found guilty of marijuana violations were in for a shock. After dipping to a low of 28 months in 1975, judges started meting out average sentences of twice that length in 1983.

It seems to be having some effect. Consecutive polls of high school seniors show marijuana, hashish, and amphetamines are still easy to score but that all drugs became less available in 1983 than they were in previous years.

THE LEGALIZATION ALTERNATIVE

Many people equate advocacy of legalization with immorality and licentiousness. However, the issue has more to do with politics, economics, and civil liberties.

The present conservative climate does not lend itself to a pragmatic approach to the drug problem. However, the budget-slashing fervor that comes with it will force a reevaluation of spending priorities. An increasingly educated and politically moderate population could well conclude that our drug bans are too expensive to sustain.

During earlier periods in our history, drug abuse was concentrated among the powerless. In the last century and the early part of this one, it was women. More recently, it was lower-class males. Now, however, it has ensnared the upwardly mobile, politically active, and affluent. Even in the absence of a pro-repeal groundswell among the masses, opinion leaders will help tip the balance toward more productive tactics in the drug war.

Arizona's idea of a license and tax stamp—if implemented minus the self-incrimination trap—is a pragmatic approach. Combined with decriminalization of drug use, it can reverse a host of criminogenic forces. Lowered drug costs reduce the impetus for drug-related stealing. Reduced profits make the drug trade less attractive to organized crime. Profits are visible, making them subject to taxation. Licensing enhances quality control, cutting down on overdose hazards. Law enforcement expenditures are confined to pursuing those dealers who adulterate their products or evade taxes. And the user's habit is between him, his doctor, and his God.

A free society is based on the premise that human beings are rational and can be trusted to make informed choices. Just as it is with cigarettes, caffeine, cholesterol, alcohol, sugar—and all the other substances that we know are harmful to us but which, nonetheless, remain legal—so it must be with drugs.

CRIMEWARPS

- As physical fitness grows in social value, a stigma will attach to adolescents who indulge in drug use.
- The current ballooning of drug use among young adults reflects a corresponding blip in usage among late 1970s high school seniors. Recent cohorts of high school seniors, because they are using significantly less drugs than earlier cohorts, will reduce the usage among young adults as they enter the drug-prone eighteen to twenty-five years.
- Marijuana and alcohol are the drugs most likely to sustain their popularity.
- Methadone maintenance and other heroin-blocking programs will help reduce the incidence of drug-related street crimes.
- As drug use shifts toward the middle class, drug-related street crimes will decrease but white-collar crimes, like embezzlement and forgery, will increase.
- Securing international cooperation in eliminating drugs at the source will become increasingly difficult as third world revolutions disrupt existing agreements.
- Big-time drug traffickers will purchase major influence in legitimate governments.
- The Mafia, which is said to control about half the U.S. heroin traffic and little of the cocaine, marijuana, or pill trade, will decline as a factor in the drug business. Rising groups such as Colombians, Cubans, Mexicans, and Orientals will dominate the illegal market.
- Drugs with elastic demands, such as marijuana, will remain in the hands of independents and be resistant to organizing.
- The illicit drugs favored by middle-class users will be decriminalized.
- The first experiments in legalizing heroin will take place on the West Coast, which historically has pioneered drug decriminalization legislation and where the demographics favor those who support legalization of other drugs.
- Blacks and fundamentalists will be the strongest forces against decriminalization of narcotics.
- The states will pass decriminalization legislation earlier than the federal government.
- Decriminalization of use and possession of drugs will occur before decriminalization of selling.

Crimewarp V

The Ups and Downs
of Big Brother

When Raymond Lee Stewart murdered six people in Rockford, Illinois, he left no witnesses and no clues. Police Chief Delbert Peterson had no idea where to begin looking for him. But then pictures of the murder scene were sent to the psychological profiling team at the FBI Academy. From those shots, they were able to deduce the following description of the killer:

RACE Black
SEX Male
AGE Late 20's
PERSONALITY Quiet, loner
RELATIONSHIP TO VICTIMS Knew first victim
RESIDENCE Lives nearby
DRESS Dark clothes
JOB Semiskilled night work
TRANSPORTATION Car with a shortwave radio
PETS Large dog

The profile was one of the team's 15 percent that are right on target. Stewart was nabbed and convicted.

The profiling program combines police work with psychology. Using what they know about repeat offenders, profilers employ known patterns to analyze new crimes. Most of the time, the profiles are at least helpful to local investigators; often, as in their profile of Raymond Lee Stewart and convicted Atlanta child murderer Wayne Williams, they hit a bull's-eye.

The crackerjack FBI men who worked up Stewart's description are in the process of feeding their know-how into a computer. By the year 2000, a machine will be doing the work of skilled investigators.

Computerized psychological profiling is just one of the technologies that will alter the way we respond to crime in the future. Effective law enforcement—like our new crimes—will break free of its reliance on personal contact. Judicious management of high-tech surveillance, information processing, and physical force will be the keys to crime control.

However, even as the criminal justice system becomes more efficient, we will become less dependent on it for protection. The next century will see us returning to a preindustrial model of self-help. Private police, community-level watches, and a full panoply of futuristic security hardware will equip us to take care of ourselves.

We will be supported by environments carefully designed to have crime prevention built in. "Defensible space" architecture will reduce opportunities for assaults, robberies, and burglaries, while promoting a twenty-first-century version of circling the wagons. Spatial arrangements will encourage neighbors to watch out for each other and their territories.

Big Brother's technologically feasible ascendance, however, will be legislatively restrained. In the process of fighting his advancement in state and federal government, we will fail to notice the rise of myriad miniature Big Brothers at the block and neighborhood level. Our pockets of privacy will become smaller and more vulnerable to prying.

16

Pyrotechnic Policing

In 1980, Miami officials were feeling nervous about crimes against elderly residents. But the fear wave keeping honest people off the streets was even more worrisome than the crimes themselves. In mid-1982, the city tried out a new solution: *video cops.*

Lincoln Road and Washington Avenue became the beats for a platoon of twenty video cameras posted at strategic locations to survey the street. For a time, they worked—purse snatchings declined and people were less scared.

But eventually the mechanical eyes turned out to be a bust. What with maintenance problems, bored monitor-watchers, and residents yelling "invasion of privacy," it just wasn't worth it. In July 1984, the cameras were retired. However, the new era of policing that they represented was not.

Routine video surveillance has long been a part of traffic control in Tokyo and is now becoming routine in New York. Banks, embassies, apartment houses, and corporate headquarters use it to detect intruders. As the twenty-first century unfolds, pyrotechnic electronic surveillance—both visual and auditory—will enhance police penetration of our lives.

□ □ □

In 1982, Terry Dean Rogan was an unemployed part-time college student. Sitting in class in Michigan, he had no idea that two murders and two robberies were being committed by someone in California who was using his name. In June of that year, the Los Angeles police put out a warrant for Rogan's arrest. In October they nabbed him. It was the first of five arrests for four crimes Terry never committed.

Saginaw police had been summoned when Rogan was having a loud fight with his girlfriend. While responding to the dispute call, they did what they're supposed to do: They made a routine computer check with the FBI's National Crime Information Center (NCIC) to see whether their quarry had outstanding warrants against him anywhere in the country. In Rogan's case, they came up with a "hit" and carted him off to the county jail.

Rogan had lost his wallet during a 1981 visit to Detroit and was nowhere near Los Angeles when the crimes in question had taken place. Using his stolen driver's license and other identity cards, an imposter was on the loose killing and robbing people. A fingerprint check with the FBI confirmed that Terry was not their man.

But that didn't mean Rogan was home free. He was trapped in an electronic maze which led to four more searches and arrests at gunpoint—three in Michigan and one in Texas. Each began with a routine traffic check. There was no place in the United States where the computer couldn't reach him. The NCIC services about 64,000 criminal justice agencies and processes some 400,000 information requests a day. Its record for accuracy is abysmal. An Office of Technology Assessment audit found that half the records sampled were incomplete or inaccurate. The FBI admits that at least 12,000 erroneous reports are transmitted *every day*. But trying to unravel the mistakes is a no-win game. Local agencies are responsible for the accuracy of the information they enter into the NCIC computers. As Terry Rogan learned, police encounter tremendous obstacles in trying to remove flawed records from the system.

Because of the growing anonymity of crime and unlimited mobility of criminals, the future of law enforcement lies in information networks. The FBI wants to expand its vast NCIC files to include white-collar felons—and even mere "associates" who are suspected of no crime themselves. The potential for expansion is infinite. It's all a matter of how much freedom and privacy we're willing to trade off for how much law enforcement efficiency.

□ □ □

Five days before Christmas 1976, Virginia Bonsignore, a Queens, New York, housewife, was getting ready for work in the bedroom of her row house. Then she happened to look up at her mirror. What she saw there would alter not only her life, but the practices of police departments throughout the country.

Reflected in the glass was her husband, Blase, a twenty-four-year veteran of the New York City Police Department. His hand held an off-duty revolver, which law required him to keep twenty-four hours a day. He voiced the words, "I'm going to kill you."

This is a joke, thought Virginia.

Blase moved her to the bed and Virginia saw him raise the gun. The next thing she remembers is lying in a pool of blood, believing she was dead.

She wasn't, but her husband was. After pumping five bullets into her brain, leg, lower torso, and hip, her mate of seventeen years shot himself and put an end to what had been a steadily deteriorating marriage and career.

This aggravated assault/suicide was predictable and preventable, but those responsible for intervening had neglected what was happening before their eyes. Blase, ordinarily a fastidious man who took enormous pride in dressing well and looking good, became unkempt. He started drinking heavily and losing weight. His guns became casual playthings. On the job, he became reclusive, fearful—a decorated officer, he now saw himself as a loser and a loner.

At home, he paid nocturnal visits to his younger daughter's room and sat on the bed, staring at her. Linda would wake up, terrified. But that was nothing compared to the harrowing visits to her grandmother's grave that Blase made his older daughter, Polly, endure. As his sanity crumbled, he grew increasingly violent at home and suspicious of his wife. He had her followed, checked up on her when she visited friends, and wrote her accusatory notes. He charged her co-worker in a bookstore—a college student—with having an affair with her. And Blase was no longer having sex with her or even sleeping in the same room.

What happened on December 20, 1976, was the collision of three powerful vectors. On the one hand, a traditional wife and mother was testing the waters of liberation by getting a job. On the other, a traditional male was undergoing bizarre behavior changes, exacerbated by jealousy and rage over his wife's new independence. Behind it all was a police "code of silence," which allowed an officer charged with the power of life and death to keep his guns and proceed with business as usual despite an obvious nervous breakdown.

In 1981, Virginia's tragedy became the basis of a landmark civil rights suit, *Bonsignore v. the City of New York.* The plaintiff's lawyer, James Sawyer, called me in as an expert witness. I took the stand and testified for seven hours about the psychological hazards of police work, the perils of making a gun the symbol and implement of police authority, and the innovative programs that could keep a battle-weary officer from exploding.

The tall, middle-aged woman—with a comet's tail of bullet fragments trailing from the brain stem to the center of her cognitive and motor functions—won her case. Her battle established a precedent. Police departments can now be held liable for tracking the psychological state of their officers and taking remedial actions before sending stressed-out cases on the street with a gun.

Bonsignore has a larger significance for the future. Recent Supreme Court decisions limit police use of guns and affirm that, where wrongful acts are the result of agency policies rather than isolated incidents, the government is liable for those acts.

The growing recognition of the misuse of deadly force by police and the wrenching stresses under which they must work, is leading to an array of changes in police procedure: restrictions on use of firearms; psychological monitoring and removal of guns for burnt-out cops; ethical training in the consequences of deadly force; substitution of guns with nonlethal alternatives; and early warning systems to detect troubled police and intervene before they hurt themselves, their families, fellow officers, or the public.

□ □ □

It was a brisk autumn at Arden House, the majestic Harriman estate in upstate New York. On this day in the early 1970s, I had been flown there by helicopter as personal consultant to the Police Commissioner. The occasion was a management retreat conference with a group of officers from the New York City Police Department. I, along with an associate, had recently introduced the Full Service Model of policing, which we had developed for NYPD Commissioner Patrick Murphy and his successor, Donald Cawley.

The Full Service Model was a total systems approach to organizational development. Its goal was to shift the basis of police authority from militarism, authoritarianism, and force to social service, professionalism, and psychological skill. We wanted to deemphasize the "John Wayne Syndrome" and upgrade the use of human relations techniques in resolving conflict. The arrests-and-summons "numbers game" which had long ruled policework was to be tempered with an emphasis on quality of services rendered. Community members, along with rank and file officers, were to be given an enhanced role in making police policy. Minority and female officers were an important part of the game plan. So was careful attention to the psychological health of all officers.

Unlike some previous police reforms, the Full Service Model was designed to expose police to a consistent set of expectations from day of recruitment to day of retirement. Its underlying principle: to coordinate all key parts of the police socialization process—recruitment, entry tests, training, performance evaluation, promotions, rewards, management style, psychological services—and bring them into harmony with the progressive goals of NYPD.

Our approach to police change won considerable national attention in law enforcement circles and in 1975, the federal government adopted our model as part of a National Training and Demonstration Project. Pilot programs were set up in several cities, and twelve regional conferences were held to encourage national implementation. But the era of humanistic policing was struggling through an ongoing feud in the police world—and the model was part of it.

On one side were Pat Murphy's boys—the progressives at the Police Foundation and Police Executive Research Forum. On the other were LAPD chief Ed Davis' boys—the traditionalists at the International Association of Chiefs of Police. Ed Davis came from a mold in which policemen were men and social workers were social workers. In the media he had become the sultan of S.W.A.T. (Special Weapons and Tactics). Murphy, by contrast, represented the triumph of mind over macho. He had been a prime mover in putting women on patrol, getting men off "the pad" (institutionalized collections of bribes), and promoting the service role of officers.

A monopoly on the legitimate use of civil force is the traditional basis for police authority and many were reluctant to fool with it. Despite back-to-back progressive commissioners, NYPD was no exception. One of New York's Finest was vehement in his response to the model: "It's a pinko commie plot to subvert law enforcement and turn cops into a bunch of fag social workers!" The Arden House management retreat conference was part of an ongoing series of meetings needed to overcome such resistance and lubricate the implementation of service-oriented policing.

More than a decade later, police are fighting the same philosophical battle. However, a new generation of cops is tipping the scales toward the progressives. Hiring freezes and layoffs have allowed older police to age and retire. As budgets loosen, veterans are being replaced with youngsters, gradually leaning the age distribution of police to the low end of the scale. Because of the end of the draft, today's rookies don't come in with a military background. Instead, many are products of a rock and drug culture. Younger, more educated, more liberal, and more tolerant, they face the future with a vastly different set of resources than the police of the past: transactional analysis, ethical awareness workshops, sensitivity training, and ethnic consciousness-raising.

Even the technical aspects of the job are changing. Electronic surveillance, blood spectrography, voice prints, hypnosis, polygraphs, and truth serum will become the key tools of the trade. Tasers, mace, tranquilizer bullets, and restraining nets will reduce the need for deadly force. As Dirty Harry passes into oblivion, the nature of policing will inevitably change, becoming at once more humane and more impersonal.

□ □ □

In the old days, informants, friendly shopkeepers, and cooperative neighbors provided the beat cop with the tips he needed to control his territory. Policing was a personal business having less to do with crime busting than with maintaining order. The neighborhood man in blue did everything from helping immigrants find a place to live to bringing food to the poor to greasing the local political machine.

The patrol car changed things. The work is still the same: 10 to 20 percent law enforcement; the rest, order maintenance and social service. But the *intimacy* is gone. Today's police glide by in an air-conditioned cruiser, outfitted with a public address system and microcomputer. Theoretically, they could go through an entire shift without ever getting out from behind the wheel. But that's bad public relations, so police have begun making tentative forays into an earlier era with a bunch of homey sounding programs: Park, Walk, and Talk; foot patrol; community and team policing.

The idea is if police are nice to the people, people will be nice to them. Satisfied clients will keep them posted on local conditions and indigenous bad guys. It's a good idea for now. But it won't do as much good in the future when less crime occurs at the neighborhood level. Massive interacting data banks and other police departments will be the prime stool pigeons of the Information Age.

We will need fewer police in the future. Computers, like the NCIC that put Terry Rogan in jail, and video cameras, like the ones that surveyed Miami Beach's Lincoln Road, will cover more territory than a beat cop ever could. Lower rates of conventional crime and the trend toward reduced government spending will make it hard to justify increased staffing.

Between 1971 and 1974, the number of criminal justice employees grew at a rate of about 5.5 percent a year. Since then, growth has shrunk to 3 percent or less per year. In preinflation dollars, expenditures have grown at about the same pace. With only 2.8 percent of the public pie, criminal justice ranks pretty low compared to other government functions. Only space research gets less funding.

More than half of all justice expenditures are for police. A mere 1.5 percent of public funds supports close to 20,000 federal, state, and local police agencies and their 724,000 employees. About three quarters are "sworn"—full-fledged cops complete with uniform, badge, and gun—1 of them for every 408 of us. The rest are civilians.

The ratio of cops to people is highest in the largest cities and in the South- and Mid-Atlantic states. Because of population shifts, big city departments won't grow much in the future. But the state and county agencies that service rural and suburban areas will expand rapidly. The agencies in rural boomtowns like Gillette, Rock Springs, and Evanston, Wyoming, (which you read about in Chapter 5) attest to this trend.

□   □   □

Overall, police employment has been growing at a much faster rate than the population. Do we need more? Anthony Bouza, Minneapolis' maverick police chief, dares to say no: "The rarely acknowledged reality is that most departments have too many cops rather than too few, and the difficulty lies in our inability to manage resources effectively."

The proof of Bouza's assertion is found in San Jose. With the help of a computer-aided dispatch system, CAPSS, the police department runs lean and mean. Chief Joe McNamara explains: "The average concentration of police officers to civilian population is about 2.6 per thousand nationwide. Here in San Jose, largely because of CAPSS, we can operate with a ratio of only 1.3 officers per thousand."

Effective resource management means maximum prevention, detection, and apprehension with minimum danger to police and the public. It also means that policing must adapt to the white-collar and gray-market crimes of the future. Like the high-tech task force in Silicon Valley, cops must be savvy in the ways of microcircuits and sophisticated accounting.

In the future, police resources will be more mechanical and electronic than human. Computer-assisted information processing, electronic surveillance, advanced lie detectors, biochemical forensic tests, and nonlethal weapons will alter the methodology of law enforcement.

INFORMATION POSSES

Our most innovative crime-fighting strategies are predicated on free-flowing intelligence. The Violent Criminal Apprehension Program, for example, was established to detect patterns that might tie random victims to specific serial murderers. VI-CAP's stock in trade is information. The program is essentially a clearinghouse for unsolved murders, sexual assaults and miscellaneous disappearances.

The idea makes sense. Serial killer Henry Lee Lucas confessed to murdering 188 people in 24 states. But if he hadn't confessed, only a cross-tabulation of national data could have connected him to such far flung crimes. Convicted murderer Ted Bundy was suspected of killings covering at least four states in every corner of the country. Kenneth Bianchi, the Hillside Strangler, didn't confine his murders to the canyons of Los Angeles but continued his spree in Bellingham, Washington. It takes information to connect geographically remote crimes.

The FBI's magnificent psychological profiling program, which yielded up serial murderer Gary Lee Stewart, would not have worked without information. The computer analysis that described the killer didn't pull his traits out of a hat. After searching extensive files of criminal history and modus operandi, it combined variables in such a way that a pattern emerged. The *known* was manipulated to identify the *unknown*. Indeed, the current rash of serial murders would not have been discovered at all if not for exchanges of facts among police departments.

□ □ □

The Congressional Office of Technology Assessment recently identified 85 computerized law enforcement, investigative, and intelligence record systems. The government uses these systems to file 288 million records on 114 million people—about half the U.S. population. Much of the information resides in the FBI's NCIC, which stores national data on outstanding warrants, criminal histories, stolen property, and missing persons. With a prompt from the NCIC, even a routine traffic stop can net a serial killer. But the inaccuracies ensnare innocent people, too.

Terry Rogan of Michigan, who was mistakenly arrested five times, is one computer casualty; Willie Jones of New York is another.

A petty criminal, Jones sat in jail for three months just because he has the same name as a major offender. Jones was caught trying to beat the fare in a subway station and was released on a conditional discharge. When the district attorney sent for his "rap" sheet, two came back. The first was Willie Jones' history of seven mostly misdemeanor arrests; the second contained the records of another Willie Jones who fit the same general description as the fare beater: age early thirties, black, slim, five feet ten inches, one hundred and fifty pounds,

beard. But his rap sheet told of thirteen felony arrests for robbery, gun possession, and drug sales. More important, it bore the notation "Wanted."

So Willie Jones, free on a minor offense, was now arrested and sent to jail on
a drug charge. No one, not even his own lawyer, believed Willie when he said
that the felony record didn't belong to him. His fingerprints were never
checked, and it took three months and five hearings before the mistaken identity was discovered.

Then there was Eastern Airlines flight attendant Sheila Jackson Stossier. In
1983, Louisiana police arrested her on the basis of a warrant issued in Houston
and entered into the NCIC. The name on the warrant was similar, but not
identical, to Stossier's. A check of her passport and other ID would have
straightened the matter out, but Louisiana officials never bothered.

The Houston warrant was for a misdemeanor. It didn't belong in the FBI's
system in the first place. Misdemeanor suspects are not ordinarily eligible for
extradition from one state to another. So even if Stossier *was* the real suspect,
she shouldn't have been locked up for three days.

Sometime later, she testified at a House of Representatives hearing on a
Justice Department proposal to expand the reach of the fallible NCIC: "As a
result of this incident I have suffered from medical difficulties, stress, and inability to sleep, and I have become subject to rumors."

□   □   □

Despite such mix-ups, the justice system of the future will not be able to
function without access to information. But don't expect an instant computer
revolution at your stationhouse. Even with available technology, only about one
tenth of the nation's police departments have adopted some form of computer
service, and most of those are being used for prosaic functions: as a way to keep
count of arrests and summonses; or worse, a souped-up calculator to add up
crime complaints. Fewer than two thirds are exploiting their equipment's capacity to aid in police deployment, long-term planning, and crime analysis. Only
about one tenth—with catchy acronyms like ARJIS, CASS, CATCH, MO-
TION, POSSE—are deputizing their computers for fingerprint searches, MOs,
organizing investigations, and tracking offenders.

Part of the problem is that most administrators have not yet figured out how
to utilize information. In a slyly incisive article, law enforcement expert Louis
Mayo discerns that police leaders are flying blind: "In many cases, sophisticated
mathematics camouflage foggy thinking and yield highly precise misinforma-
tion. Computers have compounded the problem by facilitating complex analysis
of doubtful data about misleading questions. Precision without perception is
counterproductive to meaningful research."

In contrast to the federal system, the local computer connection has fallen
flat. For manufacturers, it simply doesn't pay to develop highly specialized applications for law enforcement. Our fewer than 20,000 domestic law enforcement
agencies are a paltry market "compared to the 100,000 hospitals, 500,000 ho-

tels, and millions of individual businesses," observes a Washington, D.C., computer consultant.

Most of the alphabet soup, whiz-bang software police use today is a carryover from the 1970s. Big money provided by the now-defunct Law Enforcement Assistance Administration sparked its development. With the money gone, police computing is languishing—a pity when you see what computer cops can do.

In San Diego, for example, it took two thirds of a second to get a description of a suspect in a stabbing. One woman, after fatally knifing another, drove off in a blue Pontiac with a man wearing a Hell's Angels jacket. As they took off, a witness heard the woman call him "Dirt." The watch commander punched "Hell's Angels" and "Dirt" into his ARJIS terminal and up came what he termed a "real bad guy." In addition to a long string of arrests, the file contained a providential item: he hung out with a woman who owned a blue Pontiac. ARJIS also spewed out her address. "I got on the radio, dispatched a patrol car, and we were waiting to arrest them before they got home," says the commander with satisfaction.

□ □ □

In the process of investigating a specific crime, ARJIS stumbled on a habitual criminal. The 12–23 percent of criminals who chronically commit felonies are responsible for the majority of serious crimes. Our best hope for controlling crime is to get them off the street and we have a means to do it—the career criminal program. But at present, we lack adequate information systems with which to support it.

Career criminal programs—which target serious repeat offenders for intense surveillance, investigation, prosecution, and imprisonment—are fine in theory, but first you have to know who to go after. That means comprehensive and accurate histories, a hard thing to come by in the criminal justice world. In the case of serious youthful offenders, the problem is compounded by the sealing of juvenile records. When crimes have occurred across jurisdictions, it's even more difficult. Not only do you need access to local criminal history records, but you need those of other states—and even the federal government.

The distribution of information proceeds at a snail's pace. Any teenage "hacker" with a modem can instantly transmit gossip, announcements, and programming tips anywhere in the country. Many police and prosecutors, however, still wait weeks to get fingerprint and criminal history information sent by mail across state lines.

Even though many law enforcement agencies now have automated files, their format is not standardized across jurisdictions. Exchanging incompatible data wipes out the benefits of automation. With them the early identification of a career criminal and an opportunity for well-informed decisions as he moves through the system are lost.

Minneapolis' controversial Target 8 program, which has surmounted these constraints, identifies its quarries by searching all available records. The multistage selection process starts with field cops, who make suggestions based on informal knowledge of their beats. In-house backup documentation is assembled. Then come formal checks of local, state, and federal records. The data are boiled down, digested, and spit out in the form of a career criminal score for each candidate. The ones who pass get to be one of eight felons selected for intense surveillance by the police.

The Target 8 program relies on an old form of police surveillance—patrol. Rory Rowles, a Target 8 subject whom I interviewed while he was confined in St. Cloud Prison, complained: "I was noticing more patrol cars around my house and a little harassment on the street by being pulled over. . . . They put a label on me. . . . This guy's a habitual criminal. Just harass him as much as possible. . . . To get away from the harassment, I will have to move."

Rowles didn't like it, but the intense surveillance worked. Bouza points with pride to the fact that, in the program's first year, none of the targets was rearrested for a felony.

ELECTRONIC SURVEILLANCE

In the past, police surveillance was limited by the boundaries of human seeing and hearing. Today a cornucopia of electronic marvels broadens their reach. Wiretaps, for instance, which pick up suspects' private conversations, have become increasingly popular and sophisticated.

No more than one fifth of the public likes the idea of electronic bugs infesting our lives. However, between 1974 and 1982 public approval of wiretapping grew by close to 20 percent. Those most likely to approve have a paradoxical blend of liberal and conservative traits: white, male, Republican, college-educated, farmer or professional or businessperson, income over $15,000, older than thirty years of age.

Court orders for wiretaps and hidden microphones peaked during the Nixon years, reaching a high of about 875 in 1973. After the Watergate scandals, authorizations sank steadily to a low of under 575 in 1979. But since then, it's been an unbroken upward climb. As of 1983, court authorizations numbered around 650. More than two thirds of the bugs invaded that most private of all places—someone's home—and stayed an average one month. Half were extended to a second month.

As repugnant as electronic visitors may be, it's often the only way to catch big-time crooks. In 1984, nearly 2,400 suspects were arrested and 649 convicted as a result of that year's court-ordered interceptions—a ten-year high.

Electronic interceptions involve massive invasions of privacy—not only the suspect's, but everyone who has contact with him. The problem is acute when a public official is being investigated. Hundreds of legitimate but sensitive calls can be unnecessarily violated. Because the privacy issue is so real, a high order of cause is required to get a court's consent for an interception. Often, there's little more than rumors and unreliable informants to substantiate wiretap requests. Most judges find that unacceptable. But there's one form of eavesdropping that doesn't require a judge's go-ahead: secretly recorded conversations with government agents. This exception clears the way for what has come to be known as a "sting."

In a sting, undercover agents wearing wires gain the confidence of their target and appeal to his inclination to commit a crime. Audio- and/or videotapes then record and transmit the crime as it is taking place. In the case of Carmine Persico, reputed head of the Colombo crime family, the crime was bribery.

In 1978, undercover agent Richard Annicharico got close to Victor Puglisi, the crime family's conduit for payoffs and "fixes." Surreptitious recordings of his conversations with Puglisi revealed that Persico had offered the agent a $250,000 bribe to help him get an early prison release for a hijacking conviction. In 1984, based on this and other evidence, the attorney general of the United States announced Persico's indictment along with that of the entire top echelon of his organization. The investigation had been carried out over a period of years and included "undercover operations and extensive court-approved electronic surveillance." The trial took place in 1985, and the seven-year-old tapes were introduced as evidence. They showed that he had offered bribes to an IRS agent to drop tax investigations as well as perform other favors.

The celebrity stings of the past decade—Abscam, John DeLorean—have upset civil libertarians. But Frank Tuerkheimer, U.S. attorney in Wisconsin during the height of the controversy, says stings are the only way to deal with certain kinds of crime: "White collar offenders have means to commit crimes more subtly than violent street criminals. . . . if we rely on standard law enforcement techniques designed to combat street crime, we will for the most part be prosecuting crimes committed by poor people." Tuerkheimer finds stings to be less intrusive and more effective than the alternatives.

☐ ☐ ☐

"Wired" G-men, hidden room mikes, and pen registers that track every call dialed from a given phone, seem almost primitive compared to the other surveillance tools now being used by one fourth of federal agencies. Conversations transmitted by microwave towers and satellites, or those conducted on cordless and cellular telephones, fall through a crack in the law. These can literally be snatched out of the air and intercepted at will—and they are, especially in international espionage.

A whole industry has grown up around big business's, big crime's, and big government's attempts to cling to their secrets. An assortment of bug detectors, electronic handkerchiefs, masking tone emitters, and computer and voice scramblers stands ready to obstruct the unwelcome bug. But technology always seems to one-up itself, and some forms don't lend themselves to easy defeat.

For example, the super-helicopters—Blue Thunder and Airwolf—are not figments of a Hollywood producer's imagination. Similar helicopters can fly at 6,000 feet and track a small beeper attached to a car over a 250-mile radius. A loophole in the law allows such tracking devices to be used with little restriction.

Tracking can be quite dramatic. The Trakatron system used in the movie *Andromeda Strain* is not science fiction: It exists and it's in use. A badge pinned to a subject—employee or crime suspect—allows his movements to be monitored on a remote television screen. When the person wanders outside a designated area, security people can close it off by remote control or move in on him.

The Sensitrace system, another surveillance aid, is attached to objects instead of people. For $3,000 a month, one brokerage house installed Sensitrace to crack down on stock thefts. They coated all the certificates with a film that emits neutrons when exposed to electromagnetic radiation. Detector panels were installed in the office's only entryway. Any unauthorized person passing through with certificates would be caught stealing.

Even the pedestrian surveillance camera is undergoing some flashy reincarnations. Miami's monitor-watchers got bored with the blurred gray street images they had to track day in and day out. But they didn't have "Mac Private Eye" to help them.

This new video digitizer was introduced in early 1985. Its claim to fame is its ability to convert video signals into high-resolution, real-time, moving images on the thirty-two-bit, lightning fast Macintosh computer. Camera adjustments can be made through the computer, eliminating the need for a television monitor. Without resorting to freeze frames or stationary images, the new-tech toy captures each frame individually, allowing it to be studied, manipulated, filed, and transmitted—all through the computer's software and peripherals.

Then there's the video camera that poses as a peephole. Mounted behind a door, it's no bigger than a door chime. The camera transmits images to a desktop control center, complete with monitor, two-way speaker, and electronic door release. The wide-angle lens allows the operator to see everything on the other side of the door without ever having to leave his seat or letting people know they're being watched.

HIGH-TECH FORENSICS

All these forms of surveillance make police privy to outward behavior. But there are forms of monitoring which give them access to more private domains: polygraphs, voice stress analyzers, hypnosis, truth serum, physical trace evidence.

Lie detectors and truth-telling devices need improving. Although they're still unreliable and beatable, that hasn't discouraged police from using them as investigative aids. Despite admitted imperfections, they are a great boon in bogged-down inquiries. An eyewitness under hypnosis, for example, can recall crucial details that might be lost otherwise. While the leads that come out of such techniques are useful, the interrogations themselves are not admissible as evidence in most courts of law.

However, the analysis of physical trace evidence is evolving in ways that make up for that loss. In the years since 1966, the number of crime laboratories in this country has more than doubled. In the future, physical trace evidence will become the dominant means of investigating and convicting offenders.

Crimes are becoming more impersonal and less localized, and eyewitnesses who can immediately identify a perpetrator are becoming more scarce. In the dearth of eyewitnesses and confessions, the setting that "Quincy" made famous is fast becoming the most reliable adjunct to criminal investigations and trials: Polygraph and voice stress analyses are subject to interpretation, but an electron spin resonance test of gun powder is far less open to debate. Eyewitness identification is notoriously fickle, but a laser-fluoresced latent fingerprint doesn't lie or change its mind. A confession can always be thrown out because a suspect wasn't read his rights, but an ultraviolet bloodstain spectrograph doesn't need rights. A knife from a suspect's kitchen can be excluded from evidence because it was seized without a warrant, but an analysis of the polypeptides in the hairs clutched by a rigor-mortised hand doesn't require a court order.

Microscopic traces of saliva, blood, hair, and fiber are often the only links between a crime and a criminal. In Oakland, California, a series of rapes had the police worried. Semen and blood specimens taken from a half dozen victims indicated that a single assailant was responsible. But who? The crime lab used genetic markers found in body fluids to develop a biological profile of the rapist.

That profile fit only 2 percent of the population. Several suspects already in custody were typed. Their blood types didn't match, and they were released. But a sample taken from an injured burglary suspect who was getting first aid came up positive. The genetic match was sufficient grounds to issue a search warrant. When clothing belonging to the rape victims was found in his home, the crimes were solved. Forensic science had not only exculpated the innocent but indentified the guilty.

Many authorities advocate a greater reliance on physical evidence. In his landmark *Escobedo* decision in 1964, Justice Arthur Goldberg declared: "We have learned the lesson of history, ancient and modern, that a system of criminal law enforcement which comes to depend on 'confession' will, in the long run, be less reliable than a system which depends on extrinsic evidence independently secured through skillful investigation."

NONDEADLY FORCE

By curtailing coercive confessions and arbitrary searches, growing skill in developing physical evidence will allow police to better safeguard our civil liberties. But there is one right that, until 1979, police took away an average of 310 times a year. It is the basis of all our freedoms—life itself.

In October 1984, New York police responded to a call to evict Eleanor Bumpurs, a sixty-six-year-old EDP (emotionally disturbed person, in police jargon) from her apartment in a Bronx housing project. The enraged and frightened woman lashed out at the officers with a knife and one of them shot her dead.

It's unfair to engage in Monday-morning quarterbacking when that kind of split-second decision is at stake. Events happened quickly. The officer felt threatened. And New York State law—as well as NYPD standard operating procedure—allows police to shoot in self-defense. However, the death might not have occurred if the officers on the scene had been equipped with the nonlethal weapons that will arm the police of the future.

Technology is helping to make policing less violent. Unnecessary shootings will be reduced as the available arsenal of nonlethal weapons grows.

For example, Eleanor Bumpurs might have been restrained with a taser, an electric dart gun effective at ranges up to twelve feet—suitable for defense in an apartment vestibule.

Another option is the leg grabber—an eight-foot metal pole with pincers at the end. After getting the pincers around her legs, a pull handle would have knocked Mrs. Bumpurs off her feet. Embarrassing, but not deadly.

Or how about the "immobilizer"? Two poles linked by chains could have confined her legs and arms before she could wreak any havoc. Very effective at close range—and Eleanor Bumpurs' knife was at very close range.

In the outdoors, where there's lots of room to maneuver, large nets, slippery "super-banana-peel" liquids, CN gases, and "shortstop" bullets are all ways to throw dangerous people off balance without using a firearm.

□ □ □

Not everyone who has stared down the barrel of a police service revolver is dangerous. New York, Los Angeles, Houston, and Philadelphia—cities with large minority populations—are among those that have suffered major scandals over shootings of civilians. In many cases they involved killings of unarmed youths who were fleeing the scene of a crime.

New York boasted one of the classic cases. In 1973, Police Officer Thomas Shea shot and killed a young black, Clifford Glover, in Jamaica, Queens. The boy was unarmed. The police brass didn't support Shea and neither did the prosecutor. Shea was charged with murder—the first time in the history of the department that an officer had been brought up on criminal charges for a line-of-duty shooting—and acquitted. But in a Department trial, he was dismissed from his job on grounds of reckless endangerment and wanton disregard of life.

Many thought Shea had been railroaded because of pressure from the black community, but Police Commissioner Donald Cawley, who always had the courage to go against the tide, felt there was a real problem. He ordered a search of Shea's records and found that there was a history of violence. Why, he asked, didn't we flag this guy before he killed a child?

Cawley called me and my associate into his office to join a top-level, top-secret parley on identifying trigger-happy cops before they did any damage. The outcome was the establishment of a review panel to scan personnel records. Our goal was to find the closet Thomas Sheas, get them off the streets and into counseling. Many variables were considered:

• A trail of civilian complaints? They could be very active cops *or* ones with a penchant toward abuse of authority. Maybe both.
• Frequent "resisting arrest" charges on activity reports? Perhaps they beat up on their prisoners.
• Patrol cars often banged up? They could be overly aggressive.
• Marginal performance ratings? There may be an attitude problem.

• Too many transfers from precinct to precinct? Maybe nobody wants to work with them.
• Line of duty injuries? Could be an overzealous officer.
• A drinking problem? Strain at home? Over their head in debt? Possible stress case.

The early warning system was employed but not computerized, so a comprehensive analysis could never be achieved. While many stressed-out, violence-prone cops were identified and helped, many others slipped through the cracks. Blase Bonsignore was one. Now he's dead, his wife is maimed, his daughters are traumatized, and the department has lost what was once a good policeman.

However, one unqualified lifesaver did come out of the Shea incident—Interim Order 118, which refined existing statutes and orders. I.O. 118 called for minimizing force and restricting use of firearms to those situations in which a suspect posed an immediate danger to the life of innocent bystanders or officers.

In 1985, the Supreme Court of the United States echoed the provisions of I.O. 118 in *Garner v. Tennessee*—a stunning decision striking down outdated fleeing-felon statutes.

The circumstances of *Garner* were eerily similar to the Shea shooting. On the night of October 3, 1974, about one year after the death of Clifford Glover, Edward Garner broke into a neighbor's home in Memphis and stole a purse containing $10. Police were summoned to look for a prowler.

While Officer Leslie White radioed the dispatcher to report that the team had arrived on the scene, his partner Elton Hymon went around to the back of the house. There, he heard a door slam and saw Garner—a slight, fifteen-year-old black youth—running across the yard. Hymon saw no sign of a weapon and called out, "Police! Halt!" But Garner started to climb the fence. Knowing that he would lose Garner if the thief got over the fence, Hymon pulled a gun and shot him in the head. Garner later died on the operating table.

Officer Hymon had not violated the law by shooting. Tennessee allowed police to gun down escaping suspects. However, fleeing-felon statutes are archaic carryovers inherited from England. They originated in an era when all felonies were punishable by death, so it didn't much matter if you were hung by the King on a public gallows or if you were mowed down by a constable in the street.

Those were days in which unarmed civilians were rallied by a hue and cry. It was each man's duty to join the posse and chase dangerous felons through the countryside. Because the felon faced death anyway, he had nothing to lose by trying to kill his pursuers. The fleeing-felon law was a protective device for giving the good guys a leg up.

But these conditions don't exist today. Most crimes don't carry the death penalty, and civilians aren't charged with chasing crooks. We have police for that—and they're armed. Not only have fleeing-felon laws outlived their function, but they violate the Constitution in three ways:

• The failure to distinguish between a dangerous and nondangerous suspect is tantamount to unreasonable search and seizure, a violation of the Fourth Amendment.
• Administering punishment—that is, shooting—without benefit of trial violates the due process provisions of the Fifth and Fourteenth amendments.
• Killing a suspect for stealing $10 is out of proportion to the crime, abridging the Eighth Amendment ban on cruel and unusual punishments.

By ruling that a "police officer may not seize an unarmed, nondangerous suspect by shooting him dead," the Supreme Court has sent the fleeing-felon law back to the fifteenth century where it belongs.

□ □ □

There has been a general downward trend in shootings of police by civilians and civilians by police since 1974. In an average year, however, civilians are still ten times more likely to be killed by police than vice versa. Perceived misuse of force by police creates smoldering resentments that erupt into riots and sidewalk executions.

James Fyfe, of the American University School of Justice, cautions that nobody knows the precise extent of police homicides: "No one institution collects information on how often the people who are paid to protect us kill us." But the outlook is good. Many police departments have adopted administrative regulations that limit use of force much more stringently than state and federal law. Cities with the tightest restrictions have the lowest mean rate of shootings by police. Nationally, the annual average of 310 police killings between 1970 to 1979 dropped to 227 between 1980 and 1983.

Fyfe avers that restrictions on use of force have in no way diminished the ability of police to do their work. Nor have they encouraged criminals. "Anyone who argues that the frequency of police shootings had anything to do with the crime rate is completely off base." Reflecting on the 1980–83 period, Fyfe adds: "During these years, the crime rate has been going down. Fewer shootings are not encouraging crooks to go out and commit crimes because they know the cops are somehow handcuffed.

"The big issue I see now is that so many of the justifiable shootings are occurring in situations where the officer had no choice but to shoot. But he created that instance by poor tactics."

Fyfe is in a good position to know. A sixteen-year veteran of the New York City Police Department, he spent plenty of time on the street before retiring as a lieutenant and turning his considerable talents to police research.

"Police are the only emergency service that rushes into situations without having any idea of what they're getting into." By contrast, says Fyfe, fire departments know the specifications of a building before entering it to douse raging flames. Doctors know what's inside a body. The military learns the terrain before launching an attack. Only police have been getting away with operating in the dark.

"The next big issue will be on developing tactics," concludes the ex-cop.

Those tactics are likely to be nonlethal. One reason for the recent reduction in carnage is that police have learned to *talk* rather than *shoot* their way through situations. The superb work of hostage-negotiating teams is in the upper reaches of a growing repertoire of non-violent police tactics. In the future, the service revolver will be overshadowed by alternatives to deadly force. Civilian lives will be spared—and so will those of the police.

☐ ☐ ☐

Between 1973 and 1982, 1,085 police officers were killed in the line of duty. Of these, one fifth died in situations involving bar fights, deranged people, family quarrels, and other disturbances—precisely the kinds of calls that are amenable to the taser treatment. The plurality of dead police have died on the business end of a gun.

Assaults are different. When a cop is injured (as opposed to killed), a gun is rarely used. The overwhelming majority of attack weapons are the kind that could be fended off with sprays, nets, "immobilizers," and stun guns. The percentage of police injured in assaults has been declining since 1978. But like their dead colleagues, more than one third of the officers who suffer injuries are wounded during attempts to quell disturbances or subdue the mentally ill.

Cops don't like to shoot people. When they do, they suffer terribly. The trauma lasts for years: guilt, ostracism, nightmares, insomnia, gastrointestinal problems, withdrawal, sexual difficulty. By the time the press has raked them over the coals, they come out looking callous. They're not. The only place most of them have drawn a gun in their entire career is on the police practice range.

Most cops are gun shy. They're more likely to hesitate a bit too long and get hurt themselves than to empty their gun into someone's chest. But a scrupulous officer doesn't need to battle his conscience to shoot an electric dart or throw a nylon net. That's why the nondeadly weapons of the future will save their lives as well as ours.

CITIZEN PARTICIPATION

"Citizens should have a voice in damn near everything a police department does. People have a right to say how police will use force or how a S.W.A.T. team should operate. Police are simply civilians who are working for the rest of the civilians," ventures Wesley Pomeroy of the Dade County Independent Review Panel.

Them's fightin' words in the we-they world that divides police from civilians. If Pomeroy hadn't worn a badge for a quarter of a century, one might be inclined not to take such heresy seriously. But it's hard to argue with his credentials. Pomeroy, a real life veteran of CHiPs (California Highway Patrol) and the San Mateo Sheriff's Department, went on to become police chief in Berkeley and secretary of the police commission in Detroit. A law degree and vast law enforcement experience netted him White House staff positions and various other Washington plums.

His conclusion after watching policing unfold for close to fifty years is: "Formal civilian oversight entities are going to grow in number and maturity." The key to their success will be to respect police without becoming their patsy.

In Dade County, recounts Pomeroy, cops actually welcome the Independent Review Panel. "Sometimes the police themselves will refer difficult cases to us. They'll say, 'We've done everything we can, but people don't believe us. Maybe if you give this an independent, open evaluation, they'll be satisfied.' "

Pomeroy sees citizen participation as a form of "institution-building, not supplanting." "It's the job of a police chief to administer discipline and root out wrongdoers. If some outside entity takes over that function, that relieves the chief of the responsibility. And he or she is the one whose feet should be held to the fire."

Recently, Pomeroy helped found the International Association for Civilian Oversight of Law Enforcement, the first such organization in the country. He expects its fledgling membership of ombudsmen and other assorted police-monitors to grow and become an important force on the police scene.

□   □   □

The concept of citizen participation in policing isn't new; it began in 1956 with the first image-building community relations program in St. Louis, Missouri. But it took the riots and protests of the 1960s for the need to hit home. An increasing demand for service coupled with a deteriorating public image forced police to make room for civilian input. Up until now, those attempts have taken the form of public relations schemes, crime prevention programs, citizen planning councils and complaint review boards. Much of it has been window dressing.

However, the future policeperson—like the housewife—will be liberated by the computer and electronic gadgetry from much of his drudgery. Computer-directed patrols, on-line filing of reports, handling nonemergency calls by appointment or over the phone—all will free police to play a more active role in their assigned territories.

Tomorrow's policeperson will be an ombudsman, a community advocate. As the first and most visible line of government to which we turn in times of crisis, police are in a unique position to act as intermediaries between citizens and government agencies.

The twenty-first-century police agency will encompass the full spectrum of the community. Racial balances will be promoted through conscription. Higher education will seep in through college cadet programs. In fact, police agencies will function somewhat like a college, conforming to widely approved minimum standards in order to gain accreditation. Accreditation will, in turn, reduce civil liability when cops crack.

Police and their communities will become more closely intertwined even though the investigative tools of their trade will be impersonal. The changes are germinating now; they will blossom by the year 2000.

CRIMEWARPS

- There will be an overall decline in the number of sworn officers. However, the number of civilian workers will increase.
- Overall agency growth will be highest in suburban and rural areas.
- Automated surveillance, report-writing, and information systems will reduce some police functions. Among these will be fixed posts, firsthand intelligence gathering, random patrol.
- Government and private data banks will be linked up to create detailed, multipurpose dossiers on citizens.
- New laws will curtail the dissemination and utilization of dossier information.
- The number of false arrests triggered by faulty data bases will increase.
- By the late 1990s, most police departments will have access to computer services.
- The installation of court-ordered electronic interceptions will reach record levels within the next few years.
- "Stings" will remain the method of choice for developing cases where no strong probable cause exists at the outset.
- Bug detectors will become household appliances as citizens strive to ensure some measure of privacy. Phones will come equipped with voice scramblers as standard equipment.
- Physical trace evidence will become the method of choice for developing criminal cases. Confessions will become obsolete except as a form of corroboration.
- Firearms will become a specialized part of the police weapons arsenal. Nonlethal weapons will replace them as standard equipment.
- In-service psychological screening and early warning systems will become standard personnel programs in police departments.
- Police shootings of civilians will drop dramatically.
- Assaults against police officers will continue to decrease.
- Citizen-oversight groups will be an increasing factor in police policy-making.
- The law enforcement aspects of policing will grow more impersonal.
- The social service functions of police will become more community-oriented.

17

Uncrowded Courts

Wayne County Circuit Court, Detroit: On January 22, 1985, Judge Robert Colombo, Jr., unveiled the courtroom of the future. That was the day CAT crept in—invading defense counsel's desk, the prosecutor's table, the judge's bench and even the jury room. Housed in a cathode-ray tube that can instantly display the trial proceedings translated by Computer-Aided Transcription, the new technique is an adjunct to court reporting—a function that was threatened with extinction by the advent of taped proceedings. Thanks to CAT, instead of drifting into obsolescence, court reporters are rapidly becoming the information managers of the court system.

If it weren't for the computer terminals scattered around the courtroom, you wouldn't know that justice had made a great leap forward. Court reporters type testimony on the same old paper stenotype machines, just as they always did, but it doesn't stop there. It's fed directly into a computer, which converts the arcane symbols into English and instantly transcribes testimony.

With no more than a three-second delay, a judge, lawyer, juror, or deaf witness can read an ongoing examination. In one hour, one hundred and twenty-five pages of testimony can be edited, printed, and ready for review. At the end of each trial day, lawyers can have a complete transcript—quite an improvement over the thirty days it can take to get a manual one.

Nearly ten thousand court reporters now use CAT, a jump of about 60 percent since 1983. Most states have access to CAT, but the National Shorthand Reporters Association plans to computerize the majority of American courtrooms within five years. "It should improve the productivity and quality of justice for those using the legal system," predicts Thomas Rumfola of NSRA. "Over the past 10 years, a lot of laws have been enacted to speed up the trial process. This technology will allow us not only to speed up the trial process, but the appeal process. People will no longer have to languish in jail waiting for their appeal to come up. Appeals will be instantaneous." An additional enhancement allows the CAT operator to feed directly into the court's central computer. By seeing the status of each case at a glance, court administrators can make rational scheduling decisions.

In the five years between 1978 and 1983, civil and criminal case filings in state courts increased at the rate of about 4 percent a year. But the largest increase—30 percent—occurred in appeal filings. By streamlining the flow of trial and appeals information, CAT technology will make a major contribution toward uncrowding our courts.

☐ ☐ ☐

Two neighborhood kids started brawling in the street. Their mothers rushed in to break up the fight, but not without an angry bout of name-calling. Soon the peacemakers ended up wrestling each other to the ground while their now quiet children stood and watched. After dusting herself off, one of the mothers went to the police station and filed charges for assault and battery against her opponent.

The scene could have taken place anywhere at any time. But this was Columbus, Ohio, in the early 1970s. That's why the matter was settled in a unique way that has since been emulated across the country.

In 1971, Columbus was the site of a pilot project: a community dispute settlement center. Because the center functioned in the evenings and was based in the prosecutor's office, it came to be known as the Night Prosecutor Program.

Under ordinary conditions, the assault and battery case might have become one of the more than 10 million criminal cases that clog the country's state court calendars. Instead, this case became one of over 250,000 that have been referred to the NPP for mediation since 1971 and have saved Columbus millions of dollars in court costs.

The American Bar Association conservatively estimates there are two hundred dispute settlement centers nationwide. Interspersed among mediation programs are an assortment of youth courts and private courts. The hallmark of all these efforts is the growing voice of the victims and other private citizens in the proceedings.

In the future, our crowded courts will be reserved for only the most onerous cases. Others will be diverted to an array of specialized, small-scale, private forums. The quality of justice will be swifter and more fair than in public courts, but it will be removed from the public eye and the jury of peers envisioned by the Constitution.

SHORTCUTTING JUSTICE

Our court system is designed around constitutional demands for fair and open trials, representation, due process, and an impartial jury. As such, it's one of the most American institutions we've got. But according to a 1981 poll, most of our compatriots don't like it: They feel it's unsound and needs overhauling.

It's not because they have hard feelings about judges. On the contrary, among ten occupations, federal justices are seen as the most likely to act in the public interest. Nor is it because they think judges have become too powerful, biased, or subjective. The majority of those polled see judges as fair and honest. And it's not because they disagree with the outcome of cases. Sixty percent of those surveyed think most cases come out the way they should.

The cause of the public's discontent is not judges but sentences. Over the past twenty years, a growing part of the public has felt that courts have been too easy on criminals. By 1981, nearly 90 percent of us were screaming for tougher prison terms—especially if we were white and over sixty. Most of us were even willing to make end runs around the Bill of Rights. Majorities favored preventive detention, access to juvenile records in federal investigations, and accepting illegally seized evidence as long as police act in good faith.

Our newfound bloodthirstiness is partly a function of misconceptions about the courts. Plea bargaining, sentencing, and appeals are the subjects of some of our most prevalent myths about crime.

□ □ □

"He copped a plea," say our television detectives, usually with a disgusted sigh. That's our signal that another street thug is about to get off easy. By pleading guilty to a lesser charge, the animal who killed the old lady will get fifteen years for manslaughter instead of the chair for murder one. Or the small-time thief will be bargained down from a felony to a misdemeanor. If so, he'll do no more than one year's time.

The stereotype is correct in one respect: A lot more cases are decided by guilty plea than by trial. In 1979, nearly half the felony arrests ended in a guilty plea, while only 5 percent went to trial. In Portland, Oregon, there are four pleas for every trial. In Geneva, Illinois, it's thirty-seven pleas for each trial.

But there the similarity between stereotype and reality ends. A Bureau of Justice Statistics analysis reveals a shocker: In most jurisdictions, the defendant pleads guilty to the *top* charge filed by the prosecutor! Is he crazy? Why cop a plea at all?

There are benefits in pleading to the top charge. Dropping the lesser charges is one. If you commit a robbery with an unlicensed gun, some states impose a separate mandatory sentence for the weapon that can add up to five years to the time served for robbery alone. Those who are found guilty after being tried tend to get longer and harsher sentences than those who waive a trial. It used to be difficult to get twelve jurors to come up with the unanimous verdict required for a conviction, but now we have minijuries of only six, making guilty verdicts easier to come by. If you're guilty, it's usually safer to cop a plea.

□ □ □

Once guilt is established, punishment must be set. People are under the mistaken impression that judges have enormous discretion in meting out sentences. In the past they did, but they had very little control over the time actually served. Parole boards determined that.

Today, both judges and parole boards have lost much of their latitude. As of 1983, forty-eight states and the District of Columbia had enacted mandatory sentences for murder, gun crimes, drug law violations, sex crimes, or serious habitual offenders. At least nine states abolished parole. Offsetting the new toughness were forty-seven states and the District of Columbia which made provisions for reduced sentences through "good time."

The only states where judges still have fairly broad leeway in setting punishments are those with indeterminate sentences. Indeterminate sentences used to be considered the height of enlightened corrections. A convict would be given a minimum and maximum term, but the actual time he served would be determined by how quickly he became rehabilitated. But most didn't get rehabilitated. Or the prisons would get so crowded, inmates would be arbitrarily released before serving their minimum sentence.

In any case, it wasn't working. Today fewer than half the states allow indeterminate sentences. And most of those have some form of guidelines or mandatory sentence a judge must follow in setting a prison term.

Minnesota, for example, has guidelines that try to coordinate sentencing policy with available prison space. Convicts do time according to the seriousness of their current crime and their previous convictions. If they are sentenced for burglarizing a neighbor's home and they have a criminal history score of 3, they must spend 30 months in prison. If they committed the same crime but have a history score of only 1, then the sentence is reduced to only 23 months. Judges are free to depart from these guidelines, but they must put their reasons in writing.

From guidelines, it's a short step to determinate sentences, which provide a fixed term that might be reduced by good time or parole. It's these sentences— which about half the states have adopted—that have turned our prisons into sardine cans.

About one third of the states with determinate sentences go even further and allow for presumptive sentences. In this case, the sentence length is set by law and must be applied in all cases. The only exceptions are those with either mitigating or aggravating circumstances. In these, the judge can shorten or lengthen the sentence by a prescribed amount.

North Carolina is one such state. The Fair Sentencing Act, implemented in

1980, increased the predictability of prison terms. But FSA had an unanticipated consequence. There was a sharp jump in felons who copped a plea rather than taking a chance on a trial with a fixed sentence at the end. Not only were sentences equalized for those committing similar crimes, but court calendars were eased.

The FSA represents the "just desserts" approach to sentencing: That is, everyone who commits a particular crime should be similarly punished. But a contrary trend, "selective incapacitation," deems that punishments should be calibrated not only to the crime committed but to the probability that other crimes will be committed in the future. Such an approach mandates unequal punishments for equal crimes and removes the predictability of sentences. Under such a system, plea bargains are likely to increase among the youngest, most active felons and decrease among older, less serious criminals.

It's a quandary. As one observer writes, "Unfortunately, a just sentence may not be effective, and an effective one may not be just."

Despite all its apparent chaos, the court system does manage to produce fairly consistent results. The likelihood of incarceration increases with the seriousness of the crime and the defendant's criminal history.

But when it comes to sentencing, the judge's judgment is increasingly being shunted aside in favor of prescribed formuli.

□ □ □

The loss of judicial discretion in sentencing is part of a general effort to reduce the power of the courts. A favorite target is the appeals process. To be a card-carrying conservative these days, you have to frown on the seemingly endless reviews of guilty verdicts, death sentences, and habeas corpus petitions. It almost seems as if lower court decisions don't count: If they appeal enough times, anyone can get off scot-free.

As with many stereotypes, this one contains a kernel of truth: appeal filings are spreading wildly. Between 1973 and 1983, the number of state court appeals more than doubled while those in federal courts grew by 90 percent. Most were civil rather than criminal. But even so, the roughly three hundred thousand criminal appeals accounted for almost half the volume. In the 1960s, by contrast, criminal appeals made up only 10 to 15 percent of the total. The percentage increase in criminal appeals has outpaced the FBI crime index by a factor of two; grown faster than criminal filings in state courts, and until 1981 surpassed even the phenomenal ballooning of the prison population.

The more rights we give a defendant, the more we provide openings for appeals. A 1963 Supreme Court decision giving indigent defendants the right to counsel on appeal fueled the trend. A more recent ruling makes "ineffective" counsel grounds for appeal. It will add still more momentum to the groundswell.

Such decisions are one reason the New Right is attacking the Supreme Court and pushing for a narrow "original intent" interpretation of the Constitution. As a fail-safe, the conservative Reagan administration decimated the Legal Services Corporation, which provides lawyers for the poor. Without a lawyer to enforce them, the rights decided by the Supreme Court have no practical value.

Conservatives need not fear. Liberal justices have not tipped the balance in favor of criminal defendants. A one-hundred-year survey of criminal appeals shows that defendants were more likely to win an appeal at the end of the conservative nineteenth century than at any time during the liberal twentieth. In 1970, for most of the country, the odds of losing on appeal were slightly less than twice the odds of winning.

You'd think that the odds of winning would vary by region. After all, the Northeast is a stronghold of liberalism while the South is a bastion of traditional values. However, except for the 1960–70 period, the odds of winning an appeal were less in the Northeast than in the rest of the country. The South simply followed the same pattern as other regions. Conservativism and liberalism have no apparent bearing on whether a petitioner prevails on appeal.

Ideology is relevant only insofar as it expands the bases for appeal. Libertarian decisions that limit the kinds of evidence that may be introduced into a case have provided appellants with grounds for complaint. But many of those same decisions are being watered down. Illegally seized evidence may now be used under a "good faith" exception to the Exclusionary Rule. Confessions obtained without reading a subject his rights may be admitted under a "public safety" exception to the *Miranda* rule. But on balance, expanded rights prevail—and along with them, burgeoning appeals dockets.

Since the bases for appeals are not likely to undergo much shrinkage, new ways must be found to unclog the court calendars. Appeals are not instant replays of a trial; they are simply a review of the written record. Did the trial judge prejudice the jury with his instructions? Was evidence improperly introduced? Did the defendant get effective counsel?

The ability to complete an appeal on a timely basis is almost entirely a matter of how soon the record is made available. Old manual methods took up to a month just to produce a complete trial transcript. Then the lawyers had to review it to prepare arguments for appeal before submitting the record to the judge. Enter technologies like CAT. By making information instantly available, the process is short-circuited and lawyers can file arguments while the case is still fresh in their minds. CAT can speed the appeals process by 50 to 100 percent.

Technology can help in other ways: It can docket court appearances, notify jurors, monitor fines, allocate cases, and track their progress. Thanks to electronics, civil liberties need not be sacrificed on the altar of court efficiency.

PRIVATE COURTS

But computers can't relieve courts of their basic functions—processing pleas, imposing sentences, reviewing appeals. Well-known shortages of judges and funds leave our tribunals groaning under the weight of their caseloads. Yet, public outrage keeps the pressure on police to make arrests and prosecutors to prosecute. Their output is the courts' input.

The answer is to divert cases into other forums. The most successful of these turn public functions over to private citizens.

When a college student was raped on her campus in Philadelphia, she decided to seek compensatory damages from the college. But she didn't take her case to the Pennsylvania Court of Common Pleas, with its backlog of seventy-six thousand civil cases. She went instead to a private court, Judicate, which hires prominent former judges to hear cases and arrive at binding decisions. Judicate follows state laws and functions the same way as a public court. The only difference is that the rape victim's case was heard within eight weeks instead of three and a half years—and she didn't have to be exposed to the public eye.

Similarly, when a fourteen-year-old Newburgh, New York, boy was caught with a stolen hot-water heater, he wasn't taken to family or criminal court for arraignment. Rather, he was hauled off to Judge Joanna Tower's youth court. Judge Tower, age seventeen, was a high school senior.

Her fellow actors in the courtroom—prosecutors and defense lawyers—were, like Tower, volunteers recruited from local high schools. After several weeks of training, they went to work.

Tower's court was one of fourteen youth forums in New York State. She handled offenses too minor and offenders too young for the juvenile justice system to bother with. The "judge" was empowered to sentence her charges to community service and counseling.

Youth courts are a phenomenon of small cities. In large cities, the kinds of cases they try don't even make it into the system. But that doesn't mean large court systems are without relief. Neighborhood justice centers, like Columbus, Ohio's, Night Prosecutor Program are filling the need with mediation.

Mediation is an informal, nonadversarial method for dealing with disputes: A jilted fiancé who breaks into his ex's apartment to recover an engagement ring she won't return; the distraught mother-in-law who tries to snatch her deceased daughter's dog away from the widowed husband; a dishonest employer who won't pay his clerks the money they worked for; the careless tenant who damages a landlord's property; the desperate welfare mother who passes a bad check; an outraged husband who beats up his unfaithful wife; the drunken teenager who menaces his father. All of these are crimes, but they're better handled outside the criminal courts. When the issue is the countless ways we cheat, hurt, and beat up each other, it's often more constructive to arrive at a mediated settlement than to throw someone in prison. But mediated agreements have teeth. If the parties don't honor them, they go to jail.

Neighborhood dispute settlement centers have become highly professionalized. But they were founded on the principle of community participation. In the early days, trained local volunteers—law students and ordinary residents—negotiated the agreements between disputants.

Alternate courts epitomize the transformation of our judicial system. Proceedings have become privatized, shortcutting our constitutional guarantee of a public trial. The jury concept has also undergone a metamorphosis. Instead of a *jury* of one's peers, the new courts provide a *judge* of one's peers. Victims and other civilians have been given a greater voice in the administration of justice.

CRIMEWARPS

- The number of states with some form of determinate sentencing will increase. So will the states that have abolished parole.
- As determinate sentences crowd prisons, states will be forced to institute extended good time provisions to ease the congestion.
- Sentences will become standardized based on present offense, criminal history, and predictors of future criminality. Increased predictability and severity will heighten the appeal of plea bargaining for the most serious offenders and reduce it for less-serious ones.
- Increased acceptance of plea bargaining by the most serious offenders will reduce the clogging of court calendars.
- State courts are becoming active in making civil liberties decisions that form the basis of appeals claims. The number of criminal appeals in state courts will continue to increase.
- New restrictions are being imposed on the kinds of claims that can be appealed to federal courts. The number of criminal appeals going to federal courts will level off and diminish.
- Technology-accelerated appeals will open up prison space now occupied by those waiting long periods of time for their case to come up.
- A wide variety of cases will be diverted from the criminal courts into informal forums. The most prominent among these will be neighborhood arbitration centers.
- As justice becomes decentralized, it will become more individualized and personalized.
- Criminal court calendars will become less crowded.

18

Prisons Without Walls

In 1974, the late Robert Martinson, one of the slightly mad geniuses of criminology, published an explosive critique of American corrections. After reviewing hundreds of studies, he concluded that *rehabilitation was a failure.* His findings caused a furor both within and without the criminal justice world and have been vigorously debated ever since.

Martinson's work provided ample justification for those who were fed up with "soft" liberal notions of handling criminals. The pendulum of corrections swung to the right and hard-nosed, punitive theories of "incapacitation" became all the rage.

Sometime later, Martinson suggested to me a wild prescription for handling convicts. I'll paraphrase: "The only way to control crime is for each convict to be followed by a parole officer twenty-four hours a day."

I thought Martinson was raving.

But he was a visionary.

In 1983, Florida became one of the first pioneers in statewide house arrest. More than five thousand of her convicts have since been subject to twenty-four-hour surveillance—at home. Each is assigned a house arrest officer, who carries a caseload of not more than twenty "inmates" and employs team surveillance to keep his charges off guard. His wards are required to report in a minimum of four times a week and keep an hourly log of how they spend their time. They must submit to—and pay for—drug and alcohol tests on demand. With the exception of approved jobs or public service work, convicts are confined to their homes.

The system has advanced to a point where minor offenders are monitored by attache case–sized boxes that pick up signals from a transmitter they wear around their ankles. Jay Match, a traffic violator, was one of the first to be supervised by an electronic jailkeeper. The human one was miles away manning the computers that registered the signals from Jay's home. Neither the computers nor their operators belong to the state of Florida. The entire system is managed by Pride Incorporated, a private contractor.

House arrest is a good idea. It relieves the desperate overcrowding in local prisons and costs less than providing room and board at government expense. It allows the convict to work, take care of children, and stay integrated in society. Counties in Kentucky, Michigan, New Mexico, Oregon, and Utah are using the system. California, Georgia, New Jersey, New York, North Carolina, Ohio, and Texas have decided to give it a try.

The time is fast approaching when prisons will need no walls and convicts won't have to check in with a house arrest officer. Their round-the-clock parole/probation officer will be an electronic tracking device. Robert Martinson's vision will have come true.

□ □ □

In 1981, Control Data Corporation opened a new assembly plant to produce thirty-megabyte disk drives selling for $25,000 to $35,000 per unit. Its assemblers work for less money, but make components faster and with fewer errors, than those at Control Data's other facilities.

This paragon of productivity is located in four retooled rooms at Minnesota's Stillwater State Prison. The workers: long- and short-term maximum security inmates. More than a dozen have gone on to be hired as regular Control Data employees after completing their sentences.

A decade ago, Control Data's endeavor would have been unthinkable. Until 1979, federal law prohibited prisons from manufacturing goods to be shipped across state lines. That left little to make other than license plates, soap, and spartan office furniture for other state agencies. Only 10 percent of inmates were employed in prison industries, and the skills they acquired weren't marketable on the outside; the rest were idle. Out of idleness came demoralization and riots.

By 1983, the federal government had designated several private-sector pilot projects in prison industries. Minnesota's Control Data assembly line was one of seven.

• In Arizona, thirty female inmates handled room reservations on the toll-free line for Best Western International hotels.
• Nevada prisoners built satellite dishes for cable television.
• Kansas inmates manufactured mail-sorting machines and other metal products.

By 1985, nearly half the states had enacted statutes enabling private industry to put prison inmates to work. The unions don't like it because they feel jobs are being taken away from their members. Sponsors' competitors don't like it either, claiming their prices are being unfairly undercut by cheap labor.

But the wardens love it. Inmates are occupied in a way that makes sense. It's not just busywork: They're earning about twenty-five times more an hour than they would churning out license plates—and paying taxes on it, too! Some states earmark a portion of earnings for forced savings, victim compensation, and upkeep. By the time an inmate is released, he not only has a nest egg but a sense of responsibility.

Of about one-half million prison inmates, only a few hundred are working for companies like Control Data. In response to a need for cost controls in American industry and a trend toward private contracting of correctional services, the number will grow. Chief Justice Warren Burger has argued that prisons will become "factories with fences" rather than "warehouses" with walls.

□ □ □

The Silverdale Detention Center, on the outskirts of Chattanooga, Tennessee, houses convicted murderers, petty criminals, and a smattering of DWI (driving while intoxicated) cases. But the guards don't work for the state or for the county; instead, their uniform sweaters are emblazoned with the logo of the Corrections Corporation of America.

CCA, a private company, has contracted to build and operate a number of state and federal prisons. But they have competitors. Correctional workers in California, Pennsylvania, Minnesota, Tennessee, and Texas variously sport the emblems of CCA, Buckingham Security, Volunteers of America, Behavioral Systems Southwest, and RCA Service Company.

As of early 1984, fourteen contracts turned over management of federal facilities to private hands. Twenty-eight states reported privately operated adult prisons, prerelease, work release, and halfway house programs. Nearly one thousand nine hundred juvenile facilities were privately run. Enabling legislation for private jail operations was pending or had passed in several Southwestern states.

Private contractors claim they can do more with less. Free of red tape and civil service constraints, they can build prisons faster and run them cheaper than the public sector. The government, desperate to break out of its overcrowded and antiquated facilities, is turning to entrepreneurs.

The private sector charges taxpayers a daily fee for each inmate it supervises. On that basis, CCA runs Tennessee's Silverdale Detention Center for $3 less a day than the $24 it costs the county to provide the same services—and still banks on a 10-to-15-percent profit. That arrangement works out fine as long as the budget is calculated on a realistic number of inmates.

In 1985, the county budget assumed 250 Silverdale inmates. But the daily census averaged more than 300. Hamilton County found itself with cost over-runs of $200,000. With its fixed overhead, the state could have handled the unplanned inmates for only about $5 per head; but it was contractually locked into CCA's $21 figure.

Such blunders will not slow the trend. Private prison contracting is part of a general drift to disencumber government. Between 1980 and 1985, the value of publicly leased private services nearly doubled. The trend was fueled by the conservative Reagan administration, but even the most liberal Democrats endorse it.

"It is not the government's obligation to provide services, but to see that they're provided. The government doesn't have the same incentives for efficiency," as the private sector explained New York State governor Mario Cuomo in 1985.

□ □ □

At age thirty-six, after serving sixteen years for murder, Jim was granted parole. There was every sign that he would do well back in "the world." William Walsh, a prison volunteer who had befriended him, helped Jim get started in a successful business. But it wasn't long before the ex-con was arrested again—this time for killing three people.

"I knew him so well," lamented Walsh to an *Omni* writer who reported the story. "I knew it wasn't lack of love, lack of money, or a lousy environment that made him violent. It must have been something inside him."

Walsh, a chemist at Argonne National Laboratory, set out to learn what that something was. He decided to focus on hair and conducted a series of tests comparing violent and nonviolent brothers, violent criminals and law-abiding citizens.

The levels of trace metals Walsh found in the hair of impulsive and sociopathic personalities was quite distinct from that of more peaceful people. He theorized that abnormal trace-metal patterns in the hair are a reflection of treatable metabolic problems. Vitamins, minerals, and sugar reduction could turn a raging bull into a docile lamb.

Walsh hopes that his findings will not only cure some criminals but prevent criminal behavior. By screening people for trace-metal abnormalities, early intervention can short-circuit criminal tendencies.

Metabolic and biochemical manipulation is not a distant dream. Dr. Stephen Schoenthaler, a leading figure in diet and behavior research, has been consulted by forty-four states in changing the diets at educational and correctional institutions. His findings are disputed by the medical establishment. But cases such as Dan White's "Twinkie defense"—junk food-induced derangement—(for his assassination of San Francisco mayor George Moscone and supervisor Harvey Milk) have helped to give Schoenthaler's theories credence.

In the future, we will rely less on external prison controls to thwart criminals and more on internal biochemical controls. Diet will be one of the basic approaches. Where violence is caused by hereditary diseases, like Lesch-Nyhan syndrome, we will treat criminals with gene therapy. Or where a rapist is driven by raging hormones, antiandrogen drugs or surgical castration may be the sentence of choice. Sophisticated tests will detect organic brain defects that produce repetitive violent behavior.

Space shortages will not allow us the luxury of indiscriminately throwing criminals in jail. All convicts will go through psychological, metabolic, neurological, and hormonal screening to determine the most suitable level of confinement. To the horror of civil libertarians, punishment will be determined more by prognosis than by the crime actually committed.

Police are the entry point into the criminal justice process, and corrections the terminal point. Everything that happens along the way reverberates in the prison, probation, and parole system.

The crime rate has declined, but police are arresting millions of people, prosecutors are filing more cases in the courts, and judges are meting out longer and harsher sentences. The effusion of all these efforts is reflected in the record eruption of the prison population—an incredible 45.5 percent just since 1977. The accumulated impact of all this zeal has created the central reality that informs most decisions in the corrections field: overcrowding.

OVERCROWDING AND TRIAGE

State prisons are running an average of 10 percent over capacity. For federal prisons, the number is 24 percent. It has been and will continue to be impossible to keep up with the escalating demand for prison beds. Between 1981 and 1984, about 100,000 beds were added. But the number of inmates grew by more than 130,000.

Taxpayers demand tough sentences, but there's a limit to what they're willing to spend on their hunger for revenge. Even if the public trough were bottomless, we could not keep up with demand. It takes several years for the government to complete construction on a new prison, and private contractors like CCA need at least six months. But escalating demand won't wait for the concrete to be poured.

While bursting prisons await new cells, activist courts are hacking away at the limited space that already exists. The trend in Supreme Court decisions is to reduce prisoner rights. But unconstitutional and inhumane conditions are still fair game for court intervention. At the end of 1984, prison systems in seven states and the District of Columbia were run by court order or consent decree. In twenty-five other states, at least one major institution was similarly constrained. Court interventions cut the growth in inmate populations, but cause local officials to tear their own hair.

In 1985, the overcrowded, substandard Tennessee state prison system was under court order not to admit any more inmates. But convicts kept getting sentenced and judges kept shipping them off to local jails where they awaited transfer to prison. The jails were backing up, so a frustrated sheriff, Gene Barksdale, decided he was going to "Head 'em up, move 'em out." On November 13, he took twelve convicted rapists and robbers and delivered them to the West Tennessee Reception Center. When they were refused admittance to the state prison, Barksdale chained them to a fence outside the center and left them there.

The Corrections Corporation of America proposed to alleviate Tennessee's misery by expanding and upgrading the entire prison system. The governor was all for it, but entrenched interests eventually defeated the bid. Meanwhile, the governor was gored on the horns of a dilemma: on one side, rising conviction rates and lagging construction; on the other, court orders that eat up existing beds because of overcrowding and substandard conditions.

                                                                     ☐ ☐ ☐

In 1984, while the governor squirmed in Tennessee, New York was one of eight states whose conditions of confinement were not the subject of judicial ire. But I remember a time when this wasn't the case.

Seven years before, I experienced firsthand the catch-22 in which the governor of Tennessee and many other officials find themselves. During 1977–78, I was head of the criminal justice task force in New York's Office of Management and Budget. My department was charged with overseeing the finances of all the city's criminal justice operations. But it was our sprawling, five-county correctional system that gave me my worst Excedrin headaches.

New York prisons—like those of any municipality or county—house inmates awaiting trial, sentencing, or transfer to a state prison, and convicted misdemeanants serving sentences shorter than one year. In 1977, these jails—like Sheriff Barksdale's in Tennessee—were holding an overflow of convicted felons who had been crowded out of state prisons or caught on parole violations. A federal judge had closed "The Tombs"—of *Short Eyes* fame—on account of dangerous living conditions. And its alumni were causing doubling up in other jails.

We were facing ten class action suits spanning eighty separate issues—some of which had dragged on for five years. The city and the courts had promulgated a set of minimum standards dealing with overcrowding, access to libraries, inmate classification, recreation, lock-in/lock-out periods, and other exigencies of life behind bars.

Some of our prisons were yawning, empty canyons due to a shortage of personnel to run them; others were groaning with too many inmates and too little space. The House of Detention for Men on Riker's Island, one of the latter, had recently been the scene of a devastating riot.

Several years before, a system built to hold seventy-six hundred detainees had expanded to nearly twice its rated capacity. By 1977, the courts had bullied the inmate population down to seven thousand—an acceptable number—but their profile had changed drastically.

"Today our detention population consists almost entirely of accused felons," admonished the corrections commissioner in justifying his funding requests. "Ninety-four percent of those awaiting trial are charged with felonies—almost all of them are for crimes against people rather than property. Sixty-four percent are charged with Class A and B felonies—the most serious crimes in our penal code."

The Department of Corrections wanted $14 million added to its budget— and that didn't even include the cost of renovating aging facilities. If we went to full implementation of minimum standards, it would cost nearly $25 million. New York was in the midst of its famed "fiscal crisis" and we were slashing budgets, not expanding them.

The city needed money for its ailing prisons. We explored selling or leasing some of our empty beds to the state. Having recently emerged from the wreckage at Attica, state prison officials knew what overcrowding could mean. They were desperate for relief. But long hours of haggling across opposing sides of a conference table didn't produce an agreement—not during my tenure, anyway.

We had already implemented private contracting of towing illegally parked cars, but we hadn't gotten around to considering private contracting of illegally parked people—namely, those in our crumbling correctional facilities. Under New York State's constitution, privately sponsored prison industries are *verboten*. But since the governor of the state endorsed privately contracted services, that stricture presumably doesn't apply to leasing our prisons in toto.

In any case, we muddled through as best we could while being administratively drawn and quartered. With the problem unsolved, the City was eventually forced to engage in a form of triage—the premature release of high-risk suspects.

In November 1983, 613 Riker's Island detainees were freed and more than one third failed to appear for their trials. That year, 21,000 accused or convicted inmates in other states were released under similar conditions—a court order to relieve overcrowding.

☐ ☐ ☐

Triage is becoming the guiding principle of corrections. There is not, and will not be, enough room on the lifeboat to house all our prisoners; some will have to be dumped overboard. The critical question for the future is: Who?

It's a Class A dilemma. In 1980, for example, the state of Pennsylvania adopted sentencing guidelines. The goal: to increase the number of serious offenders who went to prison. The guidelines succeeded. Between 1980 and 1984, the incarceration rate for persons convicted of aggravated assault jumped from 44 percent to 69 percent. For convicted burglars, it rose from one half to two thirds. The average minimum sentence had two months added to it.

Fine. But more frequent and longer prison sentences are aggravating Pennsylvania's overcrowding problem.

"We don't want to jail large numbers of persons who are accused of lesser crimes," warned an analyst after studying the state's sentencing practices, "particularly if it means releasing serious offenders earlier."

Triage.

Illinois has been in a similar fix. It dealt with overcrowding by giving inmates extra time off for good behavior—a widely used strategy. The law allowed up to three months good time. But as prisons strained their capacity, that period stretched to eleven months. By mid-1983, 10,000 felons—none murderers, rapists, or armed robbers—had been released before completing their time. That year, the state supreme court put an end to extended good time and the prisons projected an almost 100-percent turnover in their inmate population.

Triage.

In the future, sophisticated formuli will determine who is to be incapacitated and under what conditions. The groundwork is being laid now with a concept called "selective incapacitation."

SELECTIVE INCAPACITATION

Since the demise of rehabilitation, the predominant approach to punishing criminals has been incapacitation. "Lock 'em up!" acquired respectability through the imprimatur of such noteworthy advocates as Professor James Q. Wilson, a Harvard political scientist.

In a 1979 interview, asked why other methods hadn't worked, Wilson responded: "They've been based on the optimistic and false assumption that therapy—somebody treating somebody else—will change the other person. What is best is to change the actual pattern of rewards and penalties facing an individual. Most offenders, like most citizens, are rational. Most will react in a favorable direction, but that's very different from treating them."

Wilson was advocating swiftness and certainty of punishment as the means to raise the price for committing crime. If a thief knew for sure he'd be going to prison, reasoned Wilson, he'd opt to avoid stealing and find some other way to make a living. Hence, collective incapacitation—making the punishment fit the crime and meting out like sentences for like crimes.

However, in 1979, nearly two thirds of those admitted to prison had been there before. Half of them had been incarcerated four or more times. Had they served their full sentences, nearly half the crimes they committed on the outside would not have happened.

The "certainty" of going to prison after being arrested rose by 46 percent over the next several years, but recidivism continued unabated. Collective incapacitation wasn't working either.

In looking at patterns of repeat offenses, it became clear that not every con has an equal likelihood of recidivism. The younger the convict, the more apt he is to return to prison within the first year of his release. (To be exact, the second half of the first year after release is the highest risk period for a new arrest—often on the grounds of a parole violation.) Property offenders are more likely to end up back in prison than violent ones. Males more than females. Blacks more than whites.

When compared to first timers, recidivists are more likely to have been without work and using illegal drugs at the time of their arrest. They are also more likely to have a history of imprisonment in the family.

It has become obvious that some convicts are more of a threat than others and that these are the ones to whom scarce prison space should be devoted.

□ □ □

In developing the selective incapacitation concept, the Rand Corporation studied more than two thousand inmates in California, Texas, and Michigan. Based on their self-reports, Rand developed an index for predicting future criminality. The number of positive responses to the following items determined the score:

• A prior conviction for the crime being predicted.
• Jailed for more than half of the two-year period preceding the most recent arrest.
• First conviction before the age of sixteen.
• Commitment to a juvenile detention facility.
• Use of heroin or barbiturates in the two-year period prior to the current arrest.
• Heroin or barbiturate use as a juvenile.
• Employed for less than half of the two years prior to the current arrest.

A score of 0 to 1 predicts a low offense rate; 2 to 3, a medium rate; 4 or more, a high rate. Rand believes the offenders who score higher than 4 should be assigned the longest prison sentences.

Peter Greenwood, who conducted Rand's selective incapacitation research in California, estimates that such a sentencing policy could reduce that state's "robbery rate by 20 percent with no increase in the total number of robbers incarcerated." By contrast, collective incapacitation can achieve the same reduction only by doubling, tripling, or quadrupling the current prison population.

It's a truism that locked-up criminals can't wreak havoc in the community. But we need to determine which among our 700,000 jail and prison inmates are likely to commit the most crimes if they're set free.

We can't predict this based on existing information: Official records are incomplete and often inaccurate. The Rand Corporation staff learned as much as it did only with the help of self-reports from inmates, and those are suspect. Macho convicts have been known to exaggerate their exploits; more reticent ones selectively forget the deeds they'd rather not publicize. In any case, the Rand index mistakenly labeled more than half its sample as high-rate offenders.

However, the quality of information will improve over time, and our predictors will become more refined. Electroencephalograph scalp recordings will detect the slowed alpha-wave activity that can help identify potential thieves. Genetic screening will locate the extra Y chromosome that has incorrectly been identified with violence but more accurately linked to the low IQ that triggers much delinquency. Adding physiological data to social history gives real power to predictions. Run it all through a computer, and the crime reduction potential of selective incapacitation can be realized.

All these tests are geared to detect a tendency toward the street crimes committed mostly by those who are least likely to be intimidated by prison: minorities and the poor. Experience shows that the white-collar crook, whose criminal tendencies don't show up in his genes or brain waves, is far more likely to be deterred by the prospect of prison. But all our physiological razzle-dazzle won't help us identify him.

However, there's a more troublesome issue: selective incapacitation punishes people for crimes *they have not yet committed.* Despite this sticky wicket, the Supreme Court has cleared the way for implementation. *Schall v. Martin* upholds preventive detention of violent juveniles to keep them from committing more crimes while awaiting trial. It's just a short step to applying that principle to those who have already been convicted. Rather than sentencing them for what they did, they will be sentenced for what they might do.

But there's one more caveat: Incapacitation incapacitates only those who are incapacitated. In any given year, only 1 person goes to state prison for every 273 crimes committed.

DOING TIME WITHOUT JAIL

Selective incapacitation is a rational scheme for allocating scarce prison space. The most incorrigible and dangerous criminals are locked up the longest while less serious offenders do softer time.

Most experts seem to agree that prisons should be reserved for the most barbarous among us, but there's nothing new in that. Our prisons are already filled with violent criminals. If you review each inmate's total record, you'll find that more than half the first-timers are there for a violent crime and more than half the repeaters have done time for violence somewhere in their careers.

Rapists, brawlers, and killers are responsible for only about one tenth of all crimes; something needs to be done with the others. As of 1983, a steadily rising parole and probation population surpassed the 2 million mark. In the future, that trend will continue. While the prisons fill up with the dangerous few, new forms of probation will supervise the innocuous many. Restitution to victims; cost-savings to the state; maximum freedom and responsibility for convicts, will be our watchwords.

Restitution, already in occasional use by 85 percent of juvenile courts, will be the preferred mode for dealing with delinquency. Many kids don't have the jobs or the money to directly compensate victims for burning down their home, snatching a purse, or breaking into the cash register. But they can make up for it by performing public services—cleaning up parks, escorting senior citizens, helping the handicapped. Those who complete a restitution obligation are less likely to steal, vandalize, or shoplift again.

But restitution isn't only for street kids; it's a dandy comeuppance for older, white-collar convicts. Several years ago Missouri Valley, a highway contracting company, pleaded guilty to bid-rigging. Instead of sending the principals to a country-club federal prison, the judge ordered them to endow a $1,475,000 chair of ethics at the University of Nebraska. Such punishments benefit the public and don't cost the taxpayers any money.

Lone voices, such as penal philosopher Graeme Newman, advocate a return to another cost-effective form of punishment—physical pain. In the old days, it used to be the stocks, whipping post, and dunking stool. Newman is more modern: He suggests calibrated electric shocks for no more than eight hours— and only after passing a medical examination. Not only is this form of punishment inexpensive, but it's direct, quick, and hurts only the criminal. Unlike incarceration and twenty-four-hour surveillance, family and friends are not caught in the net.

Round-the-clock electronic monitoring and other new nonjail forms of incarceration can also be low in cost, especially when the convict pays for his own GOSSline or Supervisor surveillance. Jay Match, the West Palm Beach house arrestee with a transmitter strapped to his ankle, paid Pride Incorporated $410 to monitor his house arrest for three months. Other chronic misdemeanants in Florida pay $5 a day, plus medical and probation costs, for the privilege of at-home electronic surveillance.

The Florida experiment is instructive. During its first year, the number of felony convicts shunted off to prison dropped significantly. But only one eighth of the house arrests were direct prison diversions, and about one quarter were regular probation. The rest were probation violators who might not have gone to prison at all.

"What these data suggest," writes local professor Thomas Blomberg, "is that house arrest is widening the net of social control by including many individuals who would have not been subject to prison, but were given a tougher house arrest sanction over probation."

Blomberg adds that this widened net encompasses not only the convict but his family. They, too, share in the intrusions of twenty-four-hour surveillance. He concludes, "we may well be extending discipline from prisons into the larger society, thereby contributing to what has been termed, 'a minimum security society.'"

The net of the minimum security society will spread far beyond the walls of convicts' homes and jobs. Jay Match's black box signaled Pride Incorporated if he wandered beyond the 150–200-foot radius of his transmitter. In the future, people like Jay won't be confined to their homes or to such short distances. Surgically implanted, nuclear-powered, electronic tracking devices will allow them to move freely, but a monitor will know where they are every second.

Others will monitor themselves. Biofeedback devices will teach them to recognize and control criminal impulses. Still others won't need monitoring at all. Their behavior will be altered by daily visits to medico-probation officers who will administer mandatory doses of psychoactive drugs. Others will undergo surgical procedures to modify genes, hormone levels, and other physiological crime triggers.

Of course, all these forms of probation will be voluntary. Convicts will always be free to opt for prison—and most will. Because house arrest, electronic tracking, and biochemical and surgical treatments will be self-funded, they will be beyond the reach of the poor. Criminal justice administration will, more than ever, split off into separate tracks for haves and have-nots. The affluent will have their brains manipulated in the comfort of their own home; the poor will be warehoused in prison.

But the poor will have a way out: prison industries. The Control Data assembly lines of the future will provide them with the earnings to buy their way out of prison and into minimum security programs.

The lifetime probability of going to prison has been steadily increasing. Between 1973 and 1979 alone, it rose by nearly one third. At 1979 levels, a person born in this country today has between 1 chance in 59 and 1 in 37 of serving time in a state prison. If a felon, he's likely to languish there an average of 1.5–2.5 years. It's true that most of the 40-million-plus crimes committed each year go unpunished. But imprisonment figures like these show that a huge part of our population spends at least part of its life behind bars.

The number of offenders will continue to swell, but the walls that traditionally separate the penitentiary from the wider world will be eroded by crisscrossing currents. In one direction, the prison will move into the community through new surveillance and biochemical treatment methods. In the other, the community will move into the prison in the form of private contracting and corporate prison industries. Except for the worst offenders, the prisons of the future will be prisons without walls.

CRIMEWARPS

- Over the long term, prisons will no longer be overcrowded, as convicts manageable by other means are diverted out of them.
- Prison construction will be taken over primarily by the private sector.
- Existing capacity will be increased by Supreme Court decisions that whittle away inmate rights. While current decisions focus on searches, appeals, and death sentence reviews, future decisions will deal with conditions of confinement. Restrictions on double-bunking and minimum cell size will be loosened, allowing legal crowding of existing facilities.
- Refined selective incapacitation criteria combined with sophisticated psycho-biomedical screening will be the principal way of determining punishment.
- The rehabilitation ideal will be resurrected—not in "soft" psychotherapy form, but in mechanical biochemical form.
- Prisons will house only those who are incorrigible and unmanageable by any other means.
- Electronic tracking will be the dominant means of probation and parole supervision.
- Restitution will be a component of most punishments.

· The poor will be disproportionately punished through traditional incarceration.
· Privately contracted prison industries will provide the poor with marketable skills and a financial base upon their release from prison. They will be one of our best hopes for breaking the cycle of crime and poverty.

19

Helping Those Who
Help Themselves

In early April 1985, Antonio Torres of Miami grabbed his gun and went to a trailer park to face down two men who he believed had broken into his home and stolen $50,000 worth of jewelry. It was less than four months after self-styled vigilante Bernhard Goetz stood up to four young hoods on an IRT subway train in New York City. Goetz, whose public image had seesawed between hero and knave, was loudly proclaiming the right of civilians to arm themselves. Perhaps Torres heard him.

Torres' odyssey began on March 15 when, while running an errand, his wife spotted an unfamiliar car near the house. Anna Maria Torres, who sold jewelry from their home, returned just in time to see the car pull away. Something told her its occupants were up to no good, so she quickly jotted the license number on the back of a grocery receipt.

Mrs. Torres opened her door to find the house in shambles. She called the police, but forgot to tell them about the car she had seen and the license number she had recorded. A couple of weeks later, she stumbled across the grocery receipt. But she opted against passing it on to the police.

"I knew they weren't going to do anything about it," she reasoned. "Can you imagine how many burglaries there are in Miami every day, every hour?"

She and Antonio reportedly decided to take matters into their own hands. A friend had seen the presumed getaway car in a trailer park, and Mr. Torres decided to go there to confront the driver and his companion. When he found his quarry, Torres insinuated, "Someone told me you had some jewelry to sell." He was then led to a Hialeah apartment complex, where the suspects' accomplice was waiting. Torres allegedly pulled out a gun, forced both captives into the car, and took them to his house. He released them after five hours. However, a witness had summoned the police. Torres was arrested, charged with kidnapping, held on bond, but never prosecuted—because his purported victims "disappeared."

Detective Gary Venema exclaimed, "We can't have people running around with guns. That's why we have laws, so things don't get out of hand like this."

Anna Maria Torres was incredulous. "They treated us like we were the robbers and they were the good guys."

The Torres case harks back to a tribal form of justice in which the law helps those who help themselves. As we "arm ourselves against a sea of troubles," people who are indifferent to other civil liberties staunchly defend the Second Amendment to the Constitution—the right to bear arms.

Disillusioned by the government's inability to protect us against crime, we have intensified our romance with the gun. It peaked in 1977, but now seems to be burning itself out. The percentage of people who own up to keeping guns at home has been slowly dwindling.

□   □   □

If the general public is gradually disarming itself, so are the private police who are hired to protect it.

Late in 1975, the Cajun Wharf in Little Rock hired a Guardsmark contract guard to patrol the premises. Contrary to the advice of Ira Lipman, Guardsmark's CEO, the restaurant owner insisted on an armed guard. One evening, while on duty, the guard struck up a conversation with the bartender, who in turn poured him several rounds of drinks. After a while, a friend of the guard's joined in, thought it might be fun to tease him, and tried to unholster his gun. A scuffle followed and the gun fired. When the smoke cleared, it revealed one dead friend.

Lipman vowed such a thing would never happen again and became the industry leader in lobbying to disarm private guards. More than 99 percent of his contract police now do their jobs without a gun.

Guardsmark is the sixth-largest security company among 10,000 that employ a total of more than 1 million people. The industry is growing at the rate of 10 to 15 percent a year. Private guards now outnumber sworn officers 2 to 1, and the gap is projected to grow nearly twice as wide by 1990.

Private police, like the one assigned to the Cajun Wharf restaurant, now permeate every kind of facility. The largely unregulated private security industry patrols residential streets, monitors hospitals, guards nuclear facilities, watches banks, transports payrolls—and even protects the government. Of the nation's 1.1 million private police, 36,000 secure military bases, airports, public housing projects, parks. Many direct traffic and help sworn officers conduct investigations.

Private police cost the taxpayers far less than public police. But they're more likely to be undereducated, unstable, and untrained. One study revealed that two thirds have criminal records, and a shocking number end up stealing the property they're paid to protect. Endowed with no more than the power we all have to make a citizen's arrest, they're not obliged to observe any of the constitutional restraints that allegedly tie the hands of sworn officers. If a suspect blurts out a confession without being read his rights or if evidence is improperly seized, it is all admissable in court. The Constitution, after all, is intended to protect us against excesses by *government* agents—and private guards, whose services are sometimes contracted by government, are not considered to be part of government.

However, Lipman, a sophisticated, tough-minded merchandiser, is leading the way in upgrading the quality of the guards in whose hands our well-being will increasingly be placed. He claims to put his employees through a tougher screening process than many sworn police, hiring only 1 out of 25 applicants. He polygraphs, psychologically tests, and investigates them. Then he trains them, puts them into the field, and charges top dollar for them.

Until the Lipman lead takes hold in this runaway industry, reduced government spending will leave us at the mercy of an unknown number of private police who are persons of questionable skill and character. Public safety will be managed by huge private armies and meted out according to the client's ability to pay.

□   □   □

A few years ago, I appeared on a television show to evaluate the hardware people use to shield themselves against crime. Sharing the set with me was Miklos Korodi, president of Warner Amex Security Systems. He introduced me to a newfangled multipurpose alarm which can summon police, firefighters, or emergency paramedics—and even features a portable panic button. The allegedly fail-safe system does all this through interactive cable television scanned by round-the-clock computers. (It operates on a principle similar to the systems that monitor convicts sentenced to house arrest.) In flipping through the company's promotional material, I came across a story that shows the system strutting its stuff:

A man and woman broke into the home of a diamond cutter and tried to rob him and his wife at gunpoint. The diamond cutter decided he wasn't going to play and rushed the gunman. He succeeded in knocking over the robber but got himself shot in the ear and throat in the process. Mrs. Diamond Cutter immediately reached for her remote-control alarm button. Forty seconds later, the police were there—just in time to keep the intruders from finishing the job.

The star of this show—an interactive alarm—is just one item in a phantas-magorical array of high-tech gadgetry that will help us to help ourselves in the fight against crime.

□   □   □

In late summer 1982, twenty-five families were lofting volleyballs, racing bikes, playing dominoes, and making merry in a whirl of hamburgers, hot dogs, chili, and Kool-Aid. The occasion? The first Gattling and Atlanta streets Back-to-School Block Party in Texarkana, Texas.

The carnival-like romp was fun, but it had a serious purpose: to draw each family into the neighborhood's Crime Watchers Program—one of hundreds of such programs that have formed in cities across the country.

Gattling and Atlanta streets' block project was part of a citywide effort, Awareness of Crime in Texarkana (ACT), which had been in existence for three years. ACT got its start with seed money from Commercial Union Insurance Companies.

As with any fledgling community program, ACT had some growing pains: a lack of focus, an unrepresentative board, frustration over political manipulation, unclarity over funding. But the talented group soon smoothed things out and generated the high level of support it takes to run a successful citizen program.

Texarkana was brought to CU's attention by local congressman Sam Hall, a member of the House Judiciary Committee, and Norman Carlson, director of the Federal Bureau of Prisons. But it was an idealistic local businessman, Josh Morriss, who pulled the whole project together. Morriss recruited the president of the Junior League and a local schoolteacher; together, they organized an action committee.

Texarkana is a medium-sized city straddling two states—Texas and Arkansas. Its crime rate was rising at a time when increases were larger in smaller cities than big ones. The ACT committee set up a pilot project spanning a cross section of neighborhoods typical of today's urban areas.

There was luxurious Spring Lake Park with its spacious, high-priced, single-family homes, garaging two to three cars each. In the nine months before ACT was launched, this neighborhood of just under five hundred houses experienced a grand total of four burglaries—committed by professionals.

By contrast, the low-income areas of Beverly and Rose Hill had experienced fifteen break-ins—mostly by neighborhood kids. The population had mush-roomed by nearly 25 percent since the 1970 census, and the chances of being burglarized were twice that of Spring Lake Park.

Beverly, a lower-middle-class area made up of single family units with some attached housing, was a transitional area with "for sale" signs everywhere. Un-like the houses in Spring Lake Park, many of Beverly's homes were rented rather than owned. The population was almost exclusively white and elderly.

One step further down the socioeconomic ladder was Rose Hill. Lower class, with a large welfare population, it was 90-percent black with a great many youngsters. The residents lived mostly in multiunit subsidized housing. The incidence of neighborhood burglary was low compared to national rates—and certainly too low to know whether a crime prevention project would make any difference. But the city's demographics made it ripe for the community anticrime drive that was given its shaky start by Spring Lake Park, Beverly, and Rose Hill.

By 1982, ACT was a formal nonprofit organization made up of sixty thousand card-carrying members. (The optional $10 membership fee went into a fund for materials, printing, and engraving pens.) The thirty-five-person board of directors included both Texarkana mayors, superintendents of five school systems, business and church leaders, and members of the general public. Both Texarkana police departments worked closely with the board. The Chamber of Commerce, Jaycees, Lions' Club, Kiwanis, Boy Scouts, Girl Scouts, Brownies, and other groups joined ACT as well.

In addition to having organized fifty Watch neighborhoods, ACT spun off into a number of supplementary programs. Inmates from the local federal correctional institution were brought into the local high school to talk to students about prison. Preteen ACTors got four-color, serialized anticrime comic strips featuring Officer Opossum (Texarkana's answer to the national Crime Prevention Coalition's crime-fighting canine, "Take A Bite Out of Crime" McGruff). On the back was a burglary prevention checklist. Kids who got their parents to review and sign the checklist were awarded junior deputy badges by the police. The youngest children were brought into the ACT via Commercial Union's award-winning "Play-a-Part-in-Crime-Prevention" kits. Skits and curriculum enhancements were incorporated into regular classes to teach elementary school children some advanced lessons in crime prevention.

At the time that ACT was launched, the number of ongoing community crime prevention programs filled the first ninety-one pages of a U.S. Department of Justice directory. About three hundred and fifty thousand volunteers were showing up at police stations to help catch crooks, supervise parades, haul in drunk drivers, and alert sworn officers to crimes in progress. Some nine hundred organized citizen patrols were scouring neighborhoods, blocks, and housing projects with citizen band radios, flashlights, and walkie-talkies.

Proposition thirteen fever had swept the country, and it was clear that police resources were going to be limited. Ordinary citizens all over the country were pitching in to protect themselves against crime. The trend toward citizen participation in policing, which picked up speed in the 1970s, will continue unabated into the future.

□   □   □

Self-help in crime prevention is not a futuristic notion: It's ancient. Thousands of years before the first metropolitan police were established, the family head was charged with protecting his clan. But the roots of modern self-policing hark back to 870, when King Alfred the Great organized England into tithings. Each tithing was made up of ten families who were pledged to be responsible for each other's behavior (the roots of our colonial "snooping committees") and headed by a chief tithingman. Every ten tithings were organized into groups called hundreds. The hundreds often came together to deal with criminals and other local problems. Hundreds were part of larger units called shires, which were headed by a shire-reeve (sheriff). Sheriffs supervised the tithing system and were given the power of posse comitatus—"power of the county"—to organize all able-bodied men to assist in responding to a hue and cry. The English system of self-policing was imported to the New World and preserved by our early constables. By 1800, the constabulary had evolved from a voluntary position to a quasi-professional one.

One historian noted, "Some people resisted this step, claiming that such police were threats to civil liberty, and that they performed duties each citizen should perform himself."

Bernhard Goetz, Antonio Torres, Warner Amex, the members of ACT, and Guardsmark security services share at least the last part of that observation. We have come full circle. The crime prevention self-help movement is based on the belief that citizens should share in the responsibility for law enforcement. But contrary to the fears of our nineteenth-century predecessors, it is private citizens more than public police who are likely to trample on their fellow's civil liberties.

VIGILANTES

The ultimate deprivation of civil liberties is vigilante justice—self-policing taken to an extreme. It recognizes no due process, no ban on cruel and unusual punishment, no limits on use of force. As a means for depriving people of life, liberty, and property, it is almost as arbitrary as crime itself.

When Bernhard Goetz took the law into his own hands, he acted as victim, witness, prosecutor, judge, jury, and jailer. In true *Death Wish*/Charles Bronson style, his suspects had no opportunity to confront, rebut or mitigate the evidence against themselves. The process of administering justice was short-circuited, moving directly from alleged crime to punishment with no intervening steps.

In Goetz's case, one might make excuses. The thirty-seven-year-old blond man with the wire-rimmed glasses had found himself helpless in the face of a mugging several years before. Now he was again in immediate jeopardy, surrounded by four delinquents, one of whom later admitted that they were out to rob him.

Antonio Torres is another story. He was in no present physical danger, nor had he or his wife seen his alleged abductees stealing her jewelry. Torres simply surmised that there was a link between the car in the trailer park, the driver who greeted him, the apartment in Hialeah, and the theft—circumstantial evidence that might or might not hold up in a court of law.

The crime-punishment connection becomes even more vague in other instances of vigilantism. In May 1985, a Fort Worth grand jury returned thirty-three indictments against eight honor students and athletes at Paschal High School. The all-white, all-male group was charged with belonging to the Legion of Doom, a self-styled vigilante group allegedly devoted to ridding the campus of dopers and thieves. But the zealots—who pleaded guilty to arson, aggravated robbery, and possession of a pipe bomb—had themselves become felons. They reportedly bombed a car, blew out windows with a shotgun, vandalized school property, gutted a cat, and menaced another student with a gun. They further intimidated their prey by allegedly painting swastikas and designating the school as "Nazi territory."

There's some question about whether these methods were employed purely in the service of crime-fighting. The father of one student, whose home had been shot up by the Legion of Doom, charged that "the violence was strictly personal." His son, he explained, had once dated a girl who later started seeing a Legion of Doom member. The jealous successor started harassing the boy to learn whether he and the young woman had ever had an affair. Soon harassment gave way to violence, said the father. The door of the boy's home was broken down and his new car repeatedly vandalized.

The Legion of Doom has earned the praise of neo-Nazi groups, such as the Aryan Nations. Small wonder. Neo-Nazis, the KKK, left-wing, and fundamentalist terrorists are the essence of vigilante justice, and it is among such groups that the link between alleged crime and punishment is the most tenuous. Lynchings, hijackings, and assassinations all too often target those who are guilty of no crime other than being of a certain race, nationality, or religion.

Unlike the neo-Nazis who admire them, however, Legion of Doom members were equal opportunity terrorists. The lily-white enthusiasts menaced blacks and whites alike.

The antithesis of this lily-white anticrime group is the legendary Guardian Angels. Curtis Sliwa's mostly black and Hispanic street kids are the self-appointed patron saints of New York City's subways and other crime meccas in cities across the country. People love them. When subway riders see the red berets bouncing down the aisle or peering across a train platform, they instantly feel safer.

The Angels don't hesitate to toss graffiti artists off trains and confiscate their spray paint, but they haven't quite crossed the line to vigilantism. Rather, they straddle the gap between vigilantes and more conventional neighborhood patrols like those in Texarkana.

COMMUNITY PATROLS

Police worry about civilian patrols stepping out of line. Captain Joe Cerrato of the Texarkana, Texas, police who worked with ACT in setting up its program explains: "We cannot be everywhere. We need the eyes and ears of the citizenry to call and tell us about something suspicious going on."

But, he stresses, *"We'll* go after that location and *we'll* investigate." Cerrato need not worry. Vigilantism in resident patrols occurs rarely and only under certain conditions: when the members are drawn exclusively from a clique; when their activities are unregulated by any umbrella organization; and when patrols become dull.

Ironically, a drop in the crime rate can sow the seeds of vigilantism. When things get quiet, hepped-up anticrime groups can lose their sense of direction. If there's no other rewarding outlet for organized activity, the block watchers may turn to rousting teenagers or chasing speeders. Texarkana was able to avoid these pitfalls.

□   □   □

In about half the areas reviewed by a nationwide Rand Corporation study, groups were formed where the crime rate was low—and residents wanted to keep it that way.

FBI statistics for 1980—the first year that ACT ran a full-blown program—show the Texarkana metropolitan area had one of the lowest overall crime rates of any SMSA (Standard Metropolitan Statistical Area) in the country. The choice of Spring Lake Park as one of the test sites demonstrates that crime prevention programming isn't always linked to crime rates. ACT chose the right problem but applied it to the wrong neighborhood.

A leaflet campaign had been timed to coincide with the Christmas rush. Packets containing security survey tips, "Operation ID" engraving kits, emergency information, and block watch organizing material were prepared for door-to-door distribution in the three pilot neighborhoods. Those with a *larger* crime problem resisted ACT's first venture.

In heavily black Rose Hill well-intentioned minority youngsters were recruited to give out the kits, but they ran into trouble. I was told that only about half the residents were willing to admit the canvassers. And those who did weren't very enthusiastic. The youngsters themselves felt uncomfortable in their role as police advocates. Many of the neighbors whose doorbells they rang had had bad experiences with cops; others resented the timing of the campaign. For those who were facing the holidays with no money, the anticrime kits seemed to be anti-them.

The residents of Rose Hill were the ones at greatest risk of crime. Yet, they had not been consulted in designing the early phases of the program. What were their fears? What would make them less afraid? ACT's first efforts were based on middle class values and perceptions.

There was only one thing the packet distribution did for Rose Hill, said my informants. That was to tell delinquent kids that the program was operating in only three neighborhoods; that they should stay out of Spring Lake Park and do their burglarizing somewhere else. Displacement of crime is a common occurrence in crime prevention programs.

The cross section of Texarkana's residents eventually came to be represented in ACT and blacks were brought into the process early on, but the initial ACT steering committee was almost entirely upper and middle-middle-class, with only one active black member. There was no voice from the test sites. As with many community programs, it was the better educated and more prosperous who were the activists.

The politics of neighborhood crime prevention are such that many successful crime prevention groups are not initially formed to prevent crime at all. Rather, they spin off from other programs that engage local activists.

In Texarkana, a Living Skills course taught in the Texas Independent School District and the political agenda of a congressman provided the initial vehicles for ACT. Neither group started out in the anticrime business. Nor did the Junior League, which delivered up its president, Joanne Howard, or Offenhauser & Company, which spearheaded the campaign. ACT, in the final analysis, was a coalition of broad-based voluntary associations that banded together to fight crime. Such organizations are the key to the success of neighborhood patrols: They give legitimacy and support while preventing vigilantism.

□　□　□

In contrast to Texarkana, Chicago area anticrime groups are more likely to form in lower income areas, with blacks consistently overrepresented in their memberships. Yet, individuals from relatively higher income households within those low income neighborhoods are the ones most likely to get involved. As in Texarkana, those joining anticrime groups are driven not by fear but by their general pattern of participating in broad-based voluntary associations.

An Atlanta study confirms that there is no less neighboring and membership in voluntary associations in high crime than in low crime neighborhoods. Nor is there a difference in the extent to which neighbors share the kind of information on which community anticrime programs depend. But again, it is the more prosperous neighbors who are the most active.

The responsiveness of minority communities was vividly demonstrated in an April 1982 vote in Los Angeles. The issue was Proposition A, a special excise tax to increase the city's depleted police force by 1,350 officers. The measure was trounced, 58 percent to 42 percent. In analyzing the vote, the LAPD found that their strongest vote had come from black South Los Angeles and Mexican-American East Los Angeles. The more prosperous residents, who had earlier voted in Proposition Thirteen, were the source of the defeat. Lieutenant Dan Cooke, a press officer, observed: "On every issue, our greatest support has been from the blacks and the Mexican-Americans. They recognize what crime is."

CRIME VICTIM SERVICES

The crime experiences of minorities and the poor helped launch one of the most sweeping grass-roots changes to hit criminal justice: the victim rights movement. This powerful antidote to vigilantism began as a community-based effort for dealing with the aftershocks of crime—and one which has special significance to me.

In 1971, I was invited by Morton Bard to be a planner on an action research project he was directing for the City University of New York. Our task was to examine the interfaces in the criminal justice system and find ways to improve coordination among its various parts. During one of our weekly meetings, we were brainstorming ways in which the university could work with the criminal justice system. I ventured an idea: "What about the forgotten crime victim?

Let's design a crime victim service center." Robert Reiff, who in 1973 went on to found the first federally funded crime victim service center on the East Coast, was at that meeting.

The outline of functions I submitted to our group in a proposal I wrote in April 1972 summarizes what Reiff's center set out to do—and what crime victim service centers across the country have been doing ever since:

- Counseling victims in their legal rights for restitution and providing legal aid in the case of civil suit.
- Providing emergency services such as crisis intervention for rape victims, food and money for victims with stolen welfare checks, and medical and psychological attention for battered wives and children.
- Outreach programs for unreported victimization (usually rape), counseling by professionals who are bound by rules of privileged information for victims without recourse (such as homosexuals and "johns" who are themselves engaged in illicit activity when victimized).

The center started by Robert Reiff in the Bronx ran into trouble, but it was a brave pioneering effort that taught its descendants a lot. Within a couple of years, a nationally acclaimed program, the Victim-Witness Assistance Program (V-WAP) in Brooklyn, succeeded Reiff's enterprise. A few years after that, V-WAP went citywide, incorporated as an official city agency.

Today, crime victim services are ubiquitous. Two Presidents have declared them a priority. National organizations like NOVA (National Organization for Victim Assistance) act as advocates and clearinghouses for crime victims. Thirty-seven states and the District of Columbia offer some form of monetary compensation to victims. Multifunction centers offer counseling, escort services, day care for children of witnesses, emergency repairs of forced doors and windows, status reports on cases, and telephone alerts for court dates. Victims are even being given a voice in sentencing and parole decisions.

Community volunteers often make the difference between postcrime trauma and postcrime adjustment. Many crime victim services got their start with the unpaid workers who manned rape and crisis counseling hotlines. Reiff recruited and trained several Crime Victim Advocates from the minority neighborhoods that surrounded his center on the Albert Einstein Medical School campus in the Bronx. Although the movement is becoming increasingly professionalized and institutionalized, its roots are those of self-policing and community crime prevention: private citizens looking out for each other—and caring.

SELF-DEFENSE

It would be misleading to overstate the role of volunteer crime prevention in community life. The fact is, most people don't get involved in local anticrime groups—even when they're aware of them. A goodly number lack the time and others simply aren't interested. But a solid majority—those motivated more by fear than by socializing—take some form of individual action to protect themselves against crime. Guns and fancy hardware are among the more popular measures.

About 40 percent of Americans, a number that has been shrinking since 1977, own firearms. The vast majority own rifles and shotguns (including about a half million automatic combat weapons) rather than pistols, indicating that the American love affair with the gun has more to do with sport than with crime. However, the success of firearms training schools like Solutions Incorporated of Gretna, Louisiana, attests to the multitudes who are turning to .38's for self-defense.

Solutions Incorporated was founded in 1968. As of 1986, the school had graduated twenty thousand acolytes from eight-hour courses and its owners, Tim and Diane Zufle, were getting ready to franchise their operation. Police departments all over the country offer courses teaching gun owners how to shoot straight. But the Zufles claim that theirs is the largest civilian weapons training center in the world. Walking into the average class, you might find a heart surgeon, student, police officer, and business executive lined up in shooting crouch, firing at a target. Half the students are women.

Diane Zufle, a gun-training instructor and wife of the school's founder, teaches her charges to shoot to kill: "There's no such thing as excessive deadly force. You have to take your best shot so that you can survive. So that *you* can be a winner."

Some people sign up for her courses because they're scared by what they read in the papers and see on television. One soft-spoken, feminine housewife carries her gun with her at all times. Instead of picking her purse to match her shoes, she selects it to accommodate her gun. "I'm thinking about my family," she avers. When shopping with her children, she walks down the street with her hand on her gun. It makes her feel safer.

A close friend of the housewife signed up for the course after a flasher tried to rape her in a parking lot. "If that happened today," she says, "I'd have no reservation about pulling the trigger."

□ □ □

Not everyone is equally likely to turn to guns for defense. Southerners, like Solutions Incorporated's Louisiana clients, are more inclined to pack a pistol than others. But contrary to the gun school's enrollment pattern, women as a rule are not. Pistol ownership seems to increase with age, education, income, and occupational status. Most polls show that whites are more apt to own pistols than blacks, but a recent Gallup survey says the reverse.

In any case, these traits don't fit the profile of the average street criminal— who is young, black or Hispanic, unemployed, undereducated, unmarried, and broke. Of the estimated 120 million firearms in private circulation, relatively few end up in criminal hands. For all those crimes in which guns are most likely to be used—murder, robbery, and assault—the percentage involving firearms has been dropping since 1974 and earlier, despite the fact that the number of handguns manufactured in the United States each year has been climbing steadily since that time.

□   □   □

Some would credit gun control laws with the easing of gun crimes. All states, the District of Columbia, and the federal government now have some form of restriction on bearing arms—about 20,000 laws altogether. Kansas, Kentucky, Nebraska, New Mexico, and Oklahoma are the easiest jurisdictions in which to buy, carry, and own a gun. Illinois, New York, and the District of Columbia are among the hardest. There's no consistent correlation between the number of restrictions and the rate of violent crime, although there is a modest one between mandatory penalties for illegal possession of guns and drops in gun crime.

Regardless of federal policy, states and local governments have great latitude in deciding what they want their own citizens to do about firearms. Some places reject restrictions—like Pinedale, Wyoming, when the town voted down a ban prohibiting guns in its three bars. Morton Grove, Illinois, on the other hand, banned handguns outright and was upheld by the state supreme court.

Most people approve of restrictions on firearms—within limits. Laws requiring a permit garner a solid majority, but those banning guns altogether are opposed by more people than those who approve them. Those who prefer stricter laws hold a 10-percent slimmer majority than they did in 1975, and fewer than half believe gun control would make much difference in reducing crime.

On the whole, the public opinion ratings are starting to list toward the gun advocates, but not enough to tip the scales. Polls taken since 1975 reveal that regardless of gender, race, education, job, income, age, city size, region, religion, and political party, a majority of Americans favor stricter gun laws.

The power of the gun libertarians is unraveling a bit. The National Rifle Association seems to have gone too far and alienated one of its staunchest allies —the police lobby. It started with the NRA's refusal to support the banning of armor-piercing cop-killer bullets. (After many years, the ban passed anyway.) But the chasm widened when the Senate passed the McClure/Volkmer Bill in 1985. Even the International Association of Chiefs of Police and the Police Foundation were able to overcome their historic enmity to join forces in trying to later gut the bill in the House of Representatives.

McClure/Volkmer purported to free gun owners from the burdens of the Federal Gun Control Act of 1968. But before a compromise measure was passed the law enforcement community demurred in horror. By allowing interstate sale of guns, they argued, it would be easier for criminals to bypass state and local handgun laws. If they weren't allowed to buy a gun in Denver, why, they'd just hop over to Dallas.

That, in fact, is something like what John Hinckley did in March 1981. Sarah Brady, the staunchly conservative Republican wife of Presidential Press Secretary James Brady, who was felled in Hinckley's assassination attempt on President Reagan, opposed McClure/Volkmer. She writes of her husband's nemesis:

He walked into a Dallas pawnshop, purchased a cheap "Saturday Night Special"—
no questions asked, no waiting period to see if he had a criminal or mental illness
record—and a few minutes later he was on his way, ready to shoot the President of
the United States because he thought it would make a popular actress, Jody Foster,
fall in love with him.

Had a national waiting period and background check been in effect, John Hinckley
could have been stopped. He lied about his address. . . . He was not a Texas resident. . . . A police check would have stopped him from buying a handgun in Texas.
In fact, by lying on a Federal form, John Hinckley might well have been in jail instead
of on his way to Washington.

□ □ □

Of course, Hinckley did make it to Washington, where he shot the President,
James Brady, and two security men. Whether stricter gun controls would have
intercepted him is moot, but what stands out about the incident is this: All the
President's men and their guns could not protect him from Hinckley's ambush.
That raises questions about whether guns are an effective self-help device for
potential crime victims.

When Bernhard Goetz bought a gun after being mugged on the subway
steps, he obviously felt it would protect him. In his case, it did. Antonio Torres'
gun, however, didn't protect his house from a burglary. That occurred while no
one was home. Without the gun, he probably would not have pursued the
suspected jewel thieves. Nor would he have had to face the possibility of a life
sentence for kidnapping.

On a popular television talk show in Detroit, "Kelly & Company," I had the
pleasure of debating an articulate, thoughtful spokesperson for the NRA. I took
the extreme pro-control position. My opponent argued the Second Amendment,
which reads: "A well-regulated militia, being necessary to the security of a free
State, the right of the people to keep and bear arms shall not be infringed."

That amendment was written at a time when our new nation had no standing
army and each citizen was expected to fight in the militia. In order to do so, he
needed to be armed.

Some maintain that the Second Amendment refers to states' rights. They say
that with the advent of standing armies, national guards, and police agencies,
the individual right to bear arms is an anachronism. My opponent on "Kelly &
Company" took the other position. Whenever the word "people" appears in the
Constitution, he parried, the Supreme Court has interpreted it to refer to individual rights; therefore, the right of each of us to carry a gun is inviolate.

About halfway into the program, a man in the audience stood up. He described two experiences in which he had been victimized. In the first, he had
chased a teenage thief into an alley. When he got there, he found an accomplice
waiting. Brought up short, he aborted the chase. If he'd had a gun, said the gray-
haired man, he would have kept up the pursuit. Sometime later, he was held up
by several children—ten and twelve years old. They had a gun and he had none.
He vowed never to be outgunned again. The show's host pointedly asked me

whether I would deny such a man the right to arm himself against these types of assaults. I replied that I would.

My answer is still the same, but my reasons have changed. In 1981, I argued that cutting off the supply of imported parts at the source—combined with tough laws, hard penalties, and strict enforcement—would keep guns out of the wrong hands. Then the nice gray-haired man wouldn't need to arm himself against street hoodlums.

I no longer believe that.

What I do believe is this: Guns are usually futile as defensive weapons. Tim Zufle, founder of Solutions Incorporated, maintains that "the average gun encounter lasts no more than 2.5 seconds." In the time it takes to speed-type a short sentence, a victim must get to his gun, aim it, and fire it. The kinds of situations in which most violent crimes take place simply don't allow for that to happen.

Most violent crimes take place indoors—at home, the office, school, a friend's house—or the driveway next to the house. Only robberies take place more often on the street or in a park, and then only by a slim majority. On the streets, it's easy to be prepared for a crime and walk along with one hand at the ready. But at home, where one third of all rapes take place, it's much harder. Do the gun advocates propose that you wash the dishes holding a gun?

Diane Zufle tells her students to unload their guns at home so that a curious child or an angry lover doesn't cause an accidental death. But then what happens when the neighborhood cat burglar comes through the window? How are you going to find your gun, load it, and shoot it—all in 2.5 seconds? Even storing a gun in every room won't necessarily save you.

The criminal almost always has the element of surprise on his side. No matter how well-trained a marksman you are, it's almost impossible to protect yourself against an ambush. And most gun owners are probably not well-trained. Even hired guns, like private guards, usually have little to no formal training in handling a weapon.

Stiff gun controls won't reduce crime, but neither will open season on firearms. For every Bernhard Goetz who saves himself by standing up to four street hustlers, scores of innocent lives will be taken or maimed. Using the kind of analyses conservatives are fond of, it's clear that the costs outweigh the benefits. The Supreme Court sometimes employs cost/benefit analyses in its rulings. The Second Amendment is a good candidate for just such an approach.

□ □ □

There are plenty of nonlethal ways for people to protect themselves. The risk-benefit ratio for "target hardening" is far more attractive than it is for guns. Target hardening, as self-help, refers to the hardware and techniques that render people and property less vulnerable to crime. These devices reduce access, fool the criminal, and increase the odds of his capture.

ACT, and the multitude of community crime prevention programs it resembles, have raised our consciousness. We've learned to look at ourselves and our property the way a criminal would—and take steps accordingly. In 1982, the rate of household burglaries hit a ten-year low. The decline may, at least partly, reflect our new security consciousness.

Over that period, nearly half of all burglaries involved no forced entry. Thieves simply climbed in through an open window or walked through an unlocked door. In cases like this, security hardware doesn't do any good. However, the rate of such break-ins declined more steeply than forced entries— meaning that people are indeed becoming more careful. With access more difficult in more places, burglars are forced to find less well-fortified hunting grounds.

Clear demographic patterns make it possible to predict where those hunting grounds will be:

Those with incomes under $7,500 living in structures of four to nine units suffer the highest rate of burglary. Studies show that homeowners—whatever their income—are more likely to secure their property than renters. That may be one reason owner-occupied residences have lower rates of burglary, and why single-family houses—whether owned or rented—have lower rates than multi-unit structures.

Blacks and other minorities are more likely than others to install alarms, window bars, and/or special locks. Perhaps that's why black households have the highest rate of burglaries—both completed and attempted—involving forced entry.

The elderly, on the other hand, seem to favor indoor electrical timing devices as a means of target hardening. They use these to automatically turn on radios, televisions, and lights when their home is unoccupied. This method relies on fooling rather than foiling the burglar.

The better-educated and younger adults have still another pattern. They lean toward engraving their valuables, "Operation ID"-style. That device can speed the return of stolen property to its rightful owner—*if* it's ever found—but it's highly oversold as a means of preventing it from being stolen in the first place.

Single women are more likely to install security hardware than single men. But single-person households of either sex are less likely than multiple-person ones to use home protection measures.

All the devices mentioned so far are rather primitive compared to the interactive alarm that saved Warner Amex's smitten diamond cutter. But the super-alarm is only part of a dazzling arsenal of keyless locks, voice decoders, portable alarms, video digitizers, video peepholes, bomb blankets, and bulletproof portfolios that will become increasingly available to everyone with a few thousand dollars to spend.

In the future, like police, we will have access to electronic surveillance and information processing. How far we go in defending our fortresses will be a matter of how much we're willing to isolate ourselves behind high-tech barricades and how much we're willing to cut into our own and other people's privacy in the process.

□ □ □

The most powerful—and often most reassuring—scarecrow in our field of self-defenses is the private guard. World War II, with its insatiable appetite for munitions, created a demand for people to guard defense contractors. That catalyst launched the boom in the private security business. After the war, private police proliferated throughout the economy.

Conditions are ripe for another thrust forward. The demand for large increases in defense spending anticipates another spurt of private contracts that need to be protected—not only from outsiders, but from inside spies. Street crime rates have dropped and will continue to do so, but white-collar crime will increase. And white-collar crimes are particularly amenable to private investigations. The tax revolt is stalled for the time being, but its consequences are not. Reductions in government spending—like the Gramm-Rudman-Hollings deficit reduction law—can cut into the ability of public police to service us. Contract guards are filling the gap.

In short, we are entering a time in which the demand for private police will outstrip the supply. Higher pay, better training, and paraprofessional status will attract more qualified personnel. Like the paralegals and paramedics before them, our parapolice will acquire the status and discipline to curb the abuses identified with today's guards. Once the job climbs higher on the socioeconomic ladder, greater selectivity will weed out felons and the emotionally disturbed.

Ira Lipman at Guardsmark is leading the way in molding the future parapoliceman. But there's one problem he can't solve: the issue of our rights. Our private partners in crime prevention will have the power to watch us, track us, and hurt us. What will become of our rights when we are protected by those who are under no constraint to honor them?

CRIMEWARPS

· Vigilantism will increase as the crime rate drops—especially among extremist groups.
· The rapid expansion of the victim services movement will offset tendencies toward vigilantism among more moderate groups.
· Decreases in public services and an emphasis on volunteerism will lead to an increase in neighborhood patrols and other community crime prevention programs—especially in more affluent black suburbs and minority communities.
· Constant levels of fear will lead to an increase in individual protective measures.
· As the population ages and becomes more educated, handgun purchases will increase. A declining percentage will be owned by females.
· Tighter gun controls are supported by both the powerful and the less-powerful socioeconomic groups as well as the areas with the largest population

concentrations. Despite New Right opposition, gun control laws will become more strict.

· An outright ban of guns will not be supported either by the general population or by a conservative Supreme Court. Therefore, it will not happen at the federal level.

· As nondeadly weapons technology becomes more reliable and ripples down to the public, it will displace firearms as self-protective devices.

· Private citizens will carry tracking devices as a means to protect themselves against street crime when they travel between stops. The devices will be activated by a call to a private guard, police, or a friend. If the wearer veers off the planned route, an alarm will be raised.

· Highly sophisticated space alarms will detect movement and signal the property owners that their space has been violated, taking the element of surprise away from the intruder.

· Target hardening devices will proliferate.

· The growth in single person and elderly households will leave a growing proportion of homes poorly defended.

· Private police will attain paraprofessional status and their quality will be upgraded. Crimes committed by them will decrease.

· The vast majority of private police will be disarmed. As they take over a larger proportion of law enforcement and order maintenance duties, the number of civilians killed or injured by police agents' guns will decline.

Defensible Space

In 1973, North Asylum Hill, Connecticut, was an area in transition. Hugging Hartford's deteriorating core, it was the hub of a major commuter's route that brought in daily waves of transients. By 1976, it was a full-fledged slum. In only three years, the robbery rate had shot up by 89 percent and burglary by 145 percent. Prostitutes and drug pushers monopolized the park, and law-abiding residents were afraid to venture out in their own neighborhood.

Then along came the Hartford Institute of Criminal and Social Justice. Armed with a federal grant, they set out to explore how team policing, community action, and physical changes in the environment—a combination that had never been tried before—would impact on crime.

Physical changes were the most visible aspect of the experiment. Residents' yards were fenced in and eleven modifications were made on public streets: some through streets were narrowed; a two-way street became a one-way street; other streets emerged as cul-de-sacs, defined by attractive redwood planters filled with shrubs and trees. The alterations amounted to about $100 a house.

The design changes cut down traffic. Less accessible streets and better defined neighborhood boundaries said "Keep Out" to street thugs. By 1977, burglaries and robberies had dropped by more than one third. With all the locals watching, "johns" became uncomfortable about cruising North Asylum Hill for a pickup. The center of the fifteen-square-block area was purged of its prostitutes, and mothers with baby carriages reclaimed the park. Once-threatening streets became quiet and safe. But most important, residents stopped being so scared. Neighbors got to know each other better. Hobnobbing across the fence in their yards and venturing out into the public park, they began to keep a casual watch on each other's homes and children.

In 1979, the government took a second look at North Asylum Hill; this time, the picture didn't look so rosy. The team policing component was nullified by budget cuts and politics. The scarcity of visible police created the impression that there were more drunks on the street, more teenagers hanging out, more front-yard drug deals being made. Arrests dropped precipitously. Burglary and robbery rose to levels consistent with citywide trends.

But even in the face of all this, the fear of crime kept ebbing. Neighbors banded together in block patrols more strongly than before. Much to the chagrin of local merchants, physical changes stayed in place and kept the flow of traffic at a low ebb. The streets were defined as local turf, enabling people to recognize strangers and take action.

Design changes nurtured a community of interest. Its presence was weak in the initial evaluation, conducted just eight months into the project. But three years later, it had taken hold. It was the first time that the link between crime, spatial design, and social behavior had been demonstrated.

Of the three approaches—team policing, community action, and environmental design—the last proved to be the catalyst for enhanced social control and reduced levels of fear. What happened in North Asylum Hill is simple. With the help of security-conscious architects, people learned to use space to manage crime and forge protective links with their neighbors. The result is aptly named "Defensible Space."

Defensible space is, in a sense, a reversion to self-policing in an age where our role in taking care of ourselves has become critical. In the future, architecture will make or break our efforts to control the streets.

Natural Surveillance

Staggering under the weight of escalating crime, the people of North Asylum Hill *might have* barricaded themselves behind triple-locked doors and stayed trapped in fortresses of their own making. Instead, they learned that crime is not evenly distributed in space; that some places are more crime-prone than others. Isolated, anonymous, uncared-for, and/or unwatched spots are good bets for mayhem.

Early in this decade, I went to Quincy, Massachusetts, to help set up a crime prevention program. After being picked up at Logan Airport, I was driven through town. I had never been there before, but was immediately able to discern the most crime-prone spots. I remember driving past the mass transit depot—a hulking, dark concrete structure. I said to my hosts, "You must have a lot of rapes and muggings in there." Slightly startled, they acknowledged that those were a constant worry in the terminal.

It was predictable. The terminal had no relationship to the business area that surrounded it. Its interior was closed off from view by massive concrete obstructions and a dearth of windows. The staircases were a maze of blind spots. There was no reason for either residents or the daily flood of commuters to take any interest in it. At the end of the work day, the area was abandoned. It was an anonymous space with anonymous traffic.

In her 1961 classic, *The Death and Life of Great American Cities*, architectural critic Jane Jacobs postulated the link between design and crime: "eyes on the street" declared Jacobs, keep criminals off. Safe neighborhoods combine living, working, shopping, and entertainment. Activity keeps people watching the street. The design of the Quincy depot and its single-use surroundings did nothing to promote that kind of curiosity.

□ □ □

The role of informal surveillance is nowhere more vivid than at your local convenience store—a favorite target of robbers. In 1968, architect Shlomo Angel discovered why. They're open late and located near major traffic arteries, but remote from other businesses. The result is isolation and anonymous traffic. *No one is watching*, so robbers feel free to make late-night raids on vulnerable tills.

Angel proposed clustering high-risk establishments like gas stations, liquor stores, and all-night markets into evening town squares. That way enough traffic would flow into the area to cut down its desolation, and mutual surveillance among the businesses would offset anonymity.

For surveillance to work, you need to have a clear line of vision. Southland Corporation, parent of the omnipresent 7-Eleven stores, learned that the hard way. For years, the chain had been prime holdup bait. In addition to the thousands of dollars that had been ripped off, a number of clerks had been badly hurt. The chain of five thousand mom-and-pop stores was unsafe. So the nation's sixth-largest retailer decided to hire a resident robber.

Ray Johnson had spent twenty-five years in prison, much of it doing "hard time" at Folsom and San Quentin. "Before I was released from prison in 1968 for the last time, I'd devoted most of my life to figuring out ways to separate people like you from their money," admits Johnson unabashedly.

But when Southland hired him in 1976, he made use of his criminal's-eye view of its stores to help them hold on to their money. During his sojourns in prison, Johnson had run into a lot of 7-Eleven alumni, so he knew exactly what they looked for in a heist.

Johnson used inside information to help crimeproof the outlets. He told them to remove obstructive displays and signs from the windows so that passersby—including police—could have a clear line of vision into the store. Cash registers were moved up front so that everything going on around them was open to view. Large signs announced that clerks had only small amounts of money in the registers and that the rest was kept in lock-boxes to which cashiers had no access. The heights of display cases were lowered and aisles rearranged, reducing the opportunities for concealment. Community taxi patrols added new "eyes on the street."

When I met Johnson in the early 1980s, he was a tough-talking, rollicking ex-convict. But he had reduced Southland's robberies by 62 percent during a time that the national robbery rate was sky high. Not one for fancy jargon, Johnson didn't give his miracle a name, but, in fact, he had successfully applied the principles of defensible space.

☐ ☐ ☐

The notion of designing physical spaces to prevent crime was developed simultaneously, but separately, by architect Oscar Newman and sociologist C. Ray Jeffery in 1971. Newman called it "defensible space," while Jeffery dubbed it "crime prevention through environmental design (CPTED)." The defects of the Quincy depot and the pre-Johnson 7-Eleven stores support their insights. But the rebirth of North Asylum Hill was the direct product of their ideas.

Defensible space and CPTED are based on a simple syllogism: Crime is a form of behavior. Space is the arena within which all human behavior takes place. Therefore, changes in the design of space will produce changes in crime.

Think about some common crimes in North Asylum Hill and other urban areas—burglary, robbery, rape, vandalism:

• Burglary occurs most frequently in empty apartments, offices, or buildings.
• Robberies are crimes of anonymous streets, empty elevators, hidden stairwells, and poorly designed stores.
• Rapes happen mostly indoors under cover of night.
• Vandalism—also a nighttime crime—sullies unwatched, unlit spaces.

These crimes are the product of desire, opportunity, and perceived risk. All three elements have a spatial dimension—privacy. Amos Rapoport, an environmental behaviorist, defines privacy as the "control of unwanted interaction." In the case of crime, unwanted interaction cuts two ways. The victim wants to be protected from the intrusion of a criminal and the criminal wants to be protected from observation by witnesses and police. The way spaces are defined determines whose purpose gets served. Spaces designed to limit access and open activities to public view suffer less crime. Spaces that are freely accessible and closed off from view invite it.

Designing spaces to enhance natural surveillance and territoriality can reduce a predator's opportunities and increase his risks while, at the same time, boosting the public's sense of safety.

☐ ☐ ☐

Natural surveillance is what Jane Jacobs meant by "eyes on the street." It's the kind of casual watching we do in the course of going about our business. If we drive past a 7-Eleven store on the way home from a late poker game, that's surveillance. When Ray Johnson tells store owners to clear their display windows of obstructions, it's because he wants a masked figure with a gun to be visible to passing cars. Conversely, if a customer is being held up in the parking lot, he wants the clerk to be able to see it and call the police. In North Asylum Hill, the "eyes on the street" were created by residents lolling in their fenced-in yards or pedestrians browsing the newly closed-off streets.

Most street criminals aren't very mobile. Studies show that burglars, robbers, and rapists travel an average of two miles or less to commit their crimes. In a three-quarter-square-mile area like North Asylum Hill, it's a good bet that most of the troublemakers are the residents' own neighbors. In theory, if a local delinquent can be seen breaking into a corner house, the odds are high that he will be recognized and caught. "Eyes on the street" are a powerful weapon against neighborhood criminals.

TERRITORIALITY

In the future, however, street criminals will be more mobile and a larger share of neighborhood crime will be committed by strangers. To defend against these forays, we need to be able to spot outsiders.

In North Asylum Hill, designers did that by using planters and fenced-in yards to break up large, anonymous spaces into more intimate assigned spaces. The cul-de-sacs made public streets feel private, giving residents a feeling of ownership. The feeling is called "territoriality."

One way to foster territoriality is to keep out the people who don't belong. North Asylum Hill diverted transient through traffic out of the community. Rerouted streets and cul-de-sacs turned off anonymous drivers and burglars looking for escape routes. Strangers were noticed because residents knew who didn't belong.

If an intruder wanders into a "privatized" street, he is immediately spotted and concerned residents put on the alert. In getting away, he is forced to go through a central access point, where "eyes on the street" can jot down license numbers and call the police. Forcing a getaway car weighted with purloined television sets to make a U-turn and drive over a speed bump slows its escape and increases the odds of capture. Reduced access reduces crime. But access should not be eliminated entirely, because that leads to dangerous isolation. When Shlomo Angel proposed evening town squares, it was because it would bring more traffic to otherwise secluded stores. Interdependent merchants looking out for each other and their joint space are poor robbery prospects.

In North Asylum Hill, as in Angel's town squares, the sense of turf was more than just a screen against strangers. Making more use of their yards, streets, and park forged a positive link among neighbors. Socializing and information-sharing became the basis for block patrols, the most active component of their crime prevention efforts.

□ □ □

There is widespread debate about how much, if at all, territoriality reduces the crime rate. In North Asylum Hill, burglaries and robberies shot back up after two years, despite a strong communal feeling and the subdivision of formerly anonymous spaces. But whatever the impact on crime itself, it's clear that physical changes are the fastest way to reduce fear of crime.

In Capitol Hill, a tiny section of Denver, new streetlights illustrate the point. The district housed only about 8 percent of the city's residents, but its heavily traveled tree-lined streets accounted for one quarter of Denver's rapes, one fifth of its robberies, and a hefty percentage of its burglaries and assaults. Although pedestrians poured through the area at night, the dimly lit six-hundred-foot-long blocks had streetlamps only at the corners. Then a CPTED grant added thirty-foot lights at midblock. Residents felt safer. Some even started going out more at night. Violent crime tapered off. And the activities of a new police motorcycle patrol were rendered more effective by virtue of being visible.

An area's land use is more critical to the actual level of crime than the quality of its lighting. Studies of several Atlanta communities show that—contrary to Jacobs' theory—low-crime neighborhoods are mainly residential, while their high-crime partners mix business with housing. Small home-lined streets and a dearth of major thoroughfares are the key to keeping criminals away.

The private streets of St. Louis, Missouri, are a case in point. Like the cul-de-sacs in North Asylum Hill, each private street is closed off at one end to prevent through traffic. The open end is marked by a symbolic barrier—gateposts, narrowing of the road, a change in surface from macadam to cobblestone. An occasional car meanders through. But for the most part, streets are the site of local children's ball games and strolling baby carriages.

The limited access is psychological rather than physical, but it's every bit as powerful as an electrified fence. During one seven-year period, the crime rate on Cabanne Place, a private street, was 142 percent lower than on Cates Avenue, a public street. The most dramatic contrasts were for vandalism, assaults, and thefts of car accessories—primarily crimes of anonymity.

Not only are the private streets actually safer, but people feel safer. Residents of St. Louis' private streets were two to three times more likely to feel secure on their block than those on public streets—even when they knew the rest of the neighborhood was dangerous.

ANCILLARY APPROACHES

Without proper environmental design, security hardware, block watches, and property marking are all doomed to fail. But traditional approaches to crime prevention—target hardening and social interaction—treat space as an afterthought.

Target hardening relies on security surveys to locate crime-prone areas and property-marking programs (like "Operation ID") to identify theft-prone goods. But above all, it idolizes hardware: locks, metal doors, barred windows, alarms, video cameras, tall fences—the whole range of gimmicks and gewgaws that make a home, store, or office more difficult to penetrate.

Target hardening is essentially a Band-Aid. Professionals can defeat any security device ever invented. Fortunately for us, most crimes aren't committed by professionals—they're committed by amateurs who stumble on an apartment with an open fire escape window or a car with a key in the ignition.

Most opportunistic delinquents will be foiled by target hardening devices, but fancy window locks and door guards are futile if they're obscured by thick foliage and unlit, recessed entryways. By hiding in poorly designed spaces, an intruder can take all the time he needs to get around your hardware. When shrubs are trimmed low and strong lights eliminate shadows, he loses his hiding places and won't risk hanging around to break through your crime barriers.

One way to discourage crime is to increase the odds that a perpetrator will be seen. That's where social interaction programs come in. If someone's on vacation and you know they're away, you keep an eye on their house. When this kind of behavior is formalized, it turns into a block watch, neighborhood watch, or CB patrol—all activities in which residents or merchants band together to watch each other's property.

It's a wonderful concept. The problem is, it's not going to work if the neighborhood or block is unwatchable. If high walls block your view of the entrance or if unlit roads keep you from seeing the car being cannibalized at the end of the block, or if your kitchen window faces an empty yard instead of the action on the street, your well-intentioned vigil will be so much window dressing.

COMMUNITIES OF INTEREST

Spatial design for crime prevention incorporates elements of both target hardening and social interaction. As such, claims architect Oscar Newman, it creates communities of interest in which mutual protection is a natural outgrowth of common life-styles.

To form such communities, Newman advocates a blend of integration and segregation. He would use quotas to ensure that the poor—white and black—are integrated into middle-class developments rather than being ghetto-ized in high-rise public housing. By sprinkling small clusters throughout, he argues, peer pressures would enforce law-abiding behavior. At the same time, he departs from current thinking in espousing segregation by age, work style, and family.

In planning a four-block area for Newark, he put this radical concept to work. The designer proposed placing senior citizens in their own high-rise building adjacent to row houses for families with young children. The low-rise compounds were formed into courts that provided each family with a front and backyard, while eliminating direct access from the street. The courtyard provided a play area for tots where they could be easily watched by their mothers from inside the house. A teenage basketball court was set up beyond the children's play areas in a cluster of walk-ups at the end of the development. Scattered throughout the remaining clusters were communal sitting areas and small parking lots. If oldsters wanted to be with youngsters, all they needed to do was walk through the complex. Otherwise, they were safe on their own turf, free of teenage menaces and noisy babies.

Although working adults without children are not represented in the Newark design, Newman recommends that they live in high rises. Ordinarily the apartments they abandon during the day would be prime targets for break-ins. However, with resident older people to play pinochle in the lobby during the day, there would be sufficient "eyes on the street" to guard the building.

Using space to form small clusters of people by age, work style, and family creates a community of interest. Common interests foster a natural sense of territoriality in which everyone looks out for common turf. Because their groupings are small, members get to know each other and their habits. They can instantly spot a stranger and sense when something is wrong. In short, space can be used to mold group cohesion and patterns of interaction that foster good crime control. Space can be most effective when the groups are small and composed of similar people who live in close proximity to each other.

Local building codes will incorporate the principles of defensible space into new construction. Such attempts are already under way.

In 1983 and 1984, I worked with the Insurance Information Institute and the Independent Insurance Agents of America to help the process along. I crisscrossed the country to initiate a four-city pilot project in which community volunteers evaluated selected neighborhoods against a model code for defensible space.

Pat Harris, a former Richmond, Virginia, police officer–turned–analyst with the Virginia Department of Criminal Justice Services, had become enamored of CPTED years before. When he heard about our project, he asked us to launch it in Richmond because the state was in the process of developing a building code based on defensible space criteria.

So Richmond, with its stately mansions, tree-lined avenues, and quaint (but deserted at night) downtown area, became our first case. Eighty volunteers made up of police, college students, professors, insurance agents, and building officials canvassed the test neighborhoods for signs of territoriality and natural surveillance.

At the neighborhood level, they checked for image and isolation using these criteria:

• Are buildings of similar scale clustered together? High-rise with high, low-rise with low?
• Do many of the buildings exceed the six-story height generally considered safest from crime?
• Are commercial and residential land uses segregated?
• Are there vacant lots?
• Are bus shelters and overpasses built of opaque materials?
• Do underground transverses allow for unobstructed lines of vision?

On the block level, the surveyors looked for assignment of all public spaces and control of access by outsiders:

• Are open spaces subdivided so that the grounds within thirty feet of any main building entry are related to it through the use of real or symbolic barriers?
• Are streets "privatized"?

- Is streetlighting adequate to eliminate shadows? Are the casings vandalproof?
- Are pedestrian paths cleared of surrounding obstructions within five feet in any direction?
- Are paths connecting houses located in the rear, preventing access from public streets?

The canvassers evaluated individual structures, too; here they looked for unobstructed surveillance and access control:

- Are buildings enclosed with side yards that prevent access from the street, except through a monitored main entrance?
- How about landscaping? Are trees widely spaced? Does foliage hang no closer to the ground than seven feet and do shrubs rise no higher than three? Does any object of natural or constructed landscaping obscure a door or accessible window?
- Do tall walls and fences enclose areas not open to surveillance? Are they built of materials that are at least 50-percent opaque?
- Are parking lots adjacent to, and visible from, the windows of the car owner's home or office?
- Are common halls free of blind turns?
- Are elevators equipped with vandalproof lights, metal mirrors, and large vision panels?
- Are building laundries enclosed in glass walls and located adjacent to lobbies?
- Do garage doors avoid direct access to building interiors?
- Are fire doors and fire stairs fitted with large glass panels?

In looking at individual units within structures, the local volunteers were concerned with surveillance:

- Are the most-used rooms—kitchen, den—oriented toward the street and public areas?
- Are the windows overlooking areas closed off to surveillance inaccessible?
- Are windows made up of large or fixed panes fitted with unbreakable plastics?

The surveys were completed with hundreds of volunteers covering many miles in Richmond; Cincinnati; Portland, Oregon; and De Kalb County, Georgia. When the results were analyzed, each community was asked to tailor the data to its own needs. A U.S. Army crime prevention specialist hoped to incorporate CPTED in the rebuilding of the military's outdated, World War II facilities. The University of Cincinnati decided to survey all its campuses. Developers in Henrico County, Virginia, made commitments to use CPTED in constructing a new housing development and altering an existing one. The governor of Oregon pledged an annual award to architects and developers who excel in applying defensible space principles in building design.

For the most part, the kinds of environments our surveyors were looking for haven't yet been built: They belong to the future. But by the time the project was over, some progress had been made in hastening that future.

Defensible space doesn't deter all crimes equally well—a drunken husband brutally beating his wife in the heat of the moment will not be deflected—but it is a fine foil for crimes of opportunity that call for some prior assessment of the environment. It is precisely these kinds of crimes that dominate the police blotter.

Defensible space will speed us toward the minimum security society. The crimeproof architecture of the future will be designed to maximize surveillance of public spaces while minimizing intrusion into private ones. When we get to peer behind the mask of Big Brother, we will find that he is not entirely the electronic-tracking device implanted in a furloughed convict. Nor is he the detailed dossiers of computerized policing. Big Brother will be us—as we watch each other in fear, loathing, and benign neighborliness.

CRIMEWARPS

- Crimeproofing will be holistic. Isolation, stigma, anonymity, accessibility, and hiding places will be designed out of the environment. Enhanced visibility, socializing, personalization, and mutual protection will be designed into it. Add-ons like locks, window gates, and alarms will always have a place in security, but the real deterrents will be built into the architecture.
- Urban planning will focus on "privatizing" public space, thereby making the environment less hospitable to intruders.
- Architectural design will incorporate features that preserve clear lines of vision in interior and exterior public, semipublic, and semiprivate spaces.
- Private spaces will be designed to make them less accessible than they are today.
- Housing developments, industrial parks, and commercial centers will be subdivided into small, mutually protective clusters.
- Fear of crime will be reduced in "defensible space" zones.
- Defensible space design will be implemented via local building codes. Federal codes will remain primitive due to continuing deregulation.
- Long-term oversupplies in housing and office space combined with intense crime fears will spur the private sector to incorporate defensible space as a sales incentive to buyers.

Crimewarp VI

Conclusion: Paying the Tab for the Bill of Rights

The Northeast Kingdom Community Church—a sect of Christian fundamentalists in Island Park, Vermont—recently came to national attention because of a practice that horrified their fellow Vermonters: Sect members were alleged to regularly beat their children with slender wooden rods. In one case, according to newspaper accounts, a thirteen-year-old was thrashed for seven hours. The sect's neighbors called it child abuse. The sect's Elders called it the *will of God:* "Even little babies have a fallen nature and need to be disciplined," said one member. Bible-quoting church leaders insist that children are possessed of the devil and must "serve the Lord with fear."

Eventually most of the charges against the Northeast Kingdom Community Church were dismissed. But in its admitted beliefs on punishment, the church is an extreme expression of the stern Puritan ethic that pervades our values, our politics, and our laws. The beating example illustrates the politics of crime: A single act can be simultaneously labeled as an offense or a virtue, depending on whose values are being applied.

Based on an early Christian view of man as "fallen," the Puritan ethic defines pleasure as damnation and work as salvation. This belief persists despite several evolutions in religious and social thinking. Its implicit authoritarianism sets it on a collision course with the freedom-preserving Bill of Rights, which defines the legal parameters for our response to crime. Because our liberties will be under attack in the near future, it's important to trace the links between yesterday's Puritanism and today's moral McCarthyism.

Our straitlaced image of the Puritans might well lead you to remark that they were God's frozen people—rigid, dogmatic, harsh. But they called themselves His *chosen* people: They felt God's call beckoning them to the New World across the ocean from England. They came not only in pursuit of their own religious liberty, but to found the new Zion in the Promised Land. The Puritans believed they had entered a compact to work for God's glory. In His name, the seekers cast out the Indian "heathen" and turned the colonial wilderness into an abundant land of milk and honey.

Puritans adopted the scriptures as a complete book of laws for the conduct of everyday life. Every word was taken literally. In applying the Bible's tenets to the organization of their temporal lives, they created a short-lived American theocracy. The New World Puritans organized both the state and the church to monitor and punish sin. Tithing committees kept tabs on the private lives of their members. It was their job to report transgressions so that earthly punishments—fines, whipping, the stocks, hanging, ducking, imprisonment—might be administered in anticipation of God's eternal retribution. A general court, with ultimate authority to create and enforce the colony's laws, ruled on who was keeping God's commandments. Citizens had only those rights that were spelled out in the Bible. Anyone who tried to lead the colony into forbidden theological territory was subject to banishment. The tolerance of other religions was considered heresy—a sin against God. Additional sins were: violating the Sabbath; levity; dancing (a frivolous waste of time); gambling (not industrious or honest); drunkenness (the Puritans were prodigious drinkers and blessed liquor as bounty from God, but drunkenness was deemed Satan's work); drinking of toasts (a pagan relic used to summon the devil); idleness (a misuse of God's gift of the time to be devoted to His service); lust; pride; immodesty.

Children were a particular problem. Like their spiritual descendants in the Northeast Kingdom Community Church, Puritans believed children to be innately sinful—with corporal punishment being the only antidote. If a youngster became unmanageable, any magistrate could try him and sentence him to a flogging. If he grew into a delinquent youth, he could be put to death (there is no record of this option ever having been invoked). For the average child, however, the rigor of education was discipline enough. In their basic texts, children were bombarded with the threat of fire and brimstone and the need for piety. The popular *New England Primer* formed a life lesson around each letter of the alphabet:

"A"—"In Adam's Fall, We sinned all."

"O"—"Young Obadias, David, Josias, All Were Pious."

Early on in our history, schools were employed in the service of promoting the religious beliefs of the ruling group. Despite its seeming narrowness, education was the Puritans' great gift to our nation. Puritans, like Jews, cherished learnedness and detested ignorance; they demanded literacy and scholarship in their clergy. Puritan logic was almost Talmudic in its minute weighing of alternatives. Informed by the reason of classical literature and guided by the grace of divine faith, the Puritan religion was steeped in intellect. Puritanism was a noble experiment in the merging of rationalism and religion.

Unlike their religious heirs—today's right-wing fundamentalists—Puritans did not believe that individuals could be privy to personal demonstrations from God. He had revealed himself once and for all time in the Bible, and the only route to discovering His Word was intense study and analysis. Puritan grace did not come easily. It was an unremitting, sober struggle.

That doesn't mean Puritans were humorless or joyless. They simply turned their passion to achieving grace and devoted their lives to hard work. Forswearing the wasting of either time or money, they prospered. Though the Protestant ethic is credited with the rise of capitalism, the Puritans were socialists of sorts. Advocates of a controlled economy, they set a binding just price on all goods— and inflation was kept at bay. Their educational system honed their analytic powers, making them resourceful and shrewd, and produced the leaders who formed the nation. Towns grew, pushing their boundaries ever further into the frontier. Ministers went forth and promulgated the Puritan gospel.

Any act that didn't add to the population or contribute to the gross national product was deemed idle, and therefore sinful. In the early days of our country, a prosperous farm and bags of gold were regarded as outward signs of a guaranteed ringside seat in the Hereafter. But the money was not to be used for self-indulgence: It was God's loan to be used for His work. America was built and made rich on the denial of pleasure.

The combination of industriousness, material success, learning, and crusading zeal made Puritans the dominant force wherever they went. Their beliefs became our laws—laws which would often conflict with our rights. "Blue" laws for keeping the Sabbath remain on the books of many states to this day. So do the laws criminalizing those acts which the Puritans found offensive: prostitution, gambling, homosexuality, fornication, drunkenness, lewdness. Most pleasures were coupled with punishment, guilt, fear, frustration, and sometimes violence.

By not distinguishing between minor transgressions and major violations, the Puritan code eventually began to erode. New immigrants flooded in with the Great Migration from depression-ridden England. The clannish agricultural town began to dissolve as its members pushed farther into the wilderness, losing touch with the tight-knit community that had molded them. The second generation grew up without the galvanizing memories of religious persecution or the rigid class system that guided their parents. They began to dance, wear wigs, and consort with people of all kinds. The shortage of females on the frontier gave women a measure of freedom unknown to their more plentiful sisters in Europe. Outside values intruded, and the Puritan oligarchy began to topple.

By 1650, the Massachusetts colony had grown to fifteen thousand souls—many of them non-Puritans. It had become too large and diverse to be controlled by a theocratic oligarchy. The General Court's composition had changed. Price-setting deferred to charging whatever the traffic would bear. Power shifted from the elders to the merchants, and "degeneracy" was evident in all the great ports. The thing the Puritan prized most—order—had badly deteriorated.

Old stalwarts began to search for explanations. There must be some evil they had failed to root out and it was threatening the whole group's attainment of grace. What malevolence had they overlooked?

They found witches.

The summer of 1692 was the crucible of the Salem witches. By September, 53 out of 150 suspects were indicted. It took the intervention of a secular governor to bring the hysteria to a halt. The dismissal of the witch court of Oyer and Terminer was the last gasp of the Puritan oligarchy as America began its inexorable march toward independence, secularism, and the Bill of Rights.

□ □ □

But the old orthodoxies were not to be abandoned so easily. From the 1720s to the Revolutionary War, a Great Awakening roused the populace. Renegade preachers—"enthusiasts"—espoused a chaotic, simplified theology that displaced the Puritans' cherished "unity of life" with doctrines that "subdued reason and the intellect to the passions and emotions," according to historians Perry Miller and Thomas Johnson. By the time the American Revolution was over, the fledgling nation had entered a moral slump. Church membership had dropped off dramatically. Postwar inflation had led to price gouging. Streetwalkers were observed in Philadelphia, New York, Baltimore. Large numbers of illegitimate children were born in Pennsylvania. Church records in Massachusetts revealed that one third of the couples married in a fourteen-year period admitted to engaging in premarital sex. White youths were fornicating with black slave girls. The eighteenth-century Age of Enlightenment had elevated reason to a point where it became possible to question or deny scriptural revelation.

Our early patriots, inspired by that age, had hastened the sundering of church and state. It was not the Bible, *per se*, that the Founders wrote into the Constitution, but the secular philosophers of the Enlightenment—Locke, Hume, Mill, Rousseau, Hobbes—and the classic concept of a free citizenry borrowed from ancient Greece. From these they derived a notion that had been alien to human conclaves up until the eighteenth century: liberty and inalienable rights beyond the caprice of rulers. Liberty was defined not as a thing to be earned or lost, but as an inborn privilege accruing to all humanity. (However, it was not until the nineteenth and twentieth centuries that it was extended to those humans known as "slaves" and "women.") In order to protect our liberties, the Founders created a three-tiered form of government in which each branch checked the others. But the only branch set up to protect the inalienable rights of individuals was an independent judiciary embodied in the Supreme Court of the United States.

The Bill of Rights, which enumerates the rights of individuals, was an add-on ratified by the first Congress in 1791, two years after the Constitution went into effect. It provides the remedy for the abuses colonists suffered at the hands of King George III, as enumerated in the Declaration of Independence. But in their profound respect for diversity and minority rights, the Founders didn't wait for the Bill of Rights to separate religion and government. Article VI of the Constitution declares: "no religious test shall ever be required as a qualification to any office or public trust under the United States."

The separation of religion from government was a risky business in a society accustomed to the rule of the Christian Bible. All those things offensive to the devout Puritan spirit were happening in excess: drunkenness, gambling, debauchery, blasphemy. America's soul was in mortal danger.

The nation was ripe for a religious revival—and one came—but our staid Puritan forbears would have been scandalized by the form it took. The Second Great Awakening featured holy rollers, speaking in tongues, frenzy, frothing, ostentatious breast-beating, convulsive displays of righteous terror—the demise of a scholarly clergy and a contemplative laity. The Puritan method of logic had become too demanding for a young land on the move. Frontiersmen wanted their religion simple, personal, and direct—or not at all.

"Not at all" had become a real option. By the late eighteenth century, the Protestant majority was divided into four major groups: pro forma social church-goers, orthodox Calvinists, rationalists, and Evangelicals. From the 1790s through the early 1800s, the populace was relentlessly harangued about its innate sinfulness. Evangelicalism, however, constantly affirmed the worth of the individual. As many times as a man could fall, so could he be redeemed in Christ. The forgiveness of the church was limitless. It was out of this sense of hope that revivalism inspired a host of reform movements that ranged from abolition of slavery to abolition of demon rum. Religious fervor of this period peaked in the 1830s. By the end of the nineteenth century, a Great Reversal had begun and religion retreated from the business of social reform. Right-wing fundamentalism was born out of the conflict between orthodox evangelicals, concerned only with their souls, and outer-directed activists, who preached the liberal social gospel.

Despite a fourteen-year victory in the battle for Prohibition, the first third of this century saw fundamentalists lose the war with liberalism and retreat into separatism. Industrialization, immigration, urbanization, higher biblical criticism, liberal theology, and Darwinism drove Evangelical fundamentalists underground. The Scopes trial of 1925 sealed their isolation. No longer able to sustain their orthodoxy within the mainline churches, they split off and shifted their focus to cleaning up souls rather than society. Between the 1950s and 1960s, fundamentalism went public once more. Carl McIntire and Billy James Hargis fired the opening salvos with the American Council of Christian Churches and Christian Crusade. The embattled targets were sex education in the schools and other "humanistic" conspiracies offensive to traditional Christian sensibilities. Apocalyptic warnings were reinforced by external events. U.S. Senator Joseph McCarthy had raised the specter of internal corruption by godless communism. The Supreme Court had interfered with God's will by mandating desegregation and forbidding prayer in the schools. Righteous fires were fueled by the travesties of the 1960s and 1970s: hippies, sexual revolution, drugs, antiwar protests, Black Panthers, the New Left, radical chic, civil rights agitation, abortion on demand, X-rated entertainment, and the "me" generation. Sin was once again front-page material.

Many Americans no longer recognized their country, and they were scared. Nonbelievers and true believers ran from the mainline churches, while the boosters of "old-time religion" were filling their pews at double, triple, and quadruple their previous rates. People flocked to where they could get simple answers to complex societal questions: If the nation would only *repent*, bobby socks and Ike could be resurrected and everything would be okay again. Why couldn't we sinners see that? There must be some wickedness that had yet to be ferreted out. Like the Puritans of 1692, latter-day fundamentalists found their own witches in "secular humanists."

"Secular humanism" is a term first used in an amicus curiae brief submitted to the Supreme Court by the American Humanist Association *(Torcaso v. Watkins*, 367 U.S. 488, June 19, 1961). At issue was the plaintiff's right to a notary public's license despite his refusal to take an oath vowing a belief in God. The brief reasoned that not all religions have at their center a belief in a personal God: "The First Amendment protects the Buddhist, Ethical Culturist and other nontheists no less than Protestant, Roman Catholic and Jew." In footnote 11 of Justice Hugo Black's opinion, however, this argument was rewritten to read: "Among religions in this country which do not teach what would generally be considered belief in . . . God are Buddhism, Taoism, Ethical Culture, *Secular Humanism* and others."

"Secular humanism" was never meant to be a religious appellation; it was simply a label for distinguishing one set of humanists from another. Yet, it has come to be used as a derisive reproach to those beliefs the Puritans deemed heretical: the elevation of human reason above divine revelation, locating man rather than God at the center of the cosmos, a rejection of the doctrine of original sin and belief in the innate goodness of humanity. "What the Red Menace was in the 1950s, 'secular humanism' is today," comments John Buchanan, Baptist minister and former congressman, who was run out of office by the Religious Right.

Having thus identified a common enemy, by 1976 the Fundamentalist Right consolidated its power. The bicentennial had propelled it from obscurity to patriotic respectability. After all, the Founding Fathers had conceived us as a nation "under God"—and history, claimed Jerry Falwell, shows that God was Christian.

"The incorporation of Christian principles into both the structure and basic documents of our nation is a matter of historical fact," avers Falwell in *The*

Fundamentalist Phenomenon. "The doctrine of separation of church and state simply means that the state shall not control religion and religion shall not control the state. It does not mean that the two may never work together."

☐ ☐ ☐

By 1979, when the incorporation papers for the Moral Majority were drawn up, we were well into another Great Awakening. Conservative strategist Paul Weyrich had recruited the electronic ministry into the conservative movement and put an end to the social, political, and religious separation of fundamentalism. Revivalism and populism, patriotism and politics were now blended into an all-American stew called the New Right.

The merger of the Bible Belt and Sunbelt had created a new image for the right-wing fundamentalist. No backwoods cracker, this was a zealot with a split-level ranch, two cars, a college degree, and a cause. By 1981, the new fundamentalists had been instrumental in electing two Presidents—Jimmy Carter and Ronald Reagan. For the first time since the days of the early Puritans, the morally orthodox had their hands on the reins of power and they were ready to lead.

As the 1980s progressed, however, a new schism was evident. The fundamentalists and evangelicals once again found themselves on opposite sides of a Great Divide. The former tilted right and interpreted biblical morality to mean an endorsement of laissez-faire capitalism, arms buildups, rabid anticommunism, decentralized government, and legislation of private morality. Billy Graham, the greatest evangelist of them all, remained centrist and mainstream. A tireless fighter for social justice and other world-threatening issues, he steered well clear of political aspirations. Other evangelicals tilted left and felt the scriptures commanded them to focus on the poor and hungry while fighting for disarmament, sanctuary for refugees, environmental protection, promotion of world socialism —*and* rights for gays, women, and other minorities. Young evangelicals had rediscovered their radical legacy of social reform while newly prosperous fundamentalists pumped political iron. The gospel was sending its most orthodox adherents completely opposing messages.

All our "awakenings" accompanied major dislocations in the social structure, in which the power of white, Protestant America was severely threatened. It was always at such times that the clarion call of the "good old days" was sounded. That meant a return to old-time religion and old-time morality. At such times, individual liberty suffered. Marc Tanenbaum, a religious scholar and human rights activist, forcefully argues in his writing that any examination of history would reveal the old days were never good at all. They were rife with drunkenness, exploitation, slavery, lynchings, crime, brutality, and bigotry. Old-time moralism was often little more than a thin veil for anti-Catholicism, anti-Semitism, racism, anti-urbanism, and xenophobia. One wonders whether it still is.

In his introduction to Richard Viguerie's polemic, *The New Right: We're Ready to Lead,* Falwell proclaims: "The godless minority of treacherous individuals who have been permitted to formulate national policy must now realize they do not represent the majority." He pleads with us to "no longer permit them to destroy our country with their godless, liberal philosophies."

Liberals and conservatives, Christians and secular humanists are locked in a battle for our souls—a battle in which there seems to be no in-betweens. In *Finding Inner Peace and Strength*, Falwell states: "You either belong to the family of righteousness or the family of sin. Every unregenerate person is a member of the family of darkness until there is a new birth and the old nature is expelled." That new birth comes about only through total submission to Christ. Everyone else is doomed "to live, die, and spend eternity in Christless hell." The living hell is a chasm of fear fed by "works of the flesh" that not only war "against the Holy Spirit in our members but is attempting nationally to destroy this great nation." Citing Galatians 5:19–20, Falwell goes on to catalog a roll call of sins: "Adultery, fornication, uncleanness, lasciviousness, idolatry, witchcraft, hatred, variance, emulations, wrath, strife, seditions, heresies, envyings, murders, drunkenness, revellings, and such like."

If you didn't know this was Jerry Falwell speaking, you might well have thought it was Jonathan Edwards or Cotton Mather. The issues have not changed much since the 1600s, but the techniques for enforcing moral McCarthyism have become more refined.

□   □   □

Richard Viguerie, mastermind of the fundamentalist revolution, claims to have 85-million potential recruits with whom to build a pro-family Bible-believing coalition. This vast pool of conservativism is tapped through television ministries that reach about 20 million viewers every week and a form of computer-generated guilt known as direct mail solicitations. (The Viguerie Company alone husbands a computerized list of 4.5 million names; its namesake feels confident that the next few years will bring a doubling of that number.) Fundraising efforts, through which Viguerie claims to pull in more than either the Democratic or Republican parties, are supported by a coalition of single issue groups—such as Right to Life, Right to Work, National Rifle Association—and by the burgeoning Christian school movement—the 2 million students and 125,000 faculty members involved in 18,000 Christian schools as of 1981. The New Right has taken aim at a number of targets in an attempt to enact its moral agenda and dilute the Bill of Rights, but the main vehicles for implementing its morality are the school, the family, and the political system.

In the schools, moral rectitude has been sought through the purging of secular humanist influences that teach what the New Right calls "moral relativism" and "situation ethics." Having raised secular humanism to the status of a bona fide "religion," religious-right activists can now argue for equal time in the curriculum. That means reestablishment of voluntary prayer, revision of textbooks to reflect creationism and Christian values, the Protection of Pupil Rights Amendment, book banning, proliferation of Christian schools, restriction of sex education courses, and reaffirmation of parental authority in all matters.

Anthony Podesta, President of People for the American Way, a civil liberties lobbying group, calls the view that secular humanism pervades public school curricula "a hoax concocted by the Far Right, which uses the phrase to describe anything they don't like, from the theory of evolution to the works of Homer, Hawthorne, and Hemingway." But many parents don't see it that way. At U.S. Department of Education hearings in 1984, Michael Lisac, father of a public school student at McLaughlin Junior High in Seattle, painfully described the dilemma of "humanistic" education: "Every class that our children attends [sic] has some Home Rule signs, and what they say is 'What I think.' There are no right and wrong answers. When the child comes out, I'll guarantee you, he will be autonomous, will not respect any authority, except the child's own authority. So he could kill, he could push drugs, he could rape and murder, and there are no right and wrong answers."

The New Right's solution is to reestablish the family as the final arbiter of morality. To this end, rightist fundamentalists have sought to mandate parental consent in the distribution of contraceptive devices to minors, abolish the right to abortion on demand, defeat the Equal Rights Amendment, implement the Family Protection Act, scale down government-run domestic violence programs, eliminate pornography, reduce sex and violence in the popular arts, deny legitimacy to homosexuality, promote chastity, reinforce traditional gender roles, and heighten the appeal of sex within Christian marriage.

The teachings of school and family need support in the government if they are to be effective. That's where power politics come in. The New Right is looking to elect and appoint true believers who will run the country as a Christian nation. "Only those who have been born-again by placing their faith in Jesus Christ can effectively call upon God to bless our nation," decrees Jerry Falwell.

To this end the American Coalition for Traditional Values has set up a talent bank of conservative right-wing fundamentalist job-seekers. ACTV Chairman Tim LaHaye is quoted in *Christianity Today* as calling for a 25-percent quota for fundamentalists in federal jobs. (Is this the same ideology that has called for abolition of all affirmative action quotas?)

James Watt, former secretary of the interior; William Bennett, secretary of education; and Herbert Ellingwood of the Merit System Protection Board are some of the New Right appointees who have been called to "bless our nation" at the highest levels of government. President Reagan himself used to occasionally lapse into declaring America a Christian nation—and earned Falwell's blessing in the process: "I'll tell you who I'll vote for President," thundered Falwell in his Bicentennial July Fourth service, "the man who stands before the television cameras and says to the American public this is a Christian nation and I'm a Christian—a follower of the Lord Jesus Christ . . . as long as I lead this nation, I will lead it as a Christian under orders from his Lord."

At the Republican Convention where Ronald Reagan was nominated to run for a second term, zealous bibliolators were primed to spirit copies of the New Testament into delegates' welcome kits. (The Bibles were retracted when nonfundamentalists took umbrage at this implied slight to their own scriptures and beliefs as well as the intentions of the Founding Fathers.) Jerry Falwell was honored with bestowing the benediction.

Candidates for office have been subject to the rigors of moral report cards that rate them on their voting records (liberal organizations—such as Americans for Democratic Action and Ralph Nader's Congress Watch—have employed similar devices for years) as well as religious tests for office. Even the mosquito control board is not exempt. A Florida candidate for such a position received a questionnaire from a fundamentalist radio station demanding to know her religion as well as her views on abortion, homosexuality, and prayer in the public schools.

Judges, too, now run a gauntlet of right-wing fundamentalist panels that determine whether they are "right with God" on abortion, affirmative action, school prayer, labor unions, defendant and prisoner rights, and the First Amendment before approving them for the bench. (This practice existed in the Carter administration as well, but to a much lesser extent.)

The targets may be different, points out Viguerie, but in its tactics the New Right is simply emulating the success formula of the old liberals. While religious in orientation, the political raison d'être of these strategies is to combat legislation that favors "the legalization of immorality."

☐ ☐ ☐

On June 15, 1984, Newton Estes of Kaysville, Utah, got madder than hell and decided he wasn't going to take it anymore. He tried his own method of fighting legalized immorality. When Supreme Court Justice Byron White stood up to give a speech before the Utah State Bar Association, Estes rushed up and punched him. "You brought us pornography and four-letter words . . ." shouted the fifty-seven-year-old construction job estimator.

Estes later told FBI agents, "I don't know how else to get it stopped except through the source."

After his arrest, Estes' wife Sally told reporters that her husband "is a doer. . . . He's patriotic right down to his fingertips."

The Supreme Court is charged with protecting individual freedoms, but Newton Estes felt it had gone too far in interpreting the Bill of Rights. He saw it as his patriotic duty to help bring the country back to its senses.

In lashing out against civil liberties—such as freedom of speech—Estes conveys profound misunderstanding of the principles on which our early patriots founded this nation. It is a misunderstanding that has come to be widely shared, even by a president and attorney general of the United States.

President Reagan used to declare that the separation of church and state discriminates against religion, while Attorney General Edwin Meese reinterpreted constitutional precedents to mean that the Bill of Rights was never intended to be applied to the States. These views reflect a religious-right influence that is undermining the foundations of our pluralist democracy.

Senator Mark Hatfield of Oregon finds such a stance untenable. Civil religion, "which pounds the drums and blows the bugles, leads to the dangerous political attitude that God is ratifying everything the United States does. I reject the idea of a Christian political platform." Hatfield understands that nothing is more American than our Constitution, whose First Amendment was designed to ensure freedom of dissent. It is a guarantee that our leaders remain accountable to us—the first line of defense against despotism.

Another oppression against which it protects us is dominance of one religion, or any religion at all. The First Amendment prohibits the establishment of a state religion and any state interference with individual religious practice. The early settlers, who had had a bellyful of "God"-inspired persecution, won their own religious freedom and then proceeded to do some persecuting of their own. But the drafters of the Bill of Rights decided to write partisan religion out of this government forever.

There was a time when Jerry Falwell agreed with them. In 1965, one of his most famous sermons, "Ministers and Marches," unequivocally espoused the fundamentalist doctrine of separatism: "Nowhere are we commissioned to reform externals. We are not told to wage war against bootleggers, liquor stores, gamblers, murderers, prostitutes, racketeers, prejudiced persons, or institutions, or any other existing evil as such. Our ministry is not reformation but transformation. The gospel does not clean up the outside but rather regenerates the inside. . . . I feel we need to get off the streets and back into the pulpits and in our prayer rooms."

Now, however, some religio-politicians aver that America is a "Christian" nation with a correct "Christian" position on everything from monetary policy to birth control to crime. It is not a Christianity derived from the Sermon on the Mount—a nonjudgmental gospel of love, compassion, and peace. It is a Christianity of morality plays: the children of light versus the children of darkness. All who agree with the New Right fundamentalist agenda are dubbed righteous, God-loving, moral people.

The rest are sinners. The Catholic Church, we are told, is "Babylon, Mother of Harlots." We are further instructed that "God Almighty does not hear the prayer of a Jew." The coup de grace: "If a person is not a Christian, he is inherently a failure." The principles of tolerance on which this country was founded are degenerating into smug bigotries.

Those who advocate a Christian America point to our history and say that we were once a Christian nation—and God smiled on us. They recall that the drafters of our Constitution turned to prayer when they became stalemated in crafting it. They point to the national motto on our currency, "In God We Trust." But they fail to flip to the other side of the coin, which reads, "E Pluribus Unum"—out of many, one—a paean to our diversity. They assert that although not all of the signers of the Constitution were Christian, the drafters were influenced by Christian principles.

Of course, both we and the institutions that represent us are influenced by the religious and moral codes that guide our lives. But neither the Declaration of Independence nor the Constitution are biblical documents. While the former makes several references to "God" and "Creator," these are not Christian usages but those of civil religion.

The New Rightists take credit for being the only true patriots. But they seem to be the first in line to give up the original principles of this nation. Claiming absolute truth, they are prepared to obliterate alternate thought systems. "After the Christian majority takes control," asserts Gary Potter, president of Catholics for Christian Political Action, "pluralism will be seen as immoral and evil and the state will not permit anybody the right to practice evil."

□ □ □

The New Right is a concerned response to deeply troubling currents in American life. However, moral certitude breeds its own dangers. Fundamentalist scholars fault their movement with authoritarianism, resistance to change, lack of self-criticism, and absolutism. "Approaching every conceivable issue with a totally black or white mentality," admit Ed Dobson and Ed Hindson of Liberty Baptist College, "has caused overstatement and overcriticism in many unnecessary matters." This reproof harks back to the indiscriminate punitiveness that eventually dampened the credibility of the Puritans. But it masks a much graver peril.

Marc Tanenbaum, a widely hailed pioneer in Evangelical-Jewish and intergroup relations, warns: "There is an inexorable link between verbal violence and physical violence. Verbal violence starts the process of dehumanization which empties people of their humanity and reduces them to caricatures filled with contempt. It becomes a small thing then to swing the hate-filled caricature from a lynching tree or to shove the dehumanized person into the fires of a crematorium."

American history is replete with linkages between moral fervor and physical violence. You can trace a direct line from the pious Puritans who burnt their witches to the Ku Klux Klan who burnt their crosses to contemporary Right-to-Lifers who burn abortion clinics and neo-Nazis who "burn" Jewish talk-show hosts. In each case, the "enemy" was an interloper in the traditional religious or social order. By virtue of being black, foreign, Jewish, Catholic, or liberal, a person could be branded impure, and therefore fair game for bigoted scourges.

Among our more abominable excesses have been lynchings of blacks. In their classic study, *The Mark of Oppression*, Abram Kardiner and Lionel Ovesey describe how slavery set the stage:

> Once you degrade someone in that way, the sense of guilt makes it imperative to degrade the object further to justify the entire procedure. . . . When the enslaved person is compliant and servile, this hatred can remain hidden. . . . Should the enslaved become refractory . . . the hatred can emerge clearly. . . . The reason for the hatred becomes the loss of dominance over an object that has already been degraded . . . hence a fall in status for the white.

Too valuable as chattel to be wasted on mob justice, blacks were not lynched during slavery days. But with Reconstruction, the rope became a way to intimidate newly emancipated blacks. Blacks didn't need to break the law to incite a lynch mob. Most hangings involved "moral" offenses and were concentrated in those counties that subscribed to fundamentalist strictures forbidding card-playing, dancing, and theater attendance. Hapless blacks became convenient targets for pent-up frustrations and sexual fantasies. If they winked at, or were overly "familiar" with, a white lady, that was grounds enough for immediate death.

It is the favorite device of a guilty sinner to attribute his own desires to the object of his transgressions. Despite strong taboos against miscegenation, white men freely kept black mistresses and encouraged their young sons to cool pubescent fevers with black slave girls. Given their attraction to forbidden fruit, it was easy for them to assume that the black man coveted white women equally. From there it was a short leap to the stereotype of the black man as sexual hedonist/ sexual superman. And no white man was about to be displaced in his bed by a "dirty nigger." Having relegated the victim to the status of animal, his "upright" oppressor found it easy to project onto him all his own repressed wantonness. Lynchings became the white man's weapon for protecting his women from the perceived lusts of his black victim.

About one quarter of all lynchings were for alleged sexual crimes. Even if a white woman voluntarily copulated with a black, it was called rape. It is significant that lynchings didn't stop with the tightening of a noose. Many a dangling black was found with his penis cut off and rammed into his mouth. Sometimes he was burned alive.

It's hard to talk about burning without summoning up images of white-sheeted terrorists. The Ku Klux Klan has appeared in three incarnations. The first, founded by Confederate soldiers in 1866, was a backlash against newly freed slaves. In the ten years that followed, thousands of blacks were brutalized. When power finally settled in the hands of whites, the Klan faded out at the hands of federal troops.

But, like a bad dream, it surfaced again in 1915—its resurrection heralded by the Atlanta lynching of an innocent Jew, Leo Frank, for the murder of a young gentile girl. This time the movement took the form of a fundamentalist crusade "to punish drunks, adulterers, and other violators of the traditional moral code." Membership rolls tilted heavily toward preachers and policemen. The KKK had spread beyond the provincial confines of the South to take root in small towns and migrant-bloated cities across the country. Klansmen became the "enforcers" of Prohibition and righteous denouncers of jazz, dancing, cigarettes, and wenching.

In 1926, however, the Reed Committee —a senatorial body directed to investigate election abuses—caught the KKK literally with their pants down. The Klan had become a powerful factor in American government, but the leader of its political machine was throwing drunken orgies in his own home. Even worse, local Klan leaders "had been convicted of preserving the purity of American women by trying to rape them." Rank-and-file members, who had donned the hood solely out of "moral" conviction, were chagrined. The Klan split in two: those who supported the political agenda of the order and those who insisted on a return to the "Christian, benevolent, fraternal organization—principles that the Klan stood for." The KKK declined along with other fundamentalist activism in the 1920s and remained quiescent during the 1930s. Its back was broken in 1944 when the IRS went after unpaid taxes and forced the Klan to sell its assets and go out of business.

However, the 1954 Supreme Court desegregation decision gave the Klan a new lease on life. This time, moral rectitude dictated renewed terrorizing of blacks and Jews. There were bombings, burnings, beatings, and shootings. But by 1964, it was estimated that Klan membership had dwindled to about fifty thousand. The KKK was being displaced by "respectable" White Citizens Councils, whose rolls had climbed to 1 million.

Today, the Klan reportedly numbers no more than seven thousand—a dip of about a third since 1982. Circulation of its publications and the inflow of financial contributions have dropped off as well. The Anti-Defamation League of B'nai B'rith speculates that the secret order is being upstaged by more acceptable political and religious groups—latter-day white citizens councils—which share its agenda.

Imperial Wizard Bill Wilkerson wrote in a March 1984 editorial for *The Klansman,* "There is much support for our position. We have been opposing affirmative action and forced busing since they were first dreamed up. At first we had absolutely no help from anyone. Now we have a president, a senate, and yes, the Civil Rights Commission, who agrees with us on these issues."

While the KKK is smaller in numbers, a supportive social climate has encouraged it to step up its racist and anti-Semitic violence. More than six hundred whippings, arsons, bombings, murders, and acts of intimidation have been documented since 1978—including the gunning down of five old women in Chattanooga. (One had been planting flowers in her garden when, in their need "to blow off steam," three Klansmen mowed her down.)

The Anti-Defamation League fears that the KKK is becoming more desperate and more violent. But its soulmates, five hundred or so neo-Nazi extremists, are even more worrisome. Groups like Aryan Nations, the Order, the Covenant, the Sword and the Arm of the Lord, Christian Identity, and Posse Comitatus are linked by their ultra-rightist hatred of big government, Jews, and blacks. Like the Klan and other fundamentalist groups, they define themselves as the guardians of Christian virtue in the midst of a satanic society. Before being sentenced to a twenty-five-year prison term for numerous felony firearms convictions, a key figure in the Order, Gary Lee Yarbrough, read a statement defending his actions: "I don't want to go down into the cesspool with this country. I can't conform to a system that is totally anti-Christ."

In purging the nation of the "Antichrist," the neo-Nazis espouse violence and have armed themselves accordingly. "These dragons of God have no time for pamphlets or speeches. They are the armed party which is being born out of inability of white male youths to be heard," declares an Aryan Nations bulletin. Before they were raided by the FBI and Bureau of Alcohol, Tobacco, and Firearms agents, the "dragons of God" had declared a holy war against the so-called Zionist Occupation Government (ZOG) of North America. Training in rigorous survivalist camps with vast caches of submachine guns, grenades, anti-tank rockets, and plastic explosives, they used for target practice the figure of a state trooper with a Star of David on his chest.

According to Jim Ellison, founder and spiritual leader of the Covenant, the scriptural underpinning for the groups' militarism is found in Matthew 10:34. "Think not that I am come to send peace on earth: I came not to send peace, but a sword."

They not only have "right and might" on their side, but a computer network as well. All the hate groups are within a digital pulse of each other thanks to the Aryan Liberty Net. "Imagine, if you will," read one electronic entry, "all the great minds of the patriotic Christian movement linked together and joined into one computer."

By the time these God-crazed extremists were stopped dead in their tracks, they had killed a Missouri state trooper and a Jewish Denver talk-show host; set fire to a Jewish center and a homosexual church; bombed a natural-gas pipeline; tortured and killed two group members on a Nebraska farm; held up an armored car for $3.5 million in California; and committed a slew of robberies and counterfeiting violations.

In the RICO trial of twenty members of the Order, a founder of the sect explained that the Order referred to all nonwhites as "mud people" and swore an oath to eliminate anyone "of Jewish race and white traitors who were cohorts" with "Jews in trying to destroy our race." Jews, explained this earnest Christian, are "the progeny of the devil."

He went on to tick off an unconsummated hit list that named the likes of Henry Kissinger, David Rockefeller, Baron Rothschild, Norman Lear, and heads of the major television networks. Shortly after learning of the plot against him, Lear said: "The hit list doesn't upset me. That's just another way to die. What upsets me is that my FBI—which I always thought was there to protect me—knew about it for seven months and never told me."

Despite the FBI's best efforts, trials and prison sentences alone don't stop fanaticism. The gospel of hate continues to be spread where people are most vulnerable: the agonized farm belt, a longtime fundamentalist stronghold. In August 1985, Geraldo Rivera of the ABC News show "20/20" reported a story that left even him aghast. It opened with a tirade by an Aryan Nations spokesman:

"You wonder why you're losing your farms and ranches and businesses out there," railed the speaker to an assembly of farmers. "A bunch of international communist Jews . . . have stripped your wealth and your land from you.

"Those who hate our god Jesus Christ are before us today. Kill 'em all! Wipe 'em out. There's a war coming," he rants.

Apparently the message is getting through. Midwestern gun dealers like Randy Engleken reported to Rivera that they're doing a land-office business: "A farmer came in here the other day, and he bought two of these semiautomatic nine-millimeter Heckler and Cook rifles. He said everybody is buying them and he didn't want to be the only one caught short when things happened." The

hate is palpable. One farmer bitterly hissed to interviewer Rivera: "In my opinion, the Zionist Jew is pure evil, and yes, they have designs on my farm, my
neighbor's farm, they have designs on the whole earth."

□ □ □

Each resurgence of the Klan and its kindred groups paralleled a fundamentalist moral crusade in which "infidels" were portrayed in apocalyptic terms. By
claiming a monopoly on virtue for themselves, the crusaders could impute absolute evil to the "enemy." Inevitably, violence followed in the name of God and
morality.

One of the more stunning examples of this ineluctable tie is the wave of
arsons and bombings that swept more than thirty abortion clinics and family-
planning centers from 1982 to 1985—and continued beyond that time. Referring to themselves as the Army of God, domestic terrorists pursued their quarry
with messianic zeal. Damage to people and property was written off to a higher
calling in which they pursued the "devils," "murderers," and "Hitlers" who
terminated pregnancies.

The calling seemed to come not only from God but from President Ronald
Reagan. Judy Goldsmith, then head of the National Organization for Women,
called on Reagan to "cease his irresponsible and inflammatory rhetoric." By
repeatedly comparing abortion with murder, infanticide, slavery, and the Holocaust, she charged, he only "encourages the fanatics to step up the violence."
Perceiving themselves as having received both divine and presidential dispensa-
tion, convicted abortion vigilantes waved their Bibles and claimed: "I did it for
the glory of God."

In defending four devout Christians who admitted to bombing three clinics
in Florida, an attorney referred to his clients as "passionate," "idealistic," and
"the best" of America. God, he said was "the thirteenth juror" and "an
unindicted co-conspirator" in the case. The U.S. attorney who prosecuted the
case retorted, "It's frightening to see what happens when you put religion into a
lawsuit like this. We are not the forces of Satan. Satan isn't on trial. God
certainly isn't on trial."

Bombings and arsons drew equal condemnation from the antiabortion and
pro-choice camps. John Willke, president of the National Right to Life Committee, declared, "If we were to adopt the evil tactics of those who promote
abortion by using violence ourselves, we would destroy the very ethic that is the
foundation of the prolife movement." The denunciation on the other side came
from NOW: "These alarming terrorist attacks are . . . a campaign . . .
against American women exercising their constitutional right to obtain health
care, including abortion if they so choose. Borrowing from the methods of like-
minded international terrorist groups, small bands of fanatical and dangerous
individuals are using violence and intimidation in an attempt to impose their
morality upon American women and the American people."

Feelings about abortion run strong and deep on both sides of the issue. It's
not the purpose of this book to resolve the dilemma, but only to look at its

criminal implications. As of this writing, our legal codes do not classify abortion as a crime. However, intense moral lobbying on behalf of criminalizing it has led to violence, harassment, and vandalism.

As with the other consensual acts examined in this book, the roots of our feelings about abortion derive from the Bible, which tells us that man is made in God's own image; therefore, to destroy him is sacrilege. This concept—the sanctity of human life—is the Judeo-Christian tradition's unique contribution to civilization. But the Bible's view of procreation is not uniformly benign; there is an element that is downright punitive. In telling the story of the Fall, Genesis recounts God's charge to Eve for having tempted Adam: "I will greatly multiply thy pain and thy travail. In pain thou shalt bring forth children. Thy desire shall be to thy husband and he shall rule over thee" (3:16). This passage delineates the sacred duty of woman to give birth and be subservient to her husband, but it also paints her as a temptress and seductress for whom the pain of childbirth will be an eternal punishment. To one who interprets the Bible literally, terminating a pregnancy is sacrilegious on three counts. Not only does it violate the sacred image of God, but it preempts a holy duty and a God-given punishment.

Public opinion polls make it clear that most Americans don't support a literalistic interpretation. A NBC/AP poll taken in January 1982 reported that 61 percent of its sample agreed "every woman who wants to have an abortion should be able to have one." Even among Catholic women, three quarters would consider an abortion if necessary.

Public opinion notwithstanding, antiabortion forces claim a monopoly on protecting the sanctity of unborn life. In contrasting themselves with pro-choice advocates, they would agree with the paradox posed by Richard Viguerie: "Most liberals support abortion of innocent babies. But they oppose capital punishment for convicted murderers."

Pro-choice champions also believe in the sanctity of life. However, they argue that one must also take responsibility for the quality of that life. Therefore, decisions regarding reproduction must remain in the realm of individual conscience and not be legislated by government. They do not claim to have God on their side.

Those who do claim to are working through the courts, Congress, and state legislatures to reverse the "satanic" 1973 Supreme Court decision that "made abortion on demand the law of the land." Having been thwarted in many of their attempts, the more frustrated and extreme among them have resorted to terrorism.

▢ ▢ ▢

It would be wrong to imply that all domestic terrorism comes from the right. Up until a few years ago, most of our internal terrorist attacks came from left-wing black, Puerto Rican, student, and other radical groups. Indicators of their activities—bombings, hijackings, and explosives incidents—have shown a general downward trend since the 1970s.

This stands in contrast to international terrorist incidents against Americans, which have vaulted and remained high from the 1970s through the 1980s. Much of it can be ascribed to Muslim orthodoxy in the Middle East, but some is likely to spill over onto our own soil in the future. Inspired by fundamentalism, foreign and American, domestic terror from the right will be a much greater threat than that from the left.

In a New York *Times* editorial, Flora Lewis notes continuities among extremists of every stripe: "There are certain profound similarities in the theses advanced by the Ayatollah Khomeini's wild-eyed Islamic disciples, the orthodox militants of Israel, and the Americans who call themselves the Moral Majority." The common thread is an absolutism and intolerance that admits no truth or rights but their own. A 1950 study of prejudice dubbed this syndrome "the authoritarian personality."

The original T. W. Adorno study, as well as the ones that followed it, unearthed a constellation of traits that characterize the authoritarian personality and found that they exist uniquely on the right of the political spectrum. Such a person tends to be ethnocentric, antidemocratic, and conservative, valuing religion and tradition over science and humanitarianism. The authoritarian has a bent toward blaming external forces for his problems and displacing aggression onto weaker minorities.

This person has been with us for a long time. In describing him, I hear echoes of the Puritans, the Klan, the Christian Crusade, and all the right-wing extremists who populate our history and our present. They will be in our future, too. Not trusting to individual choice and conscience, authoritarian religionists will play Jiminy Cricket to our moral choices and wage war against the Bill of Rights.

□ □ □

It's easy to understand their frustration. Our society is groaning under the weight of its complexities and contradictions. The New Right has come to realize that liberty for some can interfere with the pursuit of life, property, and happiness for others.

The mass public vociferously supports civil liberties in the abstract but repudiates them in concrete applications. Whether getting tough on criminals, or confiscating pornographic films, or forbidding a Communist from speaking, we are almost always ready to throw out the Bill of Rights when it is invoked by those whose views and practices repel us. We want the rights for ourselves, but disown them when it's time to reciprocate.

Richard Viguerie claims that liberals have been chipping away at the Bill of Rights and that conservatives have been forced to stand up for the original rights as well as some new ones. He cites the right to protect the unborn, hold a job, bear arms, live safely, maintain family privacy, pray in school, be secure from Communist subversion, preserve money and assets.

Ironically, though liberals and conservatives wage war against each other, they have a common enemy: big government. The left won't entrust the state with our liberties, but it is quite content to give it our property in the form of high taxes, regulation, and social programs. The right is enthused about letting government tell us how to make love, what to believe, and who to worship, but distrusts it to manage our property, run our businesses, and set social priorities.

"Thus divided," notes columnist William Safire, "the defenders of civil and property rights are losing to the side that holds that government knows best and does best for people. That is why the size of all levels of government has been rising and the law-demanding moralizers and journalist-jailing legislators see themselves as the waves of the future."

Safire, however, overlooks the real hope of our civil liberties—the baby boom generation. In a New York *Times* op-ed piece, David Boaz of the Cato Institute, a public policy research organization, maintains that baby boomers combine conservative economics with liberal rights concerns. Having missed out on the Depression and World War II—but having marched through Vietnam, Watergate, stagflation, and student revolution—the boomers maintain a suspicious view of government. "Government didn't solve problems of our time," writes Boaz, "it caused them." Citing pollster Pat Caddell, he adds: "The younger generation is pro-choice on everything."

As long as this largest-generation-ever of Americans is in control, our civil liberties are relatively safe. The more socially conservative—and smaller—echo generation in the wings will, by virtue of greater education and youth, uphold the banner. Polls show succeeding generations growing more supportive of civil liberties over time.

That doesn't mean the Bill of Rights won't face a constant uphill battle—especially in the face of our chronic anxiety about crime. Effective law enforcement depends on information and surveillance, but civil liberties put a premium on privacy. Stomping on crime requires free reign in investigating suspected wrongdoers, but civil liberties demand restrictions on the way evidence is ferreted out and used. Social order calls for suppression of provocative speech, but civil liberties protect freedom of expression, public debate, and checks on government.

We will always be faced with a trade-off between civil liberties and law and order. Veering toward civil liberties can mean an affirmation of pluralism, tolerance, and competing value systems—at the price of efficient law enforcement. A steep list toward law and order gives us effective crime fighting but can also lead us down the road to authoritarianism, bigotry, and domestic terrorism. But civil liberties and social order need not be mutually exclusive. The rights enshrined in the Declaration of Independence and the Constitution contain the formula for reconciling the imperatives of freedom with the requisites of law.

21

The "Christianizing" of America

April 1979. The Reverend Jerry Falwell stood on the steps of the Capitol and addressed an estimated fifteen thousand Christian activists from twenty-six states. Flanked by five senators and two representatives, in the capital of the most determinedly pluralistic nation in the world, he declared: "The key to U.S. strength is Christianity."

The Clean Up America campaign was launched.

The Religious Right's drive to clean up America is dedicated to making us a moral, God-fearing nation—purged of secular humanists and pornographers, gays and child molesters, Communists and criminals, abortionists and atheists. Rather than preaching only from the pulpit, the New Right has devoted itself to molding political platforms. That goal was realized at the 1984 Republican convention, where conservative fundamentalists wrote the plank that helped reelect Ronald Reagan.

More than a year later, the concept of the Christian candidate was still going strong. Televangelist Pat Robertson appeared on "Good Morning America" in October to discuss why he would make a good presidential candidate. He stressed his credentials as a lawyer (with a degree from Yale), an administrator, and a broadcaster. Before he was born-again, Robertson had been a trouble-shooter for W. R. Grace Company in South America, a marine combat officer in Korea, and chairman of the Stevenson-for-President campaign in Staten Island. This Phi Beta Kappa graduate with a U.S. senator father, is anything but the stereotypical Bible-thumper; yet, the business world left him empty, so he turned to the ministry.

His mother, a devout born-again Christian, was pleased but warned: "The pulpits of this nation are filled with men just like you. They want to do good for mankind. They want to help people. But they're doing it on their own power, and that's worse than nothing."

Robertson started drawing his power from God—and the Christian Broad-casting Network he founded. If all those kilowatts get beamed to the voters he could very well become the people's choice, or at least some people's. Buried in the pages of his autobiography, *Shout It from the Housetops*, is a chilling clue to what a Robertson administration might be like: "As was true of the disciples after the crucifixion, we made a practice of locking the doors to our prayer meetings, 'for fear of the Jews.'"

Driving through New Jersey in fall 1985, you could turn on your radio and tune in to a less-splashy Christian crusade. Beyond the limelight of the highly publicized gubernatorial race between incumbent Thomas Kean and upstart Peter Shapiro, an obscure third also ran. He could be heard stumping for the right-to-life of fetuses, while demanding death for child molesters. It's time to have a Christian in the state house, he declaimed. "If not now, when?" he asked, quoting not the New Testament but the great humanist sage Rabbi Hillel.

It was Thomas Kean, and not the Christian challenger, who won that election. But the attempt to use the political system for religious agendas continues unabated.

□ □ □

Kanawha County, West Virginia—nine hundred and seven square miles of mostly small communities—has the distinction of being the contemporary fore-runner of textbook controversies that have dogged our school systems for more than a decade.

In Kanawha County, almost everyone is Protestant and almost no one is black or foreign-born. But that doesn't mean there are no cultural conflicts. A major one broke out in 1974 when a school board member, the wife of a fundamental-ist minister, led a campaign to pull three hundred and twenty-five language-arts textbooks from the countywide school curriculum and libraries. Among them were the works of Dylan Thomas, Mark Twain, George Bernard Shaw, Norman Mailer, Eldridge Cleaver, Dick Gregory, and Joseph Heller. The dissident board member's objections centered on moral relativism; use of profane and vulgar language ("good Lord," "for Chrissake," "ass-whipping") and disrespect for orthodox concepts of God, the Bible, and authority. At the first school board meeting in which she raised the issue, she proposed that the "board should have stronger control over selection."

Several weeks later, the minister's wife declared, "the books lack taste, serve no real purpose, and denounce traditional institutions." Later that month she spoke against the books in the local Baptist church, and by the end of June, she had mobilized over one thousand protestors to show up at the regular school board meetings.

Over the summer, the protests gained momentum. When the school year opened in September, one quarter of the student body boycotted classes. Businesses and mines were picketed, school buses were stalled, and the schools had to be shut down for several days. It was then agreed that the controversial books would be removed pending a review by a special citizens committee. The committee recommended that all but thirty-five of the banned books be returned. That's when the real trouble began—probably more trouble than the minister's wife had intended.

· The board of education building was dynamited.
· The superintendent of schools and four board members were arrested for "contributing to the delinquency of minors."
· Christian alternative schools sprang up and siphoned pupils off the public school system.
· Upper Kanawha Valley, the hub of the protest, moved—unsuccessfully—to secede from the rest of the county.

By the end of 1974, the protestors had managed to get parents placed on textbook selection committees. But the state declared their guidelines for textbook content illegal.

The righteous brawling continued into 1976, when a number of protest leaders ran for state and national offices. Most were defeated but undaunted. The protestors turned their attention to the new school bond issue, arguing: "We can't see the need for more schools and facilities when what's being taught isn't right."

A local teenager explained, "We're not asking that they teach Christianity in the schools. We're just asking that they don't insult our faith."

Richard Viguerie observes: "Liberals tried to picture the protestors as a bunch of ignorant rednecks out to burn books. But what upset conservative parents was a passage like the following from *Blue Denim*, a play to be read aloud by 12- and 13-year-olds." Viguerie then quotes a passage in which a character describes the dilemma of a teenage boy who has made his girlfriend pregnant: a toss-up between denying his responsibility by getting other boys to say she had gone to bed with them too, or doing the "honorable" thing and getting her an abortion.

Viguerie is right. The protest was not a matter of "ignorant rednecks." True, the Ku Klux Klan, fundamentalist congregations, and rural mine and farm workers were prominent among the dissidents, but many successful business people and professionals counted themselves in too.

Two cultural systems were arrayed against each other: orthodoxy and modernism. The former cast the issue in terms of patriotism; economic individualism; taking a stand against big government, sexual license, drinking, violence, and moral uncertainty. One protestor described the offending textbooks as "an insidious attempt to replace our periods with their question marks." The modernists, however, cast the conflict in terms of censorship, academic freedom, and incursions on the First Amendment.

The Kanawha textbook controversy marked an attempt to wrest control of education from the forces undermining what was once the dominant life-style in an earlier, rural, more homogeneous America.

The most powerful weapon of the New Right fundamentalist campaign is the attempt to gain control of the processes that mold our thoughts and values. That means monitoring what schools teach, which books line library shelves, and what kinds of magazines are displayed on newsstands. Movies and rock music are equally suspect. In George Orwell's *1984*, word monitors were called "Thought Police." Their job was to ensure that the citizens of Oceania conformed both inwardly and outwardly to the pronouncements issued by the Ministry of Truth. As we rush toward 2000, we are creating our own Thought Police. One study cites a 117-percent increase in censorship incidents between 1981–82 and 1985–86. Barbara Parker of People for the American Way indicts the Far Right for promulgating the notion that "the free flow of ideas is an un-American activity."

□   □   □

In 1985, the Federal Communications Commission denied petitions to lift the license of Nellie and Charles Babbs, who operated radio station KTTL (FM)—now KMCS (FM)—in Dodge City, Kansas. Listeners could tune in any day and hear people who call themselves good Christians rant against blacks, Asians, Catholics, and Jews. One day's fare might include "cleansing the earth of black beasts." Another's might offer, "start making a dossier on every damn Jew rabbi in this land." The station preached hatred while teaching its audience guerrilla killing tactics. Yet, the ravings didn't fall under the heading of obscenity or direct incitement to violence. Despite odious oratory that borders on the psychopathic, the FCC could not legitimately revoke the station's license.

Broadcasting magazine approved. The May 6, 1985, issue carried an editorial stating, "To its lasting credit, the FCC correctly read the First Amendment. . . . There seem to be enough other ways to judge the Babbses' qualifications to remain licensees without butting up against the First Amendment."

It's not surprising that broadcasters would support freedom of speech for an operation the entire industry finds repugnant. After all, they know what it means to be interfered with. For years, the industry has been the target of right-wing campaigns by such groups as the National Federation for Decency (NFD), Fairness in Media, and Coalition for Better Television (CBTV), who want to banish sex, violence, and liberalism from the airwaves.

Crusaders like Jerry Falwell argue that television has become the "largest baby-sitting agency in the world." As such, children are "incessantly bombarded" with sexual and criminal imagery as well as humanist biases, which teach them values that "hasten society's slide toward decadence." As if in confirmation of Falwell's admonition, television violence has become a defense in criminal trials. In 1984, Nelson Molina, twenty-one, pleaded "not guilty by reason of insanity" to charges of being an accessory to a murder in Miami. "Television intoxication" made him do it, he said. Seven years earlier, Ronald Zamora, fifteen, claimed the same defense when he killed an elderly neighbor.

All of this presumes that we are what we watch or hear—a very shaky assumption, but one that seems to be growing in appeal as diverse groups go after rock video, beer and wine commercials, and Dan Rather.

□ □ □

The First Amendment guarantees freedom of religion, speech (including symbolic speech, like burning a draft card), the press, the right of peaceful assembly and petition. In defiance of Puritan tenets, it elevates individual conscience to magisterial levels and creates the mechanism whereby rulers are held accountable to the people rather than to God. In a republic that reigns with the consent of the governed, consent must be freely given—"the product of unhindered communication." Information, debate, criticism, advocacy are the lifeblood of democracy.

Freedom of thought and expression is a difficult concept to grasp. It requires tolerance of ideas and actions which inevitably antagonize some—at times, even the majority—of the people. Nevertheless, reasoned Tunis Wortman, an early American lawyer: "A liberty of investigation into every subject of thought . . . is indisposable to the progression and happiness of mankind. . . . It is impossible that the imagination should conceive a more horrible and pernicious tyranny than that which would restrain the Intercourse of Thought."

Here we run into the major conflict between the First Amendment and orthodox Christianity. The former extols human reason, while the latter condemns it as fallen and grants authority only to the Bible. The fundamentalist vision gives lie to the old taunt "Sticks and stones may break my bones but words can never hurt me." Words—and ideas—can hurt, insists the Religious Right, and they must be closely monitored.

The Constitution makes a distinction between words and actions: It's okay to preach revolution, but it's a crime to start one. You can talk about the joys of child molesting, but it's illegal to practice it. Where speech can be proven obscene or a direct incitement to violence, it enjoys no First Amendment protection.

Proving that words lead to criminal acts is extraordinarily difficult (as shown in the chapter on pornography). In recent years, the Supreme Court has used a "balancing test" to determine when free expression has intruded on other compelling interests. When speech represents a "clear and present danger" and involves *direct* incitement of illegal conduct, it has overstepped the bounds of the First Amendment. The classic constitutional example, falsely shouting "Fire!" in a crowded theater, is a clear instance of "fighting words." But teaching, sit-down strikes, and salacious movies are much more nebulous. Our highest court has traditionally upheld a narrow definition of action and given wide berth to speech.

The Religious Right advocates the reverse. They cite presumed links between words and actions as a rationale for limiting the marketplace of ideas. The alleged linkages are extensive. They assume a tie between a Budweiser commercial and a drunken teenage driver in Peoria; a crazed cocaine-snorting salesclerk on "St. Elsewhere" and the death of a junkie in Los Angeles; gang violence in *The Warriors* and a rampage in Central Park; bared genitals in *Hustler* and a raped woman in San Francisco; sexual awakening in *The Diary of Anne Frank* and promiscuity in Delaware.

EDUCATIONAL CENSORSHIP

The educational arena is a bloody First Amendment battleground. Earlier, you encountered a distraught father who testified at a U.S. Department of Education hearing in Seattle. He decried the idea of moral relativism, claiming it taught children to be criminals. By obliterating respect for ultimate authority, he argued, that idea produces children who "could kill . . . push drugs . . . rape and murder, and there are no right and wrong answers."

Because schools play a crucial role in molding young minds, the public seems particularly reluctant to tolerate the freedoms of teachers, students, and researchers. Kanawha County is a microcosm of widespread attitudes. One national study reports:

> On some items, such as the right of high school teachers to express opinions that are in conflict with the views of the community, scarcely 25 percent of the general public are willing to acknowledge this as a right. Between one half and two thirds . . . would refuse to hire a professor if he or she held unusual or extreme views on politics or racial differences . . . only 4 percent of the mass public believe that a professor should not be interfered with, and 77 percent . . . would "send someone into his classes to check on him."

These findings are based on polls conducted in the late 1970s. In 1985 a new group, Accuracy in Academia, fulfilled the prophecy of sending someone into classes to check on professors. Lashing out at the group, Dr. Joseph Murphy, chancellor of the City University of New York, charged that they use "totally offensive" methods such as recruitment of students and other auditors to act as a "corps of thought police."

In his statement, Murphy averred: "What we have before us . . . is a group that exists largely as a symptom of serious underlying problems: the frustrated national quest for simplistic truth in a confusing time. . . . It has spawned an anti-intellectualism in which our leaders give us at best a vacuous ideology . . . and an expression of anger at large and powerful institutions wrongly perceived to be antithetical to the goals of those people who define themselves as American middle class."

Monitors have found their way into lower grades as well. According to a study conducted by People for the American Way, the 1985–86 school year witnessed documented censorship incidents in 44 out of 50 states. More than 100 films, books, and pamphlets were challenged. Nearly 40 percent of the challenges succeeded and the offending materials were restricted or removed from the shelf. These join scores of titles on the American Booksellers Association roster of banned books.

Censorship attempts rose by more than one third over the previous school year and two thirds from the two years before. They promise to rise still further because of two powerful new tools: federal restrictions on use of magnet school funds for "courses of instruction the substance of which is secular humanism" and the Pupil Rights Protection Act—also known as the Hatch Amendment.

The original legislation for the Hatch Amendment requires parental permission for psychiatric and psychological tests administered to children. That seems reasonable enough. However, the law has been writ in such broad strokes that the act is now used as the basis for assaults on classroom discussions, drug abuse programs, "tolerance days," and other school activities.

In March 1984, seven hearings were held to examine the Hatch Amendment. Phyllis Schlafly, a leading conservative activist, points out that not one representative of the National Education Association—or any member of the "other side"—came to defend the educational practices that the Hatch Amendment sought to remedy. That, reasons Schlafly, is because the practices are indefensible. In her view they explain why "schools have alienated children from their parents . . . traditional morality, such as the Ten Commandments, and from our American heritage. . . ." They explain "what children have been doing in the classrooms instead of learning to read, write, spell, add, subtract," and how they have learned to be "sexually active, take illegal drugs, repudiate their parents, and rationalize immoral and anti-social conduct." People for the American Way maintains that Phyllis Schlafly and her Far Right cohorts have spearheaded "the overwhelming majority" of censorship attempts.

This represents a change from the late 1960s and early 1970s, when left-wing complaints prevailed. Works that were considered racist, sexist, or discriminatory—like *Little Black Sambo* or *The Merchant of Venice*—dominated the censors' lists. While there are still scattered attempts to do away with such materials, today's major targets are the "antifamily," "anti-American," and "obscene" pet peeves of the Moral Majority. Not content "to decide what their own children should read," parries a PFAW *Special Report,* "they want to dictate what *everyone's* children shall read and learn and discuss in school."

The threat has become acute. "Book banners have discovered the Bill of Rights," quips Daniel Jussim in writing for *Civil Liberties.* Jussim cites several cases in which the First Amendment seems to have been turned on its head:

A member of a fundamentalist parents group in Tennessee wrote to her local paper, "[We are] against censorship! That's why we oppose these readers. Traditional values have been censored out."

Other fundamentalists, such as Concerned Women for America (CWA), attempt to censor books on the ground that they are not religiously neutral. In

1980, for example, suit was brought on behalf of a CWA member in Mead, Washington. Carolyn Grove's religious beliefs were offended when Gordon Parks' *The Learning Tree* was assigned to her daughter's English class. Grove charged that the book contained "specific blasphemies against Jesus Christ, and excessive violence and murder." The book's "swearing, profanity, obscene language, explicit description of pre-marital sexual intercourse . . . other lewd behavior . . . tends to inculcate the anti-God religion of humanism."

When defeated in lower court, Grove's lawyer called the decision "a grave defeat for civil liberties." In describing his plan to take the case to the Supreme Court, he hoped "the ACLU would support us. We'll see whether the ACLU really supports religious neutrality or whether their real desire is to outlaw Christianity."

Two years later, the Supreme Court rendered a decision in *Island Trees v. Pico*, which seemed to settle such matters. To wit: school boards could not remove books "simply because they disliked the ideas contained in those books." "Our Constitution," ruled the justices, "does not permit the official suppression of ideas."

The Supreme Court leans strongly toward upholding free speech. However, even that august forum has no power to initiate suits against censors. It can only respond to issues brought before it by others. Because such litigation is costly and time-consuming, large numbers of overt and secret censorship attempts go unchallenged.

TELEVISION AND MOVIE CENSORSHIP

About 84 million American households indulge in television. On any given night, close to 96 million people are glued to their screens. The average household stays tuned a mean of seven hours a day. Children and teenagers put in twenty-five hours per week, a good deal less than their elders, but long enough to learn some good and bad social lessons. Some 24 million viewers in nearly 12,000 communities also subscribe to cable services. These not only provide them with a wide range of localized programming, but a lush array of "adult" entertainment.

Millions of avid moviegoers have made *Rambo, E.T., Star Wars, Return of the Jedi, The Empire Strikes Back, Jaws,* and *Raiders of the Lost Ark* the top cinematic money-makers of all time. How could such a slick array of Hollywood talent not inspire impressionable audiences to go out and imitate the derring-do they see executed on the screen? Certainly the gays who boycotted *Cruising*— believing that life imitates art—feared the film would unleash a rash of violence against them. The Religious Right, alarmed by the alleged consequences of television and movie sex and violence, has campaigned mightily to put an end to the dramatization of licentiousness.

Many of the most popular entertainments have *not* been paragons of wanton sex. The top syndicated TV programs—"Family Feud," "Wheel of Fortune," "M*A*S*H," "Three's Company," and "PM Magazine"—are often insipid, sometimes brilliant, but not generally offensive. Even the blockbuster movies haven't been particularly sexy. They've been either ostentatiously bloody sagas, thinly veiled religious allegories, or both. Prime TV network fare, on the other hand, is all of the above.

Any visit with the evening soaps' premier families is apt to yield a very unpretty picture of America. Some prime time shows with the largest audience shares are rife with suggested sex, stereophonic body blows, booze, drugs, greed, corruption, and mayhem. The plots of these shows are fictional. But equal amounts of electronically edited dissolution are evident on the evening news. It's no wonder that video vigilantes of the right have taken aim at prime time and the commercials that support it.

To be sure, the Religious Right is far from being the only group that has expressed unhappiness with television. Mainstream churches, the National Coalition on Television Violence, researchers at the Annenberg School of Communications, and other groups are also on the bandwagon. And 57 percent of the American public favors banning commercials that promote drinking. But only the Far Right has objected to television fare on religious grounds and pressed for prior restraint of programming.

In the front lines is Reverend Donald Wildmon, a minister from Tupelo, Mississippi. Wildmon resigned from his pastorate in 1977 to found the National Federation for Decency. His work remained obscure until Jerry Falwell joined up with him in 1981 and launched the Coalition for Better Television. CBTV set about engaging in boycotts—the all-American form of protest that hits offenders in their pocketbooks.

After a boycott against Procter & Gamble, which resulted in that top advertiser dropping some programs, the group went after NBC and its mother company, RCA. "RCA-NBC," Wildmon announced at a packed press conference, "has excluded Christian characters, Christian values, and Christian culture from their programming." The boycott would continue, he threatened, until NBC eliminated profanity and racial and religious stereotyping; downplayed violence; and modified the way it deals with drugs and sexuality.

That particular boycott bombed, but who could argue with its laudable goals? Just tune in to "Dallas," "Dynasty," "Hill Street Blues," and the many TV movies about incest, rape, adultery, and fallen clergymen. But the religious agenda comes through in other remarks, like the one made to *People* magazine by Reverend Wildmon: "Most producers are of the Jewish perspective. What they're doing is legal, moral and right." It's not sex and violence in themselves to which the reverend says he objects, but rather "the networks' entire value system." "The [television] industry is riddled with homosexuals and only fierce public, and perhaps, even economic pressure will stop homosexuals' dominance of television," Wildmon once said to the Chicago *Sun Times*.

It is not only the sponsors and networks who are hit in the pocketbook: It is the fundamentalist public. The Radical Right has found diatribes against television to be a boon for fund-raising. In a direct-mail solicitation, Televangelist James Robison warned: "Tonight, nearly every home in America will have vio-

lence, crime, sex, perversion, and filth piped directly into their families' laps."
He then proceeded to ask for a $25 contribution "to offset Satan's attack."

In the Boston *Globe*, Richard Viguerie admitted that there's a method to the madness:

". . . we can do something the networks cannot do, which is get involved in political campaigns. . . . Even if we go after them and lose . . . we will still win by waging the battle. Because, we'll bring to our cause maybe five million people we don't have now, who will then turn their attention to senators and congressmen."

The strategy is potent because it exploits the legitimate gripes that many thoughtful Americans have about television. But when you take a closer look, writes David Bollier for People for the American Way, you find that the extreme picture painted by the Far Right is slanted by hyperbole, questionable statistics, "bogus survey techniques, unnamed volunteers, secret coalition members, and not-so-hidden political goals." CBTV's assertions are often just plain factually wrong.

CBTV's obsession with sex, for instance, has led to some overblown evaluations of television's fleshiness. While cable programming may be "guilty" of explicit sex, broadcast television never shows completed sex acts. When CBTV classifies a "Donahue" program on breast-feeding as a "sex show," Bollier wonders what kinds of criteria they are using. Or when Wildmon lumps a serious documentary such as CBS's "Gay Power, Gay Politics" in the same category with television movies like *Scruples* and *Anatomy of a Seduction*, Bollier says the religio-political agenda comes through loud and clear. The war against television is not just a war against tastelessness: It's a battle to "suppress other voices and to advance their own narrow religious/political orthodoxy," asserts Bollier.

Nowhere is this more evident than in the New Right's bid to take over CBS. Early in 1985, Senator Jesse Helms expressed his frustration with what he called "the most anti-Reagan network" and its "liberal bias." It took the form of a letter on behalf of a North Carolina–based group, Fairness in Media, in which he urged nearly one million conservatives to buy CBS stock and become Dan Rather's boss.

Lou Adler, then president of the Radio-Television News Directors Association, countered that the senator's action was "a dangerous deviation from the philosophy that has provided the foundation of our free press." He cited a long-standing separation between media ownership and news reporting.

A spokesperson for CBS added: "CBS reports the news as accurately and fairly as it can, independent of any political point of view. Its sole purpose is journalism; its goal is total objectivity. To seek control of a corporation for the sole purpose of subjecting its news operations to political influence contradicts the traditions of a free and independent press."

The forces of the right were not mollified. Two months later, broadcasting's enfant terrible, Ted Turner—owner of CNN, the Atlanta Braves, and superstation WTBS—got into the act with his own takeover bid. But he held off until he got the blessing of Jesse Helms.

The tip-off to Turner's intent was evident in a speech he had made the year before to a National Conservative Foundation seminar. Turner called network programming "stupid," "violent," "antifamily," "antibusiness." He charged them with being obsessed with the negative aspects of life and contributing to the supposed 300-percent rise in crime that started in the 1960s. Network owners and executives are "guilty of treason," he charged, and current ownership should be changed.

Several months later, in a speech to broadcasters, Turner sounded more conciliatory: "We have to get away from the redneck Ku Klux Klan–type attitude that 'we'll blow anybody's head off that doesn't think the same way that we do,' and we've got to move to some kind of liberal thinking to where people can get along together through the entertainment programming produced by the people in this room . . . what good is it if you win the ratings battle and wreck the country by polluting young people's minds and the minds of people who aren't as intelligent, discerning, or well-educated as we are?"

Turner's hostile CBS bid, like Fairness in Media's, failed. It was succeeded with a non-hostile bid for CBS News by Don Hewitt, executive producer of "60 Minutes," and CBS's top on-air talent. CBS was finally saved by offering a seat on the board to Lawrence Tisch, a real estate and movie theater mogul. But the fight to preserve itself against the Right, amidst stagnating advertising revenues, drew heavily on the company's financial resources. Enormous staff cuts followed, and corporate morale collapsed.

□ □ □

The bloodiness of our media fare offends critics across the political spectrum and news vehicles are among the worst offenders. But New Right detractors seldom take aim at newscasts for the violence they feature; instead, they go after "liberal bias," an "antibusiness" stance, premature election projections, and equal time. Between the news and entertainment sides, there's plenty to complain about.

Liberals tend to dump the problem in parents' laps and say it's up to them to supervise their children's reading and viewing habits. Conservatives call on government to regulate what we see, read, and hear. (Notice that both positions represent a reversal of each side's usual ideological stance.) Boycotts, "lockboxes," scramblers, warning captions, and alternative programs assist both sides in coping with the perils of "Miami Vice" and heavy-metal rock videos. But the presence of an adult can moderate a young viewer's response to violence by giving feedback on the events flickering across the screen.

For example, if Mommy is doing ironing in the room where Junior is watching television, she might exclaim: "What a terrible thing to do!" as the psychopathic killer in *Halloween III* raises his ever-present knife once more against pristine Jamie Lee Curtis. Or, as Katherine Wentworth dies in the car she has used to kill "Dallas' " Bobby Ewing, Daddy might cry: "She had it coming to her."

Although television intoxication has emerged as a defense in murder cases, the hundreds of laboratory studies on which lawyers base its use tell us very little about the real effects of synthetic crime and violence. But this much is clear: video violence may increase real violence if viewers are angry just before watching; if the violence they're watching is justified or rewarded; and if normal inhibitors—like guilt and anxiety—are missing.

These conditions are rarely met in entertainment violence. The world of television is one of simplistic truths. Moral dilemmas are seldom resolved in controversial ways. When amniocentesis reveals that a lead character is carrying a Down's Syndrome fetus, the writers of "Dallas" don't allow her to have an abortion. She takes a hard tumble at the Southfork charity rodeo and miscarries instead.

Television worlds are unambiguously made up of good guys and bad guys: Each gets the reward or punishment he deserves. With the exception of some of prime time's white-collar villains, who always land on their feet, good usually triumphs. But then again, the lead antagonists of popular evening soap operas rarely kill or hit anyone; they just manipulate people. And that's plain good business, American style. As a rule, entertainment's comic book morality ties up everything in a neat, unambiguous bundle within 50 minutes plus commercials.

Television executives script the resolution of moral ambiguities in ways that Don Wildmon would approve. As an example, Thomas Leahy of CBS cites his network's policy toward programs involving drugs: "If characters are shown using illegal drugs, the depiction must be related to plot or character development and the adverse consequences of such actions must also be demonstrated. Drugs will not be shown in a manner that suggests it is glamorous to use substances or that such use confers any kind of advantage to the user."

□ □ □

A focus on the "negative" aspects of life is the chronic complaint of the Religious Right against the media they perceive to be controlled by the Liberal Left. An average of nearly two crimes are committed per prime time show. Because television is the sole exposure that some viewers have to the law, it would be useful if there were some fit between television crime and real life crime. But there isn't. Neither the acts, frequencies, criminals, nor law enforcement responses reflect what really goes on.

The typical video crime is brutal—70 percent involve some kind of violence. In the real world, only one tenth of all crimes are violent; most others are of the dull, penny-ante variety that wouldn't make for much action on the screen.

Television has turned the actual age and socioeconomic distribution of crime upside down. Among prime-time crooks, nearly all are white and male; more than three quarters are career criminals; 70 percent are middle and upper class. Contrary to the real world, one-inch reels of magnetic tape show "Establishment" figures—often middle-aged, middle- and upper-class businesspeople—committing the street crimes that in real life are the province of a small percentage of young, lower-class males. Remember who shot J. R. Ewing? It was no Puerto Rican street kid.

Businesspeople are second only to professional crooks as the most frequent lawbreakers on television. Richard Channing—"Falcon Crest's" racetrack operator and sometime newspaper and radio station owner—was, at one time, surely one of the most elegant heavies on the air. A 1981 study determined that half of all chief executive officers occupying television's fictional boardrooms were—like Channing—engaged in crooked activities. In "Miami Vice," the businessman-cum-barbarian attained his apotheosis. According to one study, every man of commerce shown through late October 1985 was depicted as a greedy dope-dealer, fence, or murdering swine. While in real life corporate types tend to be involved in bribery, price-fixing, negligence, and tax evasion, on television their misdeeds lean heavily toward fraud, assault, and murder.

And what of the "thin blue line" that separates the lawful from the lawless? In the world of television and movies, that line is blurred. Police are often depicted as brutal, corrupt or dumb. Television's ace crimefighters and solvers are the private eyes, lawyers, special squads, and secret agents who do end runs around the system. Witness the enforcers in once-hit series—now relegated to late-night reruns or dusty archives—like "The Million Dollar Man" and "The Bionic Woman," "Charlie's Angels" and "The Mod Squad," "Ironside" and "Quincy," and "Kojak." If NYPD regularly used the methods of "The A-Team," "Miami Vice" or *Dirty Harry*, the state's unemployment rolls would increase by 27,000 and the federal civil rights calendar would be clogged from here to eternity. The Media Institute has concluded "the American public is receiving a grossly distorted picture of what crime and law enforcement is all about."

□ □ □

Not everyone is equally influenced by the distortions. Those who take television in large doses are the ones who are most fearful of real life crime. But it's not only how *much* TV is watched, but *who* watches. Studies show that the elderly, the poor, and high school dropouts are the heaviest viewers and that blacks, more than whites, use the media as an agent of social learning.

Television (and movie) social messages tell them:

• Aggressive behavior is an acceptable way to get one's way.
• Crime is a major lower-class career option, but it permeates all levels of society.
• Successful people "made it" through crime, so crime is a legitimate way to get ahead in life.
• As age increases, so does criminality; criminals enjoy long careers.
• The trend of the future is increased violence.

Such social messages reinforce delinquent behavior while fueling the public's fear of violence and distrust of big business.

Television, however, also displays a great many role models of helpful, decent people. Take Jessica Fletcher, the Miss Jane Marple–type protagonist in "Murder, She Wrote." Or Bill Cosby's dedicated family man in the hit show bearing his name. Some researchers believe that such characters support pro-social behavior in viewers; others conclude the Richard Channings are so pervasive that they overwhelm the positive influences.

But the "largest baby-sitting agency in the world" is not the only—or even the most powerful—influence on social learning. Family and peer pressures supersede it—and the extent to which we learn life from media violence remains highly speculative. In testifying at federal hearings on family violence, social researcher Jib Fowles of the University of Houston averred: "My colleagues have generated an enormous amount of research . . . supposedly demonstrating the evil effects of [television] viewing. I have elsewhere referred to this literature as 'one of the grandest travesties in the uneven history of social science.' "

Ironically, while entertainment programming has taken most of the heat, it is news and documentaries that actually cause most of the damage. David Phillips, of the University of California at San Diego, has conducted a number of studies that examine the impact of mass media violence. His conclusions merit serious consideration because, unlike most such research, they study real life, not laboratory, effects.

In looking at car crashes, suicides, and murders, he finds that national death rates by unnatural causes rise and peak three days after highly publicized news events. Heavyweight prizefights, such as the Muhammad Ali–Joe Frazier "Thrilla in Manila," resulted in sharp increases in murders. Marilyn Monroe's suicide led to a rise in driver deaths in car crashes. Widely disseminated murder-suicides led to a rash of crashes in which both drivers and passengers were killed.

Phillips concludes that violence is partly the effect of "modeling." You're more likely to imitate an aggressor if you share his racial and social traits. You're more apt to direct offscreen aggression against a target that is like an onscreen victim. In studying children, social psychologist Seymour Feshbach has found that the same aggressive stimulus can have "diametrically opposite effects depending on whether the viewer believed it was real or fictional."

Can it be that violent, macho Mike Hammer is more benign than the evening news? Feshbach explains that news reports describe the world as it really is. That makes the images hard to discard when a child moves on to do its homework. On the news, good guys don't always prevail and bad guys don't always get their just desserts.

When children watch fantasy characters like Hammer, they can more easily draw boundaries around the experience and isolate it from real life. The world inside those borders becomes a useful device for displacing aggression, draining off frustration, delaying destructive impulses, and engaging in forbidden behaviors without fear of punishment. However, highly detailed fantasy violence comes close to reality and can be transformed into a "how-to" message that teaches fierceness to viewers.

But again, for the most part, fantasy violence is not realistic. It is the stylized stuff of *Indiana Jones and the Temple of Doom* or the high-tech heroics of "Airwolf" and *Star Wars*. Researchers Robert Kaplan and Robert Singer go so far as to say: "The television networks may have become an easy scapegoat, accepting undue blame for the violence in our world. . . . Instead of castigating the networks it might be more useful to ask why the public is so fascinated by violent programs." Contrary to the forces on the Right, Kaplan and Singer find the evidence that television causes real life violence too weak to justify restrictions in programming.

□ □ □

The future media mix of fantasy and real violence will be determined by changing age demographics. Thirty-four- to sixty-four-year-olds are the new growth market. Older audiences tend to demand more news, information, and "adult" entertainment—those kinds of communications that are rife with sex and violence.

The overall share of network audiences is eroding—fast. While today's share is in the 80-percent range, it is projected to hover around 60–70 percent in the 1990s. The defectors are turning to cable and home video. The cultural channels that were the great hope of cable television are in trouble. Many have folded due to the paucity of specialized audiences. The services that remain are more saturated with sex and violence than the networks ever were.

Attempts to censor cable are "real and serious," warns Frank Biondi of Home Box Office. What any outlet chooses to televise, he insists, should be dictated by consumer demand. Biondi's subscribers demand adult-oriented material, and HBO provides it. Home videotapes, like cable, are a free-for-all, often containing scenes cut from the original theater or TV showings.

Yet, there is some evidence that older audiences are less tolerant of gratuitous sex and violence than the younger ones. Polls show that those over fifty-five are less than half as likely to approve of the film industry making movies on any subject it chooses. And they're more than twice as likely to endorse banning sexually explicit books from high school libraries.

In 1985, recognizing such demographics, MTV—a rock video network—launched VH-1, its second nonstop music video service. In contrast to its more punk and sexually violent predecessor, says chief operating officer Robert Pittman, VH-1 was designed to appeal to an older audience whose values focus on "love and optimism, and fantasies of a great life."

But some experts predict that traditionally passive viewers will become more active, siphoning off audiences to transactional, information-oriented services. Such switches will help expand nonfantasy media offerings in the future. Even though "real" events featured on the news seem to do more behavioral damage than "fantasy" events, an information-hungry, older population will not take kindly to censoring its right to know. While the Religious Right will find some natural allies in an aging population, the struggle to limit speech will face an uphill battle—a battle that has been joined by recent political developments.

POLITICAL ADVOCACY OF CENSORSHIP

President Reagan was once asked at a press conference to explain the difference between American democracy and Communist regimes. "We believe in God," he answered.

This response is revealing. It makes no reference to the Constitution, or to our unique tradition of individual rights; nor does it recognize that our Constitution was designed to protect nonbelievers as well as believers.

Reagan was supported in his priorities by Attorney General Edwin Meese. In 1985, Meese lashed out against the Supreme Court in a way unheard of since Franklin Roosevelt attempted to pack that forum in 1937. Meese dubbed recent decisions upholding church/state separation "somewhat bizarre." He deemed rulings that bound the states to uphold the Bill of Rights to be "intellectually shaky." Advocating a vision of the Constitution confined by the "original intent" of the framers, he rejected judicial interpretations as the "personal views" of Supreme Court justices.

Summarizing the feelings of many critics, New York *Times* columnist Anthony Lewis wrote: "What really interests the . . . Attorney General is not judicial philosophy but particular political results. He wants more religion in this country. . . . He wants more government power to order people's lives. He wants the courts to get out of the way."

By confounding religion and politics at the highest level, the President and his appointees created an environment in which ideologues felt encouraged to take over a national news organization because its reporting was perceived as "anti-Reagan," and therefore, unpatriotic. From there, it was a short step to disrupting the flow of other forms of information—all in the name of God and country. That is precisely what has begun to happen.

"Under modern conditions of mass communications," writes the ACLU's Ira Glasser, "the function of free speech may be effectively diminished if no one can hear what the speaker says.

"The *procedural* rights to speak, publish, hear, and read remain intact," he continues. "But *what* we are permitted to speak about, publish, hear, and read is increasingly limited to what the government wants us to know."

In 1982, the Reagan administration attempted to tighten the Freedom of Information Act, which gives citizens access to the dossiers that contain data about them.

That same year, General William Westmoreland made a speech in which he said, "Without censorship, things can get terribly confused in the public mind." Blaming uncensored news for the collapse of the Vietnam war, the retired army general allowed that censorship might be required in a future war—not to keep information from the enemy, but to keep it from the American people. Less than one year later, a news blackout was declared when the United States invaded Grenada.

In 1983, the President promulgated a "secrecy order" requiring any government employee with access to "sensitive" information to preclear anything they plan to write (including a novel) or say about the government. The order applies even after federal employees leave their jobs. Glasser calls this "a lifetime curtailment of speech . . . an unprecedented system of official censorship." (His organization ultimately succeeded in mobilizing Congress to get the executive order rescinded.)

The Reagan government redirected the intent of the Export Administration Act—designed to regulate the outflow of industrial goods—by applying it to ideas. The new application called on scientists to clear any work that might someday be useful to a foreign government before publishing it. "In addition to being a frontal attack on academic freedom," charges Glasser, "the action was . . . without legislative authority."

Invoking the McCarran-Walter Act, the Reagan administration regularly denied visas to controversial foreign writers, politicians, and others. Because these figures were unable to speak here, Americans were deprived of some independent viewpoints that could help them evaluate government policies.

These devices attempt to restrict the flow of information coming into, leaving, and circulating within the country. Because they are achieved by fiat rather than legislative process, they short circuit public debate that might raise First Amendment issues. When they do reach the Supreme Court, the results are not encouraging. In recent terms, the justices have shown "a disturbing tendency to uphold restrictions on free speech in the absence of showing of improper motives by the government," write civil libertarians Burt Neuborne and Carl Loewenson, Jr.

"None of these proposals may seem all that serious a matter," cautions Walter Cronkite, "but, taken together, they form a pattern that we should be worrying about. It is a pattern of restriction."

Cushioned in patriotic homilies, the restrictions pit those patriots who support the First Amendment against those who lobby for God and country. Would the *real* Americans please stand up?

CRIMEWARPS

- Federal legislation and mini-Hatch amendments at the state level will increase the level of censorship incidents in schools. Because conservatives tend to be more politically active than other groups, traditional values will be reflected in those attempts.
- The decimation of the Legal Services Corporation by Religious Right influences will reduce the judicial recourse of the poor and powerless in redressing censorship attempts.
- Recourse will come primarily through professionals on state and local education boards. The backlash against "dumbed down" books, which began in the country's largest textbook markets—Texas and California—will continue. Publishers will improve the quality of their books because it will make economic sense for them to do so.
- Advertising of alcoholic beverages will not be banned, due to effective lobbying by the beer and wine industry. Rather it will be offset with intensive educational campaigns and public service announcements.
- The movie and broadcasting industry will self-regulate itself by monitoring audience preferences. Boycotts will not be successful; the numbers of participants will be too small to make an impact.

- As audiences age, the level of fictional sex and violence will decrease. The level of "real life" sex and violence will increase as informational and news programming expands.
- Ethnic and religious stereotyping in television and movies will continue to decrease as it has in the past two decades. This will be the product of market research and sensitizing seminars such as those now held by NBC.
- Because children will form a shrinking part of the viewing audience, children's programming will be reduced. Whereas such programs were once buttressed by federal regulations, the antiregulatory mood in government will eliminate this protection.
- News programs will continue to have a "liberal" bent because journalism is a profession that sensitizes practitioners to the First Amendment. Therefore, journalists will continue to be "anti-right," so long as those forces attempt to violate civil liberties.
- Future violations of the Bill of Rights will be subtle. They will be implemented by executive order, thereby avoiding confrontations with the Supreme Court and the Legislature. By reducing avenues for checks and balances, the violations will be more difficult to redress.
- The attempt to pack the Supreme Court and other federal courts with members of the Religious Right will make violations easier, but will not guarantee their success. Judges as a group score high on civil liberties scales. Once freed of political pressures, they will support and expand the First Amendment—as they have historically done.

Reconstituting
the Constitution

In 1980, the trial of Buddy Jacobson, a big-time horse trainer and small-time real estate operator, was one of the most sensational courtroom dramas in the country. Covering one aspect of the case for *New York* magazine at the time, I had an experience that taught me a lesson in the limits of civil liberties.

Jacobson was being tried for the 1978 murder of his neighbor and tenant, John Tupper. Tupper had been shot seven times, stabbed repeatedly, and bludgeoned. His body was found in a burning crate at a Bronx dump, giving Mario Merola—that county's innovative, tough district attorney—jurisdiction.

Merola billed the murder partly as the upshot of a love triangle. The slaying had taken place two weeks after model Melanie Cain left Jacobson—with whom she had lived for five years—to move across the hall into Tupper's apartment. Enraged over the betrayal, Merola charged, Buddy exacted a brutal vengeance on her lover.

Jacobson's lawyer, Jack Evseroff, countered that the district attorney had it all backward. It was Melanie Cain who was enraged. Fed up with her former lover's infidelities, she gave biased testimony.

The trial lasted eleven weeks and ended when a long-deadlocked jury finally eked out a guilty verdict. Before he could be sentenced, Jacobson absconded to California, where he was ostensibly seeking evidence to clear his name. He was recaptured and sentenced about six weeks later. But there had been a point toward the end of the trial when the outcome did not look so certain. I had learned of a plot to manipulate evidence and cheat—maybe even kill—Buddy Jacobson. It was obvious I had stumbled onto some serious felons. Because I had an interest in remaining alive and healthy, I decided to work under a pseudonym.

According to my information, Buddy Jacobson had tried to buy the testimony of a retired police officer, Joseph Toscanini, for $100,000. Toscanini was to testify that, while looking for an apartment in the building where Tupper was killed, he saw two men beating up a third. He was to attest that Buddy Jacobson was not one of them.

The scheme fell apart when Toscanini decided not to perjure himself. But he still had a yen for Jacobson's money, so he tried to recruit an NYPD sergeant, Arthur Broughton, to engineer a false arrest in which Toscanini and Jacobson would be caught exchanging money. Jacobson would be abducted and never suspect Toscanini's double cross.

Toscanini reportedly chose Broughton because he had a reputation as a "cool" tough cop. But he was also an honest one, who immediately reported the attempted bribe to NYPD's Internal Affairs Division. IAD began an investigation. But they called Toscanini too soon, came on too strong, and scared him off. When the case was belatedly turned over to Merola, there was nothing left to hang on the bent ex-cop but a minor crime.

I tried to verify the story with the district attorney, leaving futile callback messages. I was obstructed everywhere I turned—except by Jack Evseroff. He was furious. Under the rules of due process, the prosecution is required to give the defense access to evidence, and my call was the first Evseroff had heard of the Broughton affair.

Evseroff charged into court claiming the district attorney was withholding evidence that could clear his client. He demanded that records of the investigation be produced. At first, the police department denied that such an investigation had taken place. The records materialized soon after, when the jury began deliberations, but Evseroff was not allowed to see them. As it turned out, they could only have damaged his defense. However, the revelations brought the trial to an abrupt halt.

Fearing a mistrial, Merola was seething. He quietly began a probe to find out who I was and why I was mucking up his case.

I had left an unlisted phone number for return calls. When Merola's investigators couldn't find any person by my alias, they contacted the phone company to learn my true identity and address. When the district attorney found out that the alias was really me—someone he knew and trusted—he became cooperative.

Merola later told me that he had been about to order a wiretap on my phone. I had come within a hair's breadth of that order being executed. But for a prior professional relationship with the district attorney, what I thought to be my privacy rights—mistakenly, it turns out—would have been demolished. It was my turn to be furious.

I began a correspondence with New York Telephone Company that was instructive in the Fourth Amendment. My first letter went to the president of the phone company. I explained that I had contracted for unlisted telephone service in order to protect my privacy as a journalist who sometimes does investigative pieces involving dangerous people. Because the Bronx County district attorney's office was under no obligation to keep my identity a secret, the phone company's revelation of my name could have placed me in jeopardy. I pointed out that I had not been under investigation, nor had I been the subject of a subpoena. I had merely been acting in my capacity as a journalist. "The D.A.'s office had given no case number when it requested the information from the New York Telephone Company. It was given information that I pay you not to reveal—no questions asked!" I wrote.

Two weeks later I received a response from a vice president:

> It has long been the policy of our Company that we will release non-published record information (name and address or telephone number) to federal, state and local law enforcement agencies upon their written representation, signed by a ranking officer, that the information is required in connection with an official investigation being conducted by their office.
>
> We do not consider the release of your name and address in this instance, to be an invasion of privacy or a breach of tariff conditions under which we provide non-published service. It is a record kept in the regular course of business and is subject to production upon demand of law enforcement agencies. . . .

I responded to the letter with a request for a copy of the "written representation . . . that the information is required in connection with an official investigation." What I received was a memo verifying an *oral* request for information. Attached was this hasty explanation:

". . . our procedures permit the release of such data on a verbal request from a law enforcement agency, subject to written confirmation, when the agency indicates the information is urgently required. . . ."

It sounded to me as if the "unpublished" information was revealed before any verifiable written documentation had been received. A clever impostor could have posed as a police officer, learned who I was and where I lived.

The matter closed with the phone company's pledge to provide me with notification of any such requests in the future.

"This is a first," I was assured by their representative.

But I wasn't finished with them yet. I countered that the tariff agreement for unpublished service does not specify that information was available to law enforcement authorities on request. I proposed that the phone company apprise its customers of that fact.

My pen pal, the vice president, wrote back that his company was considering adding such a stipulation to the tariff agreement. That was in 1980.

As of this writing, that stipulation was never added. The public is lulled into the mistaken belief that unpublished information is private, but it's not. It's open to the very government intrusion that the Bill of Rights ostensibly protects us against.

I had wandered into a loophole in the Fourth Amendment. Although intended to protect us against unreasonable search and seizure, the Supreme Court has ruled that such protection applies only to our homes, businesses, and our persons. It does not extend to third parties—like hospitals, libraries, credit agencies, and phone companies—who in modern life store more information about us than we keep about ourselves.

In my Jacobson adventure, I was embroiled in a tangle of conflicting rights: the prosecutor's right to bring a killer to justice on behalf of the people; the defendant's right to confront his accuser and know the full range of evidence arrayed against him; the public's right to know, via a free press; and my right to privacy as an American.

My Jacobson anecdote might be viewed two ways, depending on your ideological stance. A "law and order" conservative would focus on the criminal and say: Jacobson's a killer, a crook. Why should we coddle him and protect his rights? Did he care about Tupper's rights when he took his life? A liberal would focus on the innocent bystander—me—whose rights are infringed in the zealous pursuit of justice.

For decades—especially during the Warren Court—the second perspective prevailed. Now the trend toward expanding the scope of individual rights is backsliding. The executive branch of government is pressing the federal judiciary to interpret the Bill of Rights in increasingly narrow ways. In its alarm over crime and safety, much of the public applauds the erosion of its freedoms. They are oblivious to the government's steadily expanding net of control—a net that will continue to spread in the future.

The Bill of Rights is made up of the first ten amendments to the Constitution. Of these, five apply to the processing of criminal cases.

□ □ □

The Fourth Amendment protects us against arbitrary—"unreasonable"—searches and seizures. It mandates that no warrants will be issued without probable cause to believe that a crime has been committed. When issued, warrants must be highly specific as to the person, place and things to be searched and seized. This article of the Constitution embodies the core of our presumed right to be left alone.

Wiretaps are considered a "search." In order to eavesdrop on my phone conversations, the district attorney in the Jacobson case would have had to get a warrant undergirded by probable cause. Some supportable wrongdoing would have had to be named. The only exception is the secret recording and transmittal of conversations between a government agent and an unsuspecting accused. I could have fallen prey to this exception.

Latter-day interpretations of the Fourth Amendment have allowed for a lower order of cause—"reasonable suspicion"—to conduct a "stop and frisk" on the street and in schools.

Improperly gathered evidence is subject to the "exclusionary rule." This rule prohibits the introduction of illegally obtained evidence into a trial. When you read about a "motion to suppress" or a suspect being freed "on a technicality," it often means the Fourth Amendment has been abridged.

☐ ☐ ☐

The Fifth Amendment is probably the most familiar item in the Bill of Rights. Popularized in B-movies and congressional hearings, we've all heard someone "take the Fifth" or "be read their rights." In an article tracing the history of this Amendment, lawyer-rabbi Joseph Glaser explains: It is in this part of the Constitution that the "conflict between the interest of the state in acquiring information and a deep seated revulsion against forcing someone, guilty or not, to condemn himself" is acknowledged.

The Fifth Amendment gives a suspect the right not to incriminate himself or to be deprived of life, liberty, or property without due process of law. In the Buddy Jacobson murder trial, the defendant did not take the stand. Under the "Fifth," he could not be forced to testify against himself.

The controversial *Miranda* warning derives from this part of the Bill of Rights. It protects suspects against coerced confessions at the hands of abusive police. It gives us the right, while in custody, to remain silent and/or be interrogated in the presence of our lawyer.

In order to protect individuals from being harassed by the state, the Fifth Amendment also proscribes "double jeopardy." Had he been acquitted, Jacobson could not have been tried for Tupper's murder a second time—even if new evidence was found against him.

☐ ☐ ☐

The Sixth Amendment guarantees a speedy and public trial before an impartial jury. It gives the accused the right to be informed of the charges and to confront the witnesses against him.

Confronting witnesses is part of a broader principle of giving a defendant access to the evidence against him. Buddy Jacobson's trial was temporarily halted because it appeared that he had not been provided with full disclosure during the "discovery" phase of his prosecution.

The Sixth Amendment also establishes the right to be represented by counsel. Subsequent decisions have extended that right to the indigent and broadened its meaning to include a right to *effective* counsel. Had Jacobson not had the money to hire one of New York's ace criminal lawyers, the court would have appointed one to handle his defense. If his lawyer had mishandled the case, that would have been grounds for a subsequent appeal.

□ □ □

The Eighth Amendment protects us against arbitrary and unjust imprisonment. It assumes that we are innocent of charges until proven guilty. Therefore, excessive bail may not be imposed. Nor, once convicted, can we be subject to cruel or unusual punishments. Debates on the death penalty and preventive detention center on the Eighth Amendment, as do most lawsuits charging inhumane prison conditions.

□ □ □

The Fourteenth Amendment requires the states to uphold all the provisions of the Bill of Rights and prohibits them from making any laws that deprive a person of life, liberty, or property without due process of law. Buddy Jacobson was tried in state, not federal, court. Without a clause extending the Bill of Rights to the states, he might well have been deprived of all the protections he enjoyed during his prosecution.

THE EROSION OF DUE PROCESS

Together, Articles IV, V, VI, VIII, and XIV of the Bill of Rights define the rights of crime suspects. They protect the innocent as well as the guilty. Opponents of these rights reason that the innocent don't need protection. Having nothing to hide, counsels Attorney General Edwin Meese, "Most innocent people are glad to talk to the police."

While this tack has some homespun appeal, it denies the fallibility of a criminal justice system that has mistakenly imprisoned—and even put to death —scores of blameless people. It also fails to take into account the tremendous advantage the state has over the individual: its capacity for intimidation and the potential for abuse. Had Sergeant Arthur Broughton been less honest, the mere presence of his uniform would have been enough to draw Buddy Jacobson into a potentially fatal swindle. With long and bitter experience at the hands of unbridled tyranny, the Framers of the Constitution crafted the Bill of Rights as a bulwark against unwarranted state incursions on individual freedom.

Our rights are a painful trade-off between crime and freedom. Liberals have traditionally erred on the side of letting a few of the guilty go free in order to protect the rights of the many innocent. Voicing the New Right's frustration with liberalism, Richard Viguerie has charged: "Their policies of obsession with the rights of hardened criminals, drug pushers, the Mafia, and terrorists are primarily responsible for 141 violent crimes committed per hour in America."

Many people—including two recent attorney generals, William French Smith and Edwin Meese—share Viguerie's fallacious assumption that due process is responsible for this country's crime woes. But those who believe that rights cause crime have set about unraveling the criminal justice amendments to the Constitution—and the federal courts have cooperated. A sample of recent decisions shows that, in most cases, the justices have favored the interests of the state over those of the individual.

SEARCHES

- *U.S. v. Leon; Massachusetts v. Shephard:* Evidence gathered in "good faith," using a defective search warrant in which a magistrate has erred, may be admitted at trial.
- *Nix v. Williams:* Illegally obtained evidence may be admitted if it would "inevitably" have been discovered by lawful means.
- *New Jersey v. T.L.O.:* Public school officials may search students based on a diluted "reasonable suspicion" standard if they believe that school rules have been violated.
- *Oliver v. U.S.:* There is no reasonable expectation of privacy on the land surrounding one's home. Police may trespass fenced and guarded fields, even if in violation of state law, without abridging the Fourth Amendment.
- *California v. Carney:* Mobile homes may be searched without a warrant under the "automobile exception" to the warrant requirement of the Fourth Amendment.
- *U.S. v. Jacobstein:* Police do not need a search warrant to conduct chemical tests on suspected narcotics discovered in a private search and turned over to them for investigation.
- *U.S. v. Karo:* Warrantless monitoring and installation of an electronic beeper does not violate the Fourth Amendment so long as it reveals no information that could not have been obtained by later visual surveillance.
- *Immigration and Naturalization Service v. Delgado:* Immigration officials may conduct unannounced sweeps of factories and businesses to search for illegal aliens.
- *INS v. Lopez-Mendoza:* Illegally seized evidence may be used in immigration proceedings.

SELF-INCRIMINATION

- *New York v. Quarles:* Where there is an "overriding consideration of public safety," police may question a suspect without apprising him of his *Miranda* rights.
- *Oregon v. Elstad:* Where *Miranda* rights are later waived, a voluntary confession, made prior to the warning, is admissible evidence.

TRIALS

- *Press Enterprises v. Superior Court of California:* The right to a public trial applies to voir dire (jury selection) proceedings, but can be overridden by a compelling alternate interest.

BAIL

- *Schall v. Martin:* Preventive detention is permissible for juveniles charged with delinquency in order to stop them from committing additional crimes.

CAPITAL PUNISHMENT

• *Pulley v. Harris:* A state is under no obligation to review a death sentence for "proportionality" to other punishments meted out in similar cases in that state.

• *Caldwell v. Mississippi:* Jurors charged with determining death sentences must be given a clear sense of their task and not be falsely relieved with assurances that higher courts may later exercise mercy.

• *Spaziano v. Florida:* A judge may impose the death penalty even after a jury has recommended life imprisonment.

• *Wainright v. Witt:* Even if they say they're willing to consider it as a punishment, potential jurors may be excluded from murder trials if they express qualms about the death penalty.

PRISONS

• *Ponte v. Real:* Prison officials need not state their reasons for preventing inmates from calling witnesses at a prison disciplinary hearing.

• *Block v. Rutherford:* Pretrial detainees have no constitutional right to contact visits or to observe searches in their cells.

• *Hudson v. Palmer:* Prison inmates have no right to privacy; Fourth Amendment prohibitions on searches do not apply to prison cells.

• *U.S. v. Gouveia:* Prison inmates have no right to counsel while they are held in administrative segregation and prior to the start of any adversary proceedings against them.

A few decisions have favored individual rights:

• *Tennessee v. Garner:* Police may not shoot to kill a fleeing suspect who is neither armed nor dangerous.

• *Hayes v. Florida:* Probable cause is required before a suspect can be transported to a police station for purposes of furthering an investigation.

• *Winston v. Lee:* A prisoner cannot be compelled to submit to surgery to remove a bullet that will be used as evidence against him.

• *Evitts v. Lucey:* A defendant has the right to "effective counsel" on appeal.

• *Ake v. Oklahoma:* States are required to provide indigent defendants who wish to plead insanity with psychiatric expert assistance in preparing for trial.

In most of these rulings, the cards have been heavily stacked against the individual, and prisoners' rights have been almost obliterated. The last chapter of this book spoke of the Supreme Court's general affirmation of First Amendment church/state and free-speech issues. Clearly, this has not carried over to the due process/criminal law amendments.

The Supreme Court has echoed the most controversial recommendations of the 1981 Attorney General's Task Force on Violent Crime: preventive detention for presumably dangerous suspects not yet convicted of a crime and a "good faith" exception to the exclusionary rule. Other proposals—new restrictions on access to the Freedom of Information Act and centralized repositories for exchanges of criminal history information—were not reflected in Supreme Court rulings, but enacted legislatively instead.

Most of the recommendations, along with the court decisions and legislation that followed in their wake, sound reasonable. No draconian measures or obvious tyrannies. But they crack open doors that are better left shut.

☐ ☐ ☐

The dilution of the *Miranda* warning with "public safety" and prior voluntary confessions exceptions creates the possibility that a hostile Supreme Court might eliminate it entirely. Then we'd be back in the dark days of the "third degree." Edwin Meese seems unconcerned about that. "*Miranda* only helps guilty defendants," he declares.

When the *Miranda* decision was promulgated in 1966, the law enforcement world raised a ruckus. How could they solve crimes, they cried, with their most powerful tool taken away? But, in fact, confessions are not the way most cases get solved; most don't get solved at all. When they do, it's because police have been summoned and arrived in time to nab the suspect at the scene. Failing that, they fall back on eyewitness accounts and physical trace evidence.

If confessions were so easy to obtain prior to *Miranda*, there would have been no need to beat them out of people. The recent use of electric prods to jolt confessions out of suspects in Queens, New York, attests that—even with *Miranda*—some police are not beyond using force to develop evidence.

☐ ☐ ☐

The new limited "good faith" exception to the exclusionary rule seems perfectly logical. Why should a rule designed to curb police misconduct punish a cop when it's the judge who has erred? But some conservatives feel the current exception for duly executed search warrants doesn't go far enough. They're pressing for a warrantless exception. A swing of two votes among Supreme Court justices would be sufficient to leave us totally at the mercy of the same police whose abuses the exclusionary rule was intended to obviate.

When the exclusionary rule was first extended to the states in 1961, the forces of law and order protested: it coddled criminals, it handcuffed the police, it let dangerous criminals free on a technicality. Pressures mounted for a modification of the rule, but they were based on spurious claims.

During the years that the exclusionary rule applied only to federal agencies, the FBI functioned perfectly well—despite its judicial "handcuffs." So nonobtrusive was the rule that twenty-six states imposed it on themselves—well before *Mapp v. Ohio* made it the law of the land. But more revealing was the fact that, contrary to popular opinion, very few vicious criminals were actually being released because of suppressed evidence. A 1978 General Accounting Office study shows that a scant .4 percent of the cases coming before federal prosecutors are declined primarily on the basis of search and seizure problems. Once prosecution commences, evidence is suppressed at trial in only 1.3 percent of the cases.

More than half of the defendants whose suppression motions are granted are convicted anyway.

In the following year, a cross-city comparison of felony processing showed that the exclusionary rule accounts for only 1–9 percent of the cases rejected for prosecution. When drug charges are removed from consideration, the figure drops to less than 2 percent in each city.

A 1982 California survey is the closest we come to bad news about the unpopular rule. Nearly 5 percent of felony arrests in that state are rejected for due process weaknesses. But nearly three quarters of those involve drug charges, not violent crimes. This doesn't mean that those "freed on a technicality" aren't dangerous. Many are. Nearly half are rearrested within two years of their release and a good number are known to have long criminal careers. Nevertheless, the figures don't justify Edwin Meese's optimism that if we could only do away with that pesky exclusionary rule, we would make a major dent in our crime problem.

There is, however, one valid argument to be made against the exclusionary rule. Its stated purpose—to curb abuses by police—isn't always achieved. Norman Darwick, former executive director of the International Association of Chiefs of Police, points out: ". . . no sanctions are directed against [police] if they secure evidence improperly. . . . Nor are they apprised, in the event of an appeal, their actions were later invalidated. . . . Thus, mistakes are rarely called to the attention of the arresting officer."

Darwick emphasizes that police must make many of their searches in life-threatening situations that require split-second decisions. Under these conditions, he questions just how much of a deterrent effect the Rule can have on police. It seems to Darwick, the only ones who benefit are the guilty.

Not true. I was guilty of no crime in reporting on the Buddy Jacobson case. Yet, save for a district attorney who did the right thing in reversing himself, I would unjustly have had my most private conversations overheard by state intruders. Without strict requirements for probable cause, that phone tap might have been planted with no hesitation. By virtue of having to comply with the exclusionary rule, generations of law enforcement agents are learning to respect the rights of individuals. Those individuals, whether guilty like Jacobson or innocent like me, have no shelter against government whims but the Bill of Rights.

I'm grateful for the exclusionary rule and the Fifth Amendment. They protect me without impeding justice. The proof is in the numbers. In the years since *Miranda* and *Mapp v. Ohio*, arrests, convictions, and imprisonment rates have climbed steeply, and in some cases reached record levels. That should please everyone who supports law and order.

☐ ☐ ☐

Perhaps the most dangerous door to be opened in recent Supreme Court terms is preventive detention. On the face of it, the ruling makes sense. If a juvenile has a track record of crime and violence, why release him into the community while awaiting trial? He'll only use that time to prey on innocent people and wreak more human havoc.

Conservatives promise that preventive detention will reduce violent crime, but that belief is based on flawed assumptions. The government's own study shows that only about 10 percent of federal defendants released before trial are rearrested for new crimes, violate conditions of release, or fail to appear for trial. Less than one fifth that number are convicted of, and imprisoned for, serious crimes committed while out on bail.

The federal numbers are depressed by an unrepresentative proportion of low-risk white-collar suspects. But even at the local level, where street punks make up the bulk of those sent back to the community, the numbers are tolerable. Less than one sixth of those released are rearrested for new crimes—not all of them grave.

Those with serious prior records, a current history of drug use, poor employment histories, and weak social roots have the highest probability of messing up before trial. (Drug abusers, for example, are more than twice as likely to be rearrested before trial than abstainers. But their crimes are less serious than those who don't use drugs.) Admittedly, that is precisely the population the preventive detention rule aims to curtail.

The longer the time before trial, the greater the risk of misconduct. Therefore, a speedy trial—as mandated by the Constitution—would seem a more equitable solution than preventive detention.

To be sure, preventive detention of violent juveniles is surrounded with all kinds of legislative safeguards: hearings, lawyers, access to records, time limits, the entire panoply of due process protections. But the data on which they rely are defective. Our ability to predict violence is notoriously short of the mark, and criminal histories are outrageously inaccurate, incomplete, outdated, and unreliable.

To deter fewer than 15 percent of releasees, it scarcely seems worth violating three of our most cherished principles:

The presumption of innocence until proven guilty (which the Burger Court ruled, in 1979, does not apply to pretrial detention).

The ban on infliction of punishment without due process.

The stricture against imposition of excessive bail.

Once we allow for the preventive detention of violent juveniles, how long before a zealous administration starts hauling in homosexuals or political dissenters?

THE DISINTEGRATION OF PRIVACY

Our constitutional right to privacy was articulated in *Griswold v. Connecticut,* a landmark case decided in 1965. But the places where our privacy is sacrosanct have become constricted, leaving us vulnerable to unlimited surveillance. Our property is no longer protected, either by the walls of our house or by the limits of our land. Our private papers are usually not papers at all, but electronic bytes. As we approach the twenty-first century, home isn't where we keep our most personal property. Our comings and goings, bill payments, health problems, and census information are stored on myriad computer tapes at credit card agencies, banks, insurance companies, and government offices. Recent rulings on search and seizure leave all of these open to police inspection.

In an electronic age, the Constitution's two-hundred-year-old treatment of private papers and effects is artificially narrow. In Revolutionary War America, there were no phone company records to bear silent witness to our secrets. In a rural society whose economy was dominated by the cottage industries of the self-employed, private information was kept in the family Bible. Official records could tell you little more than an individual's date and place of birth, wedding date, and residence. In that home-centered society, the border between private and public was clear.

Modern life, however, has fluid boundaries. We live most of it outside our home in various spheres defined as public: offices, rock concerts, airports, freeways, welfare offices. Some of these places keep elaborate profiles of our habits, health, psyches, and itineraries. But, say recent rulings, in these realms we have no reasonable expectation of privacy.

The hours we spend in the public place called "school," for example, mean our lockers, desks, and persons are available for searches. In Hackensack, New Jersey, school officials sought the right to test all students for drugs. The constitutional challenge to that policy was watched by schools all over the country. A state superior court justice ruled it an invasion of privacy and unreasonable search and seizure. But the school board planned to appeal—all the way to the U.S. Supreme Court, if necessary. In Patchogue, New York, it is teachers' urine they want to search for drugs. By 1986, proposals for workplace drug testing had become a hotly debated national rage.

In response to the abuses of the Watergate years, the 1974 landmark Privacy Act established standards for fair information practices by the federal government. It demands that we be given the right to examine files for accuracy. Our written consent is required before files can be turned over to any outside agency. The government is required to notify us whenever it establishes a new system of records, and records kept for one purpose are not permitted to be used for another. The Privacy Act of 1974 and Title 28 of the Code of Federal Regulations (CFR) protect such records from incursions by nongovernment agencies, but do little to intercept the exchange of information between law enforcement agencies. (This is in line with *Paul v. Davis*, a 1976 Supreme Court decision that declined to extend the right to privacy to the dissemination of criminal justice information.) Other exceptions are legion—the Central Intelligence Agency, Congress, court orders, Freedom of Information Act requests, and confidential sources. When the government started using IRS records to track wayward fathers for defaulting on child support payments, the intention was praiseworthy. But that certainly isn't what our tax returns are designed to do. Runaway technology and exceptions such as this have rendered the Privacy Act ineffective.

Who would ever have thought that the National Rifle Association and the

American Civil Liberties Union would be on the same side of any issue? Yet, when it comes to the inadequacies of the Privacy Act, they are. Inaccurate information transmitted over the gargantuan government telecommunications network has cost people jobs, credit, licenses, and liberty.

The concept of privacy has begun to lose its meaning. The government seeks to keep broadening its access to dossier information both in its own and private data banks. At the end of 1985, the federal government asked Congress to give it direct access to information about the private insurance coverage of anyone in the United States. The stated purpose was to snare welfare cheats.

Earlier, an FBI advisory panel had recommended that the National Crime Information Center be used to transmit information—bank account numbers, social security numbers, addresses, aliases, contacts, and such—about white-collar-crime suspects and their associates. The purpose was to "promote a more coordinated approach to white-collar crime in general and massive, economic fraud-type crime in particular," attest Ira Glasser and Noel Salinger of the ACLU. In 1983, those same computers were to be used to keep track of people the FBI considered "suspicious"—even if they were not wanted for a specific crime. This catchall was to include suspected terrorists, drug traffickers, espionage agents and people "known to associate" with any of the above. The purpose was to enhance the administration's political surveillance program.

As early as 1970, the Bank Secrecy Act required that private institutions report all large transactions to the government—a powerful investigative tool to bag money launderers. But what of the rest of us who don't want our identities and copies of our checks whirring around government computers?

All of these moves had a solid law enforcement rationale. Given our corrosive fear of crime, we've been tempted to cave in to every government intrusion as long as it's labeled "law and order." With this kind of access to our privacy, the computer age is a boon to police. By assembling phone records, credit card slips, car rental contracts, and bank transactions they can develop a detailed profile of anyone's whereabouts and activities.

□   □   □

The Freedom of Information Act, established in 1966, is one of our few defenses against information abuse. Under this law, all documents kept by federal agencies must be made available for inspection by any American citizen—except those covering criminal inquiries, advice to the head of an agency, and classified matters. In 1984, nearly 248,000 FOIA requests were processed, with almost 92 percent being granted. The most open agency was Health and Human Services, with a success rate of about 99 percent. The least accessible was the State Department, which granted less than one third of the requests it received.

The State Department's low rate of compliance reflects attempts by a conservative administration to gut the FOIA. With the stroke of a pen, President Reagan did what Congress would not do: He established "the broadest security classification system in American history," making it much harder to get access to government dossiers.

"Information is power," writes David Burnham in his eye-opening book, *The Rise of the Computer State,* "and . . . organizations increase their power by learning how to swiftly collect and comprehend bits and pieces of information."

☐ ☐ ☐

The neo-conservative vision of the Constitution is one that favors government privilege over individual liberty. Federal Judge Robert Bork, a Reagan appointee who is said to be high on the list of choices to fill a Supreme Court vacancy, is representative of this vision.

Bork is responsible for a decision that is considered infamous in some circles. In upholding the right of the navy to discharge a petty officer for homosexual conduct, Bork ruled that the right to privacy should not be construed to apply to gay sex in particular or "any and all sexual behavior in general." He insisted that no court has the right to create *new* constitutional rights (but conceded that once the Supreme Court does so, lower court judges are bound by them). Bork supported his explosive decision with the assertion that there is no basis for the right to privacy in the "text, history, and structure" of the Constitution.

Bork is correct to an extent. If read literally, the Constitution makes no mention of the word "privacy." But the right is inferred from the Fourth and Fifth amendments—which protect us against government intrusions, self-incrimination, and acknowledges the primacy of private property—as well as the due process clause of the Fourteenth Amendment—which recognizes that there are areas of behavior that should be free of the prying eyes of government.

STRIPPING THE COURTS

The way issues like privacy are resolved has much to do with the shape of the judiciary. In our federal form of government, the legislative branch may amend the Constitution, but the courts are its guardian. Therefore, he who controls the courts controls the judicial interpretations that undergird our laws. As this decade closes, we stand at the threshold of a radical restructuring of the federal courts along neo-conservative lines.

The strategy calls for simultaneous packing and stripping of the courts. Of more than 600 federal judgeships, Ronald Reagan filled 164 during his first four years in office. In his second term, he had the opportunity to fill 150 more (plus a gaggle of bankruptcy judges). Compared to his predecessor, he appointed few females, Hispanics, or blacks. However, more than one quarter of Reagan's first-term choices were deemed "exceptionally well qualified" by the American Bar Association—10 percent more than Jimmy Carter's appointees. But, the quality of Reagan's second-term nominees slipped considerably.

The Religious Right introduced an ideological litmus test into the selection process: a commitment to traditional family values and the right-to-life of an unborn fetus; prayer in schools and an end to busing and affirmative action quotas. In other words, federal judges were not to neutrally weigh the complex issues that came before them. They were to prejudge them, before even donning their robes. As it is being defined today, a conservative court mandates judicial restraint over judicial activism, state's rights over a universal Bill of Rights, and ideological commitment over legal neutrality.

The plan to tip the ideological balance by packing the federal bench with extreme conservatives was heralded in a speech made by William French Smith in 1981. In condemning "subjective judicial policy-making" cum constitutional interpretation, he lobbied to bring the federal courts into line with "the groundswell of conservatism evidenced in the 1980 election."

Texas law professor Lino Graglia was one of Reagan's choices for spearheading the judicial revolution. Graglia was subsequently accused by People for the American Way of disrespect for the rule of law, denigrating the Constitution and the courts, and insensitivity to minorities. That civil liberties group then lobbied the President to drop the nomination. In August 1986, they got their wish. After a tough fight to confirm another conservative judge, Daniel Manion, the Administration dropped Graglia. But Graglia's designation remains instructive.

In 1981, Graglia was considered for a post in the Justice Department's civil rights division. But then-Attorney General William French Smith rejected him as too extreme. Apparently Ed Meese didn't agree. Graglia became candidate for the Fifth Circuit Court of Appeals.

Graglia's vehement attacks on court-ordered busing endeared him to the New Right. In separate incidents, he is reported to have referred to blacks as "pickaninnies," and characterized the Denver school board as "blacks, women, Jews, and other known subversives."

In reviewing a few pieces of Graglia's writing, his arguments against busing as a desegregation strategy seemed well-reasoned, not racist. However, many minority students were offended by him and transferred out of his classes.

As for his interpretation of the Constitution, I find his views personally repugnant, but not without foundation. Like Ed Meese, Graglia feels the judiciary has overstepped its bounds and misconstrued the Bill of Rights—especially as it applies to the states. Nowhere in that document does he find any basis for interfering with states' rights in matters of religion, abortion, sexual restraints, or desegregation. Nor does he see any reference to an "exclusionary rule."

It is true that none of those items is explicitly stated—with good reason. The Framers of the Constitution deliberately sketched its principles in broad terms. Their idea was to create a flexible document that would adapt to social changes they couldn't anticipate from their eighteenth-century vantage point.

But the Supreme Court's interpretation of the Fourteenth Amendment is particularly odious to Graglia. In his view, the Fourteenth Amendment "was adopted for the limited purpose of guaranteeing blacks certain basic rights." The Court overreached when it construed the words "nor shall any State deprive any person of life, liberty, or property without due process of law" to mean that the Bill of Rights was binding on the states, according to Graglia.

In fact, a right is hollow if it is binding only on the federal government. Our day-to-day lives are grounded in the states; our contact with the federal government, very limited. If the United States has no official religion, but the residents of Utah are bound by Mormon precepts, what does that mean to the Jews or Catholics of Salt Lake City? If we are free from arbitrary search and seizure by an FBI agent, but the Dade County sheriff can burst into our home at will, what kind of protection is that? What's the good of freedom of assembly if we're safe holding a rally in Yellowstone National Park but can get arrested for doing the same in Central Park?

Federal rights with no application to the states would splinter the nation into fifty minicountries. States' rights in 1990 cannot possibly be expected to mean the same thing it did in 1790. As it stands, the current interpretation of the Fourteenth Amendment has established only a minimum standard of rights below which the states may not fall. States are free to expand those rights, and many have done so. Besides, with a large-enough majority in both houses of Congress and the state legislatures, elected bodies are free to amend the Constitution at any time. Ira Glasser explains, "the separation of powers and the Bill of Rights were not designed to be completely impervious to democratic change. But they were designed to create an inertia in favor of liberty that no momentary majority could overcome during troubled times, or when appetite for power grew too strong."

In a scathing *National Review* piece, Graglia persists in ripping into the Fourteenth Amendment: "In the hands of the Supreme Court . . . it has become . . . a second Constitution that has swallowed the first and transferred all policymaking power not only to the Federal Government but to the unelected branch of the Federal Government, the Court itself."

Graglia is making a brilliant, but disingenuous, argument when he claims that the federal courts have usurped legislative powers without having to answer to the electorate. The Founding Fathers were much concerned with the tyranny of majorities. That's why they provided for an independent, nonelected federal judiciary. As Glasser indicates, political electorates are fickle and can't be counted on to look after the interests of unpopular minorities.

The courts, against which Graglia bears such malice, did not emerge as a remedy for civil liberties violations until 1803. The *Marbury v. Madison* decision established their power to nullify laws that exceed the limits of government authority. The Texas law professor finds this development antidemocratic and blames it for most of our social ills.

In reviewing calamitous Supreme Court decisions, Graglia rightly takes aim at the Dred Scott decision, which helped instigate the Civil War: "It is doubtful that the net contribution of the Constitution to our national well-being has been positive, and it is certain that the net contribution of judicial review has been negative." Graglia concludes: The federal bench "has effectively remade America in its own image, according to a doctrinaire ideology based on egalitarianism and the rejection of traditional notions of morality and public order. . . . Proponents of judicial review defend the power of the Supreme Court as necessary to the protection of individual liberties against government officials. . . .

In any event, federal judges have become themselves the greatest source of danger to those liberties."

If Graglia were king, the courts would be stripped of their power. A worrisome attitude in a federal judge.

□ □ □

The most dramatic court-stripping attempts have been aimed at denying the federal bench jurisdiction over cases dealing with desegregation, church/state separation, and abortion. Though unsuccessful so far, court-stripping is a serious protest against thirty years of activist Supreme Court decisions. But the odds are high that the New Right will succeed in dominating the highest court in the land.

The current roster of Supreme Court Justices is an amalgam of Eisenhower, Kennedy, Johnson, and Reagan appointments. The Nixon factor is by far the greatest. There is a solid conservative bloc, including Sandra Day O'Connor. Moderates often provide the crucial swing votes. The rest, of whom John Paul Stevens is one, hold up the libertarian end of the spectrum.

Since Supreme Court justices are appointed for life, their ages are the most telling indicators of the Court's future direction. Sandra Day O'Connor and John Paul Stevens are among the youngsters of the bench. Based on their relative youth, we can safely assume that at least one conservative and one libertarian are in for the long haul. Except for Stevens, the liberal bloc is well on in years—more so than its opposite number. Therefore, each death or retirement creates opportunities to pack the Supreme Court with conservative ideologues, tipping its delicate balance toward the Right.

Burt Neuborne, legal director of the ACLU, recognized the delicacy of the situation during Ronald Reagan's second term when he said: "if Reagan gets one Supreme Court appointment, we're in for trouble. If he gets two, we're facing disaster." That one appointment came up with the resignation of Chief Justice Warren Burger in 1986.

□ □ □

The civil liberties battles of the future, however, are not likely to be fought in the Supreme Court. Neuborne explains: "When I first came to the ACLU we were petitioners in 80 percent of our cases in the Court. Now we are respondents 80 percent of the time. Almost all of our losses in the last couple of years have come in cases that were won below and were then dragged into the Supreme Court to be reversed."

A singular inversion has occurred. In the past, the federal government and Supreme Court were the protectors of civil liberties; today, state courts and legislators are more hospitable to individual rights. In contrast to federal judges —who are appointed for life—state judges and legislators are elected. You'd think that would make them *less* likely to uphold the rights of the politically unpopular.

But in an anomalous turn of events, they've made decisions that surpass those handed down by the Supreme Court. Texas courts struck down polygraph tests for public employees. Oregon courts have provided a number of important safeguards for criminal defendants and secured free speech rights at privately owned shopping centers. Calling it a violation of the right against self-incrimination, the Montana supreme court disallowed the admission into evidence of refusals to submit to breathalyzer tests.

The U.S. Supreme Court overturned the Montana decision. But since then, it has ruled that a state court may avoid federal review if it makes a clear statement that its decision is based on state law and doesn't conflict with federal law. That gives state courts a lot of leeway and elected state judges are enjoying the role of mini–Supreme Court Justice.

Congress, also an elective body, is another surprise ally in support of individual liberties. In 1981, for example, more than forty separate bills were introduced to strip the federal courts of jurisdiction. Each of them was fought and defeated in the legislature. In 1982, Congress was successfully lobbied to save the stripped-down Legal Services Corporation, pass a stronger Voting Rights Act, and preserve an intact Freedom of Information Act. A coalition of moderates, liberals, and traditional conservatives banded together to use congressional debate procedures to derail the New Right's "Human Life" Bill, various court-stripping proposals, and a discriminatory immigration bill.

The midterm elections that year solidified the civil rights lobby. Although the National Conservative Political Action Committee had targeted a number of pro-civil rights legislators for defeat, not one lost a bid for reelection. In addition, the newly elected representatives were far more civil liberties–oriented than the Congress as a whole. Finally, the Democratic Party gained twenty-six seats in the House, more than twice the usual number of seat-shifts in a midterm election.

It seemed as if the country was rediscovering its historic centrism. Moderate state legislatures, libertarian state courts, and a moderate Congress have formed a countervailing force to increasingly conservative federal courts. But, says Mark Lynch, an attorney for the ACLU, "When you are talking with a House member or a senator, you have to be ready to negotiate and compromise; absolute positions of principle cannot always be maintained." Both neo-conservatives and libertarians are being nudged toward the center.

The fly in the ointment is the "Imperial Presidency" and its practice of rule by executive order. "A president noted for his ability to 'communicate,' " laments John Shattuck of the ACLU, "has mastered the Orwellian art of double-speak and is arguing that his executive orders are law. By definition, therefore, government by executive order is not lawless. Big Brother could not have stated the case for himself more concisely."

Instead of a government that has gotten "off the backs" of the people, it has become bigger and less accountable. Secrecy, surveillance, and enforced conformity are the biggest threats a vulnerable citizenry faces in the future.

But that citizenry is its own greatest hope for the preservation of individual freedom. "Respect for the freedom of others," explain survey researchers Herbert McClosky and Alida Brill, "is . . . furthered by greater exposure to the media, by residence in a cosmopolitan environment, and by membership in educated and sophisticated subcultures."

In a world that is thoroughly penetrated by rapid transportation and pervasive media coverage, it is difficult to remain insulated from, and ignorant of, the varieties of human experience. Contact and communication are the keys to mutual tolerance. "Human rights" is a buzzword that even the most determinedly ostrich-like American has heard.

"As each new generation matures into adulthood, the general level of freedom and tolerance in the society as a whole rises," write McClosky and Brill. Part of that has to do with education and part has to do with growing up in the decades of the "rights explosion." Even though the masses of our people tend toward political apathy and low levels of awareness, opinion leaders more than make up for that with their own libertarian orientation.

Fear of crime is the greatest inducement for sacrificing our rights. But that fear attaches mainly to the crimes of the poor. The future is bringing a shift to crimes and criminals we—rightly or wrongly—find less threatening: white-collar crimes, older and female criminals. The safer we feel, the more tenaciously will we cling to the liberties that are the hallmark of America.

CRIMEWARPS

- Population shifts from urban to rural areas will spread libertarian values of the big cities to traditionally conservative areas.
- The proliferation of extensive computerized data bases will be difficult to control. Of all our rights, the Fourth Amendment and right to privacy will be the ones most likely to suffer abuse in the future.
- Middle-class privacy rights will be enhanced. The privacy rights of the dependent poor will be steadily eroded through invasion of records that help to monitor "cheating" on government payments.
- Civil liberties remedies will become increasingly inaccessible to the poor, with the continued decimation of the Legal Services Corporation.
- Preventive detention of the accused will parallel selective incapacitation of the convicted. Predictive, rather than retributive, models will determine who remains free and who is locked up.
- The federal courts will be dominated by young conservatives, who will influence decisions for many decades to come.
- A moderate Congress will defeat the nomination of ultra–right-wing Supreme Court candidates, thereby preventing extreme shifts in the Court's composition.
- Rights restricted by the U.S. Supreme Court will be expanded by state courts and Congress.
- The availability of expanded rights will be unevenly distributed across states.

23

Sic Transit

A new climate has emerged in America. Patriotism is coming to be equated with being a fundamentalist Christian and a conservative. The clash between secular and religious forces is eroding our civil liberties and marking the way we respond to crime.

We need only look at history to see the consequences of trying to establish religious hegemony: the Crusades, the slaughter of Huguenots by Catholics in France, the Spanish Inquisition, the war between Puritans and Anglicans in England, the Muslim Jihad, the Holocaust, Belfast, Beirut, Uganda, Iran, Iraq, India, the Ku Klux Klan, neo-Nazis, abortion vigilantes. Intolerance breeds violence, leaving very little room for liberty.

Liberty is unnatural—through most of human history, people have lived without it. Psychologists know our species is more comfortable with structure than freedom. Students of social movements have recorded our readiness to abdicate responsibility for ourselves and turn it over to demagogues.

Liberty is fragile. So fragile is it that a two-thirds vote of each house of Congress and three quarters of the state legislatures could call for a Constitutional Convention, decimate the power of the Supreme Court, and revoke the entire Bill of Rights. There is considerable pressure from some conservatives for a "con-con" to establish a balanced budget amendment to the Constitution along with various court stripping proposals.

Liberty requires reciprocity. It means that we must cede to others the same privilege of independent judgment that we accord ourselves. That takes learning, tolerance, and discipline. It's much easier to quash dissent than to live with dissonance. That's why strong support for civil liberties has traditionally come from community leaders, professionals, and the educated classes.

Liberty is distributive. One person's gain is often another's loss. Bob Guccione's right to publish pictures of powdered vulvas violates Susan Brownmiller's right to dignity. Jack Abbott's right to be released from prison after due process cost an innocent Greenwich Village waiter his life. A sperm donor's right to privacy resulted in AIDS for a thirty-eight-year-old woman who was artificially inseminated with his semen. Louis Farrakhan's right to rail against Judaism robs countless Jews of their sense of safety. Affirmative action for blacks means lost opportunities for whites.

Our liberties carry a price, but polls indicate that most Americans would not even miss their rights because they never understood them. It is only after the first time that police break into their homes unannounced and warrantless that they would realize the protection they once enjoyed against unreasonable search and seizure. When thrown in jail without charges for a crime they didn't commit, they would grasp what it means to be assured of due process. After being denounced for "popery," they might comprehend the meaning of religious freedom. And when a confession is coerced out of them by means of genital shocks, the *Miranda* warning and Fifth Amendment would at last make sense.

Thanks to the hurly-burly of politics, it is unlikely that any of these scenarios will come to pass. American right-wing movements have traditionally been bound up with religion. Therefore, the fate of authoritarianism depends, to some extent, on the future direction of American religious practices.

The *1984 Yearbook of American and Canadian Churches* shows that U.S. church membership numbers about 140 million. That's slightly more than half the total population. Of those belonging to churches, more call themselves Protestant than all other American religious groups combined.

Only about 40 percent of those enrolled in religious institutions attend weekly services. For those between the ages of twenty-five and fifty-nine, church attendance was higher in the 1970s than it is now. But for those younger or older, church-going inched up a hair in this decade. Polls show that the more we age, the more we show up at our neighborhood church or shul. This bodes very well for organized religion. The sixty-plus age group will nearly double by 2025, and that means our houses of worship will be filling up. The first sputterings are being felt now. After a long period of steep decline, the National Council of Churches was pleased to report that membership losses in mainline denominations slowed in 1983 and 1984. Other churches drew more than 2.5 million new members in the same period.

Affiliated believers have not cornered the market on piety. NORC findings indicate that three quarters of us pray at least once a day, and more than 90 percent profess a belief in God. Nevertheless, despite strong religious feelings, three fifths of Americans surveyed reject the concept of "absolute moral guidelines." A decade ago, only two fifths felt that way. Kenneth Briggs, former religion editor for the New York *Times,* concludes: "Americans are turning away from the dictates of organized religion and drawing on their own spiritual feelings and conscience." Faith has been distanced from daily behavior and relegated to the realm of the mystical.

This may lead you to believe that we're a country bent on secularism. Not so, according to sociologist-priest Andrew Greeley—and he is confirmed by Gallup polls which show that those for whom "religion is very important in personal life" increased 4 percent between 1978 and 1982.

Humans have an innate need for the sacred which has persisted through umpteen scientific revolutions. The emergence of hard rock signals a primordial craving for a return to religious ecstasy. Greeley calls it "a rebellion against the new hyper-rationalist world." He goes on to quote from a religious essay of Professor Huston Smith: "the human mind stands ready to believe anything—as long as it provides an alternative to the totally desacralized mechanomorphic outlook of objective science."

The American worshiper has become, to an extent, an independent moral agent. Yet, in his search for meaning in an increasingly complex and technological world, he remains an avid consumer in the religious marketplace. The conflict between orthodox and conservative, fundamentalist and liberal, Protestant, Catholic, and Jew is not new. The place where we locate ourselves on those spectrums, interposes Greeley, is a "highly important means of social location and self-definition." The very pluralism of our creeds encourages religious affiliation.

Some would argue the opposite: Pluralism spins off so many competing ideologies that revealed "truth" loses its conviction and secularization takes over. But Greeley points out, "It is precisely in those countries where religious pluralism is most likely to be found that organized religion is also able to count on the strongest commitments"—stronger by far than in places dominated by a single official or unofficial religion. "Religious pluralism, so feared by the ardent defenders of orthodoxy," concludes Greeley, "turns out to be its best guarantee."

□   □   □

U.S. News & World Report predicts that traditional boundaries separating religions will dissolve as a result of intermarriage and ecumenism. These will be replaced by a realignment of denominations along conservative and liberal lines.

The outward-looking and egalitarian ideologies of mainline Protestants and Reform Jews will be fortified by an ever more accessible world whose woes continually impinge on our consciousness through communications and immigration. Conservative sects will attract the many who seek simplicity and certitude—a retreat from the tortuous ambiguities of modern life.

Right-wing fundamentalism will be private and emotionally intense, but not very strict. Its message will be one of practical benefits and reassurance—instant relief from illness, money troubles, guilt.

That doesn't sound very much like the politicized fundamentalism we know today. What's going to happen between now and the future that will banish the moral activists to the inner reaches of their own souls?

It's tempting to say that they will simply fall prey to the ongoing cycle of religious revival and regression that has characterized our country's social history, but that's too easy. Something has happened in this round that never existed before, counsels Marc Tanenbaum. Fundamentalists, *"as a church,"* have become hooked into the political process. As part of the New Right, they have crossed a boundary which evangelicals say violates the tenets of their professed faith. According to scholar Robert Webber, true biblical Christianity repudiates the outer world and all its institutions as fallen. While the believer "renders unto Caesar that which is Caesar's," he gives no earthly government his ultimate allegiance. The job of the church is to transmit values through its free and uninhibited witness; it must never control or get entangled with government. "If the church gains control," postulates Webber, "we can expect Christian totalitarianism which is no less desirable than a non-Christian totalitarianism."

In short, claims Webber, fundamentalism must be separatist or it ceases to be Bible-based. By putting their faith in the economic and political systems of the fallen external world, the Moral Majority and its cohorts have left the realm of biblical Christianity and crossed into that of civil religion.

There's nothing new about civil religion in our history. The relationship between it and our government has existed from the very beginning, says Webber. But civil religion, because it doesn't hold Jesus Christ at its core, is not biblical. It is simply an invoking of " 'God-words' . . . and consensus religious sentiments by the state for its own political purpose." It "blurs the distinction between church and nation and shifts faith toward a religion of nationalism."

□ □ □

Falwell and his followers have bought into a hybrid movement. "We are Catholics, Jews, Protestants, Mormons, Fundamentalists—black and white," boasts Falwell of his Moral Majority. Viguerie simultaneously takes pride in the medley of single and multi-issue groups he has put together for the New Right.

Through this confederacy, fundamentalism has entered coalition politics—whose very nature demands accommodation and compromise. Without give, all those carefully husbanded single issue groups will splinter off in their own direction and there will be little left of their Majority.

By virtue of the political strategy it has chosen, the New Right faces this dilemma: If they are to succeed in attaining power, they will have to compromise their doctrinal orthodoxies. They will, in other words, have to move toward the political center.

And that suits the tenor of the times just fine. Despite all the hoopla about ultraconservatism, Gallup polls show that a generally increasing percentage of the population defines itself as politically "middle-of-the-road." This moderate group has sustained a solid plurality since 1957. Surprisingly, the percentage of those who describe themselves as "right of center" is actually smaller now than it was in the late 1930s, late 1940s, and early 1970s. (Liberals, too, have lost percentages to moderates.)

Focus on selected demographic groups and you'll find some subtle shifts in the making:

If you belong to the country's largest religious group—Protestants—you're more likely to call yourself conservative than moderate. Within Falwell's own Baptist denomination, the largest Protestant creed, moderates hold a solid plurality. This leaves the rank-and-file Baptist somewhat out of step with his leadership in the Southern Baptist Convention, where the presidency has been held by fundamentalists since 1979.

If you look at age, you'll find that the plurality (and sometimes even the majority) of those fifty-five and older call themselves conservative rather than moderate. This is the fastest-growing segment of the population—and also the one most likely to be going to church.

Among occupational groups, the blue-, white-, and button-down collar sets all tend toward the conservative in one poll, while only executives retain their conservative plurality in the other. In both polls, the blue-collar types claim the smallest percentage of self-identified conservatives. But since the smokestack laborer is a shrinking part of our work force, he will either have to move into the expanding white-collar ranks or find himself unemployed. In the former case, he'll become more conservative; in the latter, more liberal.

Blacks, a rapidly expanding part of the population, identify with liberals and moderates.

College freshmen have, since 1970, been overwhelmingly and increasingly gravitating toward the political center, and the economic as well as moral Right. At the same time, the population as a whole has become more sexually liberal.

Religion, age, occupation, race, and education are exerting demographic pulls on political alignments, but the pulls are not going in any clear direction. If anything, these inscrutable poll results reflect the fickle jumble of American pluralism.

But there is one dimension that has some predictive strength: activism. On every measure of political action—whether writing to a congressman, attending a rally, or running for office—conservatives hold the plurality or majority. That's not surprising—since they tend to be older, more educated and more affluent—but it does augur a robust political force.

Viguerie estimates that there are some 85 million morally conservative Americans in that robust force and cites the growing conservatism of the American worker as a potential source of support. But it's a mistake to equate conservatism with fundamentalism.

Gallup polls estimate that about one quarter of the population can be considered part of the Christian Right. A high percentage of this group is evangelical, but they tend to vote more Republican than evangelicals as a whole. While the Moral Majority is the most prominent subset of this group, a goodly part is made up of those who are more moderate than right. Orbiting this bloc are evangelicals, like Billy Graham, who are neither rightists nor orthodox fundamentalists. Then there is the burgeoning Hispanic fundamentalist movement, which has produced leaders who are solidly Democratic and Liberal. Among these are former New York City Deputy Mayor Herman Badillo, a Baptist, and Bronx Representative Robert Garcia, the son of a Pentecostal minister.

Christians are far from a monolithic voting bloc. Voting for lower taxes, a strong military, and deregulation of the economy are areas where most agree with each other and the general population. However, those issues are of a different order than voting for a biblical theocracy with rigidly legislated morality. On these issues, the majority of the public is receptive to clerical guidance but rejects governmental intervention. On personal moral choices—about abortion, homosexuality, women's roles—nonevangelical Christians vote with the general population rather than their evangelical brethren; the Christian Right and non-Christian Right are similarly split. In short, Americans are individualistic enough to support conservative economic policies but too independent to abide fundamentalist-regulated morality.

Chip Prairie, a resident of Greensboro, North Carolina, addresses this distinction in a letter to the editor of his local paper. (The writer was responding to a school prayer initiative by his state's senator, Jesse Helms, after the first-term election of Ronald Reagan.)

"Legislators should understand that the people voted largely for a change in economic policy. This was not a mandate to install broad and sweeping reactionary policies.

"This new political fad group seems to contradict itself. . . . On the one hand they want 'government off the backs of the people.' On the other hand they intend to involve government in one of the dearest and most personal privileges of a free people . . . the right to follow one's own spiritual ideal. . . ."

The conservative-fundamentalist split is evident in the patterns of New Right successes and failures. In those areas where it has attempted to mandate morality, it has failed. The Supreme Court has upheld the privacy of reproductive choices, as have the states. Congress has balked at passing the Family Protection Act. The move to mandate parental notification for distribution of contraceptives to minors has been overturned. "Creationism" initiatives have been defeated. Dumbed-down, grossly simplified science textbooks are being rejected. Despite Anita Bryant's early successes, the Gay Rights Movement proceeds undaunted. Segregated Christian schools have not gained tax-exempt status. Boycotts of purveyors of sex and violence have petered out. Bible reading has not found its way back into the public schools.

The social agenda cannot succeed because every one of this nation's nine regions holds a solid moderate plurality. The U.S. House of Representatives is overwhelmingly Democratic, as are three quarters of the state legislatures and governorships. Evangelicals and conservative Christians—who make up a minority of the population—have given moral concerns their highest priority. But polls show that the rest of the country ranks these sixth after inflation, unemployment, international relations, crime, and energy problems.

The New Right has been more successful when it has addressed broader concerns. But even here, conservatives are learning that Americans always drift back to the happy middle-of-the road. The "tax revolt" has rebelled, defeating the entire round of 1984 "Proposition thirteen"–type state tax referenda. Right-wing congressmen have lost House seats along with their liberal colleagues. Mid-1986 found the Viguerie Company deep in debt, its flow of conservative cash starting to thin. At the same point in time, Jerry Falwell started a new organization, the Liberty Federation, in order to maintain his movement's flagging momentum. And most startling of all, the President that the New Right built started talking arms control to the "Commies."

The New Right has made some headway on its own terms. They've raised our consciousness about genuine rot in the foundations of our society. Deregulation is proceeding apace. A federal Equal Rights Amendment is, for the time being, routed. The Pupil Rights Amendment is giving parents a greater voice in the value training their children receive. Christian schools are a force to be reckoned with. The Education for Economic Security Act of 1984 prohibits the use of federal Magnet School funds for "any course of instruction the substance of which is secular humanism." (Secular humanism is not defined in the act.) Born-again administrators have occupied some top-level positions in the Department of Justice, Education, EPA, and the Civil Rights Commission. But the conservative agenda has not fulfilled its promise of the late 1970s.

Viewership of the electronic ministries dropped off some 10 percent between 1978 and 1980 (some say it never attracted more than a 1-percent share), and the king of televised worship has started creeping toward the political center. Falwell, after hosting archliberal Edward Kennedy on the "Old Time Gospel Hour," showed up in Miami to address rabbis at the Rabbinical Assembly convention. There, when confronted with Rabbi Marc Tanenbaum's insightful history lessons, he publicly withdrew his bid to make America a Christian nation: "I know I have been preaching the Christianization of America. I now realize that I was mistaken. . . . We are not a Christian nation. We do not want a state church. This is a pluralist society."

The mighty man from Lynchburg has allowed that abortion is a valid option if the mother's life is in jeopardy and that women are entitled to equal rights. He has even recanted his earlier segregationist stance and opened Christian schools to black children. Falwell is beginning to sound like a radical evangelical as he goes public with what his church has been doing in private: feeding the hungry, rehabilitating alcoholics and drug abusers, setting up medical and legal clinics for the poor, and dealing with environment and energy issues. The new Falwell is a product of New Right coalition politics, which demand accommodation and tolerance in a way that fundamentalism alone cannot.

It's a welcome metamorphosis. "The danger for self-righteous Christians," warns Carol Flake, author of a contemporary history of fundamentalism, "is their tendency to mistake their own intolerance for the wrath of God, to make of the Bible a bludgeon, to substitute law for love, to smite the nonconformist, to arm to the teeth and make of Armageddon a self-fulfilling prophecy."

Fundamentalism will be a factor in our future, but in a different role than today. Ed Hindson and Ed Dobson, of Liberty Baptist College, maintain that fundamentalism will prevail over left-wing evangelicalism because of its mastery of the media and concrete, image-laden "television English." However, they fail to heed the historical cycles that have always compelled fundamentalists to turn inward.

In this cycle, the reversal is being hastened by groups like People for the American Way. PFAW, spearheaded by television producer Norman Lear, is using the fundamentalists' own media tactics to reclaim patriotism for those who believe America was constituted as a pluralistic nation in which all people are free to follow their own god, free from government interference or favoritism. Joining the backlash have been a panoply of liberal groups who have adopted Viguerie's own tactics in 130 million pieces of preelection mail containing warnings about New Right abuses.

But even more toxic to right-wing fundamentalist reform is the structural centrism of American society. It usually takes a few years, but we invariably reject extremism—especially when it attempts to legislate our private behavior. In the meantime, the New Right must resolve its great ideological contradiction: how to reconcile a free market economy with government regulated morality.

Crime sits at the confluence of myriad social forces—moral discord, role conflicts, age shifts, geographic dislocations, economic movements, and technological advances. But what we define as criminal and how we respond to it is, at bottom, political. It reflects the outcome of a struggle between conflicting world views.

When we think of crime, it's almost always street crime that comes to mind. Not because it does our economy, health, and safety more damage than other kinds of offenses (it doesn't), but because those of us in the mainstream have made it a higher priority than the misdeeds of "respectable" white-collar criminals with whom we can identify. Those of us who are committed to laissez-faire economics tend not to think of the latter as criminals and resent the regulations that hamstring the operations of the free market. Those of us on the other end of the ideological continuum commiserate with the black street hustler and perceive the business criminal as an archvillain.

Then there are the other types of crimes—the ones we call "vices." Most of us wouldn't give up oral sex or penny poker games even though, in many states, we're breaking the law. Yet, others of us observe such behaviors and shrink in horror from the criminal decadence it heralds. So horrified are we that we resort to righteous violence and holy terrorism to stop it.

Crime—whether street, white collar, or vice—demands control. Our response to crime is expressed through both the formal sanctions of the criminal justice system and the informal pressures of the peer group, the school, the church, and the family. Whether the brunt of our indignation is reserved for the crooked doctor, the teenage mugger, or the corner hooker is a matter of priorities—and those priorities are set by ideology. It is in the context of a conservative-liberal battle for the national conscience that the major crimewarps will take place.

The new criminals will reflect a loss of connection with traditional structures and restraints. The decline of accountability and responsibility will produce irrational crimes among old people. The liberal drive to expand options for all social groups will promote anomie among women. While the New Right's return to an authoritarian model of family life will enhance social controls, it will contribute to domestic violence. The deterioration of social programs under conservative fiscal policies will remove many of the supports that might have deterred crime among teenagers. Juvenile criminals will be a declining presence, but the small percentage who become chronic offenders will be more dangerous. Tomorrow's normative offenders will be older, better educated, more experienced. Despite a change in the distribution of criminals, the rate of conventional crime will drop, and law and order will recede as an issue.

Recent migrations have built up the power bases of the more conservative parts of the country, but the diversity of the migrants is acting as a liberalizing force. The cataclysmic erosion of the Sunbelt's economic base will induce reverse migrations to the liberal Northeast. The new infusion of political iron to this formerly decaying region will serve as a moderating influence on national crime policies. As crime marches on, it will move to the conservative Sunbelt, invading suburbs and rural areas along the way. But our cities will become relatively more safe—despite the seething ghettoes in their midst.

The new crimes will be the kind that thrive in the deregulated atmosphere of a conservative climate. They will be less personal and more profitable. While our money and credit become more vulnerable to tampering and manipulation, our homes will be less likely crime targets. Though corporate malefaction may cause insidious health problems, our safety on the street and freedom of movement will be greatly enhanced. Ideas will be treated as property subject to stringent regulations, and work life will be dictated by security considerations. The bent toward laissez-faire crime-inducing business practices will eventually be moderated by a more sophisticated public and a powerful drive to prosecute white-collar criminals.

While technology creates new classes of white-collar crime, shifting political currents will legalize old classes of consensual crimes. A moderate public will finally reject incursions on freedom of expression and government intrusions on personal morality. We will be freer to pursue private pleasures between consenting adults—despite the growing conservatism and religiosity of the population.

Our response to crime will become tougher, but more selective, as resources shrink. In a twist of roles, the conservative influence will result in the wider casting of the government net while liberals become the champions of the individual. As we relinquish much of our privacy to computerized data banks, criminal justice efficiency will improve. Police will become more effective and impersonal, courts less crowded, prisons more exclusive. We will become more reliant on our neighbors and ourselves as a buffer against crime. The decentralization and personalization of neighborhood crime-fighting will strengthen our ties to each other. But privacy will be harder to come by. It will no longer be only big government that is watching us, but our neighbors as well.

Civil liberties will suffer—some more than others. At the federal level, court-mandated privacy and due process will be eroded by ultraconservative forces. But an increasingly middle-of-the-road Congress and more liberal state courts will more than make up for the loss. Our freedoms will be greatest where they're most meaningful—where we *live*.

Each crimewarp is made up of conflicting currents. As they tug each other toward the center, we will experience incremental changes in crime patterns. Nothing dramatic. Nothing sudden. Just a dialectical improvement of our prospects. We will live in a better-educated, better-employed, more integrated, more tolerant society. The shrinking birthrate will open up opportunities for those historically deprived of them, allowing many would-be criminals to enter the mainstream and develop a stake in the system. Street crime will decrease, abetted by changing demographics and powerful biochemical and information technologies. White-collar crimes will become easier to detect and defeat. Our personal choices for private behavior will expand. We will inherit the best of both traditions: the conservative grounding in morality, patriotism, and economic latitude; and the liberal freedom to make personal choices while maintaining a sense of responsibility, tolerance, and compassion for the larger society. As we stand at the threshold of the year 2000, there is one thing of which we can be sure: Our endemic moderateness will remain with us—reflected in our laws, our criminal justice system and our values.

Notes

The following notes contain full citations for all sources except books. Books are cited only by author's last name and, in the case of multiple listings by same author, publication date. Complete reference information for books is found in the Bibliography that follows the Notes section.

PREFACE: The Fear Wave

Parts of the Preface have been previously published in Georgette Bennett, "TV's Crime Coverage Is Too Scary and Misleading," *TV Guide*, January 5, 1985.

p. xvi VIOLENT CRIMES . . . COMMITTED MOSTLY AGAINST STRANGERS: Michael Rand, "Violent Crime by Strangers," Bureau of Justice Statistics *Bulletin*, April 1982, 1.

INTRODUCTION: The New Demographics of Crime

Parts of this chapter have been previously published in Georgette Bennett, "Crime in the Year 2000," *Virginia State Troopers Magazine*, Fall 1984.

p. 2 DROP IN VICTIMIZATION RATES SINCE 1975: "Households Touched by Crime, 1984," Bureau of Justice Statistics *Bulletin*, U.S. Department of Justice, June 1985.

p. 5   LARGE, URBAN HOUSEHOLDS MOST VULNERABLE TO CRIME: Ibid., 5.

p. 5   SELF-EMPLOYED WORKERS: U.S. Department of Justice, *Criminal Victimization 1982*, 33.

p. 8   ILL PREPARED FOR THE POST-INDUSTRIAL SOCIETY: Flake, 44. Accelerated Christian Education (ACE) is the curriculum favored by most Bible schools. When ACE students were measured on the California Assessment Program Test, their skills fell short of standards for their grade levels.

p. 8   DROPOUTS: Part of the material for this section is derived from Boyer, 239–47.

p. 11   BUSINESSMEN ARE SO OVER-REGULATED: Viguerie, 180.

p. 11   RENDER LAWS . . . MEANINGLESS . . . LEGITIMATE THE VIOLENCE . . . OF BUSINESSES: Frances Cullen et al., "Public Support for Punishing White Collar Crime: Blaming the Victim Revisited?" *Journal of Criminal Justice*, 11:6, 1983, 490–91.

p. 11   AMITAI ETZIONI: Study cited in his editorial, "Shady Corporate Practices," New York *Times*, November 15, 1985.

CRIMEWARP I: THE NEW CRIMINALS

CHAPTER 1: Women Alone

pp. 15–17   FRAN O'LEARY: Interview with author, October 25, 1979. Additional material drawn from Fran O'Leary, "Fran O'Leary Reflects on Past Life," *Fortune News*, April 1979, 6.

p. 18   UNREALISTIC EXPECTATIONS: Elizabeth Elmer, "Child Abuse and Family Stress," 62–63; Rodger Bybee, "Violence Toward Youth: A New Perspective," 7; Richard Gelles and Murray Straus, "Violence in the American Family," 30, 33. All three articles found in *Journal of Social Issues*, 35:2, 1979.

p. 18   KIND OF MOTHER . . . WE'LL BE SEEING MORE: The concept of "drift" is closely related to a sense of powerlessness. In the Introduction to Finkelhor, et al., 19, David Finkelhor makes this illuminating point about various forms of abuse: "they seem to be acts carried out by abusers to compensate for their perceived lack or loss of power. . . . Mothers resort to violence, for example, when they sense that they have lost control over their children and of their own lives."

p. 18   SHE AND HER HUSBAND ARGUED CONSTANTLY: David Ward, "Crimes of Violence By Women," in Mulvihill, Tumin, and Curtis, 883.

p. 18   SANDRA BROWN: Carey Winfrey, "White Collar Crimes by Women: Why Are They on the Rise?" New York *Times*, January 21, 1980.

p. 18   HIGH-LEVEL . . . JOB: 8 out of 1,000 figure cited by Catalyst in New York *Times*, November 25, 1984. 84 percent increase statistic from Bureau of Labor Statistics in same source.

p. 19   IMPRISONMENT RATE FOR WOMEN: Brown, Flanagan, and McLeod, 567; August 29, 1986, telephone update by Bureau of Justice Statistics.

p. 19   ROPER POLL: Ibid., 463.

p. 19   POPULATION OF THE UNITED STATES: Department of Commerce, Bureau of Census.

p. 19   ONLY 1 ARREST TO EVERY 5 ARRESTS OF MEN: Brown, Flanagan, and McLeod, 429.

p. 19   SHORTAGE OF MEN: Department of Commerce, Bureau of Census. Statistics starting with 1860 show a steady reduction in the sex ratio. The break-even point occurs in 1940 when there is a sex ratio of 100.7 men per 100 women. By 1950, the ratio has dropped to 98.6.

p. 19 MARRIAGE SQUEEZE: Guttentag and Secord, 174–79. Census tables show that the sex ratio is lowest for those who are now of marriageable age, twenty and older. For those up to nineteen years of age, the sex ratio is higher, about 104 men to 100 women. However, as Guttentag and Secord point out, when the conventional two-year age differential between marriage partners is factored in, the sex ratio drops again.

p. 19 MARRY A MAN TWO OR THREE YEARS OLDER: Ibid., 188–89.

p. 20 ONLY 81 UNMARRIED MEN FOR EVERY 100 UNMARRIED WOMEN. . . . ONE FIFTH OF WOMEN . . . HAVE NOT HAD POTENTIAL MALE PARTNER: Ibid., 17

p. 20 SKEWED DEMOGRAPHICS: Based on Department of Commerce, Bureau of Census, population projections to the year 2050.

p. 20 LITTLE INCENTIVE TO MAKE COMMITMENTS: Guttentag and Secord, 162–71.

p. 21 MAKING AN ARREST DOES MAKE A DIFFERENCE: Lawrence Sherman and Richard Berk, "The Specific Deterrent Effects of Arrest for Domestic Assault," *American Journal of Sociology*, 49:2, April 1984, 261–72.

p. 21 WOMEN LIVING ALONE: Department of Commerce, Bureau of Census.

p. 21 HOUSEHOLDS WITH NO HUSBAND PRESENT: All statistics on female-headed households taken from Bureau of Census data.

pp. 21–22 BLACK SEX RATIO: Guttentag and Secord, 201.

p. 22 ALMOST TWO BLACK WOMEN FOR EVERY MAN: Ibid.

p. 22 SELF-PERPETUATING, ESPECIALLY FOR BLACKS: For discussion of spiraling effects of low sex ratio for blacks, see Ibid., 210–11.

p. 22 BIRTHS OUT OF WEDLOCK: All statistics based on data from Bureau of Census and National Center for Health Statistics.

p. 22 DR. AARON SHIRLEY: Quoted in Nadine Brozan, "Complex Problems of Teen-Age Pregnancy," New York *Times*, March 2, 1985.

p. 22 GUTTMACHER INSTITUTE STUDY: Nadine Brozan, "Rate of Pregnancies for U.S. Teen-Agers Found High in Study," New York *Times*, March 13, 1985.

p. 23 BIRTHRATES: Department of Health and Human Services.

p. 23 INFANT MORTALITY RATES: Statistics derived from Bureau of Census and Department of Health and Human Services.

p. 23 AMERICAN BLACKS . . . THE MOST PERSISTENT AND SEVEREST SHORTAGE OF MEN: Guttentag and Secord, 199. Bureau of Census tables show shortages of black males dating back to 1860. In not one census year in all that time has the black sex ratio reached 100 men or more per 100 women. The highest point was in 1860, when the overall ratio was 99.6. The nadir was 1980, when the overall ratio dropped to 89.6. The word "overall" is important here. If the ratio were to be based only on those blacks available for marriage, it would tumble to the ratio of 73 calculated by Guttentag and Secord for the year 1970.

p. 24 JEALOUSY . . . END OF A RELATIONSHIP . . . AS MOTIVE FOR DOMESTIC VIOLENCE: G. Marie Wilt et al., "Domestic Violence and the Police," Police Foundation, 1977, 41–42.

p. 24 WOMAN SHOT HER HUSBAND . . . AFTER HE ANNOUNCED THAT HE WAS DIVORCING HER: Ward et al., 883.

p. 24 WOMEN . . . VICTIMS THREE TIMES MORE: Patsy Klaus and Michael Rand, "Family Violence," U.S. Department of Justice, Bureau of Justice Statistics, April 1984. In contradiction to the findings of Klaus and Rand and the Bureau of Justice Statistics, Gelles and Straus, 26, found that more men are physically abused by their wives than the reverse (2 million vs. 1.8 million). Both draw on self-report data bases.

BJS, however, uses victim self-reports alone, while Gelles and Straus interviewed their subjects as both victims and perpetrators.

p. 24   SIBLINGS: Klaus and Rand; also Gelles and Straus, 27.

p. 24   IN 86 PERCENT OF THE CASES: Brown, Flanagan, and McLeod, 394.

p. 24   1973 STUDY OF DOMESTIC MURDERS: Wilt et al., 9.

p. 24   SPECIAL REPORT OF NATIONAL CRIME SURVEY: Klaus and Rand, 3.

pp. 24–25   LIVING TOGETHER IS LESS DANGEROUS: Wilt et al., 30, cites findings for Kansas City study. See also Klaus and Rand, 4: "Although divorced and separated people make up on 7% of the population . . . about 75% of the spousal violence reported . . . involved persons who were divorced or separated."

p. 25   DIVORCE RATE HAS BEEN INCHING DOWNWARD: Robert Tomasson, "A Lower Divorce Rate Is Reported," New York Times, January 9, 1985. After reaching a record high of 5.3 divorces per 1,000 people, the rate declined for three straight years, reaching 4.9 per 1000 in August 1984. While the decline is considered to be significant and long-term, current levels still mean that almost half of all people marrying are getting divorced.

p. 25   WHEN WIVES KILL . . . SELF-DEFENSE: Gelles and Straus, 27. As cited in Wilt et al., 11, a Marvin Wolfgang study of 100 married couple murders found that half the victims were husbands. In Patterns of Criminal Homicide, Wolfgang developed the concept of victim-precipitated homicide. He found that about 25 percent of homicides were provoked by the victim—especially in the case of mate killings and female offenders. His findings have since been corroborated in numerous studies. In the Wilt et al. Police Foundation Detroit study, for example, the victim initiated the fatal conflict in 45.5 percent of the homicides (see p. 18).

p. 25   THEY'RE APT TO GET AWAY WITH IT: William Wilbanks, "The Female Homicide Offender in Dade County," Criminal Justice Review, 8:2, Fall 1983. See also Ward et al., 903, for profile of female homicide offender; findings show that only 1 in 11 are committed to prison.

p. 25   "BATTERED-WIFE SYNDROME" DEFENSE: Cindy Hutto case found in Steven Rittenmeyer, "Of Battered Wives, Self Defense and Double Standards of Justice," Journal of Criminal Justice, 9:5, 1981, 389. See also, N. Fiora-Gormally, "Battered Wives Who Kill—Double Standard Out of Court, Single Standard In?" Law and Human Behavior, 2:2, 1978, 133–65, for a fuller discussion of the issue.

p. 25   PMS DEFENSE: Santos case found in Nadine Brozan, "Premenstrual Syndrome: A Complex Issue," New York Times, July 12, 1982.

p. 25   REINFORCE DAMAGING STEREOTYPES: A splendid analysis of the double-edged sword of the PMS and battered-wife defenses is found in Jacoby, 213–23.

p. 25   CONFLICTS OVER SEX ROLES: Wilt et al., 19.

p. 27   VERBAL SKILLS REMAINED UNDEVELOPED: See, for example, June Andrew, "Violence and Poor Reading," Criminology, 17:3, November 1979, 361–65.

p. 27   DELINQUENCY . . . SIMILAR FOR BOYS AND GIRLS: Adler, Chapter 4; Rachelle Canter, "Sex Differences in Self-Report Delinquency," Criminology, 20:3–4, November 1982, 389; Nanci Koser Wilson, "The Masculinity of Crime—Some Second Thoughts," Journal of Criminal Justice, 9:2, 1981, 116 and 121; William Feyerherm, "Measuring Gender Differences in Delinquency: Self-Reports Versus Police Contacts," in Warren, 46–54. Feyerherm acknowledges the inconsistencies between self-reports of delinquency and arrest statistics. Self-reports generally indicate smaller male-female differences than do official records. However, he points out that self-report studies generally focus on trivial behaviors, in which male and female rates are similar.

The more serious the behaviors measured, the greater the divergence between the rates. Roy Austin, "Women's Liberation and Increases in Minor, Major, and Occupational Offenses," *Criminology*, 20:3–4, November 1982, 427, on the other hand, makes a case for the plausibility of increases in female delinquency rates. He argues that ineffective supervision by parents is one of the most important causes of delinquency. Boys have traditionally been less closely supervised than girls. Therefore, as mothers join the work force, it is girls who are most likely to be affected, with the impact being reflected in higher rates of delinquency.

p. 27   TRADITIONALLY . . . THE PROTECTION OF A MAN: Wilson, 122.

p. 27   HOMICIDE OFFENDERS . . . SINCE 1940: Ralph Weisheit, "Female Homicide Offenders: Trends Over Time in an Institutionalized Population," *Justice Quarterly*, 1:4, December 1984, 476–77.

p. 27   ROBBERY MOTIVE: Ibid., 485.

p. 27   1 OUT OF EVERY 10 VIOLENT CRIMES: Brown, Flanagan, and McLeod, 428.

pp. 27–28   GROWTH IN ADULT FEMALE VIOLENCE HAS OUTPACED THAT OF MALES: Wilson, 116. An important critique of Wilson's findings is found in Darrell Steffensmeier, "Flawed Arrest 'Rates' and Overlooked Reliability Problems in UCR Arrest Statistics: A Comment on Wilson's 'The Masculinity of Violent Crime—Some Second Thoughts,'" *Journal of Criminal Justice*, 11:2, 1983, 167–69.

p. 28   FORCIBLE RAPE: Brown, Flanagan, and McLeod, 428.

p. 28   PATRICIA JOYCE BROWN: Robert Popp, "Police Arrest Woman Suspected in 5 Holdups," San Francisco *Chronicle*, February 12, 1985.

p. 28   "M.O.": Eddyth Fortune, Manuel Vega, and Ira Silverman, "A Study of Female Robbers in a Southern Correctional Institution," *Journal of Criminal Justice*, 8:5, 1980, 323–24.

p. 28   PROFILE . . . FEMALE ROBBERS: Ibid.

p. 28   ROBBERY STATISTICS: Brown, Flanagan, and McLeod, 427; also Fortune, Vega, and Silverman, 317; August 28, 1986, telephone update by Bureau of Justice Statistics.

p. 28   43 PERCENT INCREASE IN ARRESTS: 1971–81 statistics from U.S. Department of Justice, Federal Bureau of Investigation, Uniform Crime Reports, *Crime in the United States 1980*, 195, and Brown, Flanagan, and McLeod, 430; 1960–72 statistics from Adler, 16.

p. 28   AGGRAVATED ASSAULT: 1971–81 statistics, U.S. Department of Justice, *Crime in the U.S. 1980*, 194.

pp. 28–29   ORANETTE MAYS: "Woman Is Shot After Taking Hostages on Jet," New York *Times*, January 5, 1985.

p. 29   ONE OUT OF EVERY EIGHT AGGRAVATED ASSAULTS: Brown, Flanagan, and McLeod, 427–28.

p. 29   WOMEN ARRESTED FOR MURDER: Ibid.

p. 29   NUMBER DECLINED: Ibid., 430, and U.S. Department of Justice, *Crime in the U.S. 1980*, 195.

p. 29   SIMPLE ASSAULTS: Ibid.

p. 29   HURT IS DISPLACED: Ward et al., 889.

p. 30   AN EXCESS OF CHRISTIAN ZEAL: Nicholas Hobbs quoted in Bob Frishman, "Far Right Makes a Joke of U.S. Family Week," Cleveland *Plain Dealer*, November 17, 1983.

p. 30   VIOLENCE . . . AMONG THE POOR: Gelles and Straus, 30; Klaus and Rand, 4; Finkelhor, 21.

p. 30   CHIVALRY FACTOR: Feyerherm, 47; Christy Visher, "Gender, Police Arrest Decisions, and Notions of Chivalry," 6, 10, 22 and 24; and Debra Curran, "Judicial Discretion and Defendant's Sex," 54, both in *Criminology*, 21:1, February 1983. Also, Marvin Krohn, James Curry, and Shirley Nelson-Kilger, "Is Chivalry Dead? An Analysis of Changes in Police Dispositions of Males and Females," *Criminology*, 21:3, August 1983, 418–20.

p. 31   GOING THE WAY OF THE LACE HANDKERCHIEF: Krohn, Curry, and Nelson-Kilger, 423; Candace Kruttschnitt, "Women, Crime, and Dependency: An Application of the Theory of Law," *Criminology*, 19:4, February 1982, 496–98.

p. 31   PEOPLE WHO KNOW EACH OTHER: FBI statistics for 1982 cited in Klaus and Rand, 2. In 1982, only 17 percent of reported homicides were committed by someone unknown to the victim. In another 28 percent of the murders, the relationship of the killer to the victim was unknown.

p. 31   RELUCTANT TO REPORT HAVING BEEN ON THE RECEIVING END: Maureen McLeod, "Victim Noncooperation in the Prosecution of Domestic Assaults," *Criminology*, 21:3, August 1983, 412.

p. 31   A PRIVATE MATTER: Klaus and Rand, 4.

p. 31   20 TO 34 YEAR AGE RANGE: Ibid.; also Wilt et al., 30; and Brown, Flanagan, and McLeod, 356.

p. 31   VICTIMS . . . OLDER THAN THEIR ASSAILANTS: Wilt et al., 45.

p. 31   HALF OF THE TIME, THEY END UP DEAD: Gelles and Straus, 27.

pp. 31–32   WEAPONS: Wilbanks, 13; Weisheit, 484; Wilt et al., p. 36; Ward et al., 903; and J. Sherwood Williams, Joseph Marolla and John McGrath III, "Firearms and Urban American Women," in Warren, 119–20.

p. 32   ALCOHOL: Roper survey is found in Brown, Flanagan, and McLeod, 359. Government statistics from 1971 on, found in ibid., 430 and U.S. Department of Justice, *Crime in the U.S. 1980*. One link between female drinking and violent crime is found in Williams, Marolla, and McGrath, 119–20. The authors reveal that there is a moderate correlation between overimbibing and gun ownership among women. They also report that single black urban women, living outside the South, are more likely than whites to own a gun. Alcohol and guns are present in a large percentage of homicides. Ward et al., 903, found in their study of female violence that many "had serious drinking problems"; compared to other offender categories, female killers had the "highest proportion of alcoholism." Government statistics on drunk-driving arrests also indicate a change in women's drinking habits. Since 1971, the percentage of drunk-driving arrests for women has increased at a rate three times that of men's. With the recent crackdown on that crime, the escalation will appear even steeper.

p. 32   BLACK/WHITE VICTIMIZATION RATES: Klaus and Rand, 4.

p. 32   WOMEN'S MOVEMENT: Adler quote from Tom Buckley, "Critics Assail Linking Feminism With Women in Crime," New York *Times*, March 14, 1976. One of the foremost critics of that linking is Darrell Steffensmeier in, for example, "Crime and the Contemporary Woman: Analysis of Changing Levels of Female Property Crime, 1960–1975," *Social Forces*, 57:2, December 1978, 566–84.

p. 33   INCREASE IN ARRESTS: U.S. Department of Justice, *Crime in the U.S. 1980*, 195; Brown, Flanagan, and McLeod, 430.

p. 33   TRADITIONAL CRIMES: Steffensmeier, 1978, 578–80.

p. 33   FEMINIZATION OF POVERTY: Statistics from Bureau of Census.

p. 33   FAMILIES MAINTAINED BY WOMEN: Ibid. Also see, for example, Robert Pear, "Rate of Poverty Found to Persist In Face of Gains," New York *Times*, August 3, 1984.

p. 33   CONGRESSIONAL BUDGET OFFICE ANALYSIS: *National NOW Times*, January/February 1985.

pp. 33–34   VIRGINIA AGOSTO: Jane Gross, "Cruel Odyssey of the Homeless Seeking a Bed," January 16, 1985.

p. 34   NEW YORK: Dropout rate, white-collar job statistics, etc. found in Joyce Purnick, "Poverty Worsening in City, Study Finds," New York *Times*, December 16, 1984.

p. 34   WOMEN'S INCOMES: Bureau of Census figures cited in, "Wage discrimination: the 40-cent ripoff," *National NOW Times*, January/February 1985; "Women Face Job Bias," New York *Times*, November 25, 1984.

pp. 34–35   KITT TAFT: Neal Pierce, "Women Fight Poverty With Entrepreneurship," *Public Administration Times*, January 1, 1985.

p. 35   WISCONSIN WELFARE STUDY: "Welfare Stereotype Termed Inaccurate," *Public Administration Times*, January 1, 1985.

p. 35   MARRIED-COUPLE FAMILIES . . . LABOR FORCE: Bureau of Census data on family characteristics.

p. 35   FEMALE WORKERS IN VARIOUS WORK CATEGORIES: Bureau of Labor Statistics.

p. 35   *McCall's* SURVEY: Susan Jacoby, "How 40,000 Women Feel About Their Jobs," *McCall's*, January 1985, 69.

p. 35   GROWING . . . SERVICE SECTOR: William Serrin, "Jobs Increase in Number, But Trends Are Said to Be Leaving Many Behind," New York *Times*, October 15, 1984.

p. 35   5.5 MILLION NEW JOBS . . . SERVICE SECTOR: Ibid. This figure represents job growth since 1979.

p. 35   SERVICE SECTOR POSITIONS HELD MOSTLY BY WOMEN: U.S. Department of Labor Statistics in *National NOW Times*, January/February 1985; New York *Times*, November 25, 1984.

p. 35   10 MILLION FAMILIES WHO DEPEND ON WOMEN: Bureau of Census.

p. 35   FINANCIAL INSTITUTIONS: U.S. Department of Commerce, 1977, 59.

pp. 35–36   HOSPITALS: Ibid., 67–68.

p. 36   HOTELS AND MOTELS: Ibid., 81.

p. 36   PROPERTY AND CASUALTY INSURANCE INDUSTRY: Ibid., 87.

p. 36   RETAIL STORES: Dwight Merriam, "Employee Theft," *Criminal Justice Abstracts*, September 1977, 383. "The elimination of employee theft could increase profit and dividends by 50 percent." Also, U.S. Department of Commerce, 1975, 5.

p. 36   BETWEEN 40 AND 75 PERCENT OF EMPLOYEES STEAL: U.S. Department of Commerce, 1977, 101; and Merriam, 384.

p. 36   TWO-THIRDS OF ALL NEW JOBS . . . SINCE 1979: Serrin.

p. 36   70 BY THE END OF THIS DECADE: New York *Times*, November 25, 1984.

p. 36   ECONOMIC NEED IS THE DRIVING FORCE: Merriam, 390–91.

pp. 36–37   EMBEZZLEMENT ARRESTS OF WOMEN: Adler, 16; U.S. Department of Justice, *Crime in the U.S. 1980*, 195; and Brown, Flanagan, and McLeod, 430; August 28, 1986, telephone update by Bureau of Justice Statistics.

p. 37   IF THIS TREND CONTINUES: Rita Simon quoted in Imogene Moyer, "Demeanor, Sex and Race in Police Processing," *Journal of Criminal Justice*, 9:1, 1981, 236.

p. 37   SOME WOMEN COMMITTED VIOLENT OFFENSES: Rita Simon quoted in Gest.

p. 38   THE POPULATION IS AGING: While it is likely that female violent crime will diminish with aging, there is evidence that age does not impact on female economic crime. For example, Nancy Jurik, "The Economics of Female Recidivism," *Criminology*, 21:4, November 1983, 618, reports that age did not reduce the rearrest rate of a female study population in Georgia and Texas. Also, the study of female robbers reported by

Fortune, Vega, and Silverman, 323, showed them to be somewhat older than their male counterparts. White females were older than blacks, indicating that they may have started their criminal careers at a later age.

p. 38   NEW POLICE PRACTICES: Arrests of wife-beaters have been shown to have a power-ful deterrent effect on future batterings. See Sherman and Berk, 261–72; and Richard Berk and Phyllis Newton, "Does Arrest Really Deter Wife Battery? An Effort to Replicate the Findings of the Minneapolis Spouse Abuse Experiment," *American Sociological Review,* 50:2, 253–62.

p. 38   ENGRAINED CULTURAL NORMS: Gelles and Straus, 34.

p. 38   REMOVE ASSAILANTS FROM THE SCENE: See, for example, William Greer, "City Police Have Changed Their Approach to Family Disputes," New York *Times,* March 25, 1985.

p. 38   HALF OF U.S. COUPLES COULD NOT HAVE BABIES: New York *Times,* February 11, 1985.

p. 39   WOMEN IN PROFESSIONAL, TECHNICAL, MANAGERIAL AND ADMINISTRATIVE: Growth since 1972 cited in Serrin.

CHAPTER 2: Terrible Teens

pp. 40–41   GEORGE CLANCY STORY: From John Conrad, "The Importance of Being George: Unanswered Questions About the Dangerous Juvenile Offender," in Conrad and Dinitz, 13–20.

p. 41   GARY LAUWERS, RICHARD KASSO STORY: New York *Times,* December 27, 1984, and April 10, 1985; and New York *Post,* July 6 and 9, 1984, and April 10, 1985.

p. 42   YOUNGEST DEATH-ROW INMATE: As of this writing, thirty out of twelve hundred capital convicts were juveniles at the time of their conviction. "Death Row Juveniles," *The Lipman Report,* August 15, 1984.

p. 44   VIOLENT CRIMES: Brown, Flanagan, and McLeod, 422; also U.S. Department of Justice, *Criminal Victimization 1973,* 84 and 86; and *Criminal Victimization 1982,* 47, 50.

p. 44   FIVE TO SIX TIMES MORE VIOLENT CRIMES THAN THE PREVIOUS GENERATION: Marvin Wolfgang interview with author, August 3, 1983.

p. 44   BULK OF TODAY'S CRIMINALS . . . 14 TO 24 YEARS OF AGE: Brown, Flanagan, and McLeod, 422–23, 426.

p. 44   MATURED OUT OF CRIME: A landmark study sponsored by the U.S. Department of Justice, National Institute for Juvenile Justice Delinquency Prevention, "Assessing the Relationship of Adult Criminal Careers to Juvenile Careers," and conducted by Lyle Shannon between 1974 and 1980, concludes: "Much of the concern about juvenile delinquency has been based on the premise that it leads to adult crime. . . . The few who continue to have police contacts . . . are those who become well known to the adult justice system and thus create an impression of continuity and increasing serious-ness in delinquent criminal careers." Shannon finds the normative pattern to be one of decreasing seriousness, ending after the teen years. It is only in the inner city area of his study site, Racine, Wisconsin, that he found a continuity between juvenile and adult crime—but only among half of a small hard-core group of chronic youthful offenders.

p. 44   PROFESSIONAL CRIMINALS: "Why Crime's Rapid Rise May Be Over," *U.S. News & World Report,* May 2, 1983, 41; author interview with Wolfgang; and Silberman, 49–51. See also Hamparian, 1978; and Shannon, above.

pp. 44–45   BERNHARD GOETZ'S ANTAGONISTS' CRIMINAL HISTORIES: Selwyn Raab, "4 Youths Shot by Goetz Faced Criminal Counts," New York *Times*, January 10, 1985.

p. 47   CLAUDE BROWN: "Manchild in Harlem," *The New York Times Magazine*, September 16, 1984, 40.

p. 47   PERSISTENTLY VIOLENT: Ibid., 38.

p. 47   OBTAINS THE BIGGEST GUN HE CAN FIND: Ibid., 54.

p. 48   GWYNN NETTLER: Nettler, 58.

p. 48   PUERTO RICANS AND CHICANOS: Silberman, 117–23.

p. 48   REPRODUCTIVE PRACTICES: Nettler, 82–90.

p. 49   QUESTIONABLY NURTURED CHILDREN: In 1965, when the controversial Moynihan Report was released, such assertions were considered racist and the subject of reproductive habits was avoided. Since that time, however, the problem has escalated. Black leadership organizations such as the National Urban League, Children's Defense Fund, and National Council of Negro Women have taken up the gauntlet and made reconstruction of the black family a top priority.

p. 49   MY GENERATION . . . INSTRUCTED NEVER TO CARRY A WEAPON LARGER THAN A .38: Brown, 54.

p. 49   *Psychopaths:* Harrington, 15.

p. 50   OVERALL BIRTH RATES . . . ILLEGITIMATE BIRTHS . . . BIRTHS TO WOMEN UNDER THE AGE OF 19: Bureau of Census.

p. 50   UNSUITED TO . . . THE CIVIL LIFE: Nettler, 79, 96.

p. 50   BLACKS PREY ON WHITES ABOUT TWICE AS OFTEN: U.S. Department of Justice, *Criminal Victimization 1982*, 49; *Criminal Victimization 1973*, 86.

p. 50   BLACKS HAVE VICTIMIZED OTHER BLACKS: Ibid. Also, Homer Broome, "Black on Black Homicide—Our Male Youth!" in Lee Brown (ed.), *Violent Crime: Who Are the Victims?* A symposium sponsored by the National Organization of Black Law Enforcement Executives, 1981, 33–35.

p. 50   SCARED STRAIGHT: For one evaluation, see Finkenauer.

p. 51   *U.S. Attorney General's Task Force Report on Violent Crime:* Excerpted in Needle and Stapleton, Appendix E, 71.

p. 51   L.A. GANGS: Judith Cummings, "Increase in Gang Killings on Coast Is Traced to Narcotics Trafficking," New York *Times*, October 28, 1984; and Nicole Simmons, "School Security Directors Confer on Crime, Gangs and Legal Issues," New York *Times*, July 10, 1984.

p. 51   HISPANICS IN CHICAGO: E. R. Shipp, "Chicago's Hispanic Parents Protest 70% Dropout Rate," New York *Times*, March 28, 1984; and "Chicago Police Initiate Community Gang Program," *Crime Control Digest*, March 25, 1984, 5.

p. 51   CHICAGO'S BLACK NEIGHBORHOODS: E. R. Shipp, "The Killing of a Student Athlete: A Story of 3 Chicago Families," New York *Times*, December 3, 1984.

pp. 51–52   SPRINGING UP IN ALL KINDS OF PLACES THAT YOU WOULDN'T EXPECT: Michael Bosc, et al., "Street Gangs No Longer Just a Big-City Problem," *U.S. News & World Report*, July 16, 1984; Needle and Stapleton, 6, 11. It should be noted that the most vicious of the gangs are the Big Four motorcycle gangs. The Bandidos, Hell's Angels, Pagans, and Outlaws are sophisticated organized crime networks that have taken over the amphetamine industry. With 8,000 gang members supported by 4,000 fringe members and 8,000 female associates, "these gangs are the largest and most well-armed criminal organization in the country," says Phillip McGuire of the Bureau of Alcohol, Tobacco and Firearms. But these are not kids, and you're not likely to encounter them on a streetcorner in Peoria.

p. 52   MULTIPLE-OFFENDER VIOLENT CRIMES: U.S. Department of Justice, *Criminal Victimization 1982*, 50–51, and *1973*, 86–87; August 28, 1986, telephone update by Bureau of Justice Statistics.

p. 52   60 DEPARTMENTS RESPONDING TO NATIONAL SURVEY: Needle and Stapleton.

p. 52   VIOLENT CRIMES INSIDE SCHOOLS: U.S. Department of Justice, *Criminal Victimization 1982*, 54; *1973*, 93.

p. 52   DISCRETION IN METING OUT PUNISHMENTS: Herbert Koppel, "Sentencing Practices in 13 States," U.S. Department of Justice, Bureau of Justice Statistics Special Report, October 1984, 1–2.

p. 53   JUVENILES TRIED IN ADULT COURTS: Donna Hamparian et al., Chapter 1.

p. 53   MARVIN WOLFGANG: "Delinquency in Two Birth Cohorts—Executive Summary," U.S. Department of Justice, Office of Juvenile Justice and Delinquency Prevention, September 1985, 7.

CHAPTER 3: Geriatric Delinquents

p. 55   ONION ROLL MURDER: Fred Cohen, "Old Age as a Criminal Defense," in Newman et al., 115.

p. 55   DOMESTIC HOMICIDE: William Wilbanks and Dennis Murphy, "The Elderly Homicide Offender," in Newman et al., 85.

p. 55   ELDERLY ASSAILANTS: Ibid., 84–85.

p. 56   WILL NEVER BE MAJOR FACTOR IN STREET CRIME: In 1981, even after years of increases in elderly arrest rates, old people still made up only 4 percent of total arrestees. Brown, Flanagan, and McLeod, 426.

pp. 56–57   DETECTIVE FRED TAYLOR: Interview with author, January 14, 1985.

pp. 56–57   FORREST SILVA TUCKER: "Florida's Over-the-Hill Gang Foiled in Jailbreak Attempt," *Crime Control Digest*, April 2, 1984, 5.

p. 57   GROWING FORCE IN SERIOUS CRIME: FBI statistics from 1966–80 show elderly increases in murder, rape, and larceny ranging from 202 to 355 percent. There were large increases in robbery, aggravated assault, and burglary as well. In these cases, however, the rate of elderly growth in the population outstripped the rate of growth of arrests for these crimes. Most minor crimes, on the other hand, showed substantial decreases in the same time period. David Shichor, "The Extent and Nature of Lawbreaking by the Elderly: A Review of Arrest Statistics," in Newman et al., 23–25.

p. 58   REDEFINING MORALITY . . . : Gary Feinberg interview with author, January 16, 1985.

p. 58   LIVING ANOTHER SIXTEEN YEARS: National Center for Health Statistics and Bureau of Census.

p. 58   GRAY YEARS AREN'T SO BLEAK AFTER ALL: Louis Harris and Associates, poll conducted for National Council on the Aging, June 15–July 31, 1981.

p. 58   GOOD OR EXCELLENT HEALTH: Roper Organization Survey, January 9–23, 1982.

p. 58   LEAST FREQUENT VICTIMS OF STREET CRIME: Brown, Flanagan, and McLeod, 329.

p. 58   THE "WELLDERLY": "How Poorly Off Are the Elderly?" *Time*, December 14, 1981, 37.

p. 59   INDEPENDENT ELDERLY: Barry Robinson, "Aging Children, Elderly Parents—And the Challenges of Growing Old Together," *Information Please Almanac 1985*, 333.

p. 59   ELLIOT STERN: Interview with Gary Phillips, January 14, 1985.

p. 59   GERIATRIC INEQUALITY . . . MEDIAN INCOMES: *Time* and Department of Commerce, Bureau of Census.

p. 60   LABOR FORCE PARTICIPATION: Department of Commerce, Bureau of Census.

p. 60   DOROTHY ROBINSON: Jane Gross, "Cruel Odyssey of the Homeless Seeking a Bed," New York *Times*, January 16, 1985.

p. 60   OLDER WOMEN LIVE ALONE: Bureau of Census.

p. 60   HEADING SOUTH: Robinson, 333. A good analysis of old-age migration patterns is found in Albert Chevan and Lucy Rose Fischer, "Retirement and Interstate Migration," *Social Forces*, 57:4, June 1979, 1365–80.

p. 60   LARGEST GERIATRIC POPULATIONS: Department of Commerce, Bureau of Census, *Current Population Reports*, May 1984.

p. 61   FLORIDA: Gary Feinberg, "Profile of Elderly Shoplifters," in Newman et al., 36–37.

p. 61   DADE COUNTY: "Geriatric Delinquency," *The Lipman Report*, April 15, 1983.

p. 61   FLORIDA'S ELDERLY THIEVES: Gary Feinberg, Sidney Glugover, and Irene Zwetchkenbaum, "The Broward County Senior Intervention Program," in Newman et al., 178 and 185; and Gary Feinberg, "Profile of the Elderly Shoplifter," ibid., 37–46.

p. 61   MORE AFFLUENT THAN MOST: Gary Feinberg interview with author, January 16, 1985.

p. 61   STEREOTYPES ABOUT OLDER LARCENISTS: Feinberg in Newman et al.

p. 62   DRIFT: "Drift" is a theory of juvenile crime developed by Matza, 28. "The delinquent exists in limbo between convention and crime, responding in terms of the demands of each . . . postponing commitment, evading decision. Thus, he drifts between criminal and conventional action." Matza theorizes that youngsters' delinquent behavior is effectively neutralized by the criminal justice system and other social control agencies that fail to attribute responsibility to the juvenile for his acts. In many ways, this parallels the response to geriatric delinquents who are either diverted from criminal processing prior to arrest or excused for their misconduct on the basis of age. Like Matza's juvenile delinquents, elderly criminals tend to drift between conventional and criminal acts.

p. 62   NATIONWIDE SURVEY OF ELDERLY PRISON INMATES: Ann Goetting, "The Elderly in Prison: A Profile," *Criminal Justice Review*, 9:2, Fall 1984, 15, 21.

p. 62   MARTHA TOZER: "Elderly Man Held in Killing," New York *Times*, February 20, 1985.

p. 62   PRESCRIPTIONS: Irving Molotsky, "Changing Patterns in Prescriptions in U.S.," New York *Times*, March 16, 1985.

p. 63   CONNECTICUT WOMAN: Cohen, 114.

p. 63   GUNS: Wilbanks and Murphy, 88.

pp. 63–64   SEXUAL ASSAULTS: Stephen Hucker, "Psychiatric Aspects of Crime in Old Age," in Newman et al., 75.

p. 64   JOAN GAGE . . . HER AGING FATHER: Joan Gage, "When Age Does Not Come Gently," New York *Times*, January 10, 1985.

pp. 64–65   MENTAL INSTITUTIONS: Material in this section comes from research for, as well as actual text of, Georgette Bennett, "Psycho City," *New York Daily News Sunday Magazine*, July 20, 1980.

p. 65   PSYCHIATRIC ASPECTS OF OLDER SEX OFFENDERS AND VIOLENT CRIMINALS: Hucker, 73.

p. 65   CON MAN, SWINDLER, CROOKED BUSINESSPERSON, MAFIA DON: Donald Newman, "Elderly Offenders and American Crime Patterns," in Newman et al., 8–12.

p. 65   UNDERWORLD LEGENDS: Fried; and Newman, 9.

p. 66   CONVICTION OF EIGHTY-TWO-YEAR-OLD INSURANCE ADJUSTER: Transcript of indictment, United States District Court, Southern District of New York, *United States of America vs. Bernard Gold, Istvan Mak, and Balint Szilagyi,* December 14, 1983.

p. 66 RICO STATUTE: "Outline of RICO Conviction, *United States v. Bernard Gold,*" press release, U.S. attorney, Southern District of New York, November 5, 1984. The Racketeering Influenced and Corrupt Organizations (RICO) statute is a device developed by the federal government to prosecute organized crime figures, who have frequently been immune to other charges, via tracking their illegal profits. This is often the only way to develop effective evidence in such cases and also allows the government to confiscate the proceeds from illegal activities, thus eliminating much of the incentive for committing major crimes. Originally designed to pursue high-level narcotics dealers, it has since been expanded to prosecute white-collar criminals as well.

p. 66 IF HE WERE A YOUNGER MAN: Transcript of sentencing, United States District Court, Southern District of New York, *United States of America vs. Bernard Gold,* January 15, 1985.

p. 67 CRIMES OF THE AGED UNDERREPORTED: Charles Cutshall and Kenneth Adams, "Responding to Older Offenders: Age Selectivity in the Processing of Shoplifters," *Criminal Justice Review,* 8:2, Fall 1983, 7. Tables in Brown, Flanagan, and McLeod, 307, show three quarters of all household larcenies and half of all assaults never come to the attention of police—including those committed by the elderly.

p. 67 SHOPLIFTING: McGarrell and Flanagan, 431.

p. 67 AGGRESSIVE PROSECUTION POLICIES: James Fyfe, "Police Dilemmas in Processing Elderly Offenders," in Newman et al., 101.

p. 67 DOMESTIC VIOLENCE: Ibid, 102–4.

p. 67 WHAT DO WE DO NOW? SET HIGH BAIL?: Cohen, 115.

p. 68 INCARCERATED BY HIS OWN ILLNESS: U.S. Southern District sentencing transcript, *U.S.A. vs. Bernard Gold,* 8.

p. 68 SPECIAL FACILITIES FOR AGED CONVICTS: Ann Goetting, "Prison Programs and Facilities for Elderly Inmates," in Newman et al., 170.

p. 68 MOST OF PRISON ELDERLY ARE THERE FOR VIOLENT CRIMES: Fran Teller and Robert Howell, "The Older Prisoner," *Criminology,* 18:4, February 1981, 549–54.

p. 68 DOCILE IN PRISON: Goetting, 1984, 20–21.

p. 68 SEGREGATED PRISONS: Ibid., 14; and Brown, Flanagan, and McLeod, 567.

pp. 68–69 BROWARD SENIOR INTERVENTION AND EDUCATION PROGRAM: Feinberg, Glugover, and Zwetchkenbaum, 177–90.

p. 69 DOROTHY ROBINSON AND FREDERICK EDWARDS STORY: Gross.

p. 70 COMMUNITY SERVICE JOBS: Jarold Kieffer, "Longer Worklives: A Strategic Policy Reversal Needed," *Public Administration Review,* 4:5, September/October 1984, 437.

p. 70 PAT CHOATE: quoted in Gloria Whitman, Roger Vaughan, and Arthur Boyd, "Creating Opportunity: Strategies for Increasing Economic Self-Sufficiency for Older Americans," *Public Administration Review,* 4:5, September/October 1984, 439.

p. 70 ADMINISTRATION ON AGING PROJECT: Ibid., 441–42.

p. 70 EMPLOYEE THEFT: The elderly have lower rates of theft and other counterproductive behaviors. From findings of National Institute of Justice study, "Theft of Employees in the Work Organization," cited in "Employee Benefit Abuse Exceeds $5 Billion," *Public Administration Times,* July 1, 1983.

p. 70 PRESENT AND FUTURE COHORTS OF OLD PEOPLE: Peter Uhlenberg, "Changing Structure of Older U.S. Population During the 20th Century," *The Gerontologist,* 17:3, June 1977.

CRIMEWARP II: THE MARCH OF CRIME

p. 73   LAFAYETTE . . . NEW YORK: "Dramatic Population Changes Reported," New York *Times*, May 19, 1984; U.S. Department of Justice, *Crime in the U.S. 1982*, 361, 366 and *Crime in the U.S. 1980*, 71, 76.

CHAPTER 4: New Megatropolises

pp. 75–76   HOUSTON: Case material drawn from reporting by Robert Reinhold for New York *Times*, "Houston Grapples With an Era of Dimmer Hopes," September 2, 1984; "The Great Oil Era Ends in Texas," September 16, 1984; "Texas Scrambles for Revenue as Oil Glut Cuts State Funds," May 22, 1985; "Rise in Bar Killings Angers Houston Hispanic Districts," May 7, 1985; also "Goodbye Gritty City—Hello Urban Utopia," *U.S. News & World Report*, May 9, 1983; and 1970 and 1980 census data.

p. 76   MALVERN: Case material based on William Stevens, "Philadelphia Pins Hopes for Economic Growth on New High Tech Corridor," New York *Times*, May 31, 1985.

pp. 76–77   PHILADELPHIA STATISTICS: 1970 and 1980 Census data; John Herbers, "Sun Belt Cities Prosper as Those in North Decline," New York *Times*, February 28, 1983; Peter Kilborn, "New York Home Prices Surge," New York *Times*, May 24, 1985; William Frey, "Lifecourse Migration of Metropolitan Whites and Blacks and the Structure of Demographic Change in Large Central Cities," *American Sociological Review*, 49:6, 815–16, 819; U.S. Department of Justice, *Crime in the U.S. 1981, 1984*.

p. 78   MIGRATE . . . UNDER 35: Frey, 805; Robert Crutchfield, Michael Geerken, and Walter Gove, "Crime Rate and Social Integration: The Impact of Metropolitan Mobility," *Criminology*, 20:3–4, November 1982, 474.

p. 79   HISPANIC FAMILIES: Data drawn from 1980 Census.

p. 79   ROMAN MARTINEZ AND RAUL CORREA QUOTE: Reinhold, May 7, 1985.

p. 80   LIBERTY CITY AND CUBAN REFUGEES: Section based on Philip Taft, Jr., "Policing the New Immigrant Ghettoes," *Police Magazine*, July 1982, 10–27; Bruce Porter and Marvin Dunn, "Under Siege in an Urban Ghetto," *Police Magazine*, July 1981, 25–46; John Katzenbach, "Overwhelmed in Miami," *Police Magazine*, September 1980, 6–16; Rafael San Juan, "Cuban Refugees Find America Offers Both Hope and Despair," *Heritage*, VI:1, October 1982, 5 and 12.

p. 80   HISPANICS . . . BEHIND BARS: U.S. Department of Justice, *Report to the Nation*, 31.

p. 81   ORIENTAL GANGS: Material based on Taft, Jr., 10–27; and Greg Gross, "The Vietnamese Crime Network," *The National Centurion*, November 1983, 23–28; William Greer, "Chinatown Youth Arrested in Shootings That Injured 7," New York *Times*, May 25, 1985; Fox Butterfield, "Chinese Organized Crime Said to Rise in U.S.," New York *Times*, January 13, 1985, and "The Shifting Picture of Crime by U.S. Vietnamese," New York *Times*, January 21, 1985.

pp. 81–82   WESTMINSTER POLICE SERGEANT: quoted in Gross, 25.

p. 82   88,000 IN THE 1970S TO 220,000 IN THE EARLY 1980S: Lena Williams, "To Blacks, the Suburbs Prove Both Pleasant and Troubling," New York *Times*, May 20, 1985.

p. 83   BLACKS . . . LARGEST DROP IN VICTIMIZATION RATES: U.S. Department of Justice, *Crime in the U.S. 1973, 1982*.

p. 83   BLACK SUBURBS: John Logan and Mark Schneider, "The Stratification of Metropolitan Suburbs, 1960–1970," *American Sociological Review*, 46:2, April 1981, 175–

86; John Herbers, "Census Data Reveal 70's Legacy: Poorer Cities and Richer Suburbs," New York *Times*, February 27, 1983; John Herbers, February 28, 1983.

pp. 83–84   DENSITY: David Shichor, David Decker, and Robert O'Brien, "Population Density and Criminal Victimization," *Criminology*, 17:2, August 1979, 189; Robert Sampson, "Structural Density and Criminal Victimization," *Criminology*, 21:2, May 1983, 278, 281.

p. 85   BLACK FAMILY DATA: Based on 1980 Census.

pp. 85–86   BLACK/WHITE MIGRATION: Frey, 804, 825.

p. 86   SOUTHERN BLACKS: Crutchfield, 474; William Doerner, "Violence and Southernness: Three Views," *Criminology*, 16:1, May 1978, 53.

p. 86   ELEANOR HOLMES NORTON: "Restoring the Traditional Black Family," *New York Times Magazine*, June 2, 1985, 93.

pp. 86–87   MIGRATING HISPANICS . . . HOUSEHOLD AND PERSONAL THEFTS: U.S. Department of Justice, *Report to the Nation*, 19–20.

p. 87   MIDDLE CLASS MIGRANTS . . . SUBURBS: U.S. Department of Justice, *Crime in the U.S. 1982*.

p. 87   SUNBELT STATES . . . SOUTH TAKES PRECEDENCE FOR VIOLENCE . . . WEST PREVAILS IN PROPERTY CRIMES: Regional and state crime statistics in ibid.; and ibid. *1984*.

p. 87   CHILD ABUSE . . . IN THE SOUTH: American Humane Association.

p. 87   OWN A GUN . . . DISAPPROVE OF GUN CONTROL: Wright, Rossi and Daly, 122.

p. 87   LOW INCOME . . . VIOLENCE: Kirk Williams, "Economic Sources of Homicide: Reestimating the Effects of Poverty and Inequality," *American Sociological Review*, 49:2, April 1984, 283–84, 288; Steven Messner, "Regional Differences in the Economic Correlates of the Urban Homicide Rate," *Criminology*, 21:4, November 1983, 480–81.

p. 87–88   SOUTHERNERS, PREFERRING FEWER CHILDREN: Changing Patterns of Fertility in the South: A Socio-Demographic Examination," *Social Forces*, 57:2, December 1978, 631, 633.

p. 88   BIRTH/DEATH RATIOS: "Population Losses Forecast in North," New York *Times*, October 16, 1984.

p. 89   NATIONAL OPINION RESEARCH CENTER: Combined findings from 1980, 1983, and 1984 General Social Surveys.

p. 89   ELDERLY MIGRATION PATTERNS: Albert Chevan and Lucy Rose Fischer, "Retirement and Interstate Migration," *Social Forces*, 57:4, June 1979, 1365–80; Kevin Fitzpatrick and John Logan, "The Aging of the Suburbs, 1960–1980," *American Sociological Review*, 50:1, February 1985, 106–17.

p. 89   CRIME AND THE ELDERLY: Hochstedler, 1981.

CHAPTER 5: Promised Lands

CASE EXAMPLES OF FARM PROBLEMS AND RURAL CRIME: Some material and quotes provided by Michael Joseloff of the MacNeil/Lehrer NewsHour; interviews of author with Joan Blundall of the Northwest Iowa Mental Health Center in Spencer and Father Norman White, director for rural life for the Archdiocese of Dubuque; interview by author with, and legal documents provided by, Tam Ormiston, assistant attorney general in charge of the Farm Division, for the state of Iowa; and Charles Swanson, "Rural and Agricultural Crime," *Journal of Criminal Justice*, 9:1, 1981, 19–29.

p. 92 RURAL LAND VALUES: "Value of Farmland Makes a Steep 12% Drop," New York *Times*, June 12, 1985.

p. 96 SOME HAVE CRIMINAL RECORDS: Swanson, 20.

p. 96 FEWER THAN ONE-TENTH . . . CALL THEMSELVES FARMERS: Beverly Cigler, "Small City and Rural Governance: The Changing Environment," *Public Administration Review*, November/December 1984, 540.

p. 98 RURAL CRIME STATISTICS AND PATTERNS: National Crime Surveys; FBI Uniform Crime Reports; John Laub, "Patterns of Offending in Rural and Urban Areas," *Journal of Criminal Justice*, 11:2, 1983, 129–39; Brent Smith and C. Ronald Huff, "Crime in the Country," *Journal of Criminal Justice*, 10:4, 1982, 271–81; Robert Lyerly and James Skipper, Jr., "Differential Rates of Rural-Urban Delinquency," *Criminology*, 19:3, November 1981, 385–99; John Herbers, "Growth in Rural Regions Brings Rapid Crime Rise," New York *Times*, November 4, 1979.

p. 99 RUSTIFICATION OF AMERICA: Frank Bryan, "Rural Renaissance: Is America On the Move Again?" *Public Opinion*, June/July 1982, 19.

p. 99 NEIGHBORLINESS: Ibid., 18.

p. 99 TOLERATE A BROADER RANGE OF BEHAVIORS: Thomas Wilson, "Urbanism and Tolerance," *American Sociological Review*, 50:1, February 1985, 122.

p. 99 BOOMTOWNS: Based on material from Philip Taft, Jr., "Keeping the Peace in the New Wild West," *Police Magazine*, July 1981, 8–17; William Freudenburg, "Boomtown's Youth: The Differential Impacts of Rapid Community Growth on Adolescents and Adults," *American Sociological Review*, 49:5, October 1984, 697–705; and Iver Peterson, "Wyoming Acts to Quell Boom-Time Upheavals," New York *Times*, March 12, 1985.

p. 101 AMONG THOSE WORKING IN THE PRIVATE SECTOR: U.S. Department of Justice, *Criminal Victimization 1983*, 33.

CRIMEWARP III: RING AROUND THE WHITE COLLAR

p. 103 ALBERT ARBURY: Brian Flanigan, "Ex-banker Admits $1.1 Million Theft," Detroit *Free Press*, May 4, 1983.

pp. 103–4 TO COVER EXPENSES OF ENTERPRISES: James Sterngold, "Tennessee Banker Is Given 20-Year Jail Term," New York *Times*, June 4, 1985.

p. 104 JACK DONNELLY GRAY: Robert Hershey, "Banker, Guilty on Loan, Is Assessed $516,235," New York *Times*, April 9, 1985.

p. 104 BANKS LOSE EIGHT TIMES MORE MONEY: U.S. Department of Commerce, 1977, 59.

p. 104 WHITE-COLLAR ARRESTS: U.S. Department of Justice, *Crime in the U.S. 1982*, 170–71.

p. 104 30 PERCENT OF CASE FILINGS: Brown, Flanagan, and McLeod, 495.

p. 104 FIVE TIMES THE NUMBER OF DEATHS CAUSED BY STREET CRIMINALS: Pepinsky and Jesilow, 15.

p. 105 BUSINESS FLOPS HAVE MORE THAN TRIPLED: Insurance Information Institute, 1984, 92; Small Business Administration, 11–13.

p. 105 SMALL BUSINESS STATISTICS: Chelimsky et al., 5; Small Business Administration.

p. 105 THREE-QUARTERS . . . BECOME THIEVES WITHIN FIVE YEARS: Dwight Merriam, "Employee Theft," *Criminal Justice Abstracts*, September 1977, 384.

pp. 105–6 RALPH NADER: Quote taken from his article, "America's Crime Without Criminals," New York *Times*, May 19, 1985.

p. 106   R. H. TAWNEY: Quoted in Geis and Meier, 5.

p. 106   U.S. SECRET SERVICE CASES: Brown, Flanagan, and McLeod, 530.

p. 106   SECURITIES AND EXCHANGE COMMISSION: Ibid., 527.

p. 106   FEDERAL COURTS . . . OFFICIALS: Ibid., 523.

p. 106   CRIMINAL ANTITRUST SUITS: Ibid., 526.

p. 106   U.S. POSTAL SERVICE: Ibid., 524.

CHAPTER 6: The Computer Catastrophe

p. 107   JANET BLAIR: Bruce Goldstein, "Electronic Fraud: The Crime of the Future," *The Police Chief*, June 1983, 50.

p. 107   3 MILLION WORKERS: Bureau of Labor Statistics.

p. 108   ROBERT MARR: Vin McLellan, "Of Trojan Horses, Data Diddling, and Logic Bombs," *Inc.*, June 1984.

p. 108   NUMBER OF COMPUTERS IN USE: Ibid., 104; and John Cira, "The Silicon Pry Bar," *The Police Chief*, September 1984, 46.

p. 109   PAYCHEX: Andrew Pollack, "Computer Disaster: Business Seeks Antidote," New York *Times*, August 24, 1983.

p. 109   APPETITE WILL GROW AT LEAST TENFOLD: The federal government is currently operating 18,000 medium and large computers at 4,500 sites. In David Burnham, "Computer Fraud in U.S. Agencies Put at Level Above 172 Cases," New York *Times*, October 27, 1983, Joseph P. Wright of the Office of Management and Budget was cited as predicting that, by the end of the decade, there would be 25,000 big computers and 250,000 to 500,000 microcomputers in federal offices.

p. 109–10   GOVERNMENT EMPLOYEES: Bureau of Labor Statistics.

p. 110   A NATIONWIDE SURVEY IN 1975: Donald Norris, "Computers and Small Local Governments," *Public Administration Review*, 44:1, January/February 1984, 70 and John King, "Local Government Uses of Information Technology: The Next Decade," *Public Administration Review*, 42:1, January/February 1982, 25.

p. 110   1983 SURVEY: Norris, 70.

p. 110   TEN YEARS AFTER THE INTRODUCTION OF TECHNOLOGY: King, 25.

p. 110   FINANCIAL MANAGEMENT TASKS: Norris, 74; King, 29.

p. 110   TWO THIRDS . . . BUY PREPACKAGED SOFTWARE: Norris, 75.

p. 110   SPECIALISTS: King, 31.

p. 111   DECENTRALIZATION: King, 30; and James Griesemer, "Microcomputers and Local Governments: New Economics and New Opportunities," *Public Administration Review*, 44:1, January/February 1984, 57–58.

p. 111   TED WEG: "P. V. Weg, Theft of Services Didn't Serve Us," *Computer Crime Digest*, September 1982.

p. 112   DISTRIBUTED SYSTEMS: King, 27, 33.

p. 112   DEPARTMENT OF HEALTH AND HUMAN SERVICES . . . 41,000 EMPLOYEES: David Burnham, "Agency Asks F.B.I. to Check Workers," New York *Times*, June 11, 1985.

p. 113   3 MILLISECONDS TO COMMIT: SRI International, "Computer Crime," Law Enforcement Assistance Administration, U.S. Department of Justice, 1979, 3.

p. 113   ANNUAL LOSSES . . . AMERICAN BAR ASSOCIATION STUDY: David Burnham, "Survey Outlines Computer Crimes," New York *Times*, June 11, 1984.

p. 114   BIOCHIPS: Stanley Wellborn, "Race to Create A 'Living Computer,'" *U.S. News & World Report*, December 31, 1984/January 7, 1985.

p. 114   COMPUTER DISASTER FACILITIES: Pollack, August 24, 1983.

p. 115   TARGETS OF TERRORISTS: Andrew Pollack, "Trust in Computers Raising Risk of Errors and Sabotage," New York *Times*, August 22, 1983. In Europe there have been at least thirty terrorist acts waged against computer facilities since 1978. Some were blown up. If that were to happen here, we could find ourselves in a vast power blackout, or without trains, or with disrupted phone service. It's not inconceivable. Americans are becoming a favorite target of terrorists.

CHAPTER 7: The Cashless Crisis

p. 117   BANK BANDIT . . . BINARY BANDIT: Value of average crime cited in Joseph Kelly, "On the Trail of the Binary Bandits," *Police Magazine*, July 1983, 48, and Edgar May, "White Collar Crime: Arrest by Appointment," *Police Magazine*, March 1980, 27.

p. 117   60 MILLION WIRE TRANSFERS: U.S. Department of Justice, Bureau of Justice Statistics, "Electronic Fund Transfer Fraud," March 1985.

p. 117   COUNTERFEITING . . . OUT OF THE STATEN ISLAND HOME: Joseph Berger, "4 Men Indicted by Grand Jury On S.I. in Credit Card Scheme," New York *Times*, March 21, 1985.

p. 117   CREDIT CARD BUYING POWER . . . LOSSES: "False Impressions: A Study of Credit Card Fraud," *The Lipman Report*, June 15, 1983; Leonard Sloane, "Fighting Fraud in Credit Cards," New York *Times*, March 27, 1984; Elizabeth Block, "Bandits Wielding Plastic," New York *Times*, May 22, 1983.

pp. 117–18   CHECK FRAUD: U.S. Chamber of Commerce, "White Collar Crime," 1974, 6, 36, and U.S. Department of Commerce, 1977, 109.

p. 118   TODAY, NO MORE THAN 100,000 HOMES . . . NEXT 50 YEARS, 80 PERCENT: Audrey Clayton of Forecasting International, cited in "A One-Stop Shopping Center In Your Home," *U.S. News & World Report*, May 9, 1983.

p. 119   1983 STUDY OF 16 BANKS: U.S. Department of Justice, March 1985.

p. 119   ATM AND CREDIT CARD CRIMES: Ibid.

p. 119   600 MILLION CREDIT CARDS . . . POTENTIAL TARGET OF FRAUD: Statistics found in *The Lipman Report;* Sloane; and Block.

pp. 119–20   CREDIT FRAUD IN NEW YORK CITY: Peter Herrick quoted in Sloane; Visa statistics and Brooklyn investigation cited in Barbara Basler, "17 in Brooklyn Seized in 'Sting' On Credit Cards," New York *Times*, December 5, 1984.

p. 120   MERCHANT COLLUSION: The Nilson Report cited in Block.

p. 120   THE DOMINICAN COCAINE RING: Chris Oliver, "Phony Credit Card Racket Busted," New York *Post*, May 17, 1985.

p. 120   DIAL-UP STOLEN CREDIT INFORMATION: Richard Esposito, "Crooks Dial Up Credit Secrets," New York *Post*, January 1, 1985.

p. 121   CHECK CHICANERY: American Management Association, "Crimes Against Business Project: Background, Findings and Recommendations," Unpublished, October 11, 1977; U.S. Chamber of Commerce, 1974, 36.

p. 121   A NET GAIN IN POTENTIAL CHECK WRITERS: According to Scott Bronstein, "A Check-Writing Nation Ignores the Debit Card," New York *Times*, October 6, 1985, the checkless society is far from here. On the contrary, as checks have become more convenient (e.g. interest-bearing accounts, drafts against brokerage and credit union accounts, telephone money transfers) usage has grown by about 7 percent a year in the past decade. By contrast, credit card usage has grown by only 3 percent a year in the same period.

p. 121   SECRET SERVICE . . . FORGED CHECKS: Brown, Flanagan and McLeod, 530–31; and Jack Taylor, U.S. Secret Service interview with author, July 24, 1985.

pp. 121–22   615 MILLION IN 1985: Figure cited in Paul Magnusson, "U.S. Checks to Get New Look," Miami *Herald*, November 9, 1985.

p. 122   BOND FORGERIES: Brown, Flanagan, and McLeod, 530; and Thayer.

CHAPTER 8: Stealing Technological Secrets

p. 126   WILLIAM WEBSTER: Quoted in Robert Lindsey, "U.S. Found to Breed Many Spies, But Even More Aren't Prosecuted," New York *Times*, December 20, 1984.

p. 126   CASPAR WEINBERGER: Quoted in "Massive Theft of U.S. Technology," *The Lipman Report*, April 15, 1984.

p. 126   ROGER MILGRAM: Quoted in Tamar Levin, "Putting a Lid on Corporate Secrets," New York *Times*, April 1, 1984.

pp. 126–27   EGGEBRECHT CASE: Vin McLellan, "Friday the 13th," *Inc.*, October 1983.

p. 127   ROHRER, HIBLER, REPLOGLE: Paraphrased in Jeanne Dorin McDowell, "Job Loyalty: Not the Virtue It Seems," New York *Times*, March 3, 1985.

p. 127   ANDREW POLLACK: "Computer Makers in Severe Slump," New York *Times*, June 10, 1985.

p. 128   JAMES CABRERA: Quoted in McDowell.

p. 130   CLASSIFIED MATERIAL AND SECURITY CLEARANCE: Statistics on contractors, clearances, and investigations taken from Richard Price, "Spy Case Shows Holes in Our Security," *USA Today*, October 20, 1983; Joel Brinkley, "Pentagon Study Faults Security of Contractors," New York *Times*, June 30, 1985; Amy Wilentz, "Spying to Support a Life-Style," *Time*, April 29, 1985; and *The Lipman Report*, April 15, 1984.

p. 130   MORTON HALPERIN: "How to Stop the Sale of Secrets: Don't Go For Easy Solutions," New York *Times*, July 22, 1985.

p. 131   TEXT ON TRADE SECRETS LAW: Pooley.

p. 132   FEDERAL GOVERNMENT . . . ENACT LEGISLATION: "Bills Offer Protection For Chips," New York *Times*, June 11, 1984.

p. 132   REDUCE MOBILITY: McDowell.

CHAPTER 9: Caveat Emptor

pp. 133–34   ORAFLEX AND SELACRYN CASES: Based on the following reports in the New York *Times*: Philip Shenon, "Lilly Pleads Guilty to Oraflex Charges," August 22, 1985; "U.S. Is Said to Have Dropped 3 Officials from Lilly Case," August 29, 1985; "SmithKline Is Fined For Failing to Report Side Effects of Drug," February 26, 1985.

p. 134   CARMEN TORRES CASE: Leonard Buder, "Woman Bilking Poor Who Seek Apartments," New York *Times*, December 9, 1984.

p. 134   HOUSING STARTS: Department of Commerce, Housing Construction Statistics.

p. 134   DRUG UTILIZATION IN THE UNITED STATES: Report and statistics cited in Irvin Molotsky, "Changing Patterns in Prescriptions in U.S.," New York *Times*, March 16, 1985.

p. 135   HOUSE SELECT COMMITTEE ON AGING: Report and statistics cited in Robert Pear, "Health Frauds Said to Prey on Elderly," New York *Times*, May 31, 1984.

p. 135   BIO HEALTH CASE: Cited in Edward Gargan, "Mail-Order Lab Sued Over Tests on Cow's Blood," New York *Times*, March 7, 1985.

p. 135   MIDWEST HEALTH RESEARCH CLINIC: Case cited in A. Lamden, "White Collar Crime—Remarks," *The Police Chief*, March 1984, 145–46.

p. 136   FRAUDULENT MEDICAL DEGREES AND ABRAHAM ASANTE CASE: Based on the following reports in New York *Times:* Richard Lyons, "Thousands Said to Have False Medical Degrees," December 7, 1984, and "House Panel Told of Bogus Doctor Who Left a Patient 'a Vegetable'," December 8, 1985; Nicholas Wade, "The Message From 1000 Quacks," December 17, 1985.

p. 136   DALE SHALLER: Appearance on "Pennsylvania Health Report," November 5 and 6, 1985.

p. 136   MEDICARE/MEDICAID FRAUDS: "GAO Survey Documents Medicare Overcharges," *Public Administration Times,* July 15, 1985; and Pepinsky and Jesilow, 50–51.

p. 137   MEDICARE ENROLLMENTS EXPANDED BY 40 PERCENT: Social Security Administration statistics show that hospital insurance enrollments in 1970 numbered 20,361 and grew to 28,067 by 1980. For medical insurance, enrollments grew from 19,584 to 27,400.

p. 138   OSHA STANDARDS REVISION: Frank Thompson, "Deregulation by the Bureaucracy: OSHA, and the Augian Search for Correction," *Public Administration Review,* 42:3, May/June 1982, 203–4.

p. 138   WORKER FATALITY AND INJURY REDUCTIONS: Computed from Bureau of Labor Statistics and National Safety Council data, 1950–81.

p. 138   COSTS OF WORK ACCIDENTS: Insurance Information Institute, 1982, 69.

p. 138   OCCUPATIONAL DISEASE: Insurance Information Institute, 1984, 85–86.

p. 139   STRIPPED OF ITS TEETH AND COMMITTED LEADERSHIP . . . PROBLEMS ROSE 12 PERCENT: "More Sick Workers, Less OSHA," New York *Times,* November 20, 1985.

p. 139   JOHN COFFEE: Quoted in Tamar Lewin, "Criminal Onus On Executives," New York *Times,* March 5, 1985.

p. 139   CIRCUITRON TOXIC DUMPING CASE: David Sanger, "Ex-Owner of L.I. Electronics Plant Indicted in Toxic Dumping Case," New York *Times,* December 4, 1984.

p. 140   ENTER THE EPA: Gregory Daneke, "The Future of Environmental Protection: Reflections on the Difference Between Planning and Regulating," *Public Administration Review,* 42:3, May/June 1982, 227–28, 232.

p. 140   *Official Deviance:* Douglas and Johnson, 209–10.

p. 140   CORPORATIONS LOBBY THEIR REGULATORS: Pepinsky and Jesilow, 76.

p. 140   THE GREATER THE NUMBER AND COMPLEXITY OF LEGAL ENACTMENTS: Paul Jesilow, "Adam Smith and White Collar Crime," *Criminology,* 20:3/4, November 1982, 322.

p. 140   NUMBER OF HOUSEHOLDS HAS SURGED: According to a HUD spokesperson, several economic factors are depressing the surging rate of household formations: housing prices are not appreciating more rapidly than the consumer price index, interest rates are high relative to inflation, and new tax legislation is making construction more difficult.

p. 141   WORTHLESS LAND SALES: Lamden, 145–46.

p. 141   JOHN ZACCARO: Ralph Blumenthal, "Judge Sentences Zaccaro to Work In Public Service," New York *Times,* February 2, 1985.

p. 142   WEST PAC CASE: Thomas Hayes, "Fraud is Denied in Mortgage Scheme," New York *Times,* February 5, 1985.

p. 143   GEORGE MORRISON AND FEATHERBEDDING: Based on reporting in New York *Times* by Selwyn Raab, "High-Pay Construction Reported Raising Housing and Office Rents," June 12, 1985; " '84 Pay for New York Construction Job: $308,651," June 13, 1985; "Extra Pay Called a Cost of Building in City," June 14, 1985.

p. 143   CONCRETE INDUSTRY: Selwyn Raab, "Suit Filed On Selling Concrete," New York *Times*, March 12, 1985.

p. 143   MOVING AND STORAGE INDUSTRY: Joseph Fried, "Movers Included in Charges of Bid-Rigging and Payoffs," New York *Times*, June 14, 1985.

pp. 143–44   ALEX LIBERMAN: Jesus Rangel, "City Sues Extorter for $4 Million," New York *Times*, January 15, 1985.

p. 144   NORTHEASTERN CITIES AND STATES . . . SOUTH AND WEST: John Herbers, "U.S. Plans To End Nationwide Code For Construction," New York *Times*, August 15, 1985.

p. 144   PERSONAL INJURY LAWSUITS: Insurance Information Institute, 1982, 43.

p. 144   INDEMNIFY OURSELVES AGAINST SUCH JUDGEMENTS: Ibid., 26. General liability premiums increased from $962,831,000 in 1960 to $7,690,281,000 in 1980. Medical malpractice premiums are included in these aggregates, but as of 1975 they were also reported separately. After 1975, malpractice premiums accounted for approximately one fifth and one sixth, respectively, of the aggregates cited above.

p. 144   INADEQUATE SECURITY: Data developed by Larry Sherman and Jody Klein, "Major Lawsuits Over Crime and Security: Trends and Patterns, 1958–1982," Unpublished draft report, Institute of Criminal Justice and Criminology, University of Maryland, September 1984.

p. 145   TIME OFF FROM JOBS: Kando, 78–81.

p. 145   AVERAGE WORK WEEK, MANUFACTURING AND NON-MANUFACTURING: Bureau of Labor Statistics.

p. 145   SHORTER WORK WEEK THE NORM FOR THE FUTURE: The Work in America Institute projects that, by 1990, the workweek will be reduced to 36 hours.

p. 145   COMPRESSED WORK WEEK: According to the Department of Labor, both the number and percent of full-time, nonfarm civilian workers working four and a half days or less per week, nearly doubled between 1973 and 1980. The increase in short workweeks was slow but steady until 1980, when the trend suddenly accelerated. The local public administration sector, which can be expected to level off or decline in the future, showed the largest percentage of workers on short weeks. In the manufacturing sector, the percentage of workers on short weeks more than doubled since 1973 but still fell below the 2.7 percent average for all industries. As with manufacturing, the percentage of short workweek arrangements increased for most industries. The Work in America Institute projects, by 1990, 5 percent of full-time nonagricultural workers will be on compressed work schedules. Another 25 percent will be on flexible work schedules, and 28 percent engaged in part-time work, job sharing and work sharing.

p. 145   VIDEO CASSETTE RECORDER STATISTICS: Katya Goncharoff, "Home Video: That's a Very Big Picture!" New York *Times*, October 14, 1984; Robert Lindsey, "VCR's Bring Big Changes in Use of Leisure," New York *Times*, March 3, 1985.

p. 145   BACKYARD EARTH STATION STATISTICS: "The New Order Passeth," *Broadcasting*, December 10, 1984, 54.

p. 145   PAY TV STATISTICS: Ibid., 44.

p. 145   LOW-POWER TV STATISTICS: Ibid., 58.

p. 145   CABLE SYSTEMS: In *Broadcasting*, "Neilson's Good News for Basic Services," April 11, 1983; "Cable Industry Is Ready to Roll" and "Critiquing Cable's Future," December 10, 1984.

pp. 145–46   CABLE TV PIRATES: In *Broadcasting*, "Taking the Offense on Theft of Services," June 11, 1984; "Florida Pirates," August 6, 1984; "Pirate Crackdown," August 20, 1984.

p. 146   NEW YORK *Times* EDITORIAL: "Fear of Flying," August 29, 1985.

p. 147   LETHAL SMOKESCREEN: In Douglas and Johnson, 246–48.

p. 147   THE AUTOMOBILE INDUSTRY IS PRONE TO CHEAT CONSUMERS: "Automakers and Dealers: A Study of Criminogenic Market Forces," in Geis and Meier, 143–48.

p. 148   SPEND MORE THAN $40 BILLION A YEAR TO MAINTAIN CARS: Paul Jesilow and Mary Jane O'Brien, "Deterring Automobile Fraud: A Field Experiment." Paper delivered at the annual meeting of the American Sociological Association, New York, August 1980.

p. 148   ADAM SMITH: Jesilow, 322.

p. 148   SATISFY PUBLIC CLAMOR: Pepinsky and Jesilow, 68.

p. 149   FEDERAL DEREGULATION WILL BE REPLACED BY STATE REGULATION: Naisbitt, 119. ". . . figures confirm that the burden of regulation has shifted to the states. . . . The single set of hateful, costly, yet standardized national regulations disintegrated into a labyrinth of contradictory state regulations—even more time-consuming and equally hateful."

CHAPTER 10: Cheating

p. 150   JAMES MASIELLO CASE: "Greenwich Swindler Gets 15 Years," New York *Times*, September 9, 1984.

p. 151   E.S.M. AND BEVILL: John Shad, "New Rules Should Be Cost-Effective," New York *Times*, July 28, 1985.

p. 151   E. F. HUTTON: Nathaniel Nash, "E. F. Hutton Guilty in Bank Fraud; Penalties Could Top $10 Million," New York *Times*, May 3, 1985.

p. 151   WILLIAM SAFIRE: New York *Times*, July 9, 1985.

p. 152   SECURITIES AND EXCHANGE COMMISSION: Susan Shapiro, "The Disposition of White Collar Illegalities: Prosecutorial Alternatives in the Enforcement of the Securities Laws," Presented at the annual meeting of the American Sociological Association, San Francisco, September 1978.

p. 152   EDWARD MARKOWITZ: Arnold Lubasch, "Promoter Is Guilty in $445 Million Tax Fraud," New York *Times*, April 16, 1985.

p. 152   ALBERT NIPON: "Fashion Designer Pleads Guilty," San Francisco *Chronicle*, February 12, 1985.

p. 153   NEW YORK STATE TAX CHEATS: Maurice Carroll, "Governor Seeks Big Crackdown On Tax Evaders," New York *Times*, March 2, 1985.

p. 153   COTTAGE INDUSTRY FORMATION HAS PERSISTED: In my September 6, 1985, interview with her, Wendy Lazar, former president of the National Alliance of Home-Based Business Owners, was confident of the growing trend in such enterprises. However, she avers that there are no reliable statistics to document it. One could use IRS records. However, as the IRS knows only too well, many home-business operators don't report their income. AT&T conducted a survey. But it sampled only home users of business equipment . . . and many cottage industries don't use any. Lazar cites the September 1985 issue of *Money* magazine, which declares that 11 million people work at home, one third full time—up 50 percent from a decade ago. That figure is about as close to cottage industry trend data as one can get as of this writing. The Small Business Administration doesn't track cottage industries at all, but it does measure sole proprietorships—many of which are home-based. In the SBA's *The State of Small Business: A Report of the President*, 313, statistics show that the number of sole proprietorships per 1,000 persons of entrepreneurial age has risen from 52 to 63 between 1977 and 1982.

p. 154   BANK OF BOSTON: "When Banks Launder Dirty Money," New York *Times,* February 15, 1985.

p. 154   *The Lipman Report:* "Laundering of Money—Part 2," *The Lipman Report,* September 15, 1983.

p. 154   UNIFORMED SERVICES DISABILITY: "Chicago Group Claims Widespread Disability Pension Abuse," *Crime Control Digest,* February 4, 1980.

p. 155   IRS ESTIMATES . . . WORST OFFENDERS: *The Lipman Report,* September 15, 1983.

p. 155 $100 BILLION IN . . . PREMIUMS: Insurance Information Institute, 1982, 21.

p. 155 $5 BILLION IN LIFE INSURANCE: American Council of Life Insurance.

p. 156   PROFITABILITY OF PROPERTY AND CASUALTY INDUSTRY: Based on corporate profits tabulations done by Citibank, Insurance Information Institute, 1982, 19.

p. 156   INVESTMENTS . . . OFFSET . . . UNDERWRITING LOSSES: In 1981, for example, underwriting losses came to more than $6 billion, but investment income totaled over $13 billion. This pattern has held true in almost every year since 1957. Ibid., 16–17.

p. 156   INVADE THE RESERVES: Marks and Craigie, flow chart on 125.

p. 156   SURPASS THE CONSUMER PRICE INDEX: In this case, the CPI refers only to those items covered by insurance—e.g., house furnishings and medical care. Insurance Information Institute, 1982, 41.

p. 157   15 TO 20 PERCENT OF ALL CLAIMS ARE FRAUDS: While no accurate measures are available, there are several frequently cited statistics. The Insurance Crime Prevention Institute sets the total bill for insurance fraud at $1.5 billion; premiums are 10 percent higher because of fraud. The Chamber of Commerce estimates that 10 percent of all claims filed are fraudulent (Carol Heimer, "Situational Causation in Executive Crime: The Case of Insurance Fraud," presented at annual meeting of American Sociological Association, August 1980). The National Auto Theft Bureau estimates that 10 to 15 percent of reported vehicle thefts nationwide may be attempts to defraud insurance companies. A state task force in Massachusetts reports that up to 25 percent of reported car thefts may be frauds (New York *Times,* November 26, 1985). The American Insurance Association uses 15 to 20 percent as their figure (New York *Times,* July 6, 1982).

p. 157   FRAUD IS RARE . . . IN THE COMMERCIAL LINES: I've found contradictory information here. According to Murt Von Leer, a claim manager for Kemper, more than half of that company's fraudulent claims now come from commercial lines. I'm inclined to go with Bud Clark's observation because he has an overview of the entire industry.

p. 157   FIVE INDUSTRY-WIDE INVESTIGATIVE BODIES: Insurance Committee of Arson Control (ICAC), National Auto Theft Bureau (NATB), Insurance Crime Prevention Institute (ICPI), Property Loss Insurance Register (PLIR) and Property Loss Research Bureau (PLRB).

CRIMEWARP IV: THE POLITICS OF PLEASURE

p. 163   SHIFTING FROM . . . CRIMINAL PROHIBITION . . . TO ADMINISTRATIVE REGULATION: Jerome Skolnick and John Dombrink, "The Legalization of Deviance," *Criminology,* 16:2, August 1978, 194.

CHAPTER 11: Upscale Hookers

Parts of this chapter have been previously published in Georgette Bennett, "Ladies of the Afternoon," *New York Daily News Sunday Magazine*, December 5, 1982.

p. 165   PART-TIME PROSTITUTES . . . BEGINNING TO DOMINATE THE FIELD: Adler, 74.

p. 166   THE MIDDLE AGES: *New Catholic Encyclopedia*, 879.

p. 166   CATHOLIC CHURCH . . . HOUSES OF ILL REPUTE: Clinard, 509.

p. 166   BY THE END OF THE 15TH CENTURY: *New Catholic Encyclopedia*, 879.

p. 166   THE MOST IMPORTANT ISSUE OF THE DAY: Miller and Johnson, 8.

p. 166   IN THE NORTH . . . IN THE SOUTH: Bell, 227.

p. 166   STEADY DECLINE CHARACTERISTIC OF A DYING BUSINESS: Adler, 65.

p. 166   BY 1967 . . . DROPPED TO ABOUT ONE-THIRD ITS 1920S LEVEL: American Social Health Association index of commercialized prostitution cited in ibid., 64.

p. 166   YOUNG SINGLE MEN IN 1972: Bell, 231.

p. 167   1 TO 6 TRICKS PER DAY: Abt Associates, 137.

p. 167   ONLY 9 PERCENT HAD EXPERIMENTED WITH DRUGS: A 1969 Paul Gehard study cited in Bell, 241.

p. 167   THE ADDICT-PROSTITUTE: An excellent analysis is found in Rosenbaum, 71–82.

p. 167   SELF-REPORTS . . . HEROIN USE: Brown, Flanagan, and McLeod, 362 and 427.

p. 167   MANY HAVE LEFT THE STREETS: Abt Associates, 126.

p. 167   1 IN EVERY 200 AMERICAN WOMEN: Abt Associates, 137–38.

p. 168   STREETWALKERS ACCOUNT FOR ABOUT ONE FIFTH: Ibid., 141.

p. 170   AN ESTIMATED 50,000 MASSAGE GIRLS: Estimate derived from Abt Associates, 137 and 141. Tables show that 25 percent of prostitutes work massage parlors. To arrive at the above estimate, the base figure of 200,000 estimated female prostitutes for 1973 was multiplied by .25.

p. 170   SATISFYING THEIR LUSTFUL DESIRES AT THE EXPENSE OF THE FAMILY: Falwell, 1981, 204.

p. 170   KATE MILLETT: Millett, 123.

p. 171   THE JOYS OF SEX FROM THE EXCLUSIVE POSSESSION OF SECULAR HUMANISTS: Flake, 82.

p. 171   WELCOME MORE ACCEPTANCE OF SEXUAL FREEDOM: Excerpted from *Time*/Yankelovich, Skelly, and White polls, latest that of June 1982.

p. 171   SEX BEFORE MARRIAGE . . . INFIDELITY AFTER MARRIAGE: NORC, General Social Surveys, 1972–83; also Gallup poll reported in New York *Times*, May 16, 1985.

p. 171   SEXUAL GUILT CORRELATES WITH BEING RELIGIOUS: Marilyn Story quoted in New York *Daily News*, January 11, 1985.

p. 171   I WOULD LIKE TO SEE A GREATER INTEREST IN OPPOSING PREMARITAL SEX AND ADULTERY: Viguerie, 208–9.

p. 171   FAMILY STUDIES: Nicholas Hahn, "Too Dumb to Know Better," *Criminology*, 18:1, May 1980, 3–25.

p. 171   1918: History of brothel banning found in *New Catholic Encyclopedia*, 879.

p. 171   PROHIBIT PERMISSIVENESS: Webber, 15.

p. 171   ENFORCE COMMUNITY STANDARDS OF RIGHT AND WRONG: Language from Washington *Post* survey cited in McClosky and Brill, 197.

pp. 171–72   POLLS . . . REGULATION APPROACH TO PROSTITUTION: Harris and Westin and *Time*/Yankelovich, Skelly, and White polls cited in ibid., 212.

p. 172   ALTHOUGH IT IS SCARCELY A SOCIALLY APPROVED FORM OF CONDUCT: Ibid., 211, 213.

p. 172   STAR RANCH: "Just a Nice Lady in Need," *Police Magazine*, March 1980, 2.

p. 172   MASSAGE PARLORS IN MARICOPA COUNTY: "Any Volunteers?" *Police Magazine*, March 1981, 2.

p. 172   WOLFENDEN REPORT: Quoted in *New Catholic Encyclopedia*, 880.

p. 172   CANADA AND PROSTITUTION: Christopher Wren, "Canadian Prostitution Report," New York *Times*, April 24, 1985.

p. 172   MARGO ST. JAMES: Quoted in Elaine Sciolino, "Off the Street Prostitution Is Flourishing," New York *Times*, November 14, 1984.

p. 173   UNREPORTED ILLEGAL INCOME: Abt Associates, 147.

p. 173   "NULLIFICATION" AND "COMMERCIAL SERVICE MODEL": Skolnick and Dombrink, 200–1.

CHAPTER 12: Homosexuals: The Road from Sodom and Gomorrah to the National Democratic Convention

p. 176   IT WAS THE FIRST TIME ANYONE COULD REMEMBER GAYS FIGHTING BACK: Prior to that time, gays tended to deal with conflicts by avoidance, repenting, and accepting a definition of themselves as deviant. A 1977 study revealed that, prior to 1970, they displayed very little physical or verbal anger. After 1970, however, gays more often used protest, force, or negotiation in the face of conflicts. They became much more assertive about and aware of civil rights violations. See Fred Minnigerode, "Rights or Repentance," *Journal of Homosexuality*, 2:4, Summer 1977, 323–26. In addition, gays were more likely to disclose their homosexuality after 1970 than before. In the same issue of *Journal of Homosexuality*, see Marcy Adelman, "Sexual Orientation and Violations of Civil Liberties," 330.

p. 176   MIDDLE-CLASS, WELL-EDUCATED, WELL-PAID: See, for example, study cited in "40% of Single Men Are Found Homosexual in San Francisco," New York *Times*, November 23, 1984.

p. 179   SODOMITES, THE "WATCHERS" AND HELLENISTIC CULTURE: Bailey, 23.

p. 179   SODOMY LAWS . . . HENRY VIII: Ploscowe, 198–99.

p. 179   MAX PERKINS AND ROBERT MCCORKLE: Cited in Harry Golden, "The Homosexual in North Carolina," New York *Mattachine Newsletter*, January 1965, 4–6.

p. 180   LOUISIANA SODOMY STATUTE: "Gay Rights," *Civil Liberties*, Winter 1985. As of this writing, similar cases were being litigated in Georgia and Texas. The Louisiana case is on hold pending the outcomes in the other two states.

p. 180   DOE V. COMMONWEALTH ATTORNEY: Dorsen, 124.

p. 180   SINGER V. U.S. CIVIL SERVICE COMMISSION: Analysis of case in "Legal Section," *Journal of Homosexuality*, 2:4, Summer 1977, 399–400.

pp. 180–81   OKLAHOMA CASE: *Board of Education v. National Gay Task Force*, No. 83–2030, cited in Linda Greenhouse, "4-to-4 Vote Upholds Teachers On Homosexual Rights Issue," New York *Times*, March 28, 1985.

p. 181   MOST OF THE CASES THAT WERE DECIDED ADVERSELY . . . WORTHY OF PROTECTION: Donald Knutson, "The Civil Liberties of Gay Persons," *Journal of Homosexuality*, 2:4, Summer 1977, 340–41.

p. 181   SIX POLLS, 1973–1982: Cited in William Schneider and I. A. Lewis, "The Straight Story on Homosexual And Gay Rights," *Public Opinion*, February/March 1984, 17.

p. 182   SCHNEIDER AND LEWIS: Ibid., 18.

p. 182   JERRY FALWELL FUND-RAISING LETTER: Quoted in Bollier, 239.

p. 182   JAMES ROBISON AND DEAN WYCOFF: Quoted in ibid., 240.

p. 182   JERRY FALWELL: "What God's Word Says About Homosexuality" pamphlet, cited in Goodman and Price, 46.

p. 183   SEXUAL PREFERENCE IS IRRELEVANT TO POLITICAL PHILOSOPHY: Dolan quote in *The Advocate*, a national gay magazine, cited in Bollier, 234.

p. 183   ROBERT BAUMAN: Goodman and Price, 53–54; Phil Gailey, "Democrats Seek Homosexuals' Votes," New York *Times*, July 25, 1983.

p. 183   NATIONAL ASSOCIATION OF GAY AND LESBIAN DEMOCRATIC CLUBS: Delegate statistics cited in Gailey.

p. 183   SEATTLE: Randy Shilts, "Police Come to Terms with the Gay Community," *Police Magazine*, January 1980, 31.

p. 183   IN SAN FRANCISCO, WHERE 40 PERCENT OF SINGLE MEN HAVE BEEN FOUND TO BE GAY: New York *Times*, November 23, 1984.

p. 183   CHARLES GAIN, DIANE FEINSTEIN: Shilts, 34–35. Gain's eccentricities described in Robert Epstein's award-winning 1984 documentary, *The Times of Harvey Milk*.

p. 184   BERKELEY: "Berkeley Grants 'Live-Ins' City Employee Benefits," *Public Administration Times*, January 1, 1985; "Berkeley May Offer Benefits to Non-spouses," *Public Administration Times*, October 15, 1984.

p. 184   LOS ANGELES: Shilts, 31; Robert Lindsey, "Vote Set on Homosexual Community," New York *Times*, November 5, 1984.

p. 184   LAGUNA BEACH: "Homosexual Politics on Coast Resort," New York *Times*, November 4, 1984.

p. 184   SERGEANT CHARLIE COCHRANE: Jim Mitteager, "NYPD's Gay Cops," *The National Centurion*, February 1984, 33.

p. 185   AIDS IS THE LEADING CAUSE OF DEATH: Statistic cited in Glenn Collins, "Impact of AIDS: Patterns of Homosexual Life Changing," New York *Times*, July 22, 1985.

p. 185   IS COMPULSIVE SEXUALITY FREEDOM?: Jim Fouratt quoted in Jane Gross, "Homosexuals Stepping Up AIDS Education," New York *Times*, September 22, 1985.

p. 185   JOHN MARTIN STUDY: Cited in ibid.

p. 185   GAYS LIVING AS COUPLES: Georgia Dullea, "Homosexual Couples Find a Quiet Pride," New York *Times*, December 10, 1984.

p. 185   THE ACCEPTABILITY OF CERTAIN BEHAVIOR TENDS TO VARY POSITIVELY WITH THE SOCIAL POSITION OF USERS: Jerome Skolnick and John Dombrink, "The Legalization of Deviance," *Criminology*, 16:2, August 1978, 197.

p. 186   IT IS NOT THE FUNCTION OF THE LAW TO INTERVENE IN THE PRIVATE LIVES: *Wolfenden Report*, 23–24.

p. 186   SAFEGUARD YOUTHS OR THE MENTALLY DEFECTIVE . . . PRESERVE PUBLIC ORDER AND DECENCY: Ibid., 44–47.

p. 186   BLACKMAIL, FAMILY LIFE: Ibid.

p. 186   IT IS HIGHLY IMPROBABLE THAT THE MAN TO WHOM HOMOSEXUAL BEHAVIOR IS REPUGNANT: Ibid., 47.

p. 186   THIS IS NOT TO CONDONE PRIVATE IMMORALITY: Ibid., 48.

pp. 186–87   SOUTH, WEST NORTH CENTRAL AND MOUNTAIN STATES: States with existing sodomy laws include Montana, Idaho, Nevada, Utah, Arizona, Minnesota, Michigan, Missouri, Kansas, Oklahoma, Arkansas, Texas, Louisiana, Mississippi, Alabama, Florida, Georgia, Tennessee, Kentucky, Virginia, North Carolina, South Carolina, Maryland, and Rhode Island; also the District of Columbia.

p. 187   INCIDENCE OF HOMOSEXUALITY: Both the National Gay Task Force and Lambda assert that the incidence of homosexuality has remained constant since first measured by Alfred Kinsey in the 1940s. However, SIECUS (Sex Information and Education Council of the United States) explains that Kinsey's figures are still referenced and that no studies on the scale of his research have been done since.

Kinsey's surveys conclude that 10 percent of males are more or less exclusively homosexual for at least three years after puberty and 4 percent are exclusively homosexual throughout their lives.

Hite, 1125, found that 11 percent of her male sample preferred sex with men. Of these, 2 percent also enjoyed sex with women (p. 811). Hite claims to have used a sampling method similar to Kinsey's (p. 1059). Therefore, it is significant that her proportion of homosexual men in the 1970s is roughly the same as Kinsey's 1940s sample.

Morton Hunt's update of the Kinsey studies, *Sexual Behavior in the 1970's*, similarly shows no evidence of an increase in homosexuality. Judd Marmor, in his 1980 book *Homosexual Behavior: A Modern Reappraisal*, concludes: "On the basis of these various studies, it is fair to conclude conservatively that the incidence of more or less exclusively homosexual behavior in Western culture ranges from 5–10 percent for adult males and 3–5 percent for adult females."

CHAPTER 13: Purveying Prurience

p. 190 $2-BILLION-TO-$4-BILLION INDUSTRY: U.S. General Accounting Office, "Sexual Exploitation of Children: A Problem of Unknown Magnitude," April 20, 1982, 4.

p. 190   FBI STATISTICS: U.S. Department of Justice, *Crime in the U.S. 1982, 1983*.

p. 190   U.S. POSTAL SERVICE STATISTICS: Brown, Flanagan, and McLeod, 522, 525.

p. 190   BLANKET CANADA WITH AMERICAN PORN: "Pornography Dealer Pleads Guilty to Shipping Lewd Tapes," New York *Times*, December 9, 1984.

p. 190   CLASS ASPECTS OF PORNOGRAPHY: See Bullough and Bullough, 161, 166–67.

p. 191   THE SONG OF SONGS . . . BANNED AS PORNOGRAPHIC: Ibid., 160–61.

p. 191   FUNDAMENTALIST RIGHT TAKE THEIR CUES FROM THE BIBLE: Webber, 50.

p. 191   FALWELL ON PORNOGRAPHY: Falwell, 1981, 189, 202.

p. 191   VIGUERIE ON PORNOGRAPHY: Viguerie, 168.

p. 191   SUPPORT FOR OUTLAWING PORNOGRAPHY: Survey reported in Brown, Flanagan, and McLeod, 302; also Michael Wood and Michael Hughes, "The Moral Basis of Moral Reform: Status Discontent vs. Culture and Socialization As Explanations Of Anti-Pornography Social Movement Adherence," *American Sociological Review*, 49:1, February 1984, 94.

p. 191   ATLANTA METROPOLITAN AREA STUDY: Margaret Herrman and Diane Bordner, "Attitudes Toward Pornography in a Southern Community," *Criminology*, 21:3, August 1983, 358–59.

p. 192   SUSAN BROWNMILLER: The feminist antipornography argument is found in Brownmiller, 441–45.

p. 192   STATE REPRESENTATIVE RICHARD WRIGHT: Cited in "North Carolina Is Cracking Down on Pornography," New York *Times*, October 13, 1985.

p. 193   DIANE RUSSELL: Russell, 23. Additional data cited 124–32.

p. 193   NORC ATTITUDE SURVEY RE: PORNOGRAPHY-RAPE CONNECTION: Brown, Flanagan, and McLeod, 301.

p. 193   LAWS SHOULD FORBID DISTRIBUTION: Ibid., 302.

p. 194 LABORATORY CONDITIONS ALLOW SUBJECTS TO ACT OUT BEHAVIORS THAT THEY WOULD BE UNLIKELY TO REPLICATE IN REAL LIFE: For comprehensive analysis of methodological weaknesses of laboratory experiments in behavioral effects of media violence, see Robert Kaplan and Robert Singer, "Television Violence and Viewer Aggression: A Reexamination of the Evidence," *Journal of Social Issues*, 32:4, 1976, 36–42.

p. 195 ELEMENTAL TRUTHS AND MALE REACTIONS TO PORNOGRAPHY: Hite, 1123–24.

p. 195 MEN'S QUOTES FROM "HITE REPORT": Ibid., 783, 785.

p. 195 MEN'S MAGAZINES SUBSET: Ibid., 1123.

p. 195 MEN WHO RAPE . . . BETWEEN 18 AND 29: Brown, Flanagan, and McLeod, 422–23.

p. 195 SENATE SUBCOMMITTEE ON JUVENILE JUSTICE HEARINGS: Testimony reported in "Senate Subcommittee Hears Pornography Damage Women's Civil Rights," *National NOW Times*, September/October 1984. Ordinances based on the civil rights model have already been developed for Minneapolis, Indianapolis, and Los Angeles County. See Pauline Bart, "Pornography: Institutionalizing Woman-Hating and Eroticizing Dominance and Submission for Fun and Profit," *Justice Quarterly*, 2:2, June 1985, 288–89 for a fuller treatment.

p. 196 NEW YORK *Times* EDITORIAL: "Censors in Feminist Garb," November 19, 1984.

p. 196 INDIANAPOLIS ORDINANCE: Stuart Taylor, "Pornography Foes Lose New Weapon In Supreme Court," New York *Times*, February 25, 1986.

p. 196 45,000 CHILDREN SEXUALLY EXPLOITED: R. B. D'Agostino, A. W. Burgess, A. J. Belanger, M. V. Guio, R. Gould, and C. Montan, "Investigation of Sex Crimes Against Children: A Survey of Ten States," *The Police Chief*, February 1984, 37.

pp. 196–97 PEDERASTY IN GREEK CIVILIZATION: Licht, 452–62.

p. 197 FEMALE PEDOPHILIA IS VIRTUALLY UNKNOWN: Russell, 237.

p. 197 "BLACK CATHY" WILSON: Greg Mitchell, "You Can't Buy Child Pornography Commercially, But a Shadowy Traffic Persists," *Police Magazine*, January 1983, 53.

p. 197 HOMEGROWN KIDDIE PORN . . . 90 PERCENT OF MARKET: Ibid., 57.

p. 197 NEW ORLEANS INVESTIGATION: Gerald Caplan, "Sexual Exploitation of Children: The Conspiracy of Silence," *Police Magazine*, January 1982, 49.

p. 197 GILBERT GAUTHE CASE: "Ex-Pastor Given 20-Year Sentence," New York *Times*, October 15, 1985.

p. 197 RENE GUYON SOCIETY CREED: Quoted in Caplan, 48.

p. 197 GROW UP TO BECOME PEDERASTS THEMSELVES: Mitchell, 53.

p. 197 RUNAWAYS: Study of runaways and pornography cited in Ronald Holmes, "Children in Pornography," *The Police Chief*, February 1984, 43; also Mitchell, 60.

p. 197 CHILD PROSTITUTION AND PORNOGRAPHY: Weisberg, 68–69.

p. 198 JUVENILE JUSTICE AND DELINQUENCY PREVENTION ACT OF 1974: U.S. Department of Justice, Law Enforcement Assistance Administration, "Children in Custody: A Report on the Juvenile Detention and Correctional Facility Census of 1974," 84–85.

p. 198 1984 STATISTICS ON STATUS OFFENDERS: U.S. Department of Justice, Office of Juvenile Justice and Delinquency Prevention, "Runaway Children and the Juvenile Justice and Delinquency Prevention Act: What Is the Impact?" *Juvenile Justice Bulletin*, undated, 2.

p. 198 PENNY AN 11-YEAR-OLD RUNAWAY: Ibid., 3–8.

p. 198 GLORIA STEINEM: Cited in Russell, 258.

p. 198 THE WAY MEN ARE BROUGHT UP: David Finkelhor cited in Russell, 237.

p. 198 15 STATES HAVE ADDED SEXUAL EXPLOITATION: Weisberg, 190, 206.

p. 198   90 PERCENT NEVER GET PROSECUTED: Debra Whitcomb, "Prosecution of Child Sexual Abuse: Innovations in Practice," National Institute of Justice *Research in Brief,* November 1985, 1.

p. 198   INNOVATIONS EASING COURTROOM CONFRONTATION: Ibid., 2–3, 5.

p. 199   MAJORITY OF THE PUBLIC IS BAN-HAPPY: Attitude survey findings cited in Mc-Closkey and Brill, 207–11.

p. 199   LAWYERS AND JUDGES: Ibid., 58–59.

p. 199   COMMUNITY LEADERS: Ibid., 419.

p. 199   LIBERTARIAN IDEOLOGY: Ibid., 290.

p. 199   MIDDLE-OF-THE-ROAD: Ibid., 286.

p. 200   TOLERANCE OF PORNOGRAPHY AND CITY SIZE: G. Edward Stephan and Douglas McMullin, "Tolerance of Sexual Nonconformity: City Size As A Situational And Early Learning Determinant," *American Sociological Review,* 47:3, June 1982, 411–15.

p. 200   RELIGIOSITY: McClosky and Brill, 406, 412.

CHAPTER 14: Upping the Ante on Gambling

p. 202   RABBINIC LITERATURE: Based on remarks of Rabbi Marc Gellman at United Jewish Appeal compulsive gambling conference, December 13, 1984.

p. 202   MEASURES OF GAMBLING IN THE U.S.: Ibid., 12–13.

p. 202   ALMOST ALL PERMIT SOME GAMBLING: Abt Associates, 80, 92; Austin Ranney, "Referendums and Initiatives 1984," *Public Opinion,* December/January 1985, 15–16.

p. 202   CHARITY BINGO IN STATES AND INDIAN RESERVATIONS: "Big Stakes Bingo Brings Them Into Oklahoma by the Busload," New York *Times,* December 27, 1984.

p. 203   PENNY ANTE BETTORS . . . HIGH ROLLERS: Maureen Kallick-Kaufmann, "The Micro and Macro Dimensions of Gambling in the United States," *Journal of Social Issues,* 35:3, 1979, 15–16.

p. 203   BIG SPENDERS . . . SPORTS BETS: Abt Associates, 109.

p. 203   LARGEST SHARE OF ALL GAMBLING ACTIVITIES: Kallick-Kaufmann, 17.

p. 203   NET OUTLAY FOR LEGAL WAGERING: Ibid., 19.

p. 203   ILLEGAL NET . . . DEMOGRAPHICS: Ibid., 16–19.

p. 203   FOUNDING FATHERS . . . PURITANS: Wertenbaker, 163–64, 179.

p. 203   COLONIAL PERIOD AND THE EARLY DAYS OF OUR NATION: G. Robert Blakey, "State Conducted Lotteries: History, Problems, and Promises," *Journal of Social Issues,* 35:3, 1979, 64–71.

p. 203   REGRESSIVE TAXATION . . . PROGRESSIVE GAMES: Daniel B. Suits, "Economic Background for Gambling Policy," *Journal of Social Issues,* 35:3, 1979, 55, 57.

p. 203   ADD REVENUES OF ONLY 4 PERCENT: Ibid., 60.

p. 203   NONGAMBLERS: Kallick-Kaufmann, 21–24; Judith Hybels, "The Impact of Legalization on Illegal Gambling Participation," *Journal of Social Issues,* 35:3, 1979, 28.

p. 203   FUNDAMENTALISTS . . . FORMAL OPPOSITION TO GAMBLING: Joyce, 154.

p. 204   SUBURBS . . . DEGREES . . . MONEY AND GAMBLING: Kallick-Kaufmann, 11.

p. 204   LEGAL AND ILLEGAL BETS ARE INTERCHANGEABLE: Ibid., 16; Hybels, 35.

p. 204   LEGAL GAMES CAN'T BEGIN TO COMPETE: Task Force on Organized Crime, 232–37.

p. 204   GAMBLING HAD BECOME BIG BUSINESS: Mark Haller, "The Changing Structure of American Gambling in the Twentieth Century," *Journal of Social Issues,* 35:3, 1979, 88–91.

p. 204   THE MOB'S HEGEMONY IS INCOMPLETE: Report of Task Force on Organized Crime, 218. Corresponding figures for regions not mentioned in the text are: Far West —29.2 percent, Midwest—47.4 percent, Southeast—35.7 percent.

p. 204   SMALLEST CONTRIBUTORS TO THE MOB'S GAMBLING REVENUES: Ibid., 221.

p. 204   SPORTS BOOKIE: Ibid.

p. 205   CUBAN-AMERICAN GAMBLING SYNDICATE: Eric Schmitt, "U.S. Panel Says Former Cubans Run a Bet Ring," New York Times, June 25, 1985.

p. 205   JUDGE IRVING KAUFMAN: Quoted in ibid.

p. 205   ORGANIZED CRIME DOESN'T LIMIT ITSELF TO ILLEGAL GAMBLING: Task Force on Organized Crime, 221–22.

p. 205   LICENSING PROBLEMS: Donald Janson, "Board Told to Ignore Economics in Casino Rulings," New York Times, February 24, 1985, and "Hilton Rejected for License To Operate a Jersey Casino," New York Times, March 1, 1985.

p. 205   COMPULSIVE GAMBLERS IN THE U.S.: Statistics cited in T. E. Dielman, "Gambling: A Social Problem?" Journal of Social Issues, 35:3, 1979, 41–42; The Christophers, "Compulsive Gambling," Christopher News Notes, No. 230, undated.

p. 206   THE FIRST CASINO TO DEBUT IN NEW JERSEY: Fried, 280.

p. 206   MONSIGNOR DUNNE: Remarks at UJA conference, December 13, 1985.

p. 206   GAMBLERS ANONYMOUS . . . AVERAGE AGE OF ITS MEMBERS DROPPING: Ward Morehouse III, "Teenage Gambling: Illegal, Spreading," Christian Science Monitor, March 6, 1978.

p. 206   DR. HENRY LESIEUR: Data based on studies conducted in early 1984. Henry LeSieur, Robert Klein, and Marty Rimm, "Pathological and Problem Gambling Among New Jersey High School Students," presented at Sixth National Conference on Gambling, Atlantic City, December 1984.

p. 207   ROBERT CUSTER: Cited in Morehouse.

p. 207   EXPOSURE TO WAGERING AS CHILDREN . . . GAMBLING IS READILY AVAILABLE: Kallick-Kaufmann, 26.

p. 207   ATLANTIC CITY CASINO REVENUES: Donald Janson, "A Bill Requiring Casinos to Help Cities Is Passed," New York Times, December 7, 1984.

p. 207   THE DOWNSIDE: Atlantic City data from Bernard Edelman, "Shaking Down Atlantic City," Police Magazine, November 1982, 41–49.

p. 207   GAMBLING ARRESTS: U.S. Department of Justice, Crime in the U.S. 1982, 171.

p. 208   GAMBLING AND LOTTERY, AND EXTORT RACKETEERING: McGarrell and Flanagan, 576.

p. 208   RESOURCES DEVOTED TO GAMBLING ENFORCEMENT . . . PUBLIC EXPECTS EXISTING LAWS TO BE UPHELD: Thomas Mangione and Floyd Fowler, "Enforcing the Gambling Laws," Journal of Social Issues, 35:3, 1979, 118–19.

p. 208   BETWEEN PERMISSIVENESS AND PROHIBITION: National Advisory Committee on Criminal Justice Standards and Goals, Report of the Task Force on Organized Crime, 232.

p. 208   BY 1982, WAGERING NEARLY FOUR TIMES THE AMOUNT: Abt Associates, 108. The conclusion in his report, prepared for the Internal Revenue Service, is based on unreported illegal income from gambling and assumes a ratio of 4 to 1 between legal and illegal wagers.

p. 208   LOTTERY BROKERS: Blakey, 68.

p. 209   50 GAMBLING REFERENDA: Kathleen Joyce, "Public Opinion and the Politics of Gambling," Journal of Social Issues, 35:3, 1979, 157–60; Ranney, 15–16; Kallick-Kaufmann, 11.

p. 209   NORVAL MORRIS: "The Law Is A Busybody," unpublished paper, 1972.

p. 210   FOUGHT BRINGING CASINOS TO HOT SPRINGS: Ranney, 15 and Joyce, 158.

p. 210   NEWLY LEGALIZED GAMBLING ATTRACTS NEW GAMBLERS: Kallick-Kaufmann, 26.

p. 210   30 PERCENT WHO REFRAIN . . . BECAUSE IT IS ILLEGAL: Ibid., 21.

p. 210   MILITARY SERVICE: Ibid., 23.

CHAPTER 15: The Demise of Drugs

p. 213   WORLDWIDE POPPY CROP HAS INCREASED: Joel Brinkley, "Rampant Drug Abuse Brings Call For Move Against Source Nations," New York Times, September 9, 1984.

p. 213   HEROIN SEIZURES: McGarrell and Flanagan, 536; Drug Enforcement Administration.

p. 213   PRICE HAS STABILIZED: Ibid., 437.

p. 213   DRUGS IN SILICON VALLEY: Quotes and information are derived from interviews for story developed by the author for the "MacNeil/Lehrer NewsHour," January–March 1984. Michael Joseloff produced the segment; Kuame Holman was the correspondent.

p. 214   NATIONAL COCAINE HOTLINE AND THEFT: Mark Gold and statistics cited in "Study Ties Cocaine to Theft," New York Times, September 20, 1983.

p. 215   DR. EDWIN KATAKEE'S PROPHECY: Silver and Aldrich, 63.

p. 215   DR. ARNOLD WASHTON: Quoted in Leslie Maitland Werner, "Crime Panel Told of Cocaine Abuse," New York Times, November 28, 1984.

p. 215 $26 BILLION IN LOST PRODUCTIVITY, MEDICAL EXPENSES, AND CRIME: Inflation-adjusted figures based on 1977 government-sponsored study by Research Triangle Institute, cited in "Taking Drugs on the Job," Newsweek, August 22, 1983.

p. 215   ARIZONA: "Pushing Pushers," New York Times, August 28, 1983; and interview of author with Attorney General Bob Corbin, November 1, 1985.

p. 215   GRAVITATED FROM THE LOWER TO THE MIDDLE CLASS: Along with that shift has come growing acceptance. Time/Yankelovich, Skelly, and White polls on the legalization of marijuana, for example, show that between 1969 and 1978, those favoring legalization rose from 13 percent to 31 percent. McClosky and Brill, 215. In 1982, however, those approving dropped to 21 percent. Public Opinion, April/May 1982, 30.

p. 216   COCAINE . . . THE PRICE TUMBLED: McGarrell and Flanagan, 437.

p. 216   RONALD BUZZEO: Remarks at 90th Annual Conference of International Association of Chiefs of Police published in The Police Chief, March 1984, 108.

p. 216   NONMEDICAL USAGE OF DRUGS: McGarrell and Flanagan, 356–57.

p. 216   THEFTS OF STIMULANTS AND DEPRESSANTS: Statistic calculated from figures for 1976 to 1982 reported in ibid., 437.

p. 216   PRICE INCREASES OF "UPPERS" AND "DOWNERS": Ibid.

p. 216   LOOK-ALIKE DRUGS: Buzzeo, 109.

pp. 216–17   NATIONAL SURVEY ON DRUG ABUSE . . . THOSE WHO HAVE EVER USED A DRUG: McGarrell and Flanagan, 356–57.

p. 217   DRUG USE . . . MONTH BEFORE SURVEY: Ibid., 356.

p. 217   HIGH SCHOOL SENIORS . . . USE OF DRUGS HAS BEEN DROPPING OFF SINCE 1982: Ibid., 353.

p. 218   FEMALE AND MALE STATE PRISON INMATES AND DRUGS: Ibid., 658–59.

p. 218   NEW YORK CITY HOMICIDES: Leonard Buder, "Almost 25% of Homicides In City in '81 Tied to Drugs," New York Times, February 18, 1983.

p. 218   DADE COUNTY: Michael Serrill, "The Violent World of the 'Cocaine Cowboys,' " *Police Magazine*, November 1982, 12.

p. 218   MONTEREY COUNTY: Greg Mitchell, "The California Marijuana Wars," *Police Magazine*, July 1982, 44, 50, 52.

p. 218   WASHINGTON, D.C.: "Ex-Officer Recalls His $500-a-Day Drug Habit and Its Effect," New York *Times*, December 2, 1984.

p. 218   BALTIMORE: Bernard Gropper, "Probing the Links Between Drugs and Crime," *NIJ Reports*, November 1984, 5.

p. 218   DETROIT: Steven Gettinger, "Is the Junkie/Burglar a Myth?" *Police Magazine*, November 1979, 44.

p. 219   CALIFORNIA: William McGlothlin, M. Douglas Anglin, and Bruce Wilson, "Narcotic Addiction and Crime," *Criminology*, 16:3, November 1978, 311.

p. 219   NATIONWIDE: Gropper, 4.

p. 219   RURAL, MIDDLE-AGED, MIDDLE CLASS, WHITE WOMEN: Susan Datesman, "Women, Crime and Drugs," in Inciardi 85, 87–88; and Rosenbaum, 3.

p. 219   200,000 OPIUM ADDICTS: Ray, 21.

p. 219   ONE OUT OF EVERY 400 AMERICANS: Ibid., 20.

p. 219   NEWSPAPER ACCOUNT OF 1899 . . . 1895 ARTICLE: Silver and Aldrich, 28, 29.

p. 220   HARRISON ACT: Datesman, 89–90.

p. 220   3 MEN FOR EACH WOMAN ADMITTED TO FEDERALLY FUNDED TREATMENT PROGRAMS: McGarrell and Flanagan, 628.

p. 220   SIX MEN ARRESTED FOR EACH WOMAN: Ibid., 475.

p. 220   IN 1982 RETAIL SALES OF $27 BILLION: Abt Associates, 61, 62.

p. 220   ILLICIT SALES . . . $75 BILLION: Buzzeo, 107.

p. 220   PALESTINE LIBERATION ORGANIZATION: Brinkley, September 9, 1984.

p. 220   CRUSADE AGAINST MARIJUANA WAS UNDERTAKEN: Silver, 52–53.

p. 220   NIXON ADMINISTRATION: Critique and Edward Jay Epstein quote in Gettinger, 43.

pp. 221–22   INTERNATIONAL SCENE: Parts of this section dealing with Southwest Asia were previously published in Georgette Bennett, "From the Golden Crescent to Eldridge Street," *New York*, October 13, 1980; also based on "Pakistan Ruler Says U.S. and West Are Too Soft on Drug Dealers," New York *Times*, August 12, 1984; Brinkley, September 9, 1984.

p. 222   PERU: Alan Riding, "Drug Region in Peru Booming Again," New York *Times*, December 29, 1984.

p. 222   PARAGUAY: Joel Brinkley, "Aides Suspect Paraguay Officials Of a Narcotics Link," New York *Times*, January 3, 1985.

p. 222   MEXICO: Joel Brinkley, "U.S. Says Nations Are Not Destroying Drug Crops," New York *Times*, September 25, 1985.

p. 222   BELIZE: David Pitt, "Belize Warily Considers Marijuana Herbicide," New York *Times*, October 27, 1985.

p. 223   OPERATION DELTA-9: "Operation Delta-9: Attorney General Meese Initiates Nationwide Marijuana Raid," *International Drug Report*, September 1985.

p. 223   JOHN LAWN: Quoted in Jon Nordheimer, "U.S. Gets Report World Heroin Trace Is Increasing," New York *Times*, February 21, 1985.

p. 223   HIP PROGRAM: Gettinger, 35–42.

pp. 223–24   UNIVERSITY OF CALIFORNIA ESTIMATES: Ibid., 36.

p. 224   DETECTIVE BEDROSIAN: Quoted in ibid., 40.

p. 224   DOCTORS HAVE HIGHEST ADDICTION RATE: Ray, 204.

p. 224   THE USUAL MEDICAL AND VOCATIONAL PROBLEMS: Ibid., 204.

p. 224   MATURE OUT: Ibid., 196; also Arnold Trebach, "Peace Without Surrender in the Perpetual Drug War," *Justice Quarterly*, 1:1, March 1984, 130.

p. 224   TWO TO TEN USERS FOR EVERY JUNKIE: 2:1 ratio found in Abt Associates, 33; 10:1 ratio found in Leon Hunt and Norman Zinberg, "Heroin Use: A New Look," *Drug Abuse Council*, "The Extent of Heroin Use: Users Versus Addicts," 1976.

p. 224   WANT TO GET HOOKED: Ray, 202.

p. 225   COSTS OF DRUG USE ARE GARGANTUAN: Gropper, 7–8.

p. 225   TREATMENT, LAW ENFORCEMENT ($1.2 BILLION): Figures cited in Peter Reuter, "The Real Drug Battlefront," New York *Times*, May 13, 1985.

p. 225   ADDICTS SHARE TRAITS WITH CRIMINALS: Duane McBride and Clyde McCoy, "Crime and Drug-Using Behavior," *Criminology*, 19:2, August 1981, 297.

p. 225   AGE OF FIRST NARCOTICS ADDICTION: McGlothlin, Anglin, and Wilson, 299.

p. 225   STEALING . . . DEALING AND FREELOADING: A study of crime rates of heroin abusers in New York shows that, of an average of 1,400 crimes committed per year by daily users, 1,116 were comprised of distribution offenses. These include steering, touting, selling, and copping. Gropper, 6–7.

p. 226   METHADONE MAINTENANCE: John Blackmore, "The Use and Abuse of Methadone," *Police Magazine*, January 1980, 47–48, 49–50.

p. 226   SIDE EFFECTS OF METHADONE: Rosenbaum, 112–15.

p. 226   NALTREXONE: Irvin Molotsky, "F.D.A. Announces New Drug to Block Craving for Heroin," New York *Times*, November 19, 1984.

pp. 226–27   ENGLAND . . . DR. RICHARD PHILLIPSON: Richard Phillipson, "Heroin Maintenance in Britain and Heroin for the Relief of Pain in the United States of America," *Justice Quarterly*, 1:2, June 1984, 290, 293.

p. 227   EDUCATION . . . CIGARETTES AND ALCOHOL: Trebach, 136, 140.

p. 227   HISTORY OF MARIJUANA USE AND LEGISLATION: James Inciardi, "Marijuana Decriminalization Research," *Criminology*, 19:1, 146, 151, 153–56.

p. 227   ELEVEN STATES DECRIMINALIZED: As of this writing, the states are Alaska, California, Colorado, Maine, Minnesota, Mississippi, Nebraska, New York, North Carolina, Ohio, Oregon.

p. 227   ALASKA . . . PERSONAL USE: Mitchell, 48.

p. 228   YOUNG PEOPLE TRYING GRASS AT LOWER RATE: McGarrell and Flanagan, 356–57. Data from Department of Health and Human Services, *National Survey of Drug Abuse: Main Findings 1982*, shows the following: In 1979, 30.9 percent of youths (12–17) reported ever having used marijuana. By 1982, the percentage had dropped to 26.7. For young adults (18–25), percentages are 68.2 in 1979 and 64.1 in 1982. For adults (26 and older), 19.6 percent in 1979 and 23.0 in 1982.

p. 228   YOUNG PEOPLE BECOMING LESS TOLERANT OF MARIJUANA: NORC General Social Surveys show that in 1973, 81 percent of the sample felt marijuana should not be legalized. In 1980 and 1983, an average of 77 percent took this position. Among those 18–24, 56 percent concurred in 1973 while 61 percent agreed in 1980, 1983. On the whole however, the older the respondents, the greater the percentage favoring criminalization.

Gallup polls of 1977 to 1982 diverge from NORC findings. They show an overall decline from 30 percent to 21 percent in those who favor legalization.

p. 228   SURVEYS OF HIGH SCHOOL SENIORS . . . SMOKING MARIJUANA IN PUBLIC AND PRIVATE: McGarrell and Flanagan, 264. Data drawn from Department of Health and Social Services, *Highlights from Drugs and American High School Students 1975–*

1983, shows the following: On the issue of private use of marijuana/hashish, 27.5 percent of the Class of 1976 and 37.8 percent of the Class of 1983 advocated criminalization. With reference to public use of marijuana/hashish, 59.1 percent of the Class of 1976 and 73.6 percent of the Class of 1983 advocated criminalization.

p. 228   SELLING IT ONLY TO ADULTS: Ibid., 265.

p. 228   1982 GALLUP POLL: McGarrell and Flanagan, 266.

p. 228   SCOTT PALLITO: Facts and quotes drawn from James Brooke, "Undercover Drug Agents Are Increasing in Schools," New York *Times*, May 25, 1985.

p. 229   HIGH SCHOOL SENIORS' PERCEPTIONS OF HARMFULNESS OF DRUGS: McGarrell and Flanagan, 263.

p. 229   "UPPERS," "DOWNERS," AND SUPPORT FOR EXISTING BANS: Ibid., 264.

p. 229   LOCAL DRUG VIOLATIONS ARRESTS: Ibid., 465.

p. 229   FEDERAL PROSECUTIONS: Ibid., 564.

p. 229   SENTENCES: Ibid., 580.

CRIMEWARP V: THE UPS AND DOWNS OF BIG BROTHER

p. 231   RAYMOND LEE STEWART: Bruce Porter, "The F.B.I. Psychological Profiling Team," *The National Centurion*, December 1983, 55–56.

p. 232   15 PERCENT ON TARGET: "The Random Killers," *Newsweek*, November 26, 1984.

CHAPTER 16: Pyrotechnic Policing

p. 233   MIAMI . . . VIDEO CAMERAS: "Miami Beach Police Drop Their Video Vigil," New York *Times*, July 22, 1984.

p. 234   TERRY DEAN ROGAN: David Burnham, "Victim Files Suit Over Error That Led to 5 Arrests," New York *Times*, February 12, 1985.

p. 234   NCIC: Statistics on member agencies, requests for information and erroneous reports cited in David Burnham, "F.B.I. Says 12,000 Faulty Reports On Suspects Are Issued Each Day," New York *Times*, August 25, 1985; and "Many FBI Files Are Inaccurate, Study Finds," *Police Magazine*, January 1983, 4.

p. 235   RECENT SUPREME COURT DECISIONS LIMIT POLICE USE OF GUNS: *Tennessee v. Garner* (1985) enjoins police officers from shooting to kill unarmed and nondangerous fleeing felony suspects. In another case decided in June of that year, the Court ruled that Oklahoma City was not liable for damages in the mistaken shooting of William Adam Tuttle by a rookie police officer. That single isolated incident was not sufficient to establish liability. However, a city is liable, ruled the Court, if it can be shown that the wrongful act derives from city policy and can be attributed to a municipal policymaker.

p. 238   1971 AND 1974 . . . 5.5 PERCENT A YEAR: U.S. Department of Justice, National Institute of Law Enforcement and Criminal Justice, Law Enforcement Assistance Administration, "The National Manpower Survey of the Criminal Justice System: Executive Summary," undated, 5.

p. 238   GROWTH HAS SHRUNK TO 3 PERCENT: Ibid.; and McGarrell and Flanagan, 27.

p. 238   EXPENDITURES HAVE GROWN: U.S. Department of Justice, *Report to the Nation*, 100.

p. 238   2.8 PERCENT OF PUBLIC PIE: "Justice Expenditure and Employment, 1982," Bureau of Justice Statistics *Bulletin*, August 1985, 1.

p. 238   MORE THAN HALF . . . FOR POLICE: Ibid.

p. 238   THREE-QUARTERS ARE SWORN: Ibid., 42.

p. 238   1 OF THEM FOR EVERY 408 OF US: Ratio based on a rate of police personnel per 1,000 population of 2.45, as cited in McGarrell and Flanagan, 56.

p. 238   LARGEST CITIES, SOUTH- AND MID-ATLANTIC STATES: Ibid., 56–57.

p. 238   BIG CITY DEPARTMENTS WON'T GROW MUCH IN THE FUTURE . . . STATE AND COUNTY AGENCIES WILL EXPAND: "The National Manpower Survey," 5.

p. 238   THE RARELY ACKNOWLEDGED REALITY: Anthony Bouza, "The Police and Police Management," *The Key*, Fall 1985, 7.

p. 238   THE AVERAGE CONCENTRATION OF POLICE: Joseph McNamara quoted in M. Daniel Rosen, "San Jose: It's Sherlock Holmes in Modern Dress," *Police Magazine*, September 1982, 19.

p. 239   OFFICE OF TECHNOLOGY ASSESSMENT: Statistics cited in David Burnham, "Agency Finds Lag in Laws to Bar Abuse of Electronic Surveillance," New York *Times*, October 24, 1985.

pp. 239–40   WILLIE JONES: Selwyn Raab, "Wrong Willie Jones Spends 3 Months in Jail," New York *Times*, November 30, 1985.

p. 240   SHEILA JACKSON STOSSIER: Burnham, August 25, 1985.

p. 240   AS A RESULT OF THIS INCIDENT I HAVE SUFFERED: Sheila Jackson Stossier quoted in David Burnham, "Proposal on Tracing Suspects Assailed at Hearing in House," New York *Times*, April 25, 1985.

p. 240   EVEN WITH AVAILABLE TECHNOLOGY: Statistics on extent and type of police use of computers cited in M. Daniel Rosen, "Police and Computers: The Revolution That Never Happened," *Police Magazine*, September 1982, 10.

p. 240   IN MANY CASES, SOPHISTICATED MATHEMATICS CAMOUFLAGE FOGGY THINKING: Louis Mayo, "Leading Blindly: An Assessment of Chiefs' Information about Police Operations," in Geller, 412.

p. 240   COMPARED TO THE 100,000 HOSPITALS: G. Thomas Steele quoted in Rosen, 12.

p. 241   SAN DIEGO: Anecdote cited in ibid., 9.

p. 241   12–23 PERCENT: Donna Hamperian, et al, "The Young Criminal Years of the Violent Few," U.S. Department of Justice, Office of Juvenile Justice and Delinquency Prevention, June 1985, 20.

pp. 241–42   TARGET 8: Selection process described in Minneapolis Police Department internal concept paper, "Field Integrated Neutralizing Information System: FINIS."

p. 242   PUBLIC APPROVAL OF WIRETAPPING: NORC poll reported in McGarrell and Flanagan, 210.

p. 242   COURT ORDERS FOR WIRETAPS: Ibid., 551.

p. 242   TWO THIRDS . . . INVADED . . . SOMEONE'S HOME: Ibid., 548.

p. 242   TEN-YEAR HIGH: Ibid., 556; and Administrative Office of the United States Courts, 27.

p. 243   CARMINE PERSICO: M. A. Farber, "Persico, on Tape, Discusses $250,000 Payoff to I.R.S. Agent," New York *Times*, November 13, 1985.

p. 243   WHITE COLLAR OFFENDERS HAVE MEANS: Frank Tuerkheimer, "Sting Operations . . . A Necessary Tool," *Police Magazine*, May 1980, 47.

p. 243   ONE-FOURTH OF FEDERAL AGENCIES: Burnham, October 24, 1985.

pp. 243–44   TRAKATRON; SENSITRACE: Dwight Merriam, "Employee Theft," *Criminal Justice Abstracts*, September 1977, 399.

p. 244   THE NUMBER OF CRIME LABORATORIES HAS MORE THAN DOUBLED: Marc Caplan and Joe Holt, "Forensics: When Science Bears Witness," U.S. Department of Justice, National Institute of Justice, October 1984, 8. In 1966, there were 110 crime labs; in 1983, 250.

p. 245   OAKLAND, CALIFORNIA: Rape example found in ibid., Introduction.

p. 245   WE HAVE LEARNED THE LESSON OF HISTORY: Justice Goldberg quoted in ibid., 2.

p. 247   GARNER V. TENNESSEE: Facts of case based on the decision by Justice Byron White as reported in New York *Times*, March 28, 1985.

p. 248   DOWNWARD TREND IN SHOOTINGS: Matulia, 49. The trend actually precedes 1974. Jack Kuykendahl, "Trends in the Use of Deadly Force By Police," *Journal of Criminal Justice*, 9:5, 1981, 360, studied the period 1949–74. He found that while the homicide rate had nearly doubled in that time, the percentage of police-caused homicides had declined by nearly half.

p. 248   LOWEST MEAN RATE OF SHOOTINGS BY POLICE: Ibid., 22–24.

p. 249   POLICE OFFICERS KILLED IN THE LINE OF DUTY: McGarrell and Flanagan, 433.

p. 249   ASSAULTS . . . GUN IS RARELY USED: Ibid., 436.

p. 250   CITIZEN PARTICIPATION IN POLICING ISN'T NEW: Material in this section based on Georgette Bennett-Sandler, "Citizen Participation in Policing: Issues in the Social Control of a Social Control Agency," in Iacovetta and Chang, 246–47, 259–260.

CHAPTER 17: Uncrowded Courts

p. 252   JUDGE ROBERT COLOMBO: "Computers May Play New Role in Court," *Journal of Commerce*, January 22, 1985; Rich Arthurs, "Computer Technology Enters Detroit Courtroom," *Legal Times*, January 7, 1985.

p. 252   COURT REPORTING OBSOLESCENCE: Arthurs.

pp. 252–53   125 PAGES OF TESTIMONY: Claudia Postell, "Computers in the Courtroom," *Trial*, January 1985.

p. 253   10,000 COURT REPORTERS . . . 60 PERCENT: Ibid.

p. 253   CASE FILINGS INCREASED 4 PERCENT A YEAR . . . 30 PERCENT . . . APPEAL FILINGS: Carla Gaskins, Eugene Flango, and Jeanne Ito, "Case Filings in State Courts, 1983," Bureau of Justice Statistics *Bulletin*, October 1984, 1.

p. 253   NEIGHBORHOOD BRAWL: Case example cited in U.S. Department of Justice, Law Enforcement Assistance Administration, National Institute of Law Enforcement and Criminal Justice, "Citizen Dispute Settlement," undated, "Program Concept."

p. 253   10 MILLION CRIMINAL CASES: McGarrell and Flanagan, 544.

p. 253   250,000 REFERRED TO NPP: Scot Dewhirst, "Columbus Night Prosecutor Program," *The Key*, 11:2, Summer 1985, 15.

p. 253   200 DISPUTE SETTLEMENT CENTERS NATIONWIDE: "Mediation and Conflict Resolution: China and America," *The Key*, 10:4, Winter 1984–85, 3.

p. 254   UNSOUND . . . OVERHAULING: Roper Organization Survey, February 14–28, 1981. The breakdown was as follows: 40 percent, system basically sound but needs improvement; 9 percent, basically sound, essentially good; 18 percent, basically unsound, needs fundamental overhauling; 33 percent, not too sound, needs many improvements.

p. 254   THE PUBLIC INTEREST: Roper Organization, August 15–22, 1981.

p. 254   FAIR AND HONEST: Poll by Los Angeles *Times*, December 16–18, 1979, shows that 54 percent believe judges have not assumed too much power; 57 percent believe judges base their decisions on interpretation of law rather than personal beliefs; and 62 percent believe judges deal fairly with everyone.

p. 254   SIXTY PERCENT . . . CASES COME OUT THE WAY THEY SHOULD: Ibid.

p. 254   GROWING PART OF THE PUBLIC HAS FELT COURTS HAVE BEEN TOO EASY: According to surveys of Louis Harris Associates, 52 percent of the public felt courts were too easy in 1967. That number rose to 83 percent in 1981.

p. 254   90 PERCENT SCREAMING FOR TOUGHER PRISON TERMS: Roper Organization Survey, January 10–24, 1981.

p. 254   BILL OF RIGHTS: Roper Organization polls for September 19–26, 1981, showed that 93 percent favored preventive detention, 83 percent favored access to juvenile records, 65 percent favored admitting illegally seized evidence.

p. 254   HALF THE FELONY ARRESTS: Barbara Boland and Brian Forst, "The Prevalence of Guilty Pleas," Bureau of Justice Statistics Special Report, December 1984, 1.

p. 254   PORTLAND . . . GENEVA: Ibid., 2.

p. 254   TOP CHARGE FILED BY PROSECUTOR: Ibid., 3.

p. 255   LONGER AND HARSHER SENTENCES: "Punishment may be more certain in high plea jurisdictions and more severe in high trial jurisdictions," ibid., 4.

p. 255   LOST MUCH OF THEIR LATITUDE: Statistics on mandatory sentences, good time, and parole cited in Herbert Koppel, "Sentencing Practices in 13 States," Bureau of Justice Statistics Special Report, October 1984, 1–2.

pp. 255–56   INDETERMINATE, DETERMINATE, AND PRESUMPTIVE SENTENCES: Statistics found in U.S. Department of Justice, Report to the Nation, 72.

p. 255   MINNESOTA: Kay Knapp, "What Sentencing Reform in Minnesota Has and Has Not Accomplished," Judicature, 68:4–5, October–November 1984, 184–85.

p. 255   NORTH CAROLINA: Based on findings cited in Stevens Clark, "North Carolina's Determinate Sentencing Legislation," Judicature, 68:4–5, October–November 1984, 146–47.

p. 256   A JUST SENTENCE MAY NOT BE EFFECTIVE: Brian Forst, "Selective Incapacitation: A Sheep in Wolf's Clothing?" Judicature, 68:4–5, October–November 1984, 155.

p. 256   APPEALS MORE THAN DOUBLED: Statistics on growth of appeals cited in Thomas Marvell and Sue Lindgren, "1973–1983 Trends: The Growth of Appeals," Bureau of Justice Statistics Bulletin, February 1985, 1–2, 4.

p. 257   100 YEAR SURVEY: James Meeker, "Criminal Appeals Over the Last 100 Years: Are the Odds of Winning Increasing?" Criminology, 22:4, November 1984, 561–65.

p. 257   APPEALS 50 TO 100 PERCENT: Interview with Thomas Rumfola by Robert Kimmel for Audio-TV Features, Inc., April 1985.

p. 258   JUDICATE: Martin Tolchin, "Private Courts With Binding Rulings Draw Interest and Some Challenges," New York Times, May 12, 1985.

p. 258   YOUTH COURT: Michael Winerip, "Youth-Run Courts in State Growing Beyond Novelties," New York Times, January 2, 1985.

CHAPTER 18: Prisons Without Walls

p. 260   MARTINSON . . . CRITIQUE OF AMERICAN CORRECTIONS: "With few and isolated exceptions, the rehabilitative efforts that have been tried so far have had no appreciable effect on recidivism." Robert Martinson, "What Works?—Questions and Answers About Prison Reform," The Public Interest, 35, Spring 1974, 25.

p. 261   JAY MATCH: Jon Nordheimer, "Jail Moves Into Probationer's Home," New York Times, February 15, 1985.

p. 261   HOUSE ARREST: Thomas Blomberg, "House Arrest in Florida," The Key, Fall 1985, 13; Daniel Ford and Annesley Schmidt, "Electronically Monitored Home Confinement," NIJ Reports, November 1985, 2–6.

p. 261   CONTROL DATA: "Prisons Becoming Manufacturing Sites," *Public Administration Times*, December 1, 1985.

p. 261   10 PERCENT . . . EMPLOYED IN PRISON INDUSTRIES: Ibid.

pp. 261–62   SEVEN PILOT PROJECTS: Edward Gargan, "The Nation's Prisoners Join the Labor Force," New York *Times*, August 28, 1983.

p. 262   ONE-HALF MILLION PRISON INMATES: Allen Beck and Lawrence Greenfeld, "Prisoners in 1984," Bureau of Justice Statistics *Bulletin*, April 1985.

p. 262   FACTORIES WITH FENCES: Warren Burger, "Prison Industries: Turning Warehouses into Factories with Fences," *Public Administration Review*, 45, Special Issue, November 1985, 754–57.

pp. 262–263   SILVERDALE DETENTION CENTER: Martin Tolchin, "Privately Owned Prisons Increase, So Do Their Critics," New York *Times*, February 11, 1985.

p. 262   PRIVATE COMPANY . . . TO OPERATE . . . PRISONS: "States Authorize Private Jail Services," *Public Administration Times*, February 1, 1985; and E. R. Shipp, "Group Aiding Ex-Convicts Begins Running a Jail," New York *Times*, February 17, 1985.

p. 262   AS OF EARLY 1984 . . . MANAGEMENT . . . TO PRIVATE HANDS: Joan Mullen, "Corrections and the Private Sector," *NIJ Reports*, May 1985, 4.

p. 263   HAMILTON COUNTY COST OVERRUNS: Martin Tolchin, "Privately Operated Prison in Tennessee Reports $200,000 in Cost Overruns," New York *Times*, May 22, 1985.

p. 263   1980 TO 1985 VALUE OF PRIVATE SERVICES: Value increased from $100.2 billion to $173 billion. Office of Management and Budget statistics cited in Martin Tolchin, "U.S. Pressing Plan to Contract Work," New York *Times*, March 11, 1985.

p. 263   IT IS NOT THE GOVERNMENT'S OBLIGATION: Mario Cuomo quoted in Martin Tolchin, "Governor's Cautious in Endorsing Private Operation of Prisons," New York *Times*, March 3, 1985.

p. 263   WILLIAM WALSH: Walsh's research and "Jim" anecdote reported in Leah Wallach, "Hair Trigger," *Omni*, June 1984, 22, 114.

p. 263   DR. STEPHEN SCHOENTHALER: Jane Brody, "Diet Therapy For Behavior Is Criticized As Premature," New York *Times*, December 4, 1984.

p. 264   LESCH-NYHAN SYNDROME: Harold Schmeck, Jr., "Agency Reports Genetic Therapy Is Near," New York *Times*, December 18, 1984.

p. 264   ANTIANDROGEN DRUGS: A brief description of activation of androgens in the system is found in Lee Ellis, "Genetics and Criminal Behavior," *Criminology*, 20:1, May 1982, 59.

p. 264   BRAIN DEFECTS: Harold Schmeck, "Brain Defects Seen in Those Who Repeat Violent Acts," New York *Times*, September 17, 1985.

p. 264   45.5 PERCENT SINCE 1977: Beck and Greenfeld, 1.

p. 264   OVERCROWDING: Statistics cited in ibid., 5.

p. 264   100,000 BEDS . . . 130,000 INMATES: Ibid., 1.

p. 264   COURT ORDER . . . CONSENT DECREE: Ibid., 4.

pp. 264–65   TENNESSEE STATE PRISON SYSTEM: Dudley Clendinden, "Tennessee and U.S. Court in a Dispute Over Crowded Prisons," New York *Times*, November 15, 1985.

p. 266   NINETY-FOUR PERCENT OF THOSE AWAITING TRIAL ARE CHARGED WITH FELONIES: Remarks of Commissioner William Ciuros, Jr. before Finance Committee/Public Safety Committee of the New York City Council/Board of Estimate, May 22, 1978.

p. 266   NEW YORK STATE'S CONSTITUTION: See Gargan.

p. 266   613 RIKER'S ISLAND DETAINEES . . . 21,000 INMATES IN OTHER STATES: Statistics cited by Senator Alfonse D'Amato and quoted in Joseph Berger, "D'Amato Calling for Private Ownership of Prisons," New York *Times,* August 9, 1984.

p. 266   PENNSYLVANIA: "Study of Guidelines Shows More Criminals Go to Prison," *ACJS* Today, September 1984, 21.

p. 266   WE DON'T WANT TO JAIL LARGE NUMBERS OF PERSONS: John Kramer quoted in ibid.

p. 267   ILLINOIS: "Illinois Prisons Threatening to Turn Away Inmates," New York *Times,* July 26, 1983.

p. 267   TWO-THIRDS . . . HAD BEEN THERE BEFORE: Lawrence Greenfeld, "Examining Recidivism," Bureau of Justice Statistics *Special Report,* February 1985, 1.

p. 267   HALF OF THEM, FOUR OR MORE TIMES: Ibid., 2.

p. 267   HALF THE CRIMES . . . WOULD NOT HAVE HAPPENED: Ibid., 4.

p. 267   46 PERCENT OVER THE NEXT SEVERAL YEARS: Ibid.

p. 267   THE YOUNGER THE CONVICT: Ibid., 3.

p. 267   SECOND HALF OF THE FIRST YEAR: John Wallerstedt, "Returning to Prison," Bureau of Justice Statistics *Special Report,* November 1984, 2.

p. 267   OFTEN A PAROLE VIOLATION: Ibid., 3.

p. 267   PROPERTY OFFENDERS: Ibid.

p. 267   MALES . . . FEMALES; BLACKS . . . WHITES: Ibid., 4–5.

p. 268   FIRST TIMERS . . . RECIDIVISTS: Greenfeld, 5.

p. 268   INDEX FOR PREDICTING FUTURE CRIMINALITY: Peter Greenwood, "Selective Incapacitation: A Method of Using Our Prisons More Effectively," *NIJ Reports,* January 1984, 6.

p. 268   POSITIVE RESPONSES . . . SCORE: "Identifying High-Risk Repeat Offenders," *Public Administration Times,* November 1982.

p. 268   20 PERCENT WITH NO INCREASE IN . . . ROBBERS INCARCERATED: Greenwood, 6.

p. 268   DOUBLING, TRIPLING, QUADRUPLING THE CURRENT PRISON POPULATION: Jacqueline Cohen, "Incapacitating Criminals: Recent Research Findings," National Institute of Justice *Research in Brief,* December 1983, 2, Table 3.

p. 268   700,000 JAIL AND PRISON INMATES: Total derived by adding 463,866 prison inmates (Beck and Greenfeld, 1) to an average of 227,541 jail inmates (McGarrell and Flanagan, 637).

p. 268   MISTAKENLY LABELED HALF ITS SAMPLE: Andrew von Hirsch, "Selective Incapacitation: Critique," *NIJ Reports,* January 1984, 5.

p. 268   ELECTROENCEPHALOGRAPH: Sarnoff Mednick, Jan Volavka, William Gabrielli, Jr., and Turan Itil, "EEG As A Predictor of Antisocial Behavior," *Criminology,* 19:2, August 1981, 221–22, 226–27.

p. 268   EXTRA Y CHROMOSOME: Ellis, 51.

p. 268   LOW IQ AND DELINQUENCY: David Rowe and D. Wayne Osgood, "Heredity and Sociological Theories of Delinquency: A Reconsideration," *American Sociological Review,* 49:4, August 1984, 526–40.

pp. 268–69   PHYSIOLOGICAL DATA: For an excellent analysis of psychophysiobiological approaches to treatment of crime, see Jeffery, Chapters 12–14.

p. 269   RUN IT THROUGH A COMPUTER: Yael Hassin, "Early Release Committee For Prisoners Versus Computer," *Criminology,* 18:3, November 1980, 393. The same process that is used to detain an inmate can also be used to release him. Early releases have become a fact of life for most states faced with overcrowded prisons. Shortening a sentence is the parole board's job, but parole decisions have a terrible track record. Using rank ordered sociodemographic and criminal history variables, computers do a better job. An Israeli study showed that while humans were better at predicting nonrecidivism, the computer's decisions were right in predicting recidivism about four times more often than early release boards.

p. 269   1 FOR EVERY 273 CRIMES COMMITTED: Ratio computed on 1979 statistics dividing 41 million victimizations and 150,000 new imprisonments. Patrick Langan and Lawrence Greenfeld, "The Prevalence of Imprisonment," Bureau of Justice Statistics *Special Report,* July 1985, 8.

p. 269   MORE THAN HALF THE FIRST TIMERS AND . . . REPEATERS HAVE DONE TIME FOR VIOLENCE: Greenfeld, 5.

p. 269   PAROLE AND PROBATION POPULATION . . . 2 MILLION: Lawrence Greenfeld, "Probation and Parole 1983," Bureau of Justice Statistics *Bulletin,* September 1984, 2.

p. 269   RESTITUTION . . . 85 PERCENT OF JUVENILE COURTS: Anne Larason Schneider and Peter Schneider, "A Comparison of Programmatic and 'Ad Hoc' Restitution In Juvenile Courts," *Justice Quarterly,* 1:4, December 1984, 529.

p. 269   STEAL, VANDALIZE, OR SHOPLIFT AGAIN: Ibid., 545.

pp. 269–70   MISSOURI VALLEY: "Nebraska Bid-Rigger Sentenced to Endow College Ethics Chair," New York *Times,* July 29, 1983.

p. 270   LONE VOICES . . . PHYSICAL PAIN: G. Newman, 16, Chapter 5, 140; also Lee Bowker's review of Newman's book, in *Justice Quarterly,* 1:2, June 1984, 296–98.

p. 270 $410 TO PRIDE, INC . . . FOR THREE MONTHS: Nordheimer.

p. 270 $5.00 A DAY: Ford and Schmidt, 3.

p. 270   WHAT THESE DATA SUGGEST: Blomberg. Blomberg's conclusion is supported in a thoughtful analysis by Bonnie Berry, "Electronic Jails: A New Criminal Justice Concern," *Justice Quarterly,* 2:1, March 1985, 6.

p. 270   150–200 FOOT RADIUS: Berry, 2.

p. 271   BEYOND THE REACH OF THE POOR: Berry, 7, 19, points out that some jurisdictions, such as Albuquerque, New Mexico, make GOSSline electronic surveillance available on a sliding fee for those who can't afford it. This, despite the fact that the city pays $100,000 per year for 25 monitor/bracelet sets with extra sets leased for $1,000 a year as of 1983. Among the jurisdictions reviewed by Ford and Schmidt, 5, Kenton County, Kentucky provides free electronic monitoring for those with net household incomes of under $100 a week.

p. 271   LIFETIME PROBABILITY OF GOING TO PRISON: Langan and Greenfeld, 5.

p. 271   AVERAGE OF 1.5 TO 2.5 YEARS: Herbert Koppel, "Time Served in Prison," Bureau of Justice Statistics *Special Report,* June 1984, 1.

CHAPTER 19: Helping Those Who Help Themselves

p. 274   I KNEW THEY WEREN'T GOING TO DO ANYTHING: Anna Maria Torres quoted in "Man Accused of Kidnapping of 2 He Said Robbed Home," New York *Times,* April 8, 1985.

p. 274   WE CAN'T HAVE PEOPLE RUNNING AROUND WITH GUNS: Detective Gary Venema quoted in "Robbed Man Faces Life Term in Kidnapping," New York *Times,* April 9, 1985.

p. 274   THEY TREATED US LIKE WE WERE THE ROBBERS: Anna Maria Torres quoted in New York *Times,* April 8, 1985.

p. 274   PERCENTAGE OF PEOPLE OWNING GUNS DWINDLING: McGarrell and Flanagan, 246, 248.

p. 274   CAJUN WHARF: Anecdote from Mary Alice Kmet, "Placing Employees for Best Results," *Security Management,* March 1979, 6.

p. 274   10,000 COMPANIES: Bernard Wysocki, Jr., "Hired Guns: One Big Security Risk Is the Security Guards, Some Companies Find," *Wall Street Journal,* August 30, 1983.

p. 274   EMPLOY MORE THAN 1 MILLION PEOPLE: Findings of Hallcrest Report cited in William Cunningham and Todd Taylor, "The Growing Role of Private Security," National Institute of Justice *Research in Brief,* October 1984, 3.

p. 274   OUTNUMBER SWORN OFFICERS 2 TO 1: Ibid.

p. 275   PROTECTS THE GOVERNMENT . . . 36,000: "Government Officials Turning to Private Guards to Fill Public Safety Posts," New York *Times,* November 29, 1985.

p. 275   TWO-THIRDS HAVE CRIMINAL RECORDS: Finding of New York Investigation Commission in 1980 cited in Selwyn Raab, "Growing Security-Guard Industry Under Scrutiny," New York *Times,* June 4, 1984.

p. 275   TOUGHER SCREENING PROCESS THAN SWORN POLICE: Ira Lipman cited in "How Guardsmark's Lipman Sells Security," *Business Week,* March 24, 1975.

p. 276   GATTLING AND ATLANTA STREETS BLOCK PARTY: Meg McKinney, "Block Party," *Texarkana Gazette,* August 29, 1982.

p. 277   ACT A NON-PROFIT ORGANIZATION: ACT statistics cited in "Texarkana: Two Cities—One Act," *Prevention Press,* Winter 1982, 7.

p. 277   U.S. DEPARTMENT OF JUSTICE DIRECTORY: Lockard et al.

p. 277   350,000 VOLUNTEERS: Dan Bernstein, "Police Volunteers," *Police Magazine,* Summer 1977, 17–18.

p. 277   900 ORGANIZED CITIZEN PATROLS: Yin et al., 38.

p. 277   BEFORE THE FIRST METROPOLITAN POLICE WERE ESTABLISHED: The history of self-policing is based on Bennett-Sandler et al., Chapter 1.

p. 278   SOME PEOPLE RESISTED THIS STEP: Evelyn Parks, "From Constabulary to Police Society: Implications for Social Control," *Catalyst,* Summer 1970, 80.

pp. 278–79   LEGION OF DOOM: "8 Youths Accused Of Vigilante Acts," New York *Times,* May 29, 1985; Wayne King, "School Vigilante Group Is Linked to 35 Felonies," New York *Times,* April 20, 1985; "Legion of Doom: Young Vigilantes?" *Newsweek,* April 8, 1985.

p. 279   GUARDIAN ANGELS: Bernard Edelman, "Does New York Need The Guardian Angels?" *Police Magazine,* 51–56.

p. 279   VIGILANTISM IN RESIDENT PATROLS OCCURS RARELY: Conditions under which vigilantism occurs are outlined in Yin et al., 59, 66–67.

p. 280   HALF THE AREAS REVIEWED, CRIME RATE WAS LOW: Rand Corporation News Release re: Yin et al., December 13, 1976.

p. 281   NOT INITIALLY FORMED TO PREVENT CRIME: Paul Lavrakas, "Factors Related to Citizen Involvement in Personal, Household, and Neighborhood Anti-Crime Measures—An Executive Summary," U.S. Department of Justice, National Institute of Justice, November 1981, 9.

p. 281   KEY TO SUCCESS OF NEIGHBORHOOD PATROLS: Yin et al., 67, 77.

p. 281   CHICAGO: Lavrakas, 9–10.

p. 281   ATLANTA: Greenberg, Rohe, and Williams, 118.

p. 281   LOS ANGELES: "We Love You LAPD, But Don't Tax Our House," *Police Magazine,* July 1981, 3.

p. 281   ON EVERY ISSUE, OUR GREATEST SUPPORT: Dan Cooke quoted in ibid.

p. 282   APRIL 1972 PROPOSAL: "The Center," submitted to Planning Committee, Action Research Program in Criminal Justice, Graduate Center, City University of New York, April 15, 1972.

p. 282   THIRTY-SEVEN STATES OFFER MONETARY COMPENSATION: U.S Department of Justice, *Report to the Nation,* 26.

p. 282   MOST PEOPLE DON'T GET INVOLVED IN ANTICRIME GROUPS: Lavrakas, 9–10. The Chicago area study revealed that only one tenth of his sample claimed to have participated in group anticrime efforts.

p. 283   40 PERCENT OWN FIREARMS: 1983 Gallup poll reported in McGarrell and Flanagan, 240.

p. 283   MAJORITY OWN RIFLES AND SHOTGUNS: Ibid.

p. 283   HALF MILLION AUTOMATIC COMBAT WEAPONS: Tom Morganthau, "Machine Gun U.S.A.," *Newsweek,* October 14, 1985.

p. 283   SOLUTIONS, INC.: Facts and statistics based on author interview with Diane Zufle, May 2, 1986.

p. 283   THERE'S NO SUCH THING AS EXCESSIVE DEADLY FORCE: Diane Zufle quoted in tape package approximately 5¾ minutes into broadcast, CBS "Up to the Minute," aired on October 19, 1981.

p. 283   I'M THINKING ABOUT MY FAMILY: "Housewife" quoted in tape package approximately 7½ minutes into broadcast, CBS "Up to the Minute," aired on October 19, 1981.

p. 283   IF THAT HAPPENED TODAY: Close friend quoted in tape package approximately 11¾ minutes into broadcast, CBS "Up to the Minute," aired on October 19, 1981.

p. 283   SOUTHERNERS . . . AGE, EDUCATION, INCOME, AND OCCUPATIONAL STATUS: 1983 Gallup poll reported in McGarrell and Flanagan, 248.

p. 283   WHITES MORE APT TO OWN PISTOLS THAN BLACKS: Ibid.; also Lavrakas, 7. Lavrakas' study showed that Chicago area minority households were most likely to report owning handguns as were higher income households, with higher-income blacks being the most likely to have handguns at home.

p. 283   120 MILLION FIREARMS IN PRIVATE CIRCULATION: Wright, Rossi, and Daly, 1.

p. 283   FEW END UP IN CRIMINAL HANDS: In Wright, Rossi, and Daly's study, 17–18, 260,000 firearms were confiscated in 1971, with 70 percent being handguns. In 1975, another year of that study, 275,000 handguns were reported stolen from private residences.

p. 283   THE PERCENTAGE HAS BEEN DROPPING SINCE 1974 AND EARLIER: McGarrell and Flanagan, 414, 424, 425.

p. 284   HANDGUNS MANUFACTURED IN THE U.S.: Ibid., 150. In 1974, there were 1.7 million handguns manufactured. In 1982, 2.6 million. By contrast, the manufacture of long guns dropped from 3.9 million in 1974 to 2.5 million in 1982.

p. 284   RESTRICTION ON BEARING ARMS: Ibid., 151.

p. 284   20,000 LAWS: Wright, Rossi, and Daly, 323.

p. 284   MANDATORY PENALTIES: Ibid., 317.

p. 284   PINEDALE, WYOMING: "Town in Wyoming Rejects Gun Ban," New York *Times,* December 4, 1984. Ban rejected December 4, 1984.

p. 284   MORTON GROVE, ILLINOIS: "The Village that Beat the Gun Lobby," New York *Times,* October 27, 1984. Ban upheld by Illinois Supreme Court in October 1984 after court battle that began in 1981.

p. 284   MOST PEOPLE APPROVE OF RESTRICTIONS—WITHIN LIMITS: Gallup poll findings cited in McGarrell and Flanagan, 250–55.

p. 284   POLLS SINCE 1975: Demographics of approval for stricter gun controls found in Gallup polls cited in ibid., 252–53.

p. 284   BY ALLOWING INTERSTATE SALE OF GUNS: In the final version of the bill, which was signed into law, interstate sale of rifles and shotguns was permitted, but interstate sale of handguns remained off-limits.

p. 285   HE WALKED INTO A DALLAS PAWNSHOP: John Hinckley narrative by Sarah Brady, "How to Deter Future Hinckleys," New York *Times*, November 8, 1985.

p. 286   THE AVERAGE GUN ENCOUNTER LASTS NO MORE THAN 2.5 SECONDS: Tim Zufle quoted in tape package approximately 9 minutes into broadcast, CBS "Up to the Minute," aired on October 19, 1981.

p. 286   MOST VIOLENT CRIMES TAKE PLACE INDOORS: McGarrell and Flanagan, 302–3.

p. 287   HOUSEHOLD BURGLARIES . . . TEN-YEAR LOW: Michael Rand, "Household Burglaries," Bureau of Justice Statistics *Bulletin*, January 1985, 5.

p. 287   NO FORCED ENTRY: Ibid., 1, 5.

p. 287   INCOMES UNDER $7,500 . . . 4 TO 9 UNITS: Ibid., 2.

p. 287   OWNERS VS. RENTERS: Lavrakas, 6; Rand, 2.

p. 287   BLACKS . . . ALARMS, WINDOW BARS, SPECIAL LOCKS: Ibid., 7.

p. 287   BLACK HOUSEHOLDS . . . HIGHEST RATE OF FORCED ENTRY: Rand, 2.

p. 287   BETTER-EDUCATED AND YOUNGER ADULTS: Lavrakas, 8.

p. 287   SINGLE-PERSON HOUSEHOLDS: Ibid.

p. 288   WORLD WAR II AS CATALYST: Task Force on Private Security, 31.

p. 288   A DECLINING PERCENTAGE WILL BE OWNED BY FEMALES: McGarrell and Flanagan, 246. A review of gun owner demographics as revealed in NORC surveys from 1973 to 1982 shows that females accounted for 43 percent of ownership in 1973, rose to 47 percent in 1977, and dipped to 39 percent in 1982.

p. 288   TIGHTER GUN CONTROLS SUPPORTED BY THE POWERFUL AND LESS POWERFUL: See Gallup polls cited in McGarrell and Flanagan, 252–53. Since 1975, males, the college educated, higher status job holders, Protestants, and those living in the largest cities have supported stricter laws. Since 1980, however, less powerful groups, such as the young and those with lower incomes, have displayed larger majorities in favor of stricter controls than older, higher-income respondents.

CHAPTER 20: Defensible Space

p. 290   89 PERCENT AND 145 PERCENT: Kevin Krajick, "Hartford: Claims of Success," *Police Magazine*, November 1979, 44.

p. 290   ELEVEN MODIFICATIONS MADE ON PUBLIC STREETS: U.S. Department of Justice, 1980, 52.

p. 290 $100 A HOUSE: "New Crime Prevention Concepts Profiled," *Crime Control Digest*, March 5, 1979.

p. 291   BURGLARIES AND ROBBERIES DROPPED BY MORE THAN ONE THIRD: U.S. Department of Justice, 1980, 54.

p. 291   PROSTITUTES: Krajick, 15.

p. 291   1979 SECOND LOOK AT NORTH ASYLUM HILL: Floyd Fowler, Jr., and Thomas Mangione, "Neighborhood Crime, Fear and Social Control: A Second Look at the Hartford Program, Executive Summary," U.S. Department of Justice, National Institute of Justice, April 1982, 22–27.

p. 291   FIRST-TIME LINK BETWEEN CRIME, SPATIAL DESIGN, AND SOCIAL BEHAVIOR: Ibid., 26.

p. 292   SHLOMO ANGEL: Cited in Jeffery, 191–92.

p. 292   SOUTHLAND CORPORATION: John P. Thompson, "Preface," in Johnson, xiii–xiv.

p. 292   RAY JOHNSON: Ibid., xviii.

p. 293   CONTROL OF UNWANTED INTERACTION: Rapoport, 193.

p. 294   STREET CRIMINALS . . . TRAVEL AN AVERAGE OF TWO MILES: Gerald Pyle's and Thomas Reppetto's findings cited in Jeffery, 195, 205, 212.

p. 294   DEBATE ABOUT HOW MUCH TERRITORIALITY REDUCES CRIME: Alan Booth, "The Built Environment as a Crime Deterrent," *Criminology*, 18:4, February 1981, 557–70. A Nebraska study, for example, found that defensible space fosters crime reduction in indoor public areas but not outdoor public areas.

p. 295   PHYSICAL CHANGES ARE FASTEST WAY TO REDUCE FEAR OF CRIME: U.S. Department of Justice, 1980, 64.

p. 295   CAPITOL HILL: Lisa Welke, "CPTED and Street Lights," *Nation's Cities*, December 1977, 24–25.

p. 295   ATLANTA: Greenberg, Rohe, and Williams, 121–22.

p. 295   ST. LOUIS: Newman, 1981, 140–43.

p. 296   NEWARK: Ibid., 217–19.

p. 297   SPACE CAN BE USED TO MOLD GROUP COHESION: Greenberg, Rohe, and Williams, 7.

pp. 297–98   MODEL CODE FOR DEFENSIBLE SPACE: The design specifications included here are derived from, but not exclusively based on, the following works of Oscar Newman: *Defensible Space;* with Stephen Johnston, "Model Security Code for Residential Areas," Institute for Community Design Analysis, 1974; *Design Guidelines for Creating Defensible Space;* with Karen Franck, *Factors Influencing Crime and Instability in Urban Housing Developments; Community of Interest.* Based on these works, a comprehensive checklist for defensible space was devised by the author for the Insurance Information Institute in New York.

p. 299   DEFENSIBLE SPACE DOESN'T DETER ALL CRIMES: Robert Sampson, "Structural Density and Criminal Victimization," *Criminology*, 21:2, May 1983, 290. "The expressive and explosive nature of assault implies less planning and fewer a priori assessments of the environment than does the crime of robbery."

CRIMEWARP VI: CONCLUSION: PAYING THE TAB FOR THE BILL OF RIGHTS

p. 302   GENERAL COURT: Gutman, 100–1.

p. 302   SINS: Wertenbaker, 159–76.

p. 302   CHILDREN WERE A PARTICULAR PROBLEM: Ibid., 166.

p. 302   *New England Primer:* Wright, 212.

p. 303   PERSONAL DEMONSTRATIONS FROM GOD: Miller and Johnson, 10.

p. 303   THE PURITAN OLIGARCHY BEGAN TO TOPPLE: The transformation of the colonies is described in Gutman, 111–14, 194–205; Wertenbaker, 182.

p. 304   ENTHUSIASTS: Miller and Johnson, 11.

p. 304   MORAL SLUMP: Wright, 97; Nye, 138.

p. 304   AGE OF ENLIGHTENMENT: Nye, 207.

p. 305   DIVIDED INTO FOUR GROUPS: Ibid., 195.

p. 306   FILLING THEIR PEWS AT DOUBLE . . . THEIR PREVIOUS RATES: Falwell, 1981, 19.

p. 306   SECULAR HUMANISM IS A TERM FIRST USED: Letters to the Editor of the New York *Times*, June 19, 1985, by Joseph Blau (author of a memo for the Ethical Union that was used as a basis for the amicus brief referred to herein) and Leo Pfeffer (attorney who argued the Torasco case before the Supreme Court).

pp. 306–7   THE INCORPORATION OF CHRISTIAN PRINCIPLES: Falwell, 1981, 192–93.

p. 307   RECRUITED THE ELECTRONIC MINISTRY: Viguerie, 56.

p. 307   THE MERGER OF THE BIBLE BELT AND SUNBELT: That turn of phrase is borrowed from Flake.

p. 307   A NEW SCHISM WAS EVIDENT: Webber, 15–16.

p. 308   MORAL MCCARTHYISM: A term coined by former Congressman John Buchanan in his public appearances on behalf of People for the American Way.

p. 308   85 MILLION POTENTIAL RECRUITS: Viguerie, 162.

p. 308   COMPUTERIZED LIST OF 4.5 MILLION NAMES: Ibid., 128.

p. 308   CHRISTIAN SCHOOL MOVEMENT: Statistics cited in Falwell, 1981, 21.

p. 309   MICHAEL LISAC: Testimony excerpted from Schlafly, 61.

p. 309   ONLY THOSE WHO HAVE BEEN BORN-AGAIN . . . CAN CALL UPON GOD: Goodman and Price, 46.

p. 309   TALENT BANK . . . 25 PERCENT QUOTA: On January 22, 1985, People for the American Way urged Congress to investigate links between Herbert Ellingwood, chairman of the federal Merit Systems Protection Board, and the American Coalition for Traditional Values. Tim LaHaye is quoted in the November 9, 1984, issue of *Christianity Today*.

p. 309   I'LL TELL YOU WHO I'LL VOTE FOR PRESIDENT: Goodman and Price, 109.

p. 310   LIBERAL ORGANIZATIONS . . . HAVE EMPLOYED SIMILAR DEVICES FOR YEARS: Burton Yale Pines, "A Majority for Morality?" *Public Opinion*, April/May 1981, 43.

p. 310   JUDGES . . . RUN A GAUNTLET: James Reston, "Reagan and the Courts," New York *Times*, September 18, 1985; Anthony Podesta, "The Theo-Politics Of The Right," St. Louis *Post-Dispatch*, April 23, 1985.

p. 310   LEGALIZATION OF IMMORALITY: Falwell, 1981, 188.

p. 310   NEWTON ESTES: New York *Times*, June 16, 1984.

pp. 310–11   SENATOR MARK HATFIELD: Quoted in Flake, 259.

p. 311   "MINISTERS AND MARCHES": Quoted in Goodman and Price, 77.

p. 311   SERMON ON THE MOUNT: Sandmel, 7, "The Gospel," commentaries. The sermon encompasses Matthew 5–7 in the New Testament. Included in the sermon are the Beatitudes, a form of praise "which . . . commends a type of behavior or attitude for which this worldly happiness is the promised reward . . . and the beatitudes become conditions for admission to the kingdom [of God]." The Beatitudes praise gentleness, mercy, peacemakers, the persecuted. They also praise the poor with the phrase, "How blest are these who know their need of God" (Matthew 5:3). Sandmel explains that this Beatitude "catches the religious dimension of a Jewish form of piety for which 'poverty' and 'utter dependence on God' were synonymous." Later in the sermon, Jesus preaches love of one's enemies and unostentatious, sincere piety. He warns, "Be careful not to make a show of your religion before men . . ." (Matthew 6:1) and "Beware of false prophets . . ." (Matthew 7:15). A review of the Sermon on the Mount, widely regarded to be the essence of Christianity, reveals the religio-political agenda of the New Right to be, in many ways, antithetical to Christianity.

p. 311   BABYLON, MOTHER OF HARLOTS: From Tim LaHaye's interpretation of revelation in *The Beginning of the End*, as quoted in Bollier, 85.

p. 311   GOD ALMIGHTY DOES NOT HEAR THE PRAYER OF A JEW: Rev. Bailey Smith as quoted in New York *Times*, April 22, 1981.

p. 311   IF A PERSON IS NOT A CHRISTIAN, HE IS INHERENTLY A FAILURE: Jerry Falwell in *Listen, America* as quoted in Bollier, 89.

p. 311   WE WERE ONCE A CHRISTIAN NATION . . . PRAYER . . . SIGNERS OF CONSTITUTION: Webber, 34–35.

p. 312   GARY POTTER: Citation by People for the American Way taken from *Moral Democracy*, June/July 1981.

p. 312   HOW SLAVERY SET THE STAGE: Kardiner and Ovesey, 379.

pp. 312–13   LYNCHINGS: History traced by Brown, 746–53.

p. 313   KU KLUX KLAN . . . THREE INCARNATIONS: Described in Lipset and Raab, 116–24.

p. 313   TO PUNISH DRUNKS, ADULTERERS, AND OTHER VIOLATORS: Ibid., 117.

p. 313   PRESERVING THE PURITY OF AMERICAN WOMEN: Sinclair, 284.

pp. 313–14   PRINCIPLES THAT THE KLAN STOOD FOR: Ibid.

p. 314   REMAINED QUIESCENT DURING THE 1930S: Post-1930s history of Klan found in Lipset and Raab, 276–77.

p. 314   THE KLAN NUMBERS NO MORE THAN SEVEN THOUSAND Material on Klan's current membership and activities based on Anti-Defamation League data reported in New York *Times*, November 4, 1984; also Joyce Johnson, "Ku Klux Klan Activity on the Rise," *National NOW Times*, May/June 1984.

p. 314   BILL WILKERSON: Excerpt from editorial cited in Johnson.

p. 314   FIVE OLD WOMEN IN CHATTANOOGA: Reported in ibid.

p. 314   GARY LEE YARBROUGH: Quoted in Wayne King, "F.B.I. Says It's 'Closing Net' on Armed Rightists' Group," New York *Times*, April 4, 1985.

p. 314   THESE DRAGONS OF GOD: Quoted in Wayne King, "Computer Network Links Rightist Groups and Offers 'Enemy' List," New York *Times*, February 15, 1985.

p. 315   JIM ELLISON: Scripture quoted in Wayne King, "Anti-Semitism Links Violent Groups," New York *Times*, April 28, 1985.

p. 315   ALL THE GREAT MINDS OF THE PATRIOTIC CHRISTIAN MOVEMENT LINKED TOGETHER: Quoted in King, February 15, 1985.

p. 315   MUD PEOPLE . . . JEWS IN TRYING TO DESTROY OUR RACE: Denver Daw Parmenter quoted in "Death List Names Given to U.S. Jury," New York *Times*, September 17, 1985.

p. 315   THE PROGENY OF THE DEVIL: Denver Daw Parmenter quoted in Wayne King, "Neo-Nazi Describes Assassination Plans," New York *Times*, September 14, 1985.

p. 316   JUDY GOLDSMITH: Quoted in "Reagan's Rhetoric Fuels Anti-Abortion Clinic Terrorists," *National NOW Times*, March/April 1984.

p. 316   I DID IT FOR THE GLORY OF GOD: Press statement by Curtis Beseda, who admitted to four arson attacks on abortion clinics in Washington. Reported in *National NOW Times*, July/August 1984.

p. 316   IN DEFENDING FOUR DEVOUT CHRISTIANS: Quotes cited in Jon Nordheimer, "2 Women Charged as Accessories In Bombing of 3 Abortion Clinics," New York *Times*, January 3, 1985.

p. 316   JOHN C. WILLKE: Quoted in New York *Times*, January 4, 1984.

p. 316   THE OTHER SIDE CAME FROM NOW: Excerpts from telegram sent to President Ronald Reagan by Judy Goldsmith, NOW president, dated March 1, 1984.

p. 317   EVEN AMONG CATHOLIC WOMEN: NORC poll cited in Elaine Sciolino, "A Time For Challenge," *New York Times Magazine*, November 4, 1984.

p. 317   ABORTION ON DEMAND THE LAW OF THE LAND: Viguerie, 203.

p. 317–18   INTERNAL TERRORIST ATTACKS . . . INTERNATIONAL TERRORIST INCIDENTS: Conclusions based on data reported in Brown, Flanagan, and McLeod, 406–9.

p. 318   FLORA LEWIS: Quoted in Goodman and Price, 61.

p. 318   THE AUTHORITARIAN PERSONALITY: An excellent review of the studies and their critiques is found in Brown, 478–544.

p. 318   LIBERALS CHIPPING AWAY AT THE BILL OF RIGHTS: Viguerie, 213–14.

p. 319   WILLIAM SAFIRE: Quote from his editorial, "The Unwitting Alliance," New York Times, December 17, 1984.

p. 319   DAVID BOAZ: From his editorial "In '88 Who'll Win the Baby Boomers?" New York Times, November 7, 1985.

p. 319   SUCCEEDING GENERATIONS . . . MORE SUPPORTIVE OF CIVIL LIBERTIES: McClosky and Brill, 400.

CHAPTER 21: The "Christianizing" of America

pp. 320–21   PAT ROBERTSON: Biographical facts found in Robertson, 14.

p. 321   THE PULPITS OF THIS NATION: Ibid., 18–19.

p. 321   AS WAS TRUE OF THE DISCIPLES: Ibid., 65.

p. 321   KANAWHA COUNTY: History and part of textbook controversy analysis drawn from Ann Page and Donald Clelland, "The Kanawha County Textbook Controversy: A Study of the Politics of Life Style Concern," Social Forces, 57:1, September 1978, 265–79.

p. 322   WE CAN'T SEE NEED . . . WHEN WHAT'S BEING TAUGHT ISN'T RIGHT: Protestor quoted in ibid., 270.

p. 322   WE'RE NOT ASKING THAT THEY TEACH CHRISTIANITY: Kanawha County teenager quoted in ibid., 274.

p. 322   LIBERALS TRIED TO PICTURE THE PROTESTORS: Viguerie, 168.

p. 323   117 PERCENT INCREASE IN CENSORSHIP: People for the American Way, "Attacks on Freedom to Learn: A 1985–86 Report," 1.

p. 323   THE FREE FLOW OF IDEAS IS AN UN-AMERICAN ACTIVITY: Barbara Parker quoted in People for the American Way press release, August 15, 1985.

p. 323   LARGEST BABY-SITTING AGENCY: Jerry Falwell quoted in Webber, 46.

pp. 323–24   INCESSANTLY BOMBARDED . . . SLIDE TOWARD DECADENCE: Ibid., 46.

p. 324   NELSON MOLINA, RONALD ZAMORA: "TV on Trial," Broadcasting, November 5, 1985.

p. 324   THE PRODUCT OF UNHINDERED COMMUNICATION: McClosky and Brill, 39.

p. 324   TUNIS WORTMAN: Quoted in ibid., 40–41.

p. 324   WORDS—AND—IDEAS CAN HURT: I am aware of an apparent contradiction between this chapter and the last. In the introductory chapter to Crimewarp VI, I argue that there is a link between verbal and physical violence. In this chapter, I seem to challenge that link. In reconciling this contradiction, it is important to note the distinction between thought and action. In the previous chapter, the various types of fanaticism I cite—lynchings, KKK, neo-Nazis, abortion vigilantes—are forms of direct violent action. In this chapter, I focus on thought and thought control. First Amendment decisions have maintained a separateness between speech or thought and direct incitement to violence. I mean to do the same. The fanatics discussed in the last chapter were not incited to violence by the mass media and schoolbooks that are examined in this chapter, but by their own peers. Indeed, peers and family are the determinants that mediate between thought and action.

p. 324   BALANCING TEST: Ibid., 44–45.

p. 325   ON SOME ITEMS, SUCH AS THE RIGHT OF HIGH SCHOOL TEACHERS: Polls reported in ibid., 54.

p. 325   DR. JOSEPH MURPHY: Quoted in Robert Suro, "Head of City U. Assails New Group, Accuracy in Academia," New York Times, November 15, 1985.

pp. 325–26   DOCUMENTED CENSORSHIP INCIDENTS: People for the American Way study.

p. 326   MORE THAN 100 FILMS, BOOKS AND PAMPHLETS: Ibid., 43–45.

p. 326   CENSORSHIP ATTEMPTS ROSE BY MORE THAN ONE THIRD . . . AND TWO THIRDS: Ibid., 1.

p. 326   PUPIL RIGHTS PROTECTION ACT: Ibid., 6; Schlafly, 12, 18.

p. 326   OVERWHELMING MAJORITY OF CENSORSHIP ATTEMPTS: People for the American Way, "Attacks on Freedom to Learn: A 1984–1985 Report," 2–3.

p. 326   FROM THE LATE 1960S AND EARLY 1970S . . . LEFT-WING COMPLAINTS PREVAILED: Michiko Kakutani, "The Famed Will Gather to Read the Forbidden," New York Times, April 5, 1982.

p. 326   BOOK BANNERS HAVE DISCOVERED THE BILL OF RIGHTS: Daniel Jussim, Civil Liberties, Spring 1985.

p. 326   [WE ARE] AGAINST CENSORSHIP: Fundamentalist parent quoted in Jussim.

p. 327   CAROLYN GROVE: Case and quotes cited in Jussim.

p. 327   A GRAVE DEFEAT FOR CIVIL LIBERTIES . . . OR WHETHER THEIR REAL DESIRE IS TO OUTLAW CHRISTIANITY: Grove's lawyer quoted in Jussim.

p. 327   ISLAND TREES V. PICO: Quoted in Jussim; also Alan Levine, "Fighting Censorship," New York Times, July 25, 1983.

p. 327   AMERICAN HOUSEHOLDS . . . TELEVISION: TV viewing statistics drawn from 1983 A. C. Nielsen Company, Nielsen Television Index Audience Estimates.

p. 327   CABLE SERVICES: U.S. Federal Communications Commission, Cable Television Revenues, annual.

p. 327   TOP SYNDICATED TV PROGRAMS: Nielsen.

p. 328   PRIME TIME SHOWS: Nielsen.

p. 328   57 PERCENT OF THE . . . PUBLIC: Result of Harris Poll cited in Michael Jacobson and Ronald Collins, "Ads Glamorize Alcohol, Hide Dangers," New York Times, April 25, 1985.

p. 328   RCA-NBC HAS EXCLUDED CHRISTIAN CHARACTERS: Wildmon quoted in "Boycott of NBC-TV and RCA Urged," New York Times, March 5, 1982.

p. 328   MOST PRODUCERS ARE OF THE JEWISH PERSPECTIVE: Wildmon quoted in Gioia Diliberto, "Sponsors Run For Cover as TV Vigilante Don Wildmon Decides it's Prime Time for a Boycott," People, June 6, 1981.

p. 328   THE TELEVISION INDUSTRY IS RIDDLED WITH HOMOSEXUALS: Bollier, 266.

pp. 328–29   TONIGHT, NEARLY EVERY HOME IN AMERICA: James Robison quoted in ibid., 268.

p. 329   WE CAN DO SOMETHING THE NETWORKS CANNOT DO: Viguerie quoted in ibid., 267.

p. 329   BOGUS SURVEY TECHNIQUES: Ibid., 270.

p. 329   CBTV'S OBSESSION WITH SEX: Ibid., 266, 268.

p. 329   SUPPRESS OTHER VOICES: Ibid., 273.

p. 329   THE MOST ANTI-REAGAN NETWORK . . . LIBERAL BIAS: Jesse Helms letter quoted in Broadcasting, January 21, 1985.

p. 329   A DANGEROUS DEVIATION: Lou Adler quoted in ibid.

p. 329   CBS REPORTS THE NEWS . . . A FREE AND INDEPENDENT PRESS: Mary Boies quoted in *Broadcasting*, January 14, 1985.

p. 329   TED TURNER . . . TAKEOVER BID: "Helms Tells of His Role in the Bid to Buy CBS," New York *Times*, March 3, 1985.

p. 330   TURNER'S . . . SPEECH . . . BEFORE NATIONAL CONSERVATIVE FOUNDATION: "Turner Delights Right," *Broadcasting*, July 2, 1984.

p. 330   WE HAVE TO GET AWAY FROM THE REDNECK KU KLUX KLAN: Ted Turner quoted in *Broadcasting*, December 10, 1985.

p. 331   THOMAS LEAHY: Quoted in "Networks Detail Efforts to Cut Down on Drug Use Seen on TV," *Broadcasting*, March 25, 1985.

p. 331   NEARLY TWO CRIMES PER PRIME TIME SHOW: "Distortion Seen in Prime Time Crime," *Broadcasting*, January 24, 1983.

p. 331   70 PERCENT INVOLVE . . . VIOLENCE: Jack Greene and Tim Bynum, "T.V. Crooks: Implications of Latent Role Models For Theories of Delinquency," *Journal of Criminal Justice*, 10:3, 1982, 181.

p. 331   AGE AND SOCIOECONOMIC DISTRIBUTION OF CRIME: Ibid., 182–83; *Broadcasting*, January 24, 1983.

p. 332   BUSINESSMAN-CUM-BARBARIAN: An analysis of the antibusiness (as well as the antifemale and racist) biases of "Miami Vice" is found in Ben Stein, " 'Miami Vice': It's So Hip You'll Want to Kill Yourself," *Public Opinion*, October/November 1985, 41–43.

p. 332   THE AMERICAN PUBLIC IS RECEIVING A GROSSLY DISTORTED PICTURE: Leonard Theberge of The Media Institute quoted in *Broadcasting*, January 24, 1983.

p. 332   NOT EVERYONE IS EQUALLY INFLUENCED BY THE DISTORTIONS: Conclusions based on work of George Gerbner and Paul Hirsch cited in *Broadcasting*, December 13, 1982; also Greene and Bynum, 179, 185.

p. 332   SOCIAL MESSAGES: Greene and Bynum, 178, 180, 186.

p. 333   MY COLLEAGUES HAVE GENERATED: Jib Fowles quoted in *Broadcasting*, October 24, 1984.

p. 333   MASS MEDIA VIOLENCE: REAL LIFE EFFECTS: David Phillips, "The Impact of Mass Media Violence on U.S. Homicides," *American Sociological Review*, 48:4, August 1983, 560, 564. For a thorough critique of Phillips as well as a review of the state of the art of violence-as-imitation theory, see James Baron and Peter Weiss, "Same Time, Next Year: Aggregate Analyses of the Mass Media and Violent Behavior," *American Sociological Review*, 50:3, June 1985, 347–63.

p. 333   DIAMETRICALLY OPPOSITE EFFECTS . . . REAL OR FICTIONAL: Seymour Fesbach, "The Role of Fantasy in the Response to Television," *Journal of Social Issues*, 32:4, 1976, 76.

pp. 333–34   THE TELEVISION NETWORKS MAY HAVE BECOME AN EASY SCAPEGOAT: Robert Kaplan and Robert Singer, "Television Violence and Viewer Aggression: A Reexamination of the Evidence," *Journal of Social Issues*, 32:4, 1976, 63–64.

p. 334   NETWORK AUDIENCE SHARE: Projections of Paul Bortz, cited in "Communications Consultant Bortz: An Economic Mentor," *Broadcasting*, December 6, 1982.

p. 334   OLDER AUDIENCES . . . GRATUITOUS SEX AND VIOLENCE: McClosky and Brill, 392.

p. 334   VH-1: Steve Schneider, "MTV's New Service Takes Aim at an Older Audience," New York *Times*, December 30, 1984.

p. 334   LOVE AND OPTIMISM: Robert Pittman quoted in ibid.

p. 334   TRANSACTIONAL . . . SERVICES: Bortz in *Broadcasting*, December 6, 1982.

p. 334 PRESIDENT REAGAN . . . PRESS CONFERENCE: Quote and analysis drawn from Norman Dorsen's Introduction to Dorsen, xii.

p. 335 INTELLECTUALLY SHAKY . . . ORIGINAL INTENT: From address by Edwin Meese to American Bar Association in Washington, July 9, 1985. Reprinted as article in Edwin Meese III, "The Attorney General's View of the Supreme Court: Toward a Jurisprudence of Original Intent," *Public Administration Review*, 45: Special Issue, November 1985, 703–4.

p. 335 WHAT REALLY INTERESTS THE . . . ATTORNEY GENERAL: Anthony Lewis, "Mr. Meese's Petard," New York *Times*, November 4, 1985.

p. 335 UNDER CONDITIONS OF MASS COMMUNICATIONS: Ira Glasser, "Making Constitutional Rights Work," in Dorsen, 15, 21.

p. 335 WITHOUT CENSORSHIP, THINGS CAN GET TERRIBLY CONFUSED: Westmoreland speech cited in "Cronkite Warns of Growing Trend of Censorship," *Broadcasting*, April 12, 1982.

p. 335 SECRECY ORDER: Glasser, 21–22.

p. 336 FRONTAL ATTACK ON ACADEMIC FREEDOM: Ibid.

p. 336 A DISTURBING TENDENCY TO UPHOLD RESTRICTIONS: Burt Neuborne and Carl Loewenson, Jr., "Supreme Court's 1984–85 Term: The Court Was More Protective of Constitutional Values Than Many Had Feared," *Civil Liberties*, Summer 1985.

p. 336 NONE OF THESE PROPOSALS MAY SEEM ALL THAT SERIOUS: Walter Cronkite speech before National Association of Broadcasters, reported in *Broadcasting*, April 22, 1982.

CHAPTER 22: Reconstituting the Constitution

p. 342 CONFLICT BETWEEN THE INTEREST OF THE STATE: Joseph Glaser, "A New/Old Look at the Fifth Amendment—Some Help From the Past," *The Touro Conference Volume* (Chico, California: Scholars Press), 1985, 31.

p. 343 MOST INNOCENT PEOPLE ARE GLAD TO TALK TO THE POLICE: Edwin Meese quoted in Philip Shenon, "Meese and His New Vision of the Constitution," New York *Times*, October 17, 1985.

p. 343 THEIR POLICIES OF OBSESSION: Viguerie, 215.

pp. 343–45 SAMPLE OF RECENT DECISIONS: Supreme Court Cases selected from the following sources: "Criminal Justice Decisions of the Supreme Court of the United States: 1983 Term," *Criminal Justice Review*, 9:2, Fall 1984, 84–88; Linda Greenhouse, "Rulings of High Court's Term Reaffirm Church-State Barriers," New York *Times*, July 8, 1985; Burt Neuborne and Charles Sims, "Supreme Court's 1983–84 Term: Americans Are Far Less Free Today Than They Were a Year Ago," *Civil Liberties*, Summer 1984; Burt Neuborne and Carl Loewenson, Jr., "Supreme Court's 1984–85 Term: The Court Was More Protective of Constitutional Values Than Many Had Feared," *Civil Liberties*, Summer, 1985.

p. 346 MIRANDA ONLY HELPS GUILTY DEFENDANTS: Edwin Meese quoted in Shenon.

p. 346 GENERAL ACCOUNTING OFFICE STUDY: Findings cited in National Institute of Justice, "The Effects of the Exclusionary Rule: A Study in California," December 1982, 6–7; Loren Siegel, "Law Enforcement and Civil Liberties: We Can Have Both," *Civil Liberties*, February 1983, 5.

p. 347 CROSS-CITY COMPARISON OF FELONY PROCESSING: Katherine Brosi, "A Cross-City Comparison of Felony Case Processing," U.S. Department of Justice, Law Enforcement Assistance Administration, April 1979, 19.

p. 347   1982 CALIFORNIA SURVEY: National Institute of Justice, December 1982, 1–2.

p. 347   EDWIN MEESE'S OPTIMISM: Meese is quoted in the New York *Times*, May 8, 1985, as saying he hoped the "good faith" exception to the exclusionary rule would "ultimately lead to the elimination of the rule."

p. 347   NO SANCTIONS ARE DIRECTED AGAINST [POLICE]: Darwick quoted in "IACP Testifies on Exclusionary Rule," *IACP Newsletter*, April 1982.

p. 348   PREVENTIVE DETENTION: Federal and state statistics on pretrial misconduct drawn from, "Pretrial Release and Misconduct," U.S. Department of Justice, Bureau of Justice Statistics *Special Report;* and Siegel, 5.

p. 348   DRUG ABUSERS MORE THAN TWICE AS LIKELY TO BE REARRESTED: Mary Toborg and Michael Kirby, "Drug Use and Pretrial Crime in the District of Columbia," National Institute of Justice *Research in Brief*, October 1984.

p. 348   LEGISLATIVE SAFEGUARDS: See, for example, legislation introduced by Senator Arlen Specter (R-PA), cited in "Preventive Detention Bill Introduced in U.S. Senate," *The Criminologist*, 9:5, October 1984, 5.

p. 348   GRISWOLD V. CONNECTICUT: Trubow, 12.

p. 349   HACKENSACK, NEW JERSEY: Alfonso Narvaez, "Jersey Judge Weighs Mandatory School Drug Tests," New York *Times*, November 13, 1985.

p. 349   CONSTITUTIONAL CHALLENGE: Robert Hanely, "Drug Tests by Jersey School Are Ruled Unconstitutional," New York *Times*, December 11, 1985.

p. 349   PATCHOGUE, NEW YORK: "L.I. Teachers Go to Court on Tests for Drugs," New York *Times*, May 23, 1985.

p. 349   PAUL V. DAVIS: Trubow, 12.

pp. 349–50   NATIONAL RIFLE ASSOCIATION AND AMERICAN CIVIL LIBERTIES UNION ON SAME SIDE: David Burnham, " '74 Privacy Law Out of Date, Disparate U.S. Groups Assert," New York *Times*, December 26, 1984.

p. 350   DIRECT ACCESS TO INFORMATION ABOUT PRIVATE INSURANCE COVERAGE: David Burnham, "White House Seeks Tax Data On Those Receiving U.S. Aid," New York *Times*, October 14, 1985.

p. 350   WHITE-COLLAR-CRIME SUSPECTS AND THEIR ASSOCIATES: David Burnham, "F.B.I. May Test Computer Index For White-Collar Crime Inquiries," New York *Times*, October 15, 1984.

p. 350   TRACK PEOPLE FBI CONSIDERED SUSPICIOUS: Ira Glasser and Noel Salinger, "Reagan's Rule: Secrecy and Surveillance Threaten Our Political Liberty," *Civil Liberties*, Summer 1984, 2.

p. 350   FOIA REQUESTS: House Subcommittee on Information statistics cited in "Assessing Freedom of Information Act," New York *Times*, August 29, 1985.

pp. 350–51   WITH THE STROKE OF A PEN . . . "THE BROADEST SECURITY CLASSIFICATION SYSTEM IN AMERICAN HISTORY": John Shattuck, "Congress and the Legislative Process," Dorsen, 55.

p. 351   INFORMATION IS POWER: Burnham, 51.

p. 351   JUDGE ROBERT BORK: Stuart Taylor, "The Reorganization of the Federal Courts," *NOW-NYS Action Report*, Winter 1985, reprinted from New York *Times*.

p. 351   600 FEDERAL JUDGESHIPS: McGarrell and Flanagan, 70.

p. 351   164 DURING FIRST FOUR YEARS . . . 150 MORE: Statistics cited in "Reagan and the Courts: His First & Second Terms," *NOW-NYS Action Report*, Winter 1985.

p. 351   FEMALES, HISPANICS, BLACKS . . . WELL QUALIFIED: McGarrell and Flanagan, 77.

p. 352   SUBJECTIVE JUDICIAL POLICY-MAKING: Smith quoted in Taylor.

p. 352   GRAGLIA WAS SUBSEQUENTLY ACCUSED: Letter to President Ronald Reagan from Anthony Podesta, president of People for the American Way, November 21, 1985.

p. 352   1981 . . . CONSIDERED FOR POST IN THE JUSTICE DEPARTMENT: "Strict Reconstructionist," Los Angeles *Times*, November 8, 1985.

p. 352   GRAGLIA'S VEHEMENT ATTACKS ON COURT-ORDERED BUSING: Full-page ad in *Austin American-Statesman*, December 1979.

p. 352   PICKANINNIES . . . BLACKS, WOMEN, JEWS: Podesta, November 21, 1985.

p. 352   ADOPTED FOR THE LIMITED PURPOSE OF GUARANTEEING BLACKS CERTAIN BASIC RIGHTS: Lino Graglia, "Was the Constitution A Good Idea?" *National Review*, July 13, 1984, 36.

p. 353   THE SEPARATION OF POWERS AND BILL OF RIGHTS: Ira Glasser, "Making Constitutional Rights Work," in Dorsen, 6.

p. 353   IT HAS BECOME A SECOND CONSTITUTION: Graglia, 36.

p. 353   MARBURY V. MADISON: Glasser in Dorsen, 6.

p. 353   IT IS DOUBTFUL THAT THE NET CONTRIBUTION: Graglia, 37.

p. 353   HAS EFFECTIVELY REMADE AMERICA IN ITS OWN IMAGE: Ibid., 38.

p. 353   PROPONENTS OF JUDICIAL REVIEW DEFEND THE POWER: Ibid., 39.

p. 354   IF REAGAN GETS ONE SUPREME COURT APPOINTMENT: Burt Neuborne, "New Appointments Would Strengthen Court's Hostility to Civil Liberties," *Civil Liberties*, Winter 1985, p. 4.

p. 354   WHEN I FIRST CAME TO THE ACLU: Ibid.

p. 354   STATE COURTS: Carl Loewenson, Jr., "ACLU Turns to State Courts and Constitutions to Protect Rights," *Civil Liberties*, Winter 1985, 7.

p. 355   FORTY SEPARATE BILLS: Shattuck, 51.

p. 355   MIDTERM ELECTIONS: Ibid., 60.

p. 355   WHEN YOU ARE TALKING WITH A HOUSE MEMBER: Mark Lynch quoted in David Burnham, "Increasing Dissent Within the A.C.L.U.," New York *Times*, August 14, 1984.

p. 355   A PRESIDENT NOTED FOR HIS ABILITY TO "COMMUNICATE": Shattuck, 67.

pp. 355–56   RESPECT FOR THE FREEDOM OF OTHERS: McClosky and Brill, 416.

p. 356   AS EACH NEW GENERATION MATURES INTO ADULTHOOD: Ibid., 435.

p. 356   POLITICAL APATHY: Ibid., 418.

CHAPTER 23: Sic Transit

p. 359   KENNETH BRIGGS: "Religious Feeling Seen Strong in U.S.," New York *Times*, December 9, 1984.

p. 359   REBELLION AGAINST . . . HYPER-RATIONALIST WORLD: Greeley, 57.

p. 359   HUSTON SMITH: Quoted in ibid., 59–60.

p. 359   IMPORTANT MEANS OF SOCIAL LOCATION: Ibid., 29.

p. 359   ORGANIZED RELIGION IS ALSO ABLE TO COUNT ON THE STRONGEST COMMITMENTS: Ibid., 28.

p. 359   RELIGIOUS PLURALISM . . . TURNS OUT TO BE ITS BEST GUARANTEE: Ibid., 97.

p. 359   *U.S. News & World Report:* "A Search for Life's Meaning in High-Tech Era," May 9, 1983.

p. 360   TRUE BIBLICAL CHRISTIANITY REPUDIATES THE OUTER WORLD: Webber, 149–50.

p. 360   CIVIL RELIGION: Ibid., 38.

pp. 360–61   GALLUP POLLS . . . MIDDLE-OF-THE-ROAD: Poll results dating back to 1937 tabulated in *Public Opinion*, April/May 1985, 35.

p. 361   SELECTED DEMOGRAPHIC GROUPS: Data drawn from NORC and Roper Organization polls assembled in ibid., 37–40. Also ibid., December/January 1984, 24, and April/May 1983, 30.

pp. 361–62   GALLUP POLLS: Material comparing voting patterns among Christians, conservatives and the general population drawn from George Gallup, Jr., "Divining the Devout: The Polls and Religious Belief," *Public Opinion*, April/May 1981; also "Opinion Roundup" in the same issue, 21–27.

p. 362   CHIP PRAIRIE: Greensboro *Daily News*, November 29, 1980.

p. 362   EVERY ONE OF THIS NATION'S NINE REGIONS HOLDS A SOLID MODERATE PLURALITY: Based on poll data assembled in *Public Opinion*, June/July 1984, 22–30.

p. 363   THE REST OF THE COUNTRY RANKS THESE SIXTH: Gallup, 41.

p. 363   AMERICANS ALWAYS DRIFT BACK TO THE HAPPY MIDDLE: This theme is deftly developed by Ben Wattenberg, "As the Dust Settles: Centrism at Work in the Participatory State," *Public Opinion*, June/July 1984.

p. 363   VIEWERSHIP . . . DROPPED OFF SOME 10 PERCENT: Flake, 235.

p. 363   THE MAN FROM LYNCHBURG . . . ABORTION . . . EQUAL RIGHTS: Ibid., 274.

p. 363   WHAT HIS CHURCH HAS BEEN DOING IN PRIVATE: Webber, 51.

pp. 363–64   THE DANGER FOR SELF-RIGHTEOUS CHRISTIANS: Flake, 214.

p. 364   HINDSON AND DOBSON: Falwell, 172.

Bibliography

This bibliography is made up of books referenced in the preceding Notes. In the Notes, books are cited only by author—also by date in cases of multiple books by the same writer —and correspond to listings in this bibliography. Articles and other sources are fully cited in the Notes themselves.

Abt Associates Inc. *Unreported Taxable Income from Selected Illegal Activities*. Washington, D.C.: U.S. Government Printing Office, September 1984.

Adler, Freda. *Sisters in Crime*. New York: McGraw-Hill, 1975.

Administrative Office of the United States Courts. *Report on Applications for Orders Authorizing of Approving the Interception of Wire or Oral Communications for the Period January 1, 1984 to December 31, 1984*. Washington, D.C.: U.S. Government Printing Office, April 1985.

Bailey, D. S. *Homosexuality and the Western Christian Tradition*. Great Britain: Longmans, Green: 1955.

Bell, Robert. *Social Deviance*. Homewood, IL: The Dorsey Press, 1976.

Bennett-Sandler, Georgette, Robert Frazier, Donald Torres, and Ronald Waldron. *Law Enforcement and Criminal Justice: An Introduction*. Boston, MA: Houghton Mifflin, 1979.

Bollier, David. *Liberty & Justice For Some.* New York: Frederick Ungar, 1982.

Boyer, Ernest. *High School: A Report on Secondary Education in America.* New York: Harper & Row, 1983.

Brown, Edward, Timothy Flanagan, and Maureen McLeod, eds. *Sourcebook of Criminal Justice Statistics—1983.* U.S. Department of Justice, Bureau of Justice Statistics Washington, D.C.: U.S. Government Printing Office, 1984.

Brown, Roger. *Social Psychology.* New York: Free Press, 1965.

Brownmiller, Susan. *Against Our Will.* New York: Bantam Books, 1976.

Bullough, Vern, and Bonnie Bullough. *Sin, Sickness and Society.* New York: New American Library, 1977.

Burnham, David. *The Rise of the Computer State.* New York: Random House, 1983.

Catholic University of America. *New Catholic Encyclopedia.* New York: McGraw-Hill, 1967.

Chelimsky, Eleanor, Frank Jordan, Jr., Linda Sue Russell, and John Strack. *Security and the Small Business Retailer.* U.S. Department of Justice, Law Enforcement Assistance Administration. Washington, D.C.: U.S. Government Printing Office, 1979.

Clinard, Marshall. *Sociology of Deviant Behavior.* New York: Holt, Rinehart & Winston, 1974.

Conrad, John, and Simon Dinitz. *In Fear of Each Other.* Lexington, MA: Lexington Books, 1977.

Dorsen, Norman, ed. *Our Endangered Rights.* New York: Pantheon Books, 1984.

Douglas, Jack, and John Johnson, eds. *Official Deviance.* Philadelphia: J. B. Lippincott, 1977.

Falwell, Jerry. *The Fundamentalist Phenomenon.* Garden City, NY: Doubleday, 1981.

———. *Finding Inner Peace and Strength.* Garden City, NY: Doubleday, 1982.

Finkelhor, David, Richard Gelles, Gerald Hotaling, and Murray Strauss, eds. *The Dark Side of Families.* Beverly Hills, CA: Sage Publications, 1983.

Finkenauer, James. *Scared Straight and the Panacea Phenomenon.* Englewood Cliffs, NJ: Prentice-Hall, 1982.

Flake, Carol. *Redemptorama.* Garden City, NY: Doubleday, 1984.

Fried, Albert. *The Rise and Fall of the Jewish Gangster in America.* New York: Holt, Rinehart and Winston, 1980.

Geis, Gilbert, and Robert Meier. *White Collar Crime: Offenses in Business, Politics, and the Professions.* New York: Free Press, 1977.

Geller, William, ed. *Police Leadership in America: Crisis and Opportunity.* Chicago: American Bar Foundation and Praeger, 1985.

Goodman, William, Jr., and James Price. *Jerry Falwell: An Unauthorized Profile.* Lynchburg, VA: Paris & Associates, 1981.

Greeley, Andrew. *Religion in the Year 2000.* New York: Sheed and Ward, 1969.

Greenberg, Stephanie, William Rohe, and Jay Williams. *Safe and Secure Neighborhoods: Physical Characteristics and Informal Territorial Control in High and Low Crime Neighborhoods.* U.S. Department of Justice, National Institute of Justice, May 1982.

Guttentag, Marcia, and Paul Secord. *Too Many Women?* Beverly Hills, CA: Sage, 1983.

Gutman, Judith Mara. *The Colonial Venture.* New York: Basic Books, 1966.

Hamparian, Donna. *The Violent Few.* Lexington, MA: Lexington Books, 1978.

———. Linda Estep, Susan Muntean, Ramon Priestino, Robert Swisher, Paul Wallace, and Joseph White. *Youth in Adult Courts: Between Two Worlds.* U.S. Department of Justice, Office of Juvenile Justice and Delinquency Prevention, 1982.

Harrington, Alan. *Psychopaths.* New York: Simon & Schuster, 1972.

Hite, Shere. *The Hite Report on Male Sexuality.* New York: Knopf, 1981.

Hochstedler, Ellen. *Crime Against the Elderly in 26 Cities.* U.S. Department of Justice, Bureau of Justice Statistics. Washington, D.C.: U.S. Government Printing Office, 1981.

Iacovetta, R.G. and Dae Chang, eds. *Critical Issues in Criminal Justice.* Durham, NC: Carolina Academic Press, 1979.

Inciardi, James, ed. *The Drugs-Crime Connection.* Beverly Hills, CA: Sage, 1981.

Information Please Almanac 1985. Boston, MA: Houghton Mifflin, 1985.

Insurance Information Institute. *Insurance Facts—1982–1983 Edition.* New York: Insurance Information Institute, 1982.

———. *Insurance Facts—1984–85 Property/Casualty Fact Book.* New York: Insurance Information Institute, 1984.

Jacoby, Susan. *Wild Justice.* New York: Harper & Row, 1983.

Jeffery, C. Ray. *Crime Prevention Through Environmental Design.* Beverly Hills, CA: Sage, 1977.

Johnson, Ray. *Ray Johnson's Total Security.* New York: Plume Books, 1985.

Kando, Thomas. *Leisure and Popular Culture in Transition.* St. Louis, MO: C. V. Mosby, 1975.

Kardiner, Abram, and Lionel Ovesey. *The Mark of Oppression.* Cleveland, Ohio: World, 1962.

Licht, Hans. *Sexual Life in Ancient Greece.* Great Britain: Barnes & Noble, 1963.

Lipset, Seymour Martin and Earl Raab. *The Politics of Unreason.* New York: Harper & Row, 1973.

Lockard, James, J. T. Skip Duncan, Robert Brenner, and Georgette Semick. *Directory of Community Crime Prevention Programs—National and State Levels.* Law Enforcement Assistance Administration, National Institute of Law Enforcement and Criminal Justice. Washington, D.C.: U.S. Government Printing Office, December 1978.

Marks, James, and John Craigie. *Sharing the Risk.* New York: Insurance Information Institute, 1981.

Matulia, Kenneth. *A Balance of Forces.* U.S. Department of Justice, National Institute of Justice. Gaithersburg, MD: International Association of Chiefs of Police, 1982.

Matza, David. *Delinquency and Drift.* New York: Wiley, 1964.

McClosky, Herbert, and Alida Brill. *Dimensions of Tolerance.* New York: Russell Sage Foundation, 1983.

McGarrell, Edmund, and Timothy Flanagan, eds. *Sourcebook of Criminal Justice Statistics—1984.* U.S. Department of Justice, Bureau of Justice Statistics. Washington, D.C.: U.S. Government Printing Office, 1985.

Miller, Perry, and Thomas Johnson, eds. *The Puritans.* New York: Harper & Row, 1963.

Millett, Kate. *Sexual Politics.* Garden City, NY: Doubleday, 1970.

Mulvihill, Donald, Melvin Tumin, and Lynn Curtis, eds. *Crimes of Violence: A Staff Report to the National Commission on the Causes and Prevention of Violence.* Washington, D.C.: U.S. Government Printing Office, 1969.

Naisbitt, John. *Megatrends.* New York: Warner, 1984.

National Advisory Committee on Criminal Justice Standards and Goals. Report of the Task Force on Organized Crime. *Organized Crime.* U.S. Department of Justice. Law Enforcement Assistance Administration. Washington, D.C.: U.S. Government Printing Office, 1976.

Needle, Jerome, and William Vaughan Stapleton. *Police Handling of Juvenile Gangs.* Washington, D.C.: U.S. Department of Justice, September 1983.

Nettler, Gwynn. *Killing Each Other.* Cincinnati, Ohio: Anderson, 1982.

Newman, Evelyn, Donald Newman, Mindy Gewirtz and Associates, eds. *Elderly Criminals.* Cambridge, MA: Oelgeschlager, Gunn and Hain, 1984.

Newman, Graeme. *Just and Painful: A Case for the Corporal Punishment of Criminals.* New York: Harrow and Heston/Macmillan, 1983.

Newman, Oscar. *Defensible Space.* New York: Collier Books, 1973.

———. *Design Guidelines for Creating Defensible Space.* U.S. Department of Justice, Law Enforcement Assistance Administration, National Institute of Law Enforcement and Criminal Justice, 1975.

——— and Karen Franck. *Factors Influencing Crime and Instability in Urban Housing Developments.* U.S. Department of Justice, National Institute of Justice, 1980.

———. *Community of Interest.* Garden City, NY: Anchor Press/Doubleday, 1981.

Nye, Russel Blaine. *The Cultural Life of the New Nation.* New York: Harper & Row, 1963.

Pepinsky, Harold, and Paul Jesilow. *Myths that Cause Crime.* Cabin John, MD: Seven Locks Press, 1984.

Ploscowe, M. *Sex and the Law.* New York: Prentice-Hall, 1951.

Pooley, James. *Trade Secrets.* Berkeley, CA: Osborne/McGraw-Hill, 1982.

Rapoport, Amos. *The Meaning of the Built Environment.* Beverly Hills, CA: Sage, 1982.

Ray, Oakley. *Drugs, Society and Human Behavior.* St. Louis, MO: C. V. Mosby, 1972.

Robertson, Pat. *Shout it From the Housetops.* Plainfield, NJ: Logos International, 1972.

Rosenbaum, Marsha. *Women on Heroin.* New Brunswick, NJ: Rutgers University Press, 1981.

Russell, Diana. *Sexual Exploitation.* Beverly Hills, CA: Sage, 1984.

Sandmel, Samuel, ed. *The New English Bible.* New York: Oxford University Press, 1976.

Schlafly, Phyllis. *Child Abuse in the Classroom.* Alton, IL: Pere Marquette Press, 1984.

Silberman, Charles. *Criminal Justice, Criminal Violence.* New York: Random House, 1978.

Silver, Gary, and Michael Aldrich. *The Dope Chronicles.* San Francisco: Harper & Row, 1979.

Silver, Isadore, ed. *The Crime Control Establishment.* Englewood Cliffs, NJ: Prentice-Hall, 1974.

Sinclair, Andrew. *Era of Excess.* New York: Harper & Row, 1964.

Small Business Administration. *The State of Small Business: A Report of the President.* Washington, D.C.: U.S. Government Printing Office, May 1985.

Task Force on Private Security, National Advisory Committee on Criminal Justice Standards and Goals. *Private Security.* U.S. Department of Justice, Law Enforcement Assistance Administration. Washington, D.C.: U.S. Government Printing Office, 1976.

Trubow, George. *Privacy and Secrecy of Criminal History Information: An Analysis of Privacy Issues.* U.S. Department of Justice, Law Enforcement Assistance Administration, National Criminal Justice Information and Statistics Service, 1978.

U.S. Department of Commerce. *Crime in Service Industries.* Washington, D.C.: U.S. Government Printing Office, September 1977.

———. *Crime in Retailing.* Washington, D.C.: U.S. Government Printing Office, August 1975.

U.S. Department of Justice, Bureau of Justice Statistics. *Criminal Victimization in the United States, 1982,* August 1984.

———. *Report to the Nation on Crime and Justice, 1983.*

————. Federal Bureau of Investigation. Uniform Crime Reports. *Crime in the United States—1980.* September 1981.

————. *Crime in the United States—1982.* September 1983.

————. *Crime in the United States—1983.* September 1984.

————. Law Enforcement Assistance Administration, National Criminal Justice Information and Statistics Service. *Criminal Victimization in the United States, 1973,* December 1976.

————. National Institute of Justice. *The Link Between Crime and the Built Environment.* Washington, D.C.: U.S. Government Printing Office, December 1980.

Viguerie, Richard. *The New Right: We're Ready to Lead.* Falls Church, VA:, the Viguerie Company, 1980.

Warren, Marguerite, ed. *Comparing Male and Female Offenders.* Beverly Hills, CA: Sage, 1981.

Webber, Robert. *The Moral Majority: Right or Wrong?* Westchester, IL: Cornerstone, 1981.

Weisberg, D. Kelly. *Children of the Night.* Lexington, MA: Lexington, 1985.

Wertenbaker, Thomas Jefferson. *The Puritan Oligarchy.* New York: Grosset & Dunlap, 1947.

Winick, Charles. *The Lively Commerce.* Chicago: Quadrangle, 1971.

Wolfenden Report. New York: Stein & Day, 1963.

Wolfgang, Marvin. *Patterns of Criminal Homicide.* Philadelphia: University of Pennsylvania Press, 1958.

Wright, James, Peter Rossi, and Kathleen Daly. *Under the Gun.* New York: Aldine, 1983.

Wright, Louis B. *Culture on the Moving Frontier.* New York: Harper & Row, 1961.

Yin, Robert, Mary Vogel, Jan Chaiken, and Deborah Both. *Patrolling the Neighborhood Beat: Residents and Residential Security.* Santa Monica, CA: Rand Corporation, 1976.

Index

, Georgette

arps